Historical and Philosophical Foundations of Western Education

SECOND EDITION

S. E. FROST, JR.

Brooklyn College
The City University
of New York (Retired)

KENNETH P. BAILEY

University of California,
Irvine

CHARLES E. MERRILL PUBLISHING COMPANY
A Bell & Howell Company
Columbus, Ohio

To My Father
SEVERE E. FROST
Historian and Master Teacher

370.9
F939L

Published by
Charles E. Merrill Publishing Co.
A Bell & Howell Co.
Columbus, Ohio

ISBN: 0-675-08970-0

Library of Congress Catalog Card Number: 72-96024

1 2 3 4 5 6 7 8 9—79 78 76 75 74 73

74.4999

Printed in the United States of America

CONTENTS

PREFACE

To a student who begins the study of the history of education, the new academic emphasis following the Russian Sputnik launching of 1958 seems meaningful; it is recent. The Dewey experiments of the 1930s are much further back; Benjamin Franklin's Academy is more remote; and early Greek experience before 3,000 B.C. seems a long time ago. Yet the 5,000 year period covered in this example represents less than one percent of the time man has been on earth. The other ninety-nine percent of man's existence we call prehistoric and ancient cultures. This text is concerned with bringing to life the many experiences of mankind in the field of education, emphasizing its continuing themes. Many times these themes have recycled but almost always at a higher level of sophistication. This book summarizes over 7,000 years of human experience, from the early stages of civilization to the contemporary problems of inner-city education. Studying how these issues have developed in the past will help the student understand the present.

In today's classes it is essential that the student find relevancy in the material being studied. It is necessary that a study of the history of education produce this kind of result. Most students enrolled in a course in the history of education plan to become teachers. The question that needs to be answered is whether or not such a course helps one to become a better teacher. Most analysts of teacher behavior recognize that a knowledge of the various stages in the development of learning allows the student to make educational decisions based upon the accumulated experiences of the world's great educators. It helps prevent reinventing the wheel. There is much to be learned in the history of education that is helpful to understanding issues of our time.

A feature of this text relates to the study made of comparative contemporary education around the world. To make certain students have available up-to-date and accurate information, visitations have been made during the last two years to the countries discussed. This has been true in terms of the study of education in the Soviet Union, England, France, West Germany, the Balkans, and Canada. The contemporary scene is the feature of part five, "Education in One World." We believe it has particular relevance to today's teacher.

Kenneth P. Bailey
University of California, Irvine

PREFACE to First Edition

Historical and Philosophical Foundations of Western Education is designed to inform and inspire those who are interested in elementary or secondary education. It offers a comprehensive view of the sweep of history, presenting helpful insights into the function of education in the process of human growth and development. Here the history of education is brought into modern perspective as the reader is shown what his past has attempted and the degree to which it has succeeded, the ideas that have been dealt with by the best minds of Western culture, and the major issues that have emerged and how they have been faced.

The book presents an overview of the developments in education from earliest known prehistoric ages to the twentieth century. Developed chronologically, the text is divided into four parts: "Life and Education in Prehistoric and Ancient Cultures," "Life and Education in Classical Cultures," "Life and Education in the Medieval World," and "Life and Education in the Modern World." This organization enables the reader to begin his study at that point in history he deems most advantageous. Some will wish to direct their thinking to the beginnings of learning at the prehuman level in the earliest ages of the earth; others will want to omit this material and start with the classical period. Still others will wish to focus attention on the modern world, giving only passing attention to earlier periods.

An innovation has been introduced into Part Two, as the Hebrew and Christian cultures, as well as the Greek and Roman, are included in the classification "classical cultures." Western culture, to be truly understood, must be seen not merely as a result of its Greek and Roman traditions, but also as an outgrowth of its Hebrew-Christian tradition. Christianity was filtered to the West through the Roman Empire, but it had roots in early Hebrew culture and these roots are important for any understanding of its contribution to the Western world. The "classical" must encompass all that is truly classical in the history of Western culture.

As the reader follows this account, he will come to appreciate the tradition of which he plans to become a part, and he will begin to understand the challenge that is his. He will gain, too, a realization that as he works with the problems of present-day society involving the young he does not stand alone; behind him are experiences of centuries, the dedication of many men and women of history, and the accumulated understandings of the ages. He will find that he holds in his hands the hopes of the present for its future.

S. E. Frost, Jr.
Brooklyn College

Part One

LIFE AND EDUCATION IN PREHISTORIC AND ANCIENT CULTURES

CHAPTER 1

In Prehistoric and Primitive Cultures

INTRODUCTION

The history of education is intensely relevant to the prospective teacher. In the face of today's demands, change is an essential ingredient for improvement of the schools. One of the more interesting phenomena of the 1970s is the recurrence or recycling of what has gone before. The tragedy is that many innovators are seemingly unaware of what has preceded. Thus, much of what could happen does not, and much of what does happen should not. What happened in Greek or Roman education has relevant value today, as does the Latin Grammar School or the development of the educational ladder.

The issues of education reassert themselves from time to time. The contemporary disciplinarian acts as if his ideas of inquiry-discovery are different from Dewey's "learning by doing." In the 1970s, the programmed-instruction advocates have forgotten the Leicester movement in English and American educational history; programmed instruction was part of the monitorial schools of the nineteenth century. Censorship, book burning, and witch hunting go back to the Greeks, and have involved every century since. The negotiating council of the 1970s had its counterpart in ancient Egypt, where employers negotiated wage contracts with the teachers. In America, the federal government has programs of matching funds, but so did the Roman emperors. Their imperial grants were often based on matching funds by local areas. The contemporary college student may be the focal point in demonstrations and strikes, but the same was true of students of the medieval university. Merit pay is now being introduced by the more daring, but the concept goes back to the charity schools of England.

Innovation is the contemporary process of bringing about change, but the innovations that are being introduced are not new. Interdisciplinary studies, team teaching, flexible scheduling, visual aids, guidance activities, parents' groups, and local parent control are all ideas out of the past. The voucher system has its roots in early American education. The contemporary academicians who have developed new physics, inquiry, or any number of activity approaches, fail to recognize they are doing, with heavy financial backing, what others tried to do half a century earlier.

Such has been the history of education. Each society has gone through a cyclical process, repeating itself over a period of time but at an ever-increasing level of sophistication. In the early stages of a society's cultural development, education tends primarily to train for economic survival and for some form of nationalistic citizenship. As society develops, the curriculum in the schools becomes more diversified, educates for the mind, for leadership, and for those things which promote national progress (i.e., science). But the history of mankind shows that as societies mature, many decline in world importance. Institutions, such as education, fail to change. They attempt to maintain the status quo when new conditions demand new approaches. Schools are tradition-bound, and become static or even reactionary. They are not relevant to the new conditions brought on by new generations. Many civilizations demonstrate this process of rise and fall. Egypt, Greece, and Rome are most notable for having "fallen," but the phenomenon is to be seen in many areas. Education, which should lead in meeting new conditions, by its institutional and support format, does not.

In its broadest sense, education has always been a factor of evolving experience. During the earliest stages of development, it is on the unconscious level. The organism interacts with its environment and, in the process, is changed or makes changes in its surroundings. As one moves along the time-line of history or the growth-line of the individual, changes become more or less conscious learnings. The organism, vaguely aware of the process of interaction, is able to anticipate outcomes. It "learns" to predict the future from the experiences of the past and of the present. Gradually it develops an awareness of process, begins to reconstruct its ideas, and creates simple institutions to serve its needs. Later, it discovers that by manipulating the environment of others, it can mold them to its desires and ideals. At this point education is conscious and teaching a deliberate undertaking.

The history of education is the story of man's continual reconstruction of his ideas and institutions, from his earliest awareness of the educative process to the present, and his varied attempts to mold each generation to them and by them. At times the forward movement has been slow, so slow indeed as to give the impression that there has been no progress. At others it is speeded up so that change takes place at all times, and education is proceeding to higher levels of involvement and achievement.

AN HISTORICAL PERSPECTIVE

As the student of history peers backward along the corridor of time and the years drop away toward the far past, his vision dims. Before the darkness closes in, he gets faint hints of man's earliest life on this planet. While the near present offers him a proliferation, and at times a confusion, of materials from which the story of man can be written, dependable evidence becomes scarcer the farther back he travels in time, until the teller of man's story has only a few rough stones, an ash here and a fossil there, a skull buried deep in coal, or, if he is lucky, a nearly complete skeleton surrounded by implements, pottery, and animal bones. From these scant pieces of evidence he must construct as best he can in imagination the life of earliest man upon this planet.

A Prelude to History

In those vast reaches of time between the vague and halting beginnings when certain forms of life, moving very slowly out of the primeval ooze, "learned" to live on dry land and the appearance of Proconsul, the earliest known link between man and the apes, many life forms evolved on this earth. Geologists, anthropologists, and archaeologists have, from the known remains of these early creatures and other pieces of evidence, cleared away some of the darkness that hides man's prehistory and made a few intelligent guesses about the kinds of beings that lived during those very early days, the environments which shaped them and, in part perhaps, they were able to shape, and the simple cultures which some of them seem to have created and passed on to their young through education.

The story these scholars tell goes like this. Sometime before 550,-000,000 B.C., clearly recognized forms of life appeared on earth. These organisms came into being, lived, and died over a period of some 350,-000,000 years. During this vast expanse of time, education, if it can be said to have existed, was unconscious biological change, the natural reconstruction of organisms through interaction with their environments. This is education in the broadest sense of the term and at its simplest.

In the Neogene period there appeared a mammalian form which anthropologists have named Proconsul, believed to be the common ancestor of apes and man. After some 15,000,000 years, a more manlike creature is known to have lived upon parts of the inhabitable earth. Scientists have named him Oreopithecus.

What was the pattern of culture these early manlike creatures fashioned? Evidence upon which to base an answer is meager and confusing. Found in the same earth formations as Oreopithecus are stone objects called eoliths, "dawn stones," which some authorities believe are the products of tool-making mammals. Others hold that these stones were shaped by natural forces, having nothing to do with tool making.

These manlike creatures developed some form of family or group life, possibly living in packs or herds, with simple rules of social life. What these rules were and how they might have been enforced are not revealed in the evidence scholars have unearthed, and we can only speculate, recognizing that our speculation may be wholly inaccurate.

Oreopithecus lived in the neighborhood of 10,000,000 B.C. After him there is a vast historical darkness. When the darkness lifted, somewhere near 750,000 B.C., there appeared, living in sections of South Africa, another manlike creature, Australopithecus, who is held to be the direct ancestor of modern man.

The earliest unmistakably human remains were discovered first near Neanderthal, a slight distance from Dusseldorf, Germany, in 1857. The creature who left us these bones has been given the name Neanderthal man and is believed to have inhabited most of Europe around 40,000 B.C.

After controlling most of the inhabitable surface of the earth for some 20,000 years, this Neanderthal race was displaced by a stronger and more clever people whom anthropologists have called Cro-Magnon. The first remains of these men were discovered in the Cro-Magnon grotto in southern France in 1868, hence the name.

All these early men and man-forms, from Oreopithecus to Cro-Magnon, lived during what anthropologists have called the Paleolithic Age, a cultural period that reaches back to at least 10,000,000 B.C. and comes to an end around 16,000 B.C. The chief characteristic of this age is the use of unpolished stone implements. During the early milleniums of this age the creatures who were modern man's ancestors did little more than select conveniently shaped stones for their use. As the age advanced, they came to shape stones, the better to meet their requirements. Later they learned to shape bone, wood, and ivory into tools they could employ to accomplish their ends. Once able to chip and shape these natural objects of their environment, prehistoric men turned to creative art, carving these materials to represent objects in their environment. Utility was very soon followed by the aesthetic, and human culture took on a depth and richness not possible earlier.

Somewhere in this far past, true man, or his forebears, discovered how to make fire. Prehistoric relics indicate that man-made fire, as distinct from natural fire, is at least 40,000 years old—from the earliest days of Neanderthal man. Later Cro-Magnon man ground bowls from the rocks, filled them with oil, and made lamps to light his night and, very possibly, to heat his cave.

Thus, in the culture of Paleolithic man were shaped stones, pieces of wood hewn for specific purposes, and ivory cut for need and beauty. There was fire for light, for warmth, and perhaps for cooking. There was an art that, toward the end of the age, reached a level of beauty and symmetry that amazes even moderns. This much we know for certain, our evidence being the remains of these early people that have been found and studied. In some ways not indicated by the materials that have come down to us these early men must have passed on this knowledge to their children—education must have been part of their culture. How this was done, what "curriculum" they developed, who taught and who "studied" we can only surmise from what we know of primitive groups.

THE TRANSITION TO HISTORY

Slowly, man learned to polish his stone implements and to shape them so that they served his needs more adequately. As he made progress in this direction, the Paleolithic Age came to an end, and there began the Mesolithic Age.

Passing through this transition period, man moved into what has become known as the Neolithic Age, beginning around 10,000 B.C. in Asia and around 5,000 B.C. in Europe. This era was characterized by changes in man's ways of living and thinking. Agriculture was replacing hunting, animals were being domesticated and bred for human use, and the arts of weaving, pottery making, healing, and architecture were being developed rapidly.

Then, somewhere in his past, man learned to prepare and use metals, probably by accident. No doubt he had known about metals long before he was able to transform them for his purpose by fire and working. There is evidence that smelting was known to man as early as 6,000 B.C. in some parts of the world, but this knowledge spread slowly and did not reach other areas until much later.

With the more extensive use of metals came the first civilizations known to modern scholars, those of Mesopotamia and Egypt. Man had come a long way from his early ancestor Proconsul, he had learned much, and he had discovered how to transmit much that he learned to his children. Cultures had developed and taken form, and education to perpetuate these cultures had become more efficient and effective.

PREHISTORIC CULTURES

LIFE IN PREHISTORIC CULTURES

The prehistoric is usually defined as all that time in the development of a people before they learned to keep written records. If we accept this definition, it becomes evident that the length of one people's prehistory may be different from that of another living in a different area of the earth's surface. The mounting mass of evidence indicates that western man developed writing somewhere between 6,000 and 5,000 B.C. Even today, however, there are people who do not have anything that can be identified as a written language, and their record keeping is most primitive.

From a study of prehistoric records—human and non-human bones, caves, tools and implements, and numerous other relics—we may assume that prehistoric men developed articulate speech and connected thought, learned to plant and harvest crops, to find and kill food animals and, at possibly a later time, to domesticate and breed these animals and care for them in herds, to catch and prepare fish for eating, to make crude clothing and bedeck their bodies, to live in groups under some social controls, to fight and destroy each other with crudely-made weapons and according to pre-established rules, to build dwellings and other structures, and to gain some control over their environments. Nevertheless, since the factors that combine to fashion the life of a people differ from place to place, we cannot assume that all people, during the prehistoric stage of their development, accomplished the same things or reached the same level of knowledge and skill.

We may assume further that, very slowly, prehistoric men learned ways of improving their skills and techniques and, therein, made "progress." It is reasonable to assume that they learned how to pass on their knowledge, skills, and techniques, along with their taboos and beliefs, to their children. Knowing what we do about children, we can assume that they learned much by just living in the group and watching what interested them. Beyond this, we can be fairly certain that their parents and other adults taught them what they deemed necessary. As far as we can learn, these early people had no schools or specialized teaching class.

PRIMITIVE CULTURES

THE NATURE OF PRIMITIVE CULTURES

Primitive signifies a relative simplicity as regards the pattern of living, a people "culturally arrested," a way of life lacking in most of those factors which in our present-day thinking constitute "civilization."

Any study of primitive cultures must include those that are known to have existed centuries ago as stages in the development of people now called "civilized," as well as those existing in undeveloped areas of the world today. Such a study, fascinating to a growing number of modern scholars interested primarily in education, reveals the fact that although cultural patterns of primitive groups are highly varied and, in many respects, dissimilar, they all have certain common characteristics which serve to identify them as primitive. These include:

1. A simplicity of structure that is thrown into bold relief when compared with the complexity of present-day industrial cultures;
2. An absence of clearly differentiated institutions for handling social needs and group functions;
3. A generalization in the areas of the arts as distinguished from the specialization found in more advanced cultures;
4. Definite limitations in the areas of social contacts to the extent that groups tend to erect barriers between themselves and others resulting in a very limited sharing of experiences;
5. A tribal social organization with all its taboos and narrowing demands;
6. A complete absence of the methods of exact science resulting in folkways, beliefs, and attitudes that, though they may serve the needs of the group at the moment and in its highly restricted environment, cannot survive in a larger environment of conflicting experiences;
7. A level of writing and reading lacking fine shades of meaning, careful determination among issues, and exact definitions;
8. A conservatism that resists change with religious zeal.

EDUCATION IN PRIMITIVE CULTURES

Although the educational picture will vary from one primitive culture to another, there are certain factors which are common to all such groups to a greater or lesser degree. The first, and in many ways the most significant factor, has to do with the *purpose* of education. Basically, education in all societies aims at orienting the individual to his social and physical environment. Since the primitive social pattern tends to be largely static, education here is a conservative and conserving force, aiming to perpetuate the *status quo* and to communicate to the young the dangers inherent in change. In general, then, primitive education aims to transmit unchanged from the adults to the young the beliefs, practices, and attitudes that have stood the test of time and proved successful in the environment in which one's ancestors have lived. In so doing, education inevitably subordinates the welfare of the individual to that of the group.

The second factor has to do with the *methodology* of primitive education. This is relatively simple and highly effective. Lacking formal schools and a designated body of individuals devoting themselves wholly to teaching, primitive societies place education in the hands of the family, the community, and the elder and more experienced members of the group. The mother and father teach their children in their homes, informally and formally. The community is a school teaching its children as they live in and interact with its total structure. At specified times in the child's development the elders of the group and those with specialized skills and knowledge instruct each child in a more formal fashion.

Further, in primitive societies educational methodology ranges all the way from incidental observation of life in the community to specific showing and telling and learning through doing. Much of the child's education comes as he watches adults going about their daily tasks— hunting, fishing, preparing food, building shelters, talking, fighting, and the many other occupations of the population. The pressures of the group plus the need to survive and to be accepted are powerful incentives to learning. In addition, because this is the child's group, he enjoys being successful in the things which his group values and is unhappy when he fails to measure up to group demands.

The third factor is concerned with the place of the *child* in the primitive community. From the point of view of the group, the child is its most precious asset. He will fish and hunt and fight and maintain the folkways of the culture when the adults grow old and die. To this end the older members of the family and of the community show and tell him how to discharge those functions necessary for group survival. The father patiently instructs his son in the accepted methods of shooting the arrow or throwing the spear. The mother, just as patiently, instructs her daughter in ways of cultivating the home garden and preparing the food the men have killed.

In some primitive communities, the time when the child matures physically is most important. He is now ready to assume adult responsibilities. At this time he is initiated in a series of "puberty rites." These include, usually, a period of careful instruction and testing extending from a few days to several years, and marked by high moments of ceremony and ritualistic pageantry designed to impress the necessary learning on the youth.

The fourth factor centers on provisions for a type of controlled *specialization* found in most primitive cultures. While there is no specialization allowed in matters of general education, as exemplified by the puberty rites, most primitive people make a place for functional specialization in their social structure. Very simple societies reveal a minimum of social differentiation, usually only the differentiation between the sexes where the female bears the children, cultivates the fields, and prepares the food while the male hunts, fishes, and fights. As societies become more complex, specialized groups appear, groups charged with specific functions necessary to the on-going of group life. These functions demand a type of instruction different from that given all members of the community, instruction in the skills, techniques, and secrets connected with the specialized function. This begins to set members of each specialized group apart from the masses as wiser and of greater importance to the whole. So separated, these members come to assume special privileges and powers over others which, in many instances, results in domination of the community by a small, specialized class of men. Included in such groups are medicine men, priests, and those skilled in predicting future events.

As each culture grows in complexity, other specialized groups appear and assume more or less a monopoly of certain occupations which develop within the society. Builders, weavers, makers of spears and arrows, animal tamers, and others, as these functions of the group become more specialized, appear. Usually instruction of novices is undertaken by older members of the specialized group and in secret. All pupils are sworn to secrecy and are threatened with dire punishment if at any time they reveal these secrets to the uninitiated. The skills of each "trade" must be kept from the masses since these have become the means by which the initiated gain and hold their privileged position in the community. The pupil to whom these secrets are revealed has, first, been chosen by members of the group as worthy of special consideration—fit to discharge his responsibilities honorably. Second, when the older members of the specialized groups are satisfied that he has learned his lessons well and has mastered the skills of the trade sufficiently to turn out work that meets the standards set by tradition, they accept him into full membership with all the accompanying privileges and immunities.

The fifth factor is a differentiated body of educational thinking and practice stemming from the growth of *secret fraternities or organiza-*

tions involving small groups of men within the larger community. Members of a community, usually youths or older men, often banded together for social activities or to observe some mystic ritual centering around a body of beliefs or tradition. In primitive communities these organizations were many and highly diverse, depending largely, it is believed, upon past experiences of the community. Usually one was admitted to one of these secret organizations only after an extended period of initiation. This included a time of study during which the novice was taught the secret doctrines of the group and other matters relative to the organization, was tested as to his specialized prowess, and was impressed with the necessity of living according to the teachings of the group and its traditions. Absolute secrecy was stressed. At times, the ritual by which some of these secrets and skills were taught was elaborate, bloody, cruel, and emotionally charged, similar, in part at least, to initiations practiced by some modern fraternities and lodges.

PRIMITIVE RELIGIOUS EDUCATION

Another type of education which looms large in primitive cultures is that growing out of the religious beliefs and conceptions of the people. Primitive man lived in an "awe-full" world, a world inspiring awe and fear at every turn. The experiences of his ancestors and his own experiences led him to believe with conviction that his environment was peopled by forces having influence upon all phases of his life.

It was impossible for every man to know all these forces and understand their ways, their likes and dislikes, and conduct himself so as to win their favor. Thus, very early in man's cultural development, there arose a specialized class of wise men or "priests" charged with the function of dealing directly with these forces. They learned the ways of the spirits and stood ready to advise others as to the proper methods of dealing with them. This resulted eventually in two patterns of "religious" education.

On the one hand, the specialists in matters spiritual taught those who were to succeed them the arts of their specialty. The priestly group accepted young men, and sometimes young women, into its ranks and instructed them in all matters related to the world of the spirits. After the novice had learned what was deemed necessary and had mastered the techniques of his chosen occupation, he was initiated into the "profession" and accepted as a fully qualified practitioner by the community. Often these initiations were accompanied by elaborate pageantry.

On the other hand, members of the priestly group instructed the young and, if necessary, the older members of the community in the ways of the spirits and powers in their environment. They taught the people how to behave under specific conditions, how to placate the unfavorable and serve the favorable, and other esoteric matters of tribal religion. This instruction was supplemented by that of parents and others with whom the child came in contact in his daily living. At times the entire community, or a gathering of several communities, participated in ritualistic dances and other ceremonies designed to influence the forces believed to control the environment. The young learned by watching these performances and, at times, by participating at the level of their ability.

Religious education, as all other education among primitive people, was one with living. The child learned so that he might live satisfactorily with those forces that peopled his environment. He was taught by just living and by the adults with whom he associated. Religious education had a wholly practical aim.

LESSONS FROM PRIMITIVE LIFE

Study of primitive cultures and their educational structures reveals not only their great diversity, but broad areas of similarity, factors that are to be found in most, if not all, early cultures. These factors are basic to all education, whether primitive or modern.

The most significant of these factors is that the education of every group is conditioned by its cultural pattern, its ways of living in its environment. Education everywhere is a means of preparing the individual to live effectively in a specific culture.

Next in importance is that the individual learns much, some would say most, by simply living in a society, seeing and hearing what goes on about him. He picks up learning as he meets the pressures of the group, discovers what is accepted and what is condemned, receives praise or blame, and experiences satisfaction in being right. Informal education is a very large part, and a most lasting part, of everyone's experience.

Third in importance is that a major educational agency in every culture is the family. Here is to be found both formal and informal education. Parents teach their children by merely living with them in the family group. They are examples which children follow instinctively. They also teach directly by telling and showing, by praising when the children conform and punishing when they fail to measure up to the standards set by the family group. The family is first in time and, in many ways, the most important teaching agency in any society.

Fourth in importance is that as societies become more complex, they create specialized groups to care for specific social functions. One of these groups is the teaching profession and the school in which it discharges its duties. There is also an educational structure designed to prepare certain members of the group to discharge this function efficiently—teacher education. Formalized education, the school, is a result of social need and develops in a group when this need is sufficiently evident.

Fifth in importance is that as the formal education structure develops, it tends to shape the culture in terms of ends and ideals which *it* has constructed. It becomes a factor in molding the young to ways of thinking and living with which the group may not agree. In very early cultures this was at a minimum, if it can be found at all. As a culture develops, conditions in the environment change, and it comes more in contact with other and different cultures. Eventually there will develop in a culture a conflict between the "conservative" and the "liberal" elements, and the "educators" will be found to line up, some on one side and some on the other. Usually, since the school is a product of the community, the majority of the people and "educators" will be found in the conservative camp.

CHAPTER 2

In the Early Stages of Civilization

INTRODUCTION

With the invention of writing, the curtain of history rises; and we are able to watch more clearly and in greater detail the drama of man's struggle to become civilized. The first scene of this drama is laid in the fertile valleys of the Tigris-Euphrates and Nile rivers where the earliest known civilizations were fashioned. In these valleys strange and fascinating cultures developed: the Sumerian, the Babylonian, the Assyrian, and the Egyptian. For generations, modern scholars knew of these cultures only vaguely from the romantic writings of early travelers or from the legends which men like to embellish and time to sanction. Lately the spades of the archaeologists have uncovered many of the cities of these people, revealing more and more of the truth of their ways of life.

From the valleys of these great rivers the scene shifts far to the east, to China, and again we are in the glow of legends which gradually give way to facts as men of the West learn more about the Orient and its ways of thinking and living.

These great civilizations were, in a sense, transitional. In them we find much that is savage, much that is barbarian, and a great deal of the primitive. We also find in them the promise of the future: a way of living together that bespeaks a civilization yet unborn, an art that struggles for beauty only sensed, and a philosophy and a religion not satisfied with anthropomorphic interpretations of the environment and crude nature gods but reaching out toward the understanding of an expanding human reason and monotheism.

While early civilizations overcame, to a degree, primitive enslavement to nature and the necessities of the present, they came under the yoke of the past and developed a deep fear of any individual freedom that might challenge this past. They were in that stage of development when the process of human social evolution had not as yet become quite conscious of itself.

IN THE TIGRIS-EUPHRATES VALLEY

History of the Valley

While primitive people no doubt lived in the great valley between the Tigris and Euphrates rivers for untold centuries, history began there around 5,000 B.C. Records have been discovered which date the *Sumerians,* the earliest people known to have inhabited the area, at or near this remote time. Their culture seems to have developed first in the bottomlands of the "Twin Rivers" with a center in *Sumer.*

Somewhere around 2,500 B.C., the area about Sumer was invaded by nomadic herdsmen and warriors coming down from Akkad under the leadership of the half-legendary king, *Sargon.* These wild, barbaric tribesmen were eventually absorbed into the Sumerian culture, and together, "native" and invader developed a fairly high civilization and a strong empire.

After several generations of rule by the Sargon dynasty, the central government weakened, and the empire of the Sumerian golden age fell apart under less skillful administration. From the ashes of this empire arose independent cities to take control and, in time, develop their own empires. One of these cities was *Ur,* the traditional home of Abraham. Here, schools are known to have existed before 2,000 B.C. Grammars and dictionaries were used in these schools, and two languages were taught—the ancient Sumerian, which had by then become the language of the "classics" of the people, and Semitic, which was used in daily conversation and trade. This education was confined to the elite and contained both theoretical and practical elements. It was typical, no doubt, of the education that was developed throughout the Sumerian empire. Indeed, it is inconceivable that the powerful government of the Sargon dynasty could have grown to such magnitude and influence without an educational system designed to train warriors, civil officers and clerks, and leaders of religion and the state.

A Sumerian city that came, in time, to dominate the Tigris-Euphrates Valley was *Babylon.* Its rule extended from about 2,000 to near 1,600 B.C., a time span during which it became the center of a fabulous empire whose fame grew into legend. One of the most forceful rulers of this empire was *Hammurabi.* Under his leadership the old Sumerian laws were collected, codified, and worked into what is now the oldest legal structure known to man. There is considerable evidence that here, too, was an elaborate system of schools for the elite, schools devoted to the education of priests, scribes, and civil servants. Here, along with the religious and the practical, was a pattern of legal education which made possible the Hammurabian code and, after the code had been formulated, an education centered on its study and interpretation.

Another thriving city that grew to power amid the ruins of the ancient Sumerian empire was *Assur.* For several centuries it lay under the heel of Babylonian rulers, but as its commercial enterprises thrived, bringing wealth and power to its people, it was able to revolt, establish itself as an independent city, and become the center of a rival empire, *Assyria.* For years Babylonia and Assyria remained rivals of equal power in the great valley of the "Twin Rivers." Then, after the tenth century B.C., Assyria was able to extend its empire to engulf Babylonia. This vast and powerful military and governmental machine rolled across the valley devouring cities and principalities, reaching the peak of its fame and greatness around 670 B.C. At that time the Babylonians united with the Medes, destroyed completely the Assyrian empire, which had become fat and soft, and restored the ancient rule and grandeur of Babylon. This renaissance of Babylonian strength lasted for more than one hundred years. Then, when the Medes, who did not appreciate the fact that theirs was a subordinate position to their companions in the overthrow of the Assyrians, allied themselves with the Persians, they were able to destroy forever this vast Babylonian empire and build a state whose power and influence reached far beyond the narrow confines of the Tigris-Euphrates.

EDUCATION IN THE VALLEY

The culture that took shape in the valley between the Tigris and Euphrates rivers created an educational structure consistent with its fundamental nature and designed to perpetuate and transmit its basic values to the young. Although differing in administration, methodology, and efficiency from city to city, state to state, and empire to empire, it was in essence the same, regardless of the political fortunes of the times. Its all-pervading aim was practical, a preparation for the professions in which the elite spent their time. Since most professions were manned by priests or controlled by them, including even the offices of king and the political hierarchy, this education has been called "priestly."

Although the records are not clear, there is enough evidence for one to assume that an elementary, or early, formal education was maintained to ground the young in the fundamentals of learning—the three R's. Having mastered these to the satisfaction of his teacher, the child was promoted to a higher school or "college" connected with a temple or library in his community, or he went away to a center of learning in a more populous community where both temple and library were larger and better equipped for advanced learning. Many technical subjects were taught, including engineering, astronomy, architecture, and medicine. Also, training in the lore and rituals of the priesthood was available for those who wished to prepare for this profession. Learning was largely a matter of memorizing materials and imitating set patterns. There was no experimentation, no practical doing, no facing up to the realities of the times. This came after schooling, when the young man entered a sort of internship to a master in his chosen profession.

Instruction was on an individual basis, there being no class teaching, and the student paid his teacher directly for his services. While elementary schools were taught by laymen, priests monopolized advanced education, giving the sanction of religion to the strange mixture of truth and folklore which the young man learned in order to merit the approval of his culture.

The culture out of which this educational structure developed was highly conventional, and the schools which this culture spawned reflected, to a marked degree, devotion to the past. Individuality was discouraged while conformity was emphasized at every stage of the child's development.

IN THE VALLEY OF THE NILE

History of the Valley

The ancient Egyptians measured their history in dynasties, often taking no account of the gaps between great ruling families, a fact which makes it next to impossible for students of Egyptian history to date with any degree of accuracy events in the early days of man's occupancy of the Nile Valley. Although the earliest hieroglyphics known to modern scholars, those found in the tomb of King Ka-ap at Abydos, have been dated near 5,650 B.C., the first event in Egyptian history that can be pinpointed with certainty is cut into the Palermo Stone, now in the museum at Palermo, and dated 4,241 B.C.

Scholars, using their own methods of determining dates, differ widely as to the time of happenings in early Egyptian history. The first dynasty, for example, is placed by Meyer at 3,315 B.C., while Petrie locates it at 5,510 B.C. If we accept Petrie's chronology, which seems to have the greatest amount of evidence in its favor, Egyptian history must be divided into the following:

The Prehistoric Age. During prehistoric times, two kingdoms developed along the shores of the Nile: Upper Egypt, including the delta at the river's northern extreme and all the northern reaches of the river, often referred to as "the black lands" because of the great fertility of the area; and Lower Egypt, including all the southern reaches of the river. Tradition tells of a great king, *Menes,* who united these two kingdoms and founded the first dynasty.

The Old Kingdom. This period includes the first through the eighth dynasties, and dates from about 5,510 to 3,787 B.C. It was during these first 2000 years of history in Egypt that the great pyramids were built and the great Sphinx constructed. The latter is placed sometime in the fourth dynasty.

The Middle Kingdom. Here Petrie places the ninth through the seventeenth dynasties, and dates the period from 3,787 to 1,580 B.C. Little is known of this 2000-year span of Egyptian history, although scholars are now digging in ruins which may in time shed more light on the life of the people who lived in this land during this great stretch of time.

The New Empire. This covers the eighteenth through the twentieth dynasties, from 1,580 to 1,090 B.C., and is the period when cracks began to appear in Egyptian strength and influence.

The Deltic Dynasties. From 1,090 to 332 B.C. the twenty-first through the thirty-first dynasties ruled Egypt, and contributed much to the eventual downfall of the empire, even though there were some strong and devoted rulers in these dynasties. During this period Egypt was weakened by corruption within and by invaders from without. Its growing weakness opened the door to the Assyrians and then to the Persians, both of whom sought to avenge themselves for past indignities as well as to extend their empires into the rich land of the Nile. It is true that during these years Egypt did enjoy fleeting moments of independence when it seemed that her former glory might return, but the strength had gone out of her; the will to rise again was weakened to death. When Alexander moved his armies to her borders, the ancient glory of tradition was little more than a memory cherished by old men, and the land fell under the yoke of these fresh, virile people from afar.

Later History. The Alexandrian rule lasted only from 332 to 323 B.C. when, at the death of Alexander, the conqueror's vast empire was divided, with Egypt falling to Ptolemy, son of Lagus, who established the Ptolemaic dynasty, which endured with some degree of success until 30 B.C. At that time Roman legions under Augustus took the kingdom as a prize of conquest and ushered in the Roman period of Egyptian history, with the land of the Nile closely interlocked in the sprawling Roman empire. Egypt had died as a great power and, for centuries, remained the pawn of strong rulers and mighty empires from the outside, a land of mystery and romance, legend and superstition, until more modern powers from the west gained control and laid a foundation for the resurgence of Egyptian influence in the world. It could be that the curtain is just now going up on a new Egypt and a revitalized period of her history.

EDUCATION IN THE VALLEY

Education in Egypt was patterned after the culture and aimed at perpetuating the values of the past while, at the same time, preparing youth to live effectively in the culture. During the Old Kingdom, the first education of the child was in the hands of the parents. The home was the school, and there was nowhere anything that could be likened to a public school. Although the evidence is not clear, there are indications that the Middle Kingdom developed three types of elementary education, or schools, all of which grew in importance and general acceptance during the New Empire. First were the temple schools, very early a part of the life of every temple, which were taught by the priests and aimed to give each pupil a mastery of writing, an art of special importance to religious functionaries. Second were court schools, established in the royal household to prepare the heir to the throne for his adult duties. Usually sons of members of the court and a few others, children of privileged persons, were admitted to these schools at the pleasure of the ruler. Here reading and writing and the customs and rituals of the court were paramount considerations. Third were department schools, conducted in each department of government to prepare boys for administrative careers in the kingdom and empire.

All elementary, or first, education was vocational. The boys (girls were trained in the home and not admitted to any of the careers of which the schools were a part) were taught to write the language, to use freely and understandingly the vocabulary of the career for which they were being trained, and to engage in other activities relevant to their future and suited to their ages. This was definitely an apprentice training. The school day ended at noon, allowing children to turn their interests to play, physical exercise, and duties of their homes. The available records of schools during the Middle Kingdom and New Empire show that, in addition to the above, boys were taught swimming, sacred songs, dancing, manners, and morals or practical ethics.

As the child grew, he moved into a more planned and structured educational program. At this "secondary" level his teachers employed copybooks to teach both writing and moral precepts. The sentences the boy was required to copy dealt with correct behavior towards gods and men. Emphasis was on style of writing, and the form followed was that of the "classics" of the Middle Kingdom.

Apprenticed in his future career and grounded in the classics of his past, a boy eventually entered a period of specific training for his chosen profession. This was wholly practical. Theory was held to be a waste of time and energy. At this stage the boy learned the secrets of his profession, secrets that had been handed down from teacher to learner, often within one family, for generations. Among the areas open to young men at this level of education were medicine, the priesthood with all its ramifications, the military, architecture, engineering, and professional writing. Those who went into the skilled trades seldom received this level of training but learned what was needed by working directly with artisans or their fathers.

At the top of the educational ladder in ancient Egypt was a "higher" education centered in the temples. Only those pupils who had the proper preliminary education were admitted to this more intensive study of ancient forms of writing, geography, cosmography, astronomy, chronology, sculpture, painting, ritualistic dancing, theory of music, law, medicine, morals, arithmetic, mensuration, hydrostatics, and the higher stages of architecture. These schools resembled, in fact, our graduate schools and universities. Talented young men carried their studies into what was then accepted as research on the frontiers of knowledge. Often graduates of temple schools made significant contributions to the advancement of a field.

In the schools that we have been discussing, boys were motivated to learn to write by the ambition to become scribes and enjoy the privileges of this highly-skilled position in Egyptian life, gain promotion to higher office, and avoid the hardships of a menial station in life. If these stimuli did not work, and at the lower levels they were often highly ineffective, the boys were encouraged to avoid the harsh punishment meted out by the teacher to the lazy. Other motivating factors came into play as one moved up the ladder of education: professional pride, love of learning, religious fervor, and the expectation of those economic rewards which successful professional men received.

Morals played a major role in ancient Egyptian education, but this was a practical and prudential morality. The fundamental qualities demanded by the culture were bravery, good character, and social and personal acceptance of responsibility. The literature used in the lower schools, and to some extent at the secondary level, was didactic. It emphasized piety toward the gods, absolute submission to the supreme and overshadowing will of the divine, and abject loyalty to the king.

Other moral and ethical principles included slavish deference to all officials, honor to parents, neighborliness especially toward the poor and needy, and self-control. Moral action was motivated almost wholly by the law of reward and favor and aimed at happiness in a worldly existence.

During the Deltic Dynasties, and until very recently, the education of Egyptians tended to take on the coloring of the powers that gained control over the land. Conquerors impressed their cultures and educational patterns upon the people, shaping them into loyal subjects of the reigning king. During those fleeting moments of independence which punctured long periods of subjugation, attempts were made to return to older forms of education or to adjust to changing and more "modern" conditions. Nevertheless, much of the ancient, highly practical program of schooling was preserved until Egypt came under the swelling power of the British Empire. Then the Egyptian was introduced to English education, which aimed to shape him into the mold of English culture. But this is a story which has no place in our study of ancient Egypt, and we will leave it for further study by those interested in later developments in the land of the Pharaohs.

IN THE VALLEY OF THE YELLOW RIVER

HISTORY OF THE VALLEY

The Chinese have a mythology reaching back into prehistory, telling of the first man, *P' an-ku,* who bore sons and established a line of wise and benevolent rulers who made the land prosperous and its enemies fearful. These legendary sovereigns were a mixture of heroism and chicanery, of naiveté and shrewdness, of strength and weakness. In fact, they represented the varied facets of the people's moral ideals and values. One characteristic seems to dominate all Chinese legend—wisdom. Even the worst of their most ancient leaders evidenced an uncanny wisdom which all people might envy.

The first historical emperor, according to Chinese tradition, was *Fu-hi,* who is said to have lived from 2,852 to 2,730 B.C. He was the great lawgiver and creator of the Chinese social order, a sort of supernatural being who mediated between the people and the divine, a son of the god but more understanding of the weaknesses of mankind than his father and thus a go-between. He was followed by *Shon-nung,* the "Divine Laborer," who taught the people how to farm. The third emperor, tradition records, was *Huang-ti,* known as the "Yellow Emperor." He was a great conqueror, overcoming neighboring nations and making them parts of an expanding empire. He gave the people many customs, beliefs, and traditions, all molded into a cultural pattern which changed little over thousands of years.

These three emperors were, most certainly, actual living persons, but much that tradition has handed down about them must, just as certainly, be classified as pure mythology. They are the heroes of Chinese legend, lending themselves to the invention of stories about their great deeds and about the times in which they lived, stories that have become part of the faith of the people among whom time and custom were shields against unbelief. Following these semi-mythological emperors is a more certain history of Chinese dynasties beginning with the *Hia,* near 2,000 B.C., and continuing to the overthrow of the Manchu dynasty, February 12, 1912, when China became a republic.

The country which was united by these leaders is, in land area, about twice the size of the United States and nurtures a population far in excess of 700,000,000 people. Although the tradition of these people is long and rich, no reliable records were kept prior to 1,200 B.C., and authentic history cannot be dated before the seventh century B.C. At this time, around 617 B.C., an educational system was established which remained substantially unchanged until well into the twentieth century.

CULTURE IN THE VALLEY

Religion has been one of the most fundamental factors in Chinese life and education. In early times the people believed that Heaven, the ultimate principle, sanctioned the tradition which all men should follow blindly. This devotion to tradition was evident in the family, where the father had absolute power to enforce obedience to himself as the carrier of tradition. The state was but an enlargement of the family, and the emperor functioned as the "Great Father" of all the people, divine in person and the absolute ruler of the nation. In him the god and tradition met, and the people worshiped their god through him. Religious observances were highly formal and based upon the foundation of ancestor worship.

Confucius, who lived between 551 and 478 B.C., the most revered of Chinese religious thinkers, saved China from degeneracy and civil war. His teachings are enshrined in the *Five Classics* and *Four Books,* which comprise the bible of Chinese religion. The second of the *Four Books* was written by *Mencius,* who lived from 372 to 289 B.C. These teachings, legends that grew about the person of Confucius, and interpretations of the master's ideas prepared by his followers, became the professed religion of the upper classes of China, the educated, while the masses embraced the idolatrous form of Buddhism, which had come down from their past, or a degenerate form of Taoism.

Until the twentieth century, China was a land of tradition and intense conservatism. Devotion to the past blocked any advance in science, the arts, and crafts. Even though there was considerable beauty and delicacy of production in their art, it was highly restrictive and imitative, lacking perspective and vigor. The language of ancient China was monosyllabic, analytic, and juxtapositive, and its literature was dry, formal, and written in a language so different from that spoken by the masses that long years of laborious study were necessary to master it. Thus, two worlds characterized Chinese culture, that of the classical past and that of the practical present. The scholar and his education were of the past, while the masses of Chinese people were in and of the present.

EDUCATION IN THE VALLEY

Chinese education aimed to conserve the past and maintain things as tradition dictated. Its paramount goal was complete uniformity; thus, it has been referred to as "static," "ancestor dominated," "family controlled," "painfully formal." Further, it prepared the student for one thing, and one thing only: to pass state examinations and thereby gain entree to a position of responsibility and honor.

China had no state system of schools nor any education that could rightly be called public. However, the state did encourage private schools as a source of young men who could pass state examinations. Women were excluded from these examinations with the result that what education they received served merely to give them a polish in social situations. Formal education was strictly for men—and for those who could pay for it.

There were three levels of ancient Chinese education: elementary, academies, and examinations. The elementary school met in the teacher's house or in the home of some wealthy patron. The hours were long and the work severe. The boy learned Chinese written characters by repeating them out loud until they were indelibly burned into his nervous system. Understanding of their meaning was not required. Having learned a few characters by this rote method, the boy gave his book to his teacher, turned away (this was called "backing the book"), and recited the lesson as loudly as he could until the teacher was satisfied. In this way, boys of ancient China learned to read and write under the guidance of teachers who, though their chief contribution to the student was mere lesson hearing, were highly revered both by pupils and their parents.

A few private academies were maintained for more advanced training of those who had completed their elementary education and wished to prepare for state examinations. These might be called "cram" or "drill" schools in which the youth studied the ancient Chinese classics more for their form than for their content, learned to write prose and verse in the classical style, and practiced the exercises that would most likely appear on the examinations.

All education beyond the elementary level led to state examinations. There were two preliminary examinations designed to weed out the less competent. Those who failed became teachers. The rest moved on to a series of three tests for degrees. Successful candidates were given state positions with the importance of the position determined by the examination passed. Every effort possible was made to protect the integrity of each examination, even to locking the student in a small room during the period of the test and passing food to him through a hole in the wall. In spite of these precautions, some officials were open to bribes, and corruption was far from unknown.

A fourth test, open only to that elect few who had passed the third test and won the coveted doctor's degree, led to membership in the Imperial Academy—the emperor's cabinet. Those who passed this test were master scholars of the realm, wise in the tradition and fitted to sit at the right hand of the emperor and advise him devotedly. This was the highest honor that could come to a Chinese.

In the elementary school, children learned to recite all the important language characters, committed to memory by rote nine sacred books, developed some skill in writing a few of the central characters so as to communicate on paper simple ideas, and were introduced to a few simple combinations in arithmetic. Literal mastery was demanded. This level of training spanned five or six years and was all the formal education most boys received, since only the most astute had even a small chance of surviving the competition of state examinations.

In the academies or secondary schools, youths translated the nine sacred books into colloquial Chinese and studied commentaries which aimed to make clear the hidden meanings of these classics. Here, emphasis was on understanding. As the pupil advanced into the higher levels of the secondary school, he was required to compose essays and poems in the style of the *Five Classics* and make final preparations for taking state examinations. At this level there was no specified time span or age limit. A student might, and often did, continue his studies throughout life or until he passed the desired examination.

The methodology at every level of Chinese education was extremely formal, emphasizing memorization and an exact reproduction of textual material. Imitation of classical examples was stressed throughout, and instruction was always on an individual basis. The classroom was a scene of confusion and ear-splitting noise as the children studied their lessons and recited aloud. The only way a teacher could tell that a child was working at his assignment was to hear his voice amid the din of dozens of other voices. Writing was learned by tracing models set by the teacher.

Most advanced education continued the formalism of the earlier level by stressing imitation of the classical style of ancient writings while suppressing all originality. The student had to memorize his books without the slightest variation and practice writing prose and verse in the style of these books. To motivate this rote memory and abject imitation, the teacher had to exert harsh discipline and resort to much artificial stimulation. All teaching methods tended to bind the student to the past and to discourage any tendencies he might have toward individuality, initiative, or creativeness.

Chinese education before the twentieth century did secure the stability of society, perpetuate the empire, and undergird the conservatism of the nation's past. It gave a thorough training in retentiveness, in application to mastery of details, and in skill in recognizing fine distinctions of form. Thus, it produced individuals who could imitate perfectly but who were devoid of initiative, inventiveness, and adaptability to new conditions. The twentieth century could come to China only after this wall of conservatism was leveled and a different pattern of education developed.

Part Two

LIFE AND EDUCATION IN CLASSICAL CULTURES

CHAPTER 3
Among the Early Hebrews

INTRODUCTION

When studying early Hebrew history, the student of western education finds problems of point-of-view. No other history is so carefully documented, authentic or not. Not only is the trustworthiness of the records challengeable, but the material is often contradictory. Available writings from the early years of these people are an aggravating mixture of legend, myth, poetry, history, and didactic pronouncements. Many of the documents which have come down to us were compiled or written by persons removed by centuries from the events which they recorded. Since accurate records were not kept in those early times, the later writings often confuse fact with fancy and truth with nostalgia. Further, the "historians" of early Judaism shaped their past to fit conceptions held at the time of writing, thereby using the past for didactic and propagandistic purposes. The Hebrew was essentially a poet and a teacher, and he saw nothing wrong in using the materials of his tradition to point a lesson or adorn a poetic inspiration.

Out of his collection of folklore, legend, poetry, drama, tall stories of giant heroes and supremely good men and women, moral tales, and accounts of actual happenings, the modern scholar must fashion a story that will, insofar as possible, stand the careful scrutiny of historical criticism.

HISTORY OF THE HEBREWS

BEGINNINGS

Palestine was a small sliver of land some 150 miles long, from Dan, on the north, to Beersheba, on the south, and twenty-five to eighty miles wide. In ancient times it was "a land flowing with milk and honey." The rains were frequent. Wells stored the water and gave it back when needed. The fields were irrigated expertly. Fruits and vegetables grew in abundance. All around the desert threatened, and as time passed and the rains became less, wells were made deeper, and the desert crept in avidly whenever the energies of the people weakened or conquerors moved the farmers from their land.

Far to the east, Ur of the Chaldees was, during the third millennium B.C., the most prosperous and powerful city of all Sumeria. The Hebrews believed that Abraham led a small band out of Ur around 2300 B.C. After wandering for some years as primitive nomads in the deserts, they entered Palestine, conquered the Canaanites who were living there, and, about 2200 B.C., began building for themselves a new life in what to many of them was the "homeland." Here they remained until 1650 B.C., when a number migrated into Egypt for reasons that are not clear. Tradition says that they were in search of grain which their lands had failed to produce.

In Egypt, they are believed to have become menial workmen or slaves. Here they lived, multiplied, and learned the ways of the great civilization that time and imagination had built in this land along the Nile. Then, possibly around 1220 B.C., under the leadership of an Egyptian priest named Moses, who had identified himself with the Hebrews as a missionary giving aid to the "lepers," they left Egypt, wandered in the desert as nomads for a time, and eventually returned to Palestine, where they settled.

YEARS IN THE "NEW" HOMELAND

After their "deliverance" from Egypt, the Hebrews settled in Palestine as farmers and herd-tenders. From Egypt they brought laws of cleanliness adapted from the code governing the priests in that land of their "captivity." Here they began developing rules and regulations fitted to a more ordered society than that of their desert experiences. Woven into these rules and regulations were principles and elements inherited from ancient Babylon and the great Tigris-Euphrates Valley community and from Egypt, as well as influences from their nomadic background.

Although there was among the Hebrews some sense of sameness, they never formed a united nation but remained twelve more or less independent tribes, each organized somewhat as a patriarchal family. Out of experiences of war among the tribes and with neighboring people arose strong men who served as leaders among the elders. Some were priests, others wise men of the people. These were known, in time, as judges. They came to exert considerable influence over the people, and their advice was respected, if not always obeyed.

When the Philistines, a powerful people to the west, threatened, the Hebrews turned to a king, to whom they were willing to give considerable power in spite of the repeated warnings of Samuel. Saul, son of Kish of the tribe of Benjamin, became their first king in 1025 B.C. He and his son, Jonathan, won notable victories over the Philistines. Although Saul reigned as the people's champion for several years, repeated attacks by the Philistines and a bloody internal war of succession led by followers of the young David weakened his power and depressed his spirits. Tradition tells us that in a violent battle with his ancient foe, Saul faced defeat and, when his lieutenants refused to slay him, fell on his own sword, leaving the kingdom to his rival, David. In David, who ruled from 1010 to 974 B.C., we see a brilliant, cruel, lustful man of the people, who, despite his savage tendencies, gave the Hebrews a reign that was destined to become the basis for their Messianic hope. In 974 B.C., David was succeeded by his son, Solomon, who ruled "wisely and justly" until 937 B.C.

Upon the death of Solomon, the ten tribes to the north formed a weak alliance which stood against the two southern tribes. This alliance eventually crystallized into Ephraim (Israel), with a capital at Samaria. The two southern tribes were called Judah, with a capital at Jerusalem.

In 733 B.C., Ephraim allied herself with Syria and began moving on Judah. To protect herself, Judah turned to her neighbor, Assyria, for help. Assyria moved in, captured Damascus, and subjected Syria, Tyre, and much of Palestine to tribute. Soon after, she returned, captured Samaria, and took some 200,000 people of those ten northern tribes as captive slaves. Although Assyria attacked Jerusalem, she was unable to bring it down. This marked the end of the power and influence of the northern tribes and left the two southern tribes to represent the Hebrews in Palestine.

YAHVEH AND HIS PROPHETS

To understand the Hebrew people, one must appreciate the place of religion in their lives and the function of their prophets as self-acclaimed representatives of Yahveh. The very early Hebrews were nomads worshiping objects of nature such as the bull, sheep, serpents, and denizens of the heavens. In their wanderings they came upon an ancient thunder god of Canaan called Yahu, whom they took as their own. Gradually, as they settled in Palestine after their return from Egypt, this Yahu took the form of a national god to whom many of the people gave allegiance.

For generations this national god, who became Yahveh, was very like the people who worshiped him. He had exaggerated human traits, was a lover of war and carnage, vengeful, sensitive to insults, and ruthless in dealing with his enemies. In time, as man's moral sensitivity was sharpened, this god took on a more moral aspect. It has been said that Moses taught Yahveh morals and eventually made him the moral conscience of the people.

With the building of the temple at Jerusalem, Yahveh had a center of worship tied to the civic life of the people. No longer was he to be worshiped along the roadside, in any forest, or by the side of any brook. Now he was at home in Jerusalem, and there his people came to do him honor and ask his forgiveness. Although he became the chief god of the Hebrews, he remained but one among many, stronger perhaps and more to be desired than the others, with a special concern for his own people, but still a god among others. Indeed, some of the people clung to the worship of the primitive gods of their tradition or gave allegiance to one or more of the gods of other people.

This state of affairs did not satisfy the priests of Yahveh. They believed that the god they served should be the only god of all the Hebrews; some saw great personal gain in wealth and power in a strict monotheism. As these priests of Yahveh became a closed social class, passing on the office to their sons, and as this class gained in wealth and power, there was increasing pressure upon the people to abandon all other gods and worship Yahveh alone. The temple at Jerusalem was a strong incentive in this direction.

As the prosperity nurtured in David's reign began to slip away toward the close of Solomon's reign and man divided against man throughout the land of Palestine, there arose a "loyal opposition," the leaders of which were called prophets. Some of these were weird fakirs who cried out against all established life and caught the fancy of the masses by their unorthodox antics. Others were more or less responsible representatives of the depressed masses, speaking out against exploitation, greed, inhumanity, degrading moral standards, and the evidences of social and moral decay that were appearing on all sides. They often represented the rural society and its moral and spiritual virtues against the flourishing industrial city life and its lack of moral fiber.

Amos, for example, was a preacher of the social gospel, crying out against the evils of a society that had forgotten the human in its lust for the material. He sought to make Yahveh the conscience of the people, a conscience that would lift moral idealism above the greed for gain that he found everywhere in the land he loved. Speaking as the voice of Yahveh, he "stood in the gate" and cried out,

> I despise your feast-days . . . . though ye offer me burnt offerings and your meal offerings, I will not accept them. . . . . Take thou away from me the noise of thy songs, for I will not hear the melody of thy viols. But let judgment run down as waters, and righteousness as a mighty stream.

Isaiah, appearing during the siege of Jerusalem, around 702 B.C., denounced economic exploitation and greed, evils of an industrial society, and cried out for man to return to justice, honesty, and love of his fellows. He dreamed of a day when a just ruler would arise to govern with wisdom and understanding.

> With righteousness shall he judge the poor, and decide with equity for the meek of the earth; and he shall smite the earth with the rod of his mouth, and with the breath of his lips shall he slay the wicked. And righteousness shall be the girdle of his waist, and faithfulness the girdle of his loins. . . . And they shall beat their swords into plough-shares, and their spears into pruning-hooks; nation shall not lift up sword against nation, neither shall they learn war any more.

He, and others like him, were endeavoring to change Yahveh from the primitive god of war and vengeance to one of love and hope, a god who championed justice for all his people and who became angry only when these "higher" virtues were denied.

They had little success. The deterioration of social and economic institutions continued, and civil strife became more violent. Yahveh and the voices of his prophets were ignored, while the people turned more and more to foreign gods. The priests of Yahveh decided to make one final stand against the divisive trends everywhere in evidence. In 639 B.C., King Josiah consented to lend his prestige to the endeavor. The plan was elaborate and ingenious. A priest, Hilkiah, announced to the king that he had "found" hidden in the secret archives of the temple a scroll upon which Moses, at Yahveh's dictation, had written laws and commandments for the people. Josiah summoned all the elders of Judah to the temple and there, in the presence of "the multitudes," read the scroll to all who could listen. This, we are told, was the "Book of the Covenant," but we are not told what its contents were. The king, the elders, and all the people, tradition says, swore to be obedient to this law forever.

This book of the people came none too soon. As economic and social conditions deteriorated within, enemies attacked from without. For centuries Palestine had been a prized stretch of land along the trade routes of the east. Whoever controlled this land could collect tribute from lavish caravans and determine the flow of goods between the great empires that arose and struggled with each other in that vast area that reached from the Tigris-Euphrates Valley to the Nile. After Josiah, Judah was subject first to Egypt and then to Babylon. Josiah's successors devised a scheme to throw off the yoke of Babylon by allying themselves with Egypt. Nebuchadnezzar discovered the plot, turned his vengeance upon Palestine, captured Jerusalem, placed Zedekiah on the throne of Judah, and took 10,000 Hebrews as slaves. When Zedekiah turned against Babylon in one final effort to gain freedom for his people, the now thoroughly angered Nebuchadnezzar poured the elite of his armed forces into the land, recaptured Jerusalem, burned the city along with its temple, brutally killed Zedekiah and his sons, and carried what was left of the population away to become slaves in Babylon.

This was the most bitter defeat in all the history of the Hebrew people, but not unexpected. They had heard Jeremiah cry out against the social evils of the city and its people. They had listened to his prophecy that Yahveh was bitterly angry and would, in time, use the Babylonians as his instrument of chastisement. The people did not obey. The Babylonians came and conquered, and the star of David sank beneath the horizon.

EXILE AND REPATRIATION

The early years in Babylon were bitter years for most of the exiles. Their temple was in ashes, and their god was far away. Out of this suffering of a people in an alien land came one of the most beautiful poems of all times:

> By the rivers of Babylon, there we sat down, yea, we wept, when we
>   remembered Zion.
> We hanged our harps upon the willows in the midst thereof.
> For there they that carried us away captive required of us a song; and
>   they that wasted us required of us mirth, saying,
> Sing us one of the songs of Zion.
> How shall we sing the Lord's song in a strange land?
> If I forget thee, O Jerusalem, let my right hand forget her cunning.
> If I do not remember thee, let my tongue cleave to the roof of my
>   mouth; if I prefer not Jerusalem above my chief joy.
>   *(Ps. 137, vss. 1–6)*

Ezekiel, the prophet of the exile, continued to hammer at the lesson taught by Jeremiah. He warned that the sins of the people were great, and Yahveh was angry. But there was a note of hope in his voice. Repentence and a determination to live by the moral law of Yahveh would, he promised, insure a return to Jerusalem and a second chance for the people. Yahveh was pictured by him as a forgiving god who had to chastise his people, whom he loved and for whom he planned better days.

When Cyrus of Persia conquered Babylon in 539 B.C., he gave the Hebrews the right to return to Jerusalem and rebuild their nation. For fifty years they had lived among the Babylonians. The great majority had found the living good and had no wish to abandon it for the uncertainties of a homeland over which others had become master. However, there were a few, whom one may think of as ancient Zionists, who still yearned for Jerusalem and preached the rebuilding of the temple and the hope of a nation all their own. Thus, more than two years after Cyrus gave them permission to leave, a small band of zealots set out from Babylon for Jerusalem. The trip was difficult and the settlers in Palestine did not welcome these invaders. The years ahead were rough, but Prince Zerubbabel and the Persian king, Darius I, gave them help, so that by 520 B.C., a new temple was completed and Jerusalem became again a Hebrew city.

HOME FROM EXILE

Fifty years is a long time to be away from home and in another land, especially if that other land is rich, prosperous, and alive with dreams of the future. Many of those who returned to Jerusalem had been born in Babylon. Others had left Palestine as children, and memories of life there were dim. Only a very few, and they were old, remembered the past vividly. Most of those returning brought with them much that was Babylonian and infused it into the new Jerusalem. But they did reach back into the past for something that would stabilize and unite the people: the book.

Persia was their master. A military state was out of the question since Judea lacked both wealth and numbers to build a strong army. Nevertheless, the Hebrews needed a binding force that would hold the people together in national unity. The answer was a theocratic state. With the temple completed, the population they found in Palestine subdued, and social and economic life restored, Ezra, a learned priest, around 444 B.C., assembled the people of Jerusalem and "from morn to midday" read to them the "Book of Law of Moses" much as Josiah had read the "Book of the Covenant" many years before. At the end of the reading the priests and the leaders of the people took a solemn oath to live by this "holy constitution" and obey its laws forever. From then until now the book has been the uniting factor in Hebrew life. This became the heart of the new Judaism and the Hebrew state became a theocracy, the people legalistic.

After the exile, Palestine remained a Persian outpost subject to the ebb and flow of world forces that shaped events in the Mediterranean area during the fifth and fourth centuries B.C. As the Macedonian empire began to take shape under Philip and his son Alexander, as Greek trade and Greek culture seeped eastward, the Persian power was shaken, and men of perception knew that the old was crumbling. There was resistance to this penetration of alien ideas and ways of living, but to little avail. Then, in 334 B.C., Alexander conquered Jerusalem, and the floodgates of Greek culture were opened. A Hellenistic party was organized in the city to transform it into a Greek outpost. Greek physical training was introduced, and the Greek language was taught everywhere. With this Hellenistic culture came licentiousness, debauchery, skepticism, and disregard of ancient religious teachings. Orthodox Hebrews fought this trend with all the intensity they could muster. A Pietistic party was formed to "purify" Hebrew life and call the people back to the ancient precepts and folkways. But a people seldom go back. Touched by new ideas from Babylon and now from Greece and the Hellenistic world, the Hebrews were irrevocably changed. Around 150 B.C. they translated their Bible into Greek, giving to the world the laws, legends, folk tales, moral teachings, and literature upon which it would build a new religion, Christianity.

HEBREW EDUCATION

BEFORE 1200 B.C.

Early education among the ancestors of the Hebrews was much like that of any primitive people. There were no formal schools; life itself served as the child's school and teacher. He learned by living in the group and participating in its activities. His parents instructed him in the skills they knew and wished him to master. When he was ready, the elders of his people gave him that instruction necessary for assuming adult responsibilities and privileges. This entire program of education must have included the crafts in which his people were proficient, skills of tracking and obtaining food, magical procedures needed to deal effectively with the unseen forces and powers of his environment, and the folklore of his tradition. The education of this period was wholly practical and tied closely to survival in both the material and social environment.

Undoubtedly, the Hebrew was tremendously influenced by the culture which he found in Egypt. Some may have even attended the schools of that country and learned to read and write. We have clear evidence that some Hebrews attained high positions in Egypt and were respected by the kings and their courts.

IN PALESTINE TO THE EXILE

Education during the nomadic years was no different from that of the "captivity" in Egypt. Informality was the method, with possibly some direct family instruction in the traditions of the people. Here the family remained the chief educational institution, and learning was all a part of living.

Once back in Palestine, the educational picture changed materially. Here it became the task of the leaders to shape into a united group a people whose spiritual identity had been severely threatened by generations of bondage to an alien culture. A tradition had to be developed, along with some real sense of national destiny. In time the experience of deliverance from Egypt, its fact and its folklore, developed into the needed tradition. All could look backward in time to those bitter but romantic days when Yahveh had delivered his people from their oppressors.

Involved deeply in this development was education, both on the family level and on that of the community. For generations the law was oral, the mores and customs of the people strengthened by experience and passed on from parent to child. But it was no less binding. The writing down of the law and the teaching of it from a book was a stage in its development, it was in no sense the beginning. The "Book of the Covenant" and the "Book of the Law of Moses" were compilations of laws and customs whose origins had been lost in antiquity. Schools were organized to teach these only when it was no longer possible to transmit them orally and informally.

This was also true regarding the sense of national destiny. A child might learn from his elders that his tribe was the strongest and that his way of living was best, but it took far more than informal living to come to the conviction that one's destiny was to carry to all the world a model code of laws and a way of living and thinking that is righteous and just. This necessitated schools, great leaders who could teach the people, and places where all might come to learn. In the case of the Hebrews, it meant that education became an integral part of religion, for what was to be taught was the people's religion in its broadest aspects.

Although schools were developed in Palestine and what the community deemed worthwhile was taught, the child lived in an environment that was intentionally educative. Monuments of stone and other materials were everywhere throughout the land memorializing great events in Hebrew history. The year was punctuated by sacred feasts commemorating important happenings or offering opportunity for the people to renew their dedication to their ideals and their god. In many of these the child was given a distinctive role to play. He was woven into family or group activity so that its meaning was brought home to him most vividly. Periodically the priests and Levites would assemble all the people, old and young, to hear the law and their interpretations. Women and children, as well as men, were among those listening and absorbing the tradition that had produced these laws. The total life in which the child grew was a school for his learning.

In the school and in the life about him the child learned religion, for religion was for the Hebrew the whole of life. He also learned a craft. It was unthinkable to the Hebrew that any boy, rich or poor, high or low class, would reach manhood without a craft to support himself. All the great leaders were craftsmen, as were the men of the streets. In addition, every boy learned the law. This basic foundation of Hebrew life was tied in with his religion as well as with his daily existence. Another element in Hebrew education was music. They were a singing people. Their history was replete with singers and musicians. Their great king, David, was a singer of sweet songs and a master of the harp. He organized musical life on a grand scale and was credited with composing many songs. The child was taught very early to sing and play an instrument so that he might take part in the life of the people and entertain himself and his friends.

Writing was becoming important in Palestine as early as the eighth century B.C., and, if we are to believe Isaiah, it was being taught to children as early as that time. But it was never thought to be of value to all. As a tool, it was confined to those who used it, the scribes. They became a special class in Hebrew society, privileged in that they possessed a skill much needed by rulers and businessmen as well as by priests and other religious functionaries. As Hebrew life became more complex and contacts with other people grew, writing increased in importance, and those who mastered its intricacies were honored and became prosperous.

With the rise of the prophets in Palestine came a need for some specialized education that would fit them for their function in society. Schools appeared to train "sons of the prophets." Since these were more or less informal and voluntary learning and teaching groupings, the term school may not fit them accurately. They usually consisted of a prophet and those young men who were attracted to him and wished to identify themselves with his reputation. In time, communities of prophets are known to have taken form and to have attracted large numbers of pupils. These communities taught the means of inducing prophetic ecstasy, the law, prayers, meditation, and rituals of worship. Samuel is believed to have founded such a school at Ramah, and other schools are known to have existed at Bethel, Gilgal, Jericho, Carmel, Gibeon, and Samaria.

In Palestine After the Exile

During the exile in Babylon, the Hebrews came in contact with a culture much superior to the one they had known in Palestine. Further, they made the transition from a predominantly agricultural people to denizens of prosperous and thriving towns. Although there were prophets crying out against evil and trying desperately to keep alive in the people's minds and hearts the memory and spirit of their homeland, priests and scribes became far more important. They gave to the people what was most needed in this land of exile but also of opportunity. When they returned from exile, these priests and scribes, teachers of the law and "the God of Heaven." became central in the new life in Palestine. It was the scribes, a combination of copyist, lawyer, and interpreter, who became the first professional teachers of the Hebrews. In time we find them organizing a sort of literary guild. Those inducted into this organization were highly trained and well versed in the law. Their education was carefully directed and covered several years of intensive and extensive preparation. No longer could one fresh from the plow and smelling of the barnyard appear in the city to teach the people and call them to obedience to Yahveh. This was now the function of the scribes and the priests. With their rise, the law became central in Hebrew life, countering the prophetic tradition that had ruled for so many generations. Jesus, representing the ancient prophetic tradition, challenged a culture that lived by the law. The legalists would punish severely all those who broke the law; Jesus told those without sin to throw the first stone.

While in exile the Hebrews were in danger of being absorbed into the culture they found there. Indeed, many of the young men, knowing nothing at first hand of their "homeland," became part of this new civilization willingly and happily. It soon became the task of the leaders to keep alive the memory of the past and to hold the exiles together in a tight little group in expectation of a return. Thus there developed in Babylon a place of meeting and worship called the synagogue. Here the books of the law were read to the people. Here they assembled to listen to their leaders talk of Yahveh and his promises. Here they found companionship and friends, a social and community life that helped to keep them distinct from their captors.

An elementary school developed within the synagogue where children were taught to read and write and to understand simple parts of the law. This institution began sometime in the third century B.C. as an answer to a need of the people. It grew in importance as its functions were increased. In time, the synagogue became a place where the scribes taught the law to all the people. Thus a "house of books" became part of the synagogue, a library and place of general education.

After the return from exile, the synagogue increased in importance. It became a center of worship and education. Scholars estimate that by 69 A.D., when Jerusalem was destroyed, no less than 400 synagogues were functioning in the city, and they were scattered in equal profusion throughout Palestine.

Sometime during the fifth century B.C. the Pentateuch—the books of Genesis, Exodus, Leviticus, Numbers, and Deuteronomy—was written down and became the heart of all Hebrew education. Students in the synagogue memorized great sections of this material in Hebrew and listened to discussions of its open and its hidden meanings. Gradually, education of the Hebrew child was becoming a matter of instruction in a book and his religion that of a book.

When, during the fourth century B.C., the people gave up Hebrew as their spoken language and turned to Aramaic, it became increasingly necessary to teach the scribes and priests the old language in which the law and other sacred works were written. Thus, instruction in Hebrew, as the language of learning, became the chief concern of schools and other educational agencies charged with the education of older boys looking to these professions.

By the third century B.C., the flood of Hellenistic culture that was engulfing the Mediterranean world reached Palestine and challenged the national culture of the people. Many wanted to turn Jerusalem into a Greek city and transform their education into a pattern more like that of the world about them. In response to this stimulus a new literature was produced, the wisdom literature, that dealt with profound social and philosophical problems. Interest turned from the books of the Mosaic law to Job, Proverbs, and Ecclesiastes. In the schools young men were turning from learning the ancient law to struggling with questions of the meaning of life, problems of suffering and prosperity, the wisdom of practical concern.

For many this trend was evil, subversive, destructive of all that was holy and right. The Pietistic party fought to maintain traditional education and protect youth from these alien ideologies. To an extent it was successful. Hebrew nationalism was reasserted, the law was returned to the schools, and the social and moral wisdom of Hellenistic penetration was subordinated. By the first century B.C., elementary schools giving instruction in reading and writing to young children were appearing in Palestine outside the synagogue. Older boys attended "academies," where they studied the oral and written literature of the Hebrew religion. Following this, a few might go on to prepare for the offices of scribe or priest. Some arithmetic and, probably, sacred music were taught in these schools. Trade education was left to the parents.

The methods used for teaching children and older boys in these schools was a combination of memorization and disputation. The pupil was expected to master the material being studied. Mastery meant ability to give it back word for word. Neither teacher nor pupil asked what should be. Their concern was with what was and had been. Failure to study or to learn was punishable by beatings and insults. Cruelty was the teacher's weapon and its results the child's motivation. It is true that some teachers did use persuasion and religious precepts, but they were in the minority.

Tradition records that Simon ben Shetach, around 75 B.C., instituted a set of reforms in education designed to spread elementary learning more widely among the people. He even made a brave attempt to institute compulsory education in Palestine. This goal was realized when Rabbi Joshua ben Gamala, in a decree of 64 A.D., made elementary education compulsory. He ordained that "teachers of young children should be appointed in each district and each town, and the children should enter school at the age of six or seven."

Although the concept of the child in the Hebrew mind changed during the centuries from primitive times to the Roman conquest, there was a fairly definite theory of the nature of the immature that pervaded Hebrew thought during historic times. This included a belief that the child was naturally willful, foolish, wild, and possibly bad. As such he needed constant discipline if he was to be trained to obedience and respect. *Ecclesiasticus* expresses this cogently: "A horse not broken becometh headstrong; and a child left to himself will be willful." *Proverbs* accents this: "A whip for the horse, a bridle for the ass, and a rod for the fool's back," and "Foolishness is bound in the heart of a child; but the rod of correction shall drive it far from him." Thus, for the Hebrew, education meant rigorous discipline by which moral and religious training could be assured. Although the father had a natural love for his child, he realized that his first duty was to save him from evil ways. The rod was applied not in wrath but in an earnest belief that such was the obligation of the father for the salvation of his child. By this method the parent and the teacher sought to instill in the child reverence for what was highest and best, respect for what was superior. For the Hebrew, strict discipline was the way of learning, knowledge, and wisdom.

HEBREW EDUCATIONAL STRUCTURE

Based on this theory, and growing out of the experiences of the Hebrew people, was an educational structure that served their needs and acculturated the youth. In this the education of the pre-school child was most important. This began at birth. Very early he learned to recite prayers, verses of scripture, proverbs, psalms, and simple material from sacred writings. As soon as possible he was taught the meanings of feasts, rituals, and customs of his people. Brighter children were taught to read, if their parents had any facility with this skill.

Between six and ten years of age the boy attended the elementary school in the synagogue, where he came under the tutelage of a scribe who taught him the written law. His textbook was the Pentateuch and his task was to memorize as much of it as possible. In addition, he learned reading, writing, and arithmetic.

At ten he passed from the elementary school of the synagogue to the Beth-hammidrash or "house of the Midrash," where he began study of the oral law and prepared for that day when he was to become a "son of the law" at about twelve or thirteen. From this day forward he was expected to obey the law and suffer all penalties prescribed for failure in this adult responsibility. He usually remained in the Beth-hammidrash until his fifteenth birthday. Then, if his parents could afford it, he was placed in the hands of a scribe who taught him further in the law and commentaries. Some boys attached themselves to individual scribes or to schools of scribes for training in the intricacies of the profession of scribe and teacher. The most famous of these advanced teachers were Hillel, Shammai, and Gamaliel.

Although Jerusalem was the center of this higher education, most of the cities of Palestine had scribes and schools of scribes prepared to carry the youth's education as far as he wished.

Before the exile, women in Palestine were equal to men and their education was similar. This equality was challenged in Babylon, and the returning exiles had learned the ways of their captors. In post-exilic Palestine, education of women was almost wholly domestic and in the home. Here we see creeping into Hebrew life the oriental idea of the subordination of women. However, although the education available to boys was more or less closed to girls, the Hebrew always respected his women highly, and his literature abounds with stories of their wisdom and skill.

IN CONCLUSION

As one studies the history of the Hebrews, he is impressed by the fact that, in many ways, their life was preparation for their future. They lost their freedom, but found themselves in a book which they began compiling during this freedom. Gradually they produced a tradition, a book, and a religion that have been able to hold them in a bond of unity through centuries of dispersion everywhere in the world. They fashioned an education by which they could pass on this tradition, this book, and this religion to their young wherever they might be. Even today, although the Hebrew is to be found everywhere and has taken on much of the culture of those among whom he lives, he is still one with his like everywhere. He has his house of worship, his book, and his god, which unite him with other Hebrews regardless of outward appearances. This is one of the miracles of history.

CHAPTER 4
Among the Early Greeks

INTRODUCTION

When Aristotle wrote his treatise on the constitutions of the Greek states, he found 158 worthy of careful study. Obviously our analysis of life and education among the early Greeks will not include all of these. For our purpose only two are of value: Sparta and Athens. These, in the first place, present a contrast between two distinct types of education, Sparta for military strength and Athens for full development of the individual. In the second place, these are roots of modern western educational thought and practice, Sparta the totalitarian and Athens the democratic.

In this study we shall avoid a mistake so often made by writers in the field, that of ignoring the time perspective. One may write a history of the Greek lands, or he may write a history of the Greek people. If he chooses the lands, he must begin his story with the islands of the Aegean and the shoreline of Asia Minor before 3000 B.C., move later to the Greek peninsula, and on to the world of Alexander the Great. If, however, he elects to write about the people, he will begin with the Dorian invasions, during the twelfth and eleventh centuries B.C., of the Peloponnesus and the Aegean Islands, and end with the Roman conquest of the Greek world. Whichever approach one takes, he will cover many centuries during which both lands and people changed from one specific pattern of culture to another several times, and life and education went through evolution and many revolutions.

To concentrate attention exclusively on the Persian wars and the Peloponnesian struggle between Athens and Sparta, leading to the Alexandrian conquest, as many have done, is to paint a false picture.

The Athenian was, in terms of western values, the Greek at his best. This is the Greek we usually read about in history and story. The Spartan, again according to western values, was the Greek at his worst. To pit the one against the other makes for good drama and easy understanding but is bad history. Both were end results of social evolution, a long and involved process of adaptation and change reaching back into the prehistoric. If the student is to gain an adequate perspective from which to view both, he must travel again this road of history and see why Sparta produced the almost-perfect soldier and Athens the highly creative minds of Plato and Aristotle.

We shall attempt to analyze both Sparta and Athens as two concepts of the good life which grew from pre-Minoan times to those of Alexander. We shall pass judgment on neither, recognizing that all judgments so made must be based on the value structure of the one making the judgment. We shall look at each in terms of its own value pattern, measuring its education against the aims which it accepted as good.

MINOAN AND MYCENAEAN CULTURES
(before 3000 to 1200 B.C.)

Scholars are constantly pushing prehistoric Greece further and further into the past. Although a century or more ago historians were dating Greek history from the first Olympiad, 776 B.C., today they find that they must go back at least to the third millennium B.C.

Archaeologists are convinced that a fairly primitive people occupied the Greek peninsula and the shoreline and islands of the Aegean before 3000 B.C. It is not known whether they were native or invaders replacing a still earlier population in a hitherto unknown past.

The earliest known invaders developed a high type of culture with Crete as its center. They organized themselves into a loose federation of cities with a king and an army, borrowed ideas and skills from Egypt and the Middle East, and maintained a relatively high degree of prosperity. Their culture is called Minoan. It flourished from before 3000 to around 1200 B.C. During these millennia, Crete became the pivot of a "civilization" commanding great material resources, producing an art comparable in many respects to that of the age of Peisistratus, and developing a thriving trade with people as far away as the Mesopotamian valley.

If we look backward for a moment, we find Argolis, on the Greek mainland, occupied by a Neolithic people of unknown origin. Sometime before the third millennium B.C., invaders from the Aegean islands and southwest Asia Minor moved into the Greek mainland and built a village atop a natural rock citadel standing in the northern corner of the Argive plain. This they named Mycenae.

EDUCATION BEFORE HOMER

The major portion of our evidence about Minoan and Mycenaean cultures is archaeological. While some mention is made of this very early period of Greek history by Homer, we must be somewhat skeptical of this source. Scholars have recently begun to decipher the ancient writing of these people, but no clear picture of their life and times is yet available.

During more than two millennia, the early people of the Aegean islands and the Greek peninsula developed language, created many kinds of art, built governments and organized themselves into patterns of social and economic life, fought wars on sea and land, built houses and palaces that challenge the ingenuity of modern architects, and thought out religions and philosophies that were controversial and intellectually challenging.

From these facts one must conclude that these people discovered ways of passing on to the young their skills, mores, and values. The children most certainly picked up much of this by just living with their elders and watching them at work and play. Parents must have taught their children many things consciously and by example. There must have been rites and ceremonies in which both children and adults participated in the process of acculturation. And, certain individuals must have devoted at least part of their time to teaching the young. These may have been religious functionaries, skilled craftsmen who took apprentices, and artists who accepted pupils. There may have been schools, places designed specifically to teach writing and reading, counting and figuring, and other phases of the intellectual and cultural wealth of the people.

THE ACHAEANS   (1300-1100 B.C.)

During the fourteenth and thirteenth centuries B.C., a Greek tribe, called Achaean, gradually infiltrated south from Thessaly into the Peloponnesus, mingled with the people there, including the Mycenaeans, and, by 1250 B.C., became rulers of Greek lands. They brought with them their language, Greek, and their religion, worship of the gods of Olympus, and imposed both upon the people they conquered.

During the years that followed they absorbed much from the cultures they found, although they were never able to attain the level of refinement or breadth of interest of the Mycenaeans. Thus, even though the culture which eventually developed was a mixture of native and invader, it was more crude, more brutal, more immoral than that of the Mycenaeans.

The *Iliad* and the *Odyssey,* the final writing of the Homeric legends, tell us of the Achaeans and their adventures. Since these poems are at least three centuries older than the period with which we are concerned, we must look at the Homeric account with a high degree of skepticism. However, since this is all we have to go by, we can only say that this is what the compilers of the Homeric poems believed the age to be.

In Achaean society the mother was the child's first teacher, instilling in him the manners, morals, and traditions of his family, clan, and tribe. There was no formal education, no teaching of letters, spelling, grammar, or counting. What of this the child needed he picked up as he grew. There were no books available. Girls were taught the arts of the home.

As boys grew older, their fathers taught them the skills of the chase and of war. From direct teaching, usually by the father, and by just living and growing in the society, the boy learned to fish, trap, farm, swim, handle animals, and fight. He learned very early how to take care of himself in his cruel and bloody society.

What little writing there was concerned only the scribes and merchants. They learned this skill from others of their professions. Since the great masses had no need for writing, it was not part of their education. They learned what was necessary for living, which could be learned accidentally by living among one's fellows or from his parents.

SPARTA: EDUCATION FOR MILITARY STRENGTH

Before Lycurgus

Among those who were to shape the destinies of Greece were the Spartans, dwellers on the plains of Laconia. Encrusted with myth, folklore, and legend, the history of these people is difficult to trace. As scholars have penetrated beneath this mass of untruth and half-truth, they have concluded that somewhere around the twelfth century B.C., the Dorians, warriors from the mountains of northern Greece, moved southward in a series of migrations, crossed the Corinthian Gulf, and pushed into Laconia where they conquered the non-Dorian population. They established their government at Argos and settled themselves in small villages through Lacedemonia. Eventually five villages, with a population of some 70,000, were brought together to compose their stronghold, Sparta.

War was their life and conquest their occupation. Driven to live the only life they knew, they subjugated the entire area, extending their rule to all the valley that lay between the Parnon Range and Taygetus mountains, a valley through which ran the Eurotas River. Then they moved out to spread their rule over most of the Peloponnesus. When, in the latter part of the eighth century B.C., they subdued the Messenians, they took thousands as slaves and laid a heavy annual tribute upon those who were left.

The invading Dorians and those non-Dorians whom they mastered slowly built the early Spartan culture, a mixture of what they brought and what they found already existing in Laconia and the Peloponnesus. Eventually a society with three clearly-defined levels took shape. At the top were the invaders who sought to maintain their uniqueness, dominating all others, the master class. These were the citizens, with all civil rights and responsibilities. The next class below these was the perioeci, or "Dwellers Around," freemen living in surrounding towns and mountain villages. They were taxed by the master class, gave military service when called, and worked as merchants and traders in the culture. They had no part in the government and were prohibited from marrying into the master class. Third in the social pattern were the helots, or slaves, the non-Dorian population which the invaders conquered, citizens of villages and cities overcome and reduced to slavery.

Before Lycurgus, these helots resembled serfs of medieval times or unskilled laborers in many parts of the world today. They were free to marry, have children, work the land on which they lived as they saw fit, enjoy village or community life, and worship their gods with rite and ceremony as they wished. They were bound to the soil, but neither they nor the soil could be sold. Each year they were required to pay a set fee to the owners of the land. Many served as domestics in the cities. Others attended their masters in war, fought for the state, and, if they conducted themselves well in battle and showed exceptional loyalty, might be given their freedom.

Having no status in the culture, helots were subject to martial law, remained constantly under surveillance of the secret police, and might be taken and killed at any time without show of cause or trial. Indeed, in spite of their modicum of freedom, helots were the restless masses, the have-nots, feared by the master class which used them but never trusted them.

Until the conquest of Messenia, when the helot population was doubled, Sparta was much like any other Greek city. It prided itself on its choral music and the teachers and composers who resided within its borders. Alcman, from Lydia, was the "hit song" writer of the seventh century B.C., immortalizing women and drinking in his ballads. Laconian pottery was famous, and the bronze work of Lacedemonia was prized throughout Greece and the Aegean islands.

Then Sparta set out upon one hundred years of intermittent war with Messenia. The first phase of the struggle extended from 725 to 705 B.C. After sixty years of an uneasy truce and galling tribute, Messenia attempted to free herself from the yoke of Sparta only to be crushed beyond recovery. Her land was divided among the Spartans and her citizens made helots.

It has been estimated that, at the time of this second Messenian war, 640-631 B.C., there were in Sparta and the surrounding areas some 32,000 Spartans—men, women, and children—who constituted the master class. The male citizens of this group were rulers of some 120,-000 perioeci and 224,000 helots. The Spartan citizens sat on a powder keg of discontent and unrest, and the only way they knew to handle the situation was to make of themselves a powerful standing army able at any moment to crush rebellion and keep the masses "in their place." Gone was the easy, free life of early Sparta, the love of music and the arts, and the friendly attitude toward those helots who served close to their masters. It was to Lycurgus that the Spartan turned for his salvation.

THE CODE OF LYCURGUS

Although most chronicles of ancient Greece accept Lycurgus as the first lawgiver of Sparta, their testimony is so conflicting and many of their accounts so apocryphal that we must approach with extreme caution this now legendary figure of Spartan history. "Authorities" place him anywhere from the ninth to the sixth century B.C. Further, if one turns to other cultures of the ancient world, including the Hebraic, he discovers legends of personal lawgivers dated during this period. Probably the code of laws which Sparta accepted after the Messenian wars was a codification of mores and customs from more ancient times reduced to writing by many hands and attributed to some legendary leader to whom the name Lycurgus was given.

Whether this theory be truth or not, the fact is that after the second Messenian war, Sparta faced social and economic problems which resulted in significant changes in the body politic and the ways of life and thought. What came to be called the Code of Lycurgus established a society dominated by the ideal of military strength and devoted to production of the finest soldiers possible.

EDUCATION OF THE SOLDIER

Sparta was an aristocratic, military state devoted to maintaining the privileged status of the citizen. All its institutions, including education, were designed to serve this end. In Sparta, the child belonged to the state, and the state accepted its responsibility by providing a complete educational system for him, a system which it controlled absolutely. The aim of this education was to make the child into the image desired by the state. The means of attaining this end was a regimen both cruel and efficient, a regimen that began at birth and ended only with death.

In a way, Spartan education began before birth. The state insisted that only the physically and emotionally fit marry and produce children. Then, when the child was born, it was presented to the *ephors,* or government administrators, who judged its fitness to live and be educated for citizenship. Those judged unfit were taken to a designated hillside, there to die or be rescued by perioeci or helots and reared as they desired. The fit were returned to their mothers who, as state nurses, reared them until the age of seven.

The early education of the child was in the home and was the responsibility of the mother. This consisted in learning very early to endure pain, be resourceful, accept want and privation, and enjoy exercises designed to toughen and strengthen the body. While yet a child, the boy was taken often to the men's club house to hear conversation and be exposed to the example of his elders. All this early education was careful indoctrination in the ideals and mores of Spartan life.

At seven, the boy was placed in a state boarding school. From this time on his education was the sole responsibility of the Spartan community, supervised carefully by the *paidonomus,* or state superintendent of schools. There he was among others who were to learn with him all the duties and skills of a citizen. He became a member of a band, usually sixty-four boys, with which he was to identify himself completely. The bravest among the group served as "herd leader." Each band was the special responsibility of an *eirene,* a young man over twenty who had to account to the state for the behavior of each boy.

The aim of education during this stage of growth was to develop a feeling of equality, comradeship, *esprit de corps.* Boys were forced to endure hardships. Their living and clothing were scant. They were taught to forage and hunt, to take care of themselves, to know the country and its demands, and to be resourceful at all times. They were whipped often, both as punishment and as a test of endurance. Fighting was encouraged as a form of exercise and a method of hardening the body. The boys' training, in addition, included dancing (as a military exercise), gymnastics, ballplaying, and a rigid schedule of other physical exercises. In all this the work was graded so as not to overtax the growing boy or hurt him physically or psychologically.

The Spartan system of education, at this level, was frankly brutalizing. In dances and choral work, military maneuvers were simulated to make the boys clever on their feet when fighting. Music and literature occupied a very subordinate place in the Spartan curriculum. Some training in music was given as a means of social and moral education for the soldier-citizen. The solemn Doric rhythms were used to inspire courage, obedience, respect for law, and self-control. Neither reading nor writing was taught, though some learned these arts privately. The Spartan disliked oratory, feeling that it was a sign of intemperance. He preferred "laconic" brevity. Some attention was given to poetry, to Homer, war songs, and ballads, insofar as they portrayed bravery and loyalty to the state. Memory was stressed as the best method of learning.

When the boy reached eighteen, he was deemed ready for strenuous military training, to which he would devote himself for the next twelve years. Bands of young men were sent out on maneuvers. Often they ambushed helots as practice for warfare. At twenty the youth took the oath of allegiance to the state, and at thirty be became a citizen, if he had proved himself worthy in all tests and performances. He was then obligated to sit in the public assembly, attend public barracks, and serve as teacher of the boys.

When the Spartan, at thirty, became a citizen, he was compelled to marry for the good of the state. He was supposed to pick a wife adequately prepared physically and psychologically to bear him children who would be efficient and effective soldiers or mothers of soldiers. Although he maintained a home for his wife and children, he spent most of his time in the public barracks as a member of the standing army, fighting for the state or supervising the education of the boys. To guard against a father's favoritism toward his own son, the state declared that all boys born over a certain period were sons of all the fathers who had sons during that time, and the men were equally responsible for all these boys. Family life and parental affection, as we know them today, were discouraged in the interest of undivided loyalty to the state.

THE SPARTAN IN LATER LIFE

When the citizen reached forty-five, he was relieved of strenuous campaigning and assigned to the "home guard." His duties were confined to local military activities and the education of the youths. At sixty, an age which very few reached since the average age of males at that time was twenty-five, he became an elder statesman, eligible to serve in the council and obligated to give wise advice to leaders of the state and to youths. Until his death, the Spartan was an instrument of the state, to do its bidding and serve its interests.

An Evaluation of Spartan Education

When we remember that the aim of Spartan education was to train the superior soldier to defend and strengthen the Spartan state and the position of its citizenry, we must recognize that the system, as developed by the leaders of Sparta, was a phenomenal success. Efficient and effective soldiers were trained, and long after other Greek states had lost their independence, Sparta was unconquered. Through her education, Sparta was able to maintain group unity and solidarity amid a general wave of individuality that inundated and finally destroyed much of Greece.

If, however, we weigh Spartan education in terms of its contribution to human welfare or in terms of its furthering democratic freedom and individual creativeness, it was a miserable failure. When Sparta became mistress of Greece, she was unable to rule wisely or with vision. She had built for war so skillfully that she was unable to function in times of peace. Her men were soldiers, not statesmen. She followed to its logical conclusion the ideal of effective education for a military state. In this she subordinated the individual to the welfare of the state so completely and thoroughly that he identified himself with the state and had no feeling that he was being repressed. He and his state were one.

ATHENS: EDUCATION FOR DEMOCRATIC LIVING

Early History

Attica, one of the smaller peninsulas of mainland Greece, was a rugged, inhospitable land. In its protected valleys and along its rocky coastline lay dozens of small cities. Living on a soil difficult to farm, with the sea never far away, and with safe harbors in abundance, the people of Attica were by circumstance traders. Shrewd, clever, and not overly scrupulous in their dealings, they were more successful than their competitors. Thus, they won the markets of the Aegean and brought wealth to their treasuries and power to their rulers.

Sometime in the prehistory of Attica, Ionians, a mixture of Pelasgo-Mycenaeans and Achaeans, fleeing invading hordes from the north, entered the area and intermarried with the population they found there. These refugees were received hospitably and became part of a single Attic stock, keen, vigorous, highly intelligent, and jealously proud of their land and accomplishments.

At the dawn of history we find these people organized in terms of blood relationships. The core of this pattern was the family, represented by its head or eldest male. Each thirty heads of families constituted a clan or *gente,* thirty clans a brotherhood or *phratry,* and three brotherhoods a *tribe.* There were in Attica four tribes or units of social relationships. In times of danger or military adventures the people were mobilized as clans and fought under their clan leaders. This arrangement crystallized an aristocracy of old and powerful families which resisted for generations all attempts at establishing a democracy.

Around 700 B.C., the cities of Attica were welded into a single political organization with Athens as its capital. This city, five miles inland from the port of Piraeus, had grown around an ancient Mycenaean acropolis. All the landowners of Attica were its citizens. The oldest families, those with the largest land holdings, held the greatest power. In times of disorder or threatened danger the people tolerated a king, who was empowered to lead the military forces. When the danger was over and peace and stability restored, the aristocracy dictated policy to the central government. Later the king was replaced by nine *archons,* each responsible for certain designated functions of the state. However, the real power rested with the well-born ruling few, the *oligarchs.*

EARLY ATHENIAN EDUCATION

There is evidence to indicate that schools were part of Attic life long before the days of Solon. The very fact that, by the sixth century B.C., Solon thought it necessary to include in his codification of Athenian law regulations governing schools proves that they were an accepted part of the social pattern. Chief among the regulations incorporated into Solon's code were that: (1) the state pledged to pay the tuition in private schools for boys whose fathers had died while fighting in the armed services; (2) parents had to see that their sons learned to read, write, and swim; and (3) a public supervisor of schools was appointed. Other laws dealt with the size of schools, hours when they might open and close, who should be admitted and how, the assignment and duties of pedagogues, contacts during school hours between the boys and older men, and access to the public gymnasium.

All these laws and regulations, it would appear, dealt with private schools. Since there is no indication that the state owned or supported schools, we can safely assume that all education in early Attica was private. Further, there is no evidence that children were required to attend school. While the state was interested in their having a basic education, it permitted parents to decide how and where they would be taught.

By the fifth century B.C., a pattern of education is evident in Attica. At its base was an "elementary" education divided among three teachers. The *grammatist* taught the child to read and write. Although his emphasis was on literary studies, at times he added arithmetic to his offerings. The *citharist* taught the child music. This included skill in playing the lyre, singing, chanting, and dancing. The aim was to develop a sense of rhythm and melody and prepare the boy to take part in various civic and religious festivals which dotted the Athenian calendar. Often the teaching of letters and music was combined under one instructor or under two instructors in one building. The *paedotribe,* or teacher of gymnastics, was the most popular. He aimed to develop grace, stamina, and good health habits.

Each teacher established himself in a community and sought to develop a clientele. Parents selected those teachers who appealed to them most, paid the required fee, and demanded results. The boy left home for school, accompanied by his pedagogue, before sunrise and did not return until after sunset. Although school occupied the boy's time seven days a week throughout the year, there were a great many religious and civic holidays to break this routine. All teaching was on an individual basis, class instruction not having been developed.

The purpose of this "elementary" education was to give a boy a grounding in that which fitted him to participate in the activities of a citizen and serve his state well. Although designed in theory for all Attic youth, only the wealthy upper classes attended these schools. They could pay the fees of the teachers and had the leisure and wealth to aspire to positions of responsibility in the state. The masses could not afford this luxury and were too much concerned with making a living to see any advantage in learning letters, music, or exercising in the gymnasium.

When the boy completed this "elementary" stage of education, he might move on to the next or "advanced" stage. This consisted largely of further physical training to which might be added two years of military instruction. At this level we find the state taking a direct interest in the education of its youth by erecting a public gymnasium, the Academy, in Athens. This building and its grounds were open to the public and were the charge of a *gymnasiarch* appointed by the state. His responsibility was to maintain a high quality of work on the part of both teachers and pupils. Since only a minority of citizens aspired to this education, and only the wealthy could afford the fees charged by instructors, the Academy catered almost exclusively to the aristocracy.

THE AGE OF PERICLES (fifth century B.C.)

Introduction. Pericles ruled Athens for only forty years, but so brilliant and creative was this period that all the fifth century B.C. has been named for him. This forty-year span (469-429 B.C.) was the culmination of forces having their origin in the years preceding the fifth century B.C., and its effects reached far into the third century B.C.

This was a time of unprecedented creativity in all areas of human interest, and Athens was the pivot. While most of the geniuses of the age were born and reached adulthood outside Athens, the freedom and stimulation of the Athenian intellectual climate drew them in their maturity like a magnet. What was the essence of this cultural structure that nourished one of the richest creative explosions known to man?

Athens, the treasury of the Delian Confederacy, was the center of a thriving trade complex. People came from all over the world to trade or transact business, and Athenian citizens traveled widely and freely, making new and challenging contacts. The citizenship of Athens included, in theory, all the freemen of Attica, the "common people" as well as the aristocracy, artisans, tradesmen, seamen, and not a few foreigners. All were able to speak and have their opinions considered. There was freedom of thought and expression in the city even though there were limits beyond which even a Socrates was not permitted to go.

The government, which had been dominated by the aristocracy for hundreds of years, was now the responsibility of the middle and lower classes. This did not eliminate the upper classes entirely, since it was they who had the wealth and leisure to devote themselves to public service. Nevertheless, it did provide opportunity for talent from among the less wealthy to be discovered and used.

During this age Athenian art reached its peak. The city's public buildings combined exquisite beauty with utility, and such artists in stone as Phidias were employed to carve their immortality upon them. Aeschylus, Sophocles, and Euripides were writing and staging their immortal dramas for all to see and hear at public expense. Herodotus and Thucydides were recording the history of the Greek people, showing both their greatness and their weakness, while Aesop was distilling the wisdom of the ages into fables that taught moral lessons. Socrates, Plato, and Aristotle were teaching philosophy and challenging Athens to think about herself honestly.

The Old Passes. This Athens of Pericles was straining against the old. Old customs, old values, old interpretations of the universe and man's place in it, old patterns of social relationships—all were being questioned and challenged. As new moral insights developed, the traditional religion with its fighting, cheating, immoral, dishonest gods became suspect. These gods, created in the image of Homeric aristocracy, were undeserving of worship by democratic Athenians. Skepticism was undermining faith.

As some Athenians studied and observed men from different cultures and realized that what they believed to be good others held to be evil, they concluded that all morals are relative. The foundations of absolutism were dissolving. Social customs, laws, and habits, they concluded, are man-made conventions designed to satisfy specific and local conditions and have no authority out of this context. There is no universal right or wrong.

Theories of evolution advanced by Heraclitus, Anaximander, and Empedocles destroyed the traditional belief that sometime in the past man had enjoyed a golden age from which he had fallen and to which he would return. In place of the golden age were earlier and more simple forms of life from which man had grown and of which he was not at all proud.

Then there was the new emphasis upon the individual. In the past, the state was the end-all of values. One's chief duty was to serve the group and insure its unity and stability. Patriotism and civic loyalty were the highest virtues. As the middle and lower classes began to demand their "rights" and win against the upper classes who represented for them the state, social stability gave way to individual aggrandizement. The poor man became wealthy and the slave the archon not because of the state but in spite of it. Freedom was not a gift of the state but the end result of a hard-fought struggle against the state.

The Sophists. Into this atmosphere, charged with confidence in the individual and distrust of anything old, came the sophists. They were, in many ways, the end result of a long history of Greek thought. Ancient Greeks had thought of the universe in terms of man. It was alive and functioning much as the human individual, but larger and more powerful. There were gods, or spirits, of everything, and man had to make his peace with them. Events in nature were caused by these spirits just as man might cause happenings in his environment.

In the seventh century B.C. there began to appear in the Greek world men who challenged this animistic interpretation of the universe. They argued that things were caused not by gods or spirits but by natural events. In place of personal and mythological causation they would substitute natural causation. They challenged men to observe nature and draw conclusions from what they saw. Thales of Miletus (640-546 B.C.) held that all things are derived from water, rain is caused by evaporation and precipitation, and the height of a pyramid can be determined by measuring the length of its shadow. Pythagoras (581?- 500 B.C.) concluded from his observations that numbers constitute the essence of all things. Others, including Xenophanes, Empedocles, and Democritus, continued this process of investigating nature. From the work of these men came a conviction that the universe was not subject to the caprice of gods but predictable in terms of a dependable cause and effect sequence.

During the fifth century B.C., thinkers began to see the possibility of applying this method of observation to man and his social relations. They turned from natural science to ethics and human relations. They raised questions of right and wrong, good and evil, honesty, loyalty— questions concerned with man's relations to his fellows personally and through the state. These were the sophists.

While hundreds of these strolling teachers roamed throughout the Greek world of the fifth century B.C., only a few names have come down to us in recognizable form and with enough data for us to characterize them. Although they were phenomenally popular in the age of Pericles and wrote widely on many subjects, their books and papers have been lost, leaving only scattered quotations from their work in the writings of others. Further, most of the accounts of them were written by their enemies, either the conservatives who felt they were destroying the very fabric of society or the radicals who were convinced that they were holding back progress. Nevertheless, we do have sufficient reliable material to draw a somewhat shadowy picture of some of them individually and all of them as a group.

Protagoras (*circa* 481-411 B.C.) came to Athens from Thrace at the invitation of Pericles in 455 B.C. He proposed to make the boys of Athens, through teaching, good citizens, successful in private affairs, and efficient in public service. His writings included treatises on education and on grammar. *On Correct Speech,* which he wrote as a textbook for his pupils, was one of the earliest attempts at a science of grammar.

Prodicus (born 465 or 450 and died around 399 B.C.) promised to teach his pupils virtue and good character. Among the subjects he was prepared to teach were ethics, natural philosophy, history of religions, and language. He strove to develop in his pupils a sense of the accuracy of words and their use. His book, *On Correct Language,* stressed use of the right word to convey the correct shade of meaning.

Hippias (fifth century B.C.) was born in Elis and came to Athens boasting that he was able to teach everything. From the pictures others have drawn of him, he was a master exhibitionist and egotist. His skill lay in his ability to popularize knowledge even if on a superficial level. He wrote on many subjects and did not hesitate to discourse at length on anything.

Gorgias (*circa* 483-375 B.C.) of Leontini was a specialist in rhetoric. While others proposed to make their pupils good individuals and good citizens, Gorgias laid claim to only one ability, to make his pupils skillful orators and users of words. He came to Athens in 427 B.C. and astonished the citizens by using prose instead of poetry, but prose often more beautiful than any poetry they had heard.

These were some of the sophists. What did they do? They were teachers of youth and investigators seeking accurate knowledge. They were comparable to modern research professors. They realized that the need in Periclean Athens for effective speech demanded precision of thought and that thinking could never be accurate without a clear understanding of language.

As a result of their investigations, the sophists reached conclusions which fascinated the youth of Athens and angered beyond measure the older men who still clung to the past and its gods. Some came to the conclusion that pleasure is the highest of human goals and the measure of all values. In pursuit of pleasure the interests of the individual are superior to those of the state.

Rebelling against the conventionality of the past, these thinkers stressed naturalism. They taught that the impulses of the individual are more to be trusted than traditional standards which may have suited a disappearing past but had little validity in the present. This led to a conviction that the individual is the source of all ethical values and that any idea of fixed principles of right and wrong is invalid.

The sophists, searching for knowledge and impelled by the forces of the world in which they lived, saw the senses as the only avenues of facts and thus the measure of all truth. What one had been told, what tradition asserted, and what the past had held to be absolute and universal had been brought into question. What could man trust? Only what he experienced. But others experienced things differently. Was there no basis for agreement? The sophists could find none. Consequently, true to their best understanding, they had to accept relativism, to make the individual man the measure of all things and his happiness the ultimate goal.

Socrates (*circa* 470-399 B.C.). This ugly, waddling figure of a man, thick-lipped, with eyes bulging from their sockets and nose flat against his face, walked among the Athenians slovenly, challenging their conceit and dropping ideas that left them uncomfortable and intellectually nude. His fellow citizens could never understand how this courageous and beautiful soul could occupy so repulsive a body.

Socrates was born in Athens. His father, Sophroniscus, was a friend of the family of the "just" Aristides. His mother acted often as a midwife. His early years were much like that of any Athenian youth. He received an education from "elementary" teachers chosen by his parents and moved on to become well versed in advanced mathematics and astronomy, a capable athlete, and a distinguished member of the city's military. In adulthood he moved in the highest circles of Periclean officialdom. He was married, apparently late in life, to Xantippe, who bore him three sons.

When he was not serving his city in its armed services or in the Assembly, he worked as a sculptor, cutting and shaping stone. In later life, driven by an "inner voice" which he could not disobey, he gave up his trade and devoted himself wholly to teaching the youth of Athens and attacking injustice and sham wherever he found it. At the palaestrae, in the market place, the gymnasiums, or just on the streets, he could be found asking questions of the lowly and the mighty, probing for answers, or just standing and thinking. A crowd of youths usually followed him, mostly to see the mighty brought low or the wise confounded. Some, however, came to ask questions and learn at the feet of the master. These latter were his pupils, young men who found in this ungainly figure of the open air a stimulation that drove them on to study and question in an effort to discover answers that even he could not give.

In an age of insatiable inquiry, Socrates was among the most persistent seekers. He believed that the very existence of the city he loved more than life itself depended upon finding answers to the questions he raised. When his pupils went from him to question others, the leaders of Athens were certain that the teacher had corrupted the pupil and was a menace to society.

While earlier Greek philosophers had been interested primarily in the world of natural phenomena and had sought to solve metaphysical problems, Socrates concentrated his genius on social problems. Piety and impiety, beauty and ugliness, the noble and the base, justice and injustice, sobriety and madness, courage and cowardice, the nature of the state and statesman, these were some of the problems with which Socrates wrestled.

Paramount among these problems, Socrates believed, was how to educate youth for good citizenship. To the extent that the educational system of a people produces good citizens, they will have a good society. To the degree that education fails, society will be weakened and in danger. Socrates saw this clearly. For him, education was man's most important undertaking. Thus he set for himself the major task of determining what constitutes a good education.

Socrates was disturbed by the dichotomy that existed in Athenian society between the positions of the conservatives and the sophists regarding virtue. On the one hand, the traditionalists held that virtue was eternal and absolute. They argued that good and bad, right and wrong, beauty and ugliness, and all other measures of man's life had been determined either by the gods or by the nature of things and that it was one's duty to discover these and live by them. On the other hand, the sophists and other "moderns" argued that these principles were relative to the situation in which they functioned. Man, they believed, had to determine right or wrong for himself in his particular situation and act on it. "Man is the measure of all things," they argued. This led to extreme individualism.

Socrates could accept neither of these positions. He knew that principles of virtue must change with changing conditions but was unable to justify an individualism that left each one free to determine virtue for himself. Eventually he came to the conclusion that thinking was the key to virtue. If one is able to think clearly and does not tire before the task is finished, he will discover virtue, not just for himself but for all men under the same conditions. In this conclusion Socrates found a permanence within change, a certainty that would transcend evolution. The human mind was, for him, the gateway to truth, and the training of this mind in the techniques of clear, accurate, and unprejudiced thinking the most important task of society.

For Socrates, this had profound educational implications. To create a society in which all men seek to do good, we must train men to think clearly. If one has been put in possession of the tools of accurate thinking, he will know the good and will do the good automatically. By teaching, Socrates held, we can make men good. He placed the teacher at the center of man's efforts to build the good society.

Thinking, for Socrates, does not take place in a vacuum. One learns to think by thinking about things that are concrete and practical. Thus Socrates was not interested in the ethereal speculations of many philosophers, in knowledge for its own sake. He wanted man to deal with that which had practical bearing on life. This is seen in the subjects which he would have the youth study. These included gymnastics for development of the body and military skill; dancing, music, and poetry to develop those qualities of grace and refinement usually associated with the gentleman; and geometry, astronomy, arithmetic, and psychology as applied to the problems of one's daily living. Most important on his list of subjects was ethics, not as theory but for effective living with and among others. When one learns to think correctly and accurately about matters in these fields, he will do what is right, act intelligently, do the good, and thereby be a good and just man.

Xenophon (430-355 B.C.). Xenophon was the arch conservative of late Periclean Athens, banished from his native city as a traitor, and an ardent admirer of the military strength of Sparta. He was conscious of the weaknesses of Athens and blamed them on the new education. To strengthen Athens and restore her former greatness, he argued, all vestiges of this new education had to be rooted out and in their place an education similar to that of Sparta established.

In the *Cyropaedia* he outlined in some detail a system of education that he believed would restore Athens to her former place of leadership among the Greek states and root out the perverse education of the sophists. Basic to this system was the conviction that education was the first business of the state and the state alone. Its aim was not to develop the individual but to produce a citizen able and willing to serve the common good at all times.

He proposed that the state erect four schools—including classrooms, exercise grounds, and living quarters—one for boys, one for young men, one for men of mature years, and one for those older men who had passed the age of military service. During the day all citizens were to spend their time learning what was necessary for service to the state. At night they would return to their homes, leaving selected youths to stand guard. Each school was to be under the supervision of twelve officers, one from each tribe of the city, chosen for their educational ability. While in school the citizens were to learn justice, self-government, a sense of gratitude to the state, obedience, temperance, courage, and endurance. When a young man reached his seventeenth birthday he was to be given intensive military training.

One might, if he wished, learn to read, write, and calculate, or go further in his literary and artistic education, but on his own time and at his expense. The business of state education was, as in Sparta, to train the soldier in the virtues of loyalty, patriotism, bodily strength and agility, and to instill hatred for the enemies of his state.

Xenophon believed that women should remain in seclusion in the home, where they would rear their children as the state wished. and manage the servants. He held that their education should aim at skill in these wifely duties and loyalty to the state. In this he adhered to the general Athenian attitude toward women in his day.

Isocrates (436-338 B.C.). Born in Athens, the son of Theodorus, Isocrates inherited both wealth and position. His father provided for him the best teachers available, and each saw in him great promise. Naturally a man of his family connections would turn to a political career. However, he had a weak voice and his physique was not commanding. When in the confusion following the Peloponnesian War he lost his fortune, he went into voluntary exile in Chios where he began teaching rhetoric. In 403 B.C., with the restoration of democracy, he returned to Athens and set himself up as a teacher of oratory.

Teaching and writing occasional speeches for the law courts, he gathered about himself pupils from among the most noted families of Greece. When, in 392 B.C., he founded his school near the Lyceum, he began a career as teacher and writer on educational and political matters. His success was equaled by no one else of his age. Pupils came to Athens from all parts of the Greek world to study with the master. So brilliant was the list of his pupils that someone wrote a book called *The Disciples of Isocrates.* Tradition has it that at the panegyric contest on the death of Mausolus of Caria in 351 B.C., all the competitors had been trained by Isocrates.

First and foremost, Isocrates was a teacher, one of the best. He devoted much of his time to training young men to follow the profession of the orator. To him, oratory was much more than skill in handling an audience. The orator was a leader of public opinion, a molder of the thinking of citizens, a key person in determining whether the city would be weak or great. His pupils were responsible for the welfare of the state and, as men of integrity and vision, must know what is good, right, and just. Using all the skill they could master, they were to lead their listeners to a devotion to these virtues.

Oratory, he taught, must get its power not from the rules or techniques of voice and rhythm but from the truth of the material spoken. Further, the education of the orator must stress the practical rather than the esoteric. A trained orator had developed a precision instrument which he must now use in the practical arena of government and world affairs. With his teacher, Socrates, he had no respect for the contention that knowledge for its own sake is good. For him, an educated man was "one who can deal with all that comes upon him day by day: who is honest and mannerly in society; who rules his desires; who is not spoiled by good fortune."

PLATO: POET-PHILOSOPHER OF EDUCATION (*circa* 428-*circa* 348 B.C.)

Introduction. Plato has been evaluated as having one of the finest minds the world has produced and as having a "foggy mind . . . forever presenting the semblances of objects which, half seen through a mist, can be defined neither in form nor dimensions." Scholars have studied and restudied his philosophy. Early Christianity made his ideas basic to its theology. Political thinkers and rulers have turned time and again to his writings for guidance. Lovers of fine literature have read and reread his dialogues for their beauty both in the original Greek and in translation. Thomas Jefferson, writing to John Adams, found reading the *Republic* "the heaviest task-work I ever went through." "I laid it down often," he said, "to ask myself how it could have been, that the world should have so long consented to give reputation to such nonsense as this?"

A challenging mind breeds both devotion and antagonism, along with a great deal of misunderstanding. Plato's was a challenging mind. He had exceptional knowledge gleaned from wide experience. He was trained by the best teachers his age produced. He had native intelligence and keenness of wit found in only a few in history. He was a restless seeker for truth, aided by an imagination that could fashion an entire system of philosophy. Added to all this was an exceptional literary skill which enabled him to write excitedly and excitingly about what he was thinking.

We are particularly interested in him because he was first and foremost a teacher. Born the same year that Pericles died, he was twenty-five years old when Athens was forced to make an ignoble peace with Sparta. A sensitive son of Athenian aristocracy, he saw Athens slipping into despair and degeneracy. As he watched the moral and spiritual decay of his native city, he became convinced, as did his teacher, Socrates, that the only hope for the restoration of her former strength and glory lay in discovering an education that would give the youth new hope and new ideals. Wrestling with the problems of education, he discovered that they could not be solved until one had solved the far larger problems of the nature of man and the world in which he must live. He saw education as an instrument for molding and shaping the individual, an instrument that could be used to produce almost any kind of individual. Thus, he turned to a study of philosophy to justify the goals of education, the ends for which the instrument would be employed.

His Life. Plato was the son of Ariston, who traced his ancestry through Codrus to the god Poseidon, and Perictione, a descendant of Solon. When his father died, his mother married Pyrilampes, a prominent figure in Pericles' government. It was in the home of his stepfather that Plato received most of his early education. Through the doors of this home came the chief figures in Athenian life at this time, including his uncle, Charmides, and his mother's cousin, Critias, both leaders in the Terror of 404 B.C.

Although the most important formative influence upon Plato's youth was Socrates, it does not appear that he considered himself a disciple of the older man, nor was he among the inner circle of his pupils. When he refers to Socrates it is as a mature "friend" for whom he had great respect. However, he was sufficiently identified with him to be shaken deeply at his death, disillusioned that democratic Athens would, under stress, behave in so undemocratic a fashion, and convinced that he would not be safe in his native city during the aftermath of this tragedy.

For the next ten years he traveled, visiting many of the centers of learning in his world and studying both philosophy and political structure wherever he could find either. When he returned to Athens, he was one of the best informed men of his day. His experiences had convinced him that education rather than politics, his first love, should command his time and devotion. Consequently, he opened a school near the Academy, the aristocratic gymnasium of Athens, and began his career of social and political reform through teaching. There he lectured, wrote epistles and dialogues, and taught the young men—from Athens and other parts of the world—who came to sit at the feet of this man with the magnetic personality and brilliant mind.

The Roots of Plato's Philosophy. The philosophical idealism, or "ideaism" as some would hold, was an outgrowth of Plato's living in the post-Periclean world of extreme individualism and moral decay. Watching Athens fall apart spiritually so that she had no stomach to resist successfully the organized might of Sparta, he could not help comparing his day with that earlier time when Athens rallied all of Greece to defeat the mighty Persian hordes and drive them from the Greek world. Despairing of the flux of human life and stung by evidence all about him of instability and degeneracy, he set about to discover that upon which he could depend, the permanent, the ideal. Only this, he believed, could give meaning to his world.

Socrates reveled in the discussion of ethical questions. This interest was passed on to his pupil, and Plato's early dialogues are little more than clever discussions of these same questions. The end of the discussion is always Socratic—by teaching, by transmitting knowledge of goodness, man will become good. Thinking, carefully and accurately undertaken, will bring the individual to a clear knowledge of virtue and, inevitably, he will shape his life accordingly.

As Plato's thinking matured, we find him digging deeper and deeper into the question of the teachableness of virtue until, in the concluding pages of the *Meno,* he faces the fact that before one can answer the question "Is virtue teachable?" he must discover the nature of virtue. It soon became evident to him that an adequate theory of the nature of virtue must rest upon the solid foundation of philosophy. Virtue is not a thing alone, standing by itself, but grows out of the fundamental nature of man and of his world and the relationships that exist between the two.

Socrates had raised the question. During his travels, after the death of Socrates, Plato examined the theories of Euclid in Megara, the idealism of the Eleatic philosophers, the ancient religious teachings of

Egypt, the mathematical studies of Pythagoras, and numerous theories of government and statecraft which he found at the capitals he visited. All of these stimulated his questioning mind and gave him leads for further investigation.

His years of teaching in his Academy, years of discussing problems and ideas with young men from all parts of the world, contributed much to the maturing of his thinking. He became increasingly convinced that the paramount function of the state was to make the best possible citizens. To give practical meaning to this conviction, he set about to develop a system of education that, if employed properly, would inculcate in men those virtues that are fundamental to goodness in both private and public life. This endeavor necessitated a careful analysis of the nature of virtue, the development of a philosophy of the good.

Plato's Theory of Education. Here we are concerned with theory, Plato's theory of education. This must not be confused with fact. Athens developed an educational structure which, as we have seen, changed with changing times. Plato was a leader of Athenian thought who happened to feel strongly that the way in which his city was educating its children was inadequate in many respects. In many of his writings he suggested improvements which he believed would remedy the mistakes of the past and bring education more in line with the needs of the present.

In two of his major works, Plato discusses education in considerable detail. The *Republic* is a sketch of an ideal state in which education is a major concern of the people. Education is the means by which children are developed into good adults devoted to the state and able and willing to advance its interests at all costs. It is education which discovers the special talents of each individual and prepares him, on the basis of these talents, to fit effectively and efficiently into the structure of the state. This is utopian, the work of a relatively young man patterning what for him is the good society.

The *Laws* is a work of an old, disillusioned man who has moved further in the direction of conservatism. He has become more realistic about man, the state, and education. He has lost his earlier faith in man's ability to reconstruct his environment. Man must be trained by those few who can know. Education has become for Plato "the particular training in respect of pleasure and pain, which leads you always to hate what you ought to hate, and love what you ought to love, from the beginning of life to the end."

To understand Plato and his thinking about education, we must keep this distinction in mind. Plato did change his point of view as he grew older. As a young man he was utopian. As an old man he was realistic.

Plato, under the influence of Socrates, began with a firm conviction that virtue is teachable, that one can be made good by education. He came to question this position, arriving at the conclusion that we must first determine the nature of virtue. After careful analysis, he concluded that there are three levels of man's nature or "soul": the appetites, the spirit, and reason or wisdom.

Is virtue teachable? Plato's answer is a guarded yes and no. In the broadest sense of the term, the individual can "learn" virtue. He learns the virtues of the appetites and the spirit by one method and that of reason by another.

Reason, in Plato's thinking, is not present in the child. It develops with adolescence. Consequently, teaching at the level of childhood cannot appeal to reason. Knowledge cannot be the ground for temperance and courage. These must be burned into the child by repeated actions which result in habit formation. Since these virtues are related to the irrational faculties, they are developed by practice resulting in fixed and automatic habits of action under all circumstances. To build these habits Plato recommends the use of pleasure and pain. Commend the child when he acts correctly, and condemn him when he fails to act correctly. This education must begin at birth and continue consistently until the right way of acting is ingrained in the very nature of the child. The drive in this direction must come from the child's entire environment. The state must be a school in which the child learns at all times. His home, the streets, the people he meets, the places he visits, all that he hears and sees, everything must teach the same lesson.

This led Plato to advocate a strict censorship within his ideal state. Poets who portray the gods as lustful, lying, crafty, and immoral were to be barred from the city. Only bold, strong, martial music could be allowed. Those rhythms that lull the senses and soften the will were not to be tolerated. Plato realized that one learns as he interacts with his environment. He also appreciated the fact that good actions are the outcome of the interaction of an individual with good natural inclinations with a good environment. This led him to demand carefully supervised procreation to insure the best possible offspring and eternal vigilance to guarantee a good environment. If the wise and good so control that rightly-endowed children are born and grow to adulthood in this purified environment, the good life is a certainty.

When Plato turned to the third virtue, wisdom, his recommendations were very different. Reason develops as the individual moves into adolescence. If his early training and habit formation have been good, his reason will recognize this fact and begin to build on it. As reason takes over, the necessity for habit formation lessens. Man begins to think, and through thinking, he comes to see that wrong action leads to unhappiness. Since no one voluntarily chooses unhappiness, the reasoning individual will chart his life course by the good which guarantees happiness. This is the Socratic doctrine of the teachableness of virtue. If one knows the good, he will live by the good. When reason develops, it is possible by appeal to this reason to show the individual what is good. As a reasoning being, he will recognize the validity of this position and will choose the good. On the level of wisdom, knowledge is virtue; to know the good is to do the good.

Plato believed that reason remains dormant until it is awakened into action. This awakening takes place through the study of mathematics. Until reason becomes active, the individual lives in a world of sense, bodily interests, custom, convention. This is the life of the child and the youth before reason is awakened. When this awakening takes place, the individual turns "from a day which is little better than night to the true day of being." He moves from the world of concrete objects to the world of abstract thought, of concepts.

For Plato, mathematics in a very unique way bridged the world of sense and the world of thought, the concrete and the abstract. Mathematics is useful in the world of material things. By it one is able to count, to measure distances and volumes, to figure accounts and keep records of stocks and money. This is the base or material phase of mathematics. Also, by using mathematics, man learns to think abstractly. He deals with the perfect circle, with $2 + 2 = 4$, with the theory of class and the null class, with equations and negative numbers. All these are of the reason, not to be found in the material world. Mathematics reaches into both worlds, that of sensation and that of abstract thought. As one studies mathematics, beginning where he is in the world of sense experiences, he moves gradually into the world of the mind; he develops general concepts which can be applied to many situations or can be manipulated free from the limitations of the material world. The mind is freed to soar among the gods, to remember those perfect ideas which were known before birth and were forgotten until recalled by the study of mathematics.

Education then for Plato is on two levels: that of the body and that of reason. The body is trained, habituated, controlled. Reason is freed to discover wisdom. Training of the body must be under compulsion. All children of citizens are to be forced to develop the virtues of temperance and courage. But reason cannot be forced. To use compulsion at this higher level is to destroy what is most important, the love of wisdom. "Bodily exercise, when compulsory," Plato says, "does no harm to the body; but knowledge, which is acquired under compulsion, obtains no hold on the mind."

Education is a means of assuring unity in the state. The state is an organism, the individual a unit. All his actions must contribute to the health of the organism lest it sicken and die. While, in the *Republic,* Plato felt that a degree of individualism was good for the state, by the time he wrote the *Laws,* he had come to believe in strict subordination of the individual to the state. "Every . . . creation," he wrote, "is for the sake of the whole, and in order that the life of the whole may be blessed; and . . . you are created for the sake of the whole, and not the whole for the sake of you." Here Plato is Spartan and totalitarian. He thinks of education as developing this totalitarian attitude, as aiming to produce an individual who will dedicate himself unreservedly to the state and forego all private interests.

Education must give the individual the where-with-all to make this attitude of devotion to the state effective. It must eventuate in both virtues and skills appropriate to the welfare of the state. In the Athens of his day, Plato realized that the efficient citizen needed accurate knowledge of the nature of government and of the state as well as military skill.

Plato hoped that education would stimulate and develop the individual so that as his reason matured he would gain a self-control that makes state regimentation and minute laws unnecessary. Here again we see Plato's concept of freedom. Discipline, regimentation, laws, all are necessary to hold material man in rein. When reason appears, man must be free to pursue the right course of action, directed by wisdom, which is the virtue of reason. He should have an inner control, developed by education, which puts him above the law, not above in the sense that he defies the law but in the sense that the law is so perfectly an expression of his will that he conforms because it is his very nature to want what the law demands. He has become the law, and the law is his naturally.

To accomplish these ends, education must be completely under the control of the state and the same for all children of the citizenry. Further, every child must receive all the education he is capable of assimilating and which is suited to his nature. Plato believed that ability was not confined to one class of men but could be found everywhere. He would have every child of every class, except the slaves, begin education together and under supervision of the state. As this mass moves forward, natural differences will appear, differences which must be recognized and dealt with through training. Eventually it will be discovered, from observation and testing, that some children have talents that fit them to become artisans who will handle the business of the state, who will buy and sell, farm and manufacture, build and manage. When this is discovered, they will be moved into an education suited to their needs and then into the world of the state. Many of the remaining will evidence talents needed by those who are to police and protect the state, the soldier class. They will be removed from the mainstream of education and given training necessary to their function in the state, that of protectors.

The remaining pupils will go on to study those matters and develop those skills necessary for governing the state. Their training will stress reason and its virtue, wisdom. Some of these will hold minor positions in the state while others will go on to higher positions. The cream, in terms of talent and wisdom, will become the "philosopher-kings," ruling the state wisely and seeing to it that justice prevails at all times.

This is a class society, but one built not on artificial differences. It is a society in which an earnest attempt is made to discover the talents of each individual, whatever his parentage or his sex, and to so train and educate him that he is able to use those talents most effectively in service to his state. Plato believed that one is happiest when he is doing that work for which he is by nature and education best equipped, and that the state is best off when each citizen is so occupied.

Basic to the educational structure recommended by Plato is the concept that training must be fitted to the developing child—not so simple that he is not challenged nor so advanced that he is put under undue strain or discouraged by failure. From birth to three years of age, the child is to be allowed to grow as his body dictates. His senses are to be stimulated so that he experiences his environment accurately and clearly. He must not be subjected to fear, and pleasure and pain must be kept at a minimum. During the nursery years, from four to six, he will be encouraged to play a great deal. He will hear, and learn, fairy tales, nursery rhymes, myths, and stories of virtuous men. He may be punished, but never in ways that will disgrace him. At this age, self-will is prominent and must be curbed, but the nurse must take care not to destroy his spirit.

The elementary school years begin when the child is six and continue until he is thirteen. At six, boys and girls are separated, both being taken from their parents to live in state quarters under the supervision of teachers appointed by the state. Since the child at this time is boisterous, wild, unruly, he must be brought under control through a program of music, play, manners, religion, and dancing. These activities are designed to teach the child dignity, poise, and smoothness of movement. Also, he must study poetry, reading, writing, singing, numbers, and geometry. At this age the child is most easily motivated by pain, pleasure, fear, desire for approval, shame, reverence, love, and hate. These the teacher will use judiciously. Since the young citizen is now more than ever aware of his environment and tends to imitate what he sees and hears, care must be taken that nothing ugly, base, or improper comes to his attention. Books he studies and contacts he has at this age are to be censored carefully. In the *Laws,* Plato puts less emphasis upon the literary and musical subjects at this age and bears down heavily on gymnastics and military training. Horsemanship and use of small weapons must be learned, graded of course to the maturity and ability of the child. When possible, boys are to be taken to the battlefield to view at first hand the bloodshed and slaughter.

During the ages thirteen to sixteen, the child masters the lyre, along with the subjects begun in the elementary years. Now that he is able, the boy begins to study the theory of arithmetic along with its more practical aspects. In addition, he memorizes as much poetry as possible and learns countless religious hymns so that he may take part in the many ceremonies sponsored by the state's religious authorities. This, Plato believed, is an important means of building loyalty to the state and to fellow men.

When the age of sixteen is reached, the boy is ready for strenuous military training and brutalizing physical exercises. No intellectual education is to be undertaken until he is twenty, so important is the physical and military at this age.

At twenty, all boys are to be given tests, the results of which determine who will end their formal education and who will go on for a ten-year study of the sciences. Whatever science the child has had to this age has been most general. Now he must come to appreciate the inner relations between the physical sciences, the integration of thinking. Another selection is made at thirty, and those showing the most promise enter upon a five-year study of dialectic and philosophy, in preparation for serving the state in the higher offices of government. Subjects studied here include ethics, psychology, theory of knowledge, government, law, and education.

At thirty-five, the young man is ready to stand for election to office. If he is successful, he serves the state until fifty. Then he is relieved from active service to the state to study higher philosophy and act as adviser to those holding office.

It will be noted that vocational training is not included in Plato's system of education. In his thinking, the slaves took care of menial tasks, and the only training needed was that which they could get in the discharging of these duties along with incidental help from other slaves. The artisans could learn their trades through an apprentice system in no way related to formal education, and the soldiers could move easily from the physical and military exercises of the regular curriculum into the arts of the professional warrior.

This pattern of education was designed to select from all the children of citizens those most capable intellectually and morally and prepare them for governing positions in the civil structure. In this way Plato hoped to give the state the best possible government, one controlled by reason and justice. He believed that when those in whom reason dominated occupied the seats of government and ruled wisely, when the bravest and most courageous policed and protected the state, and when those best fitted for the occupations necessary to support the state plied their trades well, the state would be good, the people happy, and justice found everywhere. In this way Plato proposed to save Athens from decay and shame.

The city paid little attention to him. It did listen sufficiently to make military training in a sort of Ephebic college compulsory for two years. However, the forces of disintegration were at work, and even a Plato crying bitterly to his beloved Athens to mend its ways was a voice crying in the wilderness—heard by few and obeyed by none.

ARISTOTLE: SCIENTIST-PHILOSOPHER OF EDUCATION

Introduction. There has been no man in western history who has had a more profound influence upon the thinking of all generations from his time than Aristotle. Even when men sought to ignore him or to condemn him, they found him shaping their thinking and that of those about them. Religious leaders, including Saint Thomas Aquinas, Maimonides, and Averroes, wove Aristotle into their historic creeds and produced works that became more or less authoritative for their theologies. The curricula of schools of advanced and higher education in the West were dominated for hundreds of years by the Aristotelians. Some of the bitterest battles among the intellectuals of medieval and modern times have grown out of interpretations of Aristotle's thought. Formal logic, created by Aristotle, is today practically as he left it. Fragmentary and irritatingly distorted as many of his writings are, we are dealing here with a mind so clear and so provoking that no one can ignore him, and many in all ages find themselves drawn to him with an irresistible passion.

Aristotle's Life. Aristotle was born at Stagira, a prosperous town on the northwestern shore of the Aegean, in the province of Chalcidice bordering on Macedonia, in 384 B.C. By race he was an Ionian, inheritor of the Ionian tradition in philosophy that produced many of the most significant nature philosophers of ancient times. His mother was a native of Chalcis and his father, Nicomachus, was a famous physician, a member of the guild of the "sons of Aeculapius," and for a period of years the court physician to Amyntas II, father of Philip of Macedon.

Born into a home alive with interest in science and philosophy, often surrounded by the leading figures and keenest minds of the day, Aristotle most certainly had all his native powers and talents stimulated to the utmost. In addition, he received the best education the age could provide. In his childhood and youth he learned from his parents, from those who came to his home as visitors and friends, and from the best available teachers of the area in the most competent schools that Stagira could provide.

At seventeen he went to Athens and placed himself under Plato, the most famous teacher of all Greece at that time. There, for twenty years (367-347 B.C.), he studied, taught at the Academy, and assisted the master by managing many of the activities of this busy and bustling school. At the time Aristotle came to Plato, the famous man was sixty-one years old. Although some of the earlier enthusiasm and idealistic fervor remained, this was an aging, gray-haired philosopher and teacher in the evening of his life. It was the period of the *Laws* rather than that of the *Republic.* Socrates had long since faded into the background, and concern with the analysis of ideas, logic, and scientific study dominated. During the last twenty years of Plato's life, he worked with the young student from Stagira untiringly. As a reward, the pupil became essentially a Platonist, concerned with problems the master found challenging and reaching conclusions similar to those of his teacher. He cooperated in the research undertaken by the circle of "friends" which made up the student body of the Academy, wrote essays and pamphlets clearly in line with Plato's thought at this time, and became a leading figure in all the activities of the school.

When, in his eighty-first year, Plato died, his nephew, Speusippus, became head of the Academy. Aristotle, and others closely associated with the master, felt that this younger man lacked the ability or desire to maintain the school on the same level of creative scholarship as in the past. Thus, they left Athens, and some, including Aristotle, went to Assus, on the Adramyttian gulf, where they joined a Platonic circle established much earlier by two of Plato's pupils, Erastus and Coriscus. Here Aristotle organized a school and taught for three years. From Assus, Aristotle moved to Lesbos where for two years he studied natural history and marine biology and associated with the little company of Platonists that gathered about him.

Because of his growing interest in politics, Aristotle was prevailed upon to accept the invitation of Philip of Macedon to undertake the education of his son Alexander. He saw this as a unique opportunity to have a hand in shaping the thinking of a future monarch whom he felt could become a key figure in building a more just and happy society. Thus, in 342 B.C., he took up residence at Pella to continue his teaching and to care for the education of the young Alexander for the next seven years.

After the accession of Alexander to the throne of Macedonia, 336 B.C., Aristotle saw that his mission at Pella was over and returned to Athens, where he organized a school, the Lyceum, in which he taught for the next thirteen years. Gradually, his star pupil, Alexander, moved away from his teachings, and even though the two men never lost contact, their ideas and interests became increasingly divergent. While Alexander was striving to build an empire based on equal and harmonious cooperation between Persian and Greek, an endeavor contrary to Aristotle's anti-Persian and pro-Greek convictions, Aristotle was immersing himself more and more in pure science and research. At the Lyceum we find him moving steadily away from his earlier Platonic thinking toward concern with things and events, from "the heavenly things that are the objects of the higher philosophy" to history and biology. It is from these years that we have most of his extant writings.

Alexander died in 323 B.C. Antipater, under whose protection Aristotle had worked, left Greece, making possible a resurgence of the pro-Greek party. Because he was identified with Alexander and his dream of a "united nations" of the world, including both Persia and Greece, Aristotle felt it best to flee Athens and take up residence in his mother's former home at Chalcis, on the island of Euboea. There, a year later, in 322 B.C., he died at the age of sixty-two. Thus one of the great minds of all times was placed in history to be marveled at, fought over, studied, interpreted, followed, and condemned even to the present. Wherever men think or attempt to understand their environment, Aristotle appears to assist or challenge.

Aristotle's Theory of Education. One fundamental principle of Aristotle's educational thinking is that the state must be the only educator. Private education cannot be tolerated. The existence of the state depends upon the nature of its citizens, since all citizens are to participate in the government of the state. To preserve itself the state must undertake the education of all its citizens, and it cannot tolerate any contrary or less efficient teaching.

This state-controlled education must be designed for the citizen living in the specific and particular state. No two states are alike in nature and goals. Training and education to live effectively in one will not be adequate for living in another. Nor is it possible to educate for world citizenship. One's training and education must be specific, for life in a clearly defined state.

Since education is so important for the life of the state, there is a body of common material, a general education, that all citizens of that state

must have. This must be "one and the same for all." The freedom of
Athens permitted each parent to educate his children as he saw fit and
was able. This meant that some received a fine education, while others
were given less than the necessary minimum. Economic and social
factors determined the education a child received. This, Aristotle believed, was a major reason for Athens' plight. He would change all this
by having the state see to it that every child of a citizen receive the
same basic education necessary for citizenship.

Aristotle's curriculum, in so far as he discusses this phase of education, included reading, writing, and music. The citizen must know how
to read and write if he is to perform the simple duties of a human being
in Athenian society. As he developed into a responsible participant in
government, ability to read and write became indispensable. Likewise,
gymnastics was basically necessary for the good citizen. The soul—
reason—is dependent upon a sound, healthy, well-developed body. As
soon after birth as possible, the child should begin physical exercises,
planned to follow his growth throughout life. At no time can this be
permitted to brutalize or to distort the individual. The teacher of gymnastics must understand child development so that he fits his exercises
to the abilities and needs of the pupil at each stage of growth. The end
is not, Aristotle was most emphatic, to produce an athlete able to win
at games but to produce a body fitted to nourish a sound and clear mind.
Such a body will also be adequate for military demands.

Aristotle had a good deal to say about music as a necessary part of
the child's curriculum and as a means of maintaining the good state.
He believed, as did many of the Greeks, that music has power to form
character. Rhythms and melodies exert influences over the listener
that may be good or evil. The languid music of love songs and pastoral
tunes weakens, takes away the spirit to act decisively. This undermines
the soul and must not be sanctioned by the state. The music of strong,
martial, victorious rhythms produces strength of will, determination,
and drive and must be required in the education of all citizens. The
child, in his early years, must hear good music often to develop appreciation and understanding. However, Aristotle opposed a musical education that aimed at developing skilled performers. Professionalism
seemed to him degrading. He was particularly opposed to the citizen's
learning to play the flute.

Although Aristotle's writings leave us with no clear pattern of subjects for the education of the citizen above the elementary school, we
can conjecture from what he has written on other subjects that he
would have youths and young adults study mathematics, instrumental
music, poetry, grammar, rhetoric, literature, and geography. Beyond
these, it seems reasonable to suppose that he stressed, for those inter-

ested in higher education, psychology, politics, ethics, and education. For the "post-graduate" he would recommend biology, physical sciences, and philosophy.

Aristotle was most specific when discussing the process by which the individual is to be trained. He went much beyond Plato in his condemnation of the theory that by teaching we can make one good. He emphasized his conviction that knowledge of the good does not make one good. Didactic lectures and instruction are of no value if virtue is not already present. To develop and teach theories of the good will have no effect upon the individual. In other words, the path to virtue is not through reason.

An analysis of the acquisition of virtue reveals three factors: nature, habit, and reason. Nature furnishes the individual with impulses. Virtue is not inherent in the individual. When the child is born, he is neither good nor bad, but neutral. He has potentialities which can be shaped as the environment demands. Aristotle believed that the little child is very similar to an animal in that he is driven by his appetites and emotions. But the child is more than an animal; he has potentialities far beyond those of any other living being, potentialities for shame, imitativeness, emulation, excellence, rhythm, honesty, and wonder. Here Aristotle recognized man's roots in the animal world and his uniqueness. He did not identify man with the animals, as many have attempted to do, nor did he divorce man from lower forms of life, as others have done. Rather, he saw man as part of a developing process reaching back into vegetative and animal life—the source of many of his drives and impulses—and out into the highest life of reason, the divine.

The child is not capable of reason. He is driven by his impulses. Through experiences he comes to control these impulses, to direct them toward certain ends. Here education begins. As the environment is manipulated by factors about him, his natural impulses are directed. The state, employing pain and pleasure, undertakes to direct the child toward the good. This is habit formation. It is found at all levels and in all situations: in the arts, fine and practical, when the individual learns to manipulate a tool or play an instrument, and in the areas of moral virtues, when one learns to control his appetites and passions.

What then is virtue? For Aristotle, it is a fixed habit or attitude, a "disposition of the will." One's character, then, is the sum total of all these fixed habits. Beginning as impulses in the very nature of the human being, shaped and directed by interaction with the environment, these innate factors become virtues and their totality, character.

The state must devote itself to developing its new-born citizens into good members of the community. It can do this by developing in each one good habits, and the method is pleasure and pain. This is not to be done by reasoning or telling, or lecturing. Through habit formation one develops virtues, good ways of acting. These become stronger and more dependable as one grows in a consistent environment. Thus, the state must control all education and see to it that no contradictory influences are allowed to play upon the developing child. These virtues in their sum total are one's character, directing his actions. If properly developed, the individual will automatically act as his character commands. This is moral education, the education of the individual for living the good, the moral life.

Intellectual education is another matter. The soul is dual, irrational and rational. Morality is a function of the irrational phase of the soul. Here education is habit formation. The rational is concerned with wisdom, memory, philosophy, and aptitude to learn. Here education consists of teaching, reasoning, lecturing. Again we are left with a mere suggestion. While Aristotle devoted considerable space to the discussion of moral training, he barely mentions intellectual development. Why? The answer most certainly lies in the loss of so many of his writings. It does not seem reasonable to suppose that Aristotle would have shied away from this most important phase of man's nature. If, as he holds in no uncertain terms, reason is man's uniqueness, that which distinguishes him from all other things, the development of reason and intellectual virtues must have occupied a great deal of his attention and assumed a prominent place in his teaching. Since he leaves us no clear treatment of this matter in his extant works, we must assume that we are poorer because events of history have closed many of his books to us.

THE HELLENISTIC AGE

Introduction. In 338 B.C., Philip II of Macedonia won unquestioned control of Greece at the battle of Chaeronea. For the next 192 years, from 338 to 146 B.C., all of Greece was part of the Alexandrian world. Then, with the Roman conquest, it was incorporated into the Roman world. For 675 years, Athens was a major cultural and educational center of this Roman world, until Justinian, in 529 A.D., ordered all "pagan" schools closed, turning culture and education over to the Christian world.

Long before Chaeronea, Greek culture, in the richest sense of the term, had been permeating the ancient world. As people from all parts of the civilized or partly civilized world came in contact with Greece as merchants, tourists, or scholars, the richness of Greek life was recognized and sought after avidly. As Greek colonists established themselves in far-away places, they carried with them their culture. Athens, center of a mighty empire before the Peloponnesian War, drew people from the entire world who returned home to propagate what they had experienced there. The Greek language became the language of culture and intellectual interest. The philosophies of Greece, her art, architecture, music, gymnastic exercises, all were spreading far and wide wherever men aspired to better things.

With Chaeronea, this trend was accelerated. Replicas of Athens sprang up where great cities had been built. Athenian scholars and artists were sought after and accepted enthusiastically. Athenian institutions replaced those of native origin. The world was becoming Greek, and Athens, defeated militarily, was its spiritual master.

Changes in Athenian Education. While the world was becoming Greek, significant changes were taking place at home. Although elementary education remained very much the same for several centuries, new elements were beginning to appear. Music, which had been simple, with emphasis upon the epic and the lyric, was becoming more complicated. Early concern with telling a story in tone and rhythm gave way to interest in the relations among words used, the logic of ideas expressed, and the purity of accent and pronunciation. The old music-poetry education of the child was gradually replaced by grammar, rhetoric, and oratory. Drawing was added to the elementary curriculum and became a required subject for all cultured young people.

At the secondary level, teachers multiplied in great profusion. It was becoming evident that much that had in the past been taught to young men could very well be mastered by youths. Also, as higher education became richer and more varied, it was necessary to offer youths a much broader preparation for their more advanced intellectual development. "A whole swarm of masters" appeared offering instruction in arithmetic, geometry, shorthand, horsemanship, military tactics, playing musical instruments, and anything else that youths might demand.

In addition, a new teacher appeared on the scene. First he was called a *criticos* and later a *grammaticus*. When Athens was the independent master of her Delian empire, oratory was a tool necessary for all who wished to take part in affairs of state, gather the people to a cause or an idea, or plead for themselves against charges leveled at them. After the Peloponnesian War and Chaeronea, oratory lost its practical meaning and tended to become an art for art's sake, a kind of entertainment. Nevertheless, it gained in technical interest. The Greeks began to study its construction and initiated grammar. In time this developed into a host of related interests. In addition to technical grammar, these included meter, rhythm, careful analysis and criticism of poetry both ancient and modern, and drill in correct use of words. This led to a study of what was taught by these writers—history, morals, science, and theology.

A further addition to Athenian education, at the level of young adulthood, was the so-called Ephebic College. When a young man in Athens reached the age of eighteen, he usually enlisted in the armed forces of his city for two years of military training before being accepted into full citizenship. After Chaeronea and because of the urging of such leaders as Xenophon and Plato, the Athenians, in 335 B.C., made two years of military training compulsory for all boys when they reached their eighteenth year. This was in actuality the first state-controlled school in Athens and marked a radical departure from the freedom practiced in that city for generations. During the first year, the young men served as guards around the Acropolis and policemen at the port of Piraeus and in the various districts of the city. During the second year, they patrolled the borders of Attica, took part in patriotic festivals, and learned both the code and the skills of military life. At the end of these two years they took the Ephebic Oath, received from the state a shield and a spear, and were accepted as citizens of Athens.

But the noble experiment failed. It was too late for Athens to pick up the pieces of her lost past. By 300 B.C., ephebic training was reduced to one year. Later the compulsory feature was dropped, literary subjects came to dominate the curriculum, and foreigners were admitted. Thus, from a period of compulsory military training aimed at developing a well-prepared army to defend the city, this Ephebic College became a fashionable military academy catering to the sons of the wealthy and stressing intellectual pursuits.

On the level of higher education, significant changes were taking place. The sophists were giving way to philosophical schools and established teachers supported to a degree by the cities in which they settled. The crowded conditions at the gymnasiums where early teachers had gathered their pupils made it necessary for those who could afford it to establish schools of their own in rented buildings or in structures erected for the purpose. When the founders of these institutions died, the schools were willed to their pupils and headed by some famous disciple. Gradually they became fraternities of scholars devoted almost wholly to the study and analysis of the master's writings.

Near the close of the fourth century B.C., two famous schools of philosophy were established in Athens. The school of the Stoics was founded by Zeno of Citium during the latter part of the fourth century B.C. Since he began his lectures in the Stoa, or painted corridor, on the north side of the market place at Athens, his school was called Stoic. The other school was founded in 306 B.C. at Athens by Epicurus, who purchased a garden and began teaching that pleasure is "the beginning and end of the blessed life." He did not mean that unbridled indulgence of the flesh is the road to happiness. Some pleasures are followed by "annoyances" many times in excess of the pleasure experienced. Therefore, one should seek pleasure wisely, in terms of its consequences. In this way the life of pleasure must be the life of wisdom. He admitted both men and women to his school, an act that caused many raised eyebrows and not a few scandalous stories.

These schools of philosophy continued in Athens for centuries. To them came young men from all parts of the world. In fact, some schools sent representatives to the large cities to enroll students so that competition became intense at times. Many leading thinkers and men of affairs during the Hellenistic Age had been students of these Athenian schools. Horace, Cicero, and Julius Caesar, as well as many other "noble" Romans, received some of their education at these schools in Athens.

The atmosphere was largely that of a brotherhood of scholars interested in the same things and enjoying conversations about their interests. Some of the more scholarly devoted themselves to editing and "purifying" the manuscripts left them by their masters, but little or no creative work was produced. Without doubt, the school that exerted the most influence upon later years was the Stoic. Its philosophy was incorporated to a great extent into Christianity and influenced the ethical thinking of many Christian leaders.

Education in the Alexandrian World. Chaeronea and the subsequent advances of Alexander's armies accelerated the spread of Greek, especially Athenian, culture throughout the world. Everywhere men recognized the superiority of this culture to their own; and its ideals, thought patterns, language, and institutions were embraced enthusiastically. The *Iliad* and the *Odyssey* were read throughout Asia, while the people of India and the Caucasus listened entranced to the plays of Euripides and Sophocles. The Jews, most jealous of their sacred books, were honored by the *Septuagint,* the Old Testament Scriptures translated into Greek. Greek was spoken on the streets of Egyptian cities, and copies of Greek theaters, libraries, and baths adorned communities throughout Asia and Europe. Young men from everywhere traveled to Athens to study in Greek schools. Often they returned to their homes to set up schools similar to those in Greece or to take part in the Hellenizing of their parts of the world. Greek education became the standard wherever men cherished the instruction of their children and youths.

During the third and second centuries B.C., state concern for literary education began to appear in the Alexandrian world. Sometime around the first half of the third century B.C., Polythrus, a civic-minded merchant of Teos in Asia Minor, gave his city a substantial endowment with which to organize and maintain a free system of education. The money was to support two administrators, three teachers of letters, one teacher of the lyre, and two military instructors. The administrators and teachers of letters were elected each year by the town's residents, while the teacher of the lyre and the military teachers were appointed by the administrators. Boys and girls were accepted in the school, the only requirement being that they be of citizen parents. This was elementary education; the endowment made no provision for secondary or advanced instruction.

A similar development is seen at Miletus, where Eudemus, in 210 B.C., endowed a city-controlled elementary school for boys. The income from this endowment provided for four teachers of gymnastics and four of elementary subjects, all to be chosen by popular vote each year. Rhodes, on the island of the same name, in the early part of the second century received from the king of Pergamon an endowment to finance teaching of the sons of citizens. Pergamon also endowed elementary schools in Delphi.

Gradually, city after city in most of the civilized world accepted the responsibility for the education of its children. It became a matter of state concern to provide young people with the necessary training for participation in public festivals and processions and to lay the foundation for advancement in the social structure of the age.

Higher education was usually left to private teachers and depended upon the ability of parents to pay. As admiration for Greek culture and learning increased, several large centers adopted the atmosphere of Athens, decorated their public buildings in the style of Athenian structures, and attracted scholars to establish branches of Athenian philosophical schools or create schools of their own. Athens was being transplanted in these population and trade centers.

One of the most famous of these was Alexandria, founded by the youthful conqueror in 332 B.C. to be the center of his worldwide empire. Located at the mouth of the Nile, this city was strategically placed to command the Mediterranean world and reach out from there to all that Alexander considered his own. The plans for this city were most ambitious. It was to rival Athens in every respect, to be the literary and artistic center of the world. Although Alexander did not live to realize his dream of a new Athens on the Nile (he died in 323 B.C.), his successor, Ptolemy Soter, who was as thoroughly Greek in mind and spirit as he, continued building the city according to the grandiose plans of its founder. With the help of Demetrius of Paleron, a man of wide and rich experience, Ptolemy established a library and museum in Alexandria unequaled by any in the world at that time.

At its peak, the library is said to have contained more than 700,000 rolls of manuscript, all carefully catalogued and made usable by scholars from all over the world. Here were brought the famous library of Aristotle and all his writings, as many as possible of the Greek classics that had been kept at Athens, and original manuscripts from wherever they could be found. Each roll had a biographical sketch of the author attached. Here the *Septuagint* was translated from Hebrew into Greek. Here were collected gradually the literary masterpieces of Egypt, Mesopotamia, Phonecia, and other Asiatic countries of ancient glory. Many of these were translated into Greek.

A Temple of the Muses, later called a museum, was an important part of this intellectual complex. Although some teaching did occupy the time of scholars in the museum, its chief aim was the extension of human knowledge and research. The musuem was supported by the income from a large permanent endowment, and scholars were appointed by the government and paid from the endowment. Among the facilities here were an astronomical observatory, a botanical garden, an anatomical exhibit, and a rare and exotic zoological collection. Scholars were engaged in all phases of study and research, including literary criticism, philology, textual analysis and purification, grammatical studies; they also wrote commentaries. All areas of science were explored. Studies of the human body, of the physical and social environment, of man's relation to the seen and the unseen world, were undertaken with the greatest of freedom by the best scholars the world could produce.

The significance of the Alexandrian library and museum can be appreciated if we look at some of the work that came from its environs. Euclid wrote his *Elements of Geometry* there. Ptolemy produced his *Almagest* from studies he made at Alexandria, a book which established the accepted theory on astronomy and the nature of the universe for hundreds of years, until Copernicus' *De Revolutionibus Orbium Cuelestium* was published in 1543. Here Apollonius wrote on conic sections, Eratosthenes on history, geography, and astronomy, Timoarchus on the procession of the equinoxes, and Erasistratus and Herophilus on anatomy and physiology. Here Archimedes did much of his basic research.

Alexandria was but one of many cities that, during this Hellenistic era, developed centers of research and teaching. Pergamon, responding to the desire of its king, Eumenes II (197-159 B.C.), to commemorate military triumphs by beautifying the city and drawing to it the scholars of the world, erected a famous library of some 200,000 volumes and attracted to its halls scholars in the fields of art, travel, literature, grammar, and medicine. Here Galen, the ancients' most renowned medical scientist, worked. Toward the end of the last century B.C. and during the first part of the first century A.D., Rhodes rivaled both Athens and Alexandria as a center of study and research. It trained many artists, poets, and philosophers. There the silver-tongued rival of Demosthenes, Aeschines, taught rhetoric. To Rhodes came the leaders of Roman life of the period—Mark Antony, Pompey, Julius Caesar, Cicero, Brutus, and Cassius—to learn oratory. There Dionysus Thrax wrote the first known Greek grammar.

During the Alexandrian period of the Hellenistic Age, 338-146 B.C. approximately, considerable work was done throughout the civilized world toward the formulation and classification of man's knowledge. Grammar, the science of the Greek language, interested many scholars. Working from the earlier research of the sophists, Plato, Aristotle, and the Stoics, students sought to develop this area further in the interest of clearness of thinking. The studies of Aristophanes of Byzantium (*circa* 257-180 B.C.), of Aristarchus of Samothrace (220-143 B.C.), and of Dionysius Thrax (second century B.C.) made significant contributions to this field.

Mathematics was another subject that received considerable attention during this period. Hippocrates of Chios had, in the fifth century B.C., written the first textbook on geometry. Euclid founded the school of mathematics at Alexandria in the fourth century B.C. His pupil Ptolemy, and later Apollonius, systematized knowledge in the mathematical fields and did valuable research.

Archimedes (287-212 B.C.), for some time a student and research scholar at Alexandria, made many discoveries in the field of physics and invented several of the basic tools of modern culture in his attempts to make concrete the physical principles that he and others discovered.

Geography, though no new subject to Alexandrian scholars, was systematized and advanced by Eratosthenes of Cyrene (276-194 B.C.), who collected works on the subject for the library at Alexandria and systematized the material; and Strabo (first century B.C.), who employed material from mathematics, physics, political theory, and history in interpreting the subject.

Aristarchus of Samos developed the theory that the earth moves about the sun and estimated the distances of the sun and the moon from the earth with amazing accuracy. Hipparchus (second century B.C.) discovered the procession of the equinoxes, determined the solar year accurately, and plotted the revolutions of the moon. He calculated the magnitude of many stars and fixed the duration of the year with only an error of six minutes.

CHAPTER 5
Among the Early Romans

INTRODUCTION

For many, Roman civilization is nothing more than a transmitter of culture. This interpretation misses the true genius of the Roman world. Rome gave us no creative leap forward as did Athens and Greece, but she did give to this Grecian treasure the genius that was hers. No people have ever surpassed the Romans in ability to govern vast lands and innumerable people efficiently. The large-patterned political state is uniquely Roman. Along with this, of necessity, goes Roman skill in thinking through and developing the legal structure, with its basic philosophy, which made possible this new kind of state. Other people in ancient times attempted this, but Rome excelled them all. When she boasted of an empire reaching from the Tigris and Euphrates rivers in Asia to the Firth of Forth in Great Britain, from the Pillars of Hercules to beyond the Black Sea, and from the Rhine and the Danube deep into the Sahara Desert, she could also boast of a governmental structure that staggers the imagination and a legal pattern that was just and humane.

Rome was more by far than a transmitter of Greek culture. She was a creator of culture. Her genius was practical, not contemplative. She was a builder of material marvels, not philosophical systems. She was realistic and pragmatic, not idealistic. In her way, she gave to future generations much that made them what they were and are.

The Romans began their drive to empire in Italy. As late as 509 B.C., Rome was a small Latin city-state on the peninsula now known as Italy. The Latins learned from the Greeks and Carthaginians who traded and settled there. The Romans took over Rome about 510 B.C. and established an oligarchial republic, controlled by the landed elite known as patricians. This in-group ruled until around 450 B.C., at which time the large plebeian class, composed of poor artisans and small citizen-farmers, began to demand and obtain rights and privileges. This led to the Roman Republic, which functioned successfully for over three hundred years. The Republic was at war most of the time, and its army became one of history's most successful military forces. Italy was conquered, Carthage defeated, then Greece, Asia Minor, Syria, and Egypt.

The world of the Mediterranean belonged to the Romans. Still, the Romans did not really prosper. The gap between the rich and the poor grew wider. Most lived in poverty. Reform was attempted but ended in bloodshed. In the final analysis, the Republic collapsed and the Roman Empire began. The Empire lasted for approximately five centuries. There is no exact date for its passing, but by the end of the fifth century it had disappeared.

EDUCATION IN THE PRE-GREEK PERIOD

THE ROMAN IDEAL

Education is the shaping of young life in terms of a group ideal. This fact was never more in evidence than in early Rome, before the third century B.C. The Roman wanted his son to be manly, courageous, strong, energetic. He should be able to stand among his fellows proud and unflinching, conscious of his virility, yielding to no man in loyalty and strength of character. This was the first ingredient of character for a Roman, *virtus.* Bound up with this was a second quality, *pietas.* The Roman youth learned early that he lived in a world of unseen but powerful spirits. His ancestors watched over him and demanded reverence and respect, divine beings filled his environment and were jealous of his respect and obedience, and the sacred mores hewn out of centuries of social and spiritual living demanded his scrupulous observance.

The goal of early education in Rome was inculcation of these character traits. Other "goods," growing out of a full understanding of these basic characteristics, were modesty, dignity of bearing, frugality, and a dogged perseverance. This added up to an all-consuming sense of responsibility in whatever relationship the individual found himself— responsibility to himself, to his fellows, and to the spiritual forces of his universe. Morality for the Roman was lodged in his deep respect for authority, so that all these "goods" represented this respect in some form.

The Roman Family

The Roman child was born into a Roman family. Nothing was more important in making him what he was. Here was an institution dedicated to acculturating the young; teaching them the ancient virtues and ideals; impressing upon them the importance of obedience to authority, manliness, reverence, and all the other character traits that time and experience had woven into the concept of the good man.

In the family, the father had absolute authority and was not to be questioned or challenged. About him clustered the mother, the children, all the sons' wives and children, the clients, and the slaves. Unseen, but equally important for family life, were a host of spirits of the household. This family unit was a member of a kinship group called the *gens* which was a unit in a large administrative group, the *curia*. The father was the bridge between the family and these more inclusive social groupings. It was his duty to discipline his family, see to it that they all knew their duties and discharged them well, and maintain the unity and solidarity so necessary for group strength.

In early Rome the family was the major educational unit of society. Even when the nature of the state changed and new social institutions developed, the family remained basic to education.

There may have been schools in Rome before 300 B.C. There is some evidence to this effect. If so, they were of minor significance and in no way the major educational institutions of the period. In pre-Greek Rome the child learned by living in the narrow environment of the home and the wider environment of his city. In few places in history has the child been considered more important than there. To the Roman he was the bearer of tradition, the hope of the future, and was cherished fanatically.

The mother was the child's principal teacher. She was dedicated to her children. Very early, however, the father gave major concern to the education of his son. Nothing was of more importance to him. As soon as possible the boy accompanied his father on his tours of duty, watched and learned, and received the discipline necessary. He learned the skills and obligations of a Roman gentleman. The father felt that no other could be worthy of educating his son. No slave could be allowed to discipline the boy. This would demean him in the eyes of himself and others. Even the best-intentioned teacher could not, the father thought, give his child the loving devotion necessary to his becoming the man of which the father dreamed.

The mother felt an equal responsibility for the education of the girls in the family. She schooled them in their duties as wives and mothers, trained them in mastery of the skills necessary for operating a home, and taught them to read. Beyond this, no education was provided for girls.

As devoted as the father was to his son's education, it was evident that, as society in Rome became more complex, this would not be enough. The group and the community had to supplement his efforts in areas into which it was impossible for him to accompany the boy. When old enough, the youth began participating in the rituals and ceremonial functions of the city. He attended funerals and heard orators trace the history of great men and noble families and extol the ideals by which they lived. He sat with his father in public assemblies, saw laws made and interpreted, watched and learned as priests and religious dignitaries conducted the spiritual functions of the culture, attended banquets with his father, and listened as men told of the glories of the city and sang its songs. The school was society; the subjects learned were the ways in which this society functioned and a boy's place and duties in it.

Some boys, if their family status warranted, might be "apprenticed" to a distinguished citizen who would become a sponsor and initiate them into public service. One so fortunate might move into public office and become a citizen of great distinction.

This education in the home and in society was confined almost wholly to the upper classes of Rome. The masses received a far more modest education. The father did concern himself with the education of his sons and the mother with the education of her daughters. Since, however, the child was almost certainly destined to a life far less public than that of the upper-class youth, his education was focused more upon his place in society. He learned farming, hand craft, the skills of the sailor or the soldier in the ranks, and other jobs appropriate to his function in society.

Though in matters of practical life there was a clear distinction between the education of upper-class children and those of the lower classes, basically the family education of all Roman children was the same. The virtues of manliness and reverence, obedience to constituted authority and loyalty to the state, and courage and perseverance were instilled by all fathers insofar as they were able.

GREEK LEARNING IN THE ROMAN REPUBLIC

By the third century B.C., Greece had fallen under Macedonian control. Chaeronea was history, Alexander twenty-three years dead, and Athenian culture in all its forms was charming the Mediterranean world. At Alexandria, Rhodes, Pergamon, and a hundred or more other centers of population in the civilized world, Greek scholars were teaching and founding schools at the enthusiastic urgings of the citizens. To be Greek was truly to be, and all men of refinement and culture came to drink at the fountains of Greek learning.

It was only natural that Rome should fall under the spell of Greece and open her arms to Greek scholars and teachers. While many Greeks had come to Rome in earlier times to trade or share in the growth and development of the Italian peninsula, the event that opened Rome to Greek influence was the fall of Tarentum in 272 B.C. Many Greek citizens of this city were brought to Rome as captives. A number of these were freed in time and turned their attention to translating Greek classics into Latin. Around 340 B.C. Livius Andronicus translated Homer's *Odyssey*. This was followed by the translation of Greek dramas, stories, and other writings. Soon others were busy putting in the Roman tongue the treasures of Greek literature and philosophy. Although some resented this intrusion of a "foreign" culture, most Romans knew that here was something far beyond their creative talents and cherished it lovingly. By the first century B.C. Greek culture was the master of Rome, and every educated man was its devotee.

Along with Greek scholars came Greek schools, and to these schools went Roman children. At first it was fashionable for a family of wealth and distinction to employ a Greek teacher to instruct its household in Greek language and literature. Some families accepted slaves, who were educated men captured in wars with Greek cities, to instruct their children in reading and writing. As this custom was more generally accepted, some Greeks opened schools in which they offered to teach whatever their clients wished, from the rudiments of the Greek language to philosophy and the sciences. In time, two prongs of Greek influence were clearly evident in Rome: the private teacher devoting his attention to the family of an aristocrat and the teacher operating his own school to which anyone with the fee could come and learn. Both became immensely popular.

Opposition to all this was based on the usual conservative belief that ancient values and customs were being destroyed by these foreign radicals. Cato the Censor, in 161 B.C., persuaded the Roman Senate to banish all philosophers and rhetoricians from the city. The necessary decree was issued, but it was most unpopular. Greek teachers remained, were accepted openly, and in a short time the decree was revoked, and Rome fell almost wholly under Greek influence. Even Cato, in his old age, took up the study of Greek.

Soon a complete pattern of Greek schools took shape in Rome. At the elementary level was the reading and writing school taught by a *ludi magister.* This was called the *ludus,* or play school. Next was the grammar school under the tutorship of a *grammaticus* who taught all the liberal subjects. Beginning as a Greek grammar school, this institution gradually incorporated into its curriculum the Latin language and literature as these developed in Roman life. At the peak of this educational pattern was the school of rhetoric taught by a *rhetor.* Here boys prepared to be professional advocates or lawyers. Rome had fallen completely under the spell of conquered Greece.

LATIN GRAMMAR AND LITERATURE IN THE DYING REPUBLIC

The last two centuries of the pre-Christian era were turbulent times for the Roman world. The small city-state of early days had become the center of a varied and populous empire demanding new ideas of government and economic life. The death by assassination of Tiberius Gracchus in 132 B.C. threw Rome into a period of violence and wars. Class was pitted against class as the Senate, now a self-perpetuating oligarchy, fought to destroy the popular party and its economic methods. Marius, leader of the popular party, began building a professional military machine to conquer new territories and control the Roman Empire.

While statesmen of the "old school" strove to influence the people to hold on to the virtues of the past, statesmen of the "new look" were moving inevitably in the direction of world empire. The "new frontier" would not be closed to Rome forever.

Stimulated by Greek grammar and literature, Rome was on her way to producing a Latin grammar and literature which would stand alongside Greek in a school that eventually bore the name of the Latin Grammar School. Beginning with the simple Latin grammar of Servius Nicanor and the teaching of Lucius Gallus, several noted Romans turned their attention to developing the science of Latin linguistics and producing a literature in the language. Among the names that stand out in the history of this development are Lucius Accius, Lucilius, Quintus Valerius, and Lucius Aelius Stilo Praeconinus, one a tragic dramatist, another a poet, the third a linguist, and the fourth a philologist and teacher of many of the leading Romans of the era.

One of Stilo Praeconinus' pupils, Marcus Tarentius Varro, 116-27 B.C., was an antiquarian and a profuse writer on all things Roman. Among his lost writings is a nine-book encyclopedia in which he sought to summarize the entire world of scholarship. This, scholars tell us, was named *Disciplinarum libri IX.* In its nine books he presented a compendium of all the liberal arts: grammar, rhetoric, logic, arithmetic, geometry, astronomy, music, medicine, and architecture. Five hundred years later Martianus Capella was to base his *Marriage of Philology and Mercury* on this work, producing a statement of the liberal arts that set the pattern of liberal education almost until modern times.

Along with the development of Latin grammar went the growth of a Latin literature that has served as the curriculum of scholarship down through the ages. A generation or so ago there was no scholar not thoroughly familiar with the writings of Caesar, Cicero, Lucretius, Sallus, Catulus, Virgil, Horace, Ovid, and Plautus, to name only a few.

By the time the Empire was firmly established and threats of internal war had subsided, Latin was the language of both the grammar school and the school of the *rhetor*. The small child who had been forced to learn Greek before his own language now began his instruction with Latin. The Roman citizen throughout the Empire, whatever his racial origin, had a literature he could call his own which served as a bond of scholarship wherever men of learning met. In time this was to become the language of the Roman world, to be corrupted, lolled, and twisted by unfamiliar tongues into the Romance languages of western Europe. Schools were everywhere, books flooded the market, and libraries became common possessions in cities and small hamlets loyal to Rome.

Caesar, in the first century B.C., conquered Gaul. After his murder and the victory of Octavius, Rome died as a republic and was born as an empire. Augustus became the divine Emperor in 27 B.C. The struggle between those who would perpetuate the Republic and those who would move out to Empire came to an end. No longer was the orator who could sway the Roman Senate and the people of the Eternal City the determiner of policy and the holder of power. As provincial cities came into prominence as centers of government, the army and a vast governmental bureaucracy became avenues to power and prestige. The man trained to control these or work effectively with them was the man of the hour, the master citizen.

MARCUS TULLIUS CICERO (106 43 B.C.)

Cicero was the greatest of the Roman orators, the most brilliant representative of classical republican ideals, and the principal writer in Rome's golden age of literature. Rejecting a Latin education in favor of Greek in his youth, he became a master of the Latin language.

He wrote copiously on many subjects. For his thinking on education we must turn to his treatises on rhetoric, especially his *De Oratore*. This book, he wrote to a friend, "does not deal in hackneyed rules and embraces the whole theory of oratory as laid down by Isocrates and Aristotle." The first of the three books into which this work is divided deals with the studies necessary for an orator and describes the type of man he must be.

All men, he believed, who aspire to leadership in society must have a basic liberal arts education designed to develop them completely. The advocate, in particular, is not merely one with a bag of tricks, skills of public debate, and behind-the-scenes compromise. He must be an individual thoroughly grounded in "every branch of useful knowledge." These should include philosophy, mathematics in all its branches, physics, history, music, grammar, logic, and morals.

A leader, Cicero believed, is a man with an obligation to society. This necessitates his being a good man, one imbued with the highest morality of the age. He must be honest, public-minded, devoted to the good of the people, unselfish, and pure in mind and body. He must represent the best in his times. His education and training from birth must steep him in tradition, give him a clear moral sense of right and justice, and equip him with the best that learning has to offer.

Cicero was no starry-eyed idealist. His thinking was truly pragmatic. Experience was, for him, a master teacher. He would bring up a child in the best tradition of his fathers and train him for the real world about him. The orator, for example, must be all that we have said above, and well schooled in the ways of the city, the demands of government, and the skills of his profession.

Cicero left to posterity a purity in the use of Latin which has been unexcelled, a model for orators throughout the ages, and the ideal for champions of the right. He was the last of the leaders of Rome's aristocratic republic. Energetic, devoted, and dedicated to the values that the inevitable march of history was leaving behind, he died a disappointed and bitter man. When he discovered that a price had been put on his head, he attempted to flee, but, being blown back to shore by unfavorable winds, gave up and returned to his villa saying, "Let me die in the country which I have often saved."

EDUCATION UNDER IMPERIAL CONTROL

In early Rome, the education of the child was the parents' responsibility. Custom, tradition, and pressures from the community set the pattern in which the parents moved, but there were no official regulations. Adults assumed this responsibility as part of their duty to the group and the future.

As Rome moved toward imperial status, the value of education became more apparent and the need for its encouragement evident. The stages of development are interesting and instructive. Encouraged by her model, Greece, Rome had developed a language of precision and beauty and a literature of no mean proportions. Also, the example of Greece encouraged Rome to give attention to the fine arts and the sciences. Roman cities were adorned with beautiful public buildings, giving government-sponsored work to architects and to artists in stone and wood. The right of citizenship was extended by Caesar to all physicians and teachers of the liberal arts in Rome. Even when the city was devastated by famine so that Augustus had to order all foreigners out, he made an exception of physicians and teachers.

This practice of giving preference to artists and teachers and of providing public financing for buildings, museums, libraries, and dramatic and musicial performances was continued by the emperors of Rome. Augustus employed Marcus Verius Flacus to tutor his sons and grandsons and moved him and his school into the palace. For the first time in Rome, here was a school under imperial patronage, a palace school for the education of future rulers. It amounted to recognition that a successful state must supervise closely the education of its leaders, both with money and direction.

The next step in this process was taken by Vespasian, who, in the first century A.D., provided money to pay the salaries of Latin and Greek teachers of grammar and rhetoric in designated cities. Trajan established a fund to provide education for poor children in Rome. Hadrian built a school of literature, the *Athenaeum,* in Rome and paid the salaries of many philosophers, poets, and rhetoricians. Antoninus Pius extended this practice to teachers in the provinces.

Athens, intellectual center of the Roman world, was of special interest to many Roman emperors. Young men from the imperial city and the provinces flocked to Athens to study in her philosophical schools. Hadrian was an intimate friend of many philosophers and sophists in Athens and did much to further scholarship and the fine arts there. Marcus Aurelius went to Athens in 176 A.D. to be initiated into the Eleusinian mysteries. In honor of this occasion he added to the municipal chair of rhetoric—established earlier by Antoninus Pius—another, with a much larger salary paid from the imperial treasury. He chose Herodes Atticus, a famous rhetorician of the day, as the first occupant of this chair. In addition, he provided money for the salaries of eight professors of philosophy, two to teach in each of the four schools of Athens—Academy, Lyceum, Epicurean, and Stoic. These men were to be selected by Herodes Atticus. This move established the University of Athens. Herodes was the head of the university, and the philosophers supported by the Emperor were under his direction. As other teachers received government support, they fell under control of Herodes' successors.

By the middle of the third century, this practice was general throughout the empire. Many municipalities followed the lead of Rome and began establishing schools and paying the teachers. Additional privileges and immunities were granted these new public servants. In 425 A.D., Theodosius built and staffed at public expense a great university at Constantinople.

When an emperor provided the salaries of teachers, he demanded a hand in selecting those to receive these benefits. By 362 A.D., Julian was demanding that the names of all individuals nominated for positions receiving public support be submitted to him for final determination. The people accepted this move as natural and raised only token protest as other emperors increased their authority over education. It was no surprise, then, that Theodosius was able to establish a complete monopoly in education, regulating who should be allowed to teach and what opinions and ideas they might hold.

When, in 529 A.D., Justinian wished to close all "pagan" schools and turn education over to the Christians, he had no trouble. His method was simple: issue the decree and stop all payment of salaries and subsidies.

MARCUS FABIUS QUINTILIANUS (*circa* 35-95 A.D.)

Quintilian was born at Calagurris in Spain. Coming to Rome as a youth, he was given a thorough education in the best elementary, secondary, and rhetorical schools. One of his teachers of oratory was Palaemon, and his model of the perfect orator was Cicero, in whom he could find only little faults which it pained him to mention. From 61 to 68 A.D. he lived in Spain in the retinue of Galba, the future emperor, with whom he returned to Rome. Then for twenty years he was head of the foremost school of oratory in the city and a pleader at court. Vespasian established a chair of rhetoric for him and paid his salary.

He retired in 88 A.D. to devote his time to writing one of the most famous books of all times, the *Institutio Oratoria.* After two years of retirement Domitian persuaded him to undertake the education of his two grand-nephews, whom he considered successors to his throne. As a reward, Quintilian was made a consul and received imperial favors.

The *Institutes of Oratory* was a manual dealing with the education of the young orator. Oratory in Quintilian's day had become what many are wont to call "silver Latin." Its roots lay in the excessive concentration upon poetry in the early stages of literary training. Although Quintilian preferred the Ciceronian style, he was unable to stem the tide of the new oratory which had begun even before Cicero's death. The poetizing of Latin prose continued, in spite of Quintilian and others, until it reached the *reducto ad absurdum* in the style of Fronto, an orator who strove for the startling, the quaint, the epigrammatic, and employed a thousand tricks to please and amuse his audiences.

For Quintilian the orator was a most important personage in Roman life. His old status and function no longer existed, but new conditions demanded another type of speaker. Eulogies of famous men, discussions of public matters, speeches of encouragement to armies about to enter battles, pleadings before courts of law, these and other duties made the orator a necessary part of Roman life. To assume this responsibility, Quintilian held, a man must have three qualifications not easily developed. First, he must be of good moral character. He will shape the moral conscience of the people. If he exhibits in his daily life and in his addresses integrity, devotion to high principles, and a dedication to the best interests of the state, he will serve the good of the state. Second, he must be a master of the liberal arts and sciences. His learning must be complete so that he will speak with authority and conviction. The listener will sense the uncertainty of those who do not know and refuse to follow them. On the other hand, the audience will feel confident in the presence of one who knows. Third, the orator must be able to speak well. He must study inflection, voice, gesture, facial expressions, bearing, use of the entire body, and his audiences. All that he does must serve to bring the material of his address and the audience into a unity such that response becomes automatic.

Sincerity was, for Quintilian, a major trait of the true orator. To speak simply to entertain, to make money, or to manipulate an audience was for him unworthy of the orator. The speaker, who most often would represent his client, must abide by a code of ethics which balanced his duty to his client's rights with the rights of the state. The pleader may charge a fee for his services, but one adjusted to the client's ability to pay, never excessive. This fee is to be accepted not as payment but rather "as a friendly acknowledgement of service." He must advise the client in terms of his best interest, but never at the expense of the state or justice.

While Quintilian was interested primarily in the education of the orator, he had a great deal to say about education in general. As one reads the *Institutes,* he is impressed with the modern flavor of much that this first century writer has to say. He realized that the early years of the child's education are of major importance. During these, both father and mother should supervise their children carefully, allowing nothing evil to come into their einvironment. Only the best teachers, men and women of unblemished reputations and complete dedication plus the best possible training, should be allowed to work with small children.

Quintilian was a strong believer in education in the school as against private instruction. Boys, he wrote, learn better in groups, they can profit by the example of others, and they will form friendships that may endure throughout life. Competition, learning through shared experiences, and comparison of oneself with others he believed to be good methodology. Further, a class will stimulate the teacher to do his best, while one pupil may allow the teacher to be content with less than his best. However, Quintilian was careful to stress the necessity for keeping class size small enough to allow the teacher to work effectively with individuals.

The teacher should develop his teaching in terms of the individual. Quintilian recognized individual differences and the necessity for teaching in terms of these. The teacher must study each child, learn his abilities and traits, his weaknesses and strengths, his interests and "blind spots," and shape the curriculum and methodology in terms of his findings.

A child will learn best when stimulated by praise, emulation, and rewards. Quintilian opposed corporal punishment because it disgraced the boy, was only temporary in its effect, and hardened the child. One who is punished physically will come to hate and fear both the teacher and the thing taught, will shun society and be uneasy in the presence of others who know of his disgrace, and will tend to shut himself off from learning. Rather, Quintilian would have the teacher discover the interests of the child and motivate learning as a way to satisfy these interests.

The curriculum which Quintilian suggested is basically literary. He placed little emphasis upon development of the body, feeling that there was the danger that one would become so involved in the "life . . . spent among oil . . . and . . . over wine" that he might neglect the studies of the mind. Reading and writing were basic to this curriculum. Careful training in both would lay the only possible foundation of a good education. This should be followed by the study of grammar, Greek first and then Latin. This should include syntax, linguistics, literature, and composition. Advancing from this, the pupil should devote considerable time to astronomy, philosophy, geometry, arithmetic, and music.

The young man who aspired to leadership in the state should complete his education by studying in the school of the *rhetor*. Here he should master history, literature, rhetoric, logic, professional ethics, and literary style.

PROFESSIONAL EDUCATION IN ROME

Oratory was one of the oldest professions in Rome. Its roots lay in those very early times when men sought to persuade each other in tribal councils. It developed into a necessary part of life during the Republic, creating the school of the *rhetor* and producing men of the caliber of Cicero and Quintilian. A major impetus in this direction was the Greek tradition of oratory which reached back to the *Iliad* and the *Odyssey,* possibly earlier, and culminated in the sophists. Along with the flood of Greek culture washing over the Alexandrian world came Greek oratory, Greek teachers, and Greek schools of oratory.

EDUCATION OF THE LAWYER

One of the functions of the orator in both Greek and Roman life was to represent a client before the courts. Here is the lawyer as he first appeared on the scene of western life.

In the early days of the Roman state, private teachers prepared orators who then learned their trade by watching procedures in court or working with an experienced advocate. By the time of the Empire, private schools offering to teach the law appeared. Some of these, especially those in Rome, Athens, Alexandria, and Carthage, became famous and drew students from far and wide. They developed the teaching of law into an art and had some influence upon the development of Roman law. The method was to read and memorize the law and the comments of famous jurists upon it. Often teachers lectured on shadowy points of law and gave their opinions and reasons.

Theodosius, who reigned during the late fourth century A.D., established a state monopoly of education, including legal instruction, making it a crime for public teachers to have private pupils and private teachers to teach publicly. At the same time, he established public professorships of law in Constantinople. This marked the end of private teaching of the law in the Roman Empire, since all candidates wishing to practice in the courts were required to present to the Praetorian Prefect a statement of proficiency signed by a professor in one of the public schools of law.

Justinian further limited the teaching of law by permitting only three public schools of law—those in Rome, Constantinople, and Beyrouth. In these schools the students studied for five years. They mastered the *Institutes* during the first year, the *Digest* during the next three years, and the *Code* in the fifth year. The *Novels* was studied as the decisions fitted into the material being mastered.

While the teaching of law in Rome and Beyrouth disappeared with the invasions from the north, the school at Constantinople remained strong and influential throughout the Middle Ages. With invaders everywhere, the Empire maintained sovereignty in the Exarchate of Ravenna where, in the eleventh century, the University of Bologna was to rise around the teaching of Roman law.

EDUCATION OF THE PHYSICIAN

Medicine in Rome was rooted in Greek practice and theory. The city did not have anything that could be called a science of medicine until the third century B.C., when Greek physicians were accepted. Greek medical men came to Rome and set up practices which combined the duties of physician, surgeon, and pharmacist. In time the government took an interest in their work, granted them special privileges and immunities, and at times paid them an honorarium. During the second century B. C., it became fashionable for wealthy or prominent families to employ Greek physicians as their personal doctors or to entrust these duties to slaves trained in Greek medicine.

Greek medicine was a fixture in Roman life by the first century B.C. The government was beginning to establish hospitals and to make provisions for public medicine. The armed services had their medical corps, naval hospitals were common, and cities throughout the empire were employing public physicians.

Despite all this concern with medicine, Rome never standardized medical education. A young man wishing to become a physician would place himself at the disposal of a doctor, study with him, accompany him on house calls, and assist him whenever necessary. In this way he learned his profession. During the years of apprenticeship the student read widely from Greek texts and, as Roman texts began to appear, from the works of Dioscorides, Galen, Celsus, and others.

During the Empire, regular schools of medicine appeared in large cities. Here students were taught by noted physicians, medical problems were discussed, and theoretical and practical research was undertaken. Students were encouraged to give considerable time to service in the hospitals, where they could learn through experience. Out of these schools came many of the books which were standard in the education of medieval doctors.

Interest in medicine displayed by emperors, municipal authorities, and people of wealth did at times restrict the work of doctors who might be forced to follow the wishes of those paying for their education and providing places for them to work. However, this interest did provide education, hospitals, and opportunities to do research, all of which would have been severely limited without the money made available.

Education of the Philosopher

The young man wishing to study philosophy in the ancient tradition attended a school at Athens or in one of the large cities of the Empire. Here were followers of the great thinkers of the past, studying and interpreting the writings of their masters, and in some places there were men able to add something to this inheritance. But this was only a small handful. Most Romans who studied philosophy cared little for the speculations of the past. Their interest lay in discovering ways in which they might use philosophy in their practical activities. Leaders and literary men found in philosophy enrichment, freedom, vision, and understandings valuable in the conduct of their affairs. Others were turning to the more mystical and esoteric areas of philosophy for comfort and strength to endure a world that was becoming increasingly unbearable. And there were many who looked to philosophy as a source of knowledge and wisdom they could sell to the disconsolate for a price. These latter were the professional "consultants" and "advisers" of their day. They wore the philosopher's garb, advertised their wares, and became wealthy by meeting a growing need.

These philosophers took pupils whom they trained for a fee. Some even established schools, turning out numbers of men able to set themselves up in business, serve wealthy homes as private chaplains, or devote their skills to the courts of emperors or local municipal authorities.

One must not get the impression that these philosophers were charlatans or tricksters. Some of them were, just as today some ministers, rabbis, or priests fail to live up to the high standards of their profession. The majority were dedicated men striving to fill a need in their society. As the Roman Empire grew and its power spread throughout the world, it developed many characteristics that disturbed earnest men and women. Corruption in high places, moral disintegration, weakening of the old state religion, increasing taxes, disregard of values that had seemed so basic in days gone by, selfishness, greed, all these and many more were evident in Roman culture. They caused many to give up hope in things material and turn to matters of the mind and the spirit for help and strength. It was to this growing number of men and women tottering on the edge of despair that these "philosophers" came with hope and courage.

LATIN TEXTBOOKS

We have spoken in some detail of the writings of Cicero, Quintilian, and other Romans of the first century B.C. and first century A.D. Many others wrote profusely. Some of their works are known to us directly, while most of them have been lost and have come to our attention only through references made to them by others.

A few of the books written in the fourth and fifth centuries have become classics in the history of education, in that they were the textbooks of Latin schools and Latin students almost until modern times. One of the earliest of these is the *Ars Minor* of Aelius Donatus who lived and taught around the middle of the fourth century. This book is often referred to as the *Donat*. It is a brief work dealing with parts of speech. Until well into the sixteenth century, this was the elementary Latin grammar studied by all boys. Other introductions were written, following the format and content of the *Donat*, but none attained the popularity of this fifteen-page book.

Another textbook which achieved great popularity in the Middle Ages was called the *Distiches of Cato*. Its date is unknown, although scholars tend to place it sometime in the later Roman Empire rather than, as some had supposed, at the time of Cato the Elder. It is an elementary Latin reader, teaching moral virtues by couplets which give the child a reading lesson and a lesson in right conduct.

Early in the sixth century, a grammarian at Constantinople called Priscian wrote an advanced Latin grammar. The title under which the work was published is *Institutiones Grammaticae*. It consists of eighteen books, the first sixteen treating of sounds, word formation, and inflections, the remaining two dealing specifically with syntax.

Martianus Capella, an advocate living in Carthage in the fifth century, wrote a little book which he called *The Marriage of Philology and Mercury*. Building on the earlier work of Varro, he prepared a summary of what was for him all man's worthwhile knowledge. Two of the nine books are introductory. The other seven are descriptions of grammar, rhetoric, dialectic or logic, arithmetic, geometry, astronomy, and music. It is believed that Capella omitted medicine and architecture, which Varro included, because he was writing only about those arts necessary for the gods; being immortal, they had no need of medicine or architecture. This book set the pattern for the Seven Liberal Arts, the essence of the medieval arts curriculum.

EDUCATION IN A FADING EMPIRE

Schools, developed in Rome out of ancient educational practices and Greek influences, spread throughout the Empire. In every center of population, elementary schools, Latin grammar schools, and schools of rhetoric flourished long after the days of Roman brilliance had passed.

Built on the foundations of "pagan" life and thought, these schools were gradually infiltrated by the newer Christian ideas until, in many places, their essence was Christian even though the shell resembled paganism.

For most of these schools Quintilian was the authority on pedagogy. His ideas about teaching, understanding the child, use of children's interests, class and group teaching, love and respect rather than punishment, were the ideals for which they strove. The basic texts were Cicero's speeches and writings and Virgil's poetry, plus the compendia of knowledge that were being assembled.

This learning was largely literary and was divorced from the exciting and challenging life of the times. Pupils looked to the past and strove to hold on to its values and glories while their world was changing. Constantinople was gradually becoming the true capital of the Empire, and Greek its official language. Virile, dynamic people bordering on the Empire began pushing south as they could find weaknesses in outer defenses. As they moved in, some cities and villages shrank in population and importance, and some roads and trade routes were abandoned. Many centers of population turned to independence as they found the power of the Empire unable to give them protection. Local strong men gained power as they were able to protect the populace from the invaders or make satisfactory adjustments to life with these people. Much that had been Roman disappeared, giving way to new ideas, new institutions, and a new faith.

Schools began to appear, usually under private sponsorship, to meet the needs of individuals in this new environment. Some of these were patterned after the more practical schools of the Empire, while others were new institutions for a new age. Shorthand, land surveying, architecture, medicine, law, and theology were taught as the demand warranted.

In some parts of the changing Empire, those least affected by invaders and changing conditions, schools of the Roman type grew and prospered. Scholars from all parts of Europe came to study under great teachers. There classical scholarship was preserved during the long years of transition, and centuries later when attempts were made to revive the classical tradition, scholars from these schools were sought after by princes and emperors to organize schools and teach their subjects.

The traditional idea that with the "barbarian" invasions and the "collapse" of the Roman Empire, a darkness spread over the western world, and scholarship and learning were in eclipse for hundreds of years is not rooted in fact. As we learn more about that period of history from the fourth to the tenth centuries, we realize that here was a transition age when much of the past was retained in one form or another, much was changed to meet new conditions, and new ideas and institutions were created. Only a scholar, standing in the Renaissance and looking with longing to the Age of Pericles and the Golden Age of Cicero and Virgil, a scholar with longing for a brilliant past, could forget what had happened between these two great creative eras and stigmatize the period with the name "Dark Ages" or "Middle Ages." Modern scholarship presents us with a vastly different picture of this Age of Faith.

CHAPTER 6

Among the Early Christians

INTRODUCTION

Christians held ideals on behavior and education, but often these ideals gave way to the practical realization that if there were no participation in the affairs of their community, there would not be any influence in the ultimate direction of things. The early Christians were willing to make concessions, providing they did not have to give in on any of their doctrinal tenents. Thus they were willing to participate in educational programs, providing the religious and moral issues were retained in the family. As many of the Christians saw it, the function of education was to develop techniques and evidences of learning, such as proper language usage, correct speaking, and the like. If its study included the writings of the pagans, care must be taken that the morals of the children were not affected.

These concepts are central to Christian influence on education. We must step backward in history to trace the genesis of this fourth major foundation stone of Western culture and education.

The Greeks gave the West an intellectual and artistic heritage. The Romans preserved this and passed it on, adding their own contributions in the fields of law and government. The Christians, inheriting the ethical and moral sensitivity of their Hebrew ancestry, added to this rich heritage of classical times the transcendent personality of Jesus; the consciousness of a universal, loving, and ethical god; and the belief that man, through self-sacrifice, can attain such perfection that goodness and brotherhood will reign in a "kingdom of heaven" on earth. This Christian legacy was institutionalized in the Church, and its integrity was preserved during the long generations of change and readjustment known as the Middle Ages. This Church was able to sell Christianity to the Roman Empire and new citizens moving in from the frontiers and to pass it on to our own day as one way of salvation from the fearful possibilities of this materialistic and atomic civilization.

To understand the rise of Christianity we must avoid the mistake of so many who divorce it from the times in which it was conceived and developed. Christianity was no sudden miracle bursting upon a world unprepared, a miracle fashioned and perpetrated by a heartsick divinity to save a wayward world. It was the inevitable outgrowth of the conditions of the age and of the innumerable strands of history out of which the age was woven.

Hebrew culture had developed through many generations, taking as its own along the way much that other cultures had to offer. The Jews had been pawns in many games of trade and power played by great and small states throughout the centuries. They had suffered exile and returned to rebuild their temple and worship again at their holy places. They had conceived a god who loved and cared for his own people, a god more powerful than all the others. In time he became the only god and their religion a monotheism. Their prophets had taken a god of battle and made him into a god of justice, righteousness, and love, a god who forgives the wayward and the sinful who will repent. The Hebrew had developed a law that was sacred and all-consuming, a law that regulated every minute phase of life and demanded obedience under the penalty of death. Long before Jesus' birth the people had been split into two camps, the one championing the god of the law and the other the god of the prophets, a god of justice versus a god of love.

By the first century, Jerusalem had become, in many respects, a Greek city, despite the bitter opposition of many who feared that Greek culture would destroy the moral essence of the ancient Hebrew culture. Herod, who was Greek at heart, was striving to share with Palestine all the richness which he found among the Greeks. A gymnasium was built near the temple; Greek teachers strolled through the land or settled in population centers to talk with Hebrew youths of Plato, Aristotle, Epicurus, and the Stoics. Greek ways of life and thought were not uncommon throughout the land, and young men were asking questions that disturbed the old men and the bearded rabbis.

By 63 B.C. Palestine was definitely part of the Roman world. Herod was recognized as the king of Judea by the Roman senate in 40 B.C., with the approval of Octavian and Mark Antony. His rule, lasting until 4 B.C., was a period of general prosperity during which many Roman institutions, including the Roman school pattern, were introduced into Jewish life. The years that followed saw Roman rule tightening and Roman authorities successfully shaping the life of Palestine.

It was into this atmosphere that Jesus was born. His ancestry was lower-class Hebrew. His life was spent in a narrow area of Palestine under strong Greek and Roman influence. His followers were products of this same cultural pattern. After his death, those who gave institutional structure to his doctrines were Roman citizens who took their case to Rome when they were convinced that they could not receive a just hearing in Jerusalem.

Christianity began in an environment shaped by three cultures— Hebrew, Greek, and Roman. It was a product of these cultures and worked into its theology and institutional pattern strands from all three. To forget this is to distort history and to fail to understand the meaning of Christianity for Western culture and education.

JESUS

Early Christianity was centered in the personality of Jesus. Did he actually exist? If so, who was he? What did he think? What did he say and do? All these questions have challenged scholars down the ages. Whatever the answers we give to them, we cannot escape the fact that something happened in the world of the first century that changed the history of western Europe and spread to all corners of the modern world.

Our evidence of events during these early days of Christianity is vague and frustrating. There are meager references to Jesus in the literature of the centuries that followed, but the bulk of material upon which we must base our conclusions is to be found in the New Testament and a few "sayings of Jesus" which have been discovered in more recent times. The authenticity of all this material has been challenged and championed by scholars throughout history.

How did these writings portray Jesus? They saw him as a young Jew from the lower classes. Joseph, his father, was a carpenter, a poor man who could not afford the best accommodations when his wife was about to be delivered of child. He must have received his basic education in his home and in the school of the synagogue. Whether or not he was touched by the Greek and Roman schools which were everywhere in Palestine and certainly at Jerusalem, we do not know. As a fairly bright young man of his day, he was most certainly familiar with this education and could not have remained totally unaffected.

As he grew, he came under the influence of the community synagogue school, where he learned the tradition and culture of his people. As a youth we find him in the temple at Jerusalem listening to the teachers there and asking questions of them.

We can assume, then, that his upbringing was not dissimilar to that of any other middle- or lower-class boy of the day. His parents cared for his early education. His mother taught him behavior, tradition, and simple religion. His father taught him the carpenter's trade. At the synagogue school he learned reading and writing and the basic principles of religion. He listened on the streets and in the temple to teachers and wise men but was probably never a pupil of any. Other educative forces in his environment must have contributed to his learning, since no one could live in Palestine at this time and remain wholly insulated from events that were swirling all about him.

When he reached young manhood and became sure of his mission, he too became a teacher, in the footsteps of the sophists. He strolled among the people, followed by a group of young men and women who listened to his words, asked questions, and proposed problems. Often he antagonized the legalists and persons in authority who attempted to trap him by presenting knotty issues. In this teaching he was concerned with religious and moral questions rather than philosophical issues. He did not argue or reason, but "taught with authority."

His followers were simple people of the community, not the philosophers, wise men, or authorities. He taught them in ways they could understand. He talked with them whenever they would listen. When they asked him questions, he gave them answers suited to their understanding. At times he quoted or created a proverb, a figurative statement of truth, pungent and vivid. At other times he used parables to illustrate his lessons.

In Jesus we have a sophist of a new sort. The sophists had been teachers of oratory, logic, philosophy, and ethics. They had striven earnestly to prepare young men for the demands of their age. Those who lived in the first century continued this tradition with, of course, the new emphases made necessary by the conditions of the time. Jesus saw man's need in terms of the spirit. He felt that the most pressing problems of the day were those of man's relations to his fellows and to his god. It was with these problems that he struggled, and those who came to him to learn went away comforted. Jesus was a sophist of the spirit, the others, sophists of the mind. Both were necessary in first century Roman culture.

CHRISTIANITY IN THE PAGAN WORLD

Jesus was a Jew devoted to the prophetic tradition. He taught in the synagogue, on the streets, and in private homes as the occasion permitted. He talked of God and man, sin and salvation, duty, sacrifice, the poor and unwanted, rewards and punishment. All this was within the Hebrew tradition. He did not think of himself as in any way antagonistic to or outside the best in Hebrew culture.

Many scholars believe that had it not been for Paul, Jesus' teachings would have been lost in an obscure sect of the period, just one sect among many. Saul of Tarsus was a devoutly orthodox Jew who intensely hated everything that threatened the ancient Hebrew law. He saw in this small sect of men and women devoted to the teachings and the memory of Jesus just such a threat and devoted himself to rooting it up and destroying it as completely as possible.

On the road to Damascus, "breathing threatening and slaughter against the disciples of the Lord," he suffered a traumatic experience characterized by blindness and the hearing of voices. When he recovered, he was a different man, a devoted disciple of "the Lord" and the most ardent propagandist of the movement he had so recently striven to destroy. From this moment he became Paul, missionary of Christianity, first organizer of the sect. As he preached, taught, and organized small groups in large centers of population in the Roman Empire, he discovered considerable interest in his work on the part of both Jews and non-Jews. While the movement was Jewish in origin and its development was in the hands of the followers of Jesus, Paul reached out beyond the Jewish community and brought into the groups he established many non-Jews. After much discussion of the problem of permitting non-Jews to participate and after many compromises, the Jews began dropping out, leaving the movement more and more to non-Jews. In time the transition was complete, and Christianity was left to the Gentiles.

CHRISTIAN EDUCATION IN THE PAGAN WORLD

THE HOME AS A SCHOOL

The home was the first educational institution of Christianity. Early converts to the Christian movement, both Jew and non-Jew, were adults. The feeling was that adherence to the church was a matter to be considered carefully and prayerfully. The early church had no place for children except as their parents inducted them into the Christian life. When a parent turned to the church and gave his solemn commitment to its principles, he endeavored to rear his children according to the moral and intellectual ideals demanded. The parent became the child's first teacher.

Both father and mother accepted this responsibility. The early literature often emphasizes the mother's part in her child's education to the neglect of the father's part. Timothy, beloved assistant of Paul, was first educated by his grandmother, Lois, and his mother, Eunice, both Jewesses converted to Christianity. Augustine attributed his early education to his mother, Monica. Origen was given his first training by his father, Leonidas.

PAGAN SCHOOLS

People affiliating with the early Christian church had been educated in the schools of the Roman Empire. Some had had only the barest instruction outside the home. Others had attended Latin Grammar Schools and schools of oratory. Some had been affiliated with the philosophical schools or studied with noted sophists. All this education was permeated with pagan ideas and worship of pagan gods. Jews who turned to Christianity had much of their education in the synagogue or at the feet of some rabbi.

Now that they had become Christian, they were forced to consider carefully the education of their children. Should they enroll them in pagan schools, or send them to the synagogue, or begin building a new system of education fitted to their new religious affiliation? This was no easy question to answer. Early Christianity had no elementary schools, leaving the parents to choose between pagan schools and ignorance. After all, the ability of even the most conscientious parent was limited. Could he give his child the learning necessary for success in adult life? While many parents had a deep aversion to pagan schools and could not send their children to them, they recognized that they did not have the right to deny these children the education they would need for success.

To deal with this problem the early church undertook to supply schools for the children of its members. Immediately after Jesus' death his followers expected him to return and establish his kingdom. Therefore they made no provision for education. As this belief faded, the church turned to preaching and teaching as a means for instruction of the membership and their families. The sermon became a lesson in scriptures, morals, or tradition. Classes were held by anyone who considered himself fitted to teach. In this early Christian community were "apostles, prophets, and teachers" speaking by authority of "the Lord." They exhorted, explained, related, and taught as they were able, and the people learned. They were not officials of the church, nor did they carry credentials testifying to their orthodoxy. They taught wherever they could attract a group or a class.

TEACHING CATECHUMENS

Paul could accept adult Jews and Gentiles into his nascent churches with a minimum of selectivity. They usually had the adequate moral and spiritual background and education to function in the group effectively. As the movement grew and attracted more Gentiles without this basic preparation, the problem of selection became acute. Further, Christianity became suspect among orthodox Jews and many Romans. Saul of Tarsus was not the only Jew who felt the Christian movement to be subversive, and the Romans were beginning to see in it an unpatriotic challenge to the state religion. These facts made leaders more conscious than ever of the impression the Christian made on a potentially hostile public. A devout, knowledgeable member was a definite asset, while anything else was a real danger.

Consequently, the church developed a procedure of preparing individuals, catechumens, for church membership; this procedure amounted to an education. An applicant for membership would be accepted on probation after a preliminary examination and an impressive initiatory ceremony. Then, for two years, in some cases longer, he was subject to instruction by one or more individuals designated by the congregation. During this time he was allowed to sit in on the service only during the reading of the Scriptures and the sermon. If he proved himself worthy, earnest, and able to understand the doctrines of the church, he was permitted to apply for baptism. Upon approval of the congregation, he was subject to a period of intensive instruction, fasting, and prayer. A careful appraisal of his character was made. If he was found to be acceptable in all matters, he was baptized and his name entered in the church registry.

This was one of the early schools of the Christian church. It arose in the second century, became almost universal during the fifth century, and, with the rise of the practice of accepting infants for baptism, discontinued after the ninth century. Its curriculum included church history, doctrine, and practices. More specifically, the catechumen was taught the meaning of membership in the Christian body, the creed, the significance of the sacraments, behavioral requirements of all members, and the Lord's Prayer. In some churches the bishop delivered a series of lectures to the catechumens on doctrine, articles of the creed, and morals.

It must be remembered that these catechumens were adults, mostly from the lower classes. They were men and women with little formal education beyond that of the synagogue or the Roman elementary school. As the Christian movement grew and spread in the Empire, the upper classes, with more formal education, were attracted, with the result that catechumenal instruction became more intellectual and theological.

CHRYSOSTOM ON EDUCATION

By the fourth century, Christianity had developed many schools, infiltrated ancient Roman schools, and was beginning to think in terms of an educational system. Theory and methodology were being discussed in many quarters.

At this juncture, John Chrysostom (345?-407), popular "silver-tongued" orator, wrote the first educational text of the Christian church. He sought to instruct parents in the early education of their children. Since little children are "as wax," he taught, their education should begin "from . . . (the) very cradle." While the child is impressionable, the parents should "imprint good principles in him." Unless education is begun at birth, the child will stand in danger of receiving wrong experiences that may warp him forever. At all times the child must be protected from hearing profane or vicious language, and if he is caught using such, he should be punished severely.

Education comes through the senses. Therefore all those who have anything to do with teaching the young must guard their charges as an army would guard the gates of a city. Bible stories, told with skill, will interest the child and teach him moral and spiritual truths. He must be discouraged from engaging in theatricals, mixed bathing, and other evils prevalent in the Roman world. Above all, the child must be taught that the lusts of this life, riches, worldly glory, power, even life itself, are nothing when compared to one's immortal future.

A high point of Chrysostom's treatise is his discussion of the education of youths in matters of sex and marriage. Christian union between man and woman is the goal of this instruction. The purity of sex as God's gift for creating immortal souls is stressed. Parents, ministers, and teachers must lead youth to appreciate this gift and use it to the glory of God. With marriage and the coming of children, the cycle is repeated; the new parents begin again the pure, holy, and devoted education of their children for eternal salvation.

CHRISTIAN THOUGHT IN THE GRECO-ROMAN WORLD

While Christian parents were struggling with the problem of educating their children in an environment permeated with non-Christian ideas and practices, leaders of this new religion were faced with the larger problem of the Christian attitude toward all Greco-Roman thinking. Greek literature, philosophy, and science had by the first century become an integral part of Roman intellectual life. Two extreme positions were advocated. One feared this culture, holding it to be the enemy of all that the Christian most cherished. The other believed it to be a preparation for Christian thought and cherished it lovingly. Between these two extremes were varying degrees of toleration and respect.

Western church leaders, true to their practical interpretation of Christianity as a way of life, feared and often hated everything Greek. Tertullian (160?-230?) believed that in the sin of Adam all men were perverted absolutely. Even the faculty of reason was so warped that it could never again be trusted. Since Greek thought was a product of human reason, the Christian should avoid it at all cost. "What," he argued, "indeed has Athens to do with Jerusalem? What concord is there between the Academy and the Church?"

Augustine (354-430) as a young man was a teacher of oratory and so enamored of classical Latin that he could not read Virgil without weeping. Upon his conversion to Christianity, he wrestled with his love of the classics and never really won. One, he advised, should read the literature of the pagan world with caution. Always ask the question, "What purpose does it serve?" As he grew older, we see him turning away from his first love, but never repudiating it altogether. He found in the Golden Rule all that can be discovered in classical philosophy and science and felt that man had only to live in accord with its prescriptions to know all that was necessary for salvation.

Another leader of early Christian thought, Jerome (340?-420), experienced the same struggle. As a young man he had a most high regard for Cicero and studied him religiously. As a Christian he was tormented by the feeling that his professions of love for Christ were insincere mouthings. In a dream he found himself before a judge who asked for his "condition." When he replied that he was a Christian, the judge thundered, "Thou liest; thou art a Ciceronian not a Christian. For where thy treasure is, there will thy heart be also." Although he constantly asked himself, "What has Horace to do with the Psalter, Virgil with the Gospels, and Cicero with Paul?" he could not betray his first love.

By 398, the Fourth Council of Carthage had vigorously prohibited the reading of classical literature, even by bishops of the church. Pope Gregory the Great (540-604), although educated in the best schools of his age, boasted that he knew no Greek, had written nothing in Greek, and had no respect for the oratory taught by rhetoricians of his day. "For," he said, "the same mouth cannot sing the praises of Jupiter and the praises of Christ." Grammar and fine writing, he believed, would "fetter the words of the Divine Oracle."

This feeling led church leaders to turn away from Greek and Roman literature, philosophy, and science. As the church grew, this hostility became more bitter. The West was anti-classical, fearing that Christianity could not meet the challenge of this tradition, that by reading and studying these writings church members would be won away from the faith, and that the security of the religion lay in insulating itself and its members from certain areas of human thought.

As a result of this official hostility, classical thought and classical literature were driven out of western Europe into the East to be brought back with the Renaissance, a period when men turned to ancient Greece and Rome for inspiration and an understanding of things human.

Leaders of the Greek church were very different. They objected to some of the material included in the classics—the accounts of immoralities on the part of the gods, for example—but they had no problem in integrating their love for things Greek with their loyalty to Christianity.

Paul, a scholar and student of the sophists, quoted often from Greek writings. His thinking shows a rich strain of Stoic philosophy. The author of the fourth Gospel, John, was fundamentally Greek and saw in Jesus the incarnation of the *logos.*

Clement of Alexandria (150?-220?) was before his conversion the leading Platonist of his day. He saw Christianity as the natural development of Plato's idealism and infused the teachings of his idol into Christian thought so thoroughly that later centuries were to interpret the Church and the Trinity in terms of Plato's perfect ideas. Clement believed that God had revealed himself to the Hebrews through the Old Testament, to the Greeks through philosophy, and to the Christians through Jesus. He interpreted philosophy as a "pedagogue" leading mankind to Christ.

Origen (185?-254?), a pupil and for some time assistant of Clement, held that anyone wishing to understand Christianity should delve deeply into Greek philosophy and science to gather knowledge necessary to explain the Scriptures.

Gregory of Nazianzen (329?-389?), one of the four great fathers of the eastern church, admired secular learning, believing that "as we have compounded healthful drugs from certain of the reptiles; so from secular literature we have received principles of inquiry and speculations, while we have rejected their idolatry, terror, and pit of destruction." Basil the Great (330?-379) wrote an essay entitled *Address to the Youth, How They Can Read Heathen Authors to Their Profit.* He was a friend of the sophist Libanius, who so impressed this leader of eastern Christianity that his praise of things Greek was unbounded. Basil often advised young Christians to spend some time at the feet of his friend. In later life, because of the infirmities of old age or because of a change in heart, he seems to have turned against classical scholarship. At the close of his life he wrote to his friend Libanius boasting that, "If ever I learned anything from you, I have forgotten it."

This affinity for things Greek was not unanimous among eastern church leaders. Some sided with the Romans in condemning the classics as dangerous to faith. The *Apostolic Constitution,* a document coming from Syria in the third century, advises true Christians to "abstain from all heathen books." Its authors held that the scriptures contained all the history, wisdom, laws and statutes, and music necessary for Christians.

Here, then, are two contrasting attitudes toward the treasury of Greek and Roman literature, philosophy, and science which the early Christians inherited. The West, practical and legalistic, could find in it nothing but evil. A Christian should avoid it as he would the devil himself. It was for Christianity to create in its scriptures and the writings of its faithful a literature and a theology which all could study in the home and in school safely and to the glory of God. The East, speculative and prophetic, saw in the classics a preparation for Christianity. It recognized that this material was not free of danger for the indiscriminate reader, but refused to turn its back upon so much scholarship and insight.

EDUCATION OF THE CHRISTIAN SCHOLAR

As Christianity changed from a religion of the depressed and more or less illiterate masses to a theology and way of life attractive to the intellectual and prosperous upper classes, the need for scholars able to interpret this new religion to a thinking and highly sophisticated public arose. No longer was it sufficient to preach the Gospel ardently, to appeal to the emotions of the people, and to instruct the simple and the children. In large centers of population were astute advocates of many religious and philosophical persuasions, teaching, arguing, and propagandizing. Products of Greek and Roman philosophical schools were seeking converts to their beliefs. Disciples of eastern cults were selling their wares to the thinking public. Professional consultants were making use of the latest "scientific" knowledge about human nature to give consolation and a sense of security to troubled souls.

Christianity could not escape this environment or hide for long behind a doctrine that ignorance was the way to salvation. It had to produce "apologists," men and women able to face the intellectuals of other persuasions and state their case with equal brilliance. The Christian scholar was an inevitable outgrowth of the times. Since reason was more at home in the East, it was natural that this development should begin and show its earliest strength in cities of the East.

Alexandria had become one of the world's centers of learning. It had a library and a museum second to none. There were philosophical schools, synagogues, Roman schools, and schools of many sophists. There, teachers and students gathered in abundance. There were Greek philosophers, Jewish scholars, oriental mystics, atheists, scientists, and preachers of many and strange doctrines. And there was a Christian church with its school for catechumens. In this stimulating environment, many asking admission to the church raised philosophical and theological questions, while members of the church were challenged by scholars of other persuasions to justify their convictions. Out of this situation arose the first known catechetical school of Christianity.

A highly-disputed legend tells us that Saint Mark founded the school. Far less disputed is the claim that the first catechetical instruction in Alexandria was offered in 179 by Pantaenus, a Stoic philosopher recently converted to Christianity. When Pantaenus retired in 189, his assistant and pupil, Clement, succeeded him as head of the school. This school which began with a Stoic interpretation of Christian doctrine now took on a decided Platonic flavor. Jesus, God, truth, salvation, and the nature of man and his universe were interpreted in terms of Plato's realm of perfect ideas. Here, Platonism entered Christianity, to take on added significance as Christian thought developed. When Clement was forced to retire in 202, his pupil, Origen, took over administration of the school.

By this time the school had become famous, and young men and women were enrolling from all parts of the Roman Empire to listen to lectures by the head of the school or to study elementary subjects under assistants. Gradually the curriculum was expanded from exclusively religious and doctrinal courses to include the study of all subjects constituting a general education—elementary, secondary, and higher. True to eastern belief that classical scholarship was basic to a deeper understanding of Christianity, the catechetical school at Alexandria offered courses in all systems of Greek philosophy except Epicureanism, in metaphysics, ethics, logic, physics, geometry, astronomy, anatomy, theology, doctrine, and interpretation of the rituals of the church. An advanced course was biblical exegesis.

This school continued as a major center for education of Christian scholars far into the fifth century and became a model for similar schools throughout the eastern world. Origen, after his banishment from Alexandria, established a catechetical school at Caesarea in Palestine. After his death the school lost its popularity but was revived by Pamphilus, who collected there the largest and most complete library of theological writings in existence at the time. One of his pupils was Eusebius, who, using the library for his source material, wrote the first *Ecclesiastical History,* an account of the founding and development of the Christian church.

Melchion, a famous teacher of rhetoric, founded a catechetical school at Antioch in the third century. He was succeeded by Lucian (250?-321), who gave the school a name throughout the Roman Empire and attracted students and scholars of reputation. One of the most famous teachers and heads of the school was John Chrysostom, educated in Antioch by Libanius. There he wrote his famous book on education, *Concerning the Education of Children.* During his administration of the school the generally accepted allegorical interpretation of scripture was abandoned, and in its place came an earnest endeavor to understand sacred writings in the light of their history and the intentions of the authors.

EDUCATION IN THE GROWING CHURCH

After Jesus' death, his disciples remained in and around Jerusalem, waiting for his more or less immediate return. They followed in his footsteps, gathering young men about them, and teaching and preaching haphazardly.

Paul began organizing small groups of followers in major cities of the Empire. These were the beginnings of churches, which developed slowly in spite of repeated persecution. In time, separate church buildings were erected, and various functionaries appeared, caring for the growing needs of the congregations. As a single individual emerged in each group to dominate and lead, the title of bishop became generally approved to designate his authority. All other officers were under his direction. The church in which he preached was called a cathedral.

When the congregation grew beyond the capacities of the cathedral and its staff, branch churches were established in outlying areas for the convenience of members. The central church, or cathedral, and all branch churches were considered within the bishop's see and under his jurisdiction. Here, for the first time, a pattern of church organization took form.

With cathedrals in large population centers and smaller churches in nearby communities, and with all forming administrative complexes of growing importance and responsibilities, the simple days of early Christianity became little more than nostalgic memories. Often a bishop, busy with the duties of his office and problems of his see, had to give orders, make interpretations of doctrine, and come to decisions to fit immediate situations. This resulted in a vast body of conflicting material and a growing feeling on the part of each bishop that he should be free to act as the situation demanded.

The Church had the Roman Empire as its example, and since the leaders were citizens of this Empire and Romans at heart, they yearned for order and unity. Gradually they found this order in statements of orthodoxy and in an emerging pattern of church organization. Strong, positive leaders developed in some areas, men who were able to exert influence over church councils and other ecclesiastical gatherings. After many battles of wits and power, the bishop of the church at Rome won the right to be accepted as chief bishop of all Christian churches, except those in the East, which gave their loyalty to the bishop at Constantinople. He came to be known as the pope, final authority in the western Church.

Just as recognition of the Roman bishop as pope did not still the claims of other bishops to authority, so acceptance by authoritative church councils of an orthodox scripture and creed did not quiet the claims made by individual churchmen for other writings and other doctrinal positions.

Christianity developed a pattern of organization resembling the Roman Empire, a creed and statement of doctrine, a liturgy of worship, and an organization of the clergy. These were to be accepted by many, challenged by others, changed as the church grew and expanded, and adjusted to different ages and differing cultures. Out of this was to come a basic structure accepted more or less by the clergy and members of the Church in the West.

Education became a major function within the Church. As the cathedral developed and congregations assembled to worship, a liturgy took form. This included preaching, teaching, and song. Men had to be trained for these duties. Often the bishop would accept young men whom he schooled in the various elements of the liturgy. Also, mothers would place their children under the care of the bishop and his staff for protection from the pagan environment and for schooling. As music became an important part of the Christian service, a boys' choir was essential to worship.

Here we have the school of the bishop's household, an institution growing out of the need to prepare priests, teach the young, and train boys for the choir. When branch churches were established within the bishop's see, it became necessary to prepare ministers to serve these new congregations. Thus the cathedral, seat of the bishop, became a bustling center of educational activity. In time each function developed into a separate school under the supervision of the bishop—a school for teaching young children the fundamentals of learning and religion, a school for training young ministers to assist the bishop or to staff outlying churches, and a song school to train choir boys. In addition, the bishop, or one of his assistants, had the responsibility of preparing catechumens for baptism and admission to full membership in the church.

Often a second church in the bishop's see would grow into a large institution rivaling the cathedral in membership and importance. Since there could be but one bishop in the see, and since the cathedral was his seat, there could be only one cathedral. Consequently, this second church was called a collegiate church. Here could be found many of the educational functions of the cathedral, including training of ministers. Priests in the smaller churches in the bishop's see organized parish schools for basic instruction of children of the members, song schools, and schools for instruction of catechumens.

What began as a valiant attempt to meet the needs of a young church in a pagan environment gradually developed into a prescribed educational system. The General Church Council at Constantinople, meeting in 381, ordered that schools for free education of children be established in every center of population. In 529, the Council of Vaison required that priests take into their homes unmarried men whom they would train as their successors. As congregational singing was abandoned, trained choir boys and men sang the service in the presence of the congregation. By 367 the Council of Leodicea ordered that all singing be done by regularly trained and appointed boys and men. When it became evident that many ministers were using the musical parts of the service to display their talent and "good voice" while neglecting their other duties, the Synod of Rome, under the prodding of Gregory the Great, in 595 prohibited ministers and deacons from participating in the musical part of the service. They were confined to singing only the gospel in the mass.

EDUCATION OF GIRLS AND WOMEN

The early Church made no distinction as to education and status between men and women. In the crowds that followed Jesus and his disciples were both men and women. While the classical Greek and

Roman sophists confined their teaching almost wholly to men, the Christian sophists treated men and women equally. Both male and female catechumens were instructed in the same classes. Elementary schools established in early churches accepted boys and girls on equal terms. Christianity, in its inception, went against the entire eastern attitude toward women, gave them equal privileges with men, and recognized the especial place of women in society.

As the Church grew, it restricted leadership in its congregations to men, reducing women to the lesser order of deaconesses. Paul's prohibition against women speaking in the service was taken literally. Women began to lose their equality with men, to be excluded from the important areas of church life. There remained one area in which they remained supreme, education of the young. Boys received their first instruction from their mothers, and the history of the early Church is full of instances of devout mothers training their sons in the scriptures and the faith. These boys eventually went out from their mothers' care to schools which prepared them for a man's place in life.

Girls became increasingly the responsibility of the mother as they were excluded from the activities of a man's world. By the fourth century, the Christian attitude toward women, especially in the West, had crystallized and the matter of their education taken on the aspect that was to characterize the Church for centuries. This attitude is amply revealed in the advice given by Jerome both to Laeta regarding the education of her daughter Paula and to Gaudentius instructing her in the education of her daughter Pacatula.

All girls, Jerome held, should be educated in strict dedication to Christian ideals. They were to be denied all freedom, and self-expression was to be suppressed vigorously. At all times, a maid must be accompanied by an adult female. He counseled, "Leave her no power or capacity to live without you, and let her feel frightened when she is left by herself." She must not have male companions, should be discouraged from using cosmetics or other means of making her body attractive, and instructed carefully in modesty and faith. Jerome was especially fearful of the bath. Here he was in accord with the general attitude of the Church, which feared that a young girl viewing her naked body in the bath would become vain and lustful. Only after marriage, when the girl was under the control of her husband, could she safely bathe.

The virgin's education should consist of learning handicrafts, the practical virtues, the scriptures, and morals. She should memorize psalms and proverbs praising virginity and motherhood. Her musical education should be limited to psalms and hymns.

This attitude was a reaction to the sexual laxity of the Roman world. Christians feared the lusts of the flesh and sought to protect against them even to the extent of excessively restricting their women. Many church leaders knew first hand how difficult it was to resist the fires of passion once ignited, and sought to protect their women from temptation.

MONASTIC EDUCATION

THE ASCETIC TRADITION

That the body is in some way an enemy of the soul was known to men of very ancient times. Primitive wise men and witch doctors have often been known to deny the body for the good of the soul. Priests of ancient religions practiced abstinence and self-denial to induce religious experiences or propitiate the gods. A great deal of asceticism is to be found in early Greek mystic religions and in the practices of the Pythagorean Brotherhood. Among the Jews, the Essenes were the most noted of many ascetic groups. The Therapeutae in Egypt practiced asceticism rigorously. Both the Cynics and the Neoplatonists included ascetic practices in their teachings and rituals.

To punish the body, fast, abhor pleasure, and wear disagreeable clothing have been ways of expressing spiritual devotion. Desire to escape the temptations of life has appeared in all ages and among most religions. Man's search for perfection and his desire to give undivided worship to his gods have produced the ascetic life, even its fanaticisms.

ASCETICISM IN THE EARLY CHURCH

Since the Christian stood in constant danger of martyrdom, and since the very existence of the church depended upon the ability of its members to endure persecution gloriously, it became necessary to institute a regimen of preparation to face torture and even death. Thus there appeared in many churches *schools of martyrdom.* There, members of the Church were instructed in how to answer magistrates when arrested, how to endure the torture of the whip or the rack, and how to meet death by fire or in the arena. Manuals were written instructing them how to prepare for every situation. These included physical exercises designed to harden the body and ascetic practices to turn attention of the believer from the body to the soul. Training given these early Christians was both psychological and physical. The mind was conditioned to meet persecution gladly, to view it as an opportunity to testify for the faith and receive eternal salvation. For a member to forsake his faith under torture or to cry out or show fear when persecuted blackened the Christian movement just that much. In times of stress the Church could not tolerate such weaknesses. It aimed in this schooling for martyrdom to prepare men and women who even in death would win the admiration of the Roman world.

This preparation for martyrdom was, in fact, a form of asceticism. To harden the body and prepare the mind, one had to abstain from debilitating pleasures, inure himself to self-denial and pain, refuse much that might become psychologically necessary to his well-being, and live each day as though it were his last. The ascetic who had come to value only his soul, had turned his back on all the world and this life had to offer, could face death for his faith serenely, even joyously.

Many Christians, living among their fellows and going about their daily tasks, would fast, deny themselves luxuries, and wear irritating clothes next to their skin. These practices have always been a part of orthodox Christian living for believers. The world was not aware of their concrete professions of devotion, but the Christians knew and found comfort in the knowledge.

As conditions in the Roman Empire worsened for the Christians, some found life in a normal community unbearable. Degeneracy and vice seemed to confront them on every side. Burdensome taxation, restrictive laws imposed by the imperial government, lack of public morality, and unendurable tensions caused some to withdraw to the mountains or the desert to live in solitude and away from temptation. In times of persecution many Christians fled their enemies and became hermits. As this practice increased, the hermit's life came to be regarded with special sanctity.

Beginning in Syria and Egypt, this practice of deserting the world for a hermit's serenity spread throughout the Empire. Some hermits gained special fame through their extreme austerities and grotesque forms of personal torture. They would strive to outdo each other in fasting, abstaining from water or sleep, and weighing their bodies down with heavy loads. Some were brilliant preachers and attracted others who lived in caves or under rocks nearby and came to listen at specified times. Gradually, colonies of hermits took shape about someone noted for his sanctity. This was the beginning of monasticism.

THE MONASTIC LIFE TAKES FORM

By the fourth century the lonely hermit was giving way to colonies of religious men valuing their solitude but living in groups for better care of their needs. These loose colonies gradually developed a pattern of living which included solitude, times for group devotion, communal meals, and ascetic practices. This is clearly illustrated in the case of Saint Anthony (about 250-350). Born in middle Egypt, be began practicing the ascetic life at the age of twenty. After fifteen years of living in society and denying his body, he withdrew to Pispir, a mountain along the Nile, where he lived as a hermit, fighting with the "devil" who appeared to him in many forms and used many wiles to dissuade him from the ascetic life. Early in the fourth century he was persuaded by those who had congregated about him to become their teacher. In time the group took on a more permanent organization, so that here was the first monastery. The institution never developed a regimen, but left the individual free to work, worship, or study as he wished. Each member lived a solitary life, and there was no common activity beyond stated worship periods. Later, Anthony withdrew to a mountain near the Red Sea, where today stands the monastery Der Mar Antonios. He remained there until shortly before his death, when he traveled to Alexandria to denounce Arianism.

Communal life became increasingly popular, and more or less stable groups were organized. The pattern of a true monastic community was drawn by Pachomius near 320. Born at Esna, in upper Egypt, around 292 of heathen parents, he served as an officer during one of Constantine's campaigns. When he returned to civilian life, he became a Christian and went immediately to live a hermit's life along the Nile, near Dendera. There he became a disciple of an aged hermit noted for his ascetic practices. After three years he organized a monastery and wrote a *Rule* to govern the lives of all its members. Since the first site of the monastery was at Tabennisi, the order took the name Tabennesiot. When Pachomius died, in 346, he had organized nine monasteries, with more than 3,000 monks in residence, and one nunnery.

The *Rule* which Pachomius wrote provided for a regular regimen of work, sleep, meals, study, and devotion. At the head of the order was an abbot, with complete authority over all the houses. Local groups were led by priors who looked to the abbot for instructions. Those wishing to become members of the order were required to subject themselves to a three-year probationary period.

Monasticism began in Egypt and had its first successes in the East. By the middle of the fourth century, Basil the Great, bishop of Caesarea, established a monastery near Pontus, where his parents lived. Other leaders of the Church sponsored monasteries, and the movement spread throughout the Roman Empire. What had begun as individuals seeking solitude and escape from a materialistic and godless world which they could no longer endure had, by the fifth century, become a way of life for thousands, and one of the most important institutions in Christendom.

The Order of Saint Benedict

If we can accept Saint Gregory's *Dialogues* as accurate, and if the four disciples of Saint Benedict who gave him the material were truthful, the patriarch of western monasticism, Benedict, was born of a good family in Nursia, near Spoleto in Umbria in 480. Unable to cope with the evils of his day, he retired to a lonely spot near Rome and lived in a cave as a hermit, praying and torturing his body to find peace and security. His fame spread, and the monks of a neighboring monastery persuaded him to become their leader. They were a wayward group who resented his attempt to introduce discipline into their lives. When they attempted to poison him, he withdrew to his cave, where disciples flocked to him for inspiration and instruction in the Christian way. In time he formed twelve monasteries in the area. Driven from his cave by jealous neighbors, he wandered south to Cassino, midway between Rome and Naples, where, on a mountain overlooking the city, he established a monastery which bore his name, the Benedictine Monastery.

Since this monastery was typical of many such institutions throughout Europe, it is well to examine it closely. Benedict prepared a *Rule* —or plan of life for the monastery—which governed every action of the monks and determined the nature of the order. According to this *Rule,* each monastery was an independent institution presided over by an abbot elected by the monks. He had absolute authority. Asceticism was looked upon not as an end but as a means of physical, mental, and spiritual development.

The monastery was a self-sufficient economic community in which each monk plied a trade or cared for an activity necessary to the welfare of all. In addition to work, the monks were given a detailed routine of worship, study, meals, sleep, solitude, prayer, and spiritual exercise. Every moment of the day and night was accounted for. The monks were to have no possessions; to be obedient at all times; to practice purity in thought and act, charity toward all, humility and self-effacement; and to develop scholarship to the limit of their abilities.

Education in the Monastery

The monastery was one answer to the problem which Christian parents faced in considering the education of their children in a pagan world. It needed new recruits to preserve its continuity. Adult Christians could be accepted and, after a period of instruction, initiated into membership. This did not prove adequate, and the monasteries were forced to seek recruits elsewhere. They found that many parents wished to offer their children to the monastery and its way of life. These were accepted and given a more or less complete education by the monks. Such children were called *interni* and were destined to become members of the monastic community. The education of these youngsters consisted of the fundamentals of reading, writing, arithmetic, religion, and advanced instruction to the limit of the capabilities of the member monks. The culmination of this education was initiation into the order.

Often, parents living in the vicinity of a monastery wanted to entrust the education of their children to the monks. Since there was no intention of establishing a permanent relationship with the monastery, these children were called *externi,* day pupils who lived at home and came to the monastery for instruction. Their curriculum was very similar to that of the *interni* except that the focus was not on membership in the order.

A major facility for education in the monastery was the library. Most monasteries stressed the continued intellectual development of their monks and included in their plan of living a requirement that each monk devote some time each day to reading and study. As a result of this practice the monasteries produced many of the finest scholars of the times. With few exceptions, the leading thinkers of western Europe for hundreds of years were members of monastic orders and received their education in and through monasteries.

One feature of most monasteries was the *scriptorium.* This was a large room in the monastery with writing desks and a reading desk. Each writing desk was equipped with parchment or paper, a pen, and ink. A monk with some skill in writing was seated at each desk. At the reader's desk sat a monk who read a book aloud while others in the room copied the material. When the reading was completed, the monastery had several copies of the book to exchange with other monasteries for books they had copied. In this way, libraries were built and books were made more general in the culture.

SAINT AUGUSTINE, FATHER OF CHRISTIAN PHILOSOPHY

The dominant figure in the early Church's struggle to develop its theology was the Bishop of Hippo in Africa, Aurelius Augustine (354-430). Born in North Africa of a Christian mother, he did not accept Christianity until, at thirty-three years of age, he came under the spell of the preaching of Saint Ambrose. He was educated in the best tradition of a fourth century Roman gentleman and became a rhetorician and a Latin scholar of renown. His *Confessions* details this education, throwing much light on the educational thinking of the upper classes of the period.

After his conversion he turned to developing Christian philosophy on the base of his Neoplatonism, a mystical and escapist interpretation of Plato's thinking which was prevalent in many parts of the Empire at that time. His *City of God* contrasts the earthly life of man with the ideal or heavenly existence open to him. The one, true to Plato's philosophy, is a kingdom of unreality, illusion, sin, suffering, and temptation. The other is eternal, the abode of all truth and goodness. The fall of Rome and all the evils of the Roman Empire were to him consequences of the unreality of all things material. Now, he argued, is the time for man to turn his eyes to heaven where he will find the true City of God, a city of perfection, truth, goodness. Man must strive to establish this city on earth, preparing a place in which Christ can reign when he returns.

Augustine developed his educational philosophy from the same Platonic root. All goodness, truth, and wisdom are to be found in the super-sensible world of perfect ideas. The world of sense is full of error and dangerous opinions. One can escape from this world of error into that of true knowledge by union with God, who is all truth and all goodness. As long as man depends upon sense experiences, he will not know truth. Reason will not yield truth. One who wishes true knowledge must turn to faith. Reason may lead man to an understanding that this is true, but only through faith can he make the leap from the world of sense to that of truth.

Since most men will never be able to make this leap and come face to face with truth, we must leave it to the Church to pronounce the truth and accept it on the authority of God's holy bride. If the Church is to state with an authority that cannot be questioned, then it must also determine what studies are valuable for man in his struggle to apprehend clearly this truth. For Augustine, all education is to be directed at understanding the scriptures and preparing one to accept eternal truth.

Augustine would exclude much from one's education. Mere learning for learning's sake or to make a good impression upon one's fellows should be avoided as a sin. Among the areas of learning which he recommends are philosophy, grammar, rhetoric, logic, arithmetic, and natural sciences. From these areas a man can take much that will aid him in understanding truth when it is pronounced by the Church or when he comes upon it through intuition. Learning is a handmaiden leading man to truth which is eternal.

Once possessed of this idea that all learning must be judged in relation to absolute truth and has value only as it can be employed to help one understand unchanging truth, Augustine was at the gateway of allegory. He entered with conviction. The Bible and all other spiritual material must be interpreted, he believed, in terms of its mystical and allegorical meaning. Human learning was for him a means of developing such interpretations.

Augustine believed that the road to learning could not be made easy. He sanctioned flogging as a means of both motivation and driving out evil spirits. The child is by nature evil, an offspring of Adam and inheritor of the sins of his father. He must be punished if his evil nature is to be kept under control and the good that is deep within him is to come to the surface.

This father of Christian philosophy did not trust human reason. He believed that man is evil and prone to sin. His intellect, a part of his material being, is a trap for his snaring. Only as he can escape from the material, from his reason, can he rise to the heavenly realm of truth. Studies will help in this struggle toward truth, but are also a danger. They may trap one in vain glory and pride or lead him into a belief that by mastering them he has mastered truth. Since only a few can ever hope to meet truth face to face, we must be ready at all times to accept the authoritative statements of the Church. When our education fails to lead us to truth, it must make us receptive of the truth as interpreted by the Church.

Since Augustine was a powerful figure in his day and became even more powerful as his writings and his ideas reached all parts of the early Church, he was responsible for much of the narrowing of scholarship that characterized the centuries before the Renaissance. The fear of human intellect which is to be found in much of medieval Christianity can be traced in large measure to Augustine.

Part Three

LIFE AND EDUCATION
IN THE MEDIEVAL WORLD

CHAPTER 7

In an Age of Faith

INTRODUCTION

The Age of Faith is that period in western history beginning roughly with the sixth century and ending with the close of the thirteenth.

This span of time has been given several names. Renaissance scholars received their inspiration from Greek and Roman cultures. To them, anything between the brilliant era of Rome's golden age and their day was a "middle age." Since to some this middle period was marked by an eclipse of humanistic interest, it could be nothing other than a "dark age." Still others, sensing that the period was a transition during which new interests and novel interpretations of man and his universe were taking shape, named it "medieval." From the perspective of Renaissance man, all these had validity.

Seen from the perspective of history, a perspective denied the creators of Renaissance Europe, the sixth through the thirteenth centuries were neither "middle" nor "dark." History is a development, each age carrying forward its past, changing as it goes, and moving into the future. The dominant institution of the age with which we are concerned was the Christian Church. Born at the time of the Roman Empire, in the days of its greatness, it was forced, by the steady decay of this same Empire, to grow up rapidly and take over power in an effort to maintain a degree of stability. Cast in such a role through circumstances not of its making, the Church gave its stamp to the period. It was truly an Age of Faith when men found security and hope in a religion that, while it served them in their daily living, fixed their eyes and minds on eternity. The orientation of the people, masses and elite, was religious. Even toward the end of the age when secular concerns were occupying the attention of men more and more, the Church was the dominant force in their lives.

The invaders who pushed into the dying Empire from across its northern borders recognized this power of the Church and accepted its authority while resting upon its promise of eternal life. Those rugged, virile people often showed little respect for the material values and accomplishments of the Roman world, but they knelt reverently before the altars of the Church and allowed its bishops to place the crown of authority upon their heads. This was indeed an Age of Faith.

Recognition of this fact will help dispel some of the erroneous ideas that have been propagated by certain historians of the age. The so-called Medieval Age was *not* a time of complete breakdown of organized civilization nor of chaos in human relations. The citizen of the Roman Empire did not awaken one morning to the horrible realization that his world had collapsed about him. The changes that took place were gradual, extending over hundreds of years, so gradual that most people were unaware that life had become different. It was only when the scholar looked backward over a century or more of time that the momentous changes that had taken place became evident.

As the Roman Empire spread its borders in the late pre-Christian and early Christian centuries, it incorporated many different people into its citizenry. They were diversified in culture, religion, government, and economics. In spite of their divergence they were held in check by strong emperors, supported by well-trained armies, and woven into the fabric of the Empire. No matter how far the borders were extended, there were other people beyond to harass the guards and slip past them into more fertile lands where living was stable and pleasant. When emperors were weak and armies less disciplined or loyal, these border people infiltrated farther into the Empire and in greater numbers, conquering territory that was not adequately defended and settling down to live more or less peaceably with those who had preceded them. With the general weakening of the western Roman Empire during the early centuries of this age, Germanic tribes from beyond the northern borders moved south in greater and greater numbers. Their trek toward the Mediterranean was slow and laborious. As they moved, some sacked the cities they found and destroyed much of the population, while others mingled with the conquered, intermarrying, ruling, farming, and building a new life and culture, a mixture of what was already there and what they brought from their ancient past.

What followed was a long period of transition. Gradually, much of the past disappeared, but not all. A student of history can discern a great deal that was taken over from the past and made part of the new life being created. In spite of all the assertions to the contrary, there is discernible in this span of centuries a clear continuity with the past. It is this continuity that, in many ways, is more important than the changes that took place. Ancient Roman institutions were continued and strengthened. The Roman legal structure, the wide pattern of Roman government, the Christian Church, and, in general, the schools of the Empire, were incorporated into the life of medieval man, changed to serve his needs, but carried forward into the modern world.

If we hold clearly in mind these two facts—the predominance of religion and continuity with the past—we will avoid many of the misinterpretations of this period of western history which have crept into common belief.

FEUDALISM

The Social Pattern

As the Roman Empire weakened, its ability to maintain order and security decreased, so that men were forced to turn to other means of protection. Kings and other rulers found themselves powerless to beat off raids by enemy armies or local brigands. Well-trained and loyal governors, the strength of Roman rule, were lacking, while the educated class which the Roman emperors had depended upon to staff their wide-flung bureaucracy had dwindled to a mere shadow of its former strength.

All this made necessary a new and more practical system of social and political life. This was called feudalism. Kings and other rulers made grants of land, or fiefs, to strong warriors who would maintain order within the bounds of their grants and, upon call, furnish and lead armies in support of their overlords. These fief holders would then grant land and privileges to lesser individuals in the area on much the same terms. The remainder of the population, peasants and serfs, was bound to the land to serve the lord of the area as he wished.

This proved to be a highly effective pattern of mutual protection and service. The lowly peasant or serf was helpless if left to his own devices. With no land or horses or armor, he could not hope to ward off those who might destroy him. Under feudalism, he could expect his lord to offer protection. In payment, he would work the land of his lord, care for his needs, and support him in war. Likewise, the small landowner felt more or less helpless when left to himself with no Roman legions or strong military garrison to come to his aid. When he swore allegiance to a lord, he accepted certain social, moral, and religious obligations in return for which he gained security as a member of a group pledged to help each other in times of danger. He and those loyal to him stood ready to answer the call of the lord and form an army under his leadership to march with armies furnished by other lords, all under the command of a great overlord or king.

Feudalism gave rise to a rigid class structure which characterized western Europe for many centuries. At the top was an aristocratic upper class composed of high officials of the Church and the nobility with its varying grades of feudal tenure. All the rest of the people constituted the lower classes, most of whom were unfree serfs. This was Europe's social structure until a class of merchants, traders, and craftsmen arose to take a position above the serfs and beneath the nobility. It was this class that was to challenge the power and privilege of the nobility during early modern times.

EDUCATION OF THE NOBLE

The feudal nobles constituted a social class concerned with government, management of large estates, and the profession of war. They were the mounted soldiers of the age. The term *chivalry* was used to designate the way of life of this class.

The focal point of this social and governmental arrangement was the home of the great lord. This was a fortified castle in which all the administrative functions of his fief were concentrated. The homes of the lesser nobility were called manor houses. Here were centered entertainment, sports, governmental activities, local defense, and economic activities necessary to maintain the entire complex.

Children of peasants and serfs received no formal education. Their learning consisted of working with their parents and others of like status to develop skills in the discharge of their menial duties. Whatever instruction they received was in the home. There they learned their place in the social structure, simple religion, superstitions and beliefs about their environment, and manners in relation to their equals and their superiors. Theirs was a practical education in the duties, responsibilities, and skills of a lower, menial class.

Children of the noble class were given an education specifically designed to fit them into their society. Usually the boy remained in his home for the first six years of his life. There he participated in the life of the family, absorbed a point of view and basic attitudes toward others, learned the simple skills of reading, writing, and figuring, and developed physically and socially. At seven, he might be sent to the manor house of the lord, the castle of the great lord, or the court of the king. There he served his master as a *page,* performing simple tasks and learning the code of manners of his rank. In addition, he was taught physical and intellectual skills necessary for life among the nobility. At fourteen he became a *squire,* obligated to accompany his master in the tournament or in battle and learn the profession of arms.

When he reached his twenty-first birthday, if he had learned his lessons well and acquitted himself with honor, he was initiated into the noble class with the title of *knight.* This was a solemn and impressive ceremony, usually performed in the castle of the great lord, the palace of the king, or the cathedral. The candidate was required to spend the night in prayer at an altar, upon which rested his sword. At times this was preceded by a bath, after which the young man was laid on a bed, clothed in a white robe and black hose. The bath symbolized purity, and the position in the bed symbolized death. After this preparation the boy would be taken to the king or the great lord, before whom he knelt in subjection. He would listen to a lecture dealing with his duties, make his vows to lord and Church, and be touched lightly on each shoulder by the tip of a sword and "dubbed" a knight. Rising from his knees, he received the symbols of his rank: a gold chain, sword belt, sword, and spurs. From that moment he was an adult, accepted in the society of nobles, and obligated to serve his class and his lord in the manner prescribed by long tradition.

Chivalry was the ideal to which the noble society of the age aspired. Its tenets dealt with war, religion, and gallantry. Young men, prepared for this ideal, were expected to be pure in body and soul, devoted to Church and lord even unto death, honorable and just toward their equals, skillful in the profession of arms and management of estates, and an example to all lesser men. The virtues aspired to were courage, loyalty, generosity, fidelity to the Church, obedience, chastity, courtesy, humility, and beneficence. As in so much of life, the "very perfit gentil knight" was often the exception. As a class, nobles tended to be snobbish, cruel, wild, ruthless, selfish, scheming, and untrustworthy. Often their morals were lax, even debased.

The curriculum which prepared a child of the nobility for adulthood in his class was practical and efficient. Since the noble lived by his estate, yet shunned actual work in producing the necessities for living, it was necessary that he learn in detail how to manage this estate. He had to understand farming, the raising of animals, hunting and fishing, the economics of buying and selling, and efficient direction of a large staff of workers. Although the menials did all the work, the noble could very easily fail, be cheated, or find his estate deteriorating if he did not understand its workings down to the most minute detail. Since the men were often away from the estate for long periods of time serving their lords, management of the business fell to the women who remained behind. Thus this training in handling household and lands was given equally to boys and girls. The ideal wife of a knight was one who could manage the entire complex of his holdings as efficiently and skillfully as he.

The young of the nobility, male or female, were expected to learn polite accomplishments, etiquette, and the code of social intercourse established by their class. While the young person served in the house of his lord, he was expected to watch, listen, and learn. He was encouraged to practice manners, listen carefully to instructions, and accept humbly any rebuke his superior felt necessary. In this way he was acculturated to his class. In addition, it was necessary that a noble be skilled in music, dancing, chess, falconry, the chase, dice, and backgammon. All these were taught in the lord's household by individuals charged with this responsibility. Boys were given special training in the rudiments of tilting in the tournament and in fencing on horseback, while girls were taught embroidery, sewing, and the art of cookery.

While the education of the young noble was practical and closely related to daily life, the intellectual aspect was not neglected. A ruling class must be steeped in tradition and have some acquaintance with the scholarly heritage of the race. The young noble learned Latin, read literature and developed some understanding of its meaning, mastered feudal law and customs, and was schooled in the Roman Catholic faith. While everyone did not gain a deep understanding in all these fields, there *were* scholars among the nobles, and Christian theologians were not wholly unknown.

Every boy of noble birth was expected to become proficient as a cavalryman, skilled in fighting, and knowledgeable in the courtesies of the profession. This education began in the home when the child watched and listened as the men talked about and prepared for war. As a page in the home of his lord he played at war, learned the art of jousting with a dummy figure—the *quintain*—and the art of fencing on horseback. As a squire he accompanied his master into battle and learned his skill firsthand. In addition, he was required to take instruction in the use of arms from a member of the household. His acceptance as a knight rested considerably upon his proficiency in this area.

LEARNING AND SCHOLARSHIP BEFORE CHARLEMAGNE

CELTIC EDUCATION AND CHRISTIANITY

Christianity was brought to Ireland in the third century. By the end of the fourth, it had become a power in the life of the people. When the

Saxons invaded England, many Christians fled to Ireland for refuge. When Saint Patrick came to Ireland, he found, in the fifth century, a fanatical, ascetic, and evangelistic Christianity rooted deep in the life of the people with little tolerance for outside influences. Although his Roman-type Christianity had some influence upon the people, an influence which many historians have blown up out of its true proportion, Irish Christianity remained largely independent.

Missionaries went from Ireland, during the sixth through the eighth centuries, to England, Scotland, and the continent. These men established monasteries as far away as Saint-Gall in Switzerland, brought Christianity to "barbarian" invaders, and devoted considerable energy to schools and education.

Protected from invasion because of its relative inaccessibility, Ireland developed an intellectual life and a core of scholars and literary men, called *Bards*, within her own tradition. Although there were contacts with the outside world, and from time to time scholars came to Ireland from distant lands, there was little in this to subvert the main stream of Irish intellectual life. Very early, the Druids and other literary men of Ireland attracted students who became their devoted disciples. Schools of literature, law, and military science are known to have existed early in the third century. With the coming of Christianity, many of the *Bards* attached themselves to the movement and established bardic schools. These stressed Gaelic literature, the scriptures, and ecclesiastical Latin. To graduate, a student had to spend twelve years in intense study.

An ancient custom among the Irish was fosterage, the practice of placing children in the home of a more fortunate kinsman for their education. This was almost universal among certain classes of society.

Another important source of Irish education was the monasteries, where community life was centered and education was a major activity. These became centers of high scholarship and attracted students from England and the continent. From them went missionaries to spread Christianity and establish schools throughout Latin Christendom. When kings and emperors wanted scholars to assist in establishing more advanced schools and raising the intellectual level of their realms, they turned to Ireland for help, and many of their learned men were products of Irish schools.

CHRISTIAN EDUCATION IN SPAIN

When, after the Second Punic War (201 B.C.), Rome sought to Latinize Spain, she found there an Iberian culture which showed evidence of Greek influence. For more than a century, Roman and Iberian cultures existed side by side. As Christianity took form, its influence came to be felt in Spain. With the decay of the Roman Empire and the coming of the Vandals and other "barbarian" people to Spain, cities fell into ruin, the prosperous trade in wine and olive oil disappeared, and the land reverted to its ancient differences and divisions. The Visigoths, who entered into Spanish affairs in the fifth century, brought a degree of stability to the society. This was possible because by this time Spain had come under the influence of Roman law and the Christian Church. Then, in 589, the king, Reccared, was baptized a Christian, and the third Council of Toledo proclaimed the conversion of the entire kingdom.

Meanwhile, monasteries for training the clergy had appeared throughout Spain, and Christian schools were challenging Roman and Iberian schools with roots in earlier days. The Council of Toledo, held in 531, required bishops to provide masters for the instruction of boys destined for the priesthood, prohibited ordination of illiterates, and required all priests to serve in the diocese of the bishop under whose charge they received their education.

The giant of Spanish intellectual life of the period was Isidorus Hispalensis (*circa* 570-636), better known as Isidore of Seville. Born of a noble family from Cartegena, he became archbishop of Seville, succeeding his brother, Leander, in 609. His writings on Christian doctrine, worship, duties of Christians and priests, and his commentaries on the scriptures, while highly significant, are thrown into the shadows by his masterpiece, an encyclopedia of all the knowledge of his age called *Originum sive etymologiarum libri xx,* or *Etymologies.* As the leader of Spanish Christianity, he made significant contributions to the growth of canon law and Church government. His activities in the two Councils of Toledo, 610 and 633, and the Council of Seville, 619, helped shape church policy in many areas.

The *Etymologies* covers in detail all the arts and sciences known to western man of the seventh century, including the superstitions and beliefs of different societies. Throughout the work, Isidore bows to authority, never presuming to suggest divergent opinions or take issue with scripture, or the writings of the Church Fathers or earlier scholars. For him, all nature has a hidden meaning, which the student must discover and expound. This "higher meaning" he found in allegory, which he used constantly. The sun is Christ and the thunder God's voice rebuking mortals. The number six reflects the perfection of the universe, and twenty-two turns up so often in scripture that he knows it must have a profound, hidden meaning.

Isidore believed that the natural was a subordinate realm above which reigned the supernatural. His world was peopled with hosts of spirits, good and evil; and the world and man's mind and conscience were battlegrounds on which these spirits fought for mastery of the world. He feared to trust his own observations and reason, but relied upon the word of those long dead. Knowledge was for him divorced from contemporary living.

SCHOOLS AND SCHOLARS IN EARLY ENGLAND

Britain was on the frontier of the Roman Empire, often out of touch with happenings in faraway Rome. Distant though it was from the center of things, it was not too far to escape the influence of early Christianity. As Roman authority weakened, Britain followed much the same course as Ireland, developing a Christian culture independent of Roman authority. This received a serious setback when the Saxons overran the country after 407. The native Celts were either enslaved or fled to Ireland, and the Roman-Christian culture that had been developing since the first century A.D. all but disappeared.

By the seventh century, Saxon invaders, joined by Angles and Jutes, had established a settled agricultural society and a fairly stable form of government. Missionaries from Ireland moved in to re-establish Christianity. These were soon followed by monks sent out by Pope Gregory the Great, in 597, and led by Saint Augustine. The king of Wessex, one of the three independent kingdoms formed by the Saxons, became a Christian and established Canterbury as the religious capital of his realm. The archbishop of Canterbury became the primate of the Church of Britain.

Since the Christianity in Britain was a result of both Celtic and Roman religious beliefs and practices, a Church council was called for the kingdom of Northumberland in 664 to debate issues dividing the Church. Listening to both sides, the king ruled in favor of Roman Christianity. After this, Britain moved in the direction of Latin Christianity, developing a strong Roman Church which was to control the religious life of the people until the Reformation under Henry VIII. An increasing number of missionaries traveled from Britain throughout Europe, preaching, establishing monasteries and schools, and teaching.

Following the decision of the king of Northumberland, Britain began a long period of rich scholarship and literature. Canterbury became a famous center of learning under the leadership of Theodore of Tarsus, archbishop from 669 to 690. He was assisted in his endeavors by Hadrian, abbot of the monastery at Canterbury. One of Hadrian's pupils was Aldhelm (circa 640-709), well versed in both Anglo-Saxon and Latin, especially the writings of the Church Fathers. Settling eventually at Malmesbury, where he received his early education, he wrote

Latin verse, set some of his poems to music, and founded churches and monasteries in which teaching and scholarship were stressed. Many of his songs remained among the popular music of Britain well into the tenth century.

The most famous of early English scholars was the noted historian Bede (673-735). He spent most of his life in the monastery at Jarrow, under Benedictine Rule, where he wrote commentaries on scripture, four texts for use in schools, a short description of the universe as it was conceived in his time, and an *Ecclesiastical History of the English Nation.* This has been called "one of the most valuable and one of the most beautiful of historical works." Bede had the artist's instinct for proportion, the artist's sense of the picturesque and the pathetic. It won him the title of "the Father of English History." In addition to its beauty, the book was highly accurate, a result of years of careful reading and research.

EDUCATION UNDER CHARLEMAGNE

As early as the time of Charles Martel, there existed at the royal palace of the Frankish kingdom a school for the education of children of the court. When Charlemagne ascended to the throne, he turned to this school as a focal point for a revival of education and culture. His endeavors were not newborn in a pagan and barbaric world but were rather the outgrowth of a long tradition.

Classical culture had not died, despite the decay of Roman authority. Latin was widely read and appreciated by many scholars. The writings of the Church Fathers were well known. Ireland and England had sent learned men to preach and teach. What Charlemagne did was to throw the power and prestige of his kingly office behind forces working for a better-educated and more intellectual leadership by stressing the duty of bishops and abbots to see to the education of the clergy, opening his court to scholars from all parts of the world, and demanding higher standards of education among the nobles.

The palace school became a model for schools throughout the kingdom. Alcuin (735-804), from the Episcopal school at the cathedral at York, was persuaded to head this school and become Charlemagne's minister of education. He drew to the palace many of the keenest and most productive minds of the world—Theodulphus, the poet, of Spain; Peter of Pisa; and Paul the Deacon, of Italy. These scholars wrote poetry, histories, hymns, sermons, textbooks, dialogues, and *capitularies* to the clergy and leaders on educational and governmental matters. Books were gathered from everywhere, and libraries grew in population centers and at cathedrals. One of the major undertakings of these scholars was a careful revision of the *Vulgate,* a Latin translation of the Bible made by Saint Jerome in the fourth century at Alexandria. An effort was made to detect and eliminate all the errors that had crept into the book in the more than 500 years since its publication.

Alcuin, as "schoolmaster" and chief educational advisor in the palace school, developed a method for teaching Latin and other basic subjects. Included in his contributions was an elementary syllabus which he used in teaching fundamentals to Pepin, son of Charlemagne. The syllabus is entitled *The Disputation of Pepin, The Most Noble and Royal Youth, with Albinus the Scholastic.* A sample of this syllabus follows:

1. General questions and answers

Pepin. What is writing?   Albinus. The guardian of history.

Pepin. What is language?   Albinus. The betrayer of the soul.

Pepin. What produces language?   Albinus. The tongue.

Pepin. What is the tongue?   Albinus. The whip of the air.

Pepin. What is air?   Albinus. The guardian of life.

Pepin. What is life?   Albinus. The joy of the happy, the sorrow of the evil, the expectation of death.

Pepin. What is death?   Albinus. An inevitable event; an uncertain journey; tears for the living; the probation of wills; the stealer of men.

Pepin. What is man?   Albinus. The slave of death, a transient traveler, a stranger in his place.

Pepin. What is man like?   Albinus. Like a fruit-tree.

Pepin. How is man placed?   Albinus. Like a lantern exposed to the wind.

Pepin. Where is he placed?   Albinus. Between six walls.

Pepin. Which are they?   Albinus. Above, below, before, behind, right, left.

Pepin. To how many changes is he liable?   Albinus. To six.

Pepin. Which are they?   Albinus. Hunger and satiety; rest and work.

Pepin. What is sleep?   Albinus. The image of death.

Pepin. What is the liberty of man?

Albinus. Innocence.

Pepin. What is the head?

Albinus. The top of the body.

Pepin. What is the body?

Albinus. The domicile of the soul.

2. Natural phenomena

Pepin. What is water?

Albinus. A supporter of life; a cleanser of filth.

Pepin. What is fire?

Albinus. Excessive heat; the nurse of growing things.

Pepin. What is cold?

Albinus. The feverishness of our members.

Pepin. What is frost?

Albinus. The persecutor of plants; the destruction of leaves; the bond of the earth; the source of waters.

Pepin. What is snow?

Albinus. Dry water.

Pepin. What is winter?

Albinus. The exile of summer.

Pepin. What is spring?

Albinus. The painter of the earth.

Pepin. What is autumn?

Albinus. The barn of the year.

After several years as head of the palace school, Alcuin retired to the monastery of Saint Martin at Tours, where he conducted a school and undertook to elevate the standards of education in all the monastic schools of the realm. Since these schools drew boys both destined for the monastic life and desirous of an education that would serve them in secular life, his influence was felt far beyond the education of the clergy.

Charlemagne's policy was one of Romanizing his subjects, both lay and cleric. He had been crowned by the Church and counted himself a devout Christian. As king and Christian he strove to nurture his people in the best that both Roman and Christian cultures could offer. His *capitularies* instructed and exhorted bishops, monks, and parish priests to give prayerful attention to education, "each according to his capacity." To make more books available, he instituted a vast project for copying those which were in the kingdom and sent copyists to libraries in distant lands to bring back copies of foreign treasures.

To strengthen the life of the monasteries, Charlemagne decreed that obedience to the *Rule* of Saint Benedict was obligatory for cloistered clerics. He had accurate copies of the *Rule* made and distributed among the monasteries with instructions that the abbots would be held responsible for their enforcement. He stressed in particular the intellectual and scholarly work required by the *Rule.*

Charlemagne elevated the standards of education and intellectual endeavor throughout his kingdom. The classical culture of ancient Rome was revived and avidly sought after wherever men of thought and devotion gathered. Libraries were assembled in monasteries, cathedrals, towns, and the palace. Young men, trained by Alcuin and other scholars who gathered about him at the palace, went out to teach, found schools, and encourage both civil and religious leaders to strive for higher intellectual and educational standards. Worship in the churches and chapels was made more uniform and correct. Church music took on a new dignity, and sermons were more factual and true.

After Charlemagne, the standards of scholarship declined amid quarrels over sovereign rights and the eventual break-up of the Empire, but doors had been opened that were never again to be shut, and sights had been lifted that were not to be lowered in all the generations to come.

SCHOLARSHIP AMONG THE ARABS   MUSLIMS ✓

Most of the western Church leaders feared Greek and Latin scholarship and forbade Christians to have any contact with it. Many theological battles in the early Church were over theories championed by students of the classical tradition. These were usually decided by western standards, making classical theories heresy. As a result, much of classical learning, along with the writings of Greek and Roman scholars, was driven east and into Arabic-speaking countries. As the Arabs spread their culture and language to other lands, they absorbed much of this classical culture along with the native cultures of the peoples they conquered.

Mohammed united Arabic-speaking people of the East and sent them on a mission of conquest to carry the truth, as they saw it, to all the world. As they became masters of most ancient centers of learning, they set about to encourage continued creative scholarship and education. The Caliphs who followed Mohammed could see no conflict between reason and the teachings of the Prophet and gave their patronage to scholars from China, India, Persia, Syria, Egypt, North Africa, and Spain, to name a few. Baghdad on the Tigris, founded and made the capital of eastern Mohammedanism by the Abbasid dynasty in the eighth century, and Cardova, in Spain, along with Constantinople, were vital centers of scholarship. There, and to other cities in the vast realm of the Moslems, came heretics from the western Christian world to meet and work with fellow intellectuals from as far away as China and India. There the great classics of all cultures, including those of the Greek and Roman golden ages, were translated into Arabic. While the West was virtually a stranger to its classical past, the Arabic world was assimilating classical treasures and making them part of its tradition. Paper was being manufactured, operations were being performed under anaesthesia, and streets were lighted at night. Some of the most beautiful poetry of all time was written, and rich music was composed and sung.

The Moslems were great borrowers and assimilators. Whatever they touched, they made their own. They were also creators and originators. During the ninth and tenth centuries, they brought many of the arts and sciences to a height far above anything that Europe was to know for many centuries. Caliph al-Ma'mum, in the ninth century, organized at Baghdad a *House of Wisdom,* second only to the great Alexandrian Museum. It comprised a library of immense proportions, an academy for teaching and study, and a host of translators able to take writings from all the important languages of the age and turn them into accurate and beautiful Arabic. There the works of Aristotle, Galen, Euclid, Ptolemy, and Plato; Neo-Platonic works and masterpieces in Judaic, Syriac, Coptic, Chinese, Hindu, and Persian, were made available for study by scholars who flocked there from all corners of the world.

Later the western world found the classics of its past in Spain and other Moslem lands, brought them back into western culture, and made them the source of a renaissance of the human spirit in the fifteenth century.

AT THE ENTRANCE TO
THE MEDIEVAL RENAISSANCE

The revival of scholarly interest so skillfully engineered by Charlemagne and the teaching of Alcuin and others who worked with him in the Frankish kingdom produced an intellectual atmosphere that was to remind western man of his past and set him dreaming of a better tomorrow. Social and economic developments of the tenth and eleventh centuries gave this dream a foundation in reality. Although progress was slowed by the Vikings, especially in England and Ireland, the dream had been given momentum by Charlemagne and his court that drove it on to a Medieval Renaissance.

Charlemagne left his empire to his only living son, Louis the Pious, a weak and ineffectual sovereign. Upon the latter's death, the kingdom was parceled out, under the Treaty of Verdun, to his three sons. The western part, roughly what is now France, went to Charles the Bald. The eastern part, now Germany, was ruled by Louis. A strip of land between the two was given to Lothair. Though lacking the drive and devotion of their grandfather, these rulers supported scholars, championed schools and libraries, and maintained contact with intellectual developments in other parts of the world.

HRABANUS MAGNENTIUS MAURUS (*circa* 776-856)

Alcuin had many brilliant and famous students, but none was more devoted to the ideals of his teacher and his emperor than Hrabanus, usually known as Rabanus. Recognizing his talents very early, Alcuin gave him the name "Maurus" after Saint Maur, the most brilliant pupil of Saint Benedict. Born at Mainze, Hrabanus received his education at the monastery of Fulda and then moved to Tours to study with Alcuin. For some twenty years he served as abbot of Fulda. In 847 he became Archbishop of Mainz and continued his studies there until his death.

Hrabanus was a tireless student, writer, teacher, and ecclesiastical administrator. He wrote treatises on Christian doctrine, an encyclopedia, a textbook in arithmetic, a grammar, works instructing the clergy as to their duties and privileges, and a detailed discussion of his views on education. This last he called *On the Soul*. His pupils went from his classes to occupy most of the key positions in the churches of Germany, and to gather into their schools the leading minds of the age. So influential was he in the educational development of the times that he has been called *Primus Praeceptor Germanae*, The First Teacher of Germany.

This leader of German intellectual life believed that no office could be more significant or influential than that of teacher and church leader. Those who aspire to this exalted position should be perfect in morality and knowledge. All things are part of their equipment and must be mastered. Scriptures, history, oratory, the "mystical sense of words," medicine, Christian doctrine, all branches of knowledge, and the manners and graces of gentlemen—these and others must be the standard equipment of one who would lead men to Christ and an understanding of His universe.

THE ENGLAND OF ALFRED THE GREAT

Latin was the language of scholarly Europe during the Middle Ages —not the classical Latin of Cicero but a practical Latin that had grown and changed as men's interests grew and changed and new words were either coined or taken over from the languages of the people Rome touched. As tribes from beyond the frontier moved into the Empire, they gave new words and expressions to help form medieval Latin. They also brought their own languages and dialects to mix and change and draw to themselves contributions from Latin. While scholarship held fairly closely to Latin, all Europe was a cauldron boiling with strange tongues mixing and changing to produce the vernacular languages that were to make up the speech of later national groups.

One of the first to realize the true significance of this development was Alfred the Great (848-900), king of Wessex. Even before his day, attempts had been made to develop an Anglo-Saxon tongue. Earlier kings had issued decrees and laws in the language of the people, a glossary of Saxon terms had been compiled, and Bede had begun translating the Gospel of John into the vernacular. Further, a host of religious and secular poems had appeared in the English tongue, the most memorable of which are *Beowulf* and the stories of Caedmon and Cynewulf. Added to this were tales and poems sung, but never written down, by the minstrels who entertained kings and nobles. There was also a crude but vital English drama taking shape for entertainment of the masses.

Alfred came to the throne after the ravages of the Vikings had destroyed many of the country's monasteries and schools and scattered its scholars. Libraries had fallen into disuse, and churches were reduced to rubble. He set about to repair the damage done by these invaders, stop the decay that followed, and promote knowledge and education among both the elite and the masses. His method was to encourage translation into the vernacular of as much good literature as possible and stimulate whatever creative genius the country might produce. The *Anglo-Saxon Chronicle,* written under Alfred's inspiration, is a masterpiece of Anglo-Saxon prose. To encourage learning among the clergy he had Gregory the Great's *Pastoral Care* and *Dialogues* translated and circulated among the bishops with instructions that they turn their attention to educating "all the youth now in England of freemen." These were to be taught first in "the English writing" and only later "in the Latin language."

The court of Alfred became a lively center of learning and the arts, attracting scholars from far and wide and serving as the nerve center of an intricate complex of educational activities. The king had monasteries built and schools organized in them, restored churches, commanded bishops and priests to encourage education among the people, and employed many assistants to collect and copy books to fill libraries throughout the realm.

EDUCATIONAL POLICY AND THE CHURCH

During the ninth through the eleventh centuries, the Christian Church experienced a profound change in its educational thinking. Earlier, the western Church feared scholarship. The intellectual stimulation came from civil rulers. Charlemagne and Alfred are examples of rulers who found education at low ebb, though in the hands of the Church, and used their royal prestige to infuse it with new spirit and life. It was they who had to order and cajole the bishops and other ecclesiastics to concern themselves with education. In most instances the infectious ignorance of the times could be traced to the Church and its pulpits.

By the ninth century the Church was beginning to develop an aggressive policy toward education and schools. This consisted of greater Church sponsorship of scholarship and teaching and, what is of possibly more significance, increasing effort on the part of ecclesiastical authorities to gain control of all education that had been developed by other agencies. This latter grew out of a realization that if the Church was to grow and dominate the affairs of men, it must shape and control their minds.

The Church's policy began to take form with the Council of Rome, called and chaired by Pope Eugenius II, in 826. This council resulted in an order instructing all bishops to train teachers of the liberal arts and theology to serve as needed in the diocese. A second Council of Rome, held in 853, instructed bishops to establish a school in every parish for the teaching of the elements of religion and a school in every cathedral to teach the liberal arts. Other Church councils reaffirmed these orders and stimulated the maintenance of schools for general education and the training of clerics, music schools, and schools of the liberal arts and sciences.

The ancient fear of learning was gone. Although some did resist these orders, holding that faith was the basis of salvation and that learning would destroy faith, the Church had learned a fundamental lesson from emperors, kings, and princes. To hold man's loyalty, one must hold his mind. Learning cannot be denied the human intellect. The choice is not between learning and no learning but between "false" and "true" learning. The Church was now launched on a campaign to separate the false from the true, as it saw the truth, and shape the mind toward the true. A corollary of this position was that all education must be in the hands of the Church. This was to lead to bitter fights between civil authorities and the Church as both struggled to hold the minds of men and win their loyalties.

THE MEDIEVAL RENAISSANCE
(Eleventh Through Thirteenth Centuries)

FACTORS SHAPING THE MEDIEVAL RENAISSANCE

The eleventh through the thirteenth centuries in Europe have been characterized as "the flowering of the Middle Ages," the culmination of centuries of growth and development, the finest years of an age that must give way to new and different events and forces. It was the medieval spirit, with all that that means, at its finest and most productive hour.

Several achievements helped shape the period and set in motion trends to determine the future. In 1066, William the Conqueror landed on English soil. There followed in England a long period of stability, security, and progress such as the country had not experienced in all its history. Commercial interests were expanded, agriculture was guaranteed markets, and farmers found contentment on the land. Industry grew and offered employment to all who would come and work, protected by a strong monarchy which opened sources of raw materials and expanded its consumer population. The Church was content to exert authority in spiritual matters, leaving temporal matters to the crown. A strong judicial system was developed, giving freedom and security to the people. In this atmosphere learning found stimulation and the scholar prestige and understanding.

Toledo, in Spain, was, very early in Christian history, a center of religious activity. Important church councils were held there in the fourth, fifth, and sixth centuries. In 712, Toledo was conquered by the Moors, who developed it as a prosperous center of trade and culture. From 712 to 1035 it was a provincial capital in the caliphate of Cardova; then it became an independent state. Arabic and Jewish scholars came there to establish a center of learning that was to attract intellectuals from all parts of the world. Although Christian scholars are known to have studied in Toledo for many years, it was not until the conquest of the city by the Christians, who made it the capital of the Kingdom of Castile, that the rich treasures of the Moslem world were opened to the West. Christian students flocked to its centers of learning, absorbing Arabic scholarship which, by that time, was an accumulation of the best that could be found in the ancient Greek, Hindu, Chinese, and Judaic traditions. There they discovered Arabic translations of most of the classics. These were translated into Latin and brought back into western culture.

Possibly the most significant factor effecting change from the early Middle Ages to the period of the Medieval Renaissance was the Crusades. During the twelfth century thousands of Christians from western Europe left home and estate, office and position, family and friends to travel east in a vain effort to destroy the "heathen" and "restore" the holy places of Christian tradition to the Church. Men and women of high position, peasants and freemen, and children in great numbers were caught up in the hysteria of the age and enlisted in the holy mission in the hope of eternal salvation. From a religious point of view, these expeditions were a miserable failure. Economically, they brought about greater contact between the East and West and stimulated trade in the many goods each wanted from the other. Italian cities grew rich and powerful as a result. Since many of the crusaders never returned, the social balance of Europe was distorted severely.

What is most important for our purposes, the Crusades multiplied cultural contacts with the East, established centers of learning and scholarship, and made available to the West the intellectual treasures of the East in abundance. In the Christian kingdom of Syria, for example, European scholars found treasures of Greek science and philosophy, Hindu mathematics, and classical literature of which the Arabs had been custodians for centuries. In addition, these scholars discovered the observational approach to learning. This was to challenge and eventually defeat the authoritarian approach which had shaped western scholarship throughout Christian history. As man came to trust his senses, he was far along the way toward modern scientific procedures.

A final factor which shaped the Medieval Renaissance was the rise in the thirteenth century of the orders of Friars. Saint Dominic (1170-1221), an Augustinian in the cathedral chapter of Osma, in Spain, was commissioned by Innocent III in 1205 to preach among the Albigenses. This was a heretical sect in Languedoc that had adopted an extreme form of Manichaeism. They believed that there were two gods, a god of good whose son was Christ and a god of evil whose son was Satan, battling each other for the soul of man. The little band of barefooted preachers who followed Dominic as he went from village to village preaching and teaching was eventually, in 1216, formed into the Order of Saint Dominic, or the Dominicans, by Honorius III. By the time of Dominic's death the order boasted over 500 friars in sixty friaries located in eight provinces embracing all of western Europe.

In 1206, Saint Francis of Assisi (1182-1226) left his father's house, that of a wealthy merchant, to devote himself to a life of poverty and service to the poor, the sick, and the lepers. By 1209 he had added preaching to his services. The small band of followers that joined him was eventually molded into an order of friars devoted to the ideals of their leader. With some misgivings, brought on by the fanatical austerity of the group's way of living, Innocent III gave the little band his blessing, and the Franciscans, or Friars Minor, became part of European Christianity in 1215.

In the first half of the thirteenth century there were in Italy various small congregations of hermits living in accord with many different rules. Around 1250, they were persuaded by the pope to unite and adopt the Rule of Saint Augustine. Thus they became known as the Order of Augustinian Hermits or the Augustinian Order. Almost immediately they abandoned the hermit's life for work in the towns among the poor.

Sometime around 1150, a crusader named Berthold and ten companions established themselves as hermits in a cave on Mount Carmel. Albert, Latin patriarch of Jerusalem, gave them a *rule* consisting of sixteen items in about 1210. According to this *rule* the monks were to live in separate huts; devote themselves to prayer, work, and austerity; and come together only for liturgical services. In 1226 the *rule* received papal sanction, and the Carmelite Order was officially established. Later they migrated to Cyprus and then to Sicily, France, and England. In 1247 at Aylesford the *rule* of the Order was changed to fit conditions in western lands, and the Carmelites became mendicant friars.

These orders turned their backs on monasteries and monastic seclusion to devote themselves to preaching and serving the unfortunate. They lived in complete poverty, supported by gifts from the people, and knew no task too demanding and no situation too shocking or repulsive for their services. The Dominicans and Franciscans soon turned to teaching and won commanding positions in institutions of higher education. The Augustinians, though not stressing education as strongly, had in their ranks some of the great scholars of the age. These Orders of Friars moved in where the monasteries left off. As monastic life became more contemplative and cloistered and teaching was of less interest or importance, the friars were ready to assume the responsibility. It was their scholarship and interest in the logical development of Christian doctrine that set the intellectual tenor of the Medieval Renaissance.

SCHOLASTICISM AND THE SCHOLASTICS

Christian theology by the eleventh century was a mass of contradictory and often confusing ideas, beliefs, and positions. Church councils, bishops, popes, and influential assemblies and persons had throughout the centuries made decisions and pronouncements regarding doctrine that were quite naturally conflicting. The mind, in its quest for consistency, often had to be content with faith and able to interpret inconsistency as an inherent inability of the finite to comprehend infinity.

Although both Plato and Aristotle were not unknown in the West between the fourth and the twelfth centuries, it was not until late in the twelfth century that they were understood and appreciated. After the conquest of Toledo, Sicily, and Syria, translations of their works were made available to western scholars. Aristippus of Sicily translated both the *Meno* and the *Phaedo* from Arabic into Latin. James of Venice translated Aristotle's *Posterior Analytics.* During the latter part of the twelfth century a flood of translations from Arabic and Greek was let loose upon western Europe. By 1200, Latin civilization had in its possession much of the science and philosophy of classical tradition—the works of Aristotle, Plato, Euclid, and Ptolemy, in addition to Arabic, Hindu, and Chinese works in these fields.

Those able to read and understand this vast storehouse of man's intellectual treasures could no longer be content with faith. They asked questions and demanded answers. They now had the tools for constructing answers. Already, scholars of the eastern Church, especially John of Damascus, had built a Christian theology on the foundation of Aristotelianism, and Moslem scholars had fashioned a consistent theology for Islam. Now western theologians were ready to begin the task of building a system of Christian thought from the material the centuries had handed to them and from the philosophy of Aristotle.

Scholasticism was western Christianity's attempt to employ reason in its search for truth. However, the truth was not free from authority. The Scholastics, scholars working within the movement, did not doubt the authority of the Church or the papacy. In matters of faith and morals this authority was infallible. Reason is God-given and, as such, cannot contradict God's authoritative Church. The Scholastics worked within the bounds of Christian authority and were certain that at no time would reason belie truth as revealed by God's holy Church.

These Scholastics failed to understand what they were doing. They thought that reason would inevitably lead to authoritative truth. They used logic with heads bowed and the voice of authority ringing in their ears. They reasoned honestly and expertly. When reason had exhausted the authoritative material handed to them, they began to ask questions and pose problems that challenged this authority. At first the scholars, men of devotion to the Church, were astounded, believing that they had made mistakes in logic. Then came the time when they were convinced that no mistakes had been made. At this point Scholasticism became the Church's severest critic, and a new generation of scholars employed reason to reshape men's minds outside of and often in contradiction to cherished and authoritative doctrines. Then the modern age had arrived.

RISE OF MEDIEVAL UNIVERSITIES

INTRODUCTION

The medieval university was an inevitable outgrowth of the medieval world. Given the particular social pattern which characterized the Medieval Renaissance, the university had to develop as it did.

In this period of increasing peace and stability, the restless energy of many was focused on scholarship. As a result, a body of brilliant and devoted intellectuals appeared to do further research and teaching in western Europe. Since both state and Church were expanding and in need of staffing their vast bureaucracies, there was an ever-growing demand for individuals trained to manage the affairs of men. This gave to teaching and learning a status far above anything experienced in the past. When we add the belief of the Church and its leaders that learning, especially skill in and understanding of dialectics, was the avenue to the truth of God and the knowledge necessary for eternal salvation, we can appreciate why many people came near to deifying the scholar and his skill.

In such an environment centers of teaching and learning developed naturally. The necessary conditions were there, the soil was prepared, and the medieval university was the inevitable consequence.

WHAT WAS THE MEDIEVAL UNIVERSITY?

The medieval university was an institution of western Europe. Teaching and learning centers were to be found in cities scattered throughout Christendom, each part of a great complex over which the Roman curia held a controlling hand. The student body and faculty of almost any university were international. Mobility characterized the intellectual community of Europe to the extent that citizens of distant places were to be found teaching and learning wherever a university flourished.

The fundamental goal of all medieval universities was professional training. The age demanded a host of well-prepared individuals to care for its needs, and the universities accepted this challenge enthusiastically. Law, medicine, theology, and the arts were all professions needing men of ability and schooling, and the universities were well-prepared to provide the schooling.

The university usually enjoyed a degree of independence not possible on modern campuses. Born of more or less informal teaching-learning communities, its products needed by state and church, and looking ultimately to the Church at Rome for guidance, the university was able to resist attempts on the part of cities and local communities, kings or emperors, bishops, and others to bend it to their will. So many authorities were vying for its favors that the university could shift its appeals from one to the other until it received what it thought to be its right. In the long struggle to maintain this independence, the university was granted privileges and immunities which left it almost wholly the master of its fate.

The university was an autonomous body organized into factions made necessary by the nature of its constituency and function. The Latin word *"universitas"* meant, in the Middle Ages, a corporation. Whenever men organized themselves into groups for specific purposes, they became a *universitas,* a corporation. Among the many corporations of the medieval world were guilds—organizations of workers, tradesmen, or others for protecting and maintaining standards, determining employment, protecting markets, and themselves looking after the other interests of a group.

Since the civil authority controlling a specific section or area seldom was able to reach beyond its borders, individuals who traveled were at the mercy of the authorities where they journeyed. A student from Italy studying in Paris could not call on his governor for protection if he fell into the hands of the Paris police. Further, both students and faculty had needs that only cooperation could satisfy. These facts made necessary the organization of groups with mutual interests and problems into guilds or *universitates.* These bodies usually had a leader, or *rector,* who represented them in all matters affecting their interests. The rectors were members of an over-all body which controlled the university. In some centers, usually where the students were mature men, student guilds exerted major authority. In others, where the students were boys and youths, teachers' guilds, or faculties, were in control.

Gradually, the term *universitas* was dropped by corporations in general and came to be applied only to the organizations within the teaching-learning community. Here there might be several *universitates* of students and four or more of masters or teachers. Later these dropped the general title and became *nations* or guilds when applied to students and *faculties* when applied to masters. Then, and then only, the entire institution was known as a *universitas,* or university.

The struggle of a teaching-learning community to maintain its independence resulted in many privileges and immunities which it came to guard jealously. Among these were exemption from certain taxes and military service, the right to be tried by one's professors or the bishop of the city rather than by municipal courts, the right to beg, the right to set just prices for books, lodging, and other necessities, the right to suspend lectures as a means of protest against unjust treatment, and the right to close down the institution completely or move to another city or country. When, in 1231, for example, the University of Paris fell into a dispute with the city over its right to fix the price of board and lodging charged students, Pope Gregory IX granted the university the right to suspend activities until its authority was recognized. So cherished was the university in medieval life that, at one time, the Church condemned by ban all who wronged either students or faculty. At another time, the Church decreed special spiritual rewards for all those who gave money or goods to students.

The university became the sole authority for granting licenses to teach. The Church had recognized for centuries that controlling education was necessary in order to control the minds of men. This meant controlling those who taught. Consequently, church authorities had been jealous of their right to license teachers. No one would be allowed to teach without the sanction of the Church, and before issuing a license, the proper churchman would satisfy himself that the applicant was prepared to teach as the Church demanded. It was a church monopoly of teaching.

After a long struggle with bishops and other ecclesiastics, the universities, which were actually taking over the educational functions of cathedrals, collegiate churches, and other agencies of advanced education, won the right to present candidates to the proper church authorities, who would issue the license without question. This meant that the university and not the Church became the agency to attest to one's orthodoxy and fitness to teach. When Church and university were in agreement theologically, this was nothing more than a ceremony. However, as universities became more independent of church domination and began to develop standards of their own, secular authority controlled teaching and the Church was shorn of its ancient prerogative to channel learning. As this happened, the scholar moved out from the world of orthodoxy and into one of freedom, controversy, and science.

GREAT UNIVERSITIES OF THE MEDIEVAL RENAISSANCE

As monasteries gave up teaching and turned to a cloistered life of prayer and meditation, great churches strengthened their schools to fill the intellectual vacuum. Coming at a time when Europe was at peace, prosperous, and united under the Church, these institutions were able to attract scholars and students and train young men to staff their expanding schools. As a result, many centers of population became famous as teaching-learning communities. Their fame attracted other scholars and students, and the community grew. Both scholars and students were gradually organized into guilds and *universities,* and a university took shape.

The University of Paris is typical of this development. Three schools developed in the city. One was the cathedral school of Notre Dame of Paris, which boasted a history reaching back at least to the Merovingian kings. Another was the school of the collegiate church of Sainte Genevieve, with a history lost in the past. The third was a school opened in 1113 by the canons of Saint Victor. These, all ecclesiastic in origin and control, attracted noted clerics from all parts of Europe and drew young men interested primarily in positions within the vast religious complex of the western world.

For many years it had been the custom for chancellors of the Cathedral of Notre Dame and of Sainte Genevieve to grant licenses to teach, the *licentia docendi.* Since theology was the main interest in Paris, all teachers and pupils were clerics or candidates for clerical office. Consequently the *studium* which developed in Paris was predominantly ecclesiastical. Teachers of the liberal arts, law, and medicine set themselves up in the city and attracted students. Students and teachers began to organize into guilds and faculties and demand privileges and immunities from civil and ecclesiastical authorities. There were strikes, riots, fights, picketing, and other manifestations of unrest as different groups built for themselves protections against each other, the community, civil rulers, and Church authorities. Gradually, by a series of decrees, the pope and papal courts recognized the authority of these organizations and offered them an increasing number of rights and immunities.

A major battle over who should license teachers shaped up during the early part of the thirteenth century. As the *studium* at Paris grew, the chancellor of the Cathedral of Notre Dame assumed exclusive right to license all teachers and asserted his authority over all phases of the teaching-learning community. These actions were resented bitterly by teachers and students, with the result that the struggle between these forces continued for a quarter of a century. In the end the teachers were granted the right to present qualified students to the chancellor for licensing, and he was obligated to accept them without question. Further, the chancellor was stripped of all power over any function or activity of the *studium.*

Gradually, both teacher and student organizations were drawn together in a unity called the University of Paris. In 1259, the rector of the faculty of liberal arts was recognized by the pope as head of the university. From a conglomerate mass of scholars and students, each organized and functioning more or less independently, there had been developed a university. It had status which reached all the way to the papal throne. It had privileges and immunities cherished fanatically which no civil or church authority dared question. It was now offering instruction in the liberal arts, theology, law, and medicine. Since the intellectual movement of which Abelard was the most distinguished representative—the dialectical development of theology—had its roots in the *studium* at Paris, theology outshone all other interests, and the dominant method of teaching was logical elaboration of authorities.

A somewhat different development is seen at Salerno, in southern Italy. Greek colonies had been founded here around the sixth century B.C. and the Greek language spoken until late in the thirteenth century. During the Middle Ages the area loyal to the counts of Salerno acknowledged the authority of the eastern emperors, trade exchange was carried on with the Byzantine Empire, and travel between the East and West kept contacts with Constantinople and its world open.

Of particular interest to us was the survival of Greek science, especially medicine, in and around Salerno. Early in the ninth century Salerno was famous for its doctors and medical research. During the eleventh century translations of medical works by Greek, Graeco-Roman, and Jewish writers were appearing in large numbers. Many of these, in Latin, were soon to be required reading in medical schools throughout Europe. Doctors and teachers of medicine came to Salerno and studied with noted physicians who were in residence there. These attracted students in great numbers so that, in time, a *studium,* with medicine as its major concern, developed.

Salerno never attained the status of a true university. Nevertheless it was recognized in 1230 by Frederick II, who declared that all those practicing or teaching medicine in the kingdom of Sicily had to present certificates from masters at Salerno. Other countries gave preference to physicians trained at Salerno, thereby adding prestige to its medical faculties. A student coming to Salerno for training as a physician was required to spend three years studying liberal arts and five years studying medicine.

At Bologna, in northern Italy, another pattern of advanced education developed. Many of the cities of Italy had received their charters and special privileges from Roman emperors. Although they had lost power and prestige in the early Middle Ages, they were beginning to develop into thriving centers of commerce and wealth by the Medieval Renaissance. When feudal lords or kings attempted to assert authority over them and collect revenue, they resisted strongly and appealed to their early status as justification for their position. This often resulted in a lengthy struggle, during which the issues involved were fought out in court. Thus Roman law became important.

As noted legal talents came to Bologna to practice their profession, students followed, and a *studium* took shape. Others were attracted to the city either to teach or learn. Giving body to this development were three forces of long tradition and great respect. One was a system of municipal schools of rhetoric and law dating back to Roman days and contributing to the study of law as a science. Another was a number of monastic schools concerned with theology and canon law. The third was the cathedral school stressing the teaching of the liberal arts. As these educational forces united, a university was formed, offering training in the liberal arts and the professions of law, medicine, and theology.

Teachers of civil law offered training in the works of Justinian, compendia of law since his day, and in the principles of law. Although Bologna trained skillful practitioners of the law, it also stressed understanding of the principles of legal procedure and was noted for its large number of legal scholars. Irnerius (*circa* 1050-*circa* 1130) made the city famous as a center of legal study. Originally a teacher of rhetoric, he had turned to the study of law when the Countess Matilda asked him to assist her in a dispute in which she was involved with the Holy Roman Emperor.

Bologna also became the center of church or canon law. The Christian Church had developed a body of legal precedent and decrees accepted as the basis for church law. This material needed codification and reworking if it was to continue to serve the Church in determining legal issues. Sometime before 1150, Franciscus Gratianus (Gratian), a monk and teacher at the monastery of San Felice in Bologna, issued a compilation of canon law which he called, appropriately enough, the *Concordia Discordantium Canonum (Harmony of Discordant Decrees).* This became the basic textbook in Church law in the universities of the Middle Ages. It followed closely the dialectical method of Abelard and medieval theology. Dogma was never questioned or challenged. By presenting a question and then quoting authorities, what appeared to be an unbiased search for truth became in fact a method of undergirding orthodoxy with undisputed evidence.

Irnerius and Gratian were but two among many keen legal minds teaching and writing at Bologna during the twelfth and thirteenth centuries. Naturally, students came in large numbers to study with these masters of civil and canon law. Organizations among both teachers and students took form. By 1189 these had been consolidated into a university structure with the guild of teachers holding the reins of authority.

We find in England a somewhat different development taking place. Oxford, the county town of Oxfordshire, some fifty miles from London, was typical of rural England in the Middle Ages. It was nationalistic in spirit and aligned with the aspirations of the English gentry. Robert Pullen, a theologian from Paris, is known to have lectured there in 1133. By 1163, a *studium* had developed, and teachers and students were being attracted to the community in ever-increasing numbers. During the thirteenth century, Dominicans, Franciscans, and Carmelites came to Oxford in large numbers, to be followed by Benedictines a little later. So rapid was this growth toward university status that, by the middle of the thirteenth century the deputies of Oxford, in an appeal to the king, described the community as a school second only to that in Paris.

England had a custom of long standing, that of assigning royal favorites or outstanding persons to its churches. These men usually discharged no ecclesiastical functions but received a yearly income from the churches to which they were assigned. It was often possible for one to have an income from several churches. The revenue received from each church was called a "living." Those receiving livings seldom went near the churches involved, and many spent most of their lives outside of England in centers of learning, courts of kings or emperors, or wherever life was suited to their interests. A large number of these individuals did contribute substantially to the cultural and intellectual life of their times by teaching, writing, advising rulers, or serving in key positions in Church and state.

Responding to the spirit of nationalism that was developing in England, Henry II, in 1167, ordered all individuals deriving incomes from English churches to live in England or forfeit their "revenues." In a similar move the French king ordered all foreign scholars to leave his realm. These moves resulted in an influx of teachers to Oxford, many bringing their students with them. By the end of the twelfth century, the *studium* at Oxford was one of the famous institutions of intellectual activity in the western world.

Paris seems to have been the model which Oxford followed. Both were controlled by masters. Both were organized into guilds with proctors responsible for the protection of the rights and privileges of each guild. In both the faculty of arts became the controlling group, directing over-all activities of the university.

However, there were vast differences between Oxford and other great universities. The presiding officer of the university was a chancellor appointed by the Bishop of Lincoln. He was not a member of the teachers' guilds but rather an extra-university official. Later the masters were granted the right to elect the chancellor.

A feature of Oxford not found at universities on the continent was the college. Students coming to study with masters at a *studium* lived in hotels, boarding houses, or private homes. At Oxford they began renting entire buildings and living together as more or less close-knit groups. In some instances wealthy persons would buy or erect a building and turn it over to a group of students as living quarters. These came very quickly to take on the flavor of the class of students living there. Some accepted only students of the upper classes, while others catered to the lower classes. Teachers developed the practice of coming to the living quarters of their pupils for instructional purposes. In time they took up residence in these halls and assumed responsibility for disciplining the students. Out of this grew the colleges of Oxford, units in which both students and teachers lived and worked. Each college took on an atmosphere and developed a tradition all its own, so that a man was more concerned with his college than with the university. These received endowments, special privileges, and developed an ethos such as to make each distinctive and unique among all others in the community.

Attracted by the success of these universities which had grown more or less spontaneously out of the intellectual fervor of the Medieval Renaissance, and jealous of the prestige which they brought to the communities, civil and Church authorities in the thirteenth century turned to setting up universities by official decree. In 1224, Frederick II issued a royal charter establishing the University of Naples. His purpose was to train bureaucrats for his despotism as well as to control the thinking of his subjects. Thus no one within his domain was permitted to attend another *studium,* and all teachers, students, and curricular patterns were under political control.

Around the middle of the thirteenth century, Innocent IV founded the University of the Roman Court at Rome. Here civil and canon law and theology were the major interests. In 1312 the Council of Venice decreed that Greek, Arabic, Chaldee, and Hebrew be added to the curriculum. Its chancellor was the cardinal chamberlain, and the college of doctors was governed by authority of the pope.

LIFE ON MEDIEVAL CAMPUSES

As teachers coming to centers of intellectual activity found what they considered their rights endangered and themselves individually unable to care for all their needs, they organized into guilds. One of the functions of these bodies was to determine standards for the profession and protect students from inferior teaching. Teachers' guilds set standards for admission which were enforced more or less rigidly. When a candidate was accepted as qualified, he came before the guild, took the oath of office, and received the symbols of his status, usually the scholar's cap and a book. As of that moment he was known as a master, a title similar to that conferred on those fully accepted into other trade guilds.

All holders of licenses who had been accepted into the guild of teachers were called masters. In some instances they might be known as doctors or professors, but these titles were of no real significance. In some few university communities the title of master was given to a teacher of the liberal arts and that of doctor to a teacher of law, medicine, or theology. Status eventually came to be attached to these titles, the master being of an "inferior" faculty and the doctor of a "superior" faculty, and they developed into degrees.

In time the guilds of teachers began admitting to their ranks apprentices, young men looking toward full membership in the guild. These were known as beginners, or *baccalaureus* (bachelors). It was not until well into the thirteenth century that this became an accepted degree.

Only gradually did requirements for these degrees take on a semblance of standardization in medieval universities. Standards were usually set by the guilds, and consisted of the reading of a number of books, attendance at a stated number of lectures, and participation in a required number of disputations or debates. In some university centers a system of practice teaching was developed. The candidates for the degrees of master or doctor were required to teach a specified number of classes. One who had fulfilled all the requirements was examined by a panel of masters and, if accepted, received into the guild under the proper degree and presented to the Church authority for licensing.

Many students came to university communities merely to listen to a few lectures and participate in the life of the populace gathered there. Others came to listen to the lectures of one or more select masters or doctors and broaden their learning. The vast majority came to prepare for the license to teach or a degree that would give them the necessary status in their chosen profession. These latter usually attended lectures, which were based on a prescribed pattern and conducted in accordance with an accepted method. This included the reading of the text being studied, a full explanation of the meaning of each passage, additional comments on passages of special interest, presentation of *glosses* or commentaries by other scholars, and discussion of problems involved in the text. This technique represented slavish loyalty to a book and to orthodoxy. The student was expected to understand, not to question or challenge.

Two kinds of lectures were to be found at a university. The ordinary lecture was given by a master or doctor for the purpose of teaching his students. The extra-ordinary lecture would be given by a bachelor or other student as a practice teaching device. Often students were paid by a bachelor to attend his lectures and criticize him so that he might see and rectify his mistakes.

Candidates for a degree engaged in disputations or listened to debates between masters or doctors. One form of the disputation was a lecture in which the speaker would pose a thesis and then present arguments for and against its validity. The lecturer would be judged by the thoroughness with which he marshaled all the pertinent material and by his ability to present it convincingly. Another form was the debate, which might be between two students, a teacher and a student, or two teachers. Here a thesis would be proposed, and the participants would take sides. The affirmative was first presented, then the negative; then each side would be given time to refute the arguments of the other. Finally the results would be tallied and verified conclusions reached.

Having fulfilled all requirements, the candidate would be presented by his sponsor, a master or doctor, to the proper authorities for examination. Usually he would receive from the examiners several passages from prescribed books and retire for a period of time with his sponsor to study the material and prepare himself. Then, at the appointed time, he would appear before the examiners, either privately or in public, and discuss the passages as completely and thoroughly as he was able. When he finished, the examiners would vote to determine whether or not to confer the degree. If the vote was favorable, he was ceremoniously inducted into the proper guild and given the accepted symbols and honors. If the vote was negative, he returned to his studies and was presented again at some later date, or he withdrew from the institution.

Since the medieval universities had no lecture halls, laboratories, libraries, or classrooms, teachers lectured and debated wherever they could find and assemble students. Some worked in their own homes, others rented space for their teaching, while still others met with students in their living quarters or lectured in public places or on street corners much like ancient sophists.

The medieval universities were strictly for men. The teachers were men, and the students were men. While there is some evidence that learned women lived in university centers and did some teaching, they were not recognized by the university organization. Usually they confined their teaching to the daughters of wealthy patrons in their homes. However, there were many women participating in the extracurricular life of the universities. Since a university community was made up of a very diverse lot of people, it attracted both men and women ready and willing to serve the needs and wishes of the population. Some came to study and learn, while others came to carouse and enjoy whatever the community had to offer. Others came to trade, provide food and lodging, or offer themselves as the students demanded. Begging, rough and raucous games, poaching, drinking, brawling, robbery, and debauchery were common. Attempts were made by university, Church, and civil authorities to hold the behavior of the students, and at times the teacher, within the bounds of accepted custom, but to little avail. Here was a virile, lustful, exuberant, and often brilliant mass of humanity crowded into a small area and seeking ways to enjoy the life that was theirs. Many were creative, and many were just wild. Feeling relieved that their generations were escaping from the past, they were sensing the future, when things human would crowd out things divine, and the Age of Faith would give way to the Renaissance.

SCHOOLS OF THE LATER MIDDLE AGES

EDUCATION FOR THE TRADES

The child of all ages has learned much through watching others. He "picks up" a language, values, mores, customs, and the intangibles that go to make him what he is. In earlier times he learned his trade in the same way. As the environment became more complicated, his parents supplemented this learning with direct instruction. This was followed by instruction on the part of organizations of individuals skilled in a particular trade and gathered together for the purpose of protecting the secrets of the trade, regulating practice, determining who should be allowed to enter the trade and learn its skills, setting standards, caring for the welfare of the workers and their families, and dealing with other concerns of the group involved. Such organizations were to be found very early in history, and their practices and purposes varied from trade to trade.

With the return of stability in the society of twelfth and thirteenth century Europe, demand for products of handicraft grew rapidly, and craftsmen of varied ability appeared. This stimulated interest in organizations of craftsmen, to protect both those of recognized ability from unfair competition and the consumer from shoddy workmanship. From these evolved the guilds of medieval Europe.

Both workers and merchants saw the advantages of organization for mutual assistance, and it was not long before the European economy was dominated by great numbers of craft guilds and merchant guilds, each caring for the needs of its members.

These touched education in two distinct ways. In the first place, they became concerned with the general education of children of guild members. Often guilds would provide money to strengthen and expand existing schools so as to care better for the children of members. At other times guilds would establish schools of their own, employ and pay teachers, and exercise the control necessary to obtain the education they desired for their children. These practices made increased amounts of money available for existing schools and multiplied the number of schools. They also increased the demand for teachers, thereby encouraging more young people to look toward teaching as a profession.

In the second place, guilds developed a plan for seeking out and training young people in the trade. Some guilds restricted membership to relatives of members, while others recruited new blood from the general public. In either case a young man destined for a trade would be apprenticed to a master. A contract was drawn up in which the master promised to teach the boy the trade, plus reading, writing, some figuring, and religion. He also gave him a home, food, and clothing during the time of the apprenticeship. This contract, or "articles of indenture," bound the boy to the master for a specified period. During this time he was to study and work diligently, serve the master in the trade as directed, keep all secrets of the trade hidden, and live a moral and religious life.

When the boy had learned the trade to the satisfaction of his master and members of the guild, he was free to leave and seek work in a shop as a journeyman. For this work he would receive pay according to the regulations of the guild. As he worked, he learned more of the skills of the trade and perfected himself under the watchful eye of the master. After several years as a journeyman he might, if he wished and the guild was satisfied with his work, become a master. As such he could have his own shop, take apprentices, and hire journeymen.

This was a carefully supervised system of vocational education in which a young boy might learn all that was necessary for life and his trade. The goal of this education was a man able to make a living, contribute to the economy, and discharge whatever other obligations he might have in his community.

There were many abuses of this system. Masters, in some instances, treated their apprentices as servants, caring more for their help in the shop than for their learning. At times masters would turn over their shops to their sons, even though they had not gone through the experiences of the apprentice or the journeyman. As this practice increased, the gulf between owner and worker grew, along with a lack of understanding on the part of each.

As guilds became more a part of the medieval economy, civil authorities stepped in with regulations designed to protect all persons concerned. Here we see a clear instance of public interest in an institution
which so vitally affects the economy. Such regulations reached even
into the training of new workers.

THE TOWNS' INTEREST IN EDUCATION

Many of the schools of Roman days were supported and controlled
by towns or cities. These continued to function more or less effectively
during the medieval period. Where "barbarian" infiltrations were most
destructive, town schools tended to fall into disuse or disappear. In
other places they were weakened or neglected. As Christian schools
developed, many town schools lost favor. In spite of all the factors in
medieval life unfavorable to the education they afforded, a great number of these city-operated schools continued to flourish.

As conditions became more stable and trade increased, many cities
became prosperous and turned to their schools for help in preparing
the young for life in the new age. The schools of the Church were
recognized as both unable and unwilling to serve these ends. They
thought of their function in conservative terms and quickly became
outdated. Realizing the situation, towns had no other recourse but to
set up their own schools. As a result, municipal schools were revived
throughout Europe, and new schools began to appear under control of
civil authorities. Towns built schools, determined tuition charges,
elected and paid teachers, and decided which children should attend.
With the help of kings and rulers, the towns of Germany and Scotland
were able to wrest power over education from the clergy and make
schools public in both support and control.

Since the Latin Grammar school was the strongest educational institution of the period, it attracted most interest on the part of municipal
authorities. These were looked upon as means of entry into the upper
classes of society and as preparation for business and government.
However, these schools were changed but little. In many instances the
name was changed to Berg Latin Grammar school, but the curriculum
and method of teaching remained identical with that of earlier days.
As a result one could find in most towns two schools, both Latin Grammar schools, one operated by the Church and the other by the town.
The only significant difference was that the town-controlled schools
were thought of as serving predominantly the interests of the burgher
class.

When the lower classes began to show an increasing interest in
reading and writing, neither Church schools nor Latin Grammar

schools were able to cope with the situation. These lower classes wanted instruction in the vernaculars, not in Latin. This necessitated the creation of town-controlled elementary schools for instruction in reading and writing the vernacular of business and commercial life. Brussels, in 1320, found many private teachers, without sanction of Church authorities, offering instruction in reading and writing and doing a prosperous business. When the Church sought to stop this practice, the duke of Brabant, John III, established in the town five elementary schools for boys and four for girls, supplementing the one elementary school for boys and the one for girls under Church control. All elementary schools in the town were permitted to teach in the vernacular. The same decree that established these schools prohibited any further teaching by private teachers.

Although the situation in Brussels was similar to that in most sections of medieval Europe, other towns met it in different ways. In some cities boys and girls attended the same school. In others private teachers were allowed to offer instruction in the vernacular and solicit pupils as they saw fit. Some of these teachers added simple arithmetic to their offerings.

This rapid development of municipal schools did not take place without strenuous opposition from Church authorities. The Church guarded its right to license teachers as a means of controlling education and thereby the minds of men. This new move was seen as a challenge to that monopoly. Local clergy were the writers and readers in their communities. For a fee, they would prepare contracts, draw wills, write letters of either a personal or business nature, and keep records for townspeople. Municipal schools for the teaching of reading and writing in the vernacular threatened their lucrative income as well as their power over schools and teachers, and they were prepared to fight for both. In some towns they were able to delay establishment of municipal schools. In others various compromises were effected. One such was an agreement that the town pay the *scholasticus,* the local secretary of the clergy, a sum equal to his revenue before the school was opened. Another was that all teachers in municipal schools be clerics. This usually applied only to Latin schools, leaving vernacular teaching to laymen. Still another agreement was to the effect that the tuition fees in municipal schools be split between church and city.

As many types of schools appeared to serve varied interests, and as public demand for these schools grew, it was natural that fierce competition among schools would arise. Not only did the Church fight municipal schools, but different schools fought each other, and established schools fought private teachers. Education had entered a competitive market, and each school sought to sell its product to the people by disparaging the products of its competitors. The attempt to monopolize education came to a head in England, in 1410, with the decision in the famous Gloucester Grammar School Case. For a long time the Gloucester Grammar School had been under Church control, the masters being appointed by the prior of a nearby abbey. A teacher not authorized by the prior opened his own school and reduced the price of tuition considerably. Those masters appointed by the prior and teaching in the Church school brought suit for damages. In the decision handed down by the court, it was held that the Church school could not hold a monopoly of education. Education, it was decided, was "merely an uncertain ministry" which anyone was privileged to undertake at his own risk. This established a precedent which has helped to shape thinking about education even to the present. Not only did the courts rule that any qualified person had the right to establish a school and attract pupils, but it also asserted that parents were free to place their children in the school of their choice.

EDUCATION IN ENGLAND IN THE LATER MIDDLE AGES

England was one of the main roots of colonial American life. Much early education in the United States was either a transplantation from England or an outgrowth of English influences. It is well then that at this point in our study we look especially at English schools of the late Middle Ages and the thinking that went into their development.

THE SCHOOLS OF MEDIEVAL ENGLAND

The Christian Church of medieval England was the sponsor of schools reaching almost every level of society. Song schools for choir boys; schools for teaching reading, writing, and the rudiments of Latin; Latin Grammar schools; schools for training priests—all were under the sponsorship of the leading churches of England. In addition, there were schools established by prominent persons and schools conducted by individual teachers as a means of making a living.

For centuries the chief educational force in England had been the Church. Its cathedrals and monasteries operated a variety of schools and were able to control teaching and learning in the interest of orthodoxy. In the fifteenth century a movement began to free some of the schools from complete Church control and lay the foundations for secular education.

It was a custom of long standing in the Church for one of wealth, or wealthy friends of an individual, to establish a fund to pay for masses for his soul after death. These funds were known as *chantries*. In time individuals or groups would create perpetual foundations for specific religious or charitable purposes, including in the grant the provision that the Church assign a priest to say masses for the soul of the benefactor. Since such priests would devote part of their time to teaching children gratis, the custom developed of stipulating that chantry foundations include teaching. The outcome was the chantry school, a free school on the elementary level, taught by a priest who was supported by the foundation and had other duties, specified in the grant, to perform. In some instances benefactors would make a gift specifically for a school, instructing the priest to say mass only as a minor part of his duties. The chantry schools were taught by clerics, but their support and control came from lay sources.

In discussing the rise of Oxford University, we mentioned that wealthy individuals or organizations, such as guilds, might establish a "college" on the campus to serve specified groups of boys. These were endowed and, as teachers came to associate themselves with them, cared for all expenses of the students and instructors, paying both tuition and salaries, as well as furnishing room and board. A similar custom grew, although not so extensively, outside the university pattern. In 1342, William of Wykeham, who had founded New College at Oxford, provided the endowment for a school at Winchester to be called Sainte Marye College. This was a free boarding school for boys studying Latin grammar. It was an endowed Latin Grammar school for poor but capable boys. In 1440, a similar school, with emphasis on the liberal arts, was established at Eton.

Foundations to support these schools were established by individuals, guilds—both craft and merchant—or voluntary groups of people with certain educational ideas in mind. The schoolmaster gradually moved out of the control of the church and became a professional teacher, not a priest who taught as a supplement to his religious duties. He often became a person of stature, one trained in teaching and sufficiently supported by the foundation to move in the best circles of the community.

By the fifteenth century the monopoly over English institutions exerted by Normans had been broken, and Englishmen were able to demand and get equal treatment and opportunities. The plague of 1348–1349 decimated the population so that men were needed for office and leadership regardless of their ancestry. The effect of this was to place English on a par with Latin in the schools. This led eventually to the English Grammar school and later the English public schools.

English education had been for generations a monopoly of the middle and upper classes. This was but natural since education was largely in Latin and aimed to train leaders for Church and state. The common man had no need for this kind of training. As schools turned to English as their language of instruction and began to change into the means for nationalistic indoctrination, the people came to realize the meaning of this for them. This led to attempts on the part of the lower classes to either gain entrance into established schools or develop schools for themselves. The government recognized this trend and championed it in the interest of national unity and loyalty. When, in 1391, Richard II was asked by the middle class to bar all children of "villeins" from schools or from promotion through learning, he refused, thus leaving the door to education open to all classes. Legislation was passed in 1406 granting parents the right to send their children to any school, provided that they were able to pay the tuition. The Gloucester Grammar School Case of 1410 was part of this move toward destroying any and all monopoly over education in England.

During the years to follow, English education was opened to greater numbers of people, schools multiplied throughout the land, and curricula were enriched. There was developing the philosophy of education and the school system that was to be brought to America to furnish the foundations of education in the United States. There were schools open to all who could pay the tuition, teaching open to qualified individuals, parents free to choose schools for their children, lay control of schools and teaching, and a curriculum which included the classics, English, the sciences, and political instruction. These were the schools of the people, the only schools that would serve the free democracy that was to develop on the American continent.

Part Four

LIFE AND EDUCATION
IN THE MODERN WORLD

CHAPTER 8
During the Renaissance

INTRODUCTION

The long shadow cast by the Renaissance reached over Western Europe and even to America. Its early phases represented a freeing of the individual to determine his own line of action and expression. In the medieval world, the individual was subordinated to the universal order of life. The Renaissance represented for him a freeing from the other worldliness of the Middle Ages; reason replaced unchallengeable faith. Education represented a return to the freedom of ancient Greece, placing an emphasis on ancient literature and language. To meet the new freedom, a curriculum and content developed. Innovations included the introduction of reason, development of the scientific method, and the discovery and study of the literature of classical Greece. To study past records of civilizations, it was essential to have a workable knowledge of Greek and Latin. The most advanced writing to be found in philosophy, literature, drama, poetry, science, medicine, and even agriculture was in either Latin or Greek. To be able to use Greek was essential to be a thorough student, but Latin was even more necessary. Latin was the universal language used for all formal legal, diplomatic, and scholarly writing. The well-known letter-writing romance of Arthur, son of Henry VII of England, and Catherine, daughter of Ferdinand and Isabella, was carried on in Latin. It became the language of men of all important levels of action. It was inevitable that Latin and Greek became the prime subjects in the curriculum. In the latter days of the Renaissance, religious forces narrowed the range of the liberal education curriculum, but it also added Hebrew to the classical languages studied. The Protestant Reformation placed value on one of the languages of the early Church Fathers, including the Old and New Testaments. Studying the scriptures in the original was essential to the church scholars.

Historians for centuries have given the name "Renaissance" to that period of western European history between the beginning of the fourteenth and the middle of the sixteenth centuries. To some this was an age cut off from its immediate past, a time during which a spirit and way of life dormant since Ciceronian Rome were reborn. More recent students of these centuries are convinced that this interpretation distorts the facts considerably. They discover western man continuing in his long development, growing out of his immediate yesterdays and reaching back to his ancient past for the inspiration needed to continue his march toward the present. There is here both continuity and rebirth. Much that happened in this period had roots in the eleventh and twelfth centuries. During these centuries western man was bringing back into his culture that thinking of ancient Greece and Rome from which his ancestors had turned as Christianity charmed their hearts and dominated their minds. The Renaissance was a continuation of this process, a time when man's heart and mind were more concerned with things human than things divine. As the floodgates of his past were opened wider, he was in danger of worshipping these ancient times too devoutly. In later centuries others had to attempt a balancing of things human and things divine, the mind and the heart, the material and the ideal.

The Renaissance must be seen as two very similar and yet different developments: the Italian and the northern. Both were basically extensions of forces found in the medieval Renaissance. Both were brought on by increased contacts with the eastern world accelerated by the Crusades, wealth and general prosperity, growing strength of civil governments, more general circulation of the writings of classical Greece and Rome, the invention of movable type, and the appearance of a strong and vocal middle class.

The Italian Renaissance was literary, artistic, and Roman, while the northern Renaissance was religious. The one produced unprecedented beauty, while the other produced national churches. The one had Petrarch, the other Luther and Calvin.

THE REVIVAL OF LEARNING

Definitions and Distinctions

The revival of learning was one phase of this much broader Renaissance, in which the intellectuals sought to recreate their Greek and

Latin past. It developed an overwhelming passion for ancient learning, culture, and writings. This phase is also called "Humanism," since it was characterized by a keen interest in things human as distinct from things divine. The supernatural, the ascetic, the authoritarian, and the universal no longer satisfied. The individual, his passions and dreams, his self-confidence and hope, his newly-found sense of the beauty of nature, became dominant. As he explored the classical past, he discovered there this same interest in the individual and confidence in man's nature. This led naturally to a desire to study this past exhaustively, to learn its methods of freeing the creative talents of man, and, finally, to imitate slavishly its form. Beginning as an all-possessing desire to recapture the creative past, the Revival of Learning, or Humanism, became an indiscriminate imitation and recapitulation of the empty shell of that past, an arid "Ciceronianism."

PETRARCH (1304-1374)

Francesco di Petracco, better known as Petrarch, was the truest representative of this revival of learning. Born at Arezzo of parents banished from Florence because of proscribed political activity, he studied the humanities at Carpentras and law at Montpellier. A failure at law, largely because of his lack of interest, he took ecclesiastical orders, was supported and befriended by Giacomo Colonna, a member of the famous Colonna family of Italian history, and was free to pursue his interests in literature.

Here was a man who turned in disgust from the dominating interests of the medieval past, from scholasticism with its meaningless logical exercises, from monasticism with its concern with asceticism and retreat from living, and from the deadly legalism of medieval universities. As he studied and read, he developed a sublime reverence for the ancients and a love for classical languages. He was a tireless scholar who had the energy to study long and travel far in search of new knowledge about the classical past. When others were indifferent to his work or opposed his endeavors, he showed a fearlessness that was unique for his day.

Possessed of the Renaissance mania for fame, he exerted his influence in several quarters with a view to a public coronation. King Robert of Naples accepted his bid, entertained him lavishly, and sent him to Rome with magnificent credentials. There, in April of 1340, he received from the hands of a Senator, and amid the thundering applause of the people and the patricians, the poet's crown. Gradually we see him turning away from the vernacular to devoted worship of classical Latin, especially that of Cicero. The ancients came alive for him so vividly that he felt he was living with them and they with him. He carried on a lively correspondence, actually one-sided, with Cicero, Homer, Virgil, Horace, Livy, Seneca, and Quintilian.

For the remainder of Petrarch's life he was untiring in the search for old manuscripts. In 1345, he discovered Cicero's *Familiar Letters* and immediately wrote a letter to the great Roman orator telling him the happy fact. When he had no more funds to continue the search, he turned to dukes, kings, and wealthy merchants who paid him well to get these ancient writings for their libraries. In 1363 he donated his library of some 200 volumes to the Republic of Saint Mark.

By the time of Petrarch's death the passion for collecting ancient manuscripts had gripped all Italy. Some prominent persons, such as Pope Nicholas V and Niccoli, spent their entire fortunes for manuscripts or to have rare books copied. Poggio, while attending the Council of Constance, found six orations of Cicero, as well as a complete copy of Quintilian's *Institutes of Oratory* at Saint Gall in Switzerland. In less than a century after Petrarch's death most of the Latin classics had been discovered.

Petrarch has been called "the first Renaissance man." This he may have been, but more than that he was a bridge between three worlds, the classical, the medieval, and the Renaissance. His love for Greek and Roman classics was a consuming passion, although he knew little Greek and had to depend largely upon the crude translations that existed. He was deeply religious and orthodox. At no time did he see his beloved ancients taking the place of faith and Christian doctrine. The Bible for him was concerned with man's eternal welfare, while the classics contributed to the perfection of man's intellect and the civilization of his manners. Saint Augustine was his religious mentor, and it was to this spiritual godfather that he poured forth his soul in *De contemptu mundi*. Lastly, his spirit was the new spirit of the Renaissance. His *Rime in Vita e Morte di Madonna Laura*, or the *Canzoniere* as the Italians prefer to call this collection of lyrics, reveals his skill in bringing together "perfect metrical form" and "language of the choicest and the purest." Shelley refers to these lyrics as "spells which unseal the inmost enchanted fountains of the delight which is the grief of love." Here is a man who "felt the beauties of nature keenly."

MANUEL CHRYSOLORAS (*circa* 1355-1415)

In 1393, Manuel Chrysoloras, a native of Constantinople and master of classical Greek, was sent to Italy by the Holy Roman Emperor, Manuel Palaeologus, to seek aid from Christian princes against the Turks. In 1395 he became a teacher of Greek in Florence, where he attracted pupils from Italy and the West and translated Homer and Plato.

He was but the first of a flood of scholars who were moving westward during the fourteenth and fifteenth centuries, bringing to the western mind the language of Athens and the literature of her "finest years." George of Trebizond, master of Aristotle's thought, and Theodore of Gaza, student of the philosophy of Plato and Aristotle, taught Greek and Aristotelian philosophy in Italy. In 1438, Georgios Gemistus Pletho, teacher of Chrysoloras and the most important authority of his day on the Platonic and Neo-Platonic philosophies, began lecturing in Florence on the philosophy of Plato and Aristotle. It was through his influence that Cosimo de Medici established a Platonic Academy in Florence.

Pupils of Chrysoloras were among the most ardent propagandists in Italy for all things Greek. Guarino da Verona stimulated classical interest at the University of Ferrara. When he returned from Constantinople, after five years of study with Chrysoloras, he brought some fifty Greek manuscripts. Giovanni Aurispa, who had studied with Chrysoloras in Florence, visited Constantinople and returned bearing 238 Greek classical works. Filelfo, another student of the master, had forty manuscripts. In this way the writings of Sophocles, Aeschylus, Plato, Aristotle, Xenophon, Plutarch, and other noted intellectuals of the Periclean Age drifted back into western culture.

In spite of the fact that Italian cities, such as Florence, Ferrara, and Verona, were centers of interest in Greek language and literature during the Renaissance, there was actually little interest of a sustained quality in Greek in Italy. Perhaps the language was too difficult. It is true that the Italian was more at home with Latin, the language of his ancient heritage, than he was with Greek. Some have suggested that the Italians naturally hated the Greeks and could stomach neither their language nor their literature. The fact is that as Greek exiles ceased to travel west, interest in Greek died out. As it faded in the south, scholars in the north, in England, Germany, and France, had mastered the language and turned to studying its philosophy and literature.

JOHANN REUCHLIN (1455-1522)

Reuchlin was among the greatest of Humanistic scholars, second only to Erasmus. He was born of Pforzheim in the Black Forest and studied Latin at the monastery school there and at the University of Freiburg. Charles I, margrave of Baden, chose him to accompany the young prince Frederick to the University of Paris. There Reuchlin learned Greek. From Paris he went to the University of Basel, where he received his master's degree and lectured on Aristotle in Greek. For the next several years, 1477-1481, he studied at Paris, Orleans, and Poitiers. As interpreter for Count Eberhard of Wurttemberg, he toured Italy and became acquainted with some of the leading scholars at Florence and at the papal court. In 1492 he was sent on a mission to Emperor Frederick at Linz. There he began the study of Hebrew under the emperor's Jewish physician, Jakob ben Jehiel Loans.

When Eberhard died, in 1496, Reuchlin moved to Heidelberg where he became an authority on the teaching of both Greek and Hebrew for all Germany. Two years later, Philip, elector palatine of the Rhine, employed him to direct the education of his son. In the same year he was sent on a mission to Rome, from which he returned laden with Hebrew books. From then on we find him devoting more and more of his time to the study and teaching of Hebrew. He became convinced that the Vulgate was not an accurate translation of the Bible and that a new attempt should be made to convey into Latin the true meaning of the Hebrew text. Toward this end he wrote his epoch-making *De Rudimentis Hebraicis,* a Hebrew grammar and lexicon. This was followed by the publication of two books, *De Verbo Mirifico* and *De Arte Cabbalistica,* developing the fantastical and mystical systems of Greek thought that he felt had affinity with the Cabbala, or Kabbalah, the theosophical interpretation of Hebrew scriptures.

Many of Reuchlin's contemporaries believed that the best method of converting the Jews to Christianity was to take from them their books. Johann Pfefferkorn (1469-1521) was the most vocal advocate of this strategy and Reuchlin's bitterest enemy. When summoned before Emperor Maximilian to give his views on the matter, Reuchlin proposed that there be established at every German university two chairs of Hebrew and that Jews be urged to contribute books to the libraries of these universities. This angered Pfefferkorn, who issued a tract accusing Reuchlin of accepting a bribe from the Jews to champion their cause. Reuchlin answered with the *Augenspiegel* (1511). When the opposition appealed to the universities for an opinion on the controversy, all of them, even the University of Paris, ruled against Reuchlin. Finally the battle was carried to Rome where, in July, 1516, a decision was handed down in favor of Reuchlin. This was followed by *Epistolae Obscurorum Virorum,* in which the great Hebrew scholar heaped such ridicule upon his enemies that they were crushed in Germany.

Reuchlin was forced to flee Stuttgart because of famine, civil war, and pestilence. He taught Greek and Hebrew for a while at Ingolstadt and then at Tubingen. He died at the baths of Liebenzell in June, 1522, old and weakened by his battles against obscurantism and prejudice, recognizing that the universities of Europe were still buried in the scholasticism of the medieval world and not yet ready for the Humanism of the new age. However, he had not failed. In the minds and thoughts of Renaissance men had come the realization that the classical inheritance of the western world was actually threefold: Greek, Latin, and Hebrew.

In the Language of the People

Medieval Latin was the language of scholarship in western Europe during the Renaissance. Humanists struggled to sell scholars the idea of returning to classical Latin with some use of Greek and Hebrew. Most of the universities resisted these pressures successfully. A few universities, such as Padua and Pavia, did open their arms to Humanism, and several new universities, such as Florence and Ferrara, were created for the pursuit of humanistic culture. The bulk of the universities saw Humanism as trivial when compared to the ancient traditions in theology, law, and medicine, plus the liberal arts.

Meanwhile, Europe was being stirred by the appearance of vigorous vernacular languages and the beginnings of a literature for the masses. This was producing both a reading public that clamored for books they could enjoy and writers who felt the lust and joy of the new freedom. The latter told stories often belittling the great and exalting the lowly, attacked the "betters" for their folly and sham, and showed the people how they might live their lives more fully and meaningfully.

Dante (1265-1321) wrote *Vita Nuova* to tell of his love for Beatrice, who won his heart when he was almost ten and she just nine, of the inspiration she gave him, and of his devotion to her even after death. Then he wrote the *Commedia,* called *divina* in the sixteenth century, a poem peopled with men and women known personally or by reputation to those for whom he wrote, a poem "not to delight, but to reprove, to rebuke, to exhort; to form men's characters by teaching them what course of life will meet with reward, what with penalty, hereafter."

Boccaccio (1313-1375) wrote the *Decameron,* one of the earliest works in Italian prose and one of the most famous books of all literature. His father had hopes that he would become a businessman or a student of canon law, but the boy, a brilliant student and collector of Greek manuscripts, yearned for a literary life. Sent to Naples by his father for business contacts, he was caught up in the gay life of the city, the brilliant court, and the seeming ability of the people to squeeze every drop of juice from life. It was on Holy Saturday, March 30, 1336, that he first caught sight of Maria d'Aquino, a married woman, whom he immortalized under the name of Fiammetta. His love for this woman, who accepted his advances and then betrayed him ruthlessly, filled his whole life and inspired every book he wrote before *Ninfale Fiesolano* and the *Decameron.* His poems, stories, allegories, and prose were read avidly by all of Italy. His studies of Greek and Latin classics were read by the scholars of the age and often admired. It was Boccaccio who, with the help of Leon Pilatus, translated Petrarch's Greek manuscript of Homer and thereby restored this poet to the western world.

What these writers were doing for the growing Italian language, Chaucer (1340-1400) did for English. From his youth he served in the courts of English rulers as page boy, soldier, and diplomat entrusted with missions of some importance. Among his first writings is *The Book of the Duchesse,* a poem in honor of Blanche, the wife of John of Gaunt, who had died in her twenty-ninth year. Chaucer learned from both French and Italian writers. He knew *Le Roman de la rose* as modern English poets know Shakespeare and gave it an English translation. Another French masterpiece which he rendered into English was *Le Dit du lion.* He learned plot and construction from Boccaccio and Dante and was acquainted with Petrarch's sonnets. His greatest work was *Canterbury Tales,* stories told by a band of pilgrims assembled at the Tabard Inn in Southwark. In his original plan each of the pilgrims was to tell a story which would be followed in turn with another, a total of fifty-eight stories. Actually, only twenty stories were finished, with two unfinished and two interrupted. While Chaucer did not determine the English language nor make any significant change in its direction, his decisive success in turning to poetic use the best English of the time and making it available for general reading made it "impossible for any later English poet to attain fame . . . by writing alternatively in Latin and French."

Francois Rabelais (1494-1553), monk and physician, wrote two famous books satirizing life in his day, especially the methods used for educating young people. We have two works, one called *Gargantua* and the other *Pantagruel,* in which Rabelais attacked medieval educational practices and made a strong case for humanistic studies and methodology.

Gargantua is a mighty giant, son of giant parents, crude and vulgar, reared in accord with medieval custom and taught by a highly recommended sophist called Holofernes. In five years and three months Gargantua learned his ABC's. Then, for the next fifty years, until he "died of the pox," this "master teacher" read to his pupil several standard works which the learner memorized completely. After all this learning Gargantua, when placed next to a youth trained in the humanistic fashion for only two years, was seen to be nothing but "a fool, a sot, a dolt, and blockhead." A pedagogical purgative was then administered which caused him to forget all he had previously learned. Freed from his past, he was now ready to begin learning correctly.

The method proposed by Rabelais was actually education by doing, in pleasant and stimulating circumstances. The pupil spent much time in the company of learned men, for whom he developed a lively admiration and whom he wished to emulate. Tennis and other games developed his body. While eating, he read "pleasant history of the warlike actions of former times" and discussed with his friends any matters of interest to them. Arithmetic was learned by playing cards and dice. This led to a growing interest in "numerical science," geometry, astronomy, and music. He was taught to play many musical instruments and to sing pleasant and jovial songs. Horsemanship, swordsmanship, wrestling, jumping, and swimming were part of his curriculum. At dinner, lessons were read to him and discussions followed. Whenever possible, Gargantua and his fellows visited shops of craftsmen to observe and learn about their trades and skills. There were public lectures, courts where lawyers were pleading, and churches in which ministers preached wisely. "Thus was Gargantua governed, and kept on in this course of education ... which, although at the beginning seemed difficult, became a little after so sweet, so easy, and so delightful, that it seemed rather the recreation of a king than the study of a scholar."

In due time Gargantua had a son, another giant, who was to benefit by the experiences of his father. The boy, Pantagruel, was sent to the University of Paris, where he was to shun the sterile learning of the past lest it destroy him. Gargantua outlined the curriculum he believed best for his son's development in the Renaissance world. In this, languages are most important. The student must learn Greek "as Quintilian will have it," Latin, Hebrew "for the Holy Scripture sake," Chaldee, and Arabic. He should develop his Greek style after Plato and his Latin style after Cicero. He must also learn history, geometry, arithmetic, music, civil law, and philosophy. Rabelais believed that astrology, which many were praising and studying as a science, was useless and unfounded in fact. As one reads these works carefully, he becomes impressed with the fact that Rabelais was a man of keen scientific interest and wanted the young man to study all fields of science accurately and deeply. Medicine to him was a science that young men should understand both from reading the works of "Greek, Arabian, and Latin physicians, not despising the Talmudists and Cabalists" and "by frequent anatomies." The Renaissance man was a student of the world around him and held that observation of this world was as much a part of education as reading authorities. Finally, Gargantua would have his son read the scriptures in the "original": the Old Testament in Hebrew and the New Testament in Greek. Leaving his books, the young man must become proficient in chivalry, warfare, and "the exercise of the field."

This, Rabelais believed, was the education a young man of the Renaissance should have, one freed from scholasticism and its sterile logic, from hair-splitting theological distinctions, from monastic seclusion. It was an education for living fully in an age rich in possibilities for intellectual pursuits. By means of satire, written in the language of the people, this French genius pointed education in the direction of the modern world.

These men, and many others, were writing in the language of the people. They entertained them, scolded them, and set forth morals from which they could profit. When a people have a literature in the language they speak and understand, they begin to demand schools in which they can learn to read this language. A reading public creates a demand for more writing, and literature grows and language is enriched as each new author strives to communicate his feelings, hopes, and fears. All this was true of the Renaissance.

SCHOOLS AND TEACHERS OF THE RENAISSANCE

EDUCATIONAL WRITINGS

What is education? How shall a good teacher teach? What should be taught? These and other questions of educational philosophy, methodology, and curriculum did not seem important in the Middle Ages. Then answers from the past had been given, and no problems existed. Even in the late thirteenth century when Egidio da Colonna wrote *De Regimine Principum,* the educational authority was Aristotle, and this book on education was based almost wholly on his writings. A somewhat earlier textbook on education, Vincent of Beauvais' *De Eruditione Filiarum Nobilium* was a source book of quotations from authors who wrote in Roman and early Christian times.

It was near the end of the fourteenth century before there appeared a fresh and challenging approach to educational problems. This was *De Ingenuis moribus et liberalibus* (On the Manners of a Gentleman and on Liberal Studies) by Pietrus Paulus Vergerius. This author was familiar with the works of classical authors on the subject, but presented new and controversial ideas. He advocated the inclusion of Latin literature in a liberal education. As scholars uncovered ancient manuscripts and translated them for the intellectuals of the Renaissance, it was natural that the masterworks on education from the past would become available for study. In 1411 Guarino da Verona published a translation of Plutarch's *On the Education of Children.* Then, in 1416, Poggio, while rummaging in a dump heap in a tower of the abbey of Saint Gall, discovered an undamaged text of Quintilian's *Institutes of Oratory.* Six years later Cicero's *de Oratore* was discovered at Lodi. Other writings on education or dealing in part with education began to appear. By the sixteenth century, all the classical writings on education were familiar to Renaissance scholars; and teachers, educational thinkers, and publishers were bringing out books in which "the new education" was discussed.

VITTORINO DA FELTRE (1378-1446)

In 1378, in the little village of Feltre on the southern slopes of the Alps, Vittorino Rambaldini was born. Nearby was the University of Padua, one of the great humanistic centers of learning. Petrarch had lived nearby. Before he died, he entrusted his library to the university for safekeeping. His disciples and admirers were to be found in and around the university studying and teaching Latin literature. While Vittorino was a student there, the great Barzizza was made professor of Latin rhetoric. The same year that Vittorino entered Padua, Chrysoloras began teaching Greek at Florence.

Vittorino remained a student and teacher at Padua for more than twenty-five years, drinking in the humanistic atmosphere of the place and studying with the greatest humanist scholars. When he left to establish his own school at Venice, he was famous throughout Italy as a Latinist without peer and as one of the ablest mathematicians of the day. He had thoroughly absorbed the Renaissance spirit and learning and was at home in all the arts, religion, and knightly customs.

A man of forty-five, steeped in the best humanistic learning that his age had to offer, a deeply religious man whose personal practices were within the ascetic tradition, dignified, urbane, and prosperous in his own school in Venice where students came from the finest homes and courts in Italy, Vittorino received an invitation to undertake the education of the family of Gianfrancesco Gonzaga, marquis of Mantua, one of the more intellectual of Italian despots. He refused emphatically. He had no liking for the pomp and ceremony of court life and knew himself to be ill-equipped for intrigue. He wanted to be free to teach as he saw fit, owing nothing to a selfish, ambitious lord.

Gonzaga was not to be denied. Princes vied to attract to their courts the most brilliant scholars and artists. They took great pride in their schools, which were symbols of their scholarly interests. To sponsor

poets, painters, writers, and teachers—all in the humanistic tradition
—gave them a sense of participating in greatness, even if vicariously.
Gonzaga pleaded and increased his offer. As Vittorino listened, he
began to see himself as one genuinely serving the people of Mantua and
the future of all Italy, by helping to educate the prince who would, in
time, rule. In the end he accepted the offer with the firm stipulation
that he would remain only so long as he was free to teach and work as
he believed worthy, and so long as the Marquis conducted himself
justly and rightly. On this basis the two men reached an agreement,
and Vittorino began one of the most famous teaching careers in all the
Renaissance.

Gonzaga gave him a palace adjacent to the royal residence and allowed him to rebuild it to house his school. The name of the structure
was *La Giocosa,* meaning "house of pleasure." Vittorino changed it to
La Giocosa, a word used to designate a school. He had its royal trap-
pings removed and in their place set furniture and fixtures appropriate
to a knightly academy. The spacious grounds around the building were
landscaped for sports, pleasant strolls along the river or through
shaded grasslands, and recreation. There were secluded nooks where
one might meditate, pray, or just sit and think. A model school plant
was built, designed in every detail to serve the kind of education Vittorino believed best.

To this school came the children of Gonzaga: four sons and a daughter, Cecilia. She was the only girl in the school, and her presence was
highly irregular. Wealthy and noble families from Italy and other parts
of Europe enrolled their sons to study with the master. Scholars came
to meet Vittorino, study his methods, and investigate the curriculum.
The aristocracy of all Europe looked to Mantua as the home of the best
of humanistic schools, and Gonzaga was happy. But Vittorino felt that
the education received in so aristocratic a school could not be the best.
Consequently he insisted that an equal number of poor boys be admitted to the school and that Gonzaga provide for them free tuition, food,
and clothing.

The pupils at *La Giocosa* ranged from six to twenty-seven years of
age. The curriculum ranged all the way from elementary training in
reading, writing, and arithmetic to Latin style, oratory, and the
knightly arts. Vittorino incorporated into this curriculum the three
strains that came together in fifteenth century culture. One was the
classical tradition that had been developed by the humanists. This
included Latin and Greek grammer and literature; oratory; composition; history as written by Livy, Plutarch, Sallust, and Valerius Maximus; the poetry of Virgil, Ovid, Horace, Juvenal, and Seneca; and the
prose of Caesar and Curtius. The second cultural strand was the Chri-

tian religion. The Bible, religious exercises, the writings of early Church Fathers, and sermons by local divines were studied and practiced. The third strand was inherited from chivalry and consisted of the manners and graces of the knight at his best, physical training, games of bodily skill, horsemanship, and running. Vittorino wove into the school at Mantua the best that was available for the mind, the soul, and the body.

Vittorino had learned from his reading on education and from his own experience with learners certain basic principles which he incorporated into *La Giocosa*. First, children learn best in pleasant surroundings where they can play while they are learning. He had no sympathy with the undernourished, precocious, solemn bookworm or study in dimly-lighted libraries. Health was basic to efficient learning. Second, the school must be a community in which children live and learn together in close friendship with their teachers. Vittorino could often be seen walking along the pathways that snaked through the grounds around *La Giocosa* followed by several happy, laughing children, talking and learning together. Third, he believed that a school should be a place where a child learned discipline. The child does not know right from wrong, the accepted from the unaccepted. He is not in control of himself. It is in the school that he must learn these things, and it is the teacher's duty to develop discipline. But one must never be unfeeling or abusive. Love, respect, and mutual appreciation are the keys to discipline. Fourth, he realized that children are different and must be allowed to develop as their own natures intend. He would study each child, giving him learning tasks suited to his ability and interests. With a good staff of teachers, Vittorino could spend time developing an understanding of each child and helping him to grow as nature intended. Fifth, Vittorino believed that the first goal of all education is character. Learning was important to him, but never at the expense of character building. A passionate Christian, Vittorino saw each pupil in the setting of eternity and strove to build within him goodness and righteousness, the criteria which he used to judge all else.

La Giocosa was built upon these principles. The faculty was chosen, the curriculum arranged, and the entire life of the school served these ends completely. Here was something new and exciting, and students and scholars came to learn, to emulate, and almost to worship.

GUARINO DA VERONA (1370-1460)

Guarino was a younger contemporary of Vittorino and among the finest Latin and Greek scholars of the Italian Renaissance. For five years he was a pupil of Chrysoloras in Constantinople. Returning from his studies, he brought to his native city of Verona a number of Greek manuscripts, which he translated and from which he lectured. As a *protege* of Lionel, marquis of Este, he became professor of Greek at Ferrara and acted as interpreter for the Greeks at the councils of Ferrara and Florence.

He translated Strabo and some of the *Lives* of Plutarch; wrote a compendium of the Greek Grammar of Chrysoloras; and prepared commentaries on Persius, Juvenal, Martial, and some of the works of Aristotle and Cicero.

Guarino's highest claim to fame was his teaching at the court of Ferrara. The Marquis Niccolo persuaded him to undertake the education of his son. To discharge this duty effectively, Guarino organized a palace school very similar to that of Vittorino, but with a significant difference. Mantua aimed to produce the gentleman and prince capable of living a rich, practical life. Ferrara looked toward the cultured priesthood, the professorial life, and literary production. From a school steeped in medieval tradition, Ferrara, under Guarino's guiding hand, became a showplace of Renaissance learning. Young scholars came from Germany and England to take back to their homelands the Italian humanistic learning and enthusiasm for the classics. Agricola, a pioneer of northern Humanism, spent four years at Ferrara studying with Guarino's son, Battista, who succeeded his father and wrote a treatise on education in which he developed the principles his father had championed.

While Mantua and Ferrara were the brightest stars of humanistic education in Italy, they were in a vast constellation of less famous schools that dotted Italy. Princes, dukes, and local despots strove to attract scholars, build schools, and lure to their domains students from all of Europe. As these returned to their homes, they carried with them all that Humanism had meant to the southerners, wove it into the fabric of northern life and thought, and laid the pattern of the northern Renaissance—the Reformation—and the scientific revolution that resulted.

CICERONIANISM

Growing out of the medieval world and its Christian culture, the Renaissance was characterized by man's desire to find richness and meaning in the world about him. Having looked to heaven for so many generations, the people of western Europe now began to look to their material environment and their fellows. Here they found value, security, joy, and hope for the future. Here they found their own salvation.

How could they get the most out of this new world they were discovering? Petrarch, Boccaccio, Niccoli, Poggio, and a host of other Italian scholars found the answer in the writings of ancient Greek and Roman philosophers, playwrights, and teachers. As they studied books from their ancestral past, they found a lust for life, a creative spirit, and an understanding of man and his world which charmed their imaginations and stirred them deeply. They yearned to recreate the Age of Pericles and Republican Rome in their own day.

To realize their dream, these men, with the help of their rulers and the wealthy, collected manuscripts, works of art, old coins, and inscriptions and began campaigns to preserve ancient structures, birthplaces and tombs of the great, and centers of early culture. Translation became a mania with many. To produce accurate manuscripts shorn of textual corruptions and translate these into the language of scholarship was the overweening goal. To aid in this endeavor, dictionaries, lexicons, glossaries, and grammars were produced in great numbers. History was studied in order to understand the times out of which the classics grew and appreciate their meaning for those times as well as for the Renaissance. In this activity, modern textual and historical study was born. Accuracy, understanding, and sensitive appreciation were the criteria for this work.

Many, engaged in this undertaking, came during the latter fifteenth and early sixteenth centuries to lose sight of the original purposes of this scholarship and turned to a worship of pure Ciceronian style and vocabulary. These were purists bent upon wiping out all the progress Latin had made since the days of Cicero and returning to the style, pronunciation, and phraseology of this master of classical Latin. For them, all that had happened since Cicero's day was corrupt, vulgar, uncouth. To free the language of this, schools, writers, speakers, and lexicographers must devote themselves to the form of the past. Some were so overcome by this obsession that they would use no words not found in Cicero, no phrasing not true to the master, no ideas not developed in his writings. This was rigid formalism, allowing for not the slightest deviation. Memory took the place of creative imagination. Schools caught in this mania became language mills turning out graduates who could write an elegant letter or oration just as Cicero would have written it but divorced completely from life and its realities in sixteenth century Europe.

A true representative of this purist strain in the Renaissance was Pietro Bembo (1470-1547). Born in Venice, he was taken very early to Florence, where he fell in love with the Tuscan dialect spoken in that area of Italy. From there he went to Rome with Guilio de' Medici and became secretary to Leo X. When the pontiff died, Bembo retired to

Padua to become historian of Venice and, later, librarian at Saint Mark's. Bembo was a brilliant humanist who so worshiped the classics that he became known as "the prince of stylists." He advised his friends to shun the Pauline epistles lest barbarous Greek spoil their appreciation of style. He was among that group who attempted to Latinize everything, including religious names and symbols. God was *Jupiter Optimus Maximus,* and the pope was *Pontifex Maximus.*

Ambition was one of Bembo's overriding characteristics. Purist and lover of Ciceronian Latin that he was, when Paul III offered him a cardinal's hat, he renounced the study of classical literature and devoted himself to theological and classical history. As a reward for his devotion, he became bishop of Gubbio and Bergamo. His love of pure Ciceronian Latin is seen in his *History of Venice,* his dialogues, poems and essays.

THE RENAISSANCE IN PERSPECTIVE

The Renaissance was a natural and inevitable outgrowth of the medieval world, a next stage in the history of western man. Through study of its classical past it aimed to build a way of life fitted to the new man in a new world. It succeeded remarkably. Scholarship was increased and sharpened. Man's creative genius was unbound and sent on its way toward the modern world.

This was a beginning. Much of the criticism of this period loses sight of the fact that the door to man's possibilities had only recently been opened. There was much to learn. The over-emphasis on language by some, the neglect of natural science, the inability to produce moral strength adequate to withstand the corruption of the age, the individualism, and the aristocratic emphasis—all were in no sense weaknesses of the movement. Rather, they were tasks yet to be accomplished. Man had discovered himself again and was beginning to sense the meaning of this discovery. He did go to excesses, make mistakes, and fail miserably to appreciate much. This was the "adolescence of modern European civilization," and only a fool would expect an adolescent to have the maturity and judgment of age and experience.

To appreciate the Renaissance, and the accompanying revival of learning, one must see it in perspective. He must understand from whence it came—from the womb of the medieval world—and where it went—to the Reformation; the scientific revolution; the Age of Reason; and the modern world of creativity, confidence in the common man, and democracy. The Renaissance was a beginning, a turning, a new day. It was for its descendants to make the most of it in their world.

CHAPTER 9
During the Reformation

INTRODUCTION

The Renaissance was the phase of the history of western man when the human spirit burst the shell of medievalism and reveled in its new-found freedom and a sense of strength and power. The Italian Renaissance re-opened the books of classical antiquity and read of the glorious days of Periclean Greece and Republican Rome. Its scholars studied these books, purified their texts, translated them, and finally gave them an adoration that, in some instances, resulted in sterile formalism. As the Renaissance spirit moved north, in the fifteenth and sixteenth centuries, it inspired man to declare his independence of a Church that had shaped his life for centuries, create new and more vigorous institutions for his well-being, educate for the practical world of commerce and industry, elevate the masses from abject poverty and ignorance to a position of dignity and self-respect in society, and tap the artistic veins of human imagination and sensitivity beyond anything known since the Greeks.

One part of this northern Renaissance has been called the Reformation, an open and successful rebellion against the Church, and establishment of Protestant sects in many areas of Europe. This stands out clearly and vividly as one studies the history of these centuries in western Europe. It is not, however, the whole story. There were several reformations going on simultaneously. There was the economic reformation, a product of the phenomenal increase in world trade and consequent growth of large port towns. There was the social reformation resulting from the wealth that commerce brought and the need for manpower in the manufacture and distribution of goods. There was the political reformation which came as civil authorities grew wealthy and powerful enough to express in action their long-smoldering resentment against the authority, corruption, and oppressions of the Church. To see the age in proper perspective, one must understand all these reformations, their roots and their bearing on fifteenth and sixteenth century Europe and the centuries to follow.

THE BRETHREN OF THE COMMON LIFE

The society called the Brethren of the Common Life was the most active and influential educational force of the period, reaching into the religious and scholarly life of the fourteenth and fifteenth centuries, educating the masses and many of the leading intellectuals of the age, and producing and printing the books that had most influence over thought and practice.

GERHARD GROOT (1340-1384)

Groot was born at Deventer, in Holland, and studied at the University of Paris and at Cologne. His mystical conversion in 1374 drove him into the Carthusian monastery at Munnikhuizen near Arnhem, where he spent three years in meditation. He came away from the monastery one of the great missionary preachers of his age. Churches were unable to hold the crowds that left their businesses, their meals, and their home duties to hear him preach. His theme was a return to the simplicity and purity of Christ, a theme taken up by Thomas a' Kempis who was educated by the Brethren and a resident in one of their houses throughout his life. So violent was Groot's denunciation of the sins of both lay and clergy that he was accused of heterodoxy and prohibited from preaching. Denied the pulpit, he turned to education, charity, and writing as means of furthering his ideals. Somewhere around 1381 he came under the influence of Johann Ruysbroeck, prior of the Augustinian canons at Groenendael near Brussels and the most famous mystic of the day. Although he died of the plague at Deventer, he lived long enough to preside over the first few days of the Brethren of the Common Life, an organization that embodies most of his ideas.

THE BROTHERHOOD

Groot was a mystic yearning to serve his fellow men in imitation of Christ. To accomplish this, he turned to charity that would breed self-dependence, teaching, and industry. As others listened to him preach and expressed a desire to follow his example, a brotherhood took form. Since members took no vows and lived under no rule, they differed from most religious organizations the Church had spawned. They were mystics united in their desire to seek unity with God and imitate the life of Christ. Each man earned his own living, spurning the practice of begging.

All classes and professions were accepted. They lived in communities called "houses," usually twenty to a house. Four residents of each house were priests and the others laymen. They pooled their earnings, preached, ministered to the poor and unfortunate, taught in schools near the house or in those of their own founding, and worked wherever they could find employment.

Many innovations were introduced by Groot and his followers. Sermons were not only in the vernacular but in the idiom of the people. Their charity aimed to rehabilitate, not to keep the recipients dependent or enslaved. Their schools emphasized the use of the vernaculars but did not neglect careful scholarship in both Latin and Greek. Most significant of all, the Brethren of the Common Life strove to restore the simple, devoted, and dedicated life of Apostolic days. Their example became infectious, spreading among all classes in society. When *Imitatio Christi* was translated into Dutch by Groot, it became an instant "best seller" and lay next to the Bible in most homes of Holland. As other translations appeared, its devotional passages became known throughout Christendom.

Every house of the Brethren had a *scriptorium* from which came books in profusion. When printing was developed, their *scriptoria* were replaced by presses. It is estimated that in 1490, more than sixty presses were owned and operated by the Brethren. Editions of the Bible, individual books of the Bible, devotional tracts, the *Imitatio Christi,* textbooks in Latin, Greek, and the vernaculars, guides to business practice, and a host of other works flowed from these presses. They were sold at very low prices so that even the poor might read them. Before 1500, more than 450 books were issued from the presses at Deventer alone. Other cities were equally prolific.

SCHOOLS AND TEACHERS

When the Church took away his right to preach, Groot turned to education as the best means of reforming the clergy and training the new generation along the lines of his ideals. Though no teacher himself, he stimulated interest in education, advised boys on their training, and counseled his followers who evidenced interest and talent in this area. As a result, teaching became one of the chief functions of the Brethren.

The Brethren opposed begging as a means of support and encouraged all their members to work for a living. This was carried over into education. Instead of encouraging poor students to beg, they provided homes for them in private residences or in their houses. At some schools they erected dormitories where students lived at a cost based on their ability to pay. They also provided books and other necessities on a similar basis.

In many communities the Brethren taught in the church or municipal schools sponsored by foundations or private interests. In others they erected their own schools and staffed them with their members. Demand for these schools spread quickly and Brethren were invited by municipalities to establish one or more with tax help. Beginning in Deventer, these schools spread throughout northern Europe, attracted many of the best minds, and served as models for other schools.

John Cele (d. 1417) was the first of the Brethren to become a teacher. A native of Zwolle, he received his education at Prague. Returning to his native city, he became rector of the town school at the insistence of Groot. Under his leadership, this school became one of the finest in all Europe, and a model for other famous institutions. John Sturm's school at Strassburg and Calvin's school at Geneva were copies of the Zwolle school. The Jesuits took many ideas from Cele. This school drew students from all parts of Europe, enrolling at one time as many as 1,200 pupils.

The school was divided into eight grades, with subject specialists teaching the higher grades with an eye on preparing boys for advanced education. The curriculum was practical, emphasizing especially grammar, rhetoric, logic, ethics, and philosophy, subjects which had meaning for the life the boys would lead. The school laid great emphasis upon religion, both the Old and New Testaments, prayers, lives of saints and other religious leaders, and practical use of Christian principles. Passages from the Bible, writings of churchmen, and the classics were memorized and discussed with the hope that students would come to understand them as they applied to the Christian life.

A pupil at the Zwolle school, Alexander Hegius (1443-1498), went on to Emmerich, where he taught for eight years and enrolled some 1,500 students, and then to Saint Lebuin's school at Deventer, where he attracted as many as 2,200 pupils. One of these was the most famous Humanist of the times, Erasmus. Hegius was predominantly a classicist, devoted to the styles of Cicero, Virgil, and Sallust. While acting as rector of the Deventer school, he devoted much of his time to supervising the publication of Latin and Greek texts. Even though he was devoted to the classics and in many ways resembled the humanists of the Italian Renaissance, he was fundamentally a member of the Brethren, a believer in the pious life and the simplicity of the Apostolic era. He could not approve of the worldly, ostentatious, materialistic interests of these "southerners."

Famous schools of the Brethren appeared at Utrecht, Groningen, Liege, Rostock, Cassel, Ghent, and Nijmegen. Men went out from these to teach in all types of schools in Europe or to found schools of their own.

CLASSICAL HUMANISM TRAVELS NORTH

EARLY NORTHERN HUMANISTS

Among the first "northerners" to evidence an interest in the intellectual stirrings to the south were scholars attached to the Brethren of the Common Life. They traveled from Holland, studied with noted humanists in Italy, and carried home their enthusiasm for the classics, to spread it among their fellows. Agricola (1443-1485) attended the town school of his birthplace, Groningen, and then studied at Erfurt and Louvain. Going to Italy in 1468 to study law, he came under the influence of Battista Guarino and Theodore of Gaza, studied Greek with them, and returned to Holland to spread humanism and love for the classics throughout the north. John Reuchlin (1455-1522) studied Greek at Paris and then went to Florence, where he met and studied with the leading humanists of the day. Later, as a teacher at Heidelberg, he became leader of the Rhenish Society, a group of young and very enthusiastic humanists. He added to an interest in Greek and Latin a growing desire to master Hebrew, to open wide the gates of the Old Testament. With the support of Count Eberhard of Stuttgart, he reigned as the leading humanist at the University of Tubingen, founded by the Count. John Wessel, a member of the Brethren, studied at Paris, where he came under the spell of mystics of Saint Victor. Going from there to Italy, he studied Greek with Bessarion and attained a smattering of Hebrew. His classical learning was directed toward understanding the New Testament rather than the philosophy and literature of Greece.

HUMANISM IN ENGLAND

The steps by which Italian Humanism came into England illustrate the process by which the revival of learning moved into northern lands, was transformed to fit their temperament, and helped prepare the people for the religious Reformation.

During much of the fourteenth and fifteenth centuries, English scholars were traveling to Italy and studying in humanistic centers. Chaucer was one of these. At the same time, scholars and teachers of the caliber of Chrysoloras and Poggio visited England, bringing the enthusiasm for classical studies that was rife in their homeland. This interchange of men and ideas increased as more Englishmen studied or vacationed in Italy, caught the intellectual fever that was becoming epidemic there, and returned with knowledge of classical languages, manuscripts in profusion, and a determination to turn English scholarship in this direction. Humphrey, Duke of Gloucester, son of Henry IV, and a graduate of Balliol College at Oxford, studied Latin, read its literature, dug deeply into works by Dante, Petrarch, and Boccaccio, and assembled a large collection of classical manuscripts which he presented to the Oxford library. William Grey studied at Florence, Padua, and Ferrara. He became one of the finest Greek scholars in England. His library of more than 200 manuscripts became the property of Balliol College. Christ Church, at Canterbury, received the manuscripts of William of Selling, who had learned his Humanism at Padua, Bologna, and Rome. Thomas Linacre, nephew of William, visited Rome with his uncle, remained to study the classics and medicines at Florence and Padua, and returned to serve as physician to Henry VIII, tutor Princess Mary in Latin, teach Greek and medicine, translate Galen's works, and found a college of medicine, the College of Physicians, in London.

When Cornelius Vitelli visited Oxford in 1475, he met a young tutor named William Grocyn (1446-1519). The two men became fast friends, and Vitelli first introduced his friend to Greek. This led to William's spending some four years in Florence, Rome, and Padua, where he studied Latin and Greek under the most famous scholars of the day. Returning to England, he became the first to hold a chair of Greek at Oxford.

Two of the most renowned humanistic scholars of fifteenth and sixteenth century England were John Colet (1461-1519) and William Lily (1468-1522). These, along with Linacre, Grocyn, Hugh Latimer, and Sir Thomas More, became a close-knit band of scholars responsible for introducing the revival of learning to England. They influenced Erasmus to make his residence in England. Colet was leader of this group. A graduate of Oxford, he studied canon and civil law in Paris, where he met Erasmus and Guillaume Budé (1467-1540), a leading scholar of Roman law and founder of both the *Collegium Trilingue,* later the *College de France,* and the library at Fontainebleau, which was later removed to Paris and became the nucleus of the *Bibliothèque Nationale.* After three years in Paris, Colet returned to England to lecture at Oxford on the Greek New Testament. Later, as dean of the Cathedral School at Saint Paul's in the heart of London, he preached Church reform, lectured on the Bible, and revitalized the Latin Grammar School, introducing both classical languages and literature. As a result, this school became a model of humanistic education in England, the showplace of the "new learning." As headmaster of this school from 1510 to 1522, William Lily built the curriculum of the school around the "new learning." He had graduated from Oxford, where he listened to lectures by Grocyn, had learned Greek at Rhodes and Rome, and had studied Latin with the best humanistic teachers Italy afforded. While at Saint Paul's, he wrote a Latin grammar in the manner of the new learning, a grammar which became a standard text for generations.

By the sixteenth century, Oxford had become a lively center of Humanism. It was graduating an increasing number of young men who continued their education at centers of the new learning in Italy. It was attracting to its faculty scholars imbued with enthusiasm for the classics. Its libraries were receiving Latin and Greek manuscripts in profusion, and students were busy reading them and correcting their mistakes.

In similar fashion, many of the secondary schools of England, including the so-called public schools, were feeling the glow of this new learning. As guilds began taking over some of these schools from the Church and establishing similar schools of their own, their practical concerns seemed better served by Humanism than by scholastic and medieval studies and methods.

Desiderius Erasmus (1466-1536)

In a vain attempt to characterize Erasmus, writers have called him many things. He is often referred to as "the scholars' scholar." Others have thought of him as "the Voltaire of the Renaissance." Because he refused either to cast his lot with Luther and the Reformation or to repudiate both, he has been called a "trimmer," one who vacillates between positions as the mood strikes him. One student of the Reformation thinks of him as "the apostle of common sense and of rational religion." Erasmus was seen in many lights and affected men differently. He was respected as a scholar, loved as a friend, used for commercial ends, and hated as an enemy of the Church.

He styled himself Desiderius Erasmus Roterodamus, expressing his belief that he was born in Rotterdam. There is evidence to indicate, however, that his birthplace was Gouda, his father's native city. His first schooling at Gouda under Peter Winckel was unpromising. From here he went to Saint Lebuin's church school at Deventer, where he came under the influence of Alexander Hegius and the Humanism of the Brethren of the Common Life. During his nine years as a pupil of Hegius and his assistant, Johannes Sinthius, he developed the love of letters that was to become the passion of his life.

Upon the death of his father in 1484, he was sent by his guardian to a school at Hertogenbosch to prepare for the monastic life. Although he became a monk and was ordained a priest, he hated the rigors of monastic life and the pedagogical methods used there. As an Augustinian canon in Saint Gregory's at Steyn, he was allowed to read the classics and Church Fathers to his heart's content. Finally he obtained permission to leave the monastery and attend the University of Paris. There he entered the college of Montaigu, where he found Jan Standonck, leader of the Dutch movement to purify the monastic orders. While at Paris he accepted a few pupils whom he instructed along humanistic lines. One of these was William Blount, fourth Baron Mountjoy, who invited him to visit England. In October of 1499 he was at Oxford, where he became a member of that humanistic circle led by Colet and including in its membership Linacre, Grocyn, and More. For the next few years he moved about Europe, teaching private pupils, writing, and studying Greek avidly. In his works published during this period, there is the constant plea for a return to the simplicity of primitive Christianity. He yearned to have the Church escape from dogma and ceremonials and return to the Bible and Church Fathers.

In 1505, Lord Mountjoy again invited him to England, where the king's physician, Baptista Boerio, employed him to supervise the education of his two sons. This included a visit to Italy where the lads might study with leaders of the new learning. He himself studied at Turin, where he received the Doctor of Divinity, and then at Bologna. When he completed his assignment, he decided to remain in Italy.

Returning to England later at the request of Lord Mountjoy, he wrote the famous *Moriae encomium* (The Praise of Folly). In this he ridiculed the Church and its scholasticism and struck out unmercifully at the hypocrisy, immorality, superstitions, and intolerance of churchmen, from popes to local clergy. He condemned the sale of indulgences, allegorical interpretations of scripture, the crude Latin used in sermons, pretended miracles, and the "silly" disputations that occupied the time of scholars. This amounted to a bold attack upon all medieval culture and a plea for the humanistic approach to life and religion.

In 1511 he went to Cambridge to teach and complete his Greek edition of the New Testament. This became one of the great works of the Reformation era. It was most carefully edited, based on the best sources available. It corrected many of the errors that had crept into the *Vulgate* and gave scholars of the northern Renaissance an example of beautiful Greek.

By 1514 we find him in Basle, supervising publication of his works. There he became associated with Johann Froben, owner of the most famous press in all Europe. Their relationship was both scholarly and commercial. Erasmus had leisure in which to study and write, and a press anxious to publish what he produced. As general editor and adviser to the press, he could see that his books appeared as he wanted them. On the other side, Froben had in Erasmus a name known and revered throughout Europe, especially among scholars. His name on a book, either as author or editor, was recommendation enough to attract thousands of buyers.

During these years of writing, teaching privately, publishing, and traveling, Erasmus was constantly under pressure to declare himself as to the Lutheran rebellion. Paul III dangled a cardinal's hat in front of him if he would align himself squarely with the Church and against Luther. Although he was in sympathy with Luther's work and opposed to the abuses which Luther condemned, Erasmus could not tolerate the excesses to which many Protestants went. He wrote to Melanchthon, "Is it for this that we have shaken off bishops and popes, that we may come under the yoke of such madmen as Otto and Farel?" He despised dogma but felt that the dogma of the Church was preferable to that of the Protestants.

JUAN LUIS VIVES (1492-1540)

Vives went far beyond Erasmus. He had read well the authors of classical times and knew both their meaning and their style. All this was nothing, he believed, unless it could be translated into terms meaningful for practical living. He wrote, "This is the fruit of all our studies, this is the goal. Having acquired our knowledge, we must turn it to usefulness and employ it for the common good." Vives had little use for arid speculations. They were meaningless for him. In the first book of his famous *De anima,* he attacked the ancients for involving themselves in absurd speculations. They ask, "What is the soul?" No one can know the answer and all affirmed answers are pure speculation, he held. "What the soul is, is of no concern for us to know," he writes. "What its manifestations are is of great importance." In his discussions of the mind he is concerned not with the essence of the mind, but with its actions. Here we are listening to a sixteenth century behaviorist.

Vives was born at Valencia, studied at Paris, and became professor of humanities at Louvain. He was brought to the attention of the English court when he dedicated his commentary on Augustine's *City of God* to Henry VIII. This resulted in an invitation to come to Corpus Christi College, Oxford, where he was made a Doctor of Laws and lectured on philosophy. During this time he supervised the education of Princess Mary and wrote *De ratione studii puerilis epistolae duae* (Two letters On a Plan of Studies for Youth), one for Princess Mary and the other for the son of Lord Mountjoy. Attached as he was to the Queen, he opposed the divorce of Henry VIII from Catherine of Aragon and lost his favored position in the royal household.

Forced to leave England, he went to Bruges, where he became a leader of a Spanish colony of scholars. There he lashed out at scholasticism and the worship of Aristotle's logic. Bruges seems to have been the center and source of Vives' inspiration as well as the physical pivot of all his activities. There he married, engaged in business, wrote creatively in the fields of education and psychology, and died.

Vives' *De Tradendis Disciplinis* (Concerning the Teaching of the Arts) has been called "the most thorough-going educational book of the Renaissance."[1] Add to this *De Institutione Feminae Christianae* (On the Instruction of a Christian Woman) and the letters dealing with the education of Princess Mary and Lord Mountjoy's son, and you have one of the most significant attempts of the period to approach education realistically.

Vives realized that education must begin in the home as soon as possible after the birth of the child. The mother is the first teacher, but the father plays a significant role. When the child reaches seven, he should enroll in a day school under a master carefully selected for his sound scholarship and moral integrity. This master should study each child carefully and construct a curriculum tailored to his disposition, talents, and needs. At times he should confer with other masters about the child's progress and adjust his teaching to this increasing knowledge. The master should be paid by the community, not by the pupil or his parents.

Although Vives believed that a youth should master classical languages and literature, he laid great stress upon knowledge and correct use of the mother tongue. By this time, Spanish had become a language with a grammar and literature equal in many respects to the best that could be offered anywhere in Europe. There was growing belief that effective teaching of ancient languages was dependent upon fluent and correct use of the vernacular. His advocacy of the vernacular as introductory to classical languages marked him as being far ahead of his times, as did his insistence upon the use of the direct, conversational method of teaching all languages.

---

1. Foster Watson, *Louis Vives* (Oxford: Oxford University Press, 1922), p. 100.

It is but natural that Vives, who insisted upon observation as the means of discovery and introduction to understanding, and who championed the practicality of all knowledge, should show great interest in the study of mathematics and the natural sciences. He held that these should be introduced into the curriculum when the child is ready and able to deal with them adequately.

Boys should study classical languages as necessary tools for scholarship and international communication; the vernacular, for accurate and rich intercourse with their fellows; mathematics; the natural sciences; and, as professional interests might dictate, law, medicine, architecture, political science, and war. Being a devout Catholic, Vives believed that education should be permeated with the Catholic faith and morals.

Vives' interest in the education of girls and women is seen in his writings on the subject and in his instruction of Princess Mary. He would have girls study the vernacular, Latin, religion, morals, the care of children, and household management. They would become wives and mothers charged with running homes and bringing up children. Their education should prepare them for these duties. Many of the subjects usually included in curricula for girls, such as music, dancing, and art, were omitted, as were history, politics, mathematics, and science.

An educator and theorist on education, a psychologist, and a student of the real world in which he lived, Vives could not avoid being concerned with the virulent social disease of poverty. In 1526, he wrote the first scientific work on public charity, *De subventione pauperum* (On Poor Relief), a book that influenced much advanced thinking in this field for generations to come. In this, Vives rejected almsgiving as an inefficient and degrading method of aiding the poor. Rather, he held that the community should accept responsibility for its poor and develop plans for their rehabilitation at public expense. Here we see Vives' faith in democracy. The masses to him are not an inferior race, as many Renaissance scholars held. Circumstances have denied them opportunities for development. If given these opportunities through education and public care, they can stand as men and leaders of society.

Vives sensed the times better than most. He saw that the past could no longer survive and that a new age was appearing. He did not understand all its implications, but as a realist and a student of the human individual, he realized that medievalism was no more, and that mankind, the elite *and* the masses, was marching forward. One of his most significant and prophetic statements is: "I see from the depths a change is coming. Amongst all the nations men are springing up of clear, excellent, and free intellects, impatient of servitude, determined to thrust off the yoke of their tyranny from their necks. They are calling their fellow-citizens to liberty." This could have been written yesterday.

MARTIN LUTHER (1483-1546)

Martin Luther became the focal point of the religious Reformation. Those who had attempted to rush history and start the revolution before its time were beaten down and destroyed, although they played their part in shaping the future. When the times were ripe, when the strands were ready to be tied, when the varied forces that had been building for centuries were in conjunction, Martin Luther, a monk of the Augustinian order and a scholar in the camp of William of Occam, was hurled into the midst of the quarrel between Church and civil authority to spearhead a Reformation that shook all Europe and reached deep into the thinking of the western world.

His Life

On the morning of November 10, 1483, in the town of Eisleben, Margaret Ziegler Luther, wife of Hans Luther, a free peasant and émigré from Thuringia, was delivered of a male child whom they named Martin. When the boy was six months old, the family moved to Mansfeld, where Hans found employment as a miner. The next few years were marked by struggle and a careful husbanding of resources as Hans became the lessee of several smelting furnaces and an elected member of the town council.

The home in which Martin spent his early years was deeply religious and characteristically superstitious. Hans and Margaret believed in strict discipline, the Catholic faith, and the efficacy of honest toil. They sent Martin to the town school, where he learned the Latin language, some of its literature, religious doctrines, and singing. Though the school was uninspiring and ruthlessly disciplinarian, he was a good student, applied himself well, and profited greatly from what was taught.

When he reached his fourteenth year, his parents sent him to Magdeburg to continue his education under the Brethren of the Common Life. Here he began to catch something of the spirit of the new learning. After one year he returned to his home for a short period before setting out for Eisenach, where, as ward of a wealthy burgher named Kuntz Cotta, he studied advanced Latin grammar, composition, rhetoric, and poetry in preparation for enrollment in the university. In the spring of

1501 we find him at the University of Erfurt, the most noted of all German universities, where he received both the bachelor of arts and the master's degrees with distinction. During these years at Erfurt he studied Latin grammar, logic, rhetoric, physics, philosophy, mathematics, metaphysics, and ethics under some of the most noted teachers of the day. There he came under the influence of the nominalist philosophy expounded by William of Occam in the fourteenth century. He was also schooled in the conventional scholasticism and writings of Aristotle, Cicero, Virgil, and Livy.

Now a master, with the proper recognition in intellectual circles, Luther turned to the study of law. He soon interrupted this to renounce the world and enter the monastery of the Augustinian Eremites at Erfurt. There he submitted to all the rigors of monastic training, studied theology diligently, took all the vows of the order, and was ordained a priest in 1507. During his stay in the monastery, he was sent for a year to the University of Wittenberg, where he studied and lectured on Aristotle's *Ethics*. There he became a friend of John Staupitz, professor of theology and vicar-general of his order. Back at Erfurt, he lectured and received another degree. Then, at the suggestion of Staupitz, he was sent to the monastery at Wittenberg. Even though he became sub-prior of the monastery, he continued his studies at the university and won the doctorate of theology. In 1512 he became Staupitz's successor as professor of biblical literature.

In the winter of 1512-1513, as he meditated on Romans 1:16-17, he reached the conclusion that salvation is the gift of a merciful God, not the result of works or merit. Man is saved by faith and faith alone. He is not worthy of God's grace, and nothing he can do will make him worthy.

For five years, Luther worked with this idea, lectured on its implications, discussed the matter with his friends and associates at Wittenberg, and listened to his students defend the thesis. Then, in 1517, his thinking having matured, he emerged from the academic walls of Wittenberg to hurl at the world his ninety-five theses, and to denounce the abuse of indulgences.

Luther posted the theses on the door of the chapel at Wittenberg and sent a copy to the archbishop, along with a strongly worded letter. Soon they were being read throughout Europe, and attacks by Tetzel, chief organizer of the sale of indulgences, and by the Dominican order, were being leveled at Luther. John Maier of Eck, known in history as Dr. Eck, accused Luther of heresy and of making a direct attack upon the papacy. Luther replied to these attacks, and furnished Leo X a copy. Attempts on the part of Leo and other high Church officials to mediate the dispute were met by Luther's repeated assurance that he would recant gladly if he could be convinced that the scriptures were against him. When Luther accepted the challenge of Dr. Eck to debate the issues laid down in the ninety-five theses, it became clear that he was not in agreement with the Church's doctrine of the divine right of the papacy, that he held the scriptures supreme in all matters of religion, that he believed John Huss to have been unjustly condemned, and that he was not in accord with other tenets of the Church. This led to a restudy of the whole matter in Rome and a papal Bull of Condemnation.

The Bull stirred Luther as nothing else had. He burned it, along with a copy of the canon law and other documents, and wrote three polemics that roused reform elements to a white heat. In his *Address to the German Nobility,* he urged civil rulers to undertake the much needed reformation of the Church. This proved to be a call for national churches under the authority of kings and princes and the death knell of the Universal Church pictured in Augustine's *City of God.* In *The Babylonian Captivity of the Church,* he attacked abuses of the Church, especially its system of sacraments, and championed the right of the individual Christian to break the shackles of a predatory priesthood. The *Freedom of a Christian Man* was a careful exposition of his doctrine of justification by faith.

In January, 1521, Luther was officially excommunicated. On April 16 of the same year, he entered Worms to make his case, at the suggestion and under the safe conduct of Charles V. He refused to recant unless convinced by the scriptures. "Unless I am convinced by the testimony of Scriptures," he told the diet, "or by an evident reason—for I confide neither in the pope nor in a council alone, since it is certain that they have often erred and contradicted themselves—I am held fast by the Scriptures adduced by me, and my conscience is taken captive by God's Word, and I neither can nor will revoke anything, seeing that it is not safe or right to act against conscience. God help me. Amen."

After the Diet of Worms, Luther was spirited away by the elector of Saxony and lodged in the castle of Wartburg, overlooking Eisenach, where under the pseudonym of Knight George, he remained in hiding until the spring of 1522. While at Wartburg, he completed his translation of the Greek New Testament into High German. After many revisions, the book was published in September, 1522. This was in line with his belief that each individual should read the Bible and interpret it for himself, freed from dependence upon priests. Now the people had the New Testament in their own language, could read it prayerfully in their homes, and know what God actually intended.

Wittenberg became the center of the Reformation movement and set an example for all Europe. There the radicals gained control and, with the aid of the town council and the university theological faculty, introduced changes in the communion, removed all images from the church, and sanctioned marriage of the clergy. As the situation became critical, Luther left Wartburg and resumed his public life at Wittenberg in March, 1522. To win the people to his gradualism, he wrote polemics, letters, sermons, treatises, and books. These were effective in helping to stem the tide of extremism that threatened the entire movement.

By 1524 the evangelical movement had moved into the sphere of social revolution. The peasants had become increasingly articulate and militant as increasing prosperity and the Lutheran doctrine of individualism brought their depressed conditions into bold relief. As they worked for greater freedom and civil rights, the more extreme reformers sided with them against the princes and nobility. Luther was in sympathy with the complaints of the peasants and their fight for social justice, but firmly believed in obedience to constituted authority in the state. When extremists turned to force to effect social reform, Luther issued a violent condemnation of their methods, *Against the Murderous and Thieving Peasant Bands,* and urged the princes to exterminate these malcontents. This led to a ruthless suppression of the peasants' revolt and undermined Luther's faith in the common man.

In spite of increasing ill health, during the last ten years of his life Luther continued the work of explaining and vindicating the Reformation. Others, often with views differing from his, were increasingly influential. He continued to attack the Church and the radicals. He prepared a translation of the Old Testament to accompany his earlier New Testament. He wrote hymns which have become part of Protestant worship. In 1546 he was moved to visit his birthplace, where he preached on several occasions to crowded congregations. The strain of travel and exposure to inclement weather were more than his weakened body could stand, and on February 18, 1546, he died at Eislaben. On February 22 his body was laid to rest in the castle church of Wittenberg, where his life work had been done.

HIS VIEWS ON EDUCATION

Schools in Germany, and to an extent throughout Europe, had fallen upon evil days. The economic reformation had changed the face of Europe, making much that medieval-minded schools had to offer useless. The political reformation had increased the desire of civil authorities to control education within their realms. Humanism and Protestantism made many traditional schools look ridiculous. When monasteries and cloisters were closed in Lutheran lands, their schools died. Cathedral and other Church schools disappeared. German reading and writing schools, as well as Latin schools, were unpopulated. Erfurt had 1,527 students in 1520. By 1527 it enrolled only fourteen. At Heidelberg there were as many professors as there were students. The University of Vienna had a student body of 661 in 1519. By 1532 only twelve students were sitting in its classes. Many felt that Luther was largely responsible. It was Erasmus who wrote, "Wherever Lutheranism prevails, there learning disappears."

Luther was deeply distressed by the state of the schools. He recognized the necessity for schools in any society, especially in one making a transition between two cultures. He once said that if he were not a priest, he would be a teacher. At another time he affirmed that were there no heaven or hell, schools would be necessary for life on this earth. To counter the decline of schools in Protestant lands, he wrote an earnest appeal to the *Mayors and Aldermen of the Cities of Germany,* urging them to promote schools and education to fill the gap left by the deposed Church.

As Luther studied social conditions in Germany, he was appalled by the ignorance, immorality, impiety, and delinquency which he found almost everywhere. It seemed to him that the people, freed from the paternalism of an all-pervading Church, were as children freed too soon from parental supervision, unable to live in freedom with responsibility. To point up an important phase of this responsibility, he wrote *Sermon on the Duty of Sending Children to School.* In this he emphasized the necessity of education for both the religious and the secular life.

In his *Address to the Christian Nobility,* Luther urged princes and civil rulers to establish elementary schools in which all children could be taught religion, languages, history, singing, instrumental music, and mathematics. After the Peasants' War he expressed some second thoughts about religious instruction. Where before he had advocated teaching the scriptures to all, now he placed emphasis upon the catechisms which he wrote for the purpose. This was to be the Bible for the masses, supplemented by Aesop's fables, in which he found many moral principles illustrated interestingly. Those with exceptional capabilities should go on to the Latin Grammar school which the town established and supported. There they would study Latin, Greek, and Hebrew, the scriptures and Church Fathers, history, and music. From these schools would come ministers, learned men who could teach and do research, and leaders in town and state life.

Those who completed the education offered by the Latin Grammar school and showed ability should go on to the university to study the scriptures and become bishops and priests.

In Summary

Luther was a scholar, a devout Christian, and a violent man. He saw his beloved Church prostituted, and fought to restore its purity. He loved mankind and freedom but came to realize that the use of freedom required a maturity of understanding which few had. He believed that education was the only avenue to this maturity. He gave the world a faith that set men thinking, a philosophy of education that opened new vistas, and a vernacular Bible that transformed German from a dialect into a language of power and beauty. A controversial figure in history, he changed Europe and set patterns in education, state, and church that were to determine much of the future.

THE REFORMATION AND
THE SCHOOLS OF GERMANY

Three educators, each of unique talents and specialized abilities, contributed to the development of Luther's ideas in the schools of Germany. These were Johannes Bugenhagen (1485-1558), Philip Melanchthon (1497-1560), and John Sturm (1507-1589). Under their expert guidance, town schools were reformed, princes reorganized or established schools in line with Protestant thinking, and Germany was well on its way to incorporating much of Luther's thinking into its educational structure.

Johannes Bugenhagen

Bugenhagen was the organizer of the Reformation. If princes and other civil rulers were to build and operate schools in accord with Lutheran thinking, it was necessary that they have expert guidance and direction. This Bugenhagen gave. He drew elaborate plans for school systems in Brunswick, Hamburg, Lubeck, Bremen, and in princely realms in northern Germany and Denmark. In each of these he planned an entire educational system, from reading and writing schools through Latin schools. He also made provisions for libraries and a form of adult education.

Towns of the Hanseatic League had maintained reading and writing schools long before the Reformation. These served the practical interests of the people, providing youth of the industrial and commercial classes with skills necessary for their success. These were under control of the Church. Bugenhagen insisted that they be transferred to municipal control, that teachers be appointed by civil authorities, and that although parents would support them through fees, teachers receive extra compensation for teaching church music, religion, and the cate-chism. Under this plan the traditional town school, with a faculty of clerics, came under control of the civil government and served as an instrument for developing loyal Protestants.

Above these reading and writing schools, in Bugenhagen's school ordinances, and decidedly superior to them in Protestant thinking, were Latin schools. These were under civil control and taught the classics and religion.

Bugenhagen believed, as did most reformers, that education should be available to both boys and girls. Thus, in every plan he drew, there were separate schools for each sex.

PHILIP MELANCHTHON

Here we are in the presence of the finest scholar of the Lutheran Reformation, called by many *Praeceptor Germaniae,* in erudition sec-ond only to Erasmus. Born at Bretten, near Pforzheim, he was the nephew of John Reuchlin, whose interest in Hebrew he failed to share. He received his bachelor's degree at Heidelberg when he was fifteen. While hardly more than a boy, he prepared a Greek grammar for his fellow students. Later he wrote a Latin grammar, which was circulated widely and used in both Catholic and Protestant schools. His texts on logic and rhetoric were widely used throughout Europe. Spending most of his professional life at Wittenberg, he taught every subject in the curriculum and wrote significant works in the areas of both the *trivium* and the *quadrivium.* While these contained little new material, they were the writings of a master teacher who knew how to make difficult ideas and concepts understandable to the school boy.

Melanchthon was a bridge between scholasticism and the Humanism that was spreading northward from Italy in the fifteenth and sixteenth centuries. He was a devoted colleague of Luther and a dedicated Protes-tant. At the same time, his devotion to Latin was almost fanatical. He could see no place in a boy's education for German and considered both Greek and Hebrew "not merely useless but detrimental."

Melanchthon, like Bugenhagen, was an educational counselor to princes and civil authorities. Although he participated in many school surveys and had a hand in preparing several school codes, his most significant contribution to the development of state-controlled educa-tion in Germany was the Saxon Code. Written by Melanchthon and revised and edited by Luther, this code set a pattern for much Protes-tant educational thinking. It insisted that civil authorities assume their sacred obligation to establish and support schools to prepare young men for leadership in state and church.

The Saxon Code prohibited the teaching of the vernacular in reading and writing schools. Latin was the only language tolerated throughout formal education. The child could learn to use the "vulgar" language in his home and among his peers. When the young person first entered school, the Code insisted, he should learn the Latin alphabet, study *Donatus* and Cato's *Disticha de Moribus,* memorize religious verses and didactic statements in Latin, and begin singing in Latin. The method of teaching was recognized as superior for that age. It consisted of readings and lengthy explanations by the teacher, memorization of long passages from Latin works, and the acquisition of a large Latin vocabulary as quickly as possible.

After several years of work at this lower level, the student turned to an exhaustive study of Latin grammar and the reading of Aesop, Erasmus' *Colloquies,* the comedies of Terance and Plautus, and other Latin books of similar difficulty. These were studied not so much for their literary value as to illustrate rules of grammar. Since a good bit of this material was memorized, the youth was given extensive training in verbatim remembering.

Following this, young men advanced to the scholarly reading of Latin classics, including Cicero, Ovid, and Virgil. They were encouraged to compose Latin prose and verse in the styles of these masters. In addition they studied rhetoric and logic.

The Saxon Code was humanistic and Lutheran. It stressed the Latin classics plus religion in the Protestant tradition. Since it became a model for other codes, these two strains permeated much of German education. Melanchthon was sought after by civil authorities, and cities often invited him to settle within their confines and direct their schools. He refused all such offers but worked diligently to find men to staff their school organizations. Many of his pupils accepted these positions, thus spreading far and wide his ideas on education. It has been estimated that at Melanchthon's death, almost every city in Protestant Germany boasted at least one of his students among its leading educators.

JOHN STURM

Sturm's classical gymnasium at Strassburg was a humanistic school with Protestant overtones, the creation of a Ciceronian who, under the spell of Martin Bucer's evangelical preaching, embraced Protestantism and wove his two loves into a school pattern which was copied by Ascham in England, Calvin in Geneva, the Jesuits, and a dozen or more cities of Protestant Europe.

Born at Schleiden, near Cologne, of a father in the employment of Count Manderscheid, he was educated in the count's home. From there he went to Liege to attend a school of The Brethren of the Common Life. This school was the model for his gymnasium. At Trilingual College, founded by Erasmus at Louvaine, Sturm learned to admire pure Ciceronian eloquence. While at Louvaine, he taught Latin and established a press with which he printed Greek and Latin texts for students of the college.

In 1537, Sturm was prevailed upon to accept the rectorship of the new gymnasium at Strassburg. There he labored for forty years, developing his ideas of what a school should be, teaching the sons of princes and kings and young men of promise from the new merchant and industrial classes, and sending from the campus leaders who were to reshape education throughout Europe.

Three Latin schools were being operated in Strassburg with a total of not more than 300 students. These were typical grammar schools of medieval tradition but with a slight humanistic flavor. Sturm recommended that they be abolished and a single school founded along the lines of the Brethren's school at Liege. The plan which he submitted to the town authorities and which was eventually adopted by them proposed a school of ten classes or grades, each with its own teacher. Boys were accepted at the age of five or six. After graduation at fifteen or sixteen, they would continue their education for five more years in a humanistic college or university.

Sturm had a clear conception of what a school should do and worked this into a plan of studies and a curriculum that was specific and detailed. To him Latin was the essence of learning. The educated man was the cultured man. This man must know and know that he knows, he must be a master of pure and elegant diction and use Latin skillfully, and he must be religious. Religion, Greek and Latin, and logic were the basic subjects of his curriculum. All these should produce the "cultured man," one who could use Cicero's Latin with eloquence.

The one exception to his exclusive emphasis upon speaking and reading Latin in the schools came at the beginning of the educational cycle, when the child was permitted to memorize the Lutheran catechism in the vernacular. Later he was required to translate this catechism into Latin. This was followed by reading Saint Paul's writings in Greek and then translating them into Ciceronian Latin. Instruction in religion was given only on weekends, with the exception that psalms in both Latin and Greek were sung each morning.

Sturm prepared a detailed syllabus for each class, stating what should be taught each day and the proper method of teaching it. He left nothing to chance or the teacher's discretion. The school was a lock-step institution; all boys moved along at the same pace under the same techniques. The famous *Ratio Studiorum* of the Jesuits was modeled after these syllabi. Sturm wrote texts for some of the classes, discussed his method and curriculum with educators and other interested persons who came to see him from all parts of Europe, corresponded widely on educational matters, and never tired of proclaiming Latin, as Cicero wrote and spoke it, the true mark of an educated man.

At one time more than 3,000 pupils were studying at Strassburg. These included noblemen, counts, barons, and princes. Kings and other civil rulers honored Sturm. His pupils established gymnasia throughout Europe and held prominent positions in state and church. School ordinances were written around his ideas and methods, his Humanism was infused into Protestant education, and northern Europe began again to appreciate Cicero's style, in spite of Erasmus' vitriolic attack upon Ciceronianism.

THE NEW GERMAN EDUCATION

The Reformation meant, among other things, that cities and states held buildings and considerable wealth formerly in the hands of the Church. At the behest of Protestant leaders, these resources were devoted to education. Civil leaders were persuaded that education was basic to all that the Reformation sought to accomplish. Luther's *Letter to the Mayors and Aldermen* influenced many cities to undertake a reorganization of their schools along Protestant lines. As most of these school patterns took shape, Latin became the chief subject, with some Greek and Hebrew added. In preparation for this work, boys were sent to reading and writing schools under municipal control. Girls usually began their education in vernacular schools.

In most communities where Protestantism took root, private schools were prohibited because of the belief that civil control of education was the only way to civil control of the mind. With civil control came, insofar as such was possible, civil support. While in some instances a small fee was charged, most Protestant education in Germany was free. Further, earnest efforts were made to discover boys of high potential and provide them with schooling at civil expense. The vast revenues which now came to cities and states from former properties of the Roman Catholic Church made this possible. Some places even went so far as to provide public lectures in a number of subject areas free to all who wished to attend. This was a sixteenth century form of adult education.

Since the Protestant Reformation was fundamentally religious, it was natural that religion would become a major interest of the schools.

The Bible in Latin or Greek was part of the curriculum of German schools. Further, since churches were reorganized along Lutheran lines, pastors were required to teach the catechism and give religious instruction to all children. Often reading and writing were added to these pastoral schools. When the pastor found himself too busy to care for this responsibility, he either employed a teacher who became part of the church's staff or turned the work over to the sexton or sacristan. In time, examinations were set up for teachers in these church schools, supervised by municipal officials.

At the college level, Protestant Germany made significant advancements. Established universities were scholastic and, in most instances, resisted both Humanism and Protestantism. This led Protestants to organize new universities in which their beliefs would be dominant. In 1527 the University of Marburg was organized from plans drawn by Melanchthon. By the end of the century, Konigsberg, Jena, and Helmstedt had appeared, and were on their way to becoming the chief centers of learning in Germany. Since these were Protestant-inspired, religion occupied a place of great importance in their curricula. Their function was to prepare pastors and leaders for a religious oriented culture, and no "heresy" could be tolerated.

Protestant Germany was education conscious. Luther's fear that overthrow of the Church might lead to educational apathy was a stimulus to him and to others in the organizing and putting under state control schools and universities which would prepare young men to continue the Reformation beyond their day. While some few Protestant areas were drawn back into the Church by vigorous counter-Reformation activities, these new schools were able to prepare the people of Germany to hold tightly to the gains they had made.

THE REFORMATION IN ENGLAND

THE NEW LEARNING

Since England was an island and her people less susceptible to waves of change than the nations on the continent, no great flood of early Humanism swept over her lands. She was something of a spectator of the Renaissance, watching it from its earliest, tumultuous days, through those years when it was drifting north and being woven into the Reformation, to its maturity in men of the caliber of Erasmus. Consequently, the Renaissance, the Reformation, and the Counter-Reformation had their impact upon England almost simultaneously.

Henry VIII became king on April 22, 1509, as a youth of eighteen. He had been educated under the influence of the Renaissance, one of his tutors being the poet Skelton. Bright, imaginative, quick to learn, he became an accomplished scholar, fluent in Latin, French, Italian, and Spanish, a musician of considerable skill, and an athlete. As king he bestowed his favors on humanistic writers, teachers, and artists, to the joy of Renaissance communities appearing in England. One of his interests was the chair of Greek, which he founded at Corpus Christi College, Oxford.

HENRY'S REFORMATION

England was not anti-Catholic. The people of England despised the clergy but were loyal to Catholicism. Chapuys, an envoy of Charles V, Holy Roman Emperor and King of Spain (as Charles I), reported from London in 1529, "Nearly all the people here hate the priests." Erasmus' *Letters of Obscure Men* was "read everywhere" and enjoyed in England possibly because it was a bitter satire on the monks. At the same time Henry was condemning Luther so violently that he earned from the pope the title of Defender of the Faith. Heretical books were burned in Saint Paul's churchyard, and four heretics were burned in the diocese of Lincoln. While Dr. Barnes, the prior of the Austin Friars, was being forced to recant his heresies, Lutheran groups were forming at Oxford and Cambridge. A year later the king was asking the Church for permission to divorce Catherine of Aragon and marry Anne Boleyn so that he might have a legitimate heir to the throne.

Political issues caused the papacy to delay decision on Henry's request for a divorce. As Cardinal Wolsey lost power over the king and it became evident that the throne of England was more powerful than Rome, a break with Catholic authority was inevitable. Finally the king, with the help of Parliament, effected a Reformation that was purely political. The Act of Supremacy, 1534, made the king head of the Church of England. The Treasons Act strengthened the king's hand against all opponents to his power. The Act of Uniformity, 1552, required clergy, teachers, and all people to accept the established church or suffer severe penalties. By the time this act was passed, Henry VIII had died (1547), Edward VI had obeyed his iconoclastic advisers and effected reforms more ambitious than Henry's, and an English liturgy and Protestant confession of faith had been drawn up.

When Edward died in 1553, Mary I, known as Catholic Mary and Bloody Mary, ascended the throne. Almost immediately she sought to wipe out all evidence of the Church of England and lead England back into the arms of Rome. Her methods were violent and bloody. Hundreds of Protestants were executed, and repressive measures were used to erase all traces of rebellion. The people were not with her. When John

Rogers, her first victim, went to the gallows, the crowds cheered him so loudly that "he seemed to be going to his marriage." When Elizabeth I came to the throne, the people were ready for "the papacy without the pope." Her reign united the best in the Renaissance, the Reformation, and the genius of England. She stood as head of both state and church, benevolent toward opponents, and arbiter of a culture seldom seen in the western world.

The English Reformation was not a violent reaction against clerical abuses as in Germany. It was political. Henry wanted supreme power and could not tolerate a superior force in his realm. Neither could he stomach the draining of the wealth of his kingdom for the benefit of Rome. In the end, the Church of England remained Catholic in doctrine and spirit, but its head was the civil ruler, king or queen.

Educationally, the English Reformation was humanistic. Among the many scholars influential in shaping the schools were Sir Thomas Elyot, Roger Ascham, and Richard Mulcaster. Each in his own way interpreted the Renaissance to Englishmen and wove its spirit into the education of the nation's leaders.

SIR THOMAS ELYOT (*circa* 1490-1546)

Elyot's early life is a matter of considerable dispute. We cannot be certain when or where he was born. Both Sainte Mary Hall, Oxford, and Jesus College, Cambridge, claim him as a student, while he tells us that he was educated at home and taught himself from the age of twelve. His father was Sir Richard Elyot, judge of the court of common pleas. Early in life, Thomas mastered Latin and Greek and was translating some of the classics from both languages. He was a humanist and a strong advocate of royal supremacy, able to help his sovereigns employ the New Learning to build their power and prestige.

Among the significant translations which Elyot published are Isocrates' *Doctrinal of Princes,* Pico della Mirandola's *Rules of a Christian Life,* and Plutarch's *The Education or Bringing up of Children.* His own writings included books on education, religion, morals, and collections of wise sayings from the Church Fathers.

The Boke Named the Governour, published in 1531, was the first educational work to appear in English. Its popularity was almost immediate, and no less than ten editions appeared before the close of the century. Here Elyot states his ideas about the moral and cultural education of a ruler.

The best state is one ruled by a monarch whose authority is undisputed. Around him must be members of an aristocracy able to offer advice. Others in the realm must accept their status in the social hierarchy and serve the monarch as their estate demands. From birth to seven years of age the young sovereign must be reared in a home where all speak Latin elegantly and where the manners and bearing of each are of the best. No base or vulgar influence shall be permitted to touch the child.

At seven he should be turned over to a tutor who will teach him music, drawing, painting, carving, and Greek. Latin must be the only language of conversation. The books he will read during his early education are Aesop's fables, Lucian, Homer, Hesiod, Virgil, Horace, and other Latin poets. All teaching must be interesting to the child, lest he develop a dislike of books. From these easier works the child will move on to Demosthenes, Cicero, Plato, and Aristotle. From these he learns logic, rhetoric, and oratory. Those who plan to enter the higher professions of the commonwealth will study law and politics diligently.

Interwoven with these studies must be extensive physical training, since the efficient "governor," whether he sits on a throne or gives advice to the king, must possess a body capable of responding to all commands of the mind. This training should include wrestling, running, swimming, riding, hunting, dancing, archery, and the use of arms. Elyot believed that archery was the best exercise for coordinating all muscles of the body.

Elyot advocated dancing for its moral value. Here he was a disciple of Plato, who thought of dancing as a symbolic art, an introduction to "prudence," the first moral virtue. When this virtue has been established, all others will follow: honor, fear, love, and "the mean." As the young person proceeds with his dancing, he will become provident, industrious, circumspect, and modest. Dancing was for Elyot the root of character education.

While Elyot was of the aristocracy and believed no one fit to rule who had not been born a "gentleman" and educated to his station, he recognized that some men of lesser estate have the ability, character, and education fitting them for leadership. These he would assign to lower official positions.

ROGER ASCHAM (1515-1568)

Ascham was born at Kirby Wiske, a small village near Northallerton, and educated in the house of Sir Humphrey Wingfield, speaker of the House of Commons. The chief sport of youths assembled at Sir Wingfield's was archery. This stimulated Ascham to write for Henry VIII *Toxophilus,* a book in English praising the sport and discussing its physical and moral value. It is a Platonic dialogue between Toxophilus and Philologus and is the model from which Izaak Walton wrote his *Compleat Angler.*

From Sir Humphrey's, Ascham went to Saint John's College, Cambridge, taking his degree and becoming, in 1540, the first regius professor of Greek at the college. Professing Protestantism shortly after Edward VI became king, he was chosen in 1548 as tutor for Princess Elizabeth, a position which he held for two years. When Mary ascended to the throne, he was appointed Latin secretary to the queen despite his religious profession, a profession which most probably he did not champion vigorously at the time. In 1555 we see him back at his earlier task of educating the princess for her royal position.

Sometime in 1563, he was dining with Sir William Cecil, secretary of state, and other ministers, when they began to discuss a scandal that had erupted at Eton. Several boys had run away from the school because of incessant floggings. A debate followed between the "floggers" and the "non-floggers." The outcome of the discussion was that Ascham was invited by Sir Richard Sackville to suggest a tutor for his son and write a treatise on "the right order of teaching." The book was *The Schoolmaster.* This was not intended as an exhaustive discussion of education but rather a "plaine and perfite way of teachying children to understand, write, and speake in Latin tong." It was not intended as a text for schools but "specially prepared for the private brynging up of youth in gentlemen and noblemens houses." Although the book was circulated among Ascham's friends, it was not published until two years after his death.

Ascham's perfect method for learning Latin consisted of double translation. The book suggested for this exercise was Sturm's *Select Letters of Cicero.* The pupil was encouraged to translate this book, or some other that his tutor might choose, into English. Then, after a time had elapsed, he translated the English back into Latin. The tutor then compared the boy's Latin with that of the original, showing him his errors. In this way boys were able to learn Latin much more quickly and interestingly than before. A chief concern of the book was to make learning so interesting that flogging or cruel punishment would not be necessary. When the boy had attained some proficiency in Latin, he was encouraged to write poems and essays in English and translate them into Ciceronian Latin.

Although Ascham was criticized by many, he succeeded in making English reputable as a language for gentlemen and scholars. He argued that what "the best of the realm think it honest to use" he "ought not to suppose it vile for him to write."

RICHARD MULCASTER (*circa* 1530-1611)

The son of a family of some importance, Mulcaster was educated in the aristocratic tradition at Eton, King's College at Cambridge, and Oxford. In 1558 he was appointed headmaster of the Merchant Taylors'

School, newly founded in London by the guild of merchant tailors for the "proper education" of boys of the middle class. Here for twenty years he worked with a select group of youths, developed his educational theory, and published his two major works on schooling, *Positions* (1581) and *Elementarie* (1582). During these years his salary was ten pounds a year. He taught from dawn to dusk six days a week with only twenty free days a year. He could be dismissed at any time without warning but had to give his employer a year's notice if he wished to resign. That he was satisfactory to the guild is attested to by the fact that he remained in his position for twenty years and built up an enrollment of 300 boys, fifty more than the charter allowed. One of his famous pupils was Edmund Spenser, author of the *Faerie Queen.*

When, after twenty years of distinguished service to Merchant Taylors' School, Mulcaster asked for a raise, he was turned down with the admonition that he should be thankful for the opportunity to teach in that school. This caused him to remark, "The faithful servant is an everlasting fool," and resign. For five years he dropped out of sight, to turn up as a teacher in Saint Paul's School and rector of a small parish. After twelve years, he resigned and lived out the remainder of his life as a village rector.

Mulcaster believed with Plato that the only aristocracy worth considering was one of intellect and talent. He sought to prepare leaders for society—men of intellectual and social capacities—and realized that these might be found in all classes of society. A fanatical believer in the monarchy and a patriot to the extreme, he held that children should be educated to literacy by parish priests. When they were able to read and write sufficiently to discharge their duties as members of the church and citizens of the community, their education should stop. Lest too many be educated beyond this minimum and overcrowd the market for public servants, only those of the most promising mind and character should be allowed to go on to advanced and higher education appropriate to a gentleman. Education should be determined by the needs of the state. Here is the concept of a planned society in which the state should determine its needs and educate only enough people to serve them effectively. The individual must use his education for the benefit of society, not for himself.

Mulcaster had extensive opportunity to observe children at work and came to understand them clearly. He was a self-taught child psychologist, recognizing that children are different and must be educated in terms of these differences. Begin the education of the child when he is ready and then proceed at his speed. All education should be "according to the strength of their bodies and the quickness of their wits jointly."

Education should be public and universal. However, he would not have the same education for all. That of boys would differ from that of girls, and boys of skill should be encouraged to study far beyond those of duller wit. Discipline should be fitted to accomplishing the task desired. Children should be led to learning by kindness and good example. To beat a boy who lacks the capacity to learn is "worse than madness," but there are boys who can learn and need the lash to encourage them.

Mulcaster's feeling for English was typical of the Elizabethan era. He realized that it had become a "proper tongue" for both the soil and faith. The child, he held, should learn to read the language he spoke.

If we are to have good education, we must have good teachers. This led, in his thinking, to agencies for training teachers who would be on a par professionally with doctors and lawyers. Along with preparation, there must be adequate compensation. He held that the first years of schooling should be under master teachers who received a salary commensurate to their competence. If the school is to demand the entire time of the teacher, it should pay him adequately, thereby making other work unnecessary. "I consider," he wrote, "that in our universities there should be a special college for the training of teachers."

OUTCOMES OF THE ENGLISH REFORMATION

While the Reformation in England was political in nature, it had profound effects upon the nation's education. Song schools in parish churches, monastic schools, and schools at the courts of abbots and bishops were closed. Funds diverted from monasteries, nunneries, shrines, and chantry foundations were used to support grammar schools, endowed schools, and Oxford and Cambridge. Scholasticism and dialectic tended to disappear in favor of Humanism, grammar, and literature. The state took charge of both the church and the schools so that all applicants for degrees and all personnel of these institutions were required to swear allegiance to the crown and were kept under strict supervision. In many of the schools in England the vernacular was substituted for Latin, and books for study began to appear.

THE REFORMATION IN FRANCE

THE RENAISSANCE AND FRANCE

Southern France lay alongside Italy and was a natural avenue for the Renaissance as it moved north. Guillaume Bude (called Budaeus) late in the fifteenth century came under the influence of this new learning at the University of Orleans and carried it to Paris and the court of Francis I. In 1516 he wrote *De l'Institution du Prince* to outline his ideas on Renaissance education. His constant propagandizing and his persuasive personality influenced Francis to establish, in 1530, the *Collegium Trilingue*, a humanistic college in which Latin, Greek, and Hebrew were taught and the faculty and students permitted great freedom of thought. This later became the *College de France*. Bude's influence is also seen in the national library which the state began assembling. These advances put France in the forefront of the northern Renaissance and laid the foundation for the reform activity that was beginning to challenge the Church.

THE FRENCH REFORMATION

These humanistic interests were gradually destroying medieval conventions in France. The concordat of 1516 placed the French Church under royal authority and weakened the power of the priesthood. In 1512, Jacques Lefevre anticipated Luther's theory of grace and his denial of transubstantiation in the commentary that he added to his Latin translation of the letters of Saint Paul. With the help of Briconnet, Bishop of Meaux, and others concerned with moral and religious reformation, Lefevre established a school of students and evangelistic preachers interested in both learning and religious reform.

As Lutheran ideas spread through France, the work of these men came under close scrutiny and evoked ruthless repression by Church and court. Lefevre's books were burned; he and his friends saved their lives by fleeing; and Francis decreed that anyone suspected of Lutheranism be burned, although, only a little later, he signed a secret treaty with the princes of Germany. Excesses committed by extremists against priests and the Church caused the French populace to turn against the reformers and side with the conservatives. Heretics were rounded up by the hundreds, and many were burned. Lefevre died in 1536 feeling that his efforts at true religious reform had failed.

This evaluation was only partially true. With the publication of Calvin's *Institutes of the Christian Religion,* French Protestantism took on new life, and in spite of repeated burnings and an inquisition along Spanish lines, a political party was taking shape based on Calvinist thinking. When attempts at compromise and mutual toleration failed, France was plunged into a series of religious wars that turned the French Reformation into a political struggle and muted its religious voices.

PETER RAMUS (1515-1572)

A poor boy, son of a charcoal burner, Ramus worked his way through the College of Navarre in Paris and became the leading educational reformer in France. His thesis for the master's degree defended the proposition: "Everything that Aristotle taught is false." This was published in 1543 and was followed by works attacking scholastic logic and advocating a scientific approach to learning. These works aligned him against the Church and the entire scholastic method upon which stood the philosophy, science, and theology of the Roman Catholic Church. After graduating, he established himself as a teacher at the University of Paris and began advocating educational reform. His ideas and the vigor with which he championed them angered the authorities so that he was three times forbidden to lecture. Then, in 1546, Henry II came to the throne, and Ramus' radical ideas received a more sympathetic hearing. Five years later he was appointed to the faculty of the College of France, where he was free to effect some of his educational reforms. This led eventually to his becoming a Protestant and, after twenty years of teaching and Reformation activities, to his murder on the third day of the massacre of Saint Bartholomew.

The philosophy of education upon which Ramus based his ideas for reform was simple but inclusive: Experience is the source of all knowledge. The student must study the world about him rather than meaningless formulae. All that is true comes from one's observation of the world in which he lives. This knowledge must be organized under basic laws of existence. These are (1) a truth is always a truth and cannot change to fit the will of authority; (2) fields of knowledge must be maintained so that no one area is allowed to encroach upon another; (3) teaching must begin with the general and proceed to the specific, which has its meaning only as it is related to the general; and (4) all knowledge must be put to use, not stored away. This is pragmatic, learning for practical life. It is utilitarian; we learn best what we can make use of.

Ramus was breaking new ground in thinking and in education. His logic was championed at Leyden, in Scottish universities, and at Cambridge. Descartes and the Port Royalists were influenced significantly by his thinking. Gradually his followers were installed in chairs of philosophy in German universities. Here was a true modern looking about him for truth, while insisting that the value of the classics lay not so much in beauty of word and form as in understanding obtained by a perceptive study of men and things.

MICHEL DE MONTAIGNE (1533-1592)

Pierre Equem de Montaigne, a herring merchant who had held many municipal offices in Bordeaux, married Antoinette de Louppes, of a noted family of Spanish Jews. The Montaignes had nine children. The third child, Michel, became head of the family upon the death of his brothers. Anxious that his son have the best possible education, Pierre placed the youth with a German family who spoke only Latin. As a result, when Michel entered the College of Guienne at six years of age, he was speaking Latin fluently. Montaigne came to hate the cruel and stupid teachers under whom he was forced to study, and his experience at college embittered him against all formal education. Graduating at thirteen, he turned to the study of law, probably at Toulouse. He was a favorite at court, a fast liver, and a man with many friends who gave him minor offices and simple court duties in exchange for his company.

Montaigne was an essayist whose writings were read widely and influenced a great deal of French thinking. Among his writings are discussions of education, schools, and teachers. Chief among these are *Of Pedantry, Of the Education of Children,* and *Of the Affection of Fathers to Their Children.*

From his childhood experiences, Montaigne came to believe that the first education of the child is most important and that the selection of a nurse and a tutor set the pattern of one's basic education. Parents, nurses, and tutors should employ love and understanding, not beating and violence, in dealing with children. All the child's early experiences should be pleasant so that he may be led easily and gently to love learning and pursue it avidly.

Sensitive to the fact that the accepted education of his day was too often concerned with filling the memory while leaving "the conscience and understanding empty," he stressed the need for developing prudence and good judgment. In some of his writings he expressed the belief that those least educated were better men and women. Education comes through habits properly built, and the school or tutor must concentrate on correct habits. Only when these have been developed should the student turn to logic, physics, geometry, and rhetoric. His model was Sparta as envisioned by Lycurgus, a society which instilled in its young habits of contempt for fear and love for valor, temperance, prudence, and justice. Ethics was of more concern to him than abstract reasoning.

Montaigne saw education in terms of usefulness. His was a truly pragmatic approach that stressed the functional concept of mind and knowledge. All that is not useful is mere ornament and useless. The teacher must impart knowledge through action. Good habits are not learned by listening to lectures or reading books but rather by living the action desired.

THE CALVINIST REVOLUTION

INTRODUCTION

From very early days, Roman Catholics believed that the earth and all that is on it belongs to God. As the papacy developed, the theory grew that the pope is God's vicar on earth, charged with the responsibility of administering affairs of this world according to God's laws. Thus, in theory, all rule is in the hands of God. The pope, as God's administrator, delegates authority to civil rulers only so long as they obey the will of God as interpreted by the Church. This is theocracy. If a civil ruler does not obey, he can be divested of all authority and another appointed in his place.

The events of the German Reformation led Luther to the position that it is the duty of civil authorities to govern and church authorities to counsel on spiritual matters. It was but a short step from this to the theory that God had given supreme authority to the civil ruler and that each national church is subject to the sovereign. In the attitudes of the princes of Germany are the roots of the theory of the divine right of kingship. National churches are institutions that the ruler uses to build loyalty and shape policy.

The English Reformation developed yet a third theory as to the relation of church and state. A largely political movement, the break from the Roman Church made Henry VIII head of both church and state. Neither was subordinate to the other, but each was equal in the person of the sovereign.

Calvin accepted the Roman Catholic theory, but substituted his church for the Roman Church. Geneva, under his direction, became a theocracy. God was the ruler, and Calvin was "the pope of Geneva." The church represented God on earth, and the state was its civil arm, reponsible for enforcing its decrees. For Calvin and the Calvinists, the education of all the people was church-inspired and religious in essence, and the state enforced all laws regarding instruction of the people.

JOHN CALVIN (1509-1564)

Gerard Calvin and his wife, the former Jeanne le Franc, had a son whom they named Jean. The boy was born on July 10, 1509, at Noyon in Picardy. Destined for the priesthood, he was educated in the household of the noble family of Hangest de Montmor. In 1523 we find him an "out-student" at the *Collège de la Marche* in Paris. This institution was under the regency of Mathurin Cordier, who became a lifelong friend and collaborator of Calvin. From there he went to the *Collège de Montaigu,* where he studied theology.

After this he studied law both at Orleans and Bruges. While in Bruges he studied with the brilliant Italian, Andrea Alciati, whose humanistic interests greatly influenced his most promising student. Upon the death of his father in 1531, Calvin returned to Paris, where the new learning had taken over from medieval scholasticism. There he studied both Greek and Hebrew. Calvin, in tune with the times and caught up in the Renaissance spirit, broke with the Roman Church in 1532-1533 and, finding the atmosphere of Paris somewhat unhealthy for Protestants, left the city and traveled among friends and intellectual cohorts. In August, 1536, he settled in Geneva to become city pastor.

Francis I wavered between the Lutheranism which was penetrating France and the Roman Church. He wished to suppress heresy but feared antagonizing the Protestant princes of Germany. Calvin felt that with the right stimulus, his king could be persuaded to the Protestant cause. In an attempt to furnish this stimulus, he wrote a reasoned defense of Protestantism under the title *Institutes of the Christian Religion.* This work was begun in 1534 in the library of Louis du Tillet at Angouleme. Shortly after it was published, Calvin translated it into French for wider reading. In this work, which shows his dependence upon Luther and Martin Bucer, Calvin, at the age of 26, gave Europe its first scholarly statement of the Protestant faith.

Geneva had thrown off obedience to Rome before Calvin accepted the position of the city's pastor, but the revolt was largely a political move against the duke of Savoy. The city was "but imperfectly enlightened in divine knowledge." To effect this enlightenment, Calvin prepared a statement of twenty-one articles of faith to which all citizens were required to swear allegiance. This was followed by forced attendance at schools located throughout the city, where a catechism drawn up by Calvin and his aides was a major part of the curriculum. Calvin was determined to educate the people to his kind of Protestantism. Fanatical teachers and members of heretical groups in the city rebelled against the rigidity of this procedure. Others resented Calvin's attempt to place the state under control of the church. When, on Easter Sunday, 1538, Calvin refused to administer the sacrament with unleavened bread, a riot broke out, and he and his colleagues were banished from the city.

For the next several years he traveled through Switzerland and France, serving the cities he visited in minor capacities. During his stay at Strassburg, he studied at the gymnasium of Sturm and began developing in his mind a school system that was later to take concrete form in Geneva. During this period he married, and continued to write in an attempt to explain further his conception of Protestant Christianity.

Meanwhile, Geneva was beset with disorder and irreligion. An attempt to restore Catholicism failed, largely as a result of a letter which Calvin wrote, at the request of the authorities, in which he gave a thorough explanation of his position. As his enemies lost power or were unable to control the situation, sentiment for Calvin's return grew. Finally, on September 13, 1541, he re-entered the city to the enthusiastic shouts of the populace—and on his own terms. For twenty-three years he ruled Geneva with an iron hand, made the city into the "Rome of Protestantism," reorganized its education, drew students and interested parties from all Europe, and spread his doctrines of Christianity throughout the western world. Preaching, writing, conferences, administration—all were eventually too much for his frail body, and on the evening of May 27, 1564, he died in the arms of his friend Theodore Beza. The next day he was buried without pomp in a public cemetery called Plain-palais.

Calvin's Educational Theory. Calvin drew his philosophy of education from his theology. Man is inherently evil and by nature prone to sin. If left to himself he will inevitably become corrupt. His only hope lies in an environment that polices him from the day of his birth until his coffin is closed in death. Calvin sought to make Geneva such an environment. In Calvin's Geneva, parents, friends, associates, the government, and the church were of one mind. Wherever the child turned, he saw goodness. Whenever he felt the urge to do evil, he found an authority devoted to rightness admonishing him severely. This was truly a theocratic state, bent on protecting the child from evil and holding the adult in the clutches of the good.

In Calvin's thinking, church, state, school, and family were one institution devoted to disciplining, instructing, and training the citizenry according to the will of God. At home each parent was obligated to teach the catechism and principles of Christian living to all children residing therein. A *consistorium* supervised this phase of education, inspecting each home as often as necessary to see that no alien ideas or false interpretations crept in. The church was a place for worship and instruction in the catechism. The state was molded by the church so that all its laws and procedures supported the puritanical ideas of the pastors.

THE SCHOOLS OF GENEVA

Calvin was a humanist who could not bring himself to accept the vernacular as a language of scholarship. The many vernacular schools in Geneva were reduced to four, one in each quarter of the city, and only boys who could not learn Latin were allowed to attend. Education of girls was left in the home, where they learned the catechism and as much religion as the parents thought fit. Should a parent wish to give his daughters more instruction, he employed a tutor who came into the home. The state required that this come under its supervision in order to protect the mothers of future citizens from evil.

For Calvin, an educational system was essential to the life of any city. From his return to Geneva in 1541 until 1559, he struggled to build in the city a model school system. The weak Latin Grammar schools that had enjoyed municipal support for many years were abolished, and in their place appeared a school structure consisting of a gymnasium and an academy. The former was modeled after Sturm's gymnasium at Strassburg. It was a Latin preparatory school of seven grades (Sturm's had ten). Although it was supervised by the city and its teachers employed by the authorities, it was supported by tuition fees. The curriculum was humanistic. While Calvin insisted that all children be instructed in the correct religion in their homes, he never envisaged advanced education for all. The academy was for those superior students who would become leaders in church and state, an intellectual elite.

The academy contained the advanced grades of this consolidated school. It offered instruction in Greek, Hebrew, mathematics, physics, ethics, logic, rhetoric, oratory, and poetry. Ten professors staffed this academy. Among these was Mathurin Cordier, a friend of Calvin from his college days.

This school became famous throughout the western world. Students came from all over Europe, and from it went young men trained to spread Calvinism in other lands. The University of Leyden in Holland, Edinburgh in Scotland, Emmanuel College at Cambridge, and Harvard College in Massachusetts were replicas of Calvin's school.

Calvin made Geneva into a school of Protestantism and an environment every phase of which was dedicated to acculturating the child to Christianity. His school was but one institution of a social complex ruled by the church. There a city was remade into a religious community along Calvinistic lines, and from its borders went men to make Calvinism the religion of much of western culture for many generations.

THE SPREAD OF CALVINISM

Although Calvinism began in Geneva as a theocratic state, it was not allied to any government or reigning monarch. It was carried to Switzerland, France, England, Scotland, the Netherlands, Germany, and the American colonies. It gave birth to the Reformed Church that recognized no geographic boundaries. Wherever it went, men turned to an educational system steeped in religion and morals and to an intellectual leadership that could be nourished only in the finest of schools.

John Knox (*circa* 1505-1572) was a Scottish priest, historian, and, by 1547, preacher of a fully developed Protestantism at Saint Andrews. When Saint Andrews fell to the French fleet in June, 1547, Knox was thrown into the galleys, to be released nineteen months later through the influence of Edward VI of England. Then followed years of preaching and travel. This included a period when he found a congenial pastorate in Geneva where he was completely converted to Calvinism. Though he was exiled from Scotland and once condemned to be burned should he ever come home, conditions changed as the Protestants became more militant and the authorities less adamant. In the end he was allowed to reside in his homeland and preach more or less freely.

When, in 1560, long-standing disagreements between England and Scotland were settled, Knox, who had become the leading Protestant in all Scotland, led Parliament to a decree abolishing the Roman Church and making Calvinism, as expressed in the Presbyterian Church, the religion of the land. In December of 1560, Knox drafted the *First Book of Discipline,* a plan for an autonomous church and a government similar to that in Geneva. This church would control the state and all its functions, including education.

In this guide to a Calvinist Scotland, Knox put religion and morals in control of the church. To insure obedience to the church's standards, he proposed a graded system of education with an elementary school in every church, a secondary school in every town, and a university in every city. He further proposed that all the wealth of monasteries and churches and all tithes be devoted to supporting this educational structure and to erasing poverty. Knox was eager to reproduce Geneva on Scottish soil, but the lords of Scotland would not agree. They were not averse to church control of elementary education, but demanded that secondary schools be left in the hands of the towns. The Presbyterian Church did become the established church of Scotland, but the educational pattern so dear to the heart of Knox and his followers was not to take form for many years to come.

The Netherlands was divided, with Catholicism in the south and the Protestant Dutch Republic in the north. In 1576 the Prince of Orange made all religious persuasions equal, and Holland became a refuge for the persecuted from every land. This heralded an age of prosperity and creative development seldom matched in all history. Soon Calvinism was the most popular faith and its devotion to schools ingrained in the lives of the people.

The University of Leyden, established in 1575, soon became the center of progressive teaching and learning in Europe. Its faculty was Protestant. As the very efficient pre-Reformation schools were taken over by Protestantism, the appropriated revenues of Catholic agencies were channeled into the support of common schools. The Dutch Reformed Church, Calvinistic in theology, cooperated with state authorities in all matters of education, often furnishing the push necessary for action.

As a result, there grew in Holland a three-tiered educational structure. At its base were common schools for the masses. These were designed to prepare individuals for the thriving and expanding commercial life of the towns, ground the young in those principles of democracy that had become basic to Dutch government, and insure correct moral and religious training for the young. The second tier was the Latin Grammar school, under control of municipal authorities and designed to prepare boys for entrance into the professions. Latin and Greek were usually taught here. Some schools added French, mathematics, and philosophy. The third tier was the university, an institution most truly expressive of the progressive, free intellectual life of the Republic. It was a free school and university, an intellectual haven for creative minds from Holland, France and England. It is estimated that during the seventeenth century more than 2,000 students from England enrolled in classes at the university at Leyden alone.

THE CATHOLIC COUNTER-REFORMATION

INTRODUCTION

Luther, Calvin, and other leaders of the Protestant movement were members of the Roman Catholic Church who came to believe, after much soul-searching, that the highway to the future lay outside the traditional Church. It must be recognized that others, equally distressed at conditions within and without the Church, believed that a reformation of the Church was possible and necessary. They realized that feudalism was giving way to a new social and political order, that the Renaissance with its emphasis upon classical civilization and literature was a challenge to medieval Christianity, that scholasticism could not contain the new knowledge that was filling men's minds, that many of the practices of the Church's hierarchy were in need of rethinking, and that the time had come for a thorough overhauling of Catholic theology. These people were sensitive to the problems that Protestants held in focus but felt that abandonment of the ancient Church was not the solution.

The Roman hierarchy recognized that nationalism was no longer a thing to be ignored, but a force reshaping the face of Europe. One world under Christ was the goal of the Church, and it would remain so. No longer could the Church ignore national loyalties and the desire arising everywhere for freedom, economic independence, and national self-containment. Roman Christianity had to come up to the times or perish. This was a time for realistic thinking and action, and many leaders were ready.

Even before the Protestant revolt, the Church had begun to move into the modern world. Much of the Renaissance was absorbed into the Church, and churchmen became its sponsors. The new learning crept into schools and religious orders and into the papacy itself. Often a priest or bishop was a scholarly gentleman, quoting the ancients and espousing their virtues. Church orders incorporated classical scholarship and made it central in their school curricula.

The Council of Trent, called in 1545, was the culmination of a long period of agitation by churchmen for a general council of the Church, with authority to recommend reforms of morals, doctrine, and administration. The council failed to do much that was needed, forces of conservatism were everywhere in evidence, and agreement was often made impossible by the greed and self-seeking of some powerful prelates. In spite of all its failures, the Council did develop a clear statement of Catholic doctrine that became the basis for future action. It was effective in correcting some of the abuses of authority about which the Protestants complained. The licentiousness of the clergy was condemned, and a new call was made for spiritual devotion to principles of primitive Christianity.

At the same time, the Church recognized the seriousness of the Protestant revolt, and some Church devotees turned to bloody repressive measures to stamp out the movement. The Spanish Inquisition aimed to suppress heretical ideas, while the *Index Expurgatorius* was designed to keep such ideas from spreading. The Duke of Alva, with the blessing of Philip II, led a vicious war against Protestantism in the Netherlands between 1567 and 1609 in an attempt to crush all revolt against the Church. After several cruel and bloody years, the Netherlands was split to form Holland, which remained liberal and Protestant, and Belgium, which was held within the Church. The Thirty

Years' War, 1618-1648, devastated Moravia and embittered thousands who could not justify in their hearts the persecutions, cruelties, and vengeance done in the name of Christian love. While Protestants were busy building a new approach to the religious life in a new political, economic, and social world, the Roman Church was equally busy reforming itself and striving to suppress revolt where it had already broken out, while appeasing those forces elsewhere that might lead eventually to open rebellion. While there was much bigotry, selfishness, insensitivity, and self-seeking on both sides, the main stream of development was characterized by the work of earnest men striving to adjust the Christian tradition to a changing world. They disagreed in doctrine and in method, but their goal was the same.

THE SOCIETY OF JESUS

Among the many efforts to reform the Roman Church during the sixteenth century was the Society of Jesus, usually known as the Jesuit Order. To understand the Society, its aims and methodology, one must know Ignatius of Loyola.

Inigo Lopez was born at the castle of Loyola in the province of Guipuzcoa, Spain, in 1491. A product of both feudalism and a noble family of chivalric background, the boy was sent at an early age to serve as page at the court of Ferdinand and Isabella. There he received his education in the tradition of Spanish nobility. At twenty-six he took service with the duke of Najera and began a career of arms. Fighting in the French attack on Pampeluna, the capital of Navarre, he was wounded in the leg and hospitalized for a considerable time. During his convalescence he read *Flowers of the Saints* and a *Life of Christ* by Ludolphus of Saxony. These, and the realization that he would never again be able to lead armed forces because of his injury, caused a crisis in his life. After a period of self-searching, punctuated by visions and other spiritual experiences, he determined to turn his back on his family and his noble state and consecrate himself to the service of the Church. He made a pilgrimage to Jerusalem in 1523 to help rescue the Holy Land from the Turks. Fear that the fanatical Turks might destroy all Christians in Jerusalem if aggravated by any attempt to challenge their authority caused the Franciscans in charge of the holy places to order him back to Spain.

After four years of study and travel in Spain, during which he met the famous Spanish scholar, Juan Luis Vives, Ignatius went to the University of Paris where he joined a group of devoted scholars, who with him, at the Feast of the Assumption in 1534, assembled in the crypt of the church of Sainte Mary on Montmartre and dedicated themselves to the services of the Church. On September 27, 1540, after several unsuccessful attempts to return to the Holy Land and after a series of unusual spiritual experiences which brought charges of heresy, Ignatius and his little band of followers were recognized by Paul III as the Society of Jesus. Ignatius was chosen general and the organization planned along military lines. A constitution governing the order was written, and Ignatius completed his *Book of Spiritual Exercises,* one of the world's most moving books.

Ignatius remained in charge of the order until shortly before his death, when ill health and infirmities made it necessary for him to turn over his administrative duties to others. Stricken by a fever, he died suddenly in Rome, July 31, 1556.

The Jesuit Order was organized along military lines with a general who had absolute authority over all members. His only superior was the pope. Each member had to take orders from his superior without question. Obedience was a cardinal virtue of the order. The Jesuits divided the world into provinces, and over each province reigned a *provincial* who was appointed by the general.

The pope saw in the new order an effective weapon against Protestantism. Consequently, the Jesuits were ordered to move throughout Europe to combat Protestant ideas wherever found, to win back rebellious lands if possible, and to hold within the folds of the Church those areas not yet contaminated by revolt.

While the Society acceded to the will of its superior, the pope, and became the Church's most effective weapon against Protestantism, it also moved into the realm of reform. Ignatius, a military man at heart, could not tolerate the laxity, immorality, and ostentation that he found prevalent in many of the holy orders and among the clergy. He saw the Church in need of many reforms if it was to meet the challenge of Protestantism. Those who succeeded him in command of the Order were relentless in their demands for a pure, dedicated, and militant Church. Some felt that this was too fanatical, and a bitter struggle developed between the Order and other Church organizations. The power of the order within the Church and at Catholic courts, doctrinal differences that developed as the order shaped its theological platform, and the deistic thinkers among Catholic intellectuals who hated the ultramontane teachings of the order led eventually to pressures which the papacy could not resist. In 1773, Clement XIV found it necessary "to cut down the mast to save the ship." In his *Brief of Suppression* he wrote, "For the sake of peace, and because the Society can no longer attain the aims for which it was founded, and on secret grounds which we enclose in our heart, we suppress the said Society." While this decree of the pope was accepted by most of the Church, Frederick II of Prussia and Catherine II of Russia protected the Society. When Frederick's successor exiled the brothers and confiscated the wealth of the order, Catherine became their sole protector. After fifty years of more or less clandestine existence, the Jesuits were restored to favor by Pius VII in 1814. From that moment the order grew in power and importance, attracting men of unusual talents and abilities, teaching and preaching throughout the world, winning an increasing number of converts to Catholicism from among the intellectuals, and publishing polemical and apologetic literature in almost all languages of the world.

THE JESUITS AND EDUCATION

When a Jesuit was accepted into the society, he swore "a special concern for the education of boys." As the order moved against Protestantism to save Catholic Europe from "contamination," it became evident to many that the most effective weapon in the struggle was education. When a careful survey of the educational facilities of the Church was made, it was discovered that while many agencies were concerned with elementary education and were doing effective teaching on this level, the Church was weak on the secondary level and in the whole area of college education. It was here that the Jesuits decided to concentrate their efforts.

The task which the society accepted was exacting and challenging, taxing the ingenuity and understanding of the best minds that could be recruited. Future clerics were being educated in schools where licentious living was unrestricted. The Renaissance was winning even the clergy to a love of paganism and a disrespect for the austerity and simplicity of the Christian life. The task of education, as the Jesuits conceived it, was to weave this Renaissance spirit and the ancient classics into the Christian ideal of obedience and submission to the Church, to turn the new individualism born of Renaissance thinking to God's service. They saw much good in the new learning and the creative urge which it was releasing, but recognized that it had to be incorporated into the concept of a universal Church that demanded abject submission to its divine will.

To meet this challenge, the Jesuits began one of the most remarkable ventures in education, construction of the *Ratio Studiorum* or Plan of Studies. A group of skilled educators was assembled to write a guide to teachers that would incorporate the ideals of the order, present a curriculum, and develop a methodology consistent with the goals of the order and the best educational thinking of the times. When completed, this was circulated among Jesuit schools, with instructions to try it out over a period of time, discover weaknesses, and report the findings to the central office. These reports were used as bases for revisions of the document. After a period of experimentation and constant rewriting in the light of actual classroom experience, the order issued a final draft in 1599. This was a detailed book of instructions dealing with educational aims of the order, course of study, administration, methods of teaching, discipline, and education of teachers. Not even in modern times, with all our knowledge of child development and teaching techniques, has a plan been developed with more care and scientific understanding. Today the *Ratio Studiorum,* with some minor revisions made in 1832, is still the basis for Jesuit education.

The Jesuits called their schools "colleges" and built them to cover two levels of instruction. The lower college accepted boys at ten and carried them through five or six years of instruction. There were three grammar classes, a class in the humanities, and one in rhetoric. From there the boys moved into the higher college or university, where they studied philosophy, mathematics, and natural science. Religion dominated every level of this education.

Each college was self-supporting, having an endowment sufficient for all its needs. Instruction was free, but gifts were always accepted. Only carefully trained Jesuits were allowed to teach in these institutions. At the head of each college was a *rector* appointed by the pope and responsible directly to the provincial in whose area the college was located. The rector was assisted by a "prefect of studies" and a "prefect of discipline." They carefully supervised all teaching, examinations, discipline, and life among the students.

Latin was the only language of instruction in Jesuit colleges. Greek was subordinate, and the vernacular was forbidden at all times. Texts were carefully edited to cull out any pagan influence that might warp the thinking of the students, and notes were inserted explaining all passages from the Christian viewpoint. Subject matter, methods of teaching, and other school matters were explained in detail, and no departures from the *Ratio* were permitted.

Education, according to the Jesuits, should be made as easy and pleasurable as possible. This was most difficult since a great deal that was taught had little or no bearing upon the daily life of the pupils. Teachers surmounted this difficulty by introducing rivalry as the major motivating device. Each pupil was pitted against another of similar ability, each class was assigned a rival, each school sought to top another school, and each teacher had his opponent whom he strove to outstrip. In addition to rivalry, the Jesuits used the sense of duty, love, desire for praise, fear of disgrace, reward and punishment, prizes, badges of honor, and positions of leadership. In short, these educators knew many methods for stimulating boys to learn.

The most used method was memory. The mind, they believed, should be stored with knowledge in abundance, and repetition was the best way to attain this goal. The teacher would explain in great detail the lesson for the following day, anticipating difficulties that might arise and clearing away any possible misunderstandings. Then the student learned the lesson verbatim. At lesson time he recited the material, discussed it until clear ideas developed, and was helped to see its relationship to all that he had learned before. Daily, weekly, monthly, and yearly reviews were employed to hold the learned material in the minds of the pupils. Thoroughness, exactness, and understanding were combined in this teaching method.

Jesuit teachers received the most careful and thorough training of any instructors at the time. Young men wishing to teach were accepted at the close of their work in the lower college. There followed two years of moral and spiritual discipline, during which the novitiate searched his soul and sought to develop self-control. Having succeeded at this level, the candidate was sent back to school for one to three years to learn the subjects he would teach. During this time he observed master teachers and came to understand their methodology. This *juniorate* was followed by three years of study in the fields of philosophy, mathematics, and natural science at a university of the Jesuit Order. At last the candidate was ready to begin teaching in the lower college under the supervision of a trained teacher who corrected and encouraged him. After three or four years of teaching, he would enter the *house of studies* in his province to devote four years to intensive theological study and the practice of spiritual exercises. Only then was he ready for ordination and complete control of a class. This was a long, rigorous, and thorough training for teaching. It left nothing to chance or individual judgment.

Did Jesuit education succeed? This has been debated for generations, and many positions have been taken. It must be recognized that the Jesuits accepted a specialized task, a war against the spread of Protestantism. In discharging this task, they felt no concern for the education of the masses of children. To them, the point of attack had to be the superior youths of the land, young men who would be leaders in their generation. Here could be the seed-beds of revolt. They were certain that those who could control the minds of elite young people during their formative years would control the destiny of Europe and the Church.

Accepting the validity of much of the criticism leveled against it down the ages, one must recognize that the Society did stop the spread of Protestantism, while training young men who were to make their mark in the world about them. Some of the finest scholars, scientists, and leaders within the Catholic Church were Jesuits, and pupils from Jesuit schools were to be found on the frontiers of every social or intellectual movement.

CHAPTER 10

Seventeenth Century
Realism and Education

THE REFORMATION LEGACY

By the close of the sixteenth century, western Europe had responded to the new political, economic, social, and religious forces that had come into being, and life in the nations of the West was never to be the same again. National interests had challenged the Church and won in many places. For great masses, this world had become more fascinating than the world to come. A consciousness of dignity, worth, and power was changing the ideological orientation of men, giving them courage to attack ancient tradition, question the most sacred authorities, and dare to invent new ways of dealing with their environment. A revolution had taken place that was to affect all areas of human living and start man upon a scientific quest that would eventually flower in the atomic and space age.

This revolution could be seen clearly in education. No longer was man willing to leave his schools in the hands of the Church. He moved to take control of them for advancement in matters of *this* world. The superior man was no longer the cleric skilled in scholastic subtleties, but the man in whom the best that classical tradition, chivalry, and Christianity could offer were integrated. The goal of education, as envisioned by most educators, was to combine Greek and Roman beauty of expression and clear thinking, chivalric sensitivity to the human, and Christian piety in a way of life that would become the ideal of the future. In pursuit of this, the Reformation had exalted the teacher far above anything known in the past. Men were encouraged to devote a lifetime to the profession. Cities and small towns sought good teachers and inaugurated them with pomp and ceremony. In search of guidelines to better education, scholars turned to Plato, Aristotle, Plutarch, Cicero, and Quintilian. Here they found basic principles of education, and curricula. From this well of understanding they drew both ideas and inspiration to nourish a new education that would serve the ends of the dawning modern age.

School surveys conducted by Reformation educators revealed many weaknesses and suggested paths to follow if schools were to be strengthened. Guided by these studies, princes, cities, and municipal units were rebuilding their schools, revising their curricula, and training their teachers. Careful and expert supervision of schools and teaching was developed. Attempts were being made to modernize school structures.

The Society of Jesus, a tool of the Roman Church in its fight against Protestantism, saw education as its best weapon. It trained teachers, erected schools, and developed curricula and methodology suited to its needs.

The Reformation era had made a beginning. It left much to be desired. Ciceronianism, disputes over theological questions that were no longer vital to men, ignorance and superstition among the masses, and a desire on the part of many Protestants to substitute their own censorship, rigid theology, and heresy hunting for that of the Roman Church, all served to retard progress. Nevertheless, a beginning had been made, and the gates of the future had been opened.

SOME SEVENTEENTH CENTURY EDUCATIONAL THEORISTS

WOLFGANG RATKE (RATICH) (1571-1635)

Ratke was educated at the gymnasium in Hamburg and the University of Rostock. An ardent Lutheran and a man of progressive thinking, he turned to educational reform after coming under the influence of Bacon's ideas concerning learning through experience. After a visit to England, he took up residence in Amsterdam, the center of scientific learning and the most prosperous and culturally oriented city in Europe at that time. Here he studied classical languages, including Hebrew, and developed a method of teaching languages that he claimed would give a student mastery of a tongue quickly and pleasantly.

In 1612, he was able to present to the electors at Frankfort a statement of his educational principles and goals. In this, he proposed to teach foreign languages better and more effectively in a much shorter time than ever before, produce textbooks in all the sciences, and organize a series of preparatory schools that would thoroughly instruct all children wishing to enter higher schools. He was outlining a basic educational structure that would revolutionize instruction, make efficient the study of the arts and sciences, and unify the people with one language, one government, and one religion.

He was so persuasive that several princes of Germany appointed committees of scholars to examine his claims and evaluate their effectiveness. Duchess Dorothea Maria of Weimar was so pleased with what was reported to her that she invited Ratke to Weimar to establish a court school in which she, her son, and her sister could learn Latin. Evidently he was highly successful, since the Duchess and her sister remained his fast friends and made it possible for him to test his plan more extensively.

Prince Ludwig von Anhalt-Kothen met Ratke through the sisters and offered him a school building, a printing press for publishing texts, type settings in six languages, and all the help and material necessary to put his method into practice. In addition, Ludwig conscripted 231 boys and 202 girls as students. The school was planned as a demonstration unit, in which teachers of the method could be instructed and prepared to teach Greek, Latin, and Hebrew "in less time . . . than could be done by any other method . . . and also with much less pain." The school consisted of three lower classes in which the vernacular was taught, a fourth in which pupils started Latin, and a sixth offering instruction in Greek. Other subjects taught in this school were arithmetic, religion, and music.

Ratke was a strange and fearful person. He believed that he had discovered a magic method of learning, which he was unwilling to disclose except for a high price. Even then he was fearful that he would be betrayed. Headed by such a man, the school failed miserably. Ratke was imprisoned and forced to sign a statement affirming that he had made claims which he knew he could not fulfill. A fanatical Lutheran who hated all other faiths, a greedy, selfish, suspicious man, he was constantly quarreling with his superiors and was fearful of his co-workers. The method never had a real chance to justify itself in practice.

What was this magic and highly secret method of teaching? Ratke was a profound student of human nature and especially of the mind. His findings led him to the conviction that good instructional methodology must be based on a clear understanding of the nature of the mind and the way the individual learns. He came to realize that traditional devotion to rote memory, devoid of understanding, was useless, and that pleasure was a more powerful force in learning than pain. From his understanding of the true nature of learning, he reasoned that all instruction must follow the course of nature, the natural order of the developing child's mind and that only one thing should be studied at a time until it is mastered, and, finally, that mastery comes after adequate repetition.

Since that which is familiar is learned more easily and quickly than that which is strange, children should begin their studies with their vernaculars and only later move to the study of foreign or classical languages. Violence, brutality, and external motivation are poor substitutes for an inherent interest in the assigned tasks.

Ratke believed that the instructor should be consistent in all his teaching, presenting similar subjects in the same way. A convert to Bacon's inductive method, he insisted that the learner first experience things, and only then move to explanations and investigations of parts. Language proceeds from things to words, and we learn something only as we see it in its proper relation to other things.

Such was the famous Ratke method of teaching and learning. In his day it was a secret to be revealed only to those who could pay his price. Today it is the method of good schools everywhere.

JOHANN AMOS COMENIUS (1592–1670)

Johann Amos Comenius has been called "the broadest-minded, the most far-seeing, the most comprehensive, and withal the most practical of all the writers to have put pen to paper on the subject of education."[1] Thus evaluated at the close of the nineteenth century, he had practically no influence on education during his lifetime. While his textbooks were used throughout the world, one being translated into twelve European languages in addition to Arabic, Persian, and Turkish, and while his theoretical works are full of the most modern and progressive ideas and understandings, educators of the seventeenth and following centuries ignored him.

HIS LIFE

Comenius, born at Nivnitz in Moravia in the kingdom of Bohemia, was an Austro-Slav. His family were members of the old church of the Moravian Brethren, followers of John Huss and related theologically to Wycliffe in England and the Waldensians of central Europe. Education was a major concern of these people. They had established the custom of teaching religion in their homes, had supported elementary and secondary schools, and had made the University of Prague the

---

1. M. W. Keatinge, *The Great Didactic of John Amos Comenius* (London: Adam and Charles Black, 1896), p. 98.

most progressive and dynamic institution of higher learning in all Europe. Although his family had some wealth, the early death of both his parents and mismanagement of the estate by his guardian left the boy destitute. At the age of twelve he was enrolled in a folk school at Straznice, where he was living with an aunt. There he learned Czech, the catechism, and a little arithmetic. Most important of all, he came to despise the methods employed in these poor village schools. He later characterized them as "so severe that schools have been looked on as terrors for boys and slaughterhouses of the mind." At sixteen he was enrolled in a Latin school at Prerov maintained by the Moravian Brethren. There he was forced to study along with boys of six or seven. The methods used were no better than those in the folk school.

At twenty, Comenius entered the College of Herborn in Nassau, intent upon becoming a minister. He met and became a fast friend of John Henry Alsted, a prodigious writer and Calvinist theologian deeply concerned with educational reform. Alsted introduced him to the ideas of Ratke and the educational progress being made in the Dutch Republic. After several short trips to centers of learning and culture, including a visit to Amsterdam, Comenius entered the University of Heidelberg, leading center of Calvinist and reform learning. There he came under the influence of Johann Valentin Andreä and David Pareus. While at Heidelberg he purchased the original manuscript of Copernicus' *De Revolutionibus Orbium Coelestium.* There also he became a friend of George Hartlib, younger brother of Samuel Hartlib, the English merchant and reformer who was influential in forming the Royal Society.

After some travel, during which he made friends with many of the leading spirits of the day, Comenius returned to Moravia, where he taught in a Latin school operated by the Moravian Brethren, and began to write theological and educational books. In 1616 he was ordained a priest in the church of the Moravian Brethren at Zeravice. This turned his energies to religious matters and was the beginning of a crusade to unite all Protestants against what he considered to be antichrist, the Roman Church. In 1618 he accepted an offer to become pastor and superintendent of schools in Fulneck, a leading center of the Brethren.

The Thirty Years' War began in 1618 when Comenius was twenty-six years of age. As Catholics and Protestants were locked in bitter combat, Europe was devastated beyond imagination. At the battle of White Mountain, the Protestant Bohemians were defeated and their leaders executed. This was followed by a period of systematic and brutal persecution of all non-Catholics, except Jews, in southern Germany, Moravia, and Bohemia. The Moravian Brethren were special targets of

Catholic forces, and every effort was made to exterminate them as the vilest of heretics. The only sin of these warm-hearted, humble, self-sacrificing, and simple people was their evangelical Protestant faith, a faith that had been anathema to militant Catholics since the burning of Huss. Comenius identified himself with his people, taught and worked among them even though he was a hunted man, became their bishop, and championed their cause wherever he could find listeners.

When persecution became excessively violent and he had lost all his property, Comenius fled Moravia with only the clothes on his back. He was forced to leave his wife, who was expecting, and his son. After the baby came, she went to live with her mother in Prerov where, in 1622, she and both children died of the plague. Meanwhile, Comenius wandered throughout Europe, seeking a home for the exiled Brethren and tutoring the children of his many protectors. Finally he settled at Leszno (Lissa) in Poland, where he became rector of the gymnasium and, for thirteen years, ministered to his people, wrote religious and educational books, and developed his new and better methods of teaching.

In 1641, at the invitation of Samuel Hartlib, English scholar and philanthropist, Comenius visited England to help establish a college that would embody many of his cherished ideas. This was a most disappointing journey. Hardly had he arrived on English soil when the Irish Rebellion broke out, and Parliament was far too busy to consider any of his proposals. However, he did voice some ideas and set in motion certain forces that contributed to the founding later of the Royal Society, a clearinghouse for scientific information and research. It was on this visit that he met John Winthrop, then governor of Massachusetts, and received a half-joking offer of the presidency of Harvard College, which he refused even to consider.

After the failure of his mission in London, Comenius accepted the invitation of Ludevic de Geer, a Hollander living in Sweden, to prepare a series of textbooks for Swedish schools. For the next six years, under the autocratic direction of Oxensteirna, the chancellor of Sweden, and John Skyte, chancellor of the University of Upsala, he wrote texts, grammars, and lexicons for the schools of Sweden.

By the time this task was completed, Comenius had become the most sought-after educator in all Europe. Cardinal Richelieu invited him to France to assist in establishing an academy of science, an invitation which he turned down. Leaders in other countries asked his help, and he was in correspondence with scholars and educators in both Europe and America. Meanwhile he was writing one book after another on education, religion, mysticism, and government.

By 1650, he decided to accept an invitation to establish a school at Sarospatak, in Hungary. This was a complete failure. After a time of wandering and persecution he settled in Amsterdam, where from 1654 until the end of his life he devoted his energies to writing, teaching, preaching, and the care of his rapidly diminishing flock of Brethren.

HIS PANSOPHIC DREAM

Science was opening windows on a fascinating and challenging world. Knowledge was growing in all directions, and the mind of man was exploring a new world of which his immediate ancestors could not even dream. Comenius, more than most scholars of his age, sensed what was happening, and was enamored of the possibilities that seemed to open before him. His imaginative mind conceived the idea of amassing all knowledge and teaching it to all men to the limit of their individual capacities. This was *pansophia.*

To Comenius, this meant a great encyclopedia to which all scholars would contribute and in which would be assembled all the knowledge man had discovered. His friend and former teacher, Alsted, had attempted this in a 120-volume work. Comenius recognized the worth of this endeavor, but realized that no man could master all knowledge and that a true compilation must be the work of many scholars. It meant, further, a great center of learning and research, where all inventions and discoveries could be assembled, where scholars would have the facilities to study and investigate, and where students could study and learn. It also meant that a new and better method of teaching had to be developed if each individual was to be able to learn from all the fields of knowledge to the limit of his capacity.

Inherent in this *pansophic* idea were two noble, if idealistic, affirmations of faith. One of these challenged the traditional doctrine of human depravity. It affirmed that mankind is capable of improvement through the development of his intellectual powers. Man comes into this world bearing the seeds of both evil and good, but he is not doomed to succumb to evil. Given proper stimulation, the seeds of virtue and piety are capable of unlimited cultivation. Man can return to his former state of purity and divinity. The other affirmation of faith was Comenius' belief that all men, even the peasant masses, can be educated. To accomplish this, all children, of whatever economic or cultural status, should be educated together, "that they may stimulate and urge on one another." All differences of sex, religion, social position, and economic advantage were to be disregarded and each individual judged on his intellectual ability.

His Writings

It would require many pages to discuss adequately all the writings of Comenius. He was a man with several missions, and wrote incessantly to further his beliefs and inform the world. Among his pamphlets and books are religious treatises, sermons, church histories, devotional material, commentaries, hymnals, catechisms, translations, works of prophecy, letters on many subjects to men in all walks of life, textbooks and guides for instruction, and major attempts at developing principles for a new and better education. We can be concerned here only with his major writings in the field of education.

Comenius' monumental discussion of educational theory and principles is the *Didactica Magna (The Great Didactic)*. This was written and revised many times over a period of years, first in Czech and finally in Latin. It was published in Amsterdam in 1657. Here he presented his mature thinking about child growth and development, about the place of education in the eternal plan for man's soul, about pansophic learning and methodology, about the several schools that comprise the educational ladder, and about "the art of education" and school management. The chief purpose of this book, he wrote, was "to seek and find a method of instruction, by which teachers may teach less, but learners may learn more."

Another theoretical work appeared under the title *The School of Infancy.* Here Comenius showed a fairly accurate understanding of the development of children from birth to six years of age. The home, he held, is the first school, and the child's education must begin at the mother's knee. This is a textbook for mothers who wish to begin their children's education correctly. It anticipates in great detail later appreciations of the value of pre-school education. At this age the child must learn to use his senses accurately, become a cooperative member of his family group, and live as a member of the religious community. Here the mother begins the pansophic education of her child in terms of his level of maturity.

In 1631 Comenius published *Januae Linguarum Reserata (Gate of Tongues Unlocked),* an introductory textbook for students beginning the study of Latin. The book attempted to arrange all the principal words of the Latin language in 1,200 sentences, each word appearing only once. After this text was used for a while, it was found to be too advanced for beginners, and Comenius wrote a more elementary text called *Vestibulum* or the *Vestibule to the Gate of Tongues Unlocked.* The aim was to simplify and grade instruction more to the child's ability, to teach each word in relation to the thing to which it referred, and to help the child identify things through Latin words.

While at Sarospatak, Comenius prepared a plan for his ideal school, *Sketch of a Pansophic School,* to guide him in developing the school he had been commissioned to organize. Although the "sketch" proposed seven graded classes, only three were ever in operation. By this time he was convinced that even his *Vestibulum* was too advanced for beginners. This led him to write one of the most famous texts of all times, *Orbis Sensualium Pictus (The World in Pictures).* Here he combined pictures, the vernacular, and Latin. On each page, covering about half the page, was a picture in which were many objects. Below the picture were two versions of a story, one in the vernacular and the other in Latin, dealing with the picture and the objects it contained. Each important Latin word was numbered, and the same number appeared on the vernacular word and on the object in the picture to which the word referred. For example, in an English version which was published in 1887, page eighty-seven contains a picture of a potter at his wheel, and about him are objects of his trade and products of his wheel. Below the picture and to the left is the story in English, beginning with "The Potter sitting over a wheel maketh Pots . . . " To the right of the page is the same story in Latin. The word "Potter" is paralleled by the Latin word "Figulas," and each is numbered "1." This same number appears on the potter in the picture. In this way Comenius sought to make the meaning of words visual.

The Aim of Education

Comenius contributed much to the easier and more pleasant method of learning languages, but words to him were only keys to open the treasures of knowledge. Education in its most complete form was preparation for life here and hereafter through the mastery of facts about the universe. We learn, he wrote, "not for the school, but for life."

Man is God's most excellent, most complete creation. His final end is beyond this life, in eternity. This life is merely preparation for eternal life. To prepare for eternity man must know all things, have power over all things, including himself, and refer himself and all things to God. The school must teach children all knowledge to the limit of their capacity, make them virtuous, and instill in them love and worship of God.

Children, he believed, are not born human. They come into this world with an innate capacity for becoming human if properly educated. Therefore education was, for him, no frill or polish that may or may not be added. It was absolutely necessary if one was to develop his human nature. Furthermore, it must begin at birth and continue until the individual has become as human as his basic nature permits. All schools with which Comenius had had experience gave the child a mass of verbiage which he had to memorize in meaningless fashion. This, to him, was less than no education. True Christian education "leads to virtue and piety." This calls for good teachers equipped with good textbooks and schooled in good methods.

THE EDUCATIONAL LADDER

Comenius envisioned a system of schools beginning with the birth of the child and continuing until adulthood, so situated that every person would have easy access to learning. He saw all subjects graded to the maturity of the child, a uniform daily and yearly schedule, a room and a teacher for each class, and hours of study determined by the child's capacity to learn. He saw each pupil studying in his properly graded class with others of his same maturity, having his own textbooks containing all the material to be learned in each class, and doing his work in the classroom under guidance of a well-trained teacher.

Since education begins at birth, every home must be a school. This he called *Schola materna* or School of the Mother's Knee. He wrote his *School of Infancy* as a handbook for mothers. It gave the mother detailed instruction in all phases of infant education: physical, mental, expressional, manual, moral, social, and religious. Here the child begins his learning of all subjects through activities suited to his interests and abilities. Woven into the book are instructions as to the use of fairy tales, Mother Goose rhymes, play, music, and construction. The mother is the child's first teacher and the home his first school.

At six, Comenius would have the child enter a *Schola vernacula* or vernacular school where he would study his native language for the next six years. Every child, regardless of rank or sex, must go to this school and receive instruction in "desegregated" classes, an almost unheard-of innovation. Children should be compelled to attend this school, located in every hamlet or village. The aim of this education was to train the sense organs, imagination, and memory through reading and writing in the vernacular, practical arithmetic, music, religion, general history, economics and politics, and the mechanical arts. Instruction must be without compulsion. Comenius was convinced that a properly motivated child would learn gladly; consequently, when one had to be beaten or forced in any way to learn, it "is the fault of no one but the teacher, who does not know how to make his pupil receptive of knowledge, or does not take the trouble to do so."

When the child had mastered the work of the vernacular school, he might progress to the *Schola Latina,* or Latin school, if he aspired "higher than the workshop." This school was divided into six classes or years: grammar, natural philosophy, mathematics, ethics, dialectic, and rhetoric. It was to be found, Comenius hoped, in every city and to be open to all who wished to learn more, regardless of their vocational plans. In this school the pupils would learn Latin, Greek, and Hebrew, and continue the study of the vernacular.

After a young person had completed the Latin school at or near the age of eighteen, he might go on to a university located in each kingdom or province. Comenius recognized that only the very few, the brightest and those of highest moral character, could profit by advanced instruction. He suggested that public examinations be instituted to select from graduates of the Latin school those fitted to continue. The university would prepare for the ministry, law, medicine, teaching, and leadership in the state. Here special concern would be taken to train the will through a curriculum that was universal, providing for the study of "every branch of human knowledge." While he recognized that a university should be a place for research, he did not believe that all the students, concerned as they were with professional competency, would have time for much original investigation.

Comenius would top off this education with extensive travel, giving the student opportunities to experience directly the world of things. Through this experience, he would come to understand and appreciate human nature and the variety of institutions man has created.

This was Comenius' educational ladder, beginning with the birth of the child and continuing into his adult years in the form of travel and mature experiences. Comenius saw no end to education. As man is continually experiencing and growing, his education can never end except with death.

His Psychological Foundation

Comenius was an appreciative observer of nature and of children. He had a keen sensitivity to his environment and seemed to understand intuitively the ways in which maturing life experiences its surroundings. But he was in no sense a modern psychologist. He was a child of his age. Yearning so to make more perfect the world in which he lived and to lead mankind to its richest possible accomplishments, he was often the dupe of his own dreams as well as of the machinations of the unscrupulous. He was a strange mixture of sagacity, acute understanding, and naïveté.

He accepted without question the reigning faculty psychology that had come down from Aristotle. He was prone to reason from analogy and put aside hard logic. These two tendencies at times distorted his clearer understanding of child nature and the ways the child grows to maturity. In spite of these defects, his psychological foundations in education were often accurate and penetrating.

All knowledge, he believed, comes through man's five senses, and there can be nothing in the mind which has not passed through these doorways. These must be trained for accuracy and clearness. If sense impressions are to be more than discrete and crude experiences of the environment, they must be taken up by the imagination, amplified, and developed. This inner sense or faculty draws out the implications of experience and brings understanding.

Comenius saw the mind as a number of faculties needing development. Memory, reason, perception, and the many other faculties were to be trained by use and activity. This was the long-honored theory of mental discipline. But Comenius was unwilling to accept this in its extreme form. Memory, for example, could be trained by daily exercise in memorizing. This, however, is not necessarily good education. Comenius realized that memory is best when the material to be memorized has come to the mind through the senses clearly and accurately, and is understood by the pupil. To accomplish this, he recommended the use of objects and a full explanation of each before any attempt is made at memorizing.

Children are different in untold ways. Comenius was sensitive to this fact and strove to develop his educational method in terms of these differences. Instruction, he constantly admonished, must be fitted to the individual child. The school must be graded so that children can be grouped in terms of their maturity and abilities, textbooks must be prepared that present knowledge in ways the child can understand, and method must be adapted to the individual child. Development is not gradual but a matter of discrete stages, each with its distinctive characteristics. The educational ladder, texts, and method all must be constructed to best care for the child at each stage of growth.

Comenius would not stop here. He attempted to carry this insight to its logical conclusion and emphasize the fact that each child is different and must be instructed in terms of *his* differences. This is most clearly seen in his emphasis upon interest in education. He believed that compulsion and force in teaching were admissions of failure and that each child could be motivated to learn if his interests were appealed to. All children want to learn. This is inherent and natural. From birth, the child has an innate desire to "see, hear, and handle everything new." He wants to know everything. The teacher must understand the child, know what in *him* furnishes the drive to learn, and use these forces skillfully. Each child has his own individual capacity to learn, some less and others more. This the teacher must realize and adapt his assignments and expectations to it at all times.

When a teacher understands the growing child and the individual child, he will teach effectively by adjusting all that he does to the one with whom he is working. He will not expect too much or too little, he will not attempt "to teach boys of two years old to dance, though they can scarcely walk," nor will he make chronological age the single criterion for teaching.

One of Comenius' basic psychological principles is expressed in these words, "what has to be done must be learned through practice"—we learn by doing. Telling, listening, and reading are important and should not be neglected, but the best learning takes place when the learner acts and repeats action until learning has become a part of the entire being, not just the mind. "In school," he wrote, "let the student learn to write by writing, to talk by talking, to sing by singing, and to reason by reasoning." This insight does not apply merely to physical activity. We learn to think by thinking, to will by willing, to appreciate by appreciating. All learning comes through acting upon what is learned.

A PANSOPHIC CURRICULUM

When Comenius affirms that everyone is "to know all things, to do all things, and to say all things," he astonishes the casual reader. This is an impossible dream. A more careful reading of Comenius will make this idea palatable to the modern mind. This was little more than a seventeenth century version of the concept of a well-rounded or many-sided education. Comenius lived in an age when the frontiers of knowledge were being explored in many directions, and areas hitherto unknown were being opened to man's mind. He realized that the narrow goals of medieval education, as well as those of Humanism, were no longer adequate. Man must travel far, to the frontiers and beyond, in the world of the intellect if he aspires to be educated. He must know many things his forefathers were denied. A well-educated man must know something about everything; he must be at home in all fields of knowledge, old as well as new. This is what Comenius meant when he aspired to have everyone "know all things, . . . do all things, and . . . say all things."

This could be done only if the curriculum were constructed correctly and a method adequate for the task devised. Comenius believed that he had discovered both.

Since much of this necessary knowledge is written in books or communicated through speaking, everyone must master languages. One must learn his own vernacular well so that he will understand what is said, appreciate fine shades of meaning and inferences, and be able to communicate his knowledge to others. He must understand other vernaculars in order to communicate with those of other lands who have knowledge to impart or wish to learn. He must be skillful in classical languages since so much of man's knowledge was gathered in days when these were the languages of common intercourse.

History was, to him, a necessary subject for a pansophic curriculum. It should be taught at all levels to reveal to man his past and the knowledge men have gained. To this should be added all the sciences and religion. As science had become the tool of all new knowledge, no one should be unacquainted with its nature and the facts it revealed. The "modern man" must be at home in the world of the sciences. Since even the "modern man" is a child of God destined for eternal life, he cannot ignore religion.

Comenius added to this the seven liberal arts, which could be studied only in the Latin tongue. He further insisted upon familiarity with manual arts and industry as the way to feel at home in man's commercial and economic environment. He did not insist that everyone be equally skilled in all these arts, but advocated enough experience to develop in the individual understanding and appreciation of this important area of human endeavor.

A PANSOPHIC METHOD

The method must grow out of the nature of child growth and follow the laws of human development. There is a time for all learning. The teacher must discover this time and teach when the child is ready. The child learns words and things together, not words first and things later, as in past methods. He learns best through understanding, as he sees the part in its relation to the whole and the whole in relation to himself. Instruction must proceed step by step, slowly, in accord with the child's growth. There can be no compulsion, since one learns best when he wants to learn.

These facts were basic to the pansophic method. Comenius expressed them in terms of analogies that he drew from nature. These analogies should not dim their luster or serve to hide the truth, which Comenius sensed in the world he was observing. From these he drew a methodology that was sound.

All teaching must appeal to the senses. The teacher will use natural objects, pictures, diagrams, models, trips to places being studied, and other objective material whenever it is available. The classroom should be decorated with visual aids to learning. Let the child see, hear, feel, taste, and manipulate his environment as much as possible.

Fit all learning to the child's ability. What is the pupil ready to learn? This must be the criterion of what is taught. Each step in learning will prepare for the next step, lay the foundation upon which future learning will build. Since nature moves from a whole to the parts, teaching must give the pupil the meaning of the unit before it explores the more minute and difficult parts.

One may think he knows and understands, but let him try to teach another. There is the real test of knowledge. Appreciating this, Comenius insisted that children learn in groups and that each one tell the others what he has learned. In this way the pupil uses his knowledge and impresses it upon himself beyond all danger of forgetting.

Learning is more efficient if correlated with similar learning. To the extent that a thing learned is related to something else learned, both will be more deeply impressed and will be remembered longer. Just as every sense should be employed in perceiving an object, so should similar materials be related in the mind so that the recall of one will stimulate recall of the other.

Such is the pansophic method, a method based on the laws of child development and learning as Comenius knew them. By these techniques the child will learn about all phases of his environment. This learning will become wider and deeper as he becomes more mature. If the teacher has wisely used interest and built the will correctly, learning will continue after he has released his charge to his own devices. In this way everyone will learn everything to the limit of his ability, and willingly.

COMENIUS IN PERSPECTIVE

We began our study of Comenius with the observation that this sensitive and understanding bishop of the Moravian Brethren had practically no influence upon the education of his day. This was due largely to the nature of the times and his place in them. The seventeenth century was an age of the divine right of kings and class distinctions. It was not ready to think in terms of education for all in schools making no divisions or provisions for rank, economic status, sex, or manner of living. Further, Comenius was identified clearly with a minority religious sect that was despised, persecuted almost to extinction, and exiled from its land and country. His people believed in freedom and resisted governmental authority, practiced Christian communism, and refused to admit to membership anyone who refused to renounce his titles and power.

Comenius wrote textbooks that were sound and right. Teachers recognized this and used them effectively. They helped to teach Latin to children of rank and power in segregated schools. There was nothing in them that contradicted the *status quo* or made propaganda for any particular religious sect or economic or social theory. It is a different story when one turns to his theoretical or religious works. Today we can read these books, recognize the clear understanding of children upon which they were written, and appreciate the soundness of their educational principles without being disturbed by their theology. People in the seventeenth century were not able to do this. Each age has its bias, against which it judges men and movements. The bias of the seventeenth century made Comenius anathema.

REALISM IN ENGLISH EDUCATION

SOME EDUCATIONAL REALISTS

Samuel Hartlib (*circa* 1599–1670) was the son of a Polish refugee merchant living at Elbing in Prussia. His mother was the daughter of a rich English merchant of Danzig. He went to England in 1628 where he lived for the remainder of his life as merchant, agriculturalist, and leader of a group of educational devotees dedicated to the reform of English education along realistic lines. He encouraged many of the leading minds of the age to write and publish works on education, printed books from his own pen and from those of friends, planned a school for the sons of gentlemen, and participated in much of the activity attendant upon Cromwell's reign in England. As a reward, Cromwell settled a pension upon him, which he lost after the Restoration.

Hartlib was an admirer of Comenius and sought to bring his ideas to the attention of Englishmen. In this endeavor he published, in 1637, *Conatuum Comenianorum praeludia* and, in 1639, *Comenii pansophiae prodromus et didactica dissertatio.* He believed that all the gains of Protestantism would be lost if diverse sects could not unite and work together. To further this idea he wrote *Ecclesiastical Peace Among Protestants* and a plan for a utopian state, *A Description of the Famous Kingdom of Macaria.* In 1647 he published *Considerations Tending to the Happy Accomplishment of England's Reformation in Church and State,* in which he advocated municipal support and control of schools in every community. This was followed, in 1656, by *A True and Ready Way to Learn the Latin Tongue.* All the ideas expressed in these educational treatises were in conflict with English tradition, which held education to be a matter of the family and not the state, and sought to maintain clear distinctions between classes and rank in the state.

One of Hartlib's highly significant proposals was an *Office of Address,* a government bureau to deal with labor, employment of the poor, relations between religious groups, education, dissemination of knowledge about scientific inventions and discoveries among scholars everywhere, and the advancement of learning.

One of Hartlib's close friends was Hezekiah Woodward (1590–1675), a Puritan teacher and strong advocate of the philosophy and methodology of Comenius. As a sense realist, he believed that teachers should use as much appeal to the senses as possible. Objects, diagrams, pictures, mock-ups, and other visual devices should be part of every lesson. He believed strongly that the teacher should study and understand the mind of the child and adapt all his teaching to the laws of this developing mind.

His masterpiece, *A Light to Grammar and All Other Arts and Sciences,* published in 1641, was dedicated to his friend Hartlib. Another important work from his pen was a pamphlet entitled *A Gate to Science.*

Hartlib's close friend, John Dury (1596–1680), was prevailed upon to write a pamphlet entitled *Reformed Schools,* published in 1650. In this he advocated the use of the senses, tradition, and reason in learning. Among the principles that he developed in his work were (1) teaching adapted to the mental level of the child, (2) no formal education before the child is nine, (3) an enriched and encyclopedic curriculum, broadening as the child advances to higher levels, and (4) all education at public expense. Dury, a Puritan clergyman, advocated closer and more harmonious relationships among the Protestants of Europe.

Probably the most noted friend and admirer of Hartlib was John Milton (1608–1674). Here was a realist of a different hue. While Comenius and the company that assembled about him have been called sense realists because of their great emphasis upon learning through the senses, Milton must be called a humanistic realist. He was a true humanist, a scholar in the classical tradition, one who believed that the best knowledge in all fields could be obtained from reading the great books of the past.

Milton was educated at Saint Paul's school in London and at Christ College, Cambridge. To complete his education, he traveled widely on the continent. Upon his return, he identified himself with the Puritan cause, taught a private school for boys in London for a number of years, and served in Parliament.

At the insistence of Hartlib, he wrote *Of Education,* published in 1644. In this he advocated that training given in Latin schools and universities be taken over by *Academies,* which should be established in each community. The Puritans liked the idea, and began founding these institutions in places out of the reach of the Anglicans, who wanted to destroy all dissenting thought and education.

Milton's basic educational thinking was Calvinist. His Academy was right out of Geneva. His statement of the aim of all education is the Calvinist aim: "I call, therefore, a complete and generous education, that which fits a man to perform justly, skillfully, and magnanimously all the offices, both private and public, of peace and war."

Elementary instruction did not concern Milton. He was thinking of a realistic, encyclopedic, thorough education that would begin when the child was twelve years of age. This would include Greek and Latin, as well as modern foreign languages, grammar, mathematics, and religion—a curriculum designed for boys of exceptional ability, those who would be leaders in government, commerce, and church. At about twenty-one the boy should leave school and travel widely to learn from experiences as broad as life itself.

Two other close friends of Hartlib who were prominent in the development of realism in English education were Sir William Petty (1623–1687) and Charles Hoole (1610–1667).

Petty's *Advice of W. P. to Mr. Samuel Hartlib For the Advancement of Some Particular Parts of Learning,* published in 1648, contained suggestions for a school system catering to English aristocracy. At the base he proposed a common school (*Ergastulum Literarium*), in which all children would learn to read and write and begin learning a trade. One might use the experience of learning a trade as the basis for making a living, for dealing with artisans who might be working for him, or just for recreation and understanding of the world of manual work. This would be followed by a trade college (*Gymnasium Mechanicum*), devoted to the advancement of all industrial pursuits. Here one might perfect his craft or come to understand the world of business and manufacture. Finally, he proposed an Academy (*Nosocomium Academicum*) similar to the university. This would include classrooms, laboratories, a library, an observatory, an art gallery, and a large aquarium.

Hoole was a practical teacher and writer on educational theory. His years as a teacher in both a town Latin school and a private school, along with thorough reading of the leading educators of the age, including Comenius, gave him a rich background upon which to base his theories and suggestions. He translated many works on education, as well as books that could be used as texts. One of the latter was Comenius' *Orbis Pictus.* Among his own writings were children's stories, a Latin grammar, and an English-Latin vocabulary.

The book that gave Hoole his greatest fame was *A New Discovery of the Old Art of Teaching School,* published in 1659, after circulating among scholars for some twenty-three years. This was the summing up of his years of teaching and study and his mature thinking about education. He suggested in the book that the child should move through a petty school and then a grammar school. All children should begin their education in the petty school, where, in groups of several hundred, they would learn to read and write in about three years. At seven or eight, children should be separated into those planning to proceed to a classical education and those who would spend some more time with English and a little arithmetic. Those looking to grammar school would study the elements of Latin for four years. These students were divided into four classes of not more than forty boys, each class under a master employed for his skill in teaching Latin by realistic methods. Hoole suggested that grammar school be administered by a master and each class taught by an usher. For three years, all boys would study Latin until they had mastered both grammar and the reading of fairly difficult passages. The fourth year gave special attention to perfecting one's knowledge of Latin grammar. It also began the study of rhetoric. Greek should begin in the fifth year and Hebrew in the sixth.

NON-CONFORMIST EDUCATION

To escape legal suppression, non-conformists turned to family education to give their children the schooling they felt necessary. This was consistent with English tradition. The aristocracy had for generations considered the home the best of all schools. It was possible for parents to teach religion, manners, and morals to their own children or to include children of neighbors and friends. This movement hatched a great number of books designed to guide parents in this educational undertaking. *The School of Infancy* by Comenius became popular. Other books of this nature included Defoe's *The Family Instructor* and *The New Family Instructor. Of Domestical Duties* by William Gouge had reached its third edition by 1634. There were also numerous catechisms which parents could use to instruct their children in true Calvinist theology.

While strict enforcement of the law against unlicensed teachers was the order of the day, dissenting elementary schools were black-market institutions, sometimes operating more or less openly and at other times diligently tracked down and abolished. After 1670, liberal courts began interpreting the law in favor of the non-conformists, and their elementary schools came out into the open in many communities throughout England. The curriculum of these schools was similar to that of realistic elementary schools under Church of England control or supervision, except that Calvinist doctrine was emphasized, and the rigid moral precepts of the Geneva tradition were drilled into the young.

The non-conformists topped their educational structure with the academy, conceived in Geneva and developed to fit English needs by John Milton. At first these schools were taught by pastors and scholarly gentlemen, dispossessed of their churches or teaching chairs by intolerant laws, in their homes or in homes of friends. After the Act of Toleration (1689), they began to appear in public more often, and to attract a wide clientele.

The academies sought to adapt instruction to the needs of the students they attracted. When preparation of students was poor, they included one or two years of elementary training in Latin. When the interest was adequate, they included a full four-year college education leading to the ministry, law, medicine, business, military and naval careers, and civil employment. Latin and Greek were stressed in most academies. Added to these subjects were usually mathematics, physics, astronomy, logic, rhetoric, ethics, and metaphysics. A few academies offered Hebrew, and some experimented with teaching modern foreign languages. Gradually the curriculum of these academies became encyclopedic or pansophic as the influence of Comenius was felt increasingly.

DANIEL DEFOE (*circa* 1659–1731)

James Foe was a butcher and a citizen of London, a non-conformist, a Calvinist who valued education above everything else. His son Daniel, who signed his name either Foe or Defoe, was educated at the famous dissenting academy conducted by Mr. Charles Morton at Stoke Newington. After completing his education, he entered business and made and lost fortunes as owner of a hosiery factory, a commission merchant dealing in Spanish and Portuguese goods, and manager and chief owner of a tile factory. His writings made him friends and enemies, brought him wealth, or contributed to his business failures. He received commissions at the hands of royalty and was pilloried and fined because of his outspoken ideas and cutting wit. *Shortest Way With the Dissenters,* published anonymously as a piece of ironical writing, caused him to be hunted down, fined, condemned to be pilloried three times, and imprisoned indefinitely. Released from prison, he continued writing pamphlets, novels, adventure yarns, and innumerable political, religious, and historical works which charmed, angered, embarrassed, tickled, and confused his reading public. His *The Life and Strange Surprising Adventures of Robinson Crusoe* and *The Fortunes and Misfortunes of Moll Flanders* are masterpieces of English literature.

In 1698, Defoe published an *Essay on Projects*. This was a collection of ideas on banks, road management, insurance societies, idiot asylums, bankruptcy, academies, military colleges, and high schools for women. Many of these ideas were far in advance of his times. Here he suggested that a national society be established to "polish and refine the English Tongue," mainly to abolish swearing. He also advocated "A Royal Academy for Military Science," an academy for the education of women, and an academy of music. It is well known that this book had tremendous influence upon Benjamin Franklin in his thinking about the Academy at Philadelphia.

REALISM IN FRENCH CATHOLIC EDUCATION

The Edict of Nantes was promulgated in April, 1598, by Henry IV, giving Protestants, mainly the Huguenots, a measure of religious liberty. Both the Catholic clergy and the French parliament disliked the edict and sought to have it repealed. The growing political power of the Huguenots during the minority of Louis XIII caused French leaders to see them as a grave danger to the state and resulted, October 18, 1685, in revocation of the edict and denial of all civil and religious liberty to French Protestants.

Although French education had remained in the hands of the Catholic Church, there was always the fear that growing Protestant influence might challenge this control. After 1685, the Church and its orders held complete control of all schools. This did not mean that scholasticism and the limited past dominated the schools. Realism was too strong and compelling a force to be denied. Further, Descartes' rationalism, with its emphasis upon clear and irrefutable truths, was ideally suited to a Church interested in reform.

ORDER OF THE ORATORY OF JESUS

At the opening of the seventeenth century in France, the Jesuits dominated secondary education. Their educational supremacy was challenged in 1614 by Cardinal de Berulle, who founded a teaching order, called the Oratory of Jesus, to raise the educational standards of the priesthood. In time the order turned to the education of youths and opened a number of colleges and seminaries throughout France, of which Juilly College, founded in 1638, was the most famous. Its pupils came largely from the French nobility.

Basic to teaching in the institutions of the order was the philosophy of Descartes. Leaders of the order, including the famous humanist father, Pere Thomassin, worked out a system of philosophical thought that combined Descartes and orthodox Catholicism and found much of Christian truth in classical literature. Many of the newer seventeenth century ideas about education, especially those on realism, were woven into the curriculum and methods of the order. The vernacular was used throughout most of the work, discipline was gentle but firm, and natural methods of motivating learning displaced the stern cruelty found in other schools of the period.

Love of the classics and a passion for scientific investigation marked the schools of the order. Classical and modern languages were taught, grammar was learned by way of the vernacular, history was emphasized, and geography was taught with the use of maps and other visual aids. Physics, chemistry, and anatomy were studied in laboratories. Algebra and arithmetic were emphasized strongly. The Cartesian love for clarity and certainty in all learning was evident wherever members of the Oratory taught.

Among the many books dealing with education that came from the Oratory were two of exceptional significance. Pere Lamy published, in 1683, *Entretiens sur les Sciences.* Here are discussions of the aim and purpose of education, methods of teaching, discipline, educational philosophy, and admonitions to teachers. Father Thomassin published, between 1681 and 1690, a series of brochures, called *Methods,* for studying languages, philosophy, and letters. In all these writings one can detect an attempt to make use of modern and progressive methods in furthering Christian education.

THE JANSENISTS AT PORT ROYAL

Cornelius Jansen (1585–1638) rose from his humble Catholic parentage at Accoy in the province of Utrecht to the bishopric of Ypres through a stormy career which included bitter battles with the Jesuits, attempts to reform the Catholic Church from within, threats of the Spanish Inquisition, and intense advocacy of Augustinianism.

His followers, the Jansenists, realized that in children rested the future of any reform movement. This became an abiding passion among them and motivated them to establish schools wherever possible. Since, as they believed, man is born in sin and is in mortal danger at all times, education must be concerned with the spiritual life of man, protecting him from sin and shaping his soul to righteousness. To accomplish this, the child must be placed in an environment from which all temptation is removed. He must be under constant supervision lest he be led astray. This the Jansenists attempted in their famous Little Schools of Port Royal.

A Cistercian abbey was founded in 1204 by Mahaut de Garlande, a few miles southwest of Paris. For centuries the abbey was under strict discipline, and served to train sisters for various functions in the Church. In 1626 the nuns were forced, because of bad health conditions in the surrounding marshes, to move to Port Royal de Paris, and the original buildings were occupied by "hermits," lay relatives of the abbess, who wished to live in solitude. Meanwhile, the nuns had come under the influence of Jean du Vergier, abbot of Saint Cyran and chief apostle of Jansenism in France. In 1648, some of the nuns returned, and the "hermits" established themselves a short distance from the abbey and set up a "little school" for sons of Jansenists. Here Racine received his education. These schools were devoted largely to the training of leaders for church and state. They were called "little" because they usually accepted no more than twenty-five pupils, and classes never consisted of more than six boys.

The chief aim of all education in the Little Schools was salvation of the soul. A secondary aim was to prepare more talented boys to become spiritual leaders. Science, literature, Latin, French, mathematics, and all other courses in the curriculum were there not for scholarship, but for moral regeneration. As devotees of the Cartesian philosophy and method, they desired clearness of thinking and certainty of understanding.

To protect the boys from temptation and to shape their characters correctly, a teacher was assigned to six youths. He never let his charges out of his sight, studied with them, taught them, participated in their recreation, and slept in the same room with them. The schools were isolated from the outside world, and the pupils were allowed only a minimum of communication with parents or relatives.

Discipline was strict but gentle. The teachers attempted to use persuasion, kindness, respect, and understanding in their dealings with children and youths.

All subjects of the curriculum were judged by their bearing on religion and their fitness for children of the age concerned. Material had to be clear, exact, and easily understood by the pupils. French was basic to all learning. Children studied the classics first in French translations. They were drilled in speaking and writing clear, precise, and eloquent French. Other subjects in the curriculum were history, which was correlated with geography, modern foreign languages, logic of the Ramus variety, mathematics, and the sciences.

The Port Royal method of teaching was based on knowledge of the growing child's mind and how it learned. The known came first and aided in understanding the unknown. Interest was made the method of motivating study. Clarity was the criterion of good teaching. Reading was taught by acquainting children with the sounds of letters in words, not letters by themselves.

The Little Schools of Port Royal lasted less than thirty years and were eventually destroyed as centers of heresy. Nevertheless, they were in the mainstream of French educational progress, so that within less than a half-century after their closing, the reforms which they advocated were made part of French education.

EDUCATION OF THE POOR

France thought of formal instruction as necessary only for the upper classes. The poor could learn what was necessary through apprenticeship. While some provisions were made to open the doors of education to a few poor boys of promise or to poor relations of influential families, the laboring classes were largely neglected.

In some instances charitable organizations or special groups of holy men, in the seventeenth century, gave thought to providing some education for the poor. In 1666, the *Congregation of Saint Charles* was founded by Father Demia to care for education of the poor in Lyons. The congregation established schools, determined curricula, and provided training for teachers to staff the schools.

One of the chief forces effecting education among the poor of France was the *Institute of the Brothers of the Christian Schools,* founded in 1648 by Jean Baptiste de la Salle (1651–1719). Born in Reims, La Salle became canon of the cathedral there and established an elementary school for the free instruction of poor children. His assistants organized themselves into a community which spread throughout France, establishing similar schools in many centers of population. As the movement began to receive popular support, the College de Saint-Yon was opened at Rouen to train teachers for their schools. Six years after La Salle's death, the community was recognized by the pope as the *Brothers of Christian Schools.*

Reading, writing, morals, manners, and religion constituted the curriculum, a course of study suited to the needs of the poor. Discipline was severe, although it became softer in later years. Children were divided into classes and these broken down into groups of bright, average, and poor students. Exercises for study were developed from the life of the pupils and included such things as writing simple letters, bills, and receipts. In many schools monitors from the advanced groups were used to teach younger children.

EDUCATION OF GIRLS

Two avenues of education were open to girls of seventeenth century France. The home could serve as their school. Parents could teach their daughters what they deemed necessary or could employ tutors to care for their education. If the home was not adequate, the girl might be sent to a convent, where her morals and religion would be attended to along with a minimum of formal instruction. As the seventeenth century progressed, women began to assume wider responsibilities. Brilliant and sophisticated women were learning much that had in the past been reserved for men and, as wives of prominent leaders, began exerting influence in crucial situations. Widows were often faced with the responsibilities of managing estates, families, and business interests. This led to increased concern for the education of girls and abandonment of the older idea that a woman's function was confined wholly to the home.

The Ursulines were founded in November, 1535, by Angela Merici (1470–1540) for the education of girls and care of the sick and needy. They received the sanction of Paul III in 1544 and of Gregory XIII in 1572, and were placed under the rule of Saint Augustine. During the seventeenth century, they established schools in France and Canada to train girls for the order or to become wives and mothers. Intellectual training was at a minimum.

While the Little Schools of Port Royal were concerned with the moral regeneration of boys, the sisters of Port Royal were holding largely to the traditions of the past. Jacqueline Pascal gives us a picture of life in a Port Royal convent in her *Regulations for Children,* published in 1657. Here we see a strong Jansenist influence. Discipline was severe. Girls spoke only in whispers and were discouraged from communicating among themselves. They were required to walk between two nuns, one before and one after, and their hands were kept busy to protect the mind from unholy thoughts. The curriculum consisted of prayers, meditation, a little reading, writing, and arithmetic. Learning was motivated by compassion for the child and devotion to her soul. Jacqueline Pascal calls her charges "little doves" for whom "we must not cease to feel pity . . . and to accommodate ourselves to them in every way that we can." Here was severity and hard discipline motivated by love and hope of salvation.

A leading figure in French education during the seventeenth century was Francois de Salignac de la Mothe Fenelon (1651–1715), archbishop of Cambria. He was educated at home and at the University of Cahors, near the chateau of Fenelon in Perigord. From there he went to the college of Saint Sulpice in Paris, where he remained until he was made superior of a "New Catholic" sisterhood devoted to the conversion of Huguenot ladies.

His *Treatise on the Education of Girls,* written in 1680 to advise the Duchess de Beauvillier on the education of her children, proved to be one of the most popular works dealing with the education of girls published during the seventeenth century. He held that a girl should be educated for her career just as carefully as a boy for his. He advocated that girls learn to read, write, understand ancient and modern history, and manage an estate. The latter included law, keeping accounts, manufacturing articles needed in the home and on the estate, trading in products of the estate, and managing servants. Girls should be given physical training for health and proper functioning of the body. The home, he believed, was better for the education of girls than the convent, where one was isolated from the realities of living.

SAINT CYR

One of the most remarkable schools for girls in all France was Saint Cyr. Francoise D'Aubigne Maintenon (1635–1719) was born in the prison at Niort of a Huguenot father and a mother who had her christened a Catholic. Relatives converted her to Protestantism, but the state took charge of her and reconverted her to Catholicism. As governess of the children of the king's mistress, she came to court and eventually became the king's mistress.

She worked with children from her youth, and was never happier than when she could help young people develop. She founded a school for poor girls at Ruil, moved it later to Noisy, and eventually made it the nucleus of the school for girls at Saint Cyr-L'Ecole, three miles west of Versailles. In 1686, the king endowed the school from the funds of the abbey of Saint Denis. To this she devoted much of her life, attending daily, sometimes arriving at six in the morning, advising and conferring with the sisters, and always planning for the education of "her children." "Nothing is dearer to me than my children at Saint Cyr," she wrote.

The history of Saint Cyr must be divided into two eras. For the first years of its existence, 1686 to 1692, it was a liberal and progressive school for the education of girls of high position. For the girls, Racine wrote *Andromaque* and *Ester,* and they acted the plays before the king and the court with considerable success. These experiences and the applause the girls received turned them to worldly and dissipated thinking and acting. It was evident that here was a school devoted to "a bold and intelligent secularization of the education of women."

To counteract this tendency, Mme de Maintenon transformed the school into a monastery and founded the Order of Saint Augustine to take charge of the work there. In deep contrition for her mistakes she wrote:

> The sorrow I feel for the girls of Saint Cyr can be cured only by time and by an *entire change* in the education that we have given them up to this hour. . . . God knows that I wished to establish virtue at Saint Cyr, but I have built on the sand. . . . Our girls have been treated with too much consideration, have been petted too much, treated too gently. We must now leave them more to themselves in their classrooms, make them observe the daily regulations, and speak to them scarcely of anything else.[2]

The new Saint Cyr received girls at six or seven years of age and kept them until marriage or until they reached their twentieth year. During this time they were in a sequestered atmosphere, allowed to visit their parents only once or twice a year and to write to them only on stated occasions. Reading, writing, and counting were taught, but little more. Only books of piety were allowed. Intellectual culture was renounced in favor of family duties, obedience to husbands, and care of children. Mme de Maintenon wrote, "Reading does more harm than good to young girls. . . . Books make witlings and excite an insatiable curiosity." Little importance was attached to history, and some went so far as to advocate prohibition of the study of French history.

Manual labor was stressed. Girls were taught to sew, embroider, knit, make tapestry, and prepare other items for the home. They did all the work of the school, including cleaning, washing, and preparing the food. "The institute," Mme de Maintenon wrote, "is intended, not for prayer, but for action."

---

2. As quoted in Gabriel Compayré, *The History of Pedagogy* (Boston: D. C. Heath, 1889), p. 220.

CHAPTER 11

In Colonial America

INTRODUCTION

To separate America from Europe and, as many have attempted in the past, to write its educational history as unique, is to distort the record and leave the reader uninstructed as to the true facts. Never since the fifteenth century have developments in America been wholly free from happenings in Europe. From the first landing of Columbus on the island of Guanahani, now identified as Watling Island in the Bahamas, in 1492, until the surrender of Cornwallis in 1781, America was a colonial possession of various European powers. Although by 1783 there was in America an autonomous community "in entire separation from European control," European influences have continued to the present.

Now that we have traced the story of life and education in the western world through the seventeenth century on the continent, we must at this point take account of the fact that in 1492, Europe began expanding to incorporate into its cultural sphere vast unknown lands to the west. What happened in those lands for centuries following Columbus was little other than an extension of European interests, attitudes, ideas, and cultural values. Failure to recognize this fact has led students in the past to miss the meaning of American history.

The Renaissance had seen the development of new kinds of schools, typically humanistic in their curriculum: the court school in Italy, the lycée in France, the gymnasium in Germany, and the Latin grammar school in England. Schools which developed in the new world were almost a direct replica of their European contemporaries. What passed for secondary education in the colonies during the colonial period was the Latin grammar school.

Those who came to America knew only the classical curriculum, and this was the area that dominated the secondary schools of colonial America. The colonial "public" considered Latin to be the chief subject to be taught in the secondary schools, and even in colleges. Greek was a strong second. This confidence in Latin as a basis of an education continued with many Americans well into the twentieth century. Ancient languages, following the European models, took up nine-tenths of the colonial secondary curriculum; it was a carry-over.

EARLY EUROPEAN INTEREST IN AMERICA

EARLY DISCOVERIES AND CONTROVERSIES

Stories of great wealth and rich cultures far to the east sifted into Europe for many centuries. The adventures of Marco Polo and others sharpened the interest of westerners in those fabulous lands. Overland trading expeditions were bringing into Europe spices, jewels, and precious metals in quantities to convince western rulers and merchantmen that an unlimited supply of things cherished and desired lay to the east waiting to be tapped. Overland transportation was dangerous, subject to bandits and other unfriendly forces. All this made men think of a water route to these areas.

Portugal first opened such a route via the offshore African islands and the Gold Coast to the west coast of India. Her rule was gradually extended through the Indian Ocean to Malacca on the southwest coast of Malaya. From there it was an easy run to the Oluccas, the famous Spice Islands about which Europeans dreamed. Along this route the Portuguese carried on a most profitable trade, bringing to Europe pepper, cloves, nutmeg, camphor, sugar, tea, coffee, and indigo. In time they pushed on to China, where they made a trade treaty and established the city of Macao as their trade center.

As a result of these explorations and the pattern of trade routes established, Pope Nicholas V, in 1454, gave the Portuguese the exclusive right of exploration and conquest on the road to the Indies.

Columbus made his landfall on October 12, 1492, touched on the coast of Cuba and Hispaniola, established a small post, and returned to Lisbon on March 4, 1493, and thence to Spain. He and all his backers, including Ferdinand and Isabella, were convinced that he had reached the eastern extremity of Asia and referred to the land as "las Indias." This naturally blossomed into a controversy between Portugal and Spain as to who could legally carry on trade with these new lands. To settle the dispute, Pope Alexander VI, a Spaniard, drew a line from north to south one hundred leagues west of the Azores and Cape Verde Islands and gave Spain free claim to all lands west of this line. The Portuguese protested and, after a conference at Tordesillas, the line was shifted to 370 leagues west of Cape Verde Islands. This has generally been considered to be the fiftieth degree of longitude west of Greenwich. "The line," as it was called, gave Portugal the bulge of South America that lies east of a line beginning at the mouth of the Amazon River and cutting south through Brazil to a point near Porto Alegre. It left to Spain most of the South American continent, all of Central America and North America.

During the years that followed, both Spain and Portugal explored these lands and came to realize that this was not the eastern extremity of Asia but a new continent separated from Asia and lying almost wholly within the sphere of influence assigned to Spain. When, in 1520, Magellan sailed south through the strait that bears his name and crossed the Pacific, the world was convinced that a new continent awaited exploration and exploitation.

EDUCATION IN SPANISH AMERICA

To the Spanish explorers and settlers the natives were savages, less than human, to be killed or enslaved as they wished. They could not be civilized. The first Spaniard to challenge this policy was Bartolome de Las Casas (1474–1566), called the "Apostle of the Indians." Born in Seville of a noble family, he was educated at the University of Salamanca and took holy orders in 1510. As a member of the Spanish expedition to Cuba under Diego Valesquez in 1511–1512, he tried vainly to check the massacre of Indians at Caonas. Returning to Spain, he protested vigorously against the cruel treatment of Indians, especially the practice of allotting them for forced labor. With the assistance of Cardinal Francisco Jimenez de Cisneros, he drew up a plan to convert and civilize the natives. This included a proposal that all Indians be gathered into settlements where churches and schools could be established for them. It also proposed that Negroes be imported from Africa as slaves. The plan failed, and he later repented his attitude toward Negroes. Throughout his life he fought to get better treatment for natives living in Spanish possessions.

While the conquistadors were brutalizing and exploiting the Indians, Catholic missionary bodies, especially the Franciscans, were struggling to teach the natives Spanish, the Christian religion, and some of the practical arts of European civilization. Discovering in the Indians a keen interest in singing, they placed considerable stress upon training the natives to participate in the musical parts of church services. They imported organs from Spain, trained choirs, and founded schools in which music was the chief attraction.

In 1551, Charles V, Holy Roman Emperor and (as Charles I) King of Spain, issued an order which served as a basis for the first universities in America. He provided money from the royal treasury for two universities, one "in the city of Lima, of the Kingdom of Peru" and the other "in the city of Mexico, of New Spain." As a result, the Universidad Mayor de San Marcos was opened in Lima in 1551, then under Dominican direction but secularized in 1571, the first and oldest university in America. Opening of the university in the city of Mexico was delayed until 1553.

From these beginnings Catholic culture and religion were spread from the Rio Grande River south to Cape Horn and north of the Rio Grande through what is now the southwestern part of the United States. Priests established missions which were churches, schools, and inns. They were usually one day's ride apart, and offered the traveler food, lodging, consolation, and instruction. The priests gathered in the native population, instructing them in the basic subjects, religion, and civilized morals—and also endeavored to keep the peace. As larger communities developed, churches and schools appeared, and definite patterns of education took form. The Spanish came first to exploit. Because of the devotion of men like Las Casas and others, they remained to convert and educate.

While Spanish Catholics were civilizing and Christianizing Central and South America and the southwestern United States, other Spaniards were exploring what is now the southern United States. Missions and schools were established in Saint Augustine, Florida, New Orleans, Louisiana, Laredo, Texas, and other places where the natives were not too hostile, and military forces could offer a minimum of protection.

PATTERNS OF LIFE IN THE AMERICAN COLONIES

The major influence shaping the culture of the United States was English. From the first permanent settlement in Virginia, English ideas of government, economics, religion, class structure, and education were basic to the development of the United States. To understand colonial America, the thirteen "plantations" which eventually became the United States, we must appreciate fully the English in the new world.

It must be remembered that the sixteenth century was an age of reformation in Europe. From the religious upheavals of the period came the Lutherans with their belief in man's freedom to read and interpret his Bible, the Calvinists convinced of the inherent evil of all men and their need for education, and the English with the Church of England, the Puritans, and the Separatists. While the Spanish, Portuguese, and French came from predominantly Catholic countries, and their effect, except for the Huguenots, was to establish Catholicism in the New World, the settlers along the east coast of the continent from New England to Virginia were Protestants who brought their protestant faiths and theories of government. These they established in their new homes, and it was they who shaped the future of the country. While some Catholics and Jews were among the early settlers, most of those who made their abode in the American colonies were Protestants.

At this point we must divest ourselves of the romantic idea that these settlers came to establish a free and democratic society. Some did dream of freedom and democracy, but they were a small minority. Settlers came to build fortunes, escape years in prison, enjoy adventure, escape religious or political persecution or restriction, establish a society more congenial to their beliefs, or work and prosper in a new and growing country. They brought their culture, its customs, mores, values, ideas, ideals, ways of thinking and acting. Gradually, a new American culture was formed, as European cultures met and made their peace in the environment of the New World.

New England

A small band of Separatists fled England for the Netherlands early in the seventeenth century. They settled around Leyden and came in contact with the Calvinists dominating the religious and intellectual life of the region. Sometime later they decided to migrate to the New World territory being developed by the Virginia Company. Speculators in London financed them, so that a band of thirty-five from Leyden and sixty-seven from London set sail in the *Mayflower*. Because of the weather or some other disaster, they landed in Massachusetts with only the Mayflower Pact to govern them. Here they established the Plymouth settlement in 1620.

The colony was never financially successful and eventually terminated all connections with the Virginia Company. Although it threw off other settlements, it was eventually, in 1691, absorbed into the larger and more powerful colony of Massachusetts Bay.

Political, economic, and religious unrest in England had stimulated many to migrate to the New World. Some 18,000 had settled in New England when, in 1629, John Winthrop and a strong financial group organized a stock company and received a charter as "The Governor and Company of the Massachusetts Bay of New England." This was primarily a trading company constituted to return a profit to its investors. Power was vested in the governor, his deputy, and the stockholders (freemen) who sat as the legislative branch of the government, the General Court.

Laws passed by the General Court to govern the colony reflected the theocratic philosophy of Calvinism. Voting privileges were given to all male landowners who were church members. The state was regarded as an arm of the church to enforce its laws and support its endeavors. Religious qualifications for voting were not withdrawn until 1691, when William and Mary transformed the colony into a royal province in line with the principles of the Act of Toleration.

New England settlers grouped themselves in towns usually built around a square of land used as common pasture and eventually called "the commons" or "the green." Facing on this central area were the church, stores, jail, schoolhouse, and other community buildings, along with homes of prominent families. Close by were homes of the other citizens and servants. Usually a stockade or similar structure was erected in the center of the "commons" for protection in times of Indian raids or other public dangers.

The king usually granted the land to the stock company, which in turn made grants to individuals for homes and farming while holding some areas for public use. Citizens went out from the town during the day to till their soil, but returned in the evening to the security of the group. As conditions improved and dangers lessened, families moved out from the center of the town to build homes and live permanently on the land which they farmed. Thus the town, beginning as a tightly organized group of people, spread out, and distances between families increased.

Class structure in New England was similar to that in England, from which most of the settlers came. At the top of the social pyramid were the aristocratic upper classes, consisting of the clergy, magistrates, landed gentry, and merchants. Beneath these were the free classes, in which could be found skilled artisans, tradesmen, freehold farmers or yeomen. At the bottom were the unfree classes, unskilled laborers, indentured servants, and a few slaves. Usually, members of this third group, since they owned no land, had no vote. Among the others, the New England town was a pure democracy, each adult male, if he belonged to the church and was orthodox in his religious belief, having a vote on all matters of group concern. Gradually the lower classes and the less orthodox gained civil rights as they increased their numbers and fought successfully against the laws and mores of the entrenched upper classes.

All New England colonies, except Rhode Island, had a state-supported religion. Taxes were levied and public lands given for support of the church. People were required to attend its services and accept its doctrines. All other churches and beliefs were illegal, and dissenters were subject to fines, jail, torture, or exile from the community. This extreme position was based on a firm belief that social unity was dependent upon religious oneness. The clergy exerted great power in the community, shaped public opinion, and set the moral and spiritual tone. The Puritans have often been referred to as "moral athletes."

THE MIDDLE COLONIES

The middle colonies were a mixture of many people with many social, religious, and political convictions. Here they found freedom and land upon which they could live without fear of persecution for their dissenting opinions. The area was settled by small communities of highly divergent people, each maintaining its own culture, values, and customs. In these settlements lived farmers, artisans, merchants, and unskilled individuals. In a sense, each community was a self-contained entity bent on preserving its tradition, its religion, and its outlook on life. In spite of some attempts to enforce a larger group control over the smaller social units, there was in these middle colonies a spirit of "live and let live." Here was truly a land of freedom for persecuted dissenters from the Old World.

THE SOUTHERN COLONIES

Virginia is representative of the development of the American coastline from the middle colonies to Spanish holdings in Florida. Between 1583 and 1588, several attempts were made to gain a foothold along the coast of what is now North Carolina. The only tangible result was the naming of the entire area Virginia in honor of "the virgin queen," Elizabeth. Glowing reports brought back to England by explorers and merchants concerning the fertility of the land and the nature of the people living there stimulated a group of financiers to fit out an expedition in 1606 to trade and establish settlements between the thirty-fourth and forty-first parallels north. On May 14, 1607, settlers and officials of the company landed at Jamestown and began establishing "plantations" along the James River. In spite of difficulties and discouragements, the colony was able to maintain itself until other boatloads of settlers arrived, and amicable arrangements could be made with the Indians. Soon colonists flowed into the area in increasing numbers, plantations sprang up along the banks of the James and Appomattox rivers, indentured servants arrived in volume, and a firm and able government took shape.

At the beginning, the colonists held land and improvements in common. This proved impractical, and in 1616 the policy was abandoned and each family received the land it was able to care for. Tobacco was the chief commercial crop, and as the demand for it grew throughout Europe, landowners became wealthy, built "great houses" which they furnished with many of the luxuries from "home," and developed a plantation culture which was to become the hallmark of southern aristocracy. By 1619, Negroes were being imported as slaves to work the plantations.

The London Company had commissioned a governor and a council to maintain civil authority and determine laws necessary for efficient community living. This structure was thought of first as a means of operating a profitable business in tobacco and other raw materials for English use. As the colony developed, it became evident that a more representative governmental structure was necessary. The governor invited planters from the plantations to meet with him to reform and remake the laws to the colony. A constitution was accepted in 1621, under which the London Company would appoint the governor and council as in the past and the people elect representatives to constitute a House of Burgesses. This body was empowered to grant supplies and originate laws, which the governor and council might revise or veto. Later the council was empowered to originate bills and sit as a supreme court to review the work of lower courts and handle certain important cases. In 1624 the king took the place and authority of the London Company.

Late in the seventeenth century the Carolinas were established with a government similar to that of Virginia. In the eighteenth century Georgia was founded. Maryland, which resembled both the middle colonies and the southern colonies, was founded by Lord Baltimore as a haven for Catholics.

While commercial interests dominated among those who first settled these southern colonies, political, religious, and other events in England during part of the seventeenth century caused many to migrate to this area. When the Church of England was in power, the Puritans were forced to live under fear of persecution or migrate to Holland or the New England colonies. Then, when these Puritans wrested control of the English government from the Church of England and established the Commonwealth, many Anglicans and royalists came to the middle and southern colonies where "they could live as Englishmen."

The economic and social structure of the southern colonies did not differ materially from that of New England. Class groupings were similar to those in England. The people coming to Virginia in the seventeenth century were mostly free landholders. Free labor was the basis for the economy. Toward the close of the century, slaves and other unfree labor groups began flowing into the colony in greater numbers, and a clear line of demarcation developed between an aristocracy and lower classes. This was a result of the increasing profits to be obtained from tobacco, the need for large land holdings to raise tobacco profitably, since the crop wore out the land quickly, and the necessity for hordes of unskilled labor to produce tobacco crops.

Many have felt that Virginia and the southern colonies should have been called "New England," since here, more than anywhere else in America, England was transplanted with the least possible change or difference. While settlers in the New England and middle colonies came in great numbers to escape religious persecution or to find a place where they could practice their dissenting faith in peace, the settlers in the South came not to escape from anything, save the Commonwealth which they considered an intruder, but to make a profit and secure themselves economically. They brought their church, their culture, their mores and customs, and their loyalty to England and its traditions. The Church of England was the established church, and ministers were sent out by the Bishop of London. These had considerable influence over political, economic, and social thinking. The people had come to America to live and prosper as they and their neighbors had in England. As soon as possible they recreated their homeland on this hospitable and pleasant soil.

THREE SOCIAL PATTERNS

Colonial America actually contained three fairly distinct patterns of culture developing out of the peculiar structure of events that determined each. New England was Calvinist, collectivist, authoritarian, and theocratic. Its life was built around the town, and its form of democracy was the town meeting in which all male landowners who were true to the faith had a voice. The middle colonies consisted of many diverse groups settling on American soil to find freedom for themselves and the right to live as they thought best. To these colonies came many nationals with many economic and religious beliefs. Each sought to preserve its past and live in peace and mutual understanding. The southern colonists came to build a new England as much like the old as possible. Here were large plantations producing tobacco and bringing wealth to their owners. Here were slaves and indentured servants in great numbers. Here each plantation was a more or less self-contained economic and social unit, producing most of what it needed and providing the necessities of life for all who lived and worked there. Here appeared an aristocracy jealous of its position and lower classes who accepted with complacency what God had so ordained.

America developed over the 170 years of colonial life three very distinct patterns of education. As men thought in terms of the life they were creating, they realized that their educational philosophy and school structure had to fit the conditions in which they found themselves and the dreams they had for the future. They borrowed much from the Old World, but shaped it into new patterns fitted to the New World and its meanings.

APPRENTICE TRAINING IN THE COLONIES

While the colonists evidenced many divergencies as they settled in New England, the middle colonies, or the South, they all came from Europe, where they had learned to share much. There were attitudes, beliefs, and customs which all settlers brought to America in common and which served to give the thirteen colonies a basic unity.

Among these was the generally accepted belief that education of all but the very wealthy consisted, in part at least, of training the child in some handicraft or vocation by means of an established relationship between apprentice and master. Intellectual accomplishments were desirable if the child's position in society made them necessary, but most children were not so fortunate. Preparation for life meant, as far as the majority was concerned, learning a trade by which they could be self-supporting.

Most children were turned over to a master very early in life. From the moment the contract was signed between parent and master, the child was responsible wholly to the master. He was pledged to work diligently, study hard, obey, keep the secrets of the trade or profession, and live a moral and Christian life. The master became responsible for the child's technical training, his board and lodging, clothes, and moral and religious upbringing. The master was also responsible for teaching the child reading and writing, or seeing that he attended a school to learn these skills.

Usually the child was apprenticed for seven years. During this time he received no wages, his keep and training being considered compensation enough. Girls completed their training by their eighteenth birthday, while boys were required to remain until age twenty-one. The apprentice system covered trades, agriculture, household service, commercial activities, shipping, merchandising, law, medicine, and teaching.

Many people migrated to America as indentured servants. Conditions in England, and in other parts of Europe during the seventeenth century, favored migration of all but the upper classes. Unemployment was increasing, poverty of the masses was distressing, labor was highly restricted by the guilds and the government, and debtors' prisons were full to overflowing. Individuals, lacking money to pay their passage to America and unable to qualify as settlers, would sign with ship captains who furnished clothes, food, and transportation, and sold them to masters or other interested persons as indentured servants. They were obligated to serve the buyer for a stated period of years, after which they were free to establish themselves in the New World.

John Harrower, a schoolmaster, sold himself to a captain in 1774 to secure his passage to America. During the voyage he kept a diary in which we find reference to the established method of handling indentured servants. "This day several came on board to purchase servant indentures, and among them were two soul drivers. They are men who make a business to go on board all ships which have either servants or convicts and buy sometimes a parcel of them as they can agree, and then drive them through the country like a parcel of sheep until they can sell to advantage."

The Virginia Company in London, in 1609, forwarded to Virginia one hundred children whom they had purchased from the poor authorities of the city. These children were transported to America and "bound" to the planters. So profitable was this venture that the supply of poor children in London and other cities was exhausted, and many were kidnapped or spirited away to supply the market.

The children, unskilled laborers, many of the poor, and those needing retraining to meet the demands of the New World, were apprenticed to masters or to those who wished to train them. The trainees would receive their keep and education for a trade, agricultural work, household duties, and even the professions. Often they were taught to. read and write. The "proper" religion was usually part of apprentice education.

In 1642, a law was passed in the Massachusetts Bay Colony to check "the great neglect in many parents and masters in training up their children in learning and labor and other employments which may be profitable to the commonwealth." This law required that public officials "take account from time to time of their parents and masters and of their children, concerning their calling and employment of their children, especially of their ability to read and understand the principles of religion and the capital laws of the country." Whenever neglect was discovered, these authorities were to take children from parents or masters and apprentice them to others. This was Calvinist in that it placed upon town authorities the duty of seeing that children received adequate education. It was also English in its evident interest in the proper apprenticing of children who were in one way or another neglected by their parents or masters.

Under this law, an apprentice was privileged to bring his complaints to court and have them adjudicated. The Plymouth Town Records of 1656 contain this item: "I, Jonathan Briggs, do most thankfully certify that I have received full satisfaction of William Hailstone of the sum of fifteen pounds, which was awarded to me by you for his neglect and wrong done to me in not instructing me in the mystery of a tailor according to his agreement."

Pennsylvania, between 1682 and 1683, passed laws requiring apprenticeship training of all children. A line from one of the laws specifies that "they be taught some useful trade or skill, that the poor may work to live and the rich, if they become poor, may not want."

The Virginia colony was typically English. Early in its history it decreed that "the Statutes for Artificers and Workmen are thought fit to be published in this colony." England held that education of children was the concern of parents and not the state. Each parent could give his child the education he thought best, to the limit of the child's ability and judgment, with no help or interference from civil authority. At the same time it was held that all children should have a trade and some learning in reading, writing, and religion. This would make them self-supporting, not a charge on society. Those children who were orphaned or whose parents were too poor to give them the basic education or whose parents neglected this education were taken by the authorities and apprenticed. This practice is seen clearly in *Oliver Twist*. The Statutes for Artificers and Workmen incorporated these ideas into law. Virginia brought this law to America.

The colony passed a law in 1646 requiring that "justices of the peace should, at their discretion, bind out children to husbandmen or tradesmen to be brought up in some good or lawful calling." Subsequent laws and regulations were along the same line. Parents were duty bound to see that their children received training in a trade or profession, plus reading, writing, and religion. When they neglected this duty or were unable to discharge it, the authorities stepped in.

The basic and most pervasive educational pattern in the American colonies was apprenticeship. Only the wealthy were exempt, on the theory that their wealth and position would free them from the necessity of working and insure more than the minimum of education. In some instances, however, even the wealthy were required to learn a trade to insure against becoming poor and indigent.

EDUCATION IN THE NEW ENGLAND COLONIES

THE TOWN SCHOOLS OF NEW ENGLAND

In 1642, Massachusetts asserted its right to force apprentice training upon children in all towns and villages in the colony. It based this right upon the needs of the "commonwealth," upon the Calvinist belief that everyone should be versed in the principles of religion, and upon the fact that those who could not read and understand "the capital laws of the country" might unknowingly commit crimes for which the death penalty was prescribed. This law of 1642 made no mention of schools, even though schools did exist at the time. It was in fact a *compulsory education law* recognizing the fact that the education of the child was possible without schools.

To understand the schools of New England, one must have a clear picture of the New England town. Most of the early settlers came to New England in groups highly selected and homogeneous. They settled in a close-knit community and built a culture consistent with their convictions and values. When individual settlers wished to join a town, they were scrutinized carefully before being admitted to membership. The General Court granted land to the entire community, usually a plot six miles square. Settlers lived in the central village on land alloted to them. As more land became available, it too was parceled out equally among the citizens.

Each town was held together as a social and economic unit by similar religious beliefs, tenure of land, common social customs, and like aspirations. Those who were not of this pattern were excluded or not permitted to become residents. Here was a nearly pure democracy in which each town had many rights that it exercised by vote of the citizens. Matters concerning the general government were decided by property owners who were members of the church. All other matters were decided by everyone, including non-freemen and non-church-members.

One of these latter matters was the town school. Half the towns of Massachusetts had established schools before 1647, while the others, with few exceptions, were hospitable to one or more private schools. Some were tuition institutions, some were supported by tax money plus a "rate bill," while others were wholly free. Some schools were held in the kitchens of housewives, where children, for a few pennies a week, learned to say the alphabet, to read a little, to sew, and to embroider "samplers." Others were schools operated by individuals able to teach reading, writing, or arithmetic. Sometimes these would all be taught by one man, but most often each was consigned to a different teacher.

Still others offered instruction in Latin and Greek in preparation for the colleges in America or Europe. The New England scene, almost from the beginning, was one of schools and churches, education and religion.

Age 15 – Fourth year added at Harvard, 1654

Ages 12-14 – College Curriculum:

Greek	Rhetoric	Geography
Latin	Oratory	Astronomy
Philosophy	Mathematics	

Ages 8-11 – In New England: Latin Grammar
    School (Secondary)

Restricted to boys: Latin
                     Greek } 1640
                     Bible
                  Arithmetic – 1745

In the South: Endowed Schools

Apprentice—usually 7 years

Ages 5-7 – Gap between Dame Schools and Latin Grammar Schools

Ages 1-4 – In New England: Town Schools, Dame Schools, Reading and
    Writing Schools, later Three R's Schools
In the South: "private," "tutorial," or charity schools

FIGURE 1

Formal Education in Colonial America

The Massachusetts law of 1642 makes no mention of schools. It instructs all who have the responsibility for children to give them apprentice training in some profitable skill plus the ability to read. In 1647, the government and General Court of the Massachusetts Bay Colony enacted the "Old Deluder Satan law," a document that has been called "the foundation of the American public school system." This law reads:

It being one chief project of that old deluder Satan to keep men from the knowledge of the scriptures, as in former times by keeping them in an unknown tongue, so in these later times by persuading from the use of tongues, (that so at least the true sense and meaning of the original might be clouded by false glosses of saint-seeming deceivers,)—[to the end] that learning may not be buried in the grave of our fathers in church and commonwealth, the Lord assisting our endeavors.

IT IS THEREFORE ORDERED, that every township in this Jurisdiction, after the Lord hath increased them to the number of 50 householders, shall forthwith appoint one within their town to teach all such children as shall resort to him, to write and read, [a teacher] whose wages shall be paid either by the parents or masters of such children, or by the inhabitants in general by way of supply [general tax] as the major part of those that order the prudential [government] of the town shall appoint: *provided,* [that] those that send their children be not oppressed by paying more than they can have them taught for in other towns. AND IT IS FURTHER ORDERED, that where any town shall increase to the number of 100 families or householders, they shall set up a grammar [i.e., Latin] school, the master thereof being able to instruct youth so far as [i.e., that] they may be fitted for the university [Harvard]. *Provided* that, if any town neglect the performance hereof above one year, that every such town shall pay £5 to the next school till they shall perform this order.

This is a *compulsory school maintenance* law. It does not require children to attend the schools provided, but insists that each town supply schools for those wishing to attend. It is the first legal assertion in America of the obligation of the government to provide the means of literary instruction. Here we are not concerned with apprenticeship education, but with learning to read and write and the study of Latin, Greek, and the seven liberal arts in preparation for college.

Most communities in the colony already maintained some form of school for the teaching of reading and writing, so that this law was merely a statement of the colony's concern for these skills. It did little more than reassert the literary provision of the law of 1642, with added emphasis upon writing, and thereby bring a few neglectful communities into line. The provision for maintaining a Latin grammar school, however, was a last-ditch attempt to bolster a fading institution. In Europe this school was the standard for those planning to go on to the university. It was confined largely to the wealthy upper classes who would be leaders in church and state. As such it was well attended and prosperous. Its function in America was tenuous. Few youths aspired to attend institutions of higher learning. Those who did usually were sent to Europe for this education. Latin, Greek, and the liberal arts had little value in the New World. Consequently, after the first few years of colonial life, the Latin grammar school was neglected for more practical and useful study. The law of 1647 was an attempt to remedy this condition, a futile attempt at best.

This law left support of schools to the judgment of the local community. At least three methods were used in the process of moving toward free schools wholly supported by the community. Many early schools were supported by voluntary contributions from those able to indulge in this form of charity. In 1636 the Boston Latin school was supported primarily by voluntary contributions of forty-five "of the richer inhabitants." As schools became more popular, towns began setting aside certain revenues for partial support of their schools. These might come from general taxes, rental of specified lands, fines, or other sources of revenue. These sources of revenue were often supplemented by a "rate bill." The town would decide the entire cost of operating its schools. Then it would designate a certain amount of public revenue for this purpose. The difference between these two amounts was divided equally among all the children attending the schools, and their parents or guardians were assessed the arrived-at amount. Those who could not pay were allowed to discharge their obligation by furnishing wood, repairing the school building, or doing other work necessary to maintain the school. Some communities ruled that "if any poor body hath children, or a child, to be put to school and not able to pay for their schooling, that the town will pay for it by rate." Here is the basis for the attitude, prevalent for so long in America, that free education is pauper education.

While this combination of public money and the "rate bill" for support of schools was adopted in many communities, others made their schools wholly tuition-supported. During the first half of the eighteenth century, Massachusetts towns gradually abandoned the "rate bill" and came to support their schools wholly by funds raised by general taxation. Here schooling became public, and the stigma of pauper education was removed. It was years later that other parts of the United States turned to free public education as a natural right of all children.

Control of schools in New England was in the hands of the selectmen or "prudential" men, who were agents for the town in all governmental affairs. The school was, in effect, a civil institution. Support, control, and supervision were matters of civic concern, not ecclesiastical. This philosophy reached even to matters of the most minute detail. Employment of teachers, where a school should be located, length of the school term, tuition rates, salaries of the master and his assistants, and methods of raising these salaries all were concerns of the town meeting in which every citizen had a vote.

This is of great significance for future development in the American colonies. As church control of the life of the people weakened, as non-church-members were admitted to citizenship, as religious freedom became the order of the day, there was no necessity for a revolution to wrest control of the schools from the church. This control had been in civil hands from the beginning, and it remained so as material and civic interests pushed ecclesiastical interests into the background.

But changes in the patterns of control developed. As towns grew and the responsibilities of the town meeting increased, it became impractical to devote time to minute details of school management. Consequently, towns designated a standing school committee responsible to the town meeting. In some cases, this committee was charged with the simple duty of inspecting the schools once a year and reporting to the people in general assembly. In others, all responsibility for schools was lodged in a committee elected by the people for a period of one year. They could be discharged at the end of the year or re-elected, depending on whether or not the people were satisfied with their stewardship. Actions of the committee could be vetoed by the town meeting. Here are the beginnings of present-day school boards elected by the people of the community, responsible for school matters, and accountable to the people at the annual school meeting and at election time.

We have been looking largely at Massachusetts as illustrative of the New England elementary and secondary school structure and philosophy. That it was truly illustrative becomes crystal clear as one turns to other New England colonies. Connecticut, organized in 1639, adopted a code of laws in 1650 including, verbatim, the Massachusetts laws of 1642 and 1647. New Haven Colony, founded in 1643, adopted a code of laws in 1656 in which the Massachusetts law of 1642 was included but much elaborated. In 1669, New Haven became part of the Connecticut Colony and thus under the Law of 1647. New Hampshire, part of the Massachusetts Colony for a time, eventually became a separate legislative unit, and in 1693 incorporated into its code the provisions of the 1647 law, with the added provision that all money for schools and churches come from a tax imposed equally upon all inhabitants of the colony. This was the first truly free school system in the colonies. Plymouth Colony erected its first town school in 1670 and experimented with several forms of support. When it became part of the Massachusetts Bay Colony in 1691, it came under the law of 1647. Maine, as part of the Massachusetts Colony during colonial days, was subject to the laws of that colony.

Two exceptions were Vermont and Rhode Island. The former was under the jurisdiction of New York and subject to its laws. The latter was so strongly individualistic and believed so earnestly in separation of church and state that it was unwilling to assert colonial authority over the schools of each community. Thus it was Massachusetts that set the pattern which eventually developed into the present-day policy of state control of public schools.

PRIVATE SCHOOLING IN NEW ENGLAND

Private schools existed in New England from the first landings of the settlers. These were of two general kinds. One was the dame school, most popular in England. The New England town pattern of community life made this school highly practical, since families lived around the town square and it was fairly easy for children to assemble in the home of some housewife who could teach them the rudiments. Since most town schools required mastery of these rudiments before admission, dame schools were in a sense preparatory. As girls were often not admitted to town schools, the dame school gave them their entire education. In towns that could not afford the town school or were not sufficiently committed to this kind of education, the dame school carried children through reading and, in some cases, even through simple writing and arithmetic. These latter were the exceptions. Some towns helped finance dame schools and even designated the number allowed and the qualifications of teachers. Most dame schools were of poor quality, taught by women with little or no education, and did little more than instruct children in the alphabet. The other type of New England school was the reading and writing school kept by a master who charged a fee for instruction. In many instances masters were given small grants from the town to help make ends meet. Smaller towns encouraged these schools and were able to point to them as fulfilling the requirements of the law of 1647. Larger towns often had several private schools competing with the town school. Masters were usually required to satisfy the town fathers as to their skill and faith. In some towns the official school would devote itself to reading, while private schools handled writing and arithmetic. Some private schools offered Latin and Greek to those wishing to advance their education beyond reading, writing, and a little arithmetic.

INSIDE NEW ENGLAND TOWN SCHOOLS

Town schools usually were open during the entire year, seven hours a day in winter and eight in summer, and met in the master's home or in a room added to his house for this purpose. Equipment was meager. Children sat on benches and the master at a rough-hewn desk. Many schools had a table or shelf attached to three walls of the room, with benches arranged so that pupils could sit and study at these tables. An open fireplace or crude stove furnished heat.

Although these schools were primarily for boys, girls were allowed to attend under specified conditions. In a few cases they were taught along with the boys. Usually, however, they were taught at different hours, during the summer months, or when the boys were at play or recreation.

Teachers were well paid and highly respected. The usual salary was £20 a year, about one-fourth that of the minister, who was the highest salaried officer in the town. Teachers in Latin grammar schools might receive £40 to £60 a year. Dames received much less, usually two shillings a year per pupil. When the town financed her school, it often gave her only cost of living. This statement found in the records of one town is typical of the people's attitude toward women teaching dame schools: "Twelve months of school taught by a female be reckoned as equivalent to four and four-fifths months of a master's school."

In New England, more than in any other section of colonial America, the schoolmaster was a professional man. This accounts for the teacher shortage and the difficulties experienced by towns in securing masters. In spite of the shortage, most of the towns maintained high standards for their teachers. In Dorchester, during the seventeenth century, of the seventy schoolmasters employed, fifty-three were graduates of Harvard, and some were physicians, assistants to the minister, or young men trained for the ministry and waiting for an appointment. Two of the great teachers of colonial New England were Elijah Corlett and Ezekiel Cheever. Corlett taught at Cambridge Latin Grammar School for at least fifty years, possibly more. Cheever (1615–1708) devoted seventy years of his long life to teaching Latin schools in New Haven, Ipswich, Charlestown, and Boston. It was he who made the Boston Latin Grammar School into the most respected secondary school in all New England.

While by and large New England schoolmasters were men of honor, devotion, and skill, there were among them unstable characters of questionable morality, "ne'er-do-wells," men who did little to enhance the public image of the teacher. Many advertisements of the following nature appeared in colonial newspapers: "Stolen on the 15th instant by one William Lloyd out of the house of Benj. Franklin, etc . . . The said Lloyd pretends to understand Latin and Greek, and has been a schoolmaster. He is an Irishman about thirty years." The paper in which the notice appeared was the *Pennsylvania Gazette.*

THE NEW ENGLAND PRIMER

Colonial common schools depended for their instructional material almost entirely upon the Bible, Psalm Books, and Testament, and upon other religious materials which were printed in primers or hornbooks. For example, the hornbook normally consisted of a single horn-covered sheet. On the sheet would be letters or numbers which would be used as the material for introducing the student to reading and arithmetic. The primer was more advanced. It consisted of a study of the alphabet, syllables, and spelling, utilizing rhymes and religious verse. Around 1660, there appeared one of the most important textbooks in all American educational history, *The New England Primer.* It became the reading book for all New England, handed to little children in the dame or reading school. It was thoroughly Calvinistic, deeply religious, and stressed on almost every page the sinfulness of man, his danger of eternal damnation, and his duties toward God and man.

The very little child was told:

> In the burying place may see
> Graves shorter there than I;
> From Death's arrest no age is free,
> Young children too may die.
> My God, may such an awful sight,
> Awakening be to me!
> Oh! that by early grace I might
> For Death prepared be.

In another place the child was warned:

> Our days begin with trouble here,
> Our life is but a span;
> And cruel Death is always near,
> So frail a thing is man.
> Then sow the seeds of Grace while young,
> That when thou com'st to die,
> Thou may'st sing forth that triumph song,
> Death, where's thy victory.

The little book expressed the New England faith in education by pointing to its humanistic and economic rewards. In a poem entitled *Good Boys at their Books,* the pupil was reminded that

> He who ne'er learns his A, B, C,
> Forever will a Blockhead be;
> But he who to his Book's inclin'd,
> Will soon a golden Treasure find.

Later in the book he was told that

> He who ne'er learns his A, B, C,
> For ever will a Blockhead be;
> But he that learns these Letters fair
> Shall have a Coach and take the Air.

The New England Primer began with the alphabet, taught the letters by pictures showing "A apple," "B bull," "C cat," etc.; verses beside pictures: "In Adam's Fall We sinned all," beside a picture of a man and woman standing under a tree; and by larger pictures with verses containing letters of the alphabet. This was followed by prayers, hymns, verses, catechisms, and John Cotton's "Spiritual Milk for American Babes, Drawn out of the Breasts of both *Testaments,* for their souls Nourishment," a catechism. The final section of the little book consisted of a dialogue between Christ, the Devil, and Youth.

There was no happiness, no joy, no love of life in this first reader for New England children. They were pictured as sinners who must be on the watch every minute, lest they doom themselves to eternal damnation. There was no separation of church and education in this book.

HARVARD COLLEGE

New England's interest in reading, writing, arithmetic, Latin, and Greek was based on a belief that the welfare of the commonwealth and of man's eternal soul demanded a degree of education. The laws of 1642 and 1647 are evidence of this fact. It was also recognized that the state and church needed leaders if they were to prosper and make progress. Even though many such leaders had migrated to the New World, this flow was in no way adequate to meet the demands of a growing society. Consequently, the colonists turned to providing their own leaders by establishing colleges suited to this purpose. In *New England's First Fruits,* published in London in 1643, is the following:

> After God had carried us safe to *New England,* and wee had builded our houses, provided necessities for our livelihood, reared convenient places for God's worship, and setled the Civill Government: One of the next things we longed for, and looked after was to advance *Learning,* perpetuate it to Posterity; dreading to leave an illiterate Ministery to the Churches, when our present Ministers shall lie in the Dust.

Facing the problem of providing educated ministers, public officials, teachers, and professional men to insure the future stability of the state, a group of one-hundred college graduates, seventy from Cambridge and thirty from Oxford, undertook the task of founding a college similar in all respects to Emmanuel College at Cambridge. In 1636, the general court of Massachusetts voted £400 towards "a schoale or colledge." The next year it ordered that the college be established at "Newetowne." In 1638, the township was renamed Cambridge, after the university from which most of the founders had come. In the same year, John Harvard, a Puritan minister who held both the bachelor's and master's degrees from Emmanuel College, died in Charlestown, bequeathing to the "wilderness seminary" half of his estate, £780, and his library of 260 books. In appreciation, the founders named the institution Harvard College.

The college was opened in 1640 and held its first commencement in 1642. Prior to 1640, only grammar school instruction was given by a "president" who taught about a dozen boys all the subjects. He was cruel, brutal, and unprincipled, collecting tuition fees from the boys and holding them virtual prisoners in his home while he taught them little or nothing and while his wife fed them food crawling with maggots. When all this was brought out in court, the poor wife broke down and confessed, asking God's forgiveness for her crime, and the "president" was dismissed and returned to England, where he is believed to have died in prison. Henry Dunster was appointed president in 1640, and gave the institution college status.

The charter of Harvard College, approved in 1650, dedicated it to "the advancement of all good literature, arts, and sciences" and "the education of the English and Indian youth . . . in knowledge and godlynes." The second building erected on the college grounds in 1654 was called the "Indian College." While English youths attended Harvard College in numbers ranging from twelve or fifteen to thirty or forty during its first years, attempts to attract Indian youths were less successful. Of the few who did enroll, only one, Caleb Cheesechaumuk, was able to weather college life and receive the bachelor's degree. In 1663, John Winthrop the younger wrote to a friend, Robert Boyle, to boast of the Latin excellence of Joel Jacoomis and Caleb, Indian students who seemed to him of outstanding ability. Joel died soon after Winthrop wrote his letter. Caleb lived to graduate in 1665, but died of tuberculosis the following year, a great disappointment to those who hoped that Harvard would become the model for an integrated college.

Control of the college was in the hands of a "board of overseers," on which sat the most prominent ministers and laity of the colony. The actual governing body of the college was "the president and fellows." These two bodies constituted the *corporation* which determined the life of the institution.

The Harvard curriculum was formulated by Dunster, a graduate of Magdalene College at Cambridge. In it he drew together the three strains of European educational development: the medieval seven liberal arts, the Renaissance and humanistic interest in the Greek and Latin classics, and the Reformation ideal of religious education. All were felt to be essential to the education of the free man who was to lead his fellows in the truth. About half the time of the student was devoted to philosophy, which included logic, ethics, and metaphysics, with probably some theology. The greater part of the remaining time was devoted to rhetoric, Greek, oriental languages, and Hebrew. Mathematics, the catechism, history, and botany were taught, but in a subordinate position. Latin was not taught because its mastery was presumed at the time of entrance, since all pupils were required to speak only the Latin tongue while within the college and all lectures were given in Latin. The disputation was a popular exercise at the college, revealing the student's knowledge and ability to use the rules of logic. Students debated everything from the best form of government to whether or not the blood circulated, from doubt as to the beginning of philosophy to whether or not Adam had an umbilical cord, from the existence of a rainbow before the deluge to whether or not the virtues of the heathen are genuine virtues.

Until the eighteenth century, a tutor was assigned to each class, with responsibility for teaching all the subjects of that class. The president tutored the senior class. Each student was responsible for his own education, meeting with and reciting to his tutor from time to time.

It was not until well along in the eighteenth century that Harvard began to break away from the European tradition of a liberal education and become more responsive to American developments. During its formative years the college was under the dominance of New England Puritanism, the major theological persuasion of the people and their leaders. As the Puritan unity of the colony weakened and a variety of intense sectarianisms, as well as the Anglican Church, made the old faith of the college insecure, there developed a bitter battle between conservative Calvinists who sought to maintain control of the board of overseers and more liberal elements who would bring into the college picture representatives from diverse religious groups. This led, in 1701, to the breakaway of some teachers and students to form Yale, which they considered a "truer school of the prophets."

EDUCATION IN THE MIDDLE COLONIES

NEW NETHERLAND

New Netherland was under Dutch control between 1609 and 1664 and between 1673 and 1674. From 1664 to 1673 it was in English hands, and after 1674 the English gained clear control. The colony was purely a commercial venture, manned and eventually settled as a trading post. After a period of time, during which the post was manned chiefly by officers and servants of the Dutch West India Company, traders, sailors, the restless, adventurous, and the shiftless, representatives of the better elements of Dutch society began to migrate to the colony. These people were more typical of the diverse population of the Netherlands, people who had taken refuge there to escape religious persecution in their homelands. Those who came to New Netherland at this time included French Huguenots, Waldensians, Moravians, Baptists, Quakers, and Jews. It has been estimated that by 1675 not fewer than fifteen languages could be heard in New Amsterdam alone.

The first school was founded in New Amsterdam in 1633 with Adam Roelantsen as its first licensed teacher. Roelantsen's image is vague on the pages of history. He was licensed to teach by the Classis of Amsterdam, sued a patron who had not paid him for "washing defendant's linen," and eventually was publicly whipped and banished from the colony. After Roelantsen there was an unbroken line of teachers licensed by the Classis of the church at Amsterdam, the court in the Dutch Reformed Church composed of ministers and ruling elders, and assigned upon request of the authorities in New Amsterdam. Their salaries were paid by the West India Company, but they were directed and supervised by the local church. The company also paid for necessary supplies, while the local government furnished the school building or, if the school was held in the master's home, paid a small stipend for maintenance. Several attempts were made to have the citizens of the colony take over its schools, but all failed.

In 1629, the patroon system was introduced into American life by the Dutch West India Company. To attract settlers and build colonies, the company would grant a petitioner an estate with sixteen miles of river or waterway frontage, extending indefinitely into the wilderness. The petitioner was obligated to "plant there within four years" a colony of fifty people fifteen years or older. For this service he was given feudal rights to rule his estate and those living on it. The Van Rensselaer estate, founded in 1630, is typical of this practice. Usually the patroon would take the place of the company and support the schools on his estate.

Other settlements in the New Netherland area followed very closely the practices in New Amsterdam. Brooklyn, granted a charter in 1646, established its first school in 1661 by joint action of the local government and the church. New Amstel, now Newcastle, in Delaware, settled by the city of Amsterdam in 1656, had a charter which read in part "that the city of Amsterdam shall send thither a proper person for schoolmaster, who shall also read the Holy Scriptures and set the psalms." Such a man was sent out with the first boatload of settlers, a house was built for him, and his salary was paid by the city of Amsterdam.

Although salaries of teachers in New Netherland were paid by the company or the city, the schools were not free. The master was permitted to supplement his salary by charging tuition, with the exception that "the poor and needy, who ask to be taught for God's sake, he shall teach for nothing." Both boys and girls attended these schools, though girls might be limited in the subjects they could study or the hours they could attend. School usually ran throughout the year, except for religious holidays, with sessions in both morning and afternoon. Subjects included "reading, writing, ciphering, and arithmetic. . . . the fundamental principles of the true Christian Religion and salvation. . . . the customary forms of prayers" and "manners."

The teacher belonged to a distinct professional class, trained to discharge his duties, but not necessarily a university man. These duties were many and varied. The duties of a teacher in Flatbush were stated clearly: he was to serve "as process-server for the schepen's court. . . . also to serve the church, leading the singing and in reading, to arrange the seats, to ring the bell, and furthermore to hold school, to dig graves, and to look after everything else that is needful thereto."

During the period of English control, 1664 to 1673, little or no changes were made in this educational picture. The government of New York maintained the school building and paid at least part of the masters' salaries. However, after 1674, when the English again wrested control of the area from the Dutch, schools were cut loose from civil authority and became parochial, supported and controlled by the Anglican Church. The city did retain authority to license teachers, but left education in all its other phases in private hands.

EDUCATION IN ENGLISH COLONIES

The Duke's Laws, formulated in 1665 for the government of the Colony of New York by the Duke of York, embodied the English attitude toward education in the colonies. Children were to be apprenticed either by their parents or guardians or by the community. Teachers were required to be licensed by some official of the established church. Beyond this, the English governments in the colonies left education in private hands or to charity organizations established for the purpose. The English did not consider education, beyond the bare necessities, a matter for state concern either in England or in the colonies. Thus, wherever the English government was in authority, all religious groups, private interests, and parents were free to select the school which they approved.

EDUCATION IN NEW JERSEY

New Jersey, founded as a colony in 1665, was from the first a land of religious freedom. As such, it attracted groups of religious devotees, who considered the school necessary to the preservation of their unity and values. West Jersey was purchased by William Penn and four other Quakers in 1677, and East Jersey came under Penn's control in 1682. The owners of these lands guaranteed religious freedom to all inhabitants. When these properties fell into English hands as part of New York in 1702, religious liberty was granted to all except "papists." Into these areas came many religious groups, including Puritans from New England, in search of greater religious freedom than was possible at "home." Because of this, each community was able to establish its own religious and educational pattern with little interference from the colonial government or from neighbors. Weak attempts to make provisions for education on a colony basis failed, with the result that in 1695 it was required that each town or community appoint three men "yearly and every year. . . . to appoint and agree with a schoolmaster." This permitted each community to have its own school, operate it as the people wished, and teach what was considered most necessary by the individuals concerned. The colonial government held onto the right of licensing teachers but was very lenient in this matter.

EDUCATION IN THE PENNSYLVANIA COLONY

Here control of schools was in the churches with little or no restrictions. Penn's *Frame of Government* placed in the governor and his council authority to "erect and order all public schools" and appoint a committee of "manners, education, and arts." In 1682, the apprenticing of children was made obligatory. In 1698, the council gave the Quakers the right to establish a school "where poor children may be freely maintained, taught, and educated in good literature, until they be fit to be put out apprentices, or capable to be masters or ushers in said schools." The Quakers were also authorized to set up a public school "where all children and servants, male and female, whose guardians and masters be willing" could attend. The Monthly Meeting, an assembly of all members of the Quaker Church in a community, was given authority to select teachers, remove them when necessary, and admit or refuse children.

The colonial government maintained its authority to license teachers, but a certificate from worthy townspeople was sufficient to meet this requirement. When a new "frame of government" replaced that of Penn, provisions for control of education that had been in the earlier document were omitted. The new one provided "that it shall and may be lawful to and for all religious societies or assemblies, and congregations of Protestants, within this province, to purchase any lands or tenements for burying grounds and for erecting houses of religious worship, schools, and hospitals." They were given the right to collect money for these purposes. Later it was enacted that money so raised and used could never be divested, even if the trustees changed their religious views.

As a result of these provisions, various religious groups in the colony developed school systems serving their constituency and propagating their religious and social views.

SECONDARY SCHOOLS IN THE MIDDLE COLONIES

The first interest of those concerned with life in the middle colonies was commercial. Reading and writing schools soon became part of the colonial structure. Although some schools offered higher instruction in Latin and Greek, and a few private Latin Grammar Schools appeared, it was not until after a long struggle that the Dutch West India Company set aside money for Latin teachers, supplied learned "professors," and founded schools at this level. Since each religious sect had the responsibility for its own schools, and since resources were often limited, little success with Latin schools was experienced in the seventeenth century. Likewise, no attempt was made to establish institutions of higher education in the middle colonies during the seventeenth century.

Education in the middle colonies during the seventeenth century was parochial, each church group establishing, maintaining, and controlling its own schools under the few laws passed by the commercial group or colony involved. This system produced a varied pattern of schools throughout the area, each championing its own cause and acculturating a specific group of children to a specialized society. Here was a high degree of freedom of education, but, except in a few wealthy communities, very poor education. Teachers were often ill-prepared, facilities were on the level of bare necessity, and standards were as varied as the schools themselves.

EDUCATION IN THE SOUTHERN COLONIES

THE SOUTHERN SOCIAL PATTERN

Virginia was typical of life and education in the southern colonies. Settlers and immigrants came to this land to better their lot, not to reform society or break away from English culture. The wealthy came to grow tobacco and grow richer. The middle classes came to ply their trades or professions where the rewards were higher. The servants came where jobs were plentiful and working conditions pleasing. All came to perpetuate the English social scheme.

England was undergoing the Industrial Revolution, with larger and larger numbers of people concentrating in towns where poverty, poor working conditions, and sub-standard living were general. This stimulated discontent, revolt, and progress. The Virginia Company and others among those with early economic interests proposed to establish in the New World English town life based on trade in silk and tea. By 1619, however, the colony was definitely committed to agriculture, especially tobacco, with its large plantations, scattered population, and clearly marked social strata. Average land holdings ranged from 450 to 900 or 1000 acres. One estate covered 200,000 acres. By the end of the seventeenth century, the population of the Virginia colony was about the same as that of London, but the land area equaled that of all England. Large landowners and officials were at the top of the social structure. The middle classes were composed of small landowners, merchants, tradesmen, and professional people. The lower classes consisted of servants and menial workers. Beneath these were the small number of Negro slaves. The Virginia colony was rural. Jamestown was its chief city in the seventeenth century, with never more than twenty houses during the century. The plantation was the real unit of population, the center of colonial life.

When Governor Berkeley was asked by his superiors in England, in 1671, "What course is taken about instructing the people within your government in the Christian religion?" his reply was, "The same course that is taken in England out of towns, every man according to his ability instructing his children." In this he was saying two things: the social structure and economic pattern in the colony were rural, and the colonists were following without change the educational thinking in England at that time.

EDUCATION OF THE LOWER CLASSES

The lower classes in the southern colonies were numerous. Throughout the seventeenth century, and even to the Revolutionary War, the servant class needed in Virginia to work the plantations and serve the upper classes amounted to half the population of the colony. Indentured servants outnumbered Negro slaves three to one. Most educational legislation in the colony dealt with the former group and aimed to include it under laws relating to orphans and apprentices. This servant class had numerous offspring. Further, a very large number of the servants were youths, who were easily trained, maintained, and controlled. They began their service at around fifteen years of age. Offspring of servants, youthful servants, and children of Negro slaves were to be apprenticed, trained, and given a minimum of education suited to their station in life. The laws dealing with orphans covered their education.

Workhouse schools attempted to provide instruction for some children of the lower classes. In England, schools had been established in "poor houses" and in "work houses" to give a bare minimum of education to children of the inmates. A school of this type was founded in Virginia in 1646, at James City. The law provided that the commissioners of each county might send two children each to the school to be trained by the colony. Each child was required to bring stated equipment furnished him by the county. This included "six barrels of corn, two coverlets, or one rug and one blanket, one bed, one wooden bowl or tray, two pewter spoons, a sow shote of six months old, two laying hens, with convenient apparel both linen and woolen, with hose and shoes." The school was in fact a joint venture of the colony and the county. In 1668, counties and parishes were given authority to erect and operate workhouse schools. The purpose was "to take poor children from indigent parents to place them to work in those houses." Some schools were built, but the lack of records on the matter indicates that the idea was not popular in the colony.

THE MINISTER AS TEACHER

Most ministers in the Virginia colony were a sorry lot. The frontier nature of colonial life, with its attendant hardships, discouraged better-trained and more devoted ministers from leaving England. Consequently the less desirable migrated to America. Nevertheless, the colony did its best to make their life comfortable. Each parish was required to support a minister, the money coming from the public treasury. Colonial laws provided that one hundred acres be set aside in each parish for the minister's use, that his salary be £200 or more yearly, and that the community make available to him a home and a church. The salary provision was excessive and was seldom met by the community.

One of the duties of the minister was "to examine, catechize and instruct the youth and ignorant persons of the parish" in the Book of Common Prayer and the catechism on every Sunday. All parents and masters were obligated to send their charges to the minister, under penalty of public censure. Ministers who neglected this duty were fined severely. When a minister could not be obtained for this education, the parish was authorized to employ a "reader," as was the custom in England, to care for church services and religious instruction of the young.

PRIVATE SCHOOLS

One of the major approaches to the education of youths in the southern colonies was private schools. A qualified teacher, usually licensed by the church or the colony, would open a school, advertise its existence, and develop a clientele. He charged a tuition fee, taught "reading, writing, and ciphering," and disciplined the children. These schools ranged all the way from very poor, "very indifferently attended by the masters," to very good, with a devoted master with more than adequate training and skill. These were often called "little schools" or "small schools."

A type of private school that became popular in the southern colonies was called "old field." The name grew out of the fact that these schools were conducted in buildings erected on land abandoned for a period of years because tobacco had exhausted the fertility. They were taught by ministers employed by parishes, ministers without a church, "readers" of the parish churches, or wandering schoolmasters who would settle in communities and make arrangements with the local people for use of the buildings available. While most of these schools provided instruction in the rudiments of reading, writing, and ciphering, some offered French, Latin, mathematics, surveying, or "finishing subjects." Now and then one would offer to prepare boys for college.

These private schools were attended, for the most part, by children of middle class families or by poor children whose tuition might be paid by the community or some philanthropic individual. Seldom was the child of an upper class family found here.

EDUCATION OF THE UPPER CLASSES

The upper classes of the South usually gave their children an education like the one they would have received had they remained in England.

Many families employed private tutors to instruct their children. Now and then two or more families would pool their expenses and hire a tutor who, at a central location or by traveling among the plantations or homes involved, would teach their children. Many of these tutors were indentured servants, bought by parents, and obligated to teach for a period of years. Ships' masters would advertise schoolmasters along with other tradesmen, and parents would buy them in terms of their needs. Other tutors were college students "working their way through school," clergymen not assigned to churches, or professional tutors. In some instances a combination home and school would be erected on a large plantation, and children from other plantations would be furnished room and board while being taught. The cost of these services was paid by parents of the children involved. Here was a carry-over from the days of feudalism, when a child of nobility would be placed at the court of a lord or higher noble for his education. Here the child would begin his education with the rudiments and proceed often to Latin, Greek, French, and other advanced studies. The curricula of these schools were determined by the desires of the parents and abilities of the tutors. In addition to developing intellectually, the child was expected to learn from his tutor manners and the attitudes and mores of his class and station in society.

Another custom, fairly widespread in the southern colonies, was that of sending children to Europe, either for all their education or, more often, to complete their professional training. Some parents, feeling that, at best, education in America would not meet their needs, sent their children to friends or relatives in England for instruction. Others provided tutorial instruction for their children, carrying them through what might be called secondary education, and then sent them to England or the continent for university and professional education. A favorite place for advanced education of colonial youths was the Middle Temple or Inns of Court, where lawyers were trained for the legal profession or leadership in the political life of the colony. Another place frequented by pupils from colonial Virginia was the University of Edinburgh, where many studied medicine.

The upper classes of the southern colonies were Englishmen in spirit and custom. They took England to Virginia and other southern colonies and sent their children home for at least their professional training. Even at the time of Thomas Jefferson (1743–1826), the question of the most advanced education was vital. His opinion was that even though America had several good colleges, an education at the best European universities was superior in many areas.

ENDOWED SCHOOLS IN THE SOUTHERN COLONIES

Following English custom, many schools were established through endowment. A philanthropic individual would set aside part of his fortune to support a school, or one might leave in his will land or other assets for this purpose. The endowment usually provided for the support of a master and a certain stated number of boys. Those who were accepted as students received free tuition and, in some cases, free board and room. Standards for admission differed according to the beliefs of the donors or the boards established to administer the endowments.

Since endowments most often consisted of land, which was plentiful in America and wore out quickly, most of the gifts soon lost value and became inadequate for support of a school. Where they consisted of land and farm stock or other assets, and the endowment was managed carefully and wisely, schools were supported for longer periods of time. However, very few were able to continue into the national period of American life.

The first of these endowed or free schools was an Indian School growing out of a gift of £500 made by an anonymous donor to support a school for a "convenient number of Indian youth." The money was given to the London Company in 1619 and turned over to the Southampton Hundred in Virginia for investing and supporting the intended school. The money was used to build and operate an iron foundry. From the proceeds of this enterprise, a building was erected and a master employed. But, in 1622, Indians attacked the small community, killed most of the settlers, and destroyed the foundry. Since the source of support was gone, no school could be maintained.

In 1620–1621, a chaplain on one of the East Indian Company's ships traveling to and from India raised a sum of money in India and other places and made a considerable contribution himself. He turned the money over to the London Company as an endowment for a school in America. It was decided to locate the school in Charles City, and the chaplain, Reverend Copeland, was made rector. While the building was being built, an Indian raid destroyed the community, and the project "came to nothing."

Benjamin Symms, a wealthy planter in Virginia, left 200 acres of land and a small herd of cattle to provide for erection of a school, support of a master and a certain number of children in Elizabeth City County, and other expenses of the school. The building was erected in Elizabeth City, and proceeds from the farm kept the school going far into the eighteenth century.

Another school, the Eaton Free School, was established in the seventeenth century at Elizabeth City to provide education for children of the community. The gift consisted of 500 acres of land, a large herd of cattle, and several Negro slaves. The minister, church wardens, and justices of the peace constituted the trustees responsible for the estate and the school. The schoolmaster was required by the terms of the will to teach "English grammar" as well as Latin. Many years later, in 1805, the Symms and Eaton schools combined to form Hampton Academy, and in the twentieth century some of the endowment was used to establish the Symms-Eaton Academy, part of the public school system of Elizabeth City.

Many endowed schools appeared in the seventeenth century. Some merely provided education for all children who could qualify, up to the limit of the school's capacity. Others made special provision for including in the student body poor children, sick or afflicted children, or other unfortunates.

HIGHER EDUCATION IN VIRGINIA

Before the Virginia colony had become a recognized settlement, attempts were made to establish a college to offer higher education to those who might become citizens and to the Indians. Sir Edwin Sandys, president of the Virginia Company in 1619, obtained a gift of 15,000 acres of land as an endowment for a college at Henrico. This institution was to serve colonial and Indian youths. Soon thereafter £1,500 were raised to endow, as a missionary branch of the college, a school for "the conversion of infidels," meaning the Indians. The idea interested many, but those in authority felt that the time was not ripe for such a venture and counseled that the colony wait until it was strong enough to guarantee support of the college "out of the revenues of the land."

Interest was continued in the project. A "Master Nicholas Ferrar" left in his will £300 "to be paid when there shall be ten of the infidels' children placed in it" (the college). In 1622, George Thorpe, a member of the King's Privy Council, came from England to become superintendent of the projected college. Hardly had he arrived at his new post when Indians fell upon the settlement at Henrico, killing 340 colonists, Mr. Thorpe, and a number of tenants. Enthusiasm for a college dedicated to Christian education of the "infidels' children" died.

In 1661, the General Assembly of Virginia passed an act enabling the colony to establish "a college of students of the liberal arts and sciences." This permissive legislation was not acted upon until 1693, when a royal charter was granted to the Virginia colony for "a certain place of universal study, or perpetual College of Divinity, Philosophy, Language and other good arts and sciences." This was the culmination of early interests in establishing a college or university in the colony and the stimulus given to the idea by James Blair. Blair was a Scot, a commissioner to the Bishop of London, and a man with enthusiasm, imagination, and courage. He was devoted to education and, arriving in America in 1685, threw himself into the drive to build a college in the colony. When he appeared before William and Mary to petition for a charter and assistance to establish the college, Attorney General Seymour objected vigorously on the grounds that the money was needed for other purposes. Blair responded by pointing out that Virginians as well as Englishmen have "souls to be saved." To this Seymour shouted, "Damn your souls; make tobacco!" The king and queen proved to be more interested in souls than tobacco: they consented to the erection of the college, contributed £2,000 to the project, and allowed their names to be used in the title. Other Englishmen and Virginians gave the college substantial donations, and the Virginia Assembly appropriated a large sum of money. As a result, the college, called William and Mary, was the wealthiest of colonial institutions of higher learning.

The purpose of the college was stated clearly when the royal grant was made in 1692: "that the Church of Virginia may be furnished with a seminary of Ministers of the Gospel, and that the youth may be properly educated in good manners, and that the Christian faith may be propagated among the Western Indians to the glory of Almighy God." The basic purpose of education was religious. It is true that then, as now, high pronouncements in official documents did not express the actual feeling of the people. Many thought of William and Mary as an avenue to class status, political prominence and power, or economic well-being.

William and Mary received support from many quarters. There were gifts of land and money, taxes from tobacco, income from surveying public lands, and direct appropriations from the legislature. Of all the colonial colleges, only William and Mary's income was adequate to meet all its needs.

Under its charter William and Mary was placed in the hands of a "board of visitors," consisting of the most prominent men among the clergy and laity. This body was largely a policy-making agency that left the actual administration of the college to "the president and fellows." The faculty consisted of two professors of divinity; one of Greek and Latin; one of mathematics, physics, and metaphysics; one of rhetoric, logic, ethics, and law; and one heading the school for the Indians.

The curriculum was similar to that of medieval colleges on the continent. Emphasis was on the seven liberal arts and classical languages and literature. Since adequate preparatory schools did not exist, considerable Latin was taught. It was not until near the middle of the eighteenth century that significant changes in the curriculum indicated that the college was coming abreast of the times.

INDIAN EDUCATION IN THE COLONIES

Indian education was of concern from the start of the colonies. The Virginia settlement had in mind immediate education of the Indians; educating and Christianizing them were both an end to civilizing them. The original Virginia charter called for a school to educate Indians.

The spot chosen was Henrico, located some fifty miles up the James River from Jamestown. The failure of the Henrico College to withstand the massacre of March 22, 1622, has been mentioned. It might be noted additionally that Henrico, established primarily to educate and christianize Indian children, was to be as much a "Collegiate School" as possible. The Virginians planned for Henrico to be an industrial school that could develop the Indians into useful members in society. They could learn farming and settle in Virginia. In turn, they could send their own members as missionaries to the unconverted Indians. Though emphasis was to be placed upon educating the "infidels," it was to be an integrated institution open to white students too. Unfortunately for the English, the Indians had no desire for this education business. On Good Friday morning, March 22, 1622, the Indians carried out a carefully conceived plan of massacre. Thus ended this "glorious experiment" in educating the Indians. After the massacre, the Virginia Company attempted once more to revive Henrico College, but in 1624 the Company lost its charter; after the colony became a royal colony, no new efforts were made to further the Indian school.

In 1701, the Society for the Propagation of the Gospel in Foreign Parts received its charter in England. One of its functions was to bring education and Christianity to the Indians. In 1712, a Giles Rainsford in North Carolina wrote of certain Chowan Indians who wanted to have their children taught to read and write. He also told of a school at Sarum (on the frontier between North Carolina and Virginia) wherein the schoolmaster, Mr. Mashburn, was anxious to teach Indians without charge. Several other accounts exist of individual Indian education in the Carolinas.

Shortly after the founding of Georgia, a school was built among the Indians. Edgar W. Knight, in his *A Documentary History of Education in the South Before 1860,* gives this description of the school as told by The Reverend Benjamin Ingham:

> The House 60 Foot long & 15 Wide. it will be divided into 3 Rooms, One at Each End, consisting of 15 Foot Square, & the School Room in the Middle as large as both the Other. Under one of the End Rooms they have dug A Cellar. The Foreside of the House faces the rising Sun, And the two Ends are due North & South. It Stands on A little Hill which we call Irene, by a Brook Side, about half a Quarter of A Mile above Tomochachees Town, where the River Savannah divides it Self into 3 Streams. This Hill has been made Some Hundred Years ago, for what Reason I can't tell; Perhaps to perpetuate the Memory of Some Illustrious Hero or famous Action. In digging the Cellar, they found Abundance of Oister Shells, and some Bones and Buck Horns. When I fixed upon this Place, the Indians ask'd me if I was not afraid to live upon A Hill, I Answer'd no. They said, the Indians were,

because they believed that Fairies haunted Hills. The Moravian Brethren out of their Zeal for the Work, Undertook the Building at a low Price; As soon as it's finish'd, which will be within A few Dayes, One of them with his Wife is to live there with me. I believe in A little Time we Shall have a good Number of Scollars. The Indians, tho' at first they would hardly be persuaded to let one child learn, yet now they are very willing to have them taught, and even Some of the Men seem to have a desire to learn.

Indian education in the colonies never amounted to much, but it was still more than the Indians wanted. The issue of Indian education continues to this day, and is one of the minority issues of our times. The Indians have never had the opportunity to be involved to any serious extent in planning their own education.

New England was equally concerned with Indian education. In the first set of instructions from the Company of Massachusetts Bay to Governor Endicott were orders to attempt to educate the Indians. About three years later, Reverend John Eliot, more famous for establishing grammar schools, began to work at educating the Indians, and for fifty years worked at Indian instruction. Eliot prepared school books in the Indian languages. Later he translated the Bible into the language of these Massachusetts Indians. In addition, he imported "common primers" and hornbooks for Indian education. Reports to England were made regularly in terms of numbers of Indian and Negro children being educated, although the terms used were more often "Heathens and Infidels."

The Indian College at Harvard has been noted elsewhere. While the college itself did not work out, Indians were to be found in Yale, Harvard, King's College, and William and Mary. Dartmouth College started as an Indian school.

DIFFERENCES BETWEEN NEW ENGLAND AND THE SOUTH

As one compares characteristics of the early settlements of New England with early pre-Revolutionary Virginia, a sharp divergence in philosophy and action between the two areas is apparent. The Puritans of New England were determined to have universal literacy, whereas in Virginia, little concern existed for education below the elite class. As Virginia and New England moved through the seventeenth and eighteenth centuries, these views sharpened. Both areas feared a decline to barbarianism, but their approaches to preventing this differed. New England would not sacrifice Puritanism to gain its educational ends;

instead, it used its religion to demand literacy. Virginia leaders were more afraid that the lower level social classes might take over—thus they chose the gentlemen's route. Here, formal schooling was of little interest; rather, Virginians were concerned about social relationships with one's equals.

Wilbur Cash, in his *The Mind of the South,* clearly delineates the significant difference between the two areas—a difference which is legendary but true. Cash characterizes the Yankee New Englander as a sober, grasping individual, with a long background of religious feuding; he was intolerant, painfully thrifty, an exhibitionist with his prowess, a supporter of privileged legislation, of convenient morals, lacking in sentimentality, a selfish seeker of personal aggrandizement. In contrast, Cash sees the Southerner as polite in manner, a sentimentalist, leading a kind of feudal life as a member of the landed gentry, adventurous, hospitable, a free and careless spender, and a lover of field sports, including racing and hunting.

The characterizations depicted by Cash are familiar ones. The Puritans preached of a God who was angry with the individual every day; Jonathon Edwards, the famed Puritan preacher, added: "In a little while you will be in eternity. How dreadful it will be to be in Hell among the devils and to know you must be there to all eternity." To today's reader, Edwards sounds morbid and sometimes sadistic. So does the New England primer from which the children studied. The Puritans believed even the humblest should learn to read the Bible. There was much early death— how horrible to die without learning to read the Bible, and thus not knowing what was right. Puritan thought was harsh because of these kinds of concepts. With considerable justification, the Puritan is often pictured as a person who opposed bear-baiting, not because of the pain and abuse to the bear, but because of the pleasure it brought the spectators.

The Southerner, on the other hand, has been pictured as engaging and exciting, not particularly because of his virtues but more literally because of the vices he slipped in. The Virginia gentleman has been fabled as a man whose lands were too extensive to fence, whose large number of slaves did the work, while the master hunted fox throughout the morning, rested in shade sipping spirits in the afternoon, danced most of the night with beautiful women, and in the meantime gambled away his heritage. Often quoted is the remark that in Virginia, it was better never to have been born than to be ill-bred. Wilbur Cash accepts this evaluation with the caution that there is a South and also many Souths. These generalizations have value, but are subject to misrepresentation.

CHAPTER 12

During Europe's
Age of Reason

INTRODUCTION

The eighteenth century was one of transition throughout Europe. Traditional patterns of life and thinking had cracked wide open during the seventeenth century, creating everywhere an atmosphere of protest against much that the past had accepted as right and just. The new century augmented this protest as there grew an abiding faith in the common man and his ability to build a better world, in the physical sciences as doors to an understanding of the environment, and in human reason as the criterion of truth and justice.

Scholars attempting to appraise the age come up with varied interpretations of its nature and significance. It has been referred to as an "age of reason," a time when man turned to human reason as his guide and judge. There was much in the century to justify this appellation. During the century, reason successfully challenged the authority of "divinely appointed" rulers, priests, prophets, the Bible, and other sacred books. Claims to truth were asked to meet tests of reason, and those that failed were branded intolerable. The conviction grew that man, if he dared to follow the dictates of reason clearly and uncompromisingly, could reform his institutions, discover social truth, and promote the welfare of all. This conviction was evident in the writings and actions of social and political thinkers, religious leaders, enlightened rulers, and educators. In many parts of Europe it was being translated into social and educational experimentation.

Some have referred to the eighteenth century as an "age of enlightenment," a time when new and challenging ideas burst upon the European mind bringing enlightenment, understanding, and dedication.

Among these ideas were the equality of all men under law, the dependability of nature, the innate goodness of man, and the superiority of natural rights over birth, privilege, and status. Twentieth century man feels at home and secure in the presence of these ideas. The Reformation, with its absolutism and authoritarianism, had been left behind. Classical Humanism, with its dependence upon Greek and Roman writings for knowledge and understanding, no longer satisfied scholars and scientists. Divine sanction of governments and rulers, demanding blind and unquestioning obedience, was challenged successfully, based on the conviction that it is man, not God, who must determine what is the best government and who is the best ruler.

Others, yearning for a security characteristic of an environment that is stable and rooted in a true and tried tradition, think of the eighteenth century as a period of decay, disintegration, "heresy," drift, and superficiality. They see revolutions that destroyed tested values of the past, tearing from the hands of the capable the reins of government and handing them to the rabble, the mobs, defying "God's just laws" by upsetting the divinely appointed social structure.

An age of transition is subject to many interpretations as men with diverse values attempt to understand its meaning. Some see in it the death of long-outmoded ways of thinking and acting, making way for new patterns better suited to new times. Others see only the passing of a time which seemed good and right. These interpretations are applied likewise to the education of the period. Since education is a product of the culture and reflects that culture in all its variety, the education of an age of transition will look both to the past and the future. It will contain much that has come to the age and is accepted as good. It will also be a growing thing, characterized by experimentation, new philosophies, new institutions, and new people. In it will remain echoes of the past. It will also give promise of the future.

JOHN LOCKE (1632-1704)

His Life

Scholar, philosopher, writer on many subjects, political figure, devotee of freedom and toleration, and educational theorist, John Locke, although he lived mostly in the seventeenth century, exerted an influence on the eighteenth, both in Europe and America, that can hardly be matched. His books, dealing with social and governmental problems and with education, expressed ideas which became sacred to many leaders of the century.

He was born August 29, 1632, at Wrighton, Somersetshire, England, son of a small landowner and attorney who, as a Puritan, fought on the side of Parliament in the Civil War. At fourteen he entered Winchester School, which was presided over by Dr. Richard Busby, the most famous flogger in all England. There he studied Latin and Greek in preparation for college. In 1652 he entered Christ Church College, Oxford, under a tutorship that he held for thirty years, until Charles II ordered him dismissed. At this time Oxford was ruled by Independents, the first group in England to advocate religious toleration. The famous Puritan, John Owen, was dean and vice-chancellor. While at Oxford, Locke received both the B.A. and M.A. degrees and served as a tutor in Christ Church College, teaching Greek, rhetoric, and philosophy.

Locke had considerable difficulty in deciding upon a career. His reading of Descartes' works stimulated an interest in philosophy. In 1664 we find him experimenting in chemistry and meteorology. His interest in theology was deadened by the fact that after the Restoration there was no place for free inquiry in the Anglican Church. Intrigued by Robert Boyle's use of the empirical method in chemistry and Sydenham's use of the same method in medicine, he prepared himself in medicine, often accompanying Sydenham on his rounds.

In 1666 he was introduced to Lord Ashley, who was to become the first earl of Schaftesbury; with this meeting, a strong friendship grew, based on their common interest in civil, religious, and intellectual freedom. The next year he took up residence in Exeter House, Lord Ashley's London home, as physician and confidential secretary. This was his home for fifteen years. There he wrote *Essay Concerning Toleration,* a book that anticipated many of the conclusions of his more mature thinking and writing.

It was at Exeter House in 1670 that Locke and "five or six friends" were discussing "principles of morality and religion" when they "found themselves quickly at a stand by the difficulties that arose on every side." This caused him to propose that he devote some time to a study of the necessary "limits of human understanding." What was thus "begun by chance, was continued by entreaty, written by incoherent parcels, and, after long intervals of neglect, resumed again as humor and occasion permitted." Twenty years later this study appeared as the *Essay Concerning Human Understanding,* one of the great formative books of British Empiricism.

While associated with Shaftesbury, Locke undertook to tutor the Earl's fifteen-year-old son. This proved to be of inestimable significance in helping to form some of Locke's ideas in the field of education. When he performed the same service for the Earl's grandson, his ideas were clarified and his convictions strengthened.

With the fall of Shaftesbury in 1675, Locke began a period of intermittent exile, when he practiced some most clever "foot work" to avoid being involved in the fate of his old friend and benefactor. Deprived of his studentship by order of the king and denied access to Oxford, he lived in Amsterdam for five years under the name of Dr. Van der Linden. Later, while in Rotterdam as a confidant of political exiles, he became known to William, Prince of Orange. William landed in England in November, 1688, and Locke followed in 1689 on the same ship that carried Princess Mary.

This was the beginning of Locke's fame in England. His *Two Treatises on Government,* a defense of the right of ultimate sovereignty in the people, appeared as an effort "to establish the throne of our great restorer, the present King William, to make good his title in the consent of the people." His *Essay Concerning Human Understanding* was published in 1690. The next year he went to live at Oates Manor in Essex, the country seat of Sir Frances Masham, where he enjoyed fourteen years of domestic peace and literary success despite his broken health. During these years he engaged in a lively battle with Jonas Proast and others over his ideas on religious toleration; gathered together letters he had written to his friend Clarke of Chipely about the education of his children and published them as *Thoughts on Education;* published *Reasonableness of Christianity as Delivered in the Scriptures* and several essays in answer to attacks upon his ideas on religion; and produced a host of writing on money and interest, the Trinity, and questions raised by readers of his *Essay Concerning Human Understanding.* These questions and Locke's answers were woven into additional chapters, which appeared in later editions of the work. After 1700 Locke devoted himself to the study of religion and prepared revised editions of some of his earlier writings. After his death, October 28, 1704, what was intended as another chapter of the famous *Essay* was published under the title *The Conduct of the Understanding.*

By 1690, the writings of this hitherto unknown Englishman began to stir the minds of the western world. His beliefs about the nature of the mind, the liberty of all men, "true" religion, and education were being discussed, attacked, and championed by scholars and the public. Locke lived in the seventeenth century, but his voice shouted out in the eighteenth and was heard by those beginning to shape a new age of toleration and freedom.

His Philosophy

Locke's philosophy is developed most fully in his *Essay Concerning Human Understanding,* which is an attempt to discover, through an introspective study of consciousness, how far the human mind can go in understanding the universe. As he looked carefully at the process of thought, he discovered the *idea,* "the term which, I think, stands best for whatsoever is the object of the understanding when a man thinks." Ideas are neither false nor true; they are mere phenomena. Further, they are not innate. The human mind, before any ideas are present, is a *tabula rasa,* a "white paper, void of all characters." In asserting that no ideas are innate, Locke is actually assuming that no idea is immune to free criticism. He believed that if there are ideas which cannot be doubted because they are innate, these must have a certainty which nothing, even human reason, can question. He feared that having once admitted the existence of innate ideas, it would be an easy step to attribute certainty to arbitrary prejudices and primitive religious beliefs.

All ideas depend upon "experience." They come either from the senses or from reflection. We receive "simple ideas" through the five senses. There is nothing in the mind except what these senses admit. Reflection is the action of the mind in arranging and elaborating these ideas into concepts. The mind receives ideas passively. Then it discriminates among them, analyzes them, draws them together in association, separates and recombines them into concepts, abstractions, new ideas, relations, and principles.

There are certain implications that can be drawn from the doctrine that there are no innate ideas. While the grounding of these in Lockian theory may be questioned, the fact that they have been so grounded cannot be denied nor can their effect upon social and educational thinking be overlooked.

First, there is implied here a definite theory of child development, which has been elaborated by many since Locke's day and which reached its *reducto ad absurdum* in "extreme behaviorism." If there are no innate ideas, the child is radically different from the adult. Both may have the same basic mental equipment, but the child has no ideas, concepts, "experience." As he develops within his own environment, his mind becomes a "furnished house," furnished with ideas that are shaped into concepts. Child development consists, among other things, in furnishing the mind through experiences which will be determined by those controlling the child's environment. The parent and the teacher thereby become determiners of the child's growing mind as they manipulate his environment. True, the nature of the *tabula rasa,* its capacities, appetites, and faculties, may differ from person to person, but beyond that each individual becomes what he is because of the ideas he receives through his senses.

Second, there is in Locke's theory some ground for the belief that "all men are born equal." Heredity, one's inherent physical being, the nature of the *tabula rasa,* and the clearness and keenness of the senses must be recognized as differing among men. In these respects men are not born equal. Beyond this, Locke's theory leads to the democratic principle of equality of opportunity. If all ideas come from experience, each individual should be free to experience as rich and full an environment as possible.

HIS EDUCATIONAL THEORY

Locke observed the world in which he lived, the world of the English gentlemen, and from his observations developed his educational theory. The results of his observations regarding education are set down in a series of writings which include *Some Thoughts Concerning Education, The Conduct of the Understanding, Some Thoughts Concerning Reading and Study for a Gentleman, Instructions for the Conduct of a Young Gentleman,* and *Of Study.*

Education, for Locke, is "the Gentleman's calling." To learn the sciences and all other intellectual matters requires "ease and leisure" possible only among the upper classes. This is not an evil, since when these classes, from which will come the leaders of men and custodians of government and morals, are properly educated, "they will quickly bring all the rest into order."

The "proper" education consists of "four things, Virtue, Wisdom, Breeding, and Learning." In this statement is to be found the heart of Locke's educational theory. Every gentleman wishes to leave his son an adequate estate. Beyond this he desires that his son be a man of *Virtue.* "I place Virtue as the first and most necessary of those endowments that belong to a man or a Gentleman; as absolutely requisite to make him valued and beloved by others, acceptable or tolerable to himself." Virtue means good character, reverence for God, love of truth, and goodwill toward others. This is the result of proper religious training. The first and most important aim of education is to produce the religious and morally good man. All else is secondary. Next to Virtue comes *Wisdom,* prudence, sound judgment, and foresight in the management of one's material affairs and in discharging those civic duties which his position in society imposes upon him. The third quality of a gentleman is *Good Breeding,* the practice of manners that was part of English tradition. A gentleman has the proper regard for himself and others. At no times does he "think meanly of himself," or "meanly of others." *Learning* is important, but not as important as Virtue, Wisdom, and Breeding. Man's highest faculty is reason, but the scholar is of less value than the gentleman. To use reason in the ethical and practical affairs of life is far more important than to amass knowledge or devote reason to the purely speculative. At one point Locke stated: "I imagine you would think him a very foolish fellow that should not value a virtuous or a wise man infinitely before a great scholar."

How shall the young man receive this education? Here again Locke's aristocratic leanings are evident. He considered both public and private education and reached the conclusion that, in spite of its shortcomings, private instruction by a tutor within the family was best. While schools such as Eton and Harrow, open to the public who could pay, might provide knowledge in a superior fashion, they could not teach morals or manners as well as the home. A tutor carefully selected by the parent or guardian, who taught the boy within the home environment, would have the advantage of parental pressure and example in matters most important. Good habits, principles of virtue and wisdom, the proper bearing, and good manners could be developed while the child learned his letters and matured intellectually.

Locke was never strong physically and spent much time traveling in search of strength and vigor. It was this lack in him that stimulated his interest in the "hardening process" and physical education. His ideal, "a sound mind in a sound body," led him to advocate play in the open air, proper hygiene, physical exposure during early life, adequate sleep, diet, and exercise. Education should concern itself with strengthening the body so that it will not hamper the mind.

A key word in Locke's thinking about education was "discipline." This applied both to body and mind. Education is a process of moral discipline by which one develops self-control. Physical exercises are to be designed to strengthen the body and bring it under absolute control of the mind. All desires and impulses are to be obedient to reason. "He that has not a mastery over his inclinations, he that knows not how to resist the importunity of present pleasure or pain for the sake of what reason tells him is fit to be done," he wrote, "wants the true principle of virtue and industry, and is in danger never to be good for any thing."

When Locke turned to consideration of the curriculum best suited to education of the gentleman, he emphasized the principle of usefulness. How will a particular study serve the best development of the individual in virtue, wisdom, breeding, and learning? He was concerned not with the child as he sits before his tutor, but with the man he will become. Since virtue is the most important characteristic of a gentleman, religion is the first and most important subject in his curriculum. This is to be followed by exploratory or introductory courses in many fields. The gentleman must manage his estate, serve his community and country whenever necessary, maintain his aristocratic status, and be well-informed in local and world matters. The gentleman is concerned with "moral and political knowledge; and thus the studies which more immediately belong to his calling are those which treat of virtue or vice, of civil society and the arts of government; and will take in also law and history."

Another curriculum principle that influenced Locke's thinking was variety. He believed that the gentleman must avoid narrowness and inflexibility of mind. When one has explored many areas, read widely, and studied many people and ways of thinking and living, he is capable of a mental freedom and elasticity not possible for one who has studied a few subjects deeply and thoroughly. "The business of education," he wrote, "as I have already observed, is not as I think to make them perfect in any one of the sciences, but so to open and dispose their minds as may best make them capable of any, when they shall apply themselves to it."

These principles of usefulness and variety caused Locke to eliminate from the curriculum of the gentleman Greek, which he considered a subject to be studied only by those who aspired to become scholars, and Latin, except the ability to read classical authors, rhetoric, logic, and disputation. He saw in much of the humanistic education mere verbalism and the "splitting of hairs" to no conceivable use.

Locke also included in his curriculum the English language, French, drawing, shorthand, geography, geometry, chronology, anatomy, natural philosophy, ethics, psychology, and manual arts. The last he thought of as recreation and a source of understanding of the work necessary about an estate.

While Locke was primarily concerned with the education of the English gentleman, as commissioner of the London Board of Trade he prepared a plan for the care and education of children from indigent families and orphans. He proposed that children of this class be taken from their parents at three years of age and kept in "working schools" until fourteen, when they could be apprenticed to learn a self-supporting trade. This would free mothers so that they could work and supplement the family income, give each child of poor parents a more wholesome environment and better discipline than he could hope for in his home, and save the community the expense of courts and jails to care for the products of slums and poverty. These children could be taught religion, handicraft, and obedience to constituted authority.

GERMAN PIETISM AND EDUCATION

While Locke was extolling freedom, teaching that the mind is a *tabula rasa,* and developing his theories of the education of the gentleman in England, Germany was watching the growth of a religious movement called Pietism, a movement that was to have a profound influence on German life, philosophy, literature, and education.

ROOTS OF PIETISM

Pietism was both a product of the late seventeenth century in Europe and an evidence of the cyclical nature of history. A careful study of religious history reveals a pattern of change and reaction. Since all religions are concerned with values, they tend to become hardened and nonprogressive in their efforts to preserve these values. This leads to a counter move on the part of those who wish to establish and defend new values more in tune with the times. After the revolution has succeeded and new values are established, they tend to become formal, stable, and nonprogressive. In time, they are attacked by a new and virile spirit which repeats the cycle.

Lutheranism, beginning as a reaction against the formalism and sterility of the Roman Church, appealed to the individual, the heart, and man's vision of sainthood. After the Thirty Years' War, this fresh approach to religion and morals had fallen under the hand of civil authorities, who wished to use it to support their governments, and autocratic theologians, who were more concerned with orthodoxy, hairsplitting theological arguments, and creedal security. What had been fresh and vital when Lutherans were attacking the Roman Church of the sixteenth century had become in the late seventeenth century formal and sterile, intellectual and ritualistic. Pietism was a rebellion against all this, a call to return to the emotional, sacrificial, and even mystical Lutheranism of the past.

Further, the rationalism of the age, plus the despair and materialism left in the wake of the war, contributed to a spiritual and moral atmosphere characterized by hopelessness and pagan bestiality. When men seek to destroy each other over long periods of time, they tend to become cynical, hardened, interested in the "flesh pots," and callous to the world of the spiritual. Pietism appeared at such a time, stressing hope, human need and understanding, a new birth, the inner light, and the separation of the individual from a corrupt and corrupting world. It condemned the ordinary pleasures of life as evidences of worldliness and called mankind to prayer, study of the scriptures, and reliance upon God.

Pietism was also in the mainstream of the realist movement of the times. Realism turned away from authority to individual experience. It stressed man's contact with the world about him and found truth in the degree of effective "relatedness" he could establish with his world. Pietism placed emphasis upon individual religious experience and practice. It was more concerned with one's relationship with God than his ability to quote authorities from the past. Pietism was the religious phase of the realism that laid the foundations of modern science. Both placed authority in experience.

PHILIP JACOB SPENER (1635-1705)

The "father of Pietism" was born at Rappoltsweiler in Upper Alsace and received his college education at Strassburg. In 1666, he was established as chief pastor of the Lutheran Church at Frankfort-on-Main, where he began to attack the churches and schools of Germany and to preach doctrines which became the foundation of Pietism. By 1686 he was court chaplain at Dresden. His preaching sorely offended the elector, John George III, who wished to dismiss him, but feared the forces that he had rallied to his cause. The problem was solved in 1691 by promoting him to the rectorship of Saint Nicholas in Berlin. In this position Spener was able to raise funds and rally support for a Pietistic university at Halle. This institution was to become one of the great seats of learning in Europe. He was also able to attack orthodox Lutheran theologians so effectively that, in 1695, the theological faculty at Wittenberg formally charged him with 264 errors.

Spener held that Lutheran schools failed to teach true virtue and piety. Their emphasis was secular and practical. While they produced graduates full of knowledge, they neglected godly living and personal devotion to God and his church. This he believed was demonstrated by the fact that Latin, the language of pagans and false religion, was stressed to the neglect of Greek and Hebrew, languages of the scriptures. Students were forced to memorize long and difficult passages dealing with obscure doctrines, while the Bible remained a book closed to many. Aristotle was stressed to the exclusion of Christian writers.

PIETISM AND THE UNIVERSITY OF HALLE

European universities of the eighteenth century were, with few exceptions, in the tradition of medieval scholarship. Instructors lectured in Latin, Aristotelianism was the reigning philosophy, truth rested on the authority of an ancient past, and theological disputations occupied much of the time of faculty and students. While the world outside was changing, the walls of the university protected a dead or dying past.

Pietism challenged this stagnation at all levels. It stressed the more modern sciences, reason, free investigation, independent thinking, and freedom of the mind to study and reach its own conclusions. This was anathema to most of the universities of Europe. The elector, Frederick of Brandenburg, a strong advocate of the educational philosophy of Pietism, sought to remedy this condition by establishing, in 1694, the University of Halle, the "first modern university." Here he collected some of the most progressive and forward-looking minds in all Europe to form his faculty. There was Christian Thomasius, professor of law, who held that all legal procedures should flow from the nature of man; Christian Wolff, professor of philosophy and mathematics, who, as a disciple of Leibnitz, held that the foundation of all philosophy is human reason; and August Hermann Francke, professor of oriental languages and religion, who believed that religious life should stem from the inner light in man's soul. These men turned from Latin to the German language as the medium of communication in class and textbooks. They abandoned ancient authorities and pledged to seek truth by the methods of science and human reason. The great difference between Halle and other universities of the time was made clear in an address delivered in 1711 by Professor Gundling. He asked, "What is the task of the university?" and answered: "to lead to wisdom, i.e., to the ability to distinguish the true and the false; but this is impossible if there be any limits imposed upon research."

Halle began with 700 pupils and grew rapidly, as it attacked the aims, methods, and curriculum of traditional universities and demonstrated the soundness of its position. In time, other universities of Germany felt the impact of these new ideas and began turning to Halle for help and inspiration. Academic freedom, so dear to the present-day university, was born at Halle and spread to inaugurate a new day for higher education.

AUGUST HERMANN FRANCKE (1663-1727)

Spener preached Pietism and attacked the schools for neglecting moral and spiritual education. Francke became the educational and missionary spearhead of the movement. Born at Lubeck of a father who served as privy councilor and justice under Duke Ernest the Pious of Gotha, Francke was orphaned at seven. His guardian saw that he received the best possible education under private tutors and at the local gymnasium, which he completed by age fourteen. Too young to enter the university, he was placed with tutors for several more years. Then he studied at Erfurt, Kiel, and Leipzig, where he was graduated and, in 1685, became a *Privatdocent.* A year later, with the help of Spener, he founded the *Collegium Philobiblicum* for the study of the Bible.

Interdicted from preaching because of his strong Pietistic emphases, Francke was appointed, through the efforts of Spener, to the chair of oriental languages and religion at the University of Halle and was made pastor in the village of Glauchau, where he established the educational complex that made his name famous throughout Europe. As one studies Francke's background from Gotha to Halle, the devotion to education that he showed is seen as inevitable. The whole atmosphere of Gotha, under Duke Ernest's personality and stimulation, was charged with a faith in education. For most of his first sixteen years Francke was in this atmosphere. While a student and instructor at Leipzig, he lectured on *The Education of Boys and Pubescents,* expressing a deep conviction as to the importance of right instruction. He was a pious man, but doubted the truths of the Christian religion. At Luneburg, while under the tutelage of Sandhagen, he experienced a sudden conversion, which brought him to the conviction that the root of all human degeneracy and unhappiness is the neglect of true Christian education from earliest childhood. This belief was strengthened during a visit to the home of Johannes Winckler, leading pastor at Hamburg, where he taught an infant school and studied schools for poor children. From this experience he became convinced that the salvation of man rested "upon the education of children to piety and Christian wisdom."

Francke was deep in the Pietistic tradition. All life for him had but one meaning, God. Man is born to honor God, to live according to his dictates, and to serve his cause at all cost. The spiritual is superior to both the physical and the intellectual. All that one will or can do must point in this direction or be abandoned. The heart is first. This is developed through good example, piety, study of the catechism, prayer, and daily reading of the Bible. Out of this should come a spirit of evangelism, a burning urge to spread the gospel to all men. While learning must always be subordinated to the Christian spirit, it is necessary for the fullest development of the Christian man. Francke realized that exclusive devotion to the intellectual led to meaningless theological disputes and doctrinal emphases, which had no relation to practical spirituality. This did not lead him to turn his back on learning and make his appeal to the uninstructed heart. Godliness and wisdom must go hand in hand. The good man is passionately devoted to God and to knowledge. This belief led him, while speaking of God and the pious life from the pulpit, to establish educational institutions providing for the instruction of children and youths at all levels of society and of all ages.

The first of these institutions was a school for poor children. While preaching at Glauchau, he established the custom of providing bread for the poor every Thursday afternoon. Upon questioning poor children and finding them ignorant of religious matters, he gave them money to attend schools in the area. When he discovered that they spent the money for other things, he organized a "poor school" and supplied books from gifts placed in the alms box. This school was so successful and superior to the schools in the community that many citizens asked that their sons be permitted to attend the classes and offered to pay for this education. These were accepted but placed in a separate school for children of burghers. When a wealthy mother of Sandershein asked Francke to recommend a tutor for her children, he suggested that she send them to him at Halle, where they could receive their instruction from a university student under his direction. This was the beginning of a third school, the *Padagogium*, for children of the nobility. Years later the king of Prussia took note of the work of this school and placed it under his patronage.

With 500 thalers donated by a friend, Francke established two orphanages, one for boys and another for girls. These were so successful and met a need so obvious that similar institutions began to appear throughout Germany. In 1697, Francke established a Latin school for boys of the upper middle class preparing for advanced education. The Latin curriculum was later broadened, and the school became an approved gymnasium. Still meeting the needs of the community as he saw them, Francke provided free board for poor university students who would volunteer to help him by teaching in his various schools. To make them more effective teachers, he was accustomed to give instruction in pedagogy at stated times. From this grew his *Teachers' Seminar,* a school for teacher education, and a special advanced school for the training of teachers for Latin schools.

To supply Pietistic literature, Francke organized the Canstein Bible Institute, which printed and sold sermons, copies of the Bible, and religious tracts in great quantities. Income from this venture was used to support the poor schools and orphanages. Later an apothecary shop was provided to furnish free medicine to deserving individuals. Those who could afford to pay were charged a fee, and the money was used to support the many charities involved in Francke's educational complex.

The aim of the entire Halle Foundation, as it has been called, was to strengthen piety and moral conviction. Realistic subjects were taught in the schools as contributing to this central objective. The sciences, Bible, catechism, religious music, Latin, prayers, and ritualistic worship were included in the curriculum of each school, the degree of difficulty suited to the maturity of the student. While Latin and Greek classics were tolerated, emphasis was placed on Greek and Hebrew as keys for unlocking the Bible.

Francke's influence was wide and deep. Frederick William I, king of Prussia, visited Halle and became a patron of the work being done there. When he established a system of elementary schools in Prussia, hc used the Halle schools as models. Orphanages similar to those at Halle were founded in many large cities of Germany, and the young men trained in the *Padagogium,* the *Teachers' Seminar,* and the *Select Seminar* were in demand as teachers, pastors, and missionaries. Many of these were to be found working in India, the American colonies, and wherever schools of the Society for the Propagation of the Gospel and the Society for the Propagation of Christian Knowledge were founded.

JOHANN JULIUS HECKER (1707-1768)

One of the most influential products of the Halle Foundation was Hecker, who was educated at the University of Halle and taught for a number of years in the *Padagogium.* In 1739 he was installed as pastor of Trinity Church in Berlin, from which he began extensive reforms in the education of poor children. Well-staffed charity schools sprang up throughout the city, and considerable money was raised to equip these adequately. By 1747, Hecker was sufficiently secure in his pulpit and trusted by the people of Berlin to open a truly realistic school, the *Oekonomisch-Mathematische Realschule.* This was designed for boys who would not benefit from the work of the gymnasium. Its curriculum emphasized arithmetic, geometry, mechanics, architecture, drawing, nature study, bookkeeping, and mining. J. F. Halm, a teacher at the school, began to use real objects and trips to factories, gardens, shops, and other places where children could see important processes in operation. Here was the "object lesson" that later became so important a part of teaching. One of the weaknesses of this school was that it placed too much emphasis upon trade training and neglected processes necessary for full development of the individual.

Hecker soon realized that the success of any educational venture rested upon the quality of teaching that could be maintained. Consequently he established a *Teachers' Seminar* especially for training personnel for elementary schools. Frederick the Great was so impressed with this venture that he required all teachers on his private domains to be graduates of this school. In 1763, he employed Hecker to draw up a school code for all Prussia, and established on the basis of this code a system of elementary schools throughout the kingdom.

PIETISTIC EDUCATION IN THE AMERICAN COLONIES

Nicolaus Ludwig Zinzendorf (1700-1760) was born at Dresden of parents devoted to Pietism. Spener was his godfather. While a student at the *Padagogium,* he lived in Francke's home and under his personal supervision. This was followed by several years at Wittenberg, where he studied law and prepared for the diplomatic service. After some years of travel and a disappointing love affair, he settled on his estate at Berthelsdorf and, with "the band of four brothers," set about to create a religious revival. He offered asylum to wandering bands of Moravian Brethren and built, on a corner of his estate, the village of Herrnhut to be their permanent home. Refugees assembled from many parts of Europe where persecution was rife. From here many went as missionaries, imbued with Zinzendorf's Pietistic zeal, to the people of the West Indies, Greenland, Livonia and the northern shores of the Baltic, Travancore in the East Indies, South Africa, Surinam; to the slaves of North Carolina and parts of South America; and to the Indians of North America. In several instances, colonies of Moravian Brethren followed the missionaries. Zinzendorf traveled widely and visited many of these outposts, spending a year in America and a somewhat longer time in London.

Zinzendorf established at Herrnhut an orphanage for girls, a school for daughters of the nobility, a home for noble ladies, a *Padagogium,* and a Latin school. As colonists from Herrnhut migrated to America, colonies were founded in Georgia and Pennsylvania, and orphanages and schools modeled after those of European Pietism were established. There were nurseries for small children, boarding schools for adolescents, and some teacher-training institutions. In all these, children were taught the traditions of their homeland, religion, and vocational skills.

Henry Melchior Muhlenberg (1711-1787) was one of the leading Pietists to carry the religious and educational ideas of the movement to America. Born at Einbeck, Hanover, he studied at the University of Gottingen and, in 1738, went to Halle, where he finished the theological studies and taught in the orphanage there. Later he became deacon at Grosshennerdorf in Upper Lusatia. Through the influence of Francke's son, who succeeded his father as head of the Halle Foundation, he was appointed to supervise the Lutheran churches in the vicinity of Philadelphia. When he arrived in America in 1742, he discovered that his duties included work with all Lutheran bodies from New York to Maryland. In 1748 he organized these churches into the first Lutheran synod in America.

With a corps of ministers and teachers from Francke's schools, he was able to develop a system of parochial schools in the German communities in the area, secure schoolmasters, and raise money to provide buildings and equipment for these schools. He personally visited most of the schools, preached sermons urging support of them by the congregations, examined pupils and teachers, and enlisted the aid of leading citizens and charity organizations. John Christopher Kunze, pastor of the Philadelphia church, was one of Muhlenberg's most ardent supporters. He organized a Latin school in Philadelphia in 1773 to provide secondary training for future pastors and teachers. As a member of the faculty of the University of Pennsylvania, Kunze introduced German language, literature, and philosophy into the curriculum. Later he was influential in bringing German culture and thought to the Columbia curriculum.

Pietism, fused with Lutheran creedal views and the discipline of the Reformed Church, moved into the small communities of eighteenth century America, communities that had their roots in the Lutheran Reformation of central Europe, and imbued them with a devotion to education and the proper care of their unfortunates.

JEAN JACQUES ROUSSEAU (1712-1778)

Rousseau was an erratic genius who influenced the modern world as did few others. For thirty-seven years he seemed dull, even stupid, erratic, delinquent, and unable to make any adjustment to normal living. Then suddenly his genius burst forth with ideas that reached into every phase of life and changed the thinking of the western world. His *Confessions,* half truth and half boasting, reveals a man in torment, a soul torn by unbearable contradictions, a mind that spilled ideas like a too-full pail, a life that baffles even the best-equipped psychiatrist.

His Life

Rousseau was born in Geneva of French parents. His father was a watchmaker, and his mother, who died when he was a week old, was the daughter of a minister. Left to his father's care almost at birth, Rousseau was brought up haphazardly. He learned to read before he was six and spent evenings with his father poring over old romances that had belonged to his mother. By seven he was reading aloud to his father from the classics and other books of weight and literary style. When he was ten, his father, having been imprisoned for a short period, left Geneva for Lyons and turned his son over to his mother's relations, who placed him under the tutorship of M. Lambercier, pastor at Boissy. In 1724, his uncle Bernard apprenticed him to a notary, who soon returned him as wholly incapable. When he was later apprenticed to an engraver, he resented the cruel treatment of his master so much that he ran away to roam through the mountains of Switzerland, learning the miseries of the peasantry, meeting people of both low and high estate, and indulging in all kinds of excesses.

At Confignon, in Savoy, he fell in with Catholic proselytizers who placed him with a young and pretty widow, Madame de Warens, to induct him into the faith. Then followed years of vagabondage, during which he was the companion of several wealthy women, a teacher of music, secretary to ambassadors and other prominent persons, an unsuccessful teacher, and a useless wanderer. Time and again he returned to Madame de Warens as her footman, lover, and toy. He seemed to enjoy this carefree relationship and showed a deep affection for her, often referring to her as "Maman." When she grew tired of the relationship and established another, Rousseau went to Paris, where he served as secretary to the Dupin family, copied music for a fee, wrote and produced an opera, *Les Muses Galantes,* and became a member of the brilliant group known as the *Encyclopaedists.* Diderot had him write articles on music and political economy for the *Encyclopedie.* Through this contact, he was introduced to most of the leading intellectuals of the day, who recognized in him a great genius but had difficulty overlooking his erratic and insane behavior.

In 1743, Rousseau met Therese le Vasseur, a servant in an inn where he was stopping. She was a woman of no beauty or education and with little understanding or sensitivity, but she had an attraction for Rousseau beyond that of any other woman he knew. They lived together for some twenty years and then were married. In this time she bore him five children, who were placed in foundling homes as soon as they were born and lost to history. Years later Rousseau wept bitter tears over the unknown fate of these children.

While Rousseau had charmed many leaders of the intellectual and social life of Paris and had been accepted as a contributor to the *Encyclopedie* during his stay in Paris, it was not until 1749 that his fame as a writer took shape. The academy of Dijon was offering a prize for the best essay dealing with the question, "Has the progress of science and the arts tended to the purification or the corruption of morals?" While traveling to Vincennes to visit Diderot, who was a prisoner in the Bastille, Rousseau chanced to see the announcement of the offer in the *Mercure de France.* This experience was cataclysmic. He tells us:

The moment I read this I saw a new world and became a new man. ... All at once I felt my senses dazzled by a thousand lights. ... Not being able to breathe and to walk at the same time, I dropped beneath one of the trees of the avenue, and there I passed half an hour in such agitation that when I arose the whole front of my coat was wet with my tears though I was not conscious of shedding them. Oh, sir, if only I could have written even a fourth-part of what I saw and felt under that tree, with what clearness would I have set forth the contradictions of our social system: with what force would I have exposed the abuses of our institutions; with what simplicity would I have shown that man is naturally good and that it is these institutions alone which make him bad.

Rousseau arose from his emotional fit, continued on to Vincennes and his visit with Diderot, and returned home to write an essay, *Discours sur les arts et sciences,* which "took the artificial and crotchety society of the day by storm," won the prize, and made him the most sought-after man in all Paris. In this essay he denounced all society and challenged man to break from his bondage and live freely and well.

During the following years, Rousseau was offered several lucrative positions in government but found himself unfitted to a sedentary and responsible life. He wrote a successful opera, *Devin du village,* an attack upon French music, *Sur la musique francaise;* and, when the academy at Dijon offered a second prize for an essay on "The Origin of Inequality," he wrote *What is the Cause of Inequality Among Men?* After establishing himself at the Hermitage, a cottage provided by Madame d'Epinay, he wrote *The New Heloise,* a discussion of marriage and family life. This novel is a collection of letters describing the loves of a man of lower position and a girl of rank, her marriage to a free-thinker of her own rank, and the partial appeasement of the lover's disappointment by noble sentiments and philanthropic endeavors.

The New Heloise appeared in 1760. In 1762, Rousseau issued two of his most famous books. From a press in Amsterdam came the *Social Contract (Contrat social),* which advocated basing all government on the consent of the governed and undermined the theory of absolute monarchy. From the Low Countries and Paris came *Emile,* which bore a subtitle *De l'Education,* a portrayal of the education of a boy from the upper classes and, in the final chapter, the education of the girl who would become his wife. These put Rousseau in the forefront of eighteenth century thinkers but involved him in bitter battles with authorities. The *Social Contract* was condemned by the monarchists as subversive, the *New Heloise* was branded as immoral, and "the profession of a Savoyard vicar" in *Emile* was attacked by the Church. On June 11, 1762, *Emile* was condemned by Parliament in Paris, and its author fled for his safety to Yverdon, in the territory of Berne, Switzerland. From here he attacked those who opposed his positions and so angered the Swiss government that the council of Geneva joined in condemning *Emile* and its author. When Rousseau leveled an attack upon the Genevan council and constitution, his home became a target for nocturnal marauders, and he was forced to flee for his life.

In 1765, he went to London under the protection of David Hume and James Boswell. There he was lionized by the English and began writing his *Confessions,* a highly dramatized story of his life. Had Rousseau been normal, he might have settled among the countryfolk of England and enjoyed the peace and quiet of a literary life. Such was not for him. Insanity was taking hold of his whole being. He came to believe that his friends were plotting his destruction and that the most casual remark was full of hidden meaning. He broke with Hume and his friends in England and, in 1770, returned to Paris and music-copying. The years that followed were full of peaceful moments followed by deep depression and fear. He wrote minor works, carried on a voluminous correspondence, and saw visitors who came to confer with him or just to meet a great man. When the periods of depression took over, he mistrusted everyone and believed that sinister plots were being hatched to destroy him and all that he counted of value. He even accused Therese, who had been loyal to him under all conditions, of an affair with a stable-boy. On July 2, 1778, he died under suspicious circumstances. The popular story was that he killed himself in a fit of depression; however, there seems to be more evidence for the belief that his death was the result of a stroke.

His Educational Theory

Rousseau effected a Copernican revolution in education when he made the child the center of the educative process. To him, the child was potentiality, and education was furnishing an environment filled with opportunities for realizing this potentiality. The teacher must forget the prejudices, preconvictions, and ideals by which he would shape the child. These will most probably distort and warp into gro- tesque shapes the child growing into manhood. Rather the teacher must learn by careful study what the child is, what his strengths and weaknesses are, where his potentials lie, and then so construct his environment that he becomes himself in the fullest measure. In the author's preface to *Emile,* Rousseau states this position clearly when he writes:

> Nothing is known about childhood. With our false ideas of it the more we do the more we blunder. The wisest people are so much concerned with what grown ups should know that they never consider what children are capable of learning. They keep looking for the man in the child, not thinking of what he is before he becomes a man. It is to this study I have given special thought in the hope that even if my method should prove chimerical and false there will always be profit in my observations. I may have gone off wrong in my view of what

is needed, but I believe I am right in my view of the person on whom
we have to work. Begin then by studying your pupils better; for
assuredly you do not know them.

Rousseau held that the child in growing from birth to adulthood
repeats the evolution of the race. This has been termed the "recapitulation theory." If we study the history of the human race and reach for
an understanding of its true development, we will have accurate knowledge of the developing child. Rousseau found that the human race had
gone through several clearly demarcated stages in its development,
each characterized by clearly discernible functions which changed
dramatically as history moved toward the present. This he saw just as
clearly in the developing human being.

Each stage is a distinct pattern with beginning, middle, and end. It is
independent of what has gone before and is in no wise preparation for
what is to follow. To treat any stage as mere preparation for the next
is to miss the whole point. At each stage the child must be encouraged
to live fully and richly as the stage demands and makes possible. Since
life is precarious and "Of all the children born a bare half survive to
adolescence . . . what are we to think of the barbarous education which
sacrifices the present to an uncertain future and makes the child miserable in order to prepare him for a remote happiness which he will
probably not live to enjoy?" Knowing the nature of each stage of development, the teacher must direct the child so that he completes every
stage fully in and for itself. Since each stage has its own needs, the
environment must serve these needs and not those of a later stage. The
best preparation for the next stage is complete development in the
present stage.

Since "everything is good as it comes from the hands of the Maker
of the world but degenerates once it gets into the hands of man," the
child is born good. The ultimate aim of education is to preserve this
natural goodness and develop the individual in terms of his potentialities. This can be done in two ways: by remaking the environment so
that it preserves man's innate goodness or by so educating the child
that he is not warped by a bad environment. Plato, in the *Republic,*
would build the good state in which the child would develop into a good
adult. Rousseau suggests the same approach in the *Discourse on Political Economy, Social Contract,* and *Considerations on the Government
of Poland.* His theme in each is that a good state will consider education as one of its most important functions. Such a state will have
compulsory education and will make available schools, tutors, and
other experiences, all aiming to produce the good citizen. When, however, the state is evil, the environment is degenerate, and anyone left

to its machinations would be destroyed, the child must be educated in isolation from the environment. This is the situation in *Emile*. By protecting the child from the evils of the environment until he is able to resist their warping influences, we can educate him according to his innate goodness. We can develop independence, judgment, under-standing, and appreciations that will insulate him from a distorting environment.

Rousseau feared education for specialization. Time and again he expressed the opinion that no one can predict the future of another. Specialized education can warp one into a form which may never be needed. Change is, for Rousseau, the most significant characteristic of society and of the environment. We do not know enough to predict what changes will take place or what skills, understandings, or learnings one will need when he matures. Therefore, the education of each child must be general and in terms of his present needs as they become known to the teacher.

In a good state, this kind of education can be given as public educa-tion. The child living in a good state will inevitably become good since he finds himself at all times in an environment that offers stimuli toward the good. Parents and others must provide these stimuli in the home and in the immediate environment of the child. Tutors and public classes continue the good environment. When a child is exposed to this good environment from birth to maturity, he will find that his inner goodness has the opportunity and the proper stimuli to develop. He becomes a good adult.

The child developing in a bad state must be protected lest its evil influences warp and distort his inner goodness. Parents must shield him from evil stimuli. He must not be forced to learn, but permitted to grow naturally. When he is ready to learn something, he can be helped to succeed. The teacher is to teach only when the right moment appears. Rousseau called this "negative education," doing nothing ex-cept protecting the growing child until such time as he is ready to learn. When this time arrives, he will learn correctly and, at maturity, his true nature will be fully developed and he will be strong, the master of himself, able to resist all the evils of a corrupt society and able to help create a better environment for his and his neighbor's children.

STAGES OF GROWTH AND EDUCATION

From birth to maturity, the individual moves through stages of growth. Each is distinct, unique, and has clearly defined characteris-tics. Education must conform to this pattern, meeting the needs of each stage and thereby developing the person to his fullest.

From birth to five years of age the primary concern of a growing body, and thus of its education, is physical development, motor activity, sense perception, and feeling. All agencies of the environment must be concentrated upon these. Since each individual is a unique complex of possibilities, no two will develop in the same way. Education must recognize individual differences. Any attempt to shape one child to fit the pattern developed by another is to deny one of the basic principles of growth. The parent, the teacher, and all others concerned with the child at this stage must respect his individuality by following the dictates of his own inner nature.

While the child is to be left alone to grow and develop as his inner nature dictates, he is not to be coddled. He must be allowed to meet hardships, act on his own in problem situations, learn by living and responding to the conditions of the environment, while being shielded from those factors in the environment that may warp or stunt his inner being. At this stage the child is amoral and asocial. He cannot be expected to act morally or socially. Rousseau had such faith in the goodness of man's basic nature that he did not fear freedom at this age. When the time comes, he held, the child will naturally develop both moral and social virtues.

Between five and twelve years of age the child is encouraged to learn from his widening environment. He is not as yet able to reason nor has he developed sex, the root of all social altruistic virtues. His model at this stage of growth should be *Robinson Crusoe,* a man living with and by his environment and succeeding as he learns from the physical world about him.

Whatever the child learns at this stage must be motivated by the demands of his nature at this time, not by the requirements of others. Here "negative education" dominates. Nature is unfolding, is reaching out into the environment for that which will satisfy its needs. Obstruction of this unfolding, no matter how well-intentioned, will distort the individual. The parent, teacher, and others must so guard and protect the child that he is not warped or prevented from living out his life as nature dictates.

The curriculum most appropriate to these years consists of activities which spring naturally from needs. The objective of education here is to develop self-assurance, contentment, health, and independence. If protected and allowed to grow naturally, the child will learn to express himself clearly and precisely as the need arises, to count accurately, to figure, and to make measurements, and he will learn about his world as he finds such learning a part of his ongoing development. No one need push him or force him to learn, since his inner nature is reaching out for satisfaction. He will learn all that is necessary to assure this satisfaction. Those people in the child's environment who are interested in his most complete and natural development will help him only when he needs their knowledge and experience to continue this natural growth and development.

The period between twelve and fifteen years of age is one of the most important for the child's development. It is here that reason emerges and begins to direct the activities of the individual. For Rousseau, reason is not an innate principle shaping life from its beginning, nor is it a product of sensation. It has its source in the emotional life of the growing youth. The infant's needs are few and simple, and his strength, though feeble, is adequate to satisfy these needs. By twelve years of age the child's strength is far greater than his needs. It is then that reason arises as a "check to strength." Reason furnishes guidance to one's passions and strengths.

Formal education begins here. Previously, the child's inner nature has been left to unfold according to its own natural laws. The parent and teacher have not interfered with these laws. Now the child must turn to study and instruction, to learning from others, to thinking. Up to this age the child reacts to physical stimuli. Now he can be reasoned with. Since in the past, authority must be avoided lest the child come to lean on the source of that authority and not learn from experience, so now authority must not be substituted for reason.

Need stimulates the activities of the body. Curiosity is the cause of reason. Rousseau made utility the principle of all learning at this stage. The youth is curious and reaches out to learn that which will satisfy his curiosity. He learns only what will be of use, not a mass of material to be stored away for possible future needs. As Robinson Crusoe needed to learn many things in order to survive in an environment free from human relationships, so the developing mind must discover knowledge in order to insure survival. Youth will, at this age, acquire physical knowledge of his environment. He will learn geography, astronomy, the physical sciences, agriculture, the manual arts and crafts.

All this learning, valuable for survival, is of the most value in developing a set of attitudes that are possible at this stage and necessary if the youth is to grow fully. These include a growing and widening curiosity, an ability to think clearly and accurately, and a knowledge of the correct methods of learning. While the youth learns science, he must be developing a taste for the sciences. While he is investigating the physical world about him, he must be developing a curiosity that will drive him to further learning. While he is studying, he must be learning correct methods of study so that he can carry forward his education without the help of others.

Learning, Rousseau believed, must be governed by three fundamental principles. First, the learner must depend on himself and his abilities. He must be encouraged to think for himself, to draw his own conclusions, to depend on his own brains rather than the judgments of others. True learning comes as the individual thinks through his problems and reaches conclusions consistent with his best knowledge and understanding. Second, everything must be learned by observation of things. Books, signs, symbols are dangerous. One can know only when he has experienced directly. All else is second-hand, vague. Third, as the youth learns, he should be encouraged to build whatever is necessary for further learning. He can observe the world about him, but he will learn most thoroughly when he constructs charts, maps, and other necessary apparatus.

The final period of growth, from fifteen to twenty years of age, is for Rousseau a new birth. At puberty sex is born, and with it comes the possibility of all the social and moral virtues of which the younger child is incapable. Before this stage the individual is limited to the physical and to the beginnings of reason. He can act and react, think and plan, direct and be directed. Now sex enters the picture by the natural unfolding of his nature. He has need of a female companion. With this may come all the higher virtues: sympathy, generosity, friendship, gratitude. He is no longer isolated, a being alone in an environment of others. He comes now to appreciate others, to realize the implications of human relationships, to reach out for others and for the author of nature. He has now become conscious of his dependence upon others and upon God.

He is ready to study all the sciences of human relationships: psychology, sociology, and ethics. The teacher, at this stage, must help the individual conquer evil passions, cruelty, malevolence, envy, covetousness, and self-centered disregard of the rights of others. He must assist in arousing the higher emotions of friendship, love, justice, philanthropy, gratitude, and sympathy. This is to be accomplished not by reading books, but through human experiences.

The curriculum at this stage consists of those areas of man's knowledge that deal with human nature and the social order. Now the individual is to be placed in situations that portray the actual relations of living men. He will learn biographies of good men, fables with a moral, social history, and the natural religion of the human heart. As these develop, he will turn to others, especially to *the* other, his mate. In her he will find fulfillment and the stimulus for all fine emotions. They will beget, another life will begin unfolding its inner nature, and the cycle will be repeated again.

THE EDUCATION OF WOMEN

Book five of *Emile* deals with the education of Sophie, who is to become the wife of Emile. Here Rousseau is traditional to the extreme. Sophie is to be trained and educated to become the wife of Emile and the mother of his children. In this, Rousseau says, "the whole education of women ought to be relative to men." At another time he asserts that "woman is made to please and to be dominated." She has no independence and thus no free development of her inner nature. Since the sexes are different, Emile is made to rule and Sophie to accept and please. Both are to develop as their sex dictates, and this demands different educations. When Sophie is trained as her sex demands, she will be the true complement of Emile; they will marry, and both will be truly happy. She will discharge her part of the marriage bargain willingly and graciously, and he will discharge his part in the same manner. Together they will form the perfect home, in which children can grow and develop normally in terms of their sex positions.

CONCLUSION

Rousseau laid the foundations for both pragmatism and progressive education. He demanded that all things be tested in terms of their use. He placed the child at the center of the educative process. He saw society as corrupt, weak, demanding, and ignorant of the true nature of the child. To protect the yet unformed individual from these evil influences, he shielded him and sought full development of his inner nature, a truly good inner nature. So shielded, the child could, he believed, unfold his innate goodness. seeking help when the task was too much for his strength or talent. After his character was fully developed, he could resist the evils of society and begin creating a good society, which would then produce the good man.

For this, and for many of the accompanying ideas and ideals, Rousseau was both worshiped and hated. Women throughout Europe turned to nursing and protecting their children. Philosophers saw in his writing the opening of the gates of prisons of both the body and the mind. Others were convinced that he was a fiend, a devil, a "wretch." Today these more violent attitudes toward him have disappeared, and modern scholars find in his writings many contradictions, inaccuracies, and exaggerations. They also find germs of some of our most modern and cherished principles.

Rousseau was a giant among men, even though his strength was not equal to the tasks he set himself. Pestalozzi, Froebel, and John Dewey were products of much of his thinking, and present-day education is, in many ways, a child of his mind.

NATIONALISM AND EDUCATION IN THE EIGHTEENTH CENTURY

The church from early times was, in the thinking of most people in Europe, the natural educator of the people. Luther had challenged this concept by his appeal to civil authorities to fill the vacuum left by the Protestant revolt. Even when they did enter the field of education, they leaned heavily upon religious institutions and talent.

By the eighteenth century, social and economic factors had produced a vast population of poor and ignorant people whose existence shamed constituted authority and challenged the moral and religious idealism of the age. Churchmen, social philosophers, and philanthropic agencies were writing and speaking out against conditions while urging that reforms be undertaken to guarantee these depressed masses their natural rights. Students of government were beginning to challenge the position that kings and emperors had divine sanction for their rule with the revolutionary idea that rulers were the instruments of the people. They held that the first duty of the ruler was to his people, to insure their welfare. Attempts of church-sponsored organizations to alleviate the steadily worsening plight of the masses were shown to be ineffectual. As a result, many turned to the state as the only institution capable of solving the problems involved.

The doctrine of natural law, which seemed so successful in the realm of the sciences, was coming to fascinate leaders of social thought. The universe, they believed, provided natural laws for the government of men and societies. These laws could be discovered by processes of thought similar to those employed in the physical sciences. Once discovered, it was the business of the state to enforce them for the good of all.

This thinking created both benevolent despotisms and democracies dedicated to the welfare of the people. The benevolent despots thought of education as a means for promoting obedience, happy and contented subjects, and efficient and prosperous producers for the group. Democrats, on the other hand, conceived of education as the method for producing intelligent citizens capable of governing themselves, for establishing civil institutions dedicated to their good. Both thought of the school as a national institution under control of the state, more or less free to all, and dedicated to molding citizens according to the intellectual and moral pattern championed by the state.

There was considerable opposition to this point of view. Churches feared it as the open door to secularism and atheism. Those with vested interests in the *status quo* opposed any change that might threaten their position. Many were convinced that it was God's will that the poor remain poor and that any attempt to change conditions would be an affront to Him. A goodly number, while granting that some education might be good for these people, wanted to confine it to the needs of their station in life and were fearful of educating them beyond their class, thereby creating discontent and civic peril.

FRENCH EDUCATION AND NATIONALISM

Jesuit education was banned in France in 1763, leaving the nation in an educational vacuum. A flood of books and pamphlets followed, advocating a national system of schools with authority centralized in the French government. Among these were *De l'Esprit* by Helvetius (1757), *Essay on National Education* by La Chalotais (1763), *Plan d'education* and *Report on Education to Parliament* by Rolland (1768), *De l'Homme* by Helvetius (1772), *Memoires* by Turgot (1775), *Provision on Education* by Diderot (1776), and *Report on the General Organization of Public Instruction Presented to the National Assembly* by Condorcet (1792).

While each of these expressed certain ideas growing out of the unique experiences and thinking of the writer, they tended to agree on basic principles. Among the areas of agreement were the following: The state must take education from the hands of the church and control it so that products of the schools will be "children of the state . . . educated by members of the state." The state cannot safely share the education of its citizens with any institution or organization not wholly under control of its authorities. All people must be educated since they are all citizens of the state. This did not mean that all should have the same education. Most writers believed that the education of the individual should be suited to his needs and his place in the social structure. This usually meant that primary education should be universal and free, while more advanced instruction should be offered to the upper classes who would lead and govern.

The central purpose of this education, all agreed, should be development of national loyalty, a sense of solidarity, and ability to serve the state. Since the state supports and promotes education for its own self preservation, it must indoctrinate civic virtues as interpreted by its leaders. Divided loyalty cannot be tolerated.

France was moving steadily in the direction of a national system of education tailored to serve national interests and to induct all citizens into the state intellectually and emotionally. It was to be a practical education, fitted to the needs of each class, and supported by the wealth of all. The state, not the individual, determined its content and method. Most of the educational leaders of the age shared the strong belief that the people could not be trusted to determine their destiny but must recognize the superior abilities and understandings of an elite. In the writings of many was a definite fear that too much education for the masses would pose a real danger to the state.

ENGLISH EDUCATION AND THE NATIONAL IMAGE

The English state during the eighteenth century did not step into education and seek to construct a school system dedicated to shaping the English citizen in the image of the state. This was not necessary, since the image was so clear and sharp that it appeared almost automatically in the educational pattern which developed.

The eighteenth century saw England moving along several lines. The upper classes became wealthy, while the masses sank deeper into poverty. Class distinctions were emphasized, with a hereditary aristocracy at the top, a fairly independent and comfortable middle class, and "inferior" classes at the bottom. English devotion to tradition, prestige, and "the will of God" kept each from interfering with the other. This social pattern existed in a politically democratic state that was economically individualistic. The state did not seek to upset this pattern. It accepted the *status quo* and turned its interests to building an empire. By 1759, England had added India and Canada to this empire, created a navy that roamed the seas unchallenged, and was well on the way to controlling explorations and trade throughout the world.

Invention of the steam engine in 1765, the mechanical shuttle in 1733, the spinning machine in 1768, and the cotton gin in 1795 placed England well on her way to the Industrial Revolution. Her coal industry in Cornwall was thriving, and coal-burning ships plied her trade in distant waters; shipbuilding became a major industry, and her villages and towns centers of a world-wide textile trade. As industry moved from the cottage and small home to large cities and mills, slums grew in number and congestion, and the middle class entrepreneur increased his wealth and power.

In this atmosphere of prosperity, security, and growing poverty, English utilitarian thought fitted nicely. Bacon and Locke had expressed it earlier. Now Adam Smith and Bentham said what was in the minds of most Englishmen. This was the belief that the good is both pleasurable and useful. Joseph Priestley (1733-1804) placed this philosophy clearly within the educational setting when he expressed the belief that the whole purpose of instruction was to produce the useful man, useful within the area of his living. Jeremy Bentham (1748-1832) developed a system of utilitarian ethics which expressed the thinking of British liberals.

None of the writers of this period felt any urge to propose a state system of education. Tradition demanded freedom in choice of school and teachers. The social philosophy of the times championed freedom over official control. Religious leaders were strong in the conviction that education and religion were inseparable and that state control of education would inevitably bring secularization of instruction. They were unwilling to entrust the teaching of religion to the state, even though the ruler of the state was head of the church. These were some of the factors which made a state system of schools impossible in England. They were also the factors which determined that English education would reflect English society and English thinking.

Education of the middle and upper classes in eighteenth century England was in the hands of parents and guardians. They were free to choose teachers and schools and determine the amount of education a child was to receive. It was expected that a father would give his son or daughter an education appropriate to his class and future duties. With few exceptions, this expectation was fulfilled. The child was educated from the parent's purse as deemed wise and necessary and in terms of his station in life. Teachers and schools were commercial ventures, free to seek patrons and offer whatever was demanded. Few restrictions were imposed.

As pauperism increased with the Industrial Revolution, resulting from the growth of large manufacturing and commercial centers and the gradual disappearance of the home craftsman and small farmer, drunkenness, debauchery, and ignorance spread among the masses. This aroused the churches, charitable agencies, and individuals to seek a remedy for these and other evils. Some realized that this social cancer could spread, to sicken and eventually destroy the whole state. Education seemed to many the only effective remedy—an education in morals, religion, and skills necessary to one's station in life.

Robert Raikes (1735-1811), a businessman of Gloucester, organized a Sunday school for poor working children in 1780. Although his was not a new idea, it had novel features which attracted other philanthropic individuals. Joseph Alleine had established Sunday schools in England in the seventeenth century, and John Wesley held Sunday classes in Savannah, Georgia, in 1737. Raikes went further than either of his predecessors by employing teachers and organizing a secular school free to children who worked six days a week and a minimum of twelve hours a day. Sunday was their holiday, a day in which they roamed the streets aimlessly committing crimes of delinquency. This Sunday school took children off the streets and made available to them reading, writing, counting, religion, the scriptures, and singing of hymns. So valuable was the idea that by 1785, a *Society for the Establishment and*

Support of Sunday Schools Throughout the Kingdom was organized to receive money and other gifts from people of all denominations and those of no religious affiliation and to establish and support Sunday schools throughout England. The Methodists and Baptists were especially enthusiastic about the movement and undertook to make it part of their church organizations. Since there was never enough money to meet all the requests for schools, volunteers were recruited as teachers, and though some were adequate, the quality of instruction suffered, and many schools were forced to close.

This lack of funds and qualified teachers threatened the Sunday school movement as well as other endeavors to provide minimum education for impoverished children. The situation was changed materially when the monitorial system was introduced into English education. Andrew Bell (1753-1832), an English divine and educator born in Saint Andrews, Scotland, was serving in 1789 as superintendent of an orphan asylum in Madras, India, when the shortage of teachers led him to conceive the idea of "mutual tuition by the pupils." He selected several bright youths from the community, taught them for part of the day, and placed each in charge of a "class" to teach the same lesson. Upon his return to London, in 1797, he published his experiences in a pamphlet, *An Experiment in Education.* Little attention was paid to this novel plan until Joseph Lancaster (1778-1838), a Quaker from Southwark, opened a school based on Bell's method but with a number of improvements. He was able to teach over a thousand children. This was the answer to the problem of mass education. One teacher and one school could give instruction to great numbers of children. It was not the best possible education, but it was better than no education, and philanthropic groups were quick to appreciate its merits.

In a very short time, similar schools were to be found throughout England. The *Royal Lancastrian Institution,* afterwards called the *British and Foreign School Society,* was founded in 1808 to gather funds and establish monitorial schools. Other organizations adopted the plan, providing teachers and books for poor schools and supervising their programs. The *National Society for Promotion of Education of the Poor in the Principles of the Established Church,* founded in the first decade of the nineteenth century, made Bell its superintendent. Monitorial schools appeared in the large cities of the United States, Mexico, South America, and many European and eastern centers. Wherever great numbers of poor children were assembled for work in manufacture, and where philanthropy sought to educate, the monitorial school grew and prospered. Though no substitute for trained teachers, the system did popularize mass education of the poor and planted in the minds of many the idea that free education for the underprivileged was both possible and necessary.

Robert Owen (1771-1858) was one of the leading philanthropists of the nineteenth century. Born at Newtown, Montgomeryshire, he was the son of a small business man, a saddler and ironmonger. He attended school in Newtown, but quit at the age of nine for an apprenticeship in a draper's shop. Leaving this after several years of training, he settled in Manchester, where, at nineteen, he was manager of a cotton mill employing 500 people. His ideas of management and treatment of workers soon shaped this plant into a showplace for all England. Later, as manager and partner in the Chorlton Twist Company at Manchester, he influenced his partners to purchase the New Lanark Mills and allow him to manage the plant. Of the more than 2,000 employees of the mill, 500 were children five or six years of age, recruited from poorhouses and charity agencies in Edinburgh and Glasgow. The workers were uneducated, their housing intolerable, sanitation nonexistent, and crime, vice, and drunkenness were rife. Owen determined to change all this.

Better houses were erected and made available to the workers at prices they could afford. Cleanliness, thrift, and decency were encouraged. A store was opened in which workers could buy goods of high quality at a few pennies above cost. The sale of liquor was put under strict supervision. New Lanark was fast becoming a model industrial community, the showplace of social enlightenment.

Owen was most successful with his program of education. He supported a monitorial school, free to all children from five to ten years of age. This he called the *New Institution*. James Buchanan, a teacher of some note and ability, undertook to organize the school and set it on its feet. His success inspired a group of philanthropists to invite him to London, where he opened the first *Infant School*. Encouraged by Buchanan, Samuel Wilderspin created more effective methods of instructing small children, organized several infant schools in the city, and was instrumental in founding the *Infant School Society*, of which he became chief agent in 1824. This agency established infant schools throughout England, collected funds for their support, and recruited teachers equipped with the best methods then known. Many philanthropic societies in England promoted schools at this level at home and in foreign countries. Among these were *The Irish Commissioners*, the *British and Foreign School Society*, and the *National Society*. The *Glasgow Infant School Society* was founded in 1826, largely for training teachers for infant schools.

Although the mill was a financial success, Owen's partners were not satisfied and wanted to return to more standard and established methods of conducting business. Finally, Owen formed a new firm with Jeremy Bentham and William Allen as partners. At the same time, he published *A New View of Society,* in which he argued that one's character is formed by environmental conditions, over which he has no control, and therefore he cannot be blamed or commended. This led him to the conclusion that to form human character rightly, one must be placed in the right environment from birth. Correct education must begin at birth and continue until one's character is firmly shaped and he can resist evil influences. His philosophy led him to advocate infant education through direct experience. He would have children learn by seeing and hearing, by walks in the country, nature study, singing and dancing, and object lessons.

Owen began factory reforms and ventures in community betterment which laid the foundation for socialism. He worked for legislation prohibiting employment of children under ten years of age and limiting their working to daylight hours and not more than ten and one-half hours each day. He proposed organizing self-contained communities of not more than 1,200 persons, who would live in one large building consisting of private apartments, a community kitchen, and mess hall. Land would be owned in common to produce food for all. Children would be left with their parents until the age of three, when they would be turned over to the community for care and education, parents having access to them at meals and other stated times. Several such communities were established. Among these were New Harmony, Indiana; Queenswood in Hants; Orbiston near Glasgow; and Ralehine in Ireland.

The questionable success of these ventures led Owen to prepare a *Report to the County of Lanark,* in which he affirmed that reform alone will not solve the problems of an industrial society; the society itself must be transformed. Essential in this transformation was an education which would indoctrinate the young as to the workers' point of view and prepare all to work effectively for the good of everyone. A leader of socialistic thought in England, Owen devoted the later years of his life to propagandizing his ideas about education, social reform, and the betterment of conditions among workers.

It was not until the beginning of the nineteenth century that the English government undertook to move into education with the passage of a weak and ineffectual compulsory education law. Tradition was strong in English thinking. The image held by the state was that of a society in which education was bought by parents or guardians or offered free by charitable agencies and philanthropy. This image dominated education in the eighteenth century and shaped an English educational system. There was growing evidence that this policy was not adequate to the demands of the new industrial age, but England moved slowly toward change, and the image remained powerful.

NATIONALISM IN GERMAN EDUCATION

Germany in the eighteenth century had reacted against religious sterility and spiritual degeneracy by turning to Pietism. Spener, Francke, and Hecker had woven it into the schools, and through them it had become part of German life and thought. The idealism permeating Pietism was natural to the Germanic nature, as was the practical interest in realism. Added to these characteristics was a deep respect for and devotion to the state, which at times amounted to servile obedience to constituted authority. Events in France, and the thinking which gave birth to them or became their product, interested many Germans but did not materially shape their thinking. The tradition of the benevolent despot was deeply engrained in German life and thought, and experience with men of the caliber of Frederick William I and Frederick the Great was proof of the soundness of this tradition. But Germany remained in the mainstream of western history, taking from the great movements of the age what it could use and rejecting that which seemed inappropriate. Frederick the Great found much in the Enlightenment that he could use profitably. Rousseau's thinking seemed of real importance to Basedow, while Rochow reached into the writings of the Physiocrats for ideas of reform. Each German leader saw his ideas as applicable to education and attempted to work out their implications in this field. German civil authorities realized very early the strategic importance of education in the life of the state and encouraged these ventures. In many instances, programs developed by these leaders were adopted in one or more German states and received financial and prestige support from governmental sources.

Johann Bernhard Basedow (1723-1790) was born at Hamburg, son of a hairdresser. Erratic and unmanageable, he left home early with little or no education. Persuaded by a friend to continue his schooling, he completed the gymnasium and entered the University of Leipzig. Later he received his master's degree from the University of Kiel. As tutor of a boy of seven in the home of Herr von Quaalen of Holstein, he became interested in education, especially the reform of current teaching methods, which he found wholly inadequate. Although he held several prominent positions in noted schools of Europe, his unstable nature and unorthodox religious views resulted in his dismissal.

In 1762, he chanced to read two of the great works on education currently attracting attention throughout Europe: Rousseau's *Emile* and La Chalotais' *Essay on National Education.* These seemed to substantiate his views on reform and convinced him that he should make every effort to popularize his own ideas about teaching. As a result, he wrote *Appeal to the Friends of Mankind and to Men of Power Concerning Schools and Studies and their Influence on Public Welfare.* This was a definite statement of his views on education and an appeal for money and backing so that he might write much-needed textbooks and establish schools dedicated to his methods. Men and institutions throughout Europe came forward with money and support. Representatives of religious persuasions, fraternal organizations, and many professions and trades gave money and their personal commendation of his ideas.

Using the funds provided, Basedow wrote, in 1770, the *Book of Methods for Fathers and Mothers of Families and for Nations.* He agreed with Comenius that education should begin at birth and in the home. He explained in simple words and in detail the methods parents might employ in the education of infants. This book was followed by the *Elementary Book.* In 1774, the two works were published in four volumes with one hundred engravings under the title *Elementarwerk,* a treatise designed to cover education from birth to eighteen years of age. The book was immediately popular throughout Europe, and Basedow was hailed as the greatest educator since Comenius, an outstanding "benefactor of mankind."

Prince Leopold of Anhalt Dessau invited Basedow to organize a school in Dessau based on his ideas of method and curriculum. He provided elaborate buildings, the salaries of all teachers and personnel, and other necessary facilities. The school was opened in 1774 and christened *Philanthropinum* to emphasize the fact that it was a product of humanity's devotion to the training of the young toward humanitarian ends. The institution became famous almost overnight. Visitors came from all over Europe to see and learn. Similar schools were established by rulers and philanthropists, and Basedow's thinking was the dominant force in much of European education.

The school's aim was to prepare upper-class boys for useful and happy living. The school should be open to youths of all religious faiths —or none—since it should be under the control of the state, which allowed divergence in religious thinking. This antagonized the orthodox and those who felt that the state should reflect a definite religious belief and enforce that belief through its schools.

Basedow's methodology was eclectic. He chose what he considered best from all the authors he read and wove a pattern that seemed to him to serve his basic educational philosophy. Everything, he held, should be taught through the senses. Objects, pictures, models, and other concrete materials should be used in place of wordy explanations, which often were meaningless to children. All languages should be taught by the conversational method. leaving grammar and rules for a time when the child had attained fluency in the spoken word. All learning must be useful, since immediate use is the most compelling motivation. What the child is asked to learn cannot be meaningful to him if it is mere preparation for a distant and meaningless future. The needs of the child today, needs that he feels and understands, are the criteria of learning. When the child wants to learn because he has a need for the learning, discipline will be unnecessary. If the child does need some discipline, it should be mild and to the point.

The *Philanthropinum* was a realistic school. Its curriculum emphasized natural history, anatomy, physics, arithmetic, geography, geometry, and physical training. Pupils were taken on field trips to factories, military camps, farms, markets, and other places where they could experience directly what they were studying. Since the pupils were from the upper classes, they were taught manners, the morals of their class, social duties and responsibilities, and skills appropriate to the life they and their parents led. Students learned this lesson by attending the courts of princes and other rulers.

Basedow recognized early, and stated so in the *Appeal,* that one of the most pressing educational needs was an adequate supply of proper textbooks. These should be written at the level of the child's comprehension and should be simple enough to be used intelligently by untrained teachers and parents. As a result of his efforts, a flood of books written for children appeared. These included books of romance, drama, history, geography, science, adventure, and many other areas of childhood interest. Since Rousseau had advocated *Robinson Crusoe* as a suitable book for youths, Basedow's followers attempted to elaborate on its theme by writing *Robinson the Younger, Swiss Family Robinson,* and other books of adventure.

Basedow became the focal point of educational reform in Germany, mobilizing philanthropic interests of the day and inspiring those with money and influence to undertake concrete experiments designed to help the less fortunate. He did more than talk about reform; he created schools which were effective in the reform movement. When it was demonstrated that education could effect reform, others copied his methods and institutions, and Basedow schools appeared throughout Germany, and their influence reached into other lands. Since the state was concerned with the deteriorating conditions among the massed poor, it was interested in Basedow's work and anxious to sponsor similar experiments. To make this work most effective, Basedow recommended establishment of a *State Superior Council for the Supervision of Public Instruction.* This influenced von Zedlitz, the Prussian minister, who, in 1787, established the *Oberschulkollegium,* by which all Prussian schools were brought under state control.

Basedow was not a man endowed with sufficient stability or social understanding to succeed. He trusted no one, fearing theft of his ideas. He quarreled with his associates and was jealous of anyone who had the talent to run the *Philanthropinum* successfully. The experiment weakened and eventually disappeared. Many who claimed to carry on his work in other places where charlatans interested in capitalizing on a popular interest for their own financial gain. The orthodox clergy, the humanists, and others devoted to traditionalism fought Basedow and his radical ideas effectively. As a result of all these factors, the *Philanthropinum* passed into history, leaving ideas and methods which were to attract educators of the nineteenth century and influence the modern trend in schooling.

Baron von Rochow (1734-1805), a wealthy German nobleman, generous, concerned with conditions of the peasant classes, sought to use the methods and ideas of Basedow to reform the education of the peasants and thereby alleviate some of their misery. He knew these people well. Many lived on his estate, afflicted with disease, vice, and ignorance. They could be helped, he believed, through proper education. In 1772, he published a teachers' manual, *School Book for Children of Country People and for the Use of Village Schools,* to direct those in charge of young children. At the same time he established a class for teachers, and required that all members of his teaching staff be graduates of this class. A later book, *Children's Friend,* put forth the contention that "children belong to the state" and that the state "must provide for their education." Other educational writings from his pen include *Schools for the Poor, Formation of National Character by Popular Schools,* and *Abolition of Public Beggary.* He also translated Mirabeau's *Discourse on National Education* into German. Baron von Zedlitz was impressed by the work and writings of von Rochow, and consulted him often as to proposed reforms of German schools.

While Basedow and von Rochow were working for the betterment of German education, proposing more effective methods, and interesting men of wealth and position in state education for the poor and disadvantaged, a new spirit was taking command of the minds and hearts of Germans everywhere. This was inspired by a revitalized interest in classical writings and ideals. Although it grew out of Greek and Roman life and culture, this "new Humanism" was in fact an attempt to emulate the classical spirit. It inspired a new German literature, an ideal of German manhood that met the needs of those coming into the modern age, and a culture that was to dominate German life and

German education well into the twentieth century. This wave of enthusiasm for esthetic values, for the fullest realization of the potentialities of the German language, and for the rich and full life transformed the schools of Germany. Baron von Zedlitz became an ardent supporter of this "new Humanism" and saw in it a challenge to the state to establish and support an educational system that would transform Germany in the image of the classical ideal. He turned to Basedow, von Rochow, and others for help and guidance. He was able to get the people to accept the school law of 1787, placing all Prussian schools under an *Oberschulkollegium* or state board of education. He organized elementary schools modeled after those on von Rochow's estate and classical secondary schools in villages, towns, and large cities similar to those established by Francke.

Soon the state was conducting *Abiturientenprufung* or "leaving examinations" for all children completing the course in the classical school. Children who passed their examinations were admitted directly to the university.

The transformation of Prussian education from a church-controlled to a state-controlled system was completed by the state education law of 1794, which affirmed that schools and universities are state institutions and that none can be established without consent of the state. It also affirmed that schools are subject to state examination and inspection at all times. Teachers became state employees, civil authorities assumed all administrative responsibilities, and the curriculum was to be shaped in terms of the Prussian ideal. This was to be the structure upon which the German state was built and the German character fashioned throughout the nineteenth and first half of the twentieth centuries.

THE BENEVOLENT DESPOT AND EDUCATION

France, England, and Prussia experienced a gradual take-over of education by the state during the eighteenth century. Those responsible were enlightened civil authorities and leaders of educational thought, concerned primarily with bettering conditions among the poor, while meeting problems created by industrialization. In the smaller countries of Europe, the benevolent despot and paternalism were more evident. Here men and women of some enlightenment sat on the thrones and took pride in bettering conditions for their people. They were in agreement with the idea that "poor subjects make a poor kingdom." However, they had no faith in democracy, nor did they wish to wipe out class distinctions. The peasantry was a necessary part of society and should be made happy, contented, and loyal, but not equal.

Fascinated by the reforms instituted by Frederick of Prussia, Empress Maria Theresa (1717-1780) attempted, against a background of diverse customs, language, and political leanings, to reform religion, finance, agriculture, and education in Austria. Her son Joseph was a believer in the doctrines of the Physiocrats. During his reign he was able to introduce a degree of religious toleration, give the serfs more freedom, and bring the schools of his kingdom more under state control. Teachers were made civil servants, despite the opposition of Catholic, particularly Jesuit, forces; the press was made subservient to the throne; and all foreign journals were banned. To produce the right kind of loyal subject, he believed, the government must control all means of public enlightenment, but it must be dedicated to making all the people prosperous, happy, contented, and secure. In this way it will remove all causes of unrest or discontent.

Thinking in much the same vein, Frederick IV of Denmark, as early as 1712, made school attendance in his realm compulsory, required children to study religion and learn to read, and made classes in writing and arithmetic available to all. Gustavus III of Sweden introduced the principles of the Physiocrats into his state. Charles Frederick of Baden was convinced that serfdom was not only unjust, but economically destructive of society. He made the economic principles of the Physiocrats basic to his social reforms and instituted a state-supported and state-controlled system of education that made Baden a showplace of enlightened bureaucracy.

Charles III of Spain (1759-1788) was one of the most honest, conscientious, and enlightened monarchs in eighteenth century Europe. He expelled the Jesuits and their inquisition, attempted to make restitution for the persecutions and inequalities of past reigns, and gave enthusiastic encouragement to trade, industry, and new developments in science and art. Following the principles of the Physiocrats, he established agricultural colonies, from which priests and monks were excluded, and simple farmers industriously tilled the soil in happiness and contentment, governed only by the laws of nature. Successful for a while, these colonies developed problems which even the best of intentions could not solve and were eventually abandoned. Dissatisfied with the education offered by the Church and private interests, Charles made schooling a function of the state, established modern schools, effected reforms in university and professional education, and required applicants for teaching positions to pass a state examination and hold a state certificate.

Charles dreamed of establishing free public education in all lands under Spanish control. In 1771, he sent a "director," who was in fact the first city superintendent of schools in America, with three teachers to New Orleans to establish and operate a free school. Even though bitterly opposed by the French inhabitants of that city, the school was fairly successful for several years. By using the Franciscan Fathers, Charles was able to establish schools in California where boys and girls were taught religion, reading, writing, and Spanish. Every boy was taught a trade. He decreed that a school should be a part of every mission established in California. In 1785, he supplied the funds with which the Franciscans opened schools in Saint Augustine, Florida, and near San Antonio, Texas.

Similar educational developments were being instituted in Switzerland, Finland, Holland, Mexico, Latin America, and the British Dominions. As the western world moved into the nineteenth century, men everywhere were beginning to sense the need for changes in education that would enable mankind to meet and make the most of the new environment that was coming into being. Foundations were being laid for the great educational structures that were to become the pride of western democracies.

CHAPTER 13

In Revolutionary America
- the Eighteenth Century

INTRODUCTION

It took about three generations of Americans to develop a population that looked to America rather than to Europe as the mother country. When the eighteenth century opened, America was European in inheritance and outlook. This was particularly true of areas south of New England. Its land was under European control. Its people were not far removed from their European ancestry, and many had received their education in European countries. When the eighteenth century closed, the thirteen colonies had formed a nation. They had drawn up a Declaration of Independence, fought a Revolutionary War, accepted a constitution, and created a government. During the time between, the "New World" was in revolution. Patterns of thought, attitudes toward man and God, ways of living and making a living, interests and outlooks, were changing radically. Motivations for these changes came both from the country the settlers had adopted as their home and from political, social, and economic theories hatched in Europe and brought to America by new immigrants and by visitors to the "Old Country." It was John Adams who first pointed out that the revolution was effected before the Revolutionary War began.

A New Nation Emerges

As the colonies became prosperous and problems of government were more than could be dealt with effectively under the original establishments, England transformed these governments into royal colonies. The king appointed a governor responsible to him. Each colony so constituted was permitted to have a legislature, consisting of an upper house appointed by the governor or king and a lower house elected by property owners. The function of both bodies was to advise the governor or transmit to him the ideas and complaints of those whom they represented.

Treatment by some of these governors, laws passed in England to regulate life in the colonies, and the proliferation of councils, commissions, and boards to handle specific matters were sources of increasing irritation to the colonists. Actions by the English caused increased bitterness, with the result that a convention was called in Philadelphia in 1774 to draw up a bill of grievances to be presented to the king. When the king failed to meet the demands of the colonists, war erupted. Lexington and Concord initiated hostilities in 1775, and the colonists issued their Declaration of Independence on July 4, 1776. This document expressed the revolutionary theories of the French Enlightenment. A Continental Congress was formed by the thirteen colonies to conduct the war. When the war was successfully concluded in 1781, the Articles of Confederation, which had governed the colonies during the years of military action, were replaced by a constitution. By April, 1789, the Constitution had been accepted by eleven states and the first Congress had been called at New York. North Carolina and Rhode Island soon joined their sister states in making ratification unanimous.

Many Americans believed that independence would serve as an impetus for the development of American art, music, literature, and education. Once prosperity was restored, it was hoped there would be time and money to develop education and the fine arts. But at least two generations of work had to elapse before there was time to develop an appreciation of the humanistic things. Still, even if nothing really great transpired in education during the postwar years, men did try. One of the first was Noah Webster, still a young school teacher in his twenties. He was determined that America had to be as free in her literature and fine arts as she was politically independent. His greatest work was his blue-backed speller. His *American Spelling Book* lasted as a prime book for over a hundred years. The young student may be interested in noting that Webster simplified American spelling from its original English form. For instance, he omitted the "u" from such English words as "labour" and "colour." Another of his simplifications was the dropping of one "g" from several words, such as "wagon."

A book which became nearly as popular as Webster's speller was a geography book by the Reverend Jedediah Morse, a Yale graduate. He wrote *Geography Made Easy,* a well-written, interesting book. It was not a mere compilation of facts and figures. Typical of its style was his condemnation of New England rum. He said it was "by no means a wholesome liquor. It has killed more Indians than their wars and sickness. It does not spare white people, especially when made into flip, which is rum mixed with small beer. . . ." Jedediah Morse's son, Samuel F. B. Morse, invented the electric telegraph.

Arithmetic also had an interesting writer. Nicholas Pike wrote a book based primarily upon American money and measurement systems.

THE SCHOOLS OF EIGHTEENTH CENTURY AMERICA

Revolutionary changes in American social, political, economic, and religious life were reflected in the schools of the century. As the colonies moved toward becoming an independent nation, they found schools imported from Europe more or less unsuited to their needs and began shaping an educational structure that would meet the demands of the people and exemplify the thinking of an emerging democratic society. New wealth made better schools possible, while profound changes in religious thinking and practice made the schools of a theocratic society wholly unsuitable. During this century some of the foundation stones of a free, tax-supported educational system were being laid, and a curriculum fitting the new national life was being shaped.

THE CHURCHES AND SCHOOLS

The established churches of early America considered education one of their prime functions. The Congregational Church in New England cooperated with town authorities to maintain schools and educate the people in the principles of the accepted religion. Various sects settling the middle colonies brought their schools from Europe and held them to be a major factor in preserving their moral and spiritual values. The Church of England gave money and support to charitable societies formed in England to establish and support schools in America free to poor children. The Society for the Propagation of the Gospel in Foreign Parts (the S.P.G.) opened and supported schools in all thirteen colonies under Anglican auspices.

This concern for education was strengthened by an increase in church membership, and the growing wealth of the various denominations made it possible for them to pour money into building schools at all levels. The eighteenth century was characterized by the great number of denominational schools under support of the traditional church groups as well as the new Protestant denominations that found a footing in America.

This was of great significance for the future of education in America. While earlier churches enjoyed a monopoly of education under state protection, the eighteenth century saw all churches free to establish schools and to compete freely for support and students. Each was jealous of its position and intolerant of any infringement on its freedom. It soon became evident that if any church group was given preference by the state, the freedom of all would to that degree be limited. This inevitably made religious toleration necessary. The first amendment to the Constitution was, in part at least, a result of this realization. Instead of looking to the state to insure an establishment of one religion over all others, the people now saw it as the guardian of the freedom of all religions and of their right to educate as they deemed fit.

PRIVATE SCHOOLS AND SECULAR EDUCATION

As America became more commercially oriented, and as business, shipping, trades, and money-making activities occupied more of the people's time and energy, there arose a demand for schools that would qualify men for positions in these areas. Teachers appeared in the towns and large cities, offering their services to a rapidly growing clientele. Soon their classes were crowded with young men wishing to become merchants, clerks, bookkeepers, accountants, mechanics, engineers, and seamen. These were private-venture schools supported wholly by tuition fees and responsible only to those willing to pay for this schooling.

The success of these new schools and growing dissatisfaction with traditional schools caused many to think more carefully about an educational structure that would better serve the needs of the colonists. They had the non-conformist academies of England as examples of schools adjusted to changes taking place in scholarship and offering training in keeping with the times. The first significant effort to establish a new kind of school resulted from the work of Benjamin Franklin. Franklin's plan originated the academy movement, but unfortunately, it did not become a model. Franklin's school was vocationally oriented, whereas the academies which followed returned to an almost purely academic approach. In 1749, Franklin (1706 1790) published a brochure entitled *Proposal Relating to the Education of Youth in Pennsylvania,* in which he urged that a school be established in Philadelphia concerned with teaching "those things that are likely to be most useful and most ornamental, regard being had to the several professions."

Franklin wanted what he called an English School to exist as an alternate school alongside the Latin Grammar School within the same institution, and with equal status. While alternatives included the same basic curriculum of reading, history, grammar, oratory, rhetoric, composition, literature, and logic, the teaching strategies differed. Most important was the use of English rather than the traditional Latin as the language of teaching. A second curriculum feature was that subjects to be taught and the material to be included were to be practical, although some "ornamental" work should be included.

Franklin's plan is worthy of study. It did not have extensive imitation in terms of the "practical" curriculum, but the concept of teaching in English had significant results. Franklin's plan, in part, is quoted here from his "Proposals Relating to the Education of Youth in Pensilvania," written in 1749:

> ... That we may obtain the Advantages arising from an Increase of Knowledge, and prevent as much as may be the mischievous Consequences that would attend a general Ignorance among us, the following Hints are offered towards forming a Plan for the Education of the Youth of Pensilvania, viz.
>
> It is propos'd, ... That a House be provided for the Academy, not far from a River, having a Garden, Orchard, Meadow, and a Field or two.
>
> That the House be furnished with Library, ... with Maps of all Countries, Globes, some mathematical Instruments, an Apparatus for Experiments in Natural Philosophy, and for Mechanics; Prints, of all Kinds, Prospects, Buildings, Machines, Ec.
>
> That the Rector be a Man of good Understanding, good Morals, diligent and patient; learn'd in the Languages and Sciences, and a correct pure Speaker and Writer of the *English* Tongue; to have such Tutors under him as shall be necessary.
>
> That the boarding Scholars diet together, plainly, temperately and frugally.
>
> That to keep them in Health, and to strengthen and render active their Bodies, they be frequently exercis'd in Running, Leaping, Wrestling, and Swimming, Ec. ...
>
> As to their Studies, it would be well if they could be taught *every thing* that is useful, and *every thing* that is ornamental; But Art is long, and their Time is short. It is therefore propos'd that they learn those Things that are likely to be *most useful* and *most ornamental.* Regard being had to the several Professions for which they are intended.
>
> All should be taught to write a *fair Hand,* and swift, as that is useful to All. ...
>
> *Arithmetick, Accounts,* and some of the first Principles of *Geometry* and *Astronomy.*
>
> The *English* Language might be taught by Grammar; in which some of our best Writers, as *Tillotson, Addison, Pope, Algernoon Sidney, Cato's Letters,* &c. should be Classicks: The *Stiles* principally to be cultivated being the *clear* and the *concise.* Reading should also

be taught, and pronouncing, properly, distinctly, emphatically; not with an even Tone which *under-does,* nor a theatrical, which *over-does* Nature. . . .

But if History be made a constant Part of their Reading, . . . may not almost all Kinds of useful Knowledge be that Way introduc'd to Advantage, and with Pleasure to the student? As Geography, by reading with Maps, and being required to point out the Places *where* the greatest Actions were done, to give their old and New Names, with the Bounds, Situation, Extent of the Countries concern'd, &c. . . .

And though all should not be compell'd to learn *Latin, Greek,* or the modern foreign Languages; yet none that have an ardent Desire to learn them should be refused; their *English,* Arithmetick, and other Studies absolutely necessary, being at the same Time not neglected. . . .

With the History of Men, Times, and Nations, should be read at proper Hours or Days some of the best *Histories of Nature,* which would not only be delightful to Youth, . . . but afterwards of great Use to them. . . .

The History of *Commerce,* of the Invention of Arts, Rise of Manufacturers, Progress of Trade, Change of its Seats, with the Reasons, Causes, &c. may also be made entertaining to Youth, and this will be useful to all. And this, with the Accounts in other History of the prodigious Force and Effect of Engines and Machines used in War, will naturally introduce a Desire to be instructed in *Mechanicks,* and to be inform'd of the Principles of that Art by which weak Men perform such Wonders, Labour is sav'd, Manufacturer expedited, &c. &c. This will be the Time to show them Prints of ancient and modern Machines, to explain them, to let them be copied, and to give Lectures in Mechanical Philosophy.

With the whole should be constantly inculcated and cultivated, that *Benignity of Mind,* which shows itself in *searching for* and *seizing* every Opportunity *to serve* and *to oblige;* and is the Foundation of what is called Good Breeding; highly useful to the Possessor, and most agreeable to all.

The Idea of what is *true Merit,* should also be often presented to Youth, explain'd and impress'd on their Minds, as consisting in an *Inclination* join'd with an *Ability* to serve Mankind, one's Country, Friends, and Family; which *Ability* is (with the Blessing of God) to be acquir'd or greatly encreas'd by *true Learning;* and should indeed be the great *Aim* and *End* of all Learning.

After many discouragements in gaining support for the idea, and after several compromises in the original plan, the Academy was opened in 1751 and chartered in 1753. In 1755, it was raised to the status of a college. As the institution grew in popularity, new courses were added, and its function as a secondary school and even as a college was abandoned in favor of broader service to the state, so that in 1779 the "College, Academy and Charitable School of Philadelphia" was transformed by legislation into the University of the State of Pennsylvania. This was the first specific legal establishment of a state university. In 1791, the institution took the name The University of Pennsylvania, but insisted that it remain under private management.

The academy very soon became the popular secondary school in America. Philanthropists, churches, enterprising teachers, and corporations organized for the purpose opened academies and found an eager clientele waiting. Usually these schools were controlled by a board of trustees, either elected by the founding bodies or self-perpetuating. Some of the earliest academies were Dummers, opened at Bayfield, Massachusetts, in 1761, Phillips Academy, opened at Andover, Massachusetts, in 1778, and Phillips Academy, opened at Exeter, New Hampshire, in 1783. After the Revolutionary War all the states boasted academies, and by 1800, it has been estimated that more than one hundred academies were thriving in the United States.

Some of these were exclusively for boys or for girls, while some were coeducational. Most were supported in part by public subscriptions or state subsidies. Massachusetts gave land to all its academies that measured up to standards laid down by the legislature. The state of New York, under laws passed in 1784 and 1787, asserted its right to supervise academies in its commonwealth by giving the Board of Regents the responsibility of setting standards and seeing that they were lived up to.

The curricula of the academies varied in terms of the specific needs of the clientele served. They usually offered instruction in Latin, Greek, English literature, oratory, arithmetic, algebra, trigonometry, surveying, geography, history, astronomy, elementary physics and chemistry, psychology, ethics, and evidences of Christianity. Girls were instructed in music, dancing, needlework, declamation, painting, and French. The academies differed in size and in the quality of their work. Some were very weak grammar schools, inefficient and poorly staffed, while others gave instruction of equal standing with that offered in the first two years of the best colleges of the nation. Graduates of the better institutions usually went on to study in the professions, to advanced work in college, or to trades or occupations for which they were qualified.

EDUCATION AND CIVIL AUTHORITIES

As the colonies moved into the eighteenth century and life became more complicated and interests more varied, the larger community had to concern itself more with the education of its children. The town school of the seventeenth century in New England became inadequate in the eighteenth. As people moved out from the highly localized town to farms and communities some distance from the school, they found it inconvenient or impossible to send their children to the school located in the center of the town. Since the New England town included all outlying rural areas as well as the central community, these people were part of the town's citizenry with a stake in the town school. The town, recognizing this problem, often instituted the "moving school." The teacher would travel from community to community, boarding in homes of citizens and teaching their children in rooms or buildings provided for the purpose. The time spent in each community was determined by the number of children to be taught. This meant that a community might receive a month of schooling each year or once every two years, a plan which proved wholly unsatisfactory.

In time, towns began hiring several teachers, each to spend full time in a community, teaching the children but receiving pay from the town treasury. This was called the "divided school." It was but a short step from this to complete local autonomy. Eventually, each community was, while remaining part of the larger town, authorized by town authorities to establish its own school, provide buildings and accommodations, raise money for the purpose, and employ its own teachers. In 1789, Massachusetts legalized this pattern. By 1800, it was the general structure of school organization and has, in most states, continued to the present.

FEDERAL CONCERN FOR EDUCATION

Educational thinking and practices varied greatly among the thirteen colonies. Civil control, church domination, and freedom of thinking were all evident among the colonists. When representatives of these people assembled to write a Constitution that all would accept, they faced the difficult problem of compromising differences. Education was a difference that defied any compromise and was not mentioned in the final draft of the federal Constitution. The Bill of Rights contained a "clean up" statement in the Tenth Amendment which stated "powers not delegated to the United States by the Constitution, or prohibited by it to the States, are reserved to the States respectively, or to the people." As a consequence, education was left in the hands of the states.

Legally barred from interfering with education within the states, the federal government turned to devious methods of providing for, supporting, and controlling numerous types of schools. When the states gave the central government lands to the west which they claimed,

Congress turned its attention to how best to utilize them. A law was passed in 1785 dividing these lands, which had become known as the Northwest Territory, into townships six miles square, with each township further divided into sections one mile square. When, in 1787, a vast area was sold to a land company for speculation and development, an ordinance was adopted which affirmed that "religion, morality, and knowledge being necessary to good government and the happiness of mankind, schools and the means of education shall forever be encouraged." That same year, Congress passed the *Northwest Ordinance,* regulating utilization of the land and stipulating that Section 16 of each township be reserved for schools and that two townships be donated for a university. As the land was sold, purchasers were required to set aside a monetary equivalent for the school lands provided in the ordinance. Here, during the first years as a nation, the federal government established an interest in education that has increased throughout the years that have followed.

This interest was a result of many forces operating in the early years of our national life. As early as 1727, Benjamin Franklin formed a society for mutual help and the debating of current issues that he called the *Junto.* In 1743, he was instrumental in founding the *Philosophical Society.* These were merged in 1769 into the *American Philosophical Society for Promoting Useful Knowledge.* This organization brought together most of the leading minds of America and Europe in discussions of scientific and political matters. In the interest of discovering "the best system of liberal education and literary instruction adapted to the genius of the Government of the United States," it offered a substantial prize, which stimulated many to write essays expressing their ideas on the matter. Two were considered of sufficient importance to cause the Society to divide the prize. These were *An Essay on Education* by Samuel Knox and *Remarks on Education* by Samuel H. Smith. They were published by the Society in 1787.

These were but two of the many essays and pamphlets that were appearing toward the close of the eighteenth century in the interest of education. Benjamin Rush wrote a classical work entitled *Thoughts Upon the Mode of Education Proper in a Republic* in 1786. Noah Webster's *Essays,* published in 1790, Joseph Priestley's *The Proper Object of Education in the Present State of the World,* published in 1791, and William Godwin's *The Enquirer, Reflections on Education, Manners, and Literature,* published in 1797, all advocated increased government concern for education as basic to a democratic society.

As Americans visited France and Frenchmen of note came to view happenings on this continent, a considerable exchange of ideas resulted. The French conviction that education is basic to any free society began to permeate American thinking. To propagate this belief, John Adams, after a visit to France, organized the *American Academy of Arts and Sciences.* John Jay and the noted French scholar, Ezra L'Hommedieu, were chief instigators of the University of the State of New York. To link America with French culture, Chevalier Quesnay de Beaurepaire, who had come to the colonies with Lafayette, fought in the Revolution, and remained to make this his second home, organized the *Academy of Fine Arts and Sciences of the United States,* which soon became an affiliate of royal societies in London, Paris, and Brussels. In 1800, at the suggestion of Thomas Jefferson, Dupont de Nemours published *National Education in the United States,* a highly influential book in the development of American education.

By the close of the eighteenth century, there was strong sentiment in the United States for establishing a national system of schools— elementary, secondary, and higher—under federal control and support, adapted to the needs of the country, and open to all. Education, it was felt, was necessary for a democracy, and must be an education free from sectarian bias and concerned with producing citizens loyal to American ideals and able to function effectively in this new world. George Washington was one of the most ardent advocates of this idea. While the national school system was never adopted, the federal government increased from time to time its involvement in education at all levels.

THE STATES AND EDUCATION

When the Constitution was ratified, the states set about to frame constitutions containing references to schools and education, some more specific than others. By 1800, seven states had made definite provisions for education in their constitutions: Pennsylvania, North Carolina, Georgia, Massachusetts, New Hampshire, Vermont, and Delaware. Others manifested interest in schools by establishing school funds, donating land, and encouraging educational agencies within their borders.

The Massachusetts constitution, adopted in 1780, ordered its legislators to "cherish the interests of literature and the sciences. . . . especially in the University of Cambridge, public schools, and grammar schools in the towns." Following much in the spirit of the law of 1647, the Massachusetts legislature made the district system legal in 1789, and required every community of fifty or more families to maintain an elementary school and towns of 150 or more families to support a grammar school. Towns failing in this matter were subject to fines.

New York made no direct reference to education in its constitution but, as early as 1784, sponsored a program of schools under Governor George Clinton. The state legislature set aside 690 acres of land in each township for the support of schools and established the Board of Regents of the University of the State of New York to supervise secondary and higher education in the state and to propagandize for better schools. In 1787, the Board's authority was extended to include "all the colleges, academies, and schools." Three years later, a state fund for education was provided by the sale of state lands and its disbursement placed in the hands of the Board of Regents.

The New York legislature passed a bill in 1795 setting aside £20,000 a year for five years, to be distributed through the counties and towns to each school district on the basis of the number of days school was in session during the year. By 1800, the state had 1,350 public schools receiving funds from its treasury. Although schools flourished under this state-aid principle, there was much opposition to its provisions, so that, in 1800, it was allowed to expire, leaving schools dependent upon local support.

Virginia was part of the pattern of southern culture based on plantation life, a tobacco and slave economy, and the English church and educational outlook. It was content to leave education in the hands of parents and guardians, and expressed concern only for children of the indigent and for orphans. These latter, as in England, were the responsibility of the state, in the interest of their becoming productive citizens and not charity wards of the community.

Thomas Jefferson represented a group which believed that state-supported education for all was basic to a democracy. In 1816, in a letter to Colonel Charles Yancey, he expressed his conviction in these words, "If a nation expects to be ignorant and free, in a state of civilization, it expects what never was and never will be." This was an affirmation of his earlier position, stated in 1786, that "it is an axiom in my mind that our liberty can never be safe but in the hands of the people themselves, and that too of the people with a certain degree of instruction. This it is the business of the state to effect, and on a general plan."

At the same time, Jefferson was an aristocrat, believing that the elite, intellectually and culturally, should hold responsible positions in government. He held that individuals were endowed by their creator with different talents and abilities and that each should be educated and trained to the fullest development of his natural endowments, a few to rule and the others to be ruled.

These two positions concerning a basic education for all and special education for the elite are incorporated into the *Bill for the More*

General Diffusion of Knowledge, which was submitted to the Virginia legislature in 1779. This provided that each county in the state be divided into "hundreds," each containing "a convenient number of children to make up a school," and that in each hundred there be established an elementary school offering free schooling to all white children in the hundred for three years. An overseer, to employ teachers and supervise their work, was to be chosen by the alderman for every ten schools. The teachers' wages and all other expenses were to be cared for by taxes levied on the inhabitants of the hundreds. In this we have evidence of Jefferson's strong belief that all citizens in a free society must have a basic education consisting of "reading, writing, and common arithmetick" plus an acquaintance with "Graecian, Roman, English, and American history." Parents who so wished might send their children to these schools beyond the three years of free education by paying tuition, but each child in the state would be guaranteed at least the fundamental three-year education necessary for citizenship.

Jefferson further proposed that grammar schools be established, one in each district consisting of several counties. These were to be boarding schools, supported both by appropriations from public funds and by tuition fees. They would offer Latin, Greek, English grammar, geography, and "the higher part of numerical arithmetick." While most of the students attending these grammar schools would pay the established tuition, each overseer was authorized to select one of "the best and most promising genius and disposition," whose parents could not afford further education, who would attend the grammar school at public expense. At the end of one year, a third of these charity students would be dropped, while the others went on for another year with public support. After a further weeding-out process, the most promising would be chosen to attend William and Mary College for three years. These "geniuses" would be given tuition, board, and clothing for their stay in college.

Jefferson was certain that ability for leadership was not confined to the wealthy who could afford to educate their children. The poor often produced children with ability and talent that did not develop because of economic conditions. He was resolved to discover as many of these as possible and provide public funds for the necessary education for their fullest growth and development.

In this, Jefferson was a "radical." The Virginia legislature was a long way from this extreme thinking and turned down the bill decisively. The aristocratic South was not ready for free public education even on this limited basis.

HIGHER EDUCATION IN EIGHTEENTH CENTURY AMERICA

The American College

The seventeenth century in America saw the rise of several colleges patterned after those in England. Harvard might well have been fitted into Cambridge University and would have felt at home on its campus. Yale was founded when Harvard became too liberal intellectually and morally for many of the "leading lights" of New England. William and Mary was a typical English college in curriculum, support, and purpose. These institutions were founded under church auspices and planned to supply the colonies with ministers and other leaders.

Better economic conditions, and the religious revival that drew thousands into the churches and opened purses for charitable and educational purposes, made possible an upsurge of interest in colleges on the part of the various denominational groups. The College of New Jersey, later to be called Princeton, was established by the Presbyterians in 1746. This was followed by the King's College, later Columbia, established by the Episcopalians in 1754; Brown, established by the Baptists in 1764; Rutgers, established by the Dutch Reformed Church in 1766; and Dartmouth, established by the Congregationalists in 1769. The only college of this period not under church control was the University of Pennsylvania, which grew out of Franklin's Academy.

English thinking about colleges dominated in all these institutions. Students were listed in terms of the rank and social position of their parents. All were required to live in dormitories, attend religious services daily, obey minute rules drawn by the masters and rector, and study with one tutor throughout their entire college career. In the thinking of most educational leaders, this was a true college education and not preparation for professional life or the trades. Conduct, morals, and character were considered of more importance than learning. Even though some changes in the pattern were introduced after the Revolutionary War, American colleges remained, well into the nineteenth century, religious institutions aiming to produce a well-defined type of man, with character and outlook suited to a ruling and cultured class.

After the Revolutionary War, these institutions began to reflect the growing democratic sentiments of the nation. Rank and social status were of decreasing importance, and strict religious requirements were gradually abolished. The curricula of these colleges became broader than before, while newer and more scientific subjects were added. French language and literature became popular as a greater exchange of ideas between France and America produced a clearer understanding of how much the two nations had in common. Other subjects added or given new emphasis in the curricula were ancient languages, psychology, logic, ethics, metaphysics, algebra, geometry, trigonometry, geography, astronomy, and government.

Control of these institutions was shifted significantly during the latter part of the eighteenth century. The early American colleges followed English thinking by placing all authority for college policy and administration in the faculty and its officers. The faculty was thought of as an autonomous, self-governing body. Gradually, non-resident boards of governors moved in to wrest control from the faculty. By the time Yale was established in 1701, the governing board consisted of ten ministers, and the president was excluded from membership in the body until 1745. While this non-resident body was made responsible for all college matters, the faculty was permitted to discharge many administrative functions. The establishment of the non-resident governing board was an attempt on the part of the churches supporting colleges to keep a firm hand on the life of the institution and its curriculum in the interest of correct morals and orthodoxy.

Another trend that began to appear after the Revolutionary War was triggered by a growing belief that the state should develop a complete system of education, including colleges. It seemed logical for the state to move in and transform private colleges into state institutions. This meant, as educational leaders saw clearly, a retreat from the denominationalism that had founded the colleges and a secularization of their activities and curricula. Harvard, William and Mary, and Yale fought this trend. When the revivalists of the period turned their attention to reshaping Yale to fit more accurately the religious outlook of the age, arguing that public money provided for its support made it in fact a quasi-public institution, President Thomas Clap fought the move vigorously and won. He argued that Yale was in fact a private, autonomous college, free to impose on its students all requirements deemed necessary to accomplish its aims. Jefferson worked to change William and Mary into a state university but was beaten. Two groups, one consisting of members of the Church of England with Tory convictions and the other representing Presbyterians, dissenters, and men with decidedly democratic leanings, fought to shape the character of King's College. The former sought to found a college under a royal charter while the latter sought to place the institution under the colonial legislature. The "church party" won, and the university's charter came from the English king, who determined the personnel of its controlling group.

New York made an attempt through its Board of Regents to bring King's College under its control. Under the law of 1784, Columbia (the new name for King's College) was placed under the Board's authority but with special privileges. By 1787 it was removed from the provisions of the law establishing the Board and permitted to function independently.

Franklin's Academy in Philadelphia came under Anglican and Tory control. An attempt was made in 1779 to convert it into a University of the State of Pennsylvania. Such an institution was set up, but the original body refused to surrender its charter and continued to function alongside the state university. After a bitter struggle and a realignment of religious and political interests in the state, the two institutions were merged and, in 1791, the new body was named the University of Pennsylvania but remained a private and independent institution.

Thus, from the beginning of statehood in America, democratic leaders, convinced of the necessity of a complete system of education, sought to transform private colleges into state-controlled and -supported institutions. This battle did not die with the eighteenth century, but continued well into the nineteenth, when the United States Supreme Court ruled, in the Dartmouth College Case, in favor of the private colleges, thereby forcing states to create new institutions to cap their educational structures.

RISE OF THE UNIVERSITY CONCEPT

With growing interest in academic matters, after the mid-point of the century some authorities began to think of expanding certain colleges into full universities offering a wider range of subjects and opportunities for professional preparation.

Repeatedly defeated in its attempt to get a charter from the Crown for a college, North Carolina made provision in 1776 for "one or more universities." A charter was granted by the legislature in 1789 and, in 1795, instruction began in the University of North Carolina, the oldest state university in the country. Vermont provided for a state university in 1777. Other states followed, so that by 1800, the concept of a university, as opposed to that of the narrow religious college of colonial days, had taken hold and was destined to bring higher education in America to a level equal to the best that European universities could offer.

This movement took two directions in the eighteenth and early nineteenth centuries. One was the expansion of certain colleges into institutions of university status or the founding of state universities. North Carolina is representative of the latter. The change of Franklin's Academy into the University of Pennsylvania illustrates the former. Harvard College became a university in 1780. In 1798, the General Assembly of Kentucky created Transylvania University which, in 1845, was reconstituted the University of Kentucky.

The other direction taken by the university movement was an attempt by some states to create a governing body to consolidate all education in the state into a University of the state. As early as 1777, the president of Dartmouth College proposed that his institution become a state university and that charity schools and academies be developed as part of the university. The charter of Georgia gave the legislature power to develop schools and encourage their support. In 1785, when the University of Georgia was chartered, its *"Senatus Academicus"* was empowered to establish, control, and supervise all public schools in the state.

New York took a similar step in 1784 when its legislature passed *An Act for establishing a university within this state.* This was the University of the State of New York, empowered to "found schools and colleges in any part of the state. . . . every such school or college being at all times to be deemed a part of the University and, as such, subject to the control and direction of the said Regents." In 1805, the legislative council of Louisiana provided for a University of New Orleans with power to establish schools and a library in each county. This venture was to be supported by two lotteries. A college was opened and functioned for a time, but the plan did not materialize, and in 1826 the project was abandoned. A similar pattern was established in 1817 by the creation of the University of Michigan, which would establish schools and other cultural agencies of the state, select, appoint, and pay teachers, and determine the curricula.

INSIDE EIGHTEENTH CENTURY AMERICAN SCHOOLS

AT THE ELEMENTARY LEVEL

The chief aim of elementary schools in eighteenth century America was literacy. Dame schools, private tutors, church schools, charity schools, and town schools all taught the child his letters and how to read simple material. In some communities this instruction was supplemented by some writing and a little arithmetic. While the reading school did, at times, add these subjects to its curriculum, usually they were taught by specialists in separate schools or rooms provided for the purpose. This concern with literacy grew out of the conviction that ability to read the Bible and basic laws of the land was necessary for effective citizenship.

Samuel Griswold Goodrich (1793–1860), a writer and publisher of children's books under the nom de plume of Peter Parley, has given us an excellent description of education in New England at the end of the eighteenth century. In his *Recollections of a Lifetime,* a kind of auto-biography, Goodrich reveals the kind of education he received as a child in rural Connecticut:

> The school-house itself consisted of rough, unpainted clapboards, upon a wooden frame. It was plastered within, and contained two apartments—a little entry, taken out of a corner for a wardrobe, and the school-room proper. The chimney was of stone, and pointed with mortar, which, by the way, had been dug into a honeycomb by uneasy and enterprising penknives. The fireplace was six feet wide and four feet deep. The flue was so ample and so perpendicular, that the rain, sleet, and snow fell direct to the hearth. In winter, the battle for life with green fizzling fuel, which was brought in sled lengths and cut up by the scholars, was a stern one. Not unfrequently, the wood, gushing with sap as it was, chanced to be out, and as there was no living without fire, the thermometer being ten or twenty degrees below zero, the school was dismissed, whereat all the scholars rejoiced aloud, not having the fear of the schoolmaster before their eyes.
>
> It was the custom at this place, to have a woman's school in the summer months, and this was attended only by young children. It was, in fact, what we now call a primary or infant school. In winter, a man was employed as teacher, and then the girls and boys of the neighborhood, up to the age of eighteen, or even twenty, were among the pupils. It was not uncommon, at this season, to have forty scholars crowded into this little building.
>
> I was about six years old when I first went to school. My teacher was Aunt Delight, that is, Delight Benedict, a maiden lady of fifty, short and bent, of sallow complexion and solemn aspect. . . .
>
> I think we had seventeen scholars—boys and girls—mostly of my own age. . . .
>
> The school being organized, we were all seated upon benches, made of what were called *slabs*—that is, boards having the exterior or rounded part of the log on one side: as they were useless for other purposes, these were converted into school-benches, the rounded part down. They had each four supports, consisting of straddling wooden legs, set into augurholes. Our own legs swayed in the air, for they were too short to touch the floor. Oh, what an awe fell over me, when we were all seated and silence reigned around!
>
> The children were called up, one by one, to Aunt Delight, who sat on a low chair, and required each, as a preliminary, to make his manners, consisting of a small sudden nod or jerk of the head. She then placed the spelling-book—which was Dilworth's—before the pupil, and with a buck-handled penknife pointed, one by one, to the letters of the alphabet, saying, "What's that?" If the child knew his letters, the "what's that?" very soon ran on thus:

"What's that?"
"A."
"Stha-a-t?"
"B."
"Sna-a-a-t?"
"C."

I looked upon these operations with intense curiosity and no small respect, until my own turn came. I went up to the school-mistress with some emotion, and when she said, rather spitefully, as I thought, "Make your obeisance!" my little intellects all fled away, and I did nothing. Having waited a second, gazing at me with indignation, she laid her hand on the top of my head, and gave it a jerk which made my teeth clash. I believe I bit my tongue a little; at all events, my sense of dignity was offended, and when she pointed to A, and asked what it was, it swam before me dim and hazy, and as big as a full moon. She repeated the question, but I was doggedly silent. Again, a third time, she said, "What's that?" I replied: "Why don't you tell me what it is? I didn't come here to learn you your letters!" . . .

I believe I achieved the alphabet that summer, but my after progress, for a long time, I do not remember. Two years later I went to the winter-school at the same place, kept by Lewis Olmstead—a man who had a call for plowing, mowing, carting manure, &c., in summer, and for teaching school in the winter, with a talent for music at all seasons, wherefore he became chorister upon occasion, when, peradventure, Deacon Hawley could not officiate. He was a celebrity in ciphering, and "Squire Seymour declared that he was the greatest arithmeticker" in Fairfield county. All I remember of his person is his hand, which seemed to me as big as Goliah's, judging by the claps of thunder it made in my ears on one or two occasions.

The next step of my progress which is marked in my memory, is the spelling of words of two syllables. I did not go very regularly to school, but by the time I was ten years old I had learned to write, and had made a little progress in arithmetic. There was not a grammar, a geography, or a history of any kind in the school. Reading, writing, and arithmetic were the only things taught, and these very indifferently—not wholly from the stupidity of the teacher, but because he had forty scholars, and the standards of the age required no more than he performed. . . .

A popular text, mentioned earlier, which appeared in 1784 and went through many editions, was Noah Webster's *Elementary Spelling Book,* called the "blue-backed speller." This was almost wholly secular. Using the phonetic method, the child learned to recognize words, spell, and read. Beginning with syllables, he moved to one-syllable words and on to words of many syllables. About a quarter of the book was devoted to short stories. These stories stressed the virtues of obedience, thrift, dependability, respect for betters, the value of money, and loyalty to one's country.

An important advance in elementary education in the eighteenth century was seen in the growing concern with teaching method at this level. Before this time, it was taken for granted that anyone with the proper learning could teach children to read, write, or figure. By 1706, the Society for the Propagation of the Gospel in Foreign Parts had come to recognize the fallacy of this belief and published, in England, a book of instruction for teachers in its schools. This prescribed the subjects to be taught: reading, writing, arithmetic, the catechism, prayers, and ritual at worship. It also listed the virtues which teachers were supposed to develop in their charges and gave many suggestions as to the treatment of children during the learning experience. A similar work by Anthony Benezet, a Quaker, stressed the fact that children learn better when their work is interesting. He urged teachers to be patient with children, to learn their natures and whims, and to adjust tasks to their abilities. Christopher Dock, a Pennsylvania schoolmaster of the Mennonite sect, was called "the pious schoolmaster on the Skippack." In 1770 he wrote *Schulordnung,* the first book on education to be composed in America. He urged that the teacher treat misconduct as a symptom of some deeper problem and seek to discover the problem rather than punish the symptom. To stimulate interest in writing, he would have the children write letters to agemates in other schools. His book was standard in many American schools of that period. Dock reminds one of Comenius because he emphasized the value of praise and commendation, sympathy, understanding, and mutual respect and love as better techniques for teaching than fear, punishment, and attempts to break the will of the child.

At the Secondary Level

The Latin grammar school continued to be an important means of secondary education in eighteenth century America. It prepared the boy for college by teaching him Greek and Latin. Since Harvard College admitted boys only after they could demonstrate ability to read Cicero at sight, speak Latin, make Latin verses, and give the forms, declensions, and conjugations of Greek nouns and verbs, these were the skills emphasized by this basic secondary school. Private-venture schools and academies, which arose in the eighteenth century in response to interests of the commercial and trading classes, turned away from the exclusively Latin and Greek curriculum to English and vocational preparation. Not bound to prepare boys for college, they could offer those newer subjects demanded by their clientele.

Many private-venture schools opened their classes to girls and provided them with instruction in reading, writing, arithmetic, geography, French, English grammar, history, Latin, bookkeeping, accounting, modern languages, drawing, painting, singing, instrumental music, sewing, and penmanship.

The academy was very similar to the private-venture school but had a greater degree of stability and public support. It offered about the same range of subjects, catered to its clientele, and attempted to take over from the Latin schools preparation for college. It aimed to educate both boys and girls, to attract support from individuals, churches, communities, states, and educational organizations, and to institute some teacher education.

As the newer subjects offered by private-venture schools and academies became popular, there arose a need for adequate textbooks—a need that was soon met by an increased flow of pamphlets, brochures, and books from the presses of the country. In 1778, Nicholas Pike brought out his *New and Complete System of Arithmetic.* Pike was master of the Newburyport, Massachusetts, grammar school and head of his own private evening school. His book explained the then-new federal money. This was followed, in 1792, by *Arithmetic, Vulgar and Decimal With the Application Thereof to a Variety of Cases in Trade and Commerce* by Isaac Greenwood, Hollis Professor of Mathematics at Harvard and private teacher of mathematics. The title indicates the practical nature of the text. The first text in English grammar to appear in America was *New Guide to the English Tongue* by Thomas Dilworth, printed first in England in 1740 and reprinted later in America. Noah Webster's *Speller* was one part of a larger project that he called *Grammatical Institute of the English Language.* The second part was a grammar and the third a reader. When the grammar appeared, Dilworth's text lost its popularity. Other popular English grammars to appear were *English Grammar,* published by Lindley Murray in 1795, and *The Young Lady's Accidence,* published by Caleb Bingham in 1799.

In 1784, Jedidiah Morse, a Congregational pastor, published *American Universal Geography.* Eleven years later he brought out *Elements of Geography.* As we have noted, these works did not confine themselves to geography, but included American history. In 1787, John McCulloch compiled *An Introduction to the History of America,* much of its content taken from an earlier work by Noah Webster. Other books for use in Latin schools, private schools, and academies kept the printers busy and brought large financial rewards to their authors and publishers. American secondary education was expanding rapidly. There was a great thirst for knowledge everywhere, and teachers, writers, and compilers were busy providing the materials necessary for better training.

AT THE COLLEGE AND UNIVERSITY LEVEL

The eighteenth century, becoming more and more sensitive to Enlightenment thinking and practices, produced changes in college and university education which amounted to a retreat from the more traditional concern with religion and the interests of the few and incorporated the ideas of rationalism and empiricism, plus a more democratic approach to higher learning. Expansion of scientific knowledge during the century made necessary a rethinking of the curriculum. The refinement of the skills needed in trade and commerce and the individualistic ideals of economic gain forced these institutions to lean more in the direction of educational utilitarianism.

Deism and Unitarianism began to affect the thinking of the leading minds on the Harvard campus, to the extent that the more orthodox Calvinists sought to force all administrators and teachers to take an oath of orthodoxy and to censor theses presented at commencement. These repressive measures did not stop the trend toward secular studies and modern sciences. Aristotle and Ptolemy were gradually displaced by Copernicus, Galileo, Kepler, and Gassendi. In 1728, Thomas Hollis endowed a professorship of mathematics and natural philosophy at Harvard and contributed many books on science and such "philosophical apparatus" as globes, skeletons, microscopes, and mechanical instruments. The first two scholars to be appointed to the chair, Isaac Greenwood and John Winthrop, were authors of works on mathematics, meteorology, natural phenomena, and astronomy and research men of no little importance. While the chief interest of Harvard remained in the areas of mathematics and the classical languages, there were increasing indications that the newer science and philosophy were commanding attention. By the close of the eighteenth century, these Enlightenment trends had become of major importance to all interested in the college.

For its first three-quarters of a century, William and Mary College held fast to its curriculum, modeled after that of Oxford, and religiously pursued its aim of training ministers and instructing youth in letters and manners, while extending Christianity to the Indians. Jefferson's proposals, made in 1779, to reform this curriculum by introducing subjects growing out of the Enlightenment and shifting the emphasis from preparing ministers to that of training leaders in public affairs, practical pursuits, and professional services, were dismissed as far too radical. This turned him to planning a state university that would be more in line with the intellectual trends of the times, and resulted in the University of Virginia, Jefferson's most prideful accomplishment, which was chartered in 1819 and opened in 1825.

Yale remained fairly loyal to the goal of its founders, which was to "supply the churches of the Colony with a learned, pious, and orthodox Ministry." Although its curriculum did turn gradually in the direction of the newer sciences and philosophy, it continued to hold to the traditional concept of a college education, to produce gentlemen versed in the classics, divinity, and the liberal arts.

King's College, later called Columbia, was founded in New York City in 1754 after a bitter struggle over what it was to be and do. The Anglican church won the argument, but was forced to soften the emphasis placed upon religion. Ministers representing the Anglicans sat alongside those from the Dutch Reformed, Lutheran, French, and Presbyterian churches on the board of trustees. The charter prohibited establishing any religious tests for entrance, study, or graduation. Samuel Johnson, the college's first president, sought to change the curriculum from that of a standard four-year college to one useful for daily life. His efforts brought little change in the plan of studies, which included Latin, Greek, grammar, literature, rhetoric, ethics, mathematics, and philosophy.

The Reverend William Smith, a graduate of the University of Aberdeen, published, in 1753, *A General Idea of the College of Mirania*. In this he drew the outlines of an ideal college in a utopian community in which youths might receive advanced training both in the learned professions and in the trades. The usual colleges, he noted, paid little attention to this latter group. Therefore, he proposed that his utopia establish a "mechanic's school" much like the school just chartered by Franklin in Philadelphia. This book attracted Franklin, who invited Smith to prepare *A Scheme of Liberal Education,* a curriculum embracing all possible subjects of interest to students of the day. This curriculum was accepted by the trustees of the academy which Franklin founded in Philadelphia. It included the usual school of classical and rhetorical studies, a school of technological studies, a school of the social sciences, and a school of the physical sciences. Students were required to attend lectures in the various schools and read a list of books and other materials during their stay at the "college."

As America moved toward the nineteenth century, the character of its higher education changed materially. The narrow concept of a liberal arts college devoted to the aristocratic training of ministers was giving way to the belief that a young man should expect from four years of advanced education a truly liberalizing experience, including the classics, philosophical studies, mathematics, the sciences, and commercially useful subjects. Those patronizing the higher institutions were in a position to demand more democratic treatment of their youths. Strict religious and moral standards were beginning to weaken, and more freedom of thought and action was allowed. The denominational colleges resisted these changes, but gradually even they were forced to recognize that changes were taking place in American life that would destroy them if they proved unable to adapt.

PROFESSIONAL TRAINING

The newer concept of a university included professional preparation for groups other than ministers, but the eighteenth century saw only a beginning in this direction. Most of the education for the ministry, law, medicine, and teaching was left to an apprentice system. A practitioner in the field would accept one or more young men as assistants and would instruct them through example and telling. He would direct their reading, discuss matters of interest with them, and, when he deemed them ready, allow them to take over part of his work.

The major colleges and universities gradually established professorships of law and medicine as part of their faculties. In 1793, Columbia University established the Kent professorship of law. As the study of the sciences grew and physicians came from France and England to America, Philadelphia, Columbia, and Harvard employed teachers of medicine who taught the subject and made use of local and visiting physicians in the laboratory.

Often young men who studied religion in college and possibly did some special work under the watchful eye of the college president would apprentice themselves to a minister for a year or more while waiting for assignment to a church.

CONCLUSION

The eighteenth century in America was one in which the colonies moved from foreign domination to a free and independent nationhood. They borrowed much from their Old World ancestry, but by the end of the century were beginning to create for themselves. Their schools, products of Old World religious struggles, began to feel the stimulus of New World conditions and needs and to turn their attention in new directions. The academy, called the only truly American school, appeared to challenge the Latin grammar school and serve the interests and needs of a new land and a new people. Ideas of freedom, equality, commercial and trade success, and a world based on science, were beginning to challenge the traditional Calvinist, aristocratic, anti-intellectual patterns that had long dominated the life of the people. These newer ideas were forcing education at all levels to reshape itself or be forgotten.

CHAPTER 14

In Nineteenth Century Europe

INTRODUCTION

Europe in the nineteenth century was a maze of conflict and intrigue. Forces that had been budding for centuries came to flower and sought to dominate the life of the people. Lines were drawn clearly, lines that in the past had been dim indications of differences, and men were forced to choose. Institutions were most sharply demarcated and set about to win the minds of men and, through their minds, their loyalty. Political, social, economic, and religious patterns united and separated the people, creating problems that challenged the best thinking and most profound understanding the age could produce.

As one looks backward from this century of change, during which much that was old crumbled into dust while the creative genius of man was building the new, he is impressed by the inevitability of it all. Given the centuries that preceded the nineteenth, their accomplishments and failures, it was "written in the stars" that certain political and economic theories would become sharply delineated. Kant would appear to save western thought from the skepticism which had grown from Locke's empiricism, as carried to its logical conclusions by Berkeley and Hume; Pestalozzi would reinterpret Rousseau and propose a new theory of social betterment; Froebel would look at the child as a flower growing in a garden, the *kinder garten;* and Herbart would create a new psychology out of the knowledge of human nature made available by the new sciences.

Each generation builds upon the foundations laid by those that preceded it. The nineteenth century in Europe is ample proof of this fact. What the new generation does is determined by what the past has accomplished or failed to accomplish. This is not a theory of arid fatalism that sees in the present nothing more than a repetition of the past —perhaps in new clothes. It is actually an affirmation of creative evolution. To the degree that the past is creative, it creates the creator who, in the new century, takes the contributions of the past and weaves them into the created new. This is more than a mere rearrangement of parts. It is a new whole that is more than and different from the sum of all its parts. In assessing any present, one must recognize all that the past has contributed, limitations as well as possibilities, and that the major contribution of this past has been the creator. This creator is a force, a factor, a being who reshapes the material given him into forms that are new in a real sense of the term.

Of all the nineteenth century thinkers, the one who saw this most clearly was Froebel, an idealist. His search for unity in the universe led him to a creative principle, which for lack of a better name he called "God," found in all nature, including man, and forever creating itself. This was one of the most challenging and fruitful concepts of the nineteenth century, a concept whose depths mankind even today has not been able to sound. When it is fully understood, we shall have the key to one world and one creative humanity in which each individual can be truly himself.

Those centuries before the nineteenth built a Europe and a world which the nineteenth inherited. This inheritance brought problems, challenges, and opportunities with which the new century had to deal. This was true in all phases of human life: political, social, religious, economic, and educational. Our concern is mainly with the educational, but to understand this fully, we must see it in the setting of all other phases of the century.

NATIONALISM IN NINETEENTH CENTURY EUROPEAN EDUCATION

In France

Nationalism dominated French education during the nineteenth century. The general opinion during the century was that national unity could be achieved only when the school system was clearly in the hands of a strong centralized government. Further, this system was designed to preserve the aristocratic nature of French society. Although the Third Republic evidenced democratic tendencies, the aristocratic ethos was strong enough to support two educational "tracks," one for the upper and one for the lower classes.

While France was bleeding from a great national revolution, its leaders made some feeble attempts to establish a national school system that would unite the people. Napoleon overthrew the Directory in 1799 and seized power in France. He is supposed to have said later, "I found the crown of France lying on the ground, and I picked it up with a sword." His first endeavor as First Consul was to strengthen national unity. The law of 1802, reflecting his favorable impression of the work of the Brothers of Christian Schools, returned elementary education to Church control. It also established a state system of secondary schools under public control. Actually Napoleon was little concerned with the ABC's. He believed that it was through secondary schools that the nation would produce its leaders, and although he permitted private secondary schools to exist, he was convinced that only as France was able to develop a strong secondary school structure under complete state control could it build strongly and effectively.

Consequently, the law of 1802 established two types of secondary schools: the *lycée* and the *collège*. The *lycée* was supported largely by the state but charged tuition of all its students. It was an aristocratic boarding school with a classical-humanistic curriculum and was located in large centers of population. The *collège* was designed for small communes, was supported largely by the local community, and took a position in French education second to the *lycée*. The law also provided for higher institutions to teach the liberal arts, sciences, and professions of theology, law, and medicine. Napoleon envisioned an educational system that would train the French aristocracy to leadership while producing men dedicated to French nationalism who could merit loyalty and respect from the masses.

This plan was furthered by the law of 1806, creating the University of France, a supreme administrative body charged with supervising all the schools of France. At its head was a grand master with a cabinet of thirty advisers, all appointed directly by the emperor. The law divided the nation into twenty-seven academies or administrative units, each presided over by a rector appointed by the grand master. Each rector was assisted by an advisory council and several inspectors.

In 1810, the state established the Superior Normal School to train teachers for the *lycée*. Thus, Napoleon erected a bureaucracy to organize a national system of education under state control, serving the interests of the state, producing citizens who would be first and above all Frenchmen.

While Napoleon's centralized state system of education remained throughout the nineteenth century largely as he designed it, the Bourbon monarchy, which held power from 1814 to 1830, made changes which favored the Catholic Church. In some places priests served as administrators and teachers of public schools, while bishops were permitted to license teachers of private schools.

This trend toward giving the Church greater influence in French education was slowed considerably during the reign of Louis Philippe,

1830 to 1848. The government which Marshal Soult formed on October 11, 1832, had as its minister of education the noted French historian and statesman François Pierre Guillaume Guizot (1787-1874). Under his instructions, Victor Cousin (1792-1867) was sent to Prussia to study what was then considered to be one of the finest educational systems in all Europe and to make recommendations for strengthening the French system. The result of this study was the school law of 1833. Under this law, each commune was ordered to establish a public primary school, erect a school building, and provide for the housing and salaries of teachers. Although these schools were "public," parents were charged tuition for their children. Only children of the very poor were allowed to attend free. In instances when the commune could not afford to meet the law's requirement, the state offered aid. While private schools were permitted to continue, their teachers had to be certified by the mayor of the commune. The power of the Church was lessened by the provision that only those children whose parents gave consent were to be taught religion.

In addition, the law authorized establishment of "higher primary schools" in towns and cities for vocational training of those who completed the work of the primary grades. To provide teachers for this system, each department was authorized to maintain a normal school.

Napoleon had centered his interest on secondary education, paying little attention to the early years of instruction. The law of 1833 gave France an equally strong system of primary schools. While these were not free or compulsory, the French state was taking giant strides in the direction of a complete school system providing each child with an education designed to develop his loyalty to the conservative social and political life of middle-nineteenth century France.

Liberal teachers were involved in the revolution of 1848. They sought to turn the national school system into a compulsory, free educational structure for all children up to their fourteenth year. This liberalizing trend, which dominated the Second Republic, was declared anathema by a law of 1850 that gave bishops and Church officials a prominent role in French education. When Louis Napoleon became emperor in 1852, he set out to rid the schools of all liberals, making them subject to discharge and possible exile. The normal schools were watched carefully lest they sow the seeds of liberalism and democracy among student teachers.

This witch-hunting came to an end with the birth of the Third Republic in 1871. As minister of public instruction in the cabinet of W. H. Waddington, Jules François Camille Ferry (1832-1893) sponsored several laws that drew the plans for French public education along democratic lines. Primary schools were made free for all children, compulsory attendance was required of those in the six to thirteen age group, and the superior council came under the domination of professional educators, who had displaced clerics. Curriculum, textbooks, certification of teachers, and payment of primary teachers' salaries were placed under the ministry of public instruction. Private and religious schools were carefully supervised by the state, members of religious orders prohibited from teaching in public schools, and religious schools forbidden to serve as public schools. In addition, *lycées* and *collèges* for girls were encouraged.

During the nineteenth century, France developed and maintained a dual educational system, with primary education confined to the lower classes and secondary education the privilege of the upper classes. As she moved into the twentieth century, higher primary, technical, and trade schools were created to care for advanced education of the masses, while the secondary schools remained upper-class oriented. By the time of the Separation Act of 1905, elementary schools were completely secularized. As French Catholics turned to religious private schools, the ministry of education increased its supervision over them, denying religious orders the right to maintain independent schools.

France had succeeded in building on firm foundations a highly centralized and nationalistic school structure, serving the state by inculcating the virtues, ideals, and mores of France and shaping the young into loyal citizens.

IN GERMANY

Frederick William III became king of Prussia in 1797. Although he set about immediately to institute reforms inside his kingdom, he had neither the strength nor the ability to deal with the difficult foreign problems that had been created by past events. Conditions worsened, and in October, 1806, war broke out between Prussia and France, resulting in the treaty of Tilsit, July 7, 1807, by which Prussia was stripped of much of her territory and left disgraced and impotent at the feet of Napoleon. In this time of deep national depression, the philosopher Fichte delivered a series of addresses, 1807-1808, in which he argued that the salvation of Prussia depended upon its ability to build a system of education adequate to prepare needed leaders and a population able to follow them intelligently. This, he held, had to be a national system imbued with the ideas and ideals of a regenerated Prussia. It should be democratic to the degree that each child might have an opportunity to get the education his talents and capacity dictated.

While the conservatives battled to maintain the social structure and aristocratic education of the time of Frederick the Great and Frederick William II, it seemed that the new king and the prominent men he was able to enlist in his service would institute educational reforms comparable to the social reforms that followed Napoleon's victory. The University of Berlin was founded on liberal principles, and Fichte became its head. The government sent a group of young men to Yverdon to study with Pestalozzi, then the most famous educator in all Europe, and bring back his ideas and methods for Prussian use. Many leaders of Prussian educational thought were influenced significantly by this Swiss reformer. As a result the elementary schools of a rejuvenated Prussia were attracting attention everywhere, and both France and the United States sent representatives to study the system with the intention of copying its virtues.

What appeared to be a nascent liberalism in education faded with the dismissal of a minister named Stein, who had been able to institute many reforms and had dreamt of a new Prussia rising out of defeat. With the rise of Hardenberg to the office of chancellor and with the death of Queen Louise, who had been the real strength behind the throne, the church and the aristocracy moved into positions of influence, and the schools of Prussia were allowed to drift under ecclesiastical domination.

Frederick William III turned from the concept of education as a means for social regeneration to the more traditional and aristocratic use of mass education to hold the common people in line while developing loyalty to the ruler and his government. As a result, a two-track system of schools was firmly established by 1830 with a *Volksschulen* and an elementary system serving 90 per cent of the people, preparing them for lesser functions in society, and a secondary system serving 10 per cent, constituting the upper classes, preparing them for higher positions and leadership. The church and the government were alert to any indication among students or teachers of liberal or "radical" tendencies.

Frederick William IV came to the throne of Prussia in 1840. Although he reversed some of the repressive measures of his father, he abhorred any idea of popular rule, thinking himself divinely commissioned to govern not only Prussia but all of Germany. His was a patriarchal monarchy which listened to advice from the various classes but acted as he saw fit, a monarchy resting on an evangelical religion. For a time he believed that the revolution of 1848 would lead to a united Germany with himself as ruler, not a democratically chosen emperor, but rather a divinely appointed one, the old Holy Roman Empire reconstituted. As this dream faded, he rebuked the teachers for encouraging the people to ask for a constitution, saying, "I will never allow to come between Almighty God and this country a plotted parchment, to rule us with paragraphs, and to replace the ancient, sacred bond of loyalty." He thought of education as an instrument for countering unauthorized social, political, and religious ideas, and teacher training schools as producers of men and women indoctrinated to teach the official doctrines of state and church.

Gradually, Frederick William IV's mind began to crack, and his brother William headed a regency to reign in his name. William was a military man interested in strengthening and reforming the Prussian army. This was opposed by the liberals, and a bitter struggle developed between conservative and liberal elements in the kingdom, with the liberals holding the upper hand. Frederick William IV died on January 2, 1861, and William became king. Unable to establish a government that would satisfy both sides and fearing a revolt led by some of his generals, he called Otto, Count von Bismarck, back to Prussia from his ambassadorial post in Paris and, on September 22, made him minister president. This was not altogether pleasing to the new king, since Bismarck was identified with the extreme conservative forces represented by the *Kreuzzeitung* group, but William I had no other choice. The powerful minister gradually came to dominate Prussian policy, and the king faded into the background. The 1870 war with France united all Germany behind the king, who on January 18, 1871, was proclaimed emperor. Though seated in this powerful chair, William left the government largely to Bismarck and lived an uneventful life, dying in 1888 to be succeeded by his son, William II.

William I believed that education should be an instrument for uniting all elements in the nation. With the help of Bismarck, a strong believer in *Kulturkampf,* the General School Regulations of 1872 were passed, giving recognition to the diverse religious groups in the empire and providing that the schools in each community should represent the dominant theological position of the area. While all schools were to be maintained by the state, they should provide for religious instruction satisfactory to the people patronizing them. Here was an attempt to silence religious conflict while maintaining a firm nationalistic hold on all education.

Meanwhile, recognition was given to the fact that Germany was becoming an industrial nation and needed schools to train skilled workers. Vocational and continuation schools were encouraged, and middle schools were made available for children of artisans, small merchants, and tradesmen who had the ability to go beyond the elementary grades but who could not attend the *gymnasium,* or secondary school.

When William II came to the throne, he continued the policy of his father, maintaining that teachers should vigorously attack both in and out of their classes the evil doctrines of socialism and communism, indoctrinating children with a belief that religion and the monarchy were the only grounds for hope among the laboring classes. At the opening of the twentieth century, Germany had developed a centralized, nationalistic educational structure, dominated by conservatism.

Its aim was to produce efficient, obedient, and loyal citizens of the fatherland, men and women willing to sacrifice themselves if demanded to do so by their leaders.

During the nineteenth century, Prussia developed a free elementary school system under state control, with teachers carefully chosen and highly trained to produce literate citizens loyal to state and emperor. When Prussia became the center of the German Empire, she was able to offer other German states the results of her successful endeavors.

Her secondary school system had become a model for the entire western world. The *gymnasium,* providing a classical education for the upper classes, was brought to a high level of efficiency during the first half of the nineteenth century. National and international developments made reforms necessary after the revolution of 1848. Tradition was strong, and any attempt at reconstruction to meet new demands was bitterly opposed. By 1870, a realistic school, the *Realgymnasium,* began preparing students for the university. William II gave this trend his blessing when he accused the classical gymnasium of producing "young Greeks and Romans," not "young Germans," and stated clearly that "the German exercise must be the center around which everything revolves." This gave greater prestige to both the *Realgymnasium* and the *Realschule.*

Young Germans who expected to attend the university and prepare for the professions or become leaders in the new scientific age were given choices regarding their education. All attended a primary school for six to nine years. Then they might enter the *gymnasium,* studying Latin, Greek, and mathematics, moving on to the university and the learned professions. If this did not appeal to them, they had the *Realgymnasium,* an in-between institution offering both classical and scientific courses. Should one wish to concentrate wholly upon modern languages and the sciences, he had the *Oberrealschule,* an institution designed to train for technical and commercial vocations. The curriculum of each school was the same for all students, since by the time one entered a particular school, he was fairly certain of his career.

During the nineteenth century, thousands of American students went to Germany, took courses in the universities, and returned home enthusiastic about what they had learned and seen. At the same time, millions of Germans migrated to America, bringing their educational ideas and methods. These immigrants exerted a tremendous influence on all levels of American education, establishing their German thinking about education into the American school system.

IN ENGLAND

English tradition made education the responsibility of parent or guardian with as little state interference as possible. Schools that existed were in private hands or under the control of religious or charitable associations. As England developed its industrial complex, and as great masses of the poor crowded into manufacturing centers to work under deplorable conditions, philanthropic measures to provide some education for the working classes were increased, and the government began to take an interest in providing help. This governmental interest was stimulated by those who feared an ignorant, undisciplined mob, and thought of education as a means for keeping the poor contented with their plight. The English government concentrated its efforts largely toward helping religious and charitable groups provide the necessary education.

As a result, virtually all religious bodies were providing charity education during the nineteenth century. Other philanthropic organizations were engaged in supporting "ragged" schools for the poor and underprivileged, orphan schools, and industrial schools, along with soup kitchens, reformatories, thrift brigades, and the like. Three important types of schools made their appearance at this time: Sunday schools, monitorial schools, and infant schools. Each had its advocates who organized societies for the spread of these schools in England and America.

Although several thousand schools were established by these societies and by private initiative, the task of providing the needed education for the masses was greater than they could handle. The Reform Act of 1832 extended suffrage to nonproperty owners. This was the first of a long series of measures which moved England along the road to true representative democracy. This act presented the state and vested interests with a menacing threat. A mass of illiterate people was being given the vote and the power that goes with it. To escape a repetition on English soil of the excesses of the French Revolution, the state had to provide education for these people wherever voluntary efforts were inadequate.

Agitation increased for more extensive governmental participation in elementary education. The voices of such men as Dickens, John Stuart Mill, Sir William Blackstone, Jeremy Bentham, and Carlyle were heard advocating tax support for schools for the working classes. The Tories were able to defeat all bills supporting this effort while they remained in power. When, in 1830, the Whigs gained control of the English government, they pushed through Parliament a bill giving £ 20,000 to the National Society and the British and Foreign Society for the construction of school buildings. Other bills followed, granting money to other societies and permitting its use for expenses other than buildings. By 1839, the money being made available for these purposes was large enough to make necessary the appointment of a committee of the Privy Council to administer the funds and provide inspectors to see that they were being spent wisely and legally. This committee became, in 1856, the Department of Education.

State support of education was, by this time, an accepted part of English policy, in spite of the bitter opposition it received from conservative and religious groups. Church societies feared that education was becoming secular, while dissenting groups were worried that the Church of England, identified closely with the English government, would gain a monopoly over all education. This opposition led to the creation, in 1858, of the Newcastle Commission to investigate the whole issue and make recommendations. The commission reached the conclusion that state support of education would lead eventually to unwarranted interference with individual rights and voted strongly against any move that would make elementary schooling free or compulsory.

This report was accepted as the will of the people until the Liberal Party came to power, with Gladstone as its most eloquent champion. In 1870 the Forster Act repudiated the Newcastle Commission and established free schools and compulsory attendance. This new law divided England into school districts to be administered by local school boards. Voluntary agencies were given one year to establish a school in every district. If this was not done, the school board was authorized to open a school supported partly by taxation and partly by fees paid by parents. All children whose parents could not meet tuition costs were admitted free. These came to be called "board schools" since they were under the jurisdiction of a school board. The law authorized the board to require attendance of all children from six to thirteen years of age. All instruction in "board schools" was secular, while voluntary schools were permitted to teach religion only to those children whose parents consented.

By the close of the nineteenth century, England was moving into state-supported, compulsory education on the elementary level. It still respected the right of private interests, both church and secular, to educate, but realized that the task of mass education was far beyond private resources and personnel. Thus a sort of cooperative pattern was developing, leaving private interests to do what they could with a minimum of regulation and stepping in when necessary to guarantee education for all.

At the secondary level, the traditional "public schools" were dominant. Such institutions as Charterhouse, Westminister, Harrow, St. Paul's, Merchant Taylor's, Eton, Winchester, Rugby, and Shrewsbury, with their classical curricula, moral and religious standards, and campus mores, set the tone for all other secondary schools. During the nineteenth century, this pattern was challenged by democratic and liberal forces who demanded more schools for the masses and greater emphasis upon the sciences. This dissatisfaction eventually influenced Parliament to appoint a series of commissions to investigate secondary education in the nation. The Clarendon Commission, while approving the classical curriculum, recommended that more attention be given to modern language, science, and social studies. Its general attitude was favorable to the English secondary school tradition as represented by the great "public schools."

Another study, by Lord Taunton and the School Inquiry Commission, was more critical of the secondary schools and made radical recommendations regarding curriculum, state supervision of standards, teacher certification, and organization. These were ignored by Parliament, which in 1869 passed the Endowed School Act, providing for a commission to assist endowed schools in their management of funds. The "public schools" continued much as they had, setting an example for other private secondary schools and maintaining rigid class distinctions within their faculties and student bodies. Some scholarships, or "free places," were made available to poor students, but these students were clearly segregated from the children of high-born parents. The classical curriculum tended to dominate all secondary education, since it provided the only means available for moving up to the colleges. English secondary schools remained dedicated to inculcating the morals and mores of the English "gentleman," even to the extent of making intellectual training of minor importance. Many held that, just as the elementary schools were a sort of apprenticeship for the masses, secondary school education was a real apprenticeship for the "gentleman."

IN OTHER COUNTRIES

As the nations of the world moved through the nineteenth century, they increasingly appreciated the fact that education was pivotal to national advancement, and took steps to develop and strengthen their public school systems. The small countries of Scandinavia were brought into the Lutheran Reformation, felt many bonds of kinship with the Germans, and often copied German policies and school organization. Acting under the inspiration of both Pestalozzi and Froebel, Uno Cygnaeus (1810-1888), in Finland, helped develop his nation's elementary education to a level that attracted the attention of all Europe and even America. He brought into this pattern "sloyd," the Swedish system of manual training. Later, Russia incorporated the system into her elementary schools, and it was from here that the United States imported it.

Just as the educational thinking and school patterns being developed in Europe were influencing the United States and Canada, so were they reaching east, to extend their influence as far as Japan. The development of this ancient country from the time Commodore Perry entered Uraga harbor on July 8, 1853, has been one of the phenomena of the modern world. From a backward feudal land, it moved rapidly to become one of the most highly industrialized and progressive nations of modern times. Feudalism was abolished in 1871 and a new social order decreed. Commissions were sent to the nations of Europe and America to study their governments, industrial complexes, and educational systems. Their recommendations produced the education code of 1872, which proclaimed that all people, both male and female, should be educated, and that anyone who failed to send his children to school was grossly neglecting his duty. Those who had the potential should continue through higher learning.

The Japanese borrowed much of their school organization, methodology, and philosophy from France, Germany, and America. They devoured avidly all new ideas, imitating much that was western but adding much from their own creative genius. It has been estimated that by the first decade of the twentieth century, ninety-eight per cent of all children of school age were in school, and that the illiteracy curve had fallen to .09 per cent, making Japan the most literate nation in the world.

IN RETROSPECT

By the opening of the twentieth century, practically every country in the "civilized" world had established some kind of public education as a result of the pressures of commercial, industrial, and humanitarian forces. The increased flow of populations from country to country, especially from England, France, and Germany, served to spread cultures, philosophies, and educational programs throughout the world. While many Europeans made their contributions to this worldwide educational ferment, it was Germany who contributed most. Its success was phenomenal. It produced a body of philosophical and educational thought that appealed to people everywhere as bases for educational structures.

We shall now turn to a study of this philosophical and educational development centered largely in the Germany of the nineteenth century.

CHAPTER 15

Educational Thought in Nineteenth Century Europe

INTRODUCTION

Three giants in educational history appeared and worked during the nineteenth century in Europe: Pestalozzi, Froebel, and Herbart. Their theories of instruction and their methodologies changed the schools of Europe, especially those for the masses, in innumerable ways, and became the foundation for much that we call modern and progressive education today.

These men, each in his own way, were educational philosophers. Their theories were influenced deeply by the philosophical systems which were being developed during that tremendously creative period that began with Spinoza and Locke in the latter half of the seventeenth century and produced during the eighteenth and first half of the nineteenth centuries Rousseau, Kant, Fichte, Schiller, Schelling, and Hegel. They took much from the rich intellectual life of their age and from the thinking of those who made it possible, but they were in no sense mere imitators. The legacies of the centuries preceding them and the contributions of their contemporaries were combined with their own thinking and observations and the whole shaped into educational patterns of unique proportions and richness.

JOHANN HEINRICH PESTALOZZI (1746-1827)

In the city of Brugg in the Swiss canton of Aargau is a bust of Pestalozzi on which is engraved the following:

Here Rests

HENRY PESTALOZZI

Born in Zurich, the 12th of January, 1746
Died at Brugg, the 17th of February, 1827

Savior of the poor at Neuhof and Stanz, father of orphans at Burgdorf
and Munchenbuchsee, founder of the popular school at Yverdon. The
educator of humanity; man, Christian, and citizen. All for others,
nothing for himself. Peace to his ashes.

TO OUR FATHER PESTALOZZI

Grateful Aargau

Who was this man, buried in a simple country churchyard under a
"rough, unhewn stone, such as I myself have always been" and, on the
one-hundredth anniversary of his death, removed to a more suitable
tomb to be remembered by the engraving just quoted?

"HARRY ODDITY OF FOOLBOROUGH"

When Pestalozzi was five years old, his father, a physician, died,
leaving his two sons and a daughter to the tender care of a mother and
a faithful servant named Babeli. The family had little money but an
abundance of love, devotion, generosity, peace, and harmony. Dominated by his mother, the nurse, and his sister, Pestalozzi became a
highly maladjusted child in whom feminine characteristics were
stronger than masculine. He was kept indoors most of the time, listening to stories and daydreaming. He did not attend school until he was
nine. He was undersized and underdeveloped, shy, awkward, absent-
minded, impractical, and intuitive.

He tells us that from childhood, he was "everybody's plaything."
Although he longed to be one of the group, he found himself "incapable
of doing what everybody does, and of enjoying what everybody enjoys."
He writes bitterly, "Although I worked hard and learned some things
well, I had none of their ability for the ordinary lessons, and so I could
not take it amiss that they dubbed me Harry Oddity of Foolborough."

Pestalozzi attended the town elementary school and then entered the
Latin school. He was depressed during these years by the realization
of his difference from others, and drifted more and more into a world
of dreams and unreality. His most memorable experiences were those
gained from visits to his grandfather, Andrew Pestalozzi, pastor at
Hoengg, near Zurich. There he could spend hours walking alone in the
woods and meditating as a child would meditate. He went with his

grandfather on his pastoral visits to the poor and downtrodden. He saw the children of the wealthy playing happily at school with their fellows, and he saw the children of the workers with hollow cheeks and sunken eyes, with misery written on their faces. He saw the extremes of great wealth and abject poverty, and developed a sense of deep pity for the poor. Even as a child, Pestalozzi began forming the aim that was to govern all his future life. He expressed this aim much later when he wrote, "Long years I lived surrounded by more than fifty beggar children. In poverty I shared my bread with them. I lived like a beggar in order to learn how to make beggars live like men." He saw the masses in poverty and degradation, shiftless, frustrated, and hopeless, with an utter lack of human dignity. "Ever since my youth," he wrote, "has my heart moved on like a mighty stream, alone and lonely, towards my one sole goal—to stop the sources of the misery in which I saw the people around me sunk."

Pestalozzi attended the University of Zurich, where he came under the influence of J. J. Breitinger, professor of Greek and Hebrew, and J. J. Bodmer, professor of history and politics. Although he showed some ability as a scholar, his college years were not marked by significant intellectual success. He developed, as a result of his professors' teachings, a passionate devotion to justice and freedom and a deep pride in the heroic history of Switzerland. He began to see that, through education, man could attain his lost dignity. During his college years he came under the spell of Johann Kasper Lavater (1741-1801), poet, theologian, and mystic, who, in 1767, aroused great patriotic enthusiasm with his ardent *Schweizerlieder,* a poem set to music, which quickly became popular.

These influences, plus the experiences of his childhood, drove the youthful and idealistic Pestalozzi to radical ideas and into movements aimed at eliminating injustices and corruption in political office and at alleviating the conditions of the poor. By the time he finished his schooling, he was branded a revolutionary, impractical visionary, and "rabble rouser."

FAILURE HEAPED ON FAILURE

As an outgrowth of his training and his desire to help others, Pestalozzi turned to the ministry to effect his life goal. His rather thick speech, nervous shyness, and self-consciousness caused him to break down in his trial sermon and realize how completely this door was shut to him. Still determined to devote himself to the poor and downtrodden, he turned to the law and politics, believing that as a statesman he could work for legislation that would in part achieve his aim. His liberal activities during his student years made him feared by those he would have helped.

At this time he read *Social Contract* and *Emile,* and became an ardent admirer of Rousseau's political and educational theories. Both books had been banned by the authorities at Zurich. This angered Pestalozzi, who, with a group of friends, published a radical paper, attacked and had removed from office certain dishonest officials, and organized the Helvetian Society for democratic action. The authorities arrested these young men, threw them in jail, and warned that they could be denied citizenship if they persisted in their activities. They were even prohibited from assembling for political discussion.

Defeated in every attempt to cure the intellectual and moral degradation of the poor, Pestalozzi turned to agriculture. He married a childhood sweetheart and, with whatever money the two could gather, bought one hundred acres of land in the canton of Aargau, built a comfortable home, and settled down to raise madder and vegetables to sell in Zurich. He christened the place Neuhof, and believed that by operating a model farm, he could teach poor, inefficient farmers how better to use their land and become prosperous tillers of the soil.

During the early years of this agricultural experiment, a son, Jacobi, was born to the Pestalozzis. The father determined to rear and educate his son as Rousseau had suggested in *Emile.* Gradually, changes were made, as Pestalozzi sensed weaknesses in Rousseau's methods and added new techniques born of his own intuitive understanding of children and how they learn. This was the beginning of the educational pattern that Pestalozzi would eventually give to the world and that would bring him both fame and disappointment.

The farm failed because of Pestalozzi's impractical nature and his lack of thorough preparation for the venture. By 1775, the now twenty-nine-year-old "Harry Oddity" had lost all the land except his home, which his creditors allowed him to keep. Defeated and almost destitute, Pestalozzi turned his home into a refuge for abandoned children. Some were vagrants picked up from the streets and highways, and others came from foundling institutions. Pestalozzi fed and clothed these waifs, gave them a home, and taught them whatever he felt their talents and abilities made possible. He believed that such children, given a home with love and care and taught informally as they lived and did household chores, would develop moral character, learn, and grow into honest, industrious citizens.

The experiment began with twenty children, who grew in a short time from undernourished, demoralized, and bewildered creatures into sturdy, competent, cheerful, and devoted workers. Many others wanted to come to Neuhof, and Pestalozzi solicited funds to provide for them.

For the next two years enough money was made available to care for thirty-seven children comfortably. Still impractical and naïve, Pestalozzi could not turn a child away, and it was not long before eighty children were living at Neuhof. The large numbers reduced personal contacts and created problems which Pestalozzi was unable to handle. Some children ran away, others returned to depraved homes, and the whole project decayed with increasing tempo. Pestalozzi had failed again, his family was bankrupt, and the home often lacked both fuel and food.

OUT OF THE DEPTHS

When hope seemed gone, Elizabeth Naef came into Pestalozzi's life. She was an uneducated servant who lived nearby and who had heard of her neighbor's troubles from her master. She moved in in spite of Pestalozzi's efforts to dissuade her, restored cleanliness and order to the home, and planted a small garden near the house; the family had food again. Elizabeth remained with the Pestalozzis, supplementing the weaknesses of Pestalozzi's idealism with her practical intelligence. Although often poor, the family was never again destitute or in danger of starving.

To bring in a little money, Pestalozzi turned to writing, but with little success. Finally he realized that he could succeed only if he wrote about what he knew, the life of the Swiss peasant. With Elizabeth as a model, he wrote *Leonard and Gertrude.* Leonard was the town drunk, and his children were waifs, degraded and uneducated. Gertrude, his wife, took over, trained and educated the children, reformed her husband, and set an example for the entire community. Pestalozzi planned the book to show how, by using his methods, children might be educated and society regenerated.

As a novel, *Leonard and Gertrude* was a huge success. The simple story of peasant life fascinated the public, and its popularity spread throughout Europe. As a work on education and social uplift, it was a failure. In the years that followed, Pestalozzi wrote three more books developing the theme of the first, edited a newspaper, and published several articles on various subjects. *Leonard and Gertrude* appeared in 1781, one year after his first unsuccessful book, *The Evening Hours of a Hermit,* a series of aphorisms and reflections.

Pestalozzi had become a close friend of Fichte, who suggested that he write his educational ideas in a scholarly book that would announce to the world his mature thinking on the whole subject of moral regeneration. The result was *My Investigations Into the Course of Nature in the Development of the Human Race,* considered by Pestalozzi his most scholarly work but largely ignored by the world of scholarship. Despite the reception of this book, Pestalozzi was convinced after the years spent in writing it that he had to become a schoolmaster.

THE ORPHANAGE AT STANZ

During the years between the failure of the Neuhof orphanage and 1799, the French Revolution had begun, developed into the Terror, and subsided. Pestalozzi was at first enthusiastic over the possibilities he saw in this move to relieve the misery of the poor, but its violence and terror revolted him, and he began to fear that Switzerland would repeat the mistakes of France. The Swiss Revolution led to the new Swiss Union, which three small districts stubbornly refused to join. French troops called in by the authorities were brutal and unfeeling. Because they were vigorously resisted by the populace, the soldiers slaughtered the people of Stanz, burned their homes, and left 111 infirm old men, 246 orphans, and 237 children who, though not orphaned, were practically homeless because of the utter destitution of their parents.

Pestalozzi was angered, and resolved to go to Stanz as a teacher and friend of the orphans. He was able to get backing from the Swiss government to open an orphanage at Stanz for fifty ragged waifs, diseased and vermin-infested. With the aid of one faithful woman servant, he worked night and day to teach and regenerate these children. Though successful to a degree, the project was under attack by the citizens of Stanz, and demands were made that Pestalozzi leave. Catholic Stanz was unhappy to have a Protestant, whom the people considered no better than an errant heretic, teaching and caring for their children. Further, Pestalozzi's methods were not orthodox, and the freedom in his school was interpreted as a result of his lack of ability to control the children.

In spite of hostility and criticism, the orphanage was proceeding rather well when a new outburst of resistance brought troops back into the district, and the building in which Pestalozzi had his school was needed for a military hospital. Exhausted and in ill health, Pestalozzi retired to a health resort, the children were sent to private homes, and the project was closed out. When, after peace was restored, the orphanage was reinstituted, it was put in the hands of a native of the district, and Pestalozzi felt he had failed again.

THE SCHOOLS AT BURGDORF AND YVERDON

Discouraged by the affront at Stanz, Pestalozzi offered his services without pay to the small village of Burgdorf. The authorities, knowing his reputation, were reluctant to give him work, but finally put him in charge of the lowest class in a school maintained for noncitizens. He succeeded so well that, in spite of much criticism of his methods, he was eventually given charge of the class of children below the entrance age of eight in a school for citizens' children. After less than a year, his children took the annual school examination and did so well that the examiners gave him a letter of deep appreciation and praise.

This caused Pestalozzi's friends to organize a *Society of the Friends of Education* to make his ideas more generally known. As part of this venture, in 1801, he wrote an exposition of his philosophy of education and methodology which he called *How Gertrude Teaches Her Children.* This interested the Swiss authorities, who founded an institute at Burgdorf in which Pestalozzi could work out his ideas with adequate help to prepare textbooks and take over some of the duties of the school. Delays, bungling, and opposition to his work in high places resulted in little money reaching him and in the deepening of his discouragement.

Nearby was a young teacher with little education and no preparation for teaching, Hermann Krusi (1775-1844), who had been given the school in his village by the authorities because he was only eighteen years old and his home was better adapted for a school than those of his competitors. His salary was one dollar a week, while one of those who sought the school job was made the policeman at one and a half dollars a week. When the French armies pillaged his village, Krusi took some of the children to Burgdorf, where he met Pestalozzi. Finding much in common, the two men combined their schools, obtained the use of an old castle, recruited two more teachers, and began a venture that was destined to change the educational thinking and practice of the western world.

Continued fighting among the Swiss cantons and Napoleon's entrance into the trouble caused Pestalozzi to move his school to Yverdon, to an old castle which seemed to fit his needs perfectly. By this time he had added to his staff a retired soldier who taught gymnastics, and a little elementary work.

Yverdon soon became a mecca for educators and others interested in social reform through education. Scholars came to study and learn the secrets of Pestalozzi's success. Pupils poured in from all over the western world. Tutors brought their charges from all countries of Europe and from America. The king gave the school official recognition. Rulers, ambassadors, teachers, professors, the wealthy, town officials, and visitors of all kinds came and went. They saw, they learned, and they marveled.

One student wrote:

> Imagine ... a very ugly man, with rough, bristling hair, his face
> scarred with smallpox and covered with freckles, a pointed, untidy
> beard, no necktie, ill-fitting trousers, stockings down and enormous
> shoes; add to this a breathless, shuffling gait, eyes either large and
> flashing or half-closed as though turned within, features expressing
> either a profound sadness or the most peaceful happiness, speech
> slow and musical, now thundering and hurried, and you will have
> some idea of the man we called "Father Pestalozzi." Such as I have
> described him to you, we loved him; yes we all loved him, for he loved
> us all; we loved him so much that when we lost sight of him for a time
> we felt sad and when he came back to us again we could not turn our
> eyes away from him.[1]

A visitor who remained with Pestalozzi for some time wrote:

> I have seen more than the paradise of Switzerland, for I have seen
> Pestalozzi, and recognized how great his heart is, and how great his
> genius; never have I been so filled with a sense of the sacredness of
> my vocation, and the dignity of human nature, as in the days that I
> spent with this noble man. I cannot think without emotion of this
> little company of brave men, struggling with the present that the
> future may be better, and finding alike their joy and their reward in
> the hope they have of raising children to the true dignity of human-
> ity.[2]

Pestalozzi remained at Yverdon for twenty years. As more pupils
came, more teachers were necessary. He could touch twenty children
with his genius and weave them into a large, loving, and trusting
family. He could not reach more than two hundred students, forty
teachers, and twenty assistants. The school had to change and leave
Pestalozzi out. Teachers began to quarrel among themselves and to
modify many of Pestalozzi's principles and methods. One of these
teachers, Schmidt by name, who had antagonized many of the teachers
by his dictatorial attitude, attacked Pestalozzi unmercifully. The
school eventually fell apart and was closed. Pestalozzi retired to Neuhof where, simple and generous soul that he was, he wrote articles
blaming himself for the school's failure and attempting to protect
Schmidt, even to being unfair to other teachers. An outsider with

---

1. As quoted in Roger De Guimps, *Pestalozzi: His Life and Work* (New York, Appleton-
Century-Crofts, Inc., 1892), p. 253.
2. *Ibid.,* p. 263.

poison pen attacked Pestalozzi vehemently and insultingly. The old educator answered these unjust accusations with the last bit of energy he had and, a few days later, died, in his eighty-first year.

A LOOK INSIDE BURGDORF AND YVERDON

The school at Burgdorf continued from 1800 to 1804. Yverdon was opened in 1805 and was finally closed in 1825. They were boarding schools for boys from six or seven to about eighteen. Most of the pupils were Swiss, but some came from almost every country of Europe and from America.

Pestalozzi was convinced that there should be no break between the home and the school, that the school should be run just as the home. He wanted to be "Father Pestalozzi," and have each child live and learn as he might in a well-ordered home where love and mutual respect abound. Although the school had a daily routine, it was often changed as the interests of the children directed. Discipline was as it might be in a home. Children were not coerced into learning. Their natural interests were encouraged, in the faith that all want to learn and will learn best that in which they are interested.

The schedule consisted of religious observances, lessons, recreation, and adequate rest. More difficult subjects were studied in the morning hours when the children were rested and fresh. Music, drawing, fencing, and manual training were reserved for the afternoon hours. Those who wished were given private lessons in languages and other subjects. Games, picnics, long walks in the forest, swimming, singing, and quiet hours—usually after the evening meal—when Pestalozzi talked to the children as a father might about God, Jesus, right, and wrong, all formed part of the life at Burgdorf and Yverdon.

PESTALOZZI'S PRINCIPLES OF EDUCATION

Pestalozzi had one, all-consuming aim—to use education to restore human dignity and a sense of individual worth to the mass of human beings living worse than animals. He realized that mere learning was not the answer. The task was one of human regeneration, of restoring hope to those who no longer had a reason to hope, of making serfs who had come to live and think like cattle into men able to accept freedom and responsibility and govern themselves. The Swiss Revolution of 1799 had liberated the masses. Now they must be prepared to live as free men.

All genuine and lasting reform, he was convinced, must begin not with the environment, but with the individual. When strength and virtue are developed in the individual, and only then, will it be possible to change the "external forms," the environment. A good state begins with good individuals.

How can this be accomplished? Only by putting into the hands of each individual the power to help himself. Paternalism, philanthropy, ready-made social reforms, weaken the individual and make him dependent. He must come to respect himself, have confidence in himself, and help himself. Anything else will inevitably fail.

Within each child are the seeds of this power. Nature reaches out to action, to self-development, to independence. These seeds must be cultivated by the proper education. Here we see Rousseau's conviction that man's inner nature is good and that the best education fosters the natural development of this innate goodness. In Pestalozzi's hands this became a faith in man, a belief that if given proper education, each individual would develop all his powers harmoniously and be able to take his place in the structure of the good society. This is a philosophy of social regeneration that makes education central.

THE LAWS OF HUMAN UNFOLDING

The individual, according to Pestalozzi, is an organism that develops according to definite laws. As the seed planted in the ground unfolds its inner self and grows into a beautiful flower, so the newborn infant, given the necessary conditions, will unfold his inherent being and grow into a well-developed and complete citizen. The business of the teacher and the student of education is to discover the laws of development and shape an educational structure that will incorporate these laws effectively.

Analysis of the individual will reveal that he is mind, heart, and body. He receives sense impressions from the environment and shapes them into ideas, concepts, thought patterns. He is related to others and to God, and from this relationship come ethical principles, moral and religious concepts and beliefs. He has inner wants, which are physical and drive him to motor activity. Education must be concerned with all three—the head, the heart, and the hand. Each develops according to its own laws and in its own way. We must discover these laws and follow them in our teaching. They will determine the methods we use and the goals we hope to attain.

The first law is that human nature is a unity. There is a oneness that must not be distorted. The head, the heart, and the hand must be developed together and interrelated lest the individual be warped and ugly. The heart is superior to the head and the hand. One must develop to the fullest his intellectual capacities. He must acquire skill in applying knowledge in constructive situations; he must be able to produce.

The end of all this, the goal that puts both head and hand in proper perspective, is one's relation to his fellows and to God. The heart, the moral and religious, correlates and unifies the self.

The second of these laws is that, although the individual must learn those vocational skills that make possible his functioning effectively in the world of work, an education that develops his fundamental capacities has priority. General education, which aims at the rich and full unfolding of man's inner self and powers, must precede vocational education, which puts its stress upon specific skills.

Third, one may know and not do. The purpose of education must always be to give the individual inner power that will result in learning and action. To merely feed the child truths others have discovered or ideas they have constructed will weaken his power of self-discovery, of free activity in his own original learning. The aim of the teacher must be "at increasing the powers of the pupil" rather than "at increasing knowledge." The teacher must "hold back" until the child has been given every opportunity to learn for himself. Only when he gives evidence that he has gone as far as he can, may the teacher step in. The true art of teaching lies in that sensitivity to children that tells the teacher when to stand aside and when to move in with needed help.

Fourth, nature strives to grow, to develop, to unfold. There are in man innate impulses that burgeon from within when the right time has come. To attempt the education of a child before he is ready is not only futile but injurious. To stimulate the child when he is ready internally is the only true education. This demands a thorough understanding of child development and of what will prove to be correct stimulation. Punishment, fear, rewards, and rivalry are not to be used as stimuli to learning. They are external and dangerous.

Fifth, all education must follow the order of nature. Education is, basically, the art of helping nature to unfold. Therefore, the teacher must understand nature and do everything he can to assist it at every step. The teacher is like the gardener "under whose care a thousand trees blossom and grow." Since the principle of growth lies in their very nature, he contributes nothing. He plants, waters, fertilizes, and prunes. "God gives the increase." In like manner, the teacher gives no power to the growing child. He is careful to see that no external force injures or disturbs the natural processes. The teacher is only interested that development proceed in accordance with its own laws. What he does is dictated by these laws, and by them alone.

Sixth, since nature makes no sudden leaps, but rather proceeds to unfold along a consistent route from birth to maturity, all instruction must be suited to this process. It must not demand more of the child than he is able to accomplish at a particular stage of growth, nor must it demand less than his capabilities indicate. This means then that education be graded to fit each stage of growth.

Seventh, Pestalozzi would have nothing to do with shoddy education. In nature the success of a particular stage of growth is dependent upon the fullest development at the preceding stage. In like manner, success in learning depends upon complete mastery of previous learning. Thoroughness, repetition, drill, practice, all are necessary if the child is to build tomorrow's learning firmly on today's. The teacher must understand how the mind of the child develops. Along with this must go a mastery of the materials of instruction and a methodology that employs the right material at the right time and insures thorough learning at each step. Since all children do not develop in the same way or at the same rate, there must be adjustments to the nature of each individual. However, there are broad and generalized techniques that can be applied to all children.

EDUCATION OF THE HEAD

The foundation of all knowledge, Pestalozzi was convinced, is sense impression. He felt, however, that the mind is no passive recipient of impressions but is rather an active force engaged in analyzing, discriminating, relating, and ordering these impressions into concepts, the true objects of knowledge.

The education of the child must begin with objects, not pictures, words, or vague generalizations. His senses must be brought into contact with real objects so that he may experience them as fully as possible and get material with which his mind can work. Only when the child begins with objects can he build clear concepts. The methodology consists of presenting to the child the right object at the right time, permitting him to work with it intimately, and allowing him to build his own concepts of its nature. This became the *object lesson* for which Pestalozzi was famous.

The child must be trained to observe, analyze, count, name, and compare objects. Merely to toss him into an environment of objects and leave him to fend for himself will result in confusion, half truths, vague concepts, and waste of time. As he discriminates among objects by seeing and touching them, he learns to count and develops the concept of numbers. As he fingers objects and compares them, he develops the concepts of measurement, from which he learns to draw. Drawing leads to writing. As he listens to the sounds of his environment, he begins to discriminate among sounds and builds a foundation for music and language. When all his experiences with an object are correlated, he is ready to attach a word to the object, *and the word has meaning.*

The object lessons, which aimed to bring the child into intimate contact with things and to help him observe them clearly and accurately, grew out of principles which have become commonplace in modern education. The child learns by moving from the known to the unknown. The traditional method of requiring children to memorize by rote Latin sentences and paragraphs without meaning was for Pestalozzi the height of stupidity. The child must know the object from direct experience; only then can its name be meaningful to him. Another principle is that all learning must begin with the concrete and move slowly to the abstract. The child cannot know the meaning of "good" until he has experienced concrete examples of goodness. Herein is involved the principle that one must understand the particular before he can know the general. One must know a particular man before he can understand the generalized term, mankind.

Pestalozzi was obsessed with beginnings. He realized that many of the mistakes of education in the past could be traced to the errors teachers made in starting children along the path to learning. If we are to avoid these mistakes, we must start right from birth and in the home. How, he asked, does the newborn child begin to learn? When we discover this, we can adjust our methodology to reality and succeed beyond anything that has been hoped for in the past. But how does the newborn begin to learn? Pestalozzi believed that he started the learning process from the logically simple and built the larger whole. This gave him hope that he could develop a method that would mechanize instruction, a method that would be so simple and easy that anyone, even an illiterate peasant mother, could employ it in teaching children. In learning language, for example, the child would first learn his letters, then syllables, then words. In learning to draw he would master the skill of drawing lines, curves, angles, dots. Then he would combine these into simple figures, and then into more complex pictures. With our better understanding of psychology, we know that this is not the way children learn, that the logically simple is not necessarily the psychologically simple. We put meaningful sentences in the place of letters and syllables and finger painting and scribbling in the place of curves and lines.

In all subjects Pestalozzi insisted that the child experience objects before anything else. From such experiences would grow the concepts of arithmetic, an understanding of maps, charts, and textbooks, and an ability to use language precisely and meaningfully. In each instance the symbols with which the individual would eventually work became meaningful. Dull routine would give way to interested understanding, and the child would be able to move from the known to the unknown efficiently and pleasantly.

EDUCATION OF THE HAND

Pestalozzi realized the need for vocational education. One must be able to do as well as think. His aim at Neuhof was to equip the individual with skills necessary for more efficient living. He believed that if the poor, inefficient farmers in the area could learn more scientific methods of doing what was required of them as farmers, they would escape from shiftlessness, degradation, immorality, and general despair. Vocational education was not an end in itself or merely a means for greater economic security. It was the means of moral and social regeneration.

As one engages in the common activities of life, he comes to experience the objects and people of his environment and learns. A narrow, ineffective life means few and unclear experiences. This may be translated into the more modern statement, "We learn what we do and by what we do." Insight comes through experience, through doing. One who has not learned how to do cannot be expected to rise above the meanest of animals.

Although Pestalozzi had some ideas about the education of the hand, he was never able to develop them into a methodology. He began his thinking, just as in the intellectual areas, with the simple and uncomplicated. He would have the mother start by exercising the hands, arms, and legs of her child. This would lead by clearly defined steps to more complex activities of the whole body. Here he was moving from the known to the unknown, from the simple to the complex, from the particular to the general.

EDUCATION OF THE HEART

Education of the head, the hand, and the heart all begin in the same way, as Pestalozzi saw it. To educate the head we must begin with objects. To educate the hand we must begin with simple body movements. To educate the heart we must begin with the simplest emotions. The moral and religious life of man is concerned with his relations with other individuals and with his creator. To prepare the child in these areas is a matter of developing the right emotions, and to develop the right emotions we must begin with the simplest, the most primitive of all emotions.

Pestalozzi found this in the relation of the child to his mother in the home. The newborn child is helpless, and for a considerable time, this helplessness will continue. Out of this comes very early the sense of dependence. This is the basic, most primitive, simplest emotion. As the child experiences his mother in many capacities and ways, he begins to develop from this emotion of dependence those more complex emotions of love, trust, gratitude, patience, and obedience. The virtues of the good life grow from these. Man first feels toward others, then comes to live virtuously with and among them. In time, dependence upon mother will decrease, and the child finds he is dependent upon others, his fellows, his teacher, those in business and the professions in his community. As he transfers this emotion of dependence to others, he develops love, trust, gratitude, patience, and obedience toward them, toward society. From this, as he matures, comes a feeling of dependence upon God, and all the emotions that he has experienced toward his mother and others are experienced toward God.

The quintessence of the art of teaching, Pestalozzi was convinced, is to be found in the ability to transfer the emotions which the little child has developed toward his mother to others in his social world, and eventually to God. This cannot be taught. Religion is not a matter of reason, as the rationalists and the orthodox theologians had held. You cannot accomplish this transfer of emotions by learning the Bible, committing to memory the catechism, or listening to reasoned sermons. Just as one learns about the world of things through experiencing objects, so here he will learn only in situations of personal relationships where he experiences others and learns through these experiences. Before the teacher talks to his classes about morality and religion, he must awaken in them the emotions of dependence and all the ramifications of this basic emotion in love, trust, gratitude, and the like.

The child comes to feel dependent upon his mother before he can talk, understand his environment, or do anything other than cry and coo. Therefore, the education of the heart begins before that of the head or the hand. If the teacher fails to recognize this fact, all other instruction will be fruitless. Here is the power and motive for all learning. By insisting upon the primacy of emotional development, Pestalozzi is making evident the fact that the child's life in the home and with his mother is basic to all else. If the mother fails, the child will suffer throughout life.

THE MAN AND HIS WORK

Pestalozzi went to his grave believing himself a failure in everything he had attempted. His early years were beset with failure. Only when he turned to teaching did he achieve success, and then only for a while. Even Yverdon crumbled and fell. The why is to be found in the nature of the man himself. Tortured by the degeneracy and ignorance in which he found his fellows living, he yearned with an all-consuming passion to help them. Driven by this passion, he became a pioneer, a radical, a revolutionary, and alienated those he would help. His first years of teaching were embittered by his own conviction that his method was correct, although those whose support he needed said he was wrong, and by the intense hatred that the Catholics in the area had toward him as a Protestant.

When at last Pestalozzi convinced the public that his methods insured success, he fell prey to fame and bigness. His idea of a perfect school was an extension of the home. He was happiest and surest of himself when, as "Father Pestalozzi," he lived in close communion with his pupils, as one big, happy, loving, trusting family. Greatness did not allow this. When kings and princes were daily visitors to Yverdon, when pupils came from all parts of the world, when he had to employ many teachers and assistants to care for the work of the school, when administrative duties became overpowering, the atmosphere of the home was lost, and Pestalozzi found himself in a strange and unfamiliar environment which he was in no way equipped to handle. He could not transform himself from a father in the midst of his family to a skillful administrator of a world-famous institution. With Pestalozzi, Yverdon had to fail.

But Pestalozzi could not see into the future. He could not see that his ideas and his faith in the child would spread throughout the world, and men of vision and understanding everywhere would look back to him for inspiration. When he died at Brugg, he saw only the ashes of a life he had sought to build. His pupils and those who came after him found in his life, his books, and his spirit, "the educator of humanity."

THE PESTALOZZIAN MOVEMENT IN EUROPE

Yverdon attracted world-wide attention. Napoleon and Talleyrand visited the school. M. A. Jullien, a knight of the Legion of Honor and a man of great wealth, paid the tuition for twenty-four selected French youths for one year's study with Pestalozzi. Karl Ritter, the noted geographer, visited Yverdon and wrote, "Pestalozzi knew less geography than a child in one of our primary schools, yet it was from him that I gained my chief knowledge of this science, for it was in listening to him that I first conceived the idea of the natural method." In 1808, the Prussian government established a fund to pay the tuition for three years for seventeen young men who were to study with Pestalozzi. These students formed a nucleus to reform the schools of Prussia and establish colleges for teacher education. Select students from Yverdon spread throughout Switzerland, revitalizing the schools and preparing teachers in the Pestalozzian method and philosophy.

Phillip Emmanuel von Fellenberg (1771-1844), a Swiss nobleman and teacher, took Pestalozzi's *Leonard and Gertrude* as the model for a school which he founded at Hofwyl for practical and vocational education. Although the usual school subjects were taught here, the stress was on such skills as tailoring, printing, shoemaking, and the like. Here Fellenberg was able to develop, in greater detail than had his master, the methodology for the education of the hand. Hofwyl became as celebrated as Yverdon and attracted visitors and selected students from all parts of the world. It served to popularize industrial and agricultural education in both Europe and America.

J. P. Greaves (1777-1842), an influential member of the Home and Colonial School Society of England, studied and worked with Pestalozzi at Yverdon. He was able to persuade the Society to draft Pestalozzianism into its infant school program. This consisted, mainly, in substituting object teaching and the training of the senses for verbal training and memorizing. At Greaves' suggestion, Pestalozzi wrote a most complete and lucid statement of his views on infant education, *Letters on the Early Education of the Child.*

Another source of Pestalozzianism in England was the Mayos, Charles (1792-1846) and his sister Elizabeth. They conducted a Pestalozzian school for boys and The Home and Colonial College for teacher education. Elizabeth was the moving spirit in the latter. They lectured on Pestalozzi's theories, published textbooks, and trained many young teachers for the English poor schools. Obsessed by Pestalozzi's idea of mechanizing instruction, they formalized Pestalozzian methods and school procedures to such an extent that all the life was squeezed from the schools they influenced.

From the work of the Mayos in England and from the writings of men and women who either studied at Yverdon or learned the Pestalozzian ideas and methods elsewhere, schools in the United States came under the influence of this Swiss educator.

So great was Pestalozzi's influence throughout the world that, in 1792, he was made a "Citizen of the French Republic," and, in 1814, was knighted by Tsar Alexander of Russia. In 1804, he was invited to come to the United States and establish a school in Philadelphia.

FRIEDRICH WILHELM AUGUST FROEBEL (1782-1852)

The Early Years

Froebel was the son of a strict, orthodox, terribly demanding German country minister who, harried by the problems of some 5,000 parishioners scattered over several villages, had no time for his family and no understanding of their needs. Froebel's mother died when he was a baby, and a stepmother was soon installed in the home. The years that followed were filled with frustration, loneliness, and neglect. The boy had a reading problem, was always at the bottom of his class, and was taken by his parents and teachers to be stupid. He soon was in stubborn revolt against his home, school, and society at large.

By the time he was ten, his stepmother could stand him no longer, and shipped him off to his mother's uncle, Pastor Hoffman, at Stadt-Ilm in Switzerland. There, for five years, he had freedom, affection, some understanding, and a normal school life. He seemed to recover from his early maladjustment, began learning as a normal boy of his age, and got along well with his agemates.

Returning home at fifteen, he was apprenticed to a forester and seemed on the way to learning a trade suited to his mentality and interest. After two years he left the position and returned home, to find himself accused for the failure of this venture and to face a complete lack of understanding on the part of his father and stepmother. The old fears, antagonisms, and frustrations returned, and the boy was disillusioned and gloomy.

THE JENA YEARS

An older brother was a student at Jena, and needed money for his expenses. Friedrich was sent with the money, found the university stimulating, and obtained permission to stay with his brother for the eight weeks remaining in the school term. When he received a small legacy from his mother's estate on his eighteenth birthday, he returned to Jena and enrolled as a student. The year was 1800.

In 1789, Schiller had accepted a professorship at Jena and established a home a few miles away at Weimar. Here lived a group of men and women who dominated the intellectual and literary life of Germany. Among these were Goethe, Schelling, Fichte, Hegel, Herder, Humbolt, and the Schlegels. By 1800, Goethe was the moving spirit at the university, seeking to attract to Jena the most stimulating minds of the age. Fichte had been teaching there since 1793. In 1798, Schelling became a member of the faculty. Hegel came to Jena in 1801. At Weimar was a theater in which Schiller's plays were staged. The Jena students were accustomed to walking to Weimar to attend these performances and to meet in their homes these geniuses of the romanticist movement. Froebel plunged into this environment, and for two years listened to lectures in philosophy, mathematics, physics, architecture, surveying, and chemistry, while absorbing the spirit and enthusiasm of his teachers. These were glorious years for a youth whose early experiences had driven him inward and caused him to distrust even himself. But they ended in sadness. He had lent some of his inheritance to a brother who refused to repay. Meanwhile, his debts piled up; his brother's refusal to honor the obligation and his father's refusal to lend him the money resulted in his spending a time in the university prison. He was eventually bailed out by his father and forced to return home in humiliation, to the old uncertainties, despondencies, and frustrations. This only increased his sense of failure and was fuel for his fires of rebellion and revolt.

YEARS OF SEARCHING

Conditions grew worse at home, and it was evident that Froebel could not remain in his father's house and retain his sanity. Introverted by his early experiences, he found the constant belittling on the part of his stepmother and his father's lack of understanding unbearable. In an effort to support himself, he worked as a farmer, a clerk, a surveyor, a private secretary and bookkeeper, and an architect. None of these seemed to satisfy him or hold his interest.

After four years as a "rolling stone," he chanced to visit a school run by a pupil of Pestalozzi and was fascinated by what he saw there. Repeated excursions to the school gave him some insight into what was being attempted, and aroused a lively interest in the children. When a teacher resigned, Froebel was offered the job and, in his twenty-third year, began his first teaching experience. He tells us that "from the first hour my occupation did not appear in the least strange to me. . . . I seemed to myself to have been a teacher already for a long while. . . . I find myself, when I am occupied with instruction, just in my element."

Though evidencing a natural talent for teaching, Froebel realized that if he were to succeed, he needed a great deal more training. To understand the aims and purposes of the school in which he was teaching, he visited Yverdon to learn from Pestalozzi. He was thrilled and inspired, but soon developed a vague sense that there was something lacking. Returning to his own school, he began to revolt against the routine and the authority of his superiors. The old frustrations returned, and although he showed great promise as a teacher, he resigned from his position and turned to the study of languages. He struggled with French, but could not master grammar, which made no sense to him.

After a few months of unsuccessful study of the language, he accepted a position as tutor of three boys, whom he took into the country and sought to educate as Rousseau had Emile. This was a saddening failure, and in desperation he took his charges to Yverdon, enrolled them in classes, and he himself became a pupil of Pestalozzi. He remained for two years studying, helping some of the teachers, and taking over some classes under Pestalozzi's supervision. There were several others serving as teacher-pupils in the school. In their more intimate discussions, they began to see the weaknesses in Pestalozzi's method and to sense that the school was falling apart because of Pestalozzi's inability to administer so large a faculty and student group.

When Froebel returned to Germany, he continued tutoring the three boys for another year. Then he enrolled at the University of Gottingen. There he was definitely searching for the principle of unity he had heard so much about at Jena many years ago, which seems to have haunted him ever since. He went back to study Hebrew and Arabic to see if in these very old languages he could discover this principle of unity, a principle that would bring order out of the chaos he found in linguistic studies. Failing here, he turned to study the sciences. He began to feel that crystallography in some way held the answer to his problem. The growing crystal was to him an expression of natural order and unification.

Froebel was not a politician, and sought to divorce himself from all nationalistic sentiments. However, by 1813, he had been caught up in the patriotic furor that was sweeping all Germany, then under the heel of Napoleon. He left his crystals, and at thirty-one became a soldier. While he was no great success in uniform, this move brought to his side two young men who became his closest friends. Wilhelm Middendorf, a handsome youth of twenty, was attractive to everyone who met him. Heinrich Langenthal was twenty-one. At this time Froebel was ten years their senior. Both learned from the "older man," and became his devoted, and highly intelligent, disciples.

THE SCHOOL AT KEILHAU

In 1816, with the support and encouragement of the widow of his elder brother, Froebel opened in Keilhau, a small village in Thuringia, a Pestalozzian-type school, which he named *The Universal German Institute.* Frau Froebel hoped that in time she and her brother-in-law would be married, and sold some of her property and silverware to establish and support the school. She entered her three sons in the school. Two sons of another brother were soon enrolled, making the school wholly a family affair. This was ideal for the Pestalozzian dream of a school. The teacher was the uncle, all the pupils were his nephews, and they were supported by the mother of three of these pupils. Here was a true family situation.

The school was pure Rousseau. The children wore simple clothes, ate simple food, worked in the fields, roamed the forest, and studied, as their needs demanded, German, geography, arithmetic, and geometry. Everything at the school was homelike and informal. While Froebel did not place as much emphasis as did Pestalozzi on sense perception, he strove to integrate the experiences of the children from within and gave a greater fluidity to the curriculum.

During the second year of the school's existence, Middendorf joined the faculty, bringing a brother of Langenthal. Later Langenthal became a member of the group. This made a most interesting and provocative faculty. Froebel was a solitary genius, crude, homely, and impractical. Froebel's sister-in-law supported the school and lived there as cook, housekeeper, and general manager.

Then Froebel generated a storm, which blew the school almost to pieces. In Berlin he had met a well-born, attractive, and wealthy widow who had an equally charming daughter. Langenthal became attracted to the daughter, and Froebel married the mother. While the three members of the faculty were delighted to have Froebel's new wife and her daughter at Keilhau, the sister-in-law flew into a rage, withdrew her support, and settled in a nearby village, embittered and resentful. The boys, especially the children of his sister-in-law, resented the new mistress of the house, who was no housekeeper and knew nothing about education or the needs of a school community. The idyllic, homelike environment was disrupted by the presence of strangers. Froebel resented this attitude and became stubborn, refusing to take advice even from his closest friends. He became tyrannical, demanding that his be the last word of authority. By 1820, the school was on the verge of collapse, when Christian Froebel, his wife, and three daughters joined the community. He was a fairly wealthy retired businessman who was able to give support to the school. His daughters married into the faculty, one becoming the wife of Middendorf.

For a while the school prospered, and enrollment grew to sixty children and youths. Froebel's arrogance increased. He demanded absolute obedience, allowing no independence on the part of other members of the community. Meanwhile, the children of his rejected sister-in-law were growing older and coming to understand what had happened to their mother. They began to disrupt the school and made public charges which created the impression that the school was a center of radicalism and treason. Though the government cleared the group of these charges, the school's image in the public eye was seriously damaged. With the school heavily in debt and under a cloud of suspicion, the enrollment shrank to five. Eventually, Christian Froebel, his daughters, and their husbands took over the school and expelled Froebel from its management. He was permitted to live there, but only as a relative.

THE SWISS YEARS

In deep despair, Froebel attempted to interest the government in his ideas about education, but failed. Then he left Keilhau for Frankfort, where he was able to interest a Swiss nobleman in his plans for a school. In a few weeks he was established in a Swiss castle and heralded as the successor to Pestalozzi. It was not long before his autocratic attitude became too much for the Swiss nobleman, and Froebel was forced to move on. He established another school, but found the attacks of the Catholics against his philosophy and the public charges being made by his embittered nephews, who now lived in Switzerland, damaging to himself and his reputation in the canton. Eventually he turned the school over to Middendorf, who had followed him to Switzerland.

FROM BURGDORF TO BLANKENBURG

Froebel took refuge in Burgdorf, the site of Pestalozzi's first school, where a strong local government dedicated to freedom protected him against the criticisms that were flying about Switzerland. He established a Pestalozzian school, and worked part-time in a local orphanage. Here were born two great ideas in Froebel's thinking. Very small children, he became convinced, needed an orderly series of experiences calculated to awaken their abilities, stimulate mental activities, and produce an inner organization of their nature. The second idea developed around the realization that the mother has an important role in the basic education of her child and the conviction that if the child is to develop correctly, the mother must be trained for this most important occupation. This gave birth to the *Mother Play and Nursery Songs,* a book to help the mother begin her child's education correctly.

Overpowered by this new interest in the preschool child, Froebel left Switzerland and went to Berlin, where he studied the nursery schools that had begun to spring up in the large cities of Europe. Eventually he rented an abandoned powder mill at Blankenburg, a village near Keilhau, with money borrowed from his youngest niece's husband, and opened the *Kleinkinderbeschaftigungsanstalt,* literally translated—"an institution where small children are occupied." Froebel was now fifty-five, a failure in everything he had attempted. The people of the village thought him slightly crazy, "an old fool who played with children." His wife had died, and his nephews lost no opportunity to attack him and accuse him of treason, radicalism, and immorality. But he had at last found himself and his talent. With some fifty children, ranging from the ages of one to seven, he developed his "gifts" and mother-play songs with almost fanatical enthusiasm.

One day, while talking to Middendorf about the school, he came of a sudden to see his little community as a garden in which children grew. This gave birth to the name *kindergarten,* a garden of children. For seven years Froebel worked with his Blankenburg children and developed a rich assortment of kindergarten material including "gifts," "occupations," and games, all designed to teach the little child in terms of his philosophy of education and of the universe. This material was prepared, boxed with printed directions for its use, and distributed throughout Germany, for mothers and for use in the kindergartens that were being established by his pupils and others.

OLD AGE

Froebel left Blankenburg in 1844 to propagate the kindergarten movement throughout Germany and to train teachers for these schools. He traveled widely, sometimes with Middendorf and sometimes alone, teaching, lecturing, founding schools, and explaining his ideas to all who would listen. During the winter months he returned to Keilhau, where he ran a teacher-training school. The first pupils at the training school were four young men. In the second year, three young women enrolled. Their success convinced Froebel that well-trained young women would make the best teachers of small children.

One of these young women was Louise Levine, an ignorant country girl, a friend of Froebel's youngest niece, who had come to Keilhau as kitchen help. She was more than thirty years younger than Froebel and, in the eyes of the feminine contingent at Keilhau, no suitable companion for a prominent man. Froebel found in her affection, understanding, and devotion, things he desperately needed. The two traveled together about Germany, founding kindergartens and demonstrating games and other kindergarten materials to parents. Froebel's family was scandalized and refused to permit him to return to Keilhau even for the winters.

At Bad Liebenstein, a well-known watering place, Froebel and Miss Levine opened a kindergarten training school and a "practice school" in which children of the peasants were taught. It was here that the Baroness von Marenholtz-Bulow (1810-1893) learned of the project, became interested, and dedicated her life to propagating kindergarten ideas and schools. A noblewoman, she was able to meet and persuade many leaders of German governmental and social life to support the kindergarten movement. She traveled in England, Italy, Switzerland, and France, lecturing, teaching, and demonstrating Froebel's teaching materials. In 1870, she founded the Froebel Seminar to train kindergarten teachers.

In 1849, Froebel was offered a handsome salary to come to Hamburg. The salary probably came from the purse of the Baroness. Middendorf was at Hamburg, and one of his daughters was working there in a kindergarten. Miss Levine was there waiting for him. This seemed the crowning opportunity of his career, but it was doomed to failure. Carl Froebel, one of the children of Froebel's rejected sister-in-law, was in Hamburg, attempting to interest the people in establishing a female university for the higher education of women and the training of teachers. He had appropriated his uncle's ideas of the kindergarten. Both men hated each other violently. To counter Froebel's popularity and initial success in Hamburg, Carl published *High Schools for Young Ladies and Kindergartens.* Many thought this to be the work of the older Froebel.

Eventually the quarrel between the two became so bitter that the older man left Hamburg for Bad Liebenstein, where the Baroness and Miss Levine had secured a hunting lodge for his school. These were happy times. Prospective kindergartners flocked to the school, visitors made daily pilgrimages to meet Froebel and see his children at play and work, and in the spring a great kindergarten festival was held at the ducal palace with Froebel the guest of honor. Later the same summer he married Miss Levine, thereby severing all ties with his family. The only people present at the wedding were Froebel, Miss Levine, the Baroness, and Middendorf. Froebel was happy, and new vigor seemed to take hold of him.

Meanwhile, Carl Froebel had become identified in the minds of many with his uncle and the kindergarten movement. He was also a leading figure in the revolutionary swell that was covering all Germany in answer to the reactionary tendencies that followed the French Revolution and Napoleonic Wars. His activities came to the attention of the Prussian minister of education, who issued a blanket condemnation of the whole kindergarten movement as "a socialistic system which is calculated to train the youth of the country to atheism" and ordered all kindergartens closed. After much work, the Baroness was able to have the decree annulled, but the battle proved too much for the aging and weakening Froebel. He was barely able to attend the children's festival in honor of his seventieth birthday and the national convention of German teachers. On the first day of summer, 1852, he died peacefully and quietly.

Middendorf had a monument erected to Froebel's memory, based upon his three "gifts," the ball, the cube, and the cylinder. Inscribed on it are the words of the poet Schiller, "Come, let us live for our children." The Baroness spent her life and fortune spreading Froebel's ideas and methods throughout Europe. Louise took over the training school, moved it to Hamburg, and continued to work for Froebelianism until her death in 1900. Middendorf intended to join the Baroness and Louise, but grew tired and dropped out of the movement. Within a year he was dead.

BASES OF THE FROEBELIAN PHILOSOPHY

In 1826, Froebel published *The Education of Man,* his major work on education, which dealt with his philosophical position and the education of children up to the age of seven. The first chapter is called "Groundwork of the Whole" and begins:

> In all things there lives and reigns an eternal law. To him whose mind, through disposition and faith, is filled, penetrated, and quickened with the necessity that this can not possibly be otherwise, as well as to him whose clear, calm mental vision beholds the inner in the outer and through the outer, and sees the outer proceeding with logical necessity from the essence of the inner, this law has been and is enounced with equal clearness and distinctness in nature (the external), in the spirit (the internal), and in life which unites the two. This all controlling law is necessarily based on an all-pervading, energetic, living, self-conscious, and hence eternal Unity. This fact, as well as the Unity itself, is again vividly recognized, either through faith or through insight, with equal clearness and comprehensiveness; therefore, a quietly observant human mind, a thoughtful, clear human intellect, has never failed, and will never fail, to recognize this Unity.
>
> This Unity is God. All things have come from the Divine Unity, from God, and have their origin in the Divine Unity, in God, alone. God is the sole source of all things. In all things there lives and reigns the Divine Unity, God. All things live and have their being in and through the Divine Unity, in and through God. All things are only through the divine effluence that lives in them. The divine effluence that lives in each thing is the essence of each thing.
>
> It is the destiny and life-work of all things to unfold their essence, hence their divine being, and, therefore, the Divine Unity itself—to reveal God in their external and transient being. It is the special destiny and life work of man, as an intelligent and rational being, to become fully, vividly, and clearly conscious of his essence, of the divine effluence in him, and, therefore, of God; to become fully, vividly, and clearly conscious of his destiny and life-work; and to accomplish this, to render it (his essence) active, to reveal it in his own life and with self-determination and freedom.
>
> *Education consists in leading man, as a thinking, intelligent being, growing into self-consciousness, to a pure and unsullied, conscious and free representation of the inner law of Divine Unity, and in teaching him ways and means thereto.*

Froebel saw education not as the transmission of cultural values or the attempt of a culture to preserve itself by shaping its young in its own image, but as part of cosmic evolution. For him the universe is a unity, a whole, one. This he called God, not the personal God of the Hebrew-Christian tradition, but "all-pervading, energetic, living, self-conscious, and hence eternal Unity." All things are this unity, this God, in different forms. The essence of all things is the same, God. God, in creating himself, creates the universe.

In man this unity, this God, becomes conscious of itself and of the process. All other creations are non-conscious; only man is conscious. Since man is God, God becomes conscious in man. Man is the highest form of this self-creating God.

As man develops from conception to death, he is growing into self-consciousness, he becomes more clearly conscious of the creative process of which he is a part. It is the function of education to lead growing, developing man "to a pure and unsullied, conscious and free representation of the inner law of Divine Unity, and in teaching him ways and means thereto." Education is part of the cosmic process by which God, the divine unity, comes to self-consciousness. The goal of all education is the individual who is clearly conscious of this process of creativity and able to create as God creates.

A philosopher who influenced Froebel greatly was Karl Christian Friedrich Krause (1781-1832), who taught that God, intuitively known, is not a personal being, since personality implies limitations, but is *an essence which contains the universe within itself.* Froebel's philosophy has often been branded pantheism, the belief that God is all and all is God. Froebel and Krause went far beyond this. All is God, they held, but God is more than all. God is creative. This does not mean that God creates out of nothing and includes this creation within himself. As God creates, he is creating himself. The creation is God, but creativity is never exhausted in its creations. God continues to create. The present is not all of God. It is contained within God, but God also is the potentiality to continue creating eternally. This Krause called *panentheism.*

An implication of this philosophy, which Froebel recognized and accepted, is that God will in the millenia ahead create things different from those now existing, just as in the past he has created things that have disappeared. Man is God's highest, his finest creation, since in man God becomes self-conscious. Millions of years in the future, God, in creating himself, will certainly create beings far superior to man in ways that man of today cannot even imagine. It is perfectly possible that the man of this century will be as primitive when compared to the man of several million years in the future as the simplest forms of life in primeval times are primitive when compared to man today. Creation for both Krause and Froebel is dynamic, never static. It does not come to a point when it can be said to be complete, but continues and will continue eternally since God is eternal. This is a form of creative evolution with "the lid off."

THE DOCTRINE OF GLIEDGANZES

Froebel held that man is God creating himself; therefore he is God, one with the totality. If this be true, then is man lost in the whole, in God? Is God a sort of ocean which swallows each drop of water and takes from it its individuality?

Thought that has attempted to relate the individual to the whole tends to destroy this individual in the interest of the whole. Then, in an attempt to preserve the individual, thought often falls into the opposite trap of extreme individualism. Krause and Froebel sought to avoid either extreme in the theory of *Gliedganzes,* the part-whole. According to this position, the individual is a unity, a living organism, but is part of the universe, which is unfolding itself and in its unfolding creates the individual. For example, each finger is a unit, an individual with a specific function all its own. At the same time, each finger is part of the hand, which is a unity, a oneness with a specific function. Neither can be truly itself without the other. The finger is not swallowed up in the hand. As long as the finger remains part of the hand, it is a finger and functions as a finger. Sever it from the hand, and it remains a fleshy object called a finger but loses its true fingerness, its functions as a finger.

In the same way, man is an individual only as he remains part of the whole. It is this membership in the whole that gives him the function of man. Sever him from the whole, and although he maintains the outward form of a man, he has lost his true manness.

God is the original unity, a living, energetic, self-conscious organism, and all the universe is God. As long as each part maintains this unity, it is truly itself and functions as such. Divorce it from the whole, and it loses this individuality. Froebel believed that in this he had solved the problem of oneness without destroying the individual.

FROEBEL'S LAW OF DEVELOPMENT

Following Pestalozzi, Froebel thought of man as a seed planted in a garden. It unfolds its inner nature, develops the fullness of its potential. This unfolding is the creative force of the universe unfolding itself and thereby creating itself. This evolutionary law of creativity is to be found in nature, in man, and in the human will and mind. Everywhere the creator is unfolding himself.

The idealist philosophers who influenced Froebel were seeking to discover a principle of unity upon which they could erect a law of development that would explain both the one and the many. Schiller held that beauty was the key to this problem. Both Fichte and Hegel believed that they had found the unity in thought and the law in the dialectic process of thesis, antithesis, and synthesis. They saw thought operating in this fashion.

Froebel was part of this movement, but neither beauty nor thought satisfied his scientifically-oriented mind. Beauty and thought seemed limited to the human being, and he sought a law that would apply to the entire universe, that would explain the creation of the physical and the spiritual, the material and the mental. To him the universe was a spiritual organism that creates itself in both the physical and the mental worlds. As he developed this concept, he came to believe that God creates himself through a dialectic that consists of action, reaction, and equilibrium. This is dynamic, not static. God acts, and this action produces reaction, which finds a dynamic relationship in equilibrium, which sets the stage for further action, reaction, and equilibrium.

In this process, self-conscious man eventually appears, a being able to understand the process and develop an education which will further the process. Man is not the end of the process. He is a stage in the ever-continuing dialectic. Froebel believed in unlimited progress. "Man," he said, is to be "looked upon not as perfectly developed, not as fixed and stationary, but as steadily and progressively growing. . . . It is unspeakably pernicious to look upon the development of humanity as stationary and complete."

Froebel was conscious of the fact that so many idealistic philosophies of oneness found themselves unable to solve the problem of evil. If the unity is good, how can it create evil? His answer was that evil is not positive, but negative. If we analyze good and evil, we find that evil is a good that has been perverted in its unfolding. This perversion may result from neglect of the development process or from a distortion of the original goodness. One is good to the extent that he is able to unfold his good inner nature to the fullest. The right education will foster this complete unfolding and eliminate any possibility of evil.

Froebel refused to be caught up in a determinism that has so often destroyed philosophies of unity. All things in the universe are God creating himself, but God is a dynamic, free principle. He cannot be determined, since there is nothing other than himself by which he can be determined. Since man is God at his best, his self-conscious self, he must be as free as God. Since the whole of God is free, his self-conscious part must also be free. Man is free to create or not to create. He is free to develop himself to the fullest or to warp, distort himself. As a self-conscious being, he can develop an education that will serve his creative nature and unfold the creative God that he is, or he can develop a static education that stunts this unfolding. He can create evil or goodness. Man is both free and dynamic, and in his own hands is his destiny.

FROEBEL'S EDUCATIONAL THEORY

Each individual, being part of a self-creating whole, comes to self-realization through self-activity. Education must lead the child "to a pure and unsullied, conscious and free representation of the inner law of Divine Unity," and it must teach the child "ways and means thereto." Education must be based on the interests and spontaneous activities of the child. He, through his own creative ability, educates himself. The teacher follows, protecting him from anything that will hinder or warp this process, and creating an environment that will stimulate and further this education. Self-activity will unfold the inner nature of the child in perfect unity within himself and with his physical and social environment. The fundamental principles of Froebel's thinking on education are freedom, self-activity, self-creativity, and unity or oneness with all that is.

As the child grows, all sides of his nature will develop in perfect harmony. He will come to know himself, others, nature, God, and the inner law that holds all these in unity. At the same time he will develop "firmness of will." The curriculum, the means for this development, is determined by the child's needs at a particular moment. Any object, lesson, assignment, or activity included in the curriculum must justify itself on the basis of what the child can do with it in achieving his own self-realization. Instruction is *not* to impart knowledge. By means of activities the child unfolds himself and through this unfolding builds habits, skills, will, and character. Knowledge is a means to these ends, not an end in itself.

This unfolding process follows a genetic order of development. Each new interest, activity, or learning grows out of an interest or activity already there. There is a clear law of inner development. The child moves from one stage to the next gradually, with no sudden leaps or cataclysmic experiences. Parents and teachers must know when the child is ready to move forward, when the old is passing and the new ready to bud. Froebel insisted that it is most important "to note the moment, the proper place, for the introduction of a new branch of instruction. . . . The whole attention of the teacher must be directed to these budding-points of new branches of instruction." The teacher must not arbitrarily say to the child, "You are six years old. It is now time for you to begin to learn to read." He must discover when the child is ready to learn to read, ready in terms of his unfolding development. Then he makes it possible for the child to begin learning to read. Froebel is pure Rousseau when he writes in *The Education of Man,* "Education . . . should necessarily be *passive, following* (only guarding and protecting), *not prescriptive, categorical, interfering."*

Froebel was most concerned with the education of children during their earliest years. His *Education of Man* carried the process to the tenth year. Within this span of years he found three stages of growth, each demanding certain specific techniques and methods: infancy, from birth to age three; childhood, from three to seven; and boyhood, from seven to ten. Although years are indicated, Froebel knew that each child develops at his own rate, and some enter each stage at ages different from others.

In infancy, the child is wholly dependent upon his mother and other members of his immediate family. Here he experiences the unity of the family group, mother, father, and child. This is his first encounter with society and social oneness. Each member of the group is unique, individual, one, but he is also a member of the whole and will develop and become himself only within this whole. The mother is responsible for the child's first education. She must exercise his limbs, train his senses, and maintain an environment that will make his own self-realization complete. To aid mothers in this most important relationship with their children, Froebel wrote his famous and highly perceptive *Mother Play and Nursery Songs with Finger Plays.* Actually the work was a joint project of Froebel, Middendorf, and others associated with the early kindergarten. The book consists of songs, verses, and illustrations designed to entertain, instruct, and help the mother. The theme is unity with home and the child's environment, mother love, the child's world, and simple morality. At the end there is a discussion of each song and plate, instructing mothers how to use each item most effectively.

During infancy the child develops simple motor skills, the sense of hearing, and the sense of sight. In these experiences are the roots of all future unfolding. His relationships with his mother and father grow in time into religion. The sense of hearing is basic to all language learning. Sight is the first avenue through which knowledge comes. The mother follows the order of nature. She assists the child as he unfolds himself, as he is self-creative.

Childhood begins when the child self-actively comes to "represent the internal outwardly," usually around three years of age. This is the kindergarten period, during which the most fundamental instincts of the child's nature awaken and begin unfolding in definite order and according to precise principles. The individual becomes able to express his inner feelings through language. This skill is developed by memorizing short poems about objects in the environment and incidents that happen in the home and the child's limited but ever-widening environment.

Froebel took Schiller's concept of play and made of it a basic technique of development and learning. He echoes Schiller when he speaks of play as "self-active representation of the inner—representation of the inner from inner necessity and impulse." As the child plays, he shapes the outer in terms of the inner, and the new shapes of the environment interact with his inner nature to stimulate its unfolding.

During this stage of development, rhythm, growing out of earlier bodily movement, and drawing assume great importance. Froebel believed that rhythm is basic to language, music, appreciation of art, and the moral qualities of firmness, moderation, and self-control. In this he is harking back to the Greeks, who saw in the dance and rhythmic movements of the body the roots of ethical and moral development.

Froebel understood that the simple drawings of the child are a means of expression. He uses this to tell what he is feeling and thinking. As the child attempts through drawing to represent what he experiences, he comes to understand himself and his environment. The perceptive teacher comes to understand the child as he watches him draw. From early attempts at drawing, the child develops language, judgment, understanding, abstract thinking, ability, and discrimination.

The child, Froebel held, unfolds his inner nature in a psychological order according to clearly defined laws. When this order is known, the teacher must provide the environment that stimulates development. This environment must consist of objects which parallel the unfolding of this inner self. Much of Froebel's later life was occupied with the construction of kindergarten materials consistent with this point of view. The result was a series of "gifts" and "occupations" keyed to the stages of the child's development.

This led Froebel into the use of symbolism in a way that is little understood by most people, and which brought much criticism down on him and the kindergarten movement. Careful observation of children and remembrances of his childhood led Froebel to the conviction that symbolism plays a major role in child development. It is the way a child conceives of his world. Fairy tales are real. A stick becomes a horse. Blocks arranged in a line are a train. The tree is a giant to be subdued. Children's games are full of imaginative symbolism, much of which is understood only by the players.

This led Froebel to believe that the process could be reversed. Instead of the child's taking from his environment an object and endowing it with meaning to fit his needs, he held that certain objects by their very nature are symbols of cosmic truths. If the child is exposed to these objects, he will be helped toward understanding the truths.

The universe is a unity, one. This the child must be led to understand. How can the mother assist her child in developing this understanding? She can give her child several soft, colored balls. The ball, round, with no edges or corners, complete in itself, *is* a symbol of unity. Within its name is the "all," b-all. As the infant plays with these balls, he will be experiencing a true symbol of God, of oneness. But he must also come to realize that wherever there is action, there is reaction; wherever he finds oneness, he also finds the many. One necessitates the other. Therefore the child must have a symbol of diversity. That Froebel found in the cube, an object that is many-sided, many-edged, with many corners. This is given to the child as a toy, a toy carefully calculated to teach the idea of many, of diversity.

To leave the child at this point would create confusion and frustration. He would come to understand oneness and diversity. Since Froebel's law of the universe is one of action, reaction, and equilibrium, he must give the child a third "gift" that symbolizes equilibrium, a "gift" that will lead him, through its symbolism, to an understanding that all seeming contradiction is cleared away in the synthesis of opposites. This he found in the cylinder. Its roundness and its flat ends are taken from the ball and the cube and symbolize this synthesis.

These three objects—ball, cube, and cylinder—were given to the child as "gifts," playthings to teach him the cosmic principles of unity, diversity, and the higher unity which brings seeming conflict into equilibrium.

Froebel developed this symbolism throughout. On the floor of every kindergarten room he would have a circle drawn, symbolizing oneness. Each morning the children would toe this circle, hold hands, pray, and sing, symbolizing their oneness as a group. The other gifts that Froebel prepared for the children consisted of large cubes cut in many ways to provide blocks. But the children were not allowed to play with these blocks as they wished. Rather, one who wished to build a house would take each individual block from the whole and construct his project. When he finished and wished to build a train, he had first to return each block to its proper place in the whole before removing blocks for the train. In this way the child would be developing the idea that diversity comes from unity and will return to unity, from the one come the many and the many are parts of the one.

Froebel was correct when he affirmed that the child in his imagination makes objects into symbols for his play. In this case, the child transfers his meaning to the object so that *for him* the object is the thing he imagines it to be. He was correct in pointing out that words are mere symbols for things and ideas. He was wrong in believing that objects carry within themselves their own symbolism. He did not realize that a ball might be an enemy to be destroyed at one time and a security symbol at another. Each individual endows objects with meaning in terms of his needs and experience. An object may symbolize different things to the same individual at different stages of development. The object does not carry its own symbolism. It becomes a symbol in a situation. This Froebel failed to see.

In addition to "gifts," Froebel created many "occupations" for kindergartners, each designed to serve the unfolding inner nature of the child. Clay modeling, paper cutting, picture coloring, weaving, sewing, sandpile play, drawing, cardboard work, all were "occupations" through which the kindergartner would learn what was necessary for his most complete development. Froebel and his associates went through Europe explaining these "gifts" and "occupations," pointing to their function in early childhood education, and training teachers to use them wisely.

Boyhood, Froebel held, is the "period of learning" in which "instruction predominates." Until about the age of six or seven, the child is developing from within, unfolding his innate nature, and must have maximum freedom for self-creativity. What he does is "for the sake of activity." Watch a small child running in circles until he is almost exhausted, and you will realize what Froebel means here. At about the age of six, the "formative instinct" appears, and activity turns to production. The child no longer runs for the pure joy of running; now he runs to get somewhere, to the next base or the goal of the game. He is acting "for the sake of results."

At this stage of growth the outer environment becomes more important. The boy works with others, drawing from the group and contributing to the group in the accomplishment of his goals. He expresses the inner in the outer as he shapes his environment to his desires. In school he should be able to devote one to two hours a day in constructive activities.

This purposefulness will carry over into the boy's games. They have significance and are, therefore, more intelligent. He no longer piles block on block, knocks the pile down, and starts making the pile again. Now he builds a castle, a fort, a compound. He no longer runs in circles, but takes part in a race. His purpose is not the mere joy he gets from running, but to win, to reach a goal, to earn the plaudits of others. From these more intelligent, more mature, and more social experiences, he begins to develop the moral qualities of "justice, moderation, self-control, truthfulness, loyalty, brotherly love . . . strict impartiality . . . courage, perseverance, resolution, prudence." These are virtues necessary for social living.

Not only should the curriculum at this level include games and play activities fitted to the boy's developmental age, but it should also make available stories of all kinds. The boy is becoming interested in the past and devours myths, legends, tales of adventure and endurance. Here is the root of history. He is gaining a sense of time and craves to know what happened in the past. As he hears and reads stories, his imagination grows, and he pictures himself in these stories. His self-consciousness becomes clearer as he imagines himself as one of the characters in the story, as he identifies himself in the story situation.

At the age of boyhood, nature becomes an impelling interest. Exploring the immediate environment, collecting natural objects, long hikes into the woods, camping trips on which boys study trees, rivers, flowers, land formations, all are of major concern and should be part of school activities. These experiences can be employed to bring the boy to an understanding of his own unity with nature and an appreciation of the fact that "all objects of nature," including himself, "are organically united members of one great living organism." This study of nature will evolve into a more thorough study of the sciences—natural history, mathematics, physics, and chemistry. Mathematics is of special importance. Through its study, the boy comes to see how God thinks mathematically. From this understanding of the mind of God, which is the mind of man, the boy comes naturally to true religion, to an understanding of God, his creation, and one's place in relation to both God and those creations who are others.

All education, Froebel held, must serve the natural unfolding of the child's inner nature. It must bring each child to an understanding of his relationship with the whole and his involvement in the totality that is God. Each step and each tool and method must be graded to serve this end. As the teacher learns about the child, he is better able to direct, stimulate, encourage, and provoke true education. At times Froebel made proposals not justified by later knowledge about child development. There were even times when he did not seem to see the educational implications of the knowledge about children available to him. Nevertheless, the central aim in all education was to assist the child to grow and develop as one with God the creator, the all-pervasive creative spirit. He believed that in the kindergarten and in the materials he had developed for the kindergartner he had found the key to this process.

The Kindergarten Movement

The kindergarten became Froebel's symbol. During his later years he devoted himself to founding kindergartens, explaining the principles underlying the school, and teaching young women to be kindergarteners. His assistants, especially the Baroness von Marenholz-Bulow and his wife, devoted themselves to spreading the ideas and practices of the master throughout Europe. Germany, partly because it identified Froebel with the revolutionary activities of his nephew and partly because it feared the liberalism and freedom permeating the kindergarten, did not take kindly to the movement. While other European countries established kindergartens, it was the United States that proved most hospitable to Froebel's ideas and methods.

The kindergarten was brought to America by Germans after the revolution of 1848. Mrs. Carl Schurz, wife of the famous German-American statesman, along with her sister, introduced Froebelianism into England. Both had been pupils of Froebel. In 1855, Mrs. Schurz opened a kindergarten in her home in Watertown, Wisconsin. Shortly after this, another student from Froebel's teachers' seminary, Caroline Frankenburg, opened a kindergarten in Columbus, Ohio. Soon these German-English schools began appearing wherever there was a heavy concentration of Germans in America. In 1860, Miss Elizabeth Palmer Peabody (1804-1894) opened the first English-speaking kindergarten in Boston, with the encouragement and blessing of Henry Barnard. She went to Europe in 1867 to study Froebelianism first hand. Upon her return she became the most vigorous exponent of the movement in America. Through training classes, lectures, articles in popular magazines, and her editorship of the *Kindergarten Messenger* from 1873 to 1877, she spread Froebelian ideas throughout the United States. Her translation of the *Mother Play Songs* is one of the best available.

William T. Harris (1835-1909) was superintendent of the St. Louis school system from 1867 to 1880. In 1873, with the help of Miss Susan E. Blow, he established the first public school kindergarten in the United States. At first the kindergartens in this country were private institutions conducted by interested teachers or parents. Then the movement became part of the program of churches and philanthropic organizations. Often they thought of kindergartens as schools for underprivileged children. Finally, school systems began reaching down into the early years of child life and making kindergartens the first stage of public education. By 1900, several hundred school systems had made the kindergarten an integral part of their public school structure.

Many changes were made in the kindergarten as it moved into American public education. Increased knowledge of psychology, biology, sociology, neurology, and hygiene brought many of Froebel's practices into question and led to revisions in method and outlook consistent with a richer understanding of child growth and development. At the same time, many of the Froebelian principles were adopted by primary teachers and by industries making games, toys, and educational materials for small children.

JOHANN FRIEDRICH HERBART (1776-1841)

Herbart was one of the major philosophers and educational theorists of the nineteenth century. Among post-Kantian thinkers, he has been ranked next to Hegel in importance. As a penetrating and exact thinker, he is on a level with Hume and Kant. He believed, with Aristotle, that politics, psychology, and education must rest on a sound metaphysics. While his philosophy never attained general acceptance in Europe, due in some degree to the Hegelians, his psychological and educational theories dominated much of European and American thinking until well into the twentieth century.

Herbart was a man of exquisite refinement, a scholar, respected but never loved. He was dignified, reserved toward strangers, commanding respect, calm, self-confident, and serious. He was alert and keenly interested when speaking about ideas that seemed important to him, but withdrew when those about him indulged in half-truths, opinions, or fragmentary inspirations. Whatever he did was done in depth. He spoke and wrote Latin perfectly, and was at home among Greek poets, sages, philosophers, and dramatists. He was in truth "the scholars' scholar." Those who knew him intimately, and they were few, saw a kindness, sympathy, and benevolence that was hidden from the world, lest it in some way betray his dedication to cold logic and exact thought.

HIS LIFE

On July 4, 1776, the Continental Congress accepted the Declaration of Independence substantially as drawn up by Thomas Jefferson. Two months before, to the day, Johann Friedrich Herbart was born in Oldenburg, a city in northwest Germany. His father was a lawyer of some local prominence who held several positions of minor importance in government and rose to the rank of privy councilor. His mother was a beautiful woman of superior intellect, energetic, ambitious, and dominating. Her unconventional life led people to brand her as eccentric. At about five years of age, young Johann fell into a tub of boiling water and was seriously injured, resulting in a delicate constitution for the rest of his days.

The boy grew and lived in a world that was alive with change and revolution. He was ten years old when the French Revolution began. He grew to maturity in the days when Napoleon was coming to power. Kant was teaching at Konigsberg, and around Jena lived the most brilliant colony of poets, dramatists, authors, and philosophers to be assembled in modern times. Pestalozzi was teaching at Burgdorf between 1800 and 1804, and then at Yverdon between 1804 and 1825. Froebel was at Jena in 1799, and, before 1814, had studied at Gottingen and Berlin. He opened his school at Keilhau in 1817 and, in 1837, began his first kindergarten at Blankenburg. These were indeed creative and disturbing years for all Europe, wonderful years for one of Herbart's intelligence to live in and develop.

Frau Herbart kept her son at home until he was twelve, teaching him herself and employing tutors for those areas she was not competent to teach. She sat in with each tutor, learning along with the boy in order to help him with his studies. Among these tutors was one, Pastor Ulzen, who believed that the one and only aim of education was to cultivate "clearness, definiteness, and continuity of thought." From ages twelve to eighteen, Herbart was a student at the Oldenburg gymnasium, where his teachers marveled at so much learning in so small a boy. At fourteen, he wrote an essay "Concerning the Doctrine of Human Freedom," and at seventeen, lectured on "The Commonest Causes that Affect the Growth and Decay of Morality in Various States." His thinking was stimulated by the American and the French revolutions and attendant political and social thought. For graduation he delivered an oration, in Latin, comparing the concepts of the "greatest good" as held by Cicero and Kant.

After Oldenburg, Herbart spent three years at the University of Jena, where he studied philosophy under Fichte and, through his mother's efforts, became a close friend of Schiller. He was a member of a group of serious students who met once a week to read and discuss papers they were writing. Although Herbart's father had hoped his son would study law at Jena and enter his profession, he was disappointed but not angry. Frau Herbart was the dominant member of the family, and she realized her son's talents for philosophy very early and did everything she could to further his development in this direction, even to accompanying him to Jena and attending his classes.

After Jena, Herbart became tutor of the three sons of the governor of Interlaken, Switzerland. He was motivated to take this step, even though he had not completed his education, by several considerations. He wanted to consolidate his learning by teaching for a while. Further, he realized that his thinking was not as yet mature enough to take the doctorate. He also wanted to establish himself in a profession that would be a source of support if he eventually decided to make philosophy his major concern. Since he was required to make monthly reports to the governor as to his sons' progress, Herbart was forced to think through his methods and the nature of instruction. As the boys were eight, ten, and fourteen years of age, his experience in education and his conclusions were applicable only to adolescents. By the time he had completed his assignment, 1800, he had become convinced that education must rest on a firm philosophical foundation and that method, subject matter, and discipline should grow out of this philosophy. He was certain that any instruction worth the price must be scientific, and that learning comes through hard work, not "soft pedagogy."

While in Switzerland, Herbart visited Pestalozzi at Burgdorf. He had great respect for this strange teacher, but had some difficulty in understanding why the children learned so much and so willingly. He could find no science, no logic in the process. While he never understood Pestalozzi, and the men were poles apart in personality and intellect, he respected fact as he found it and never ceased to analyze what he experienced. Undoubtedly, Pestalozzi stimulated Herbart to formulate a philosophy and a psychology of education based in part on what he saw at Burgdorf.

Herbart returned to Oldenburg in 1800, but was far too disturbed by the atmosphere that he found there—created by arrangements for his parents' divorce—to continue his studies. He left almost immediately for Bremen, where he remained for two years as tutor to complete work for his doctorate. By his twenty-sixth birthday, he had completed his formal education and was ready to begin his mature life's work.

From Bremen, Herbart went to the University of Gottingen, where he lectured, taught a "seminary of pedagogy," and wrote his major works on education. In the security of an academic campus he was able to think clearly and productively. From these years came *Allgemeine Padagogic* (1806) and *Hauptpunkte der Metaphysik* (1808), along with *Allgemeine praktisch Philosophie* (1808). In 1809, he was called to the chair of philosophy, occupied for so many years by the great Immanuel Kant, at the University of Konigsberg in East Prussia. No one could have been more honored. "How happy I was," he wrote, "to receive the offer of this, the most renowned chair of philosophy, the place which, when a boy, I longed for in reverential dreams, as I studied the works of the sage of Konigsberg." He remained in this position until 1833, lecturing on philosophy and pedagogy, conducting a pedagogical seminar in which students were enabled to apply the principles discussed in the classroom, and writing his most mature works on philosophy and psychology. Among the books from this period are *Einleitung in die Philosophie* (1813), *Lehrbuch der Psychologie* (1816), *Psychologie als*

Wissenschaft (1824), *Allgemeine Metaphysik* (1828), and a number of less significant publications. At Gottingen he had developed the main trends of his educational theory; the years at Konigsberg matured his psychology and sharpened his philosophy.

Herbart returned to Gottingen in 1833, where he taught, wrote the less significant works of his career, and died on August 14, 1841, of a stroke.

HIS PHILOSOPHY

Herbart was first and foremost a philosopher. His psychology and his theory of education grew out of his philosophy, and can be seen in perspective only as we understand his philosophy. This latter is no easy matter, since Herbart's philosophy is analytical and mathematical.

Kant began his thinking with an attempt to explain the possibility of *a priori* activities, activities preceding knowledge. He discovered that sensations furnish the raw material of thought, upon which the mind imposes its categories or forms. The source of these sensations is the "thing-in-itself," a cause which we must accept as existing, but which we cannot know. Fichte, Schelling, and Hegel developed the mental aspect of this position to produce German idealism. They did away with the "thing-in-itself" and equated reality with thought. Pestalozzi and Froebel were part of this tradition, developing their educational theories along the lines of idealism.

Although Herbart studied with Fichte and Schelling at Jena, he came very early in his thinking to question their position and to feel that the essence of reality is the "thing-in-itself." He, along with a growing body of scholars, came to believe that the true Kant had been warped out of all proportions by the idealism of these men and their schools of thought. In the preface to his *Allgemeine Metaphysik,* Herbart writes, "In one word, the author is a Kantian. . . . if however of the year 1828, and not of the times of the *Categories* and the *Critique of Judgment.*" Although most people did not view Kant as a realist, Herbart did, and patterned himself after this interpretation of the master.

Trained in clear and accurate analysis, Herbart insisted that all philosophy must concern itself with the reflection upon elaboration of empirical conceptions; it must begin with experience. Such reflection and elaboration led him to conclude that existence consists of independent realities or "reals." As these reals are experienced and related to each other, the mind, the will, desires, volitions, and moral character are determined.

Careful analysis of experience convinced Herbart that all the conceptions of practical life are self-contradictory. This was nothing new. Others, as far back as the Greeks, had discovered this fact, and two major theories had been developed. The Skeptics argued that there is no such thing as reality and thought cannot be trusted. Hegel had made self-contradiction the heart of his dialectic theory and out of it constructed his Absolute. Herbart could not agree with either position. For him, self-contradiction was a characteristic of phenomena, of experience, and not of reality. If we go behind experience to reality, we will find that self-contradictions disappear. Phenomena point to an independent, objective, simple reality. The categories and forms of space and time are the results of relationships among these reals.

The reasoning that seemed to Herbart to establish this position is highly analytical and mathematical, and too technical to warrant its discussion here. It is sufficient for our purpose to know that Herbart developed a metaphysics and an ontology that attracted wide attention in nineteenth century philosophical circles.

Reality is a plurality of "real" things. Herbart's philosophy is actually a "pluralistic realism." Phenomena, experiences, are the results of relations between these "reals," which are in "intellectual space," not subject to the limitations of phenomena. They have "absolute position" and do not limit one another. They come and go in "intellectual space," and we can have no knowledge of their actual relations. We can know only their relations in "phenomenal space," as they appear to us in experience.

HIS PSYCHOLOGY

Each real, according to Herbart, seeks to preserve itself, to maintain its initial integrity. When many reals coexist, they produce disturbances within each other as their integrity is challenged. The ego, or self, is a real among other reals, the "Soul-Real" striving to preserve itself and thereby suffering inner disturbances. We cannot know the "Soul-Real" in itself, but we can have immediate knowledge of its manifestations. The science of its inner reactions at being disturbed by the presence of other reals, along with its efforts at self-preservation, is psychology.

Knowledge arises from experience. When the "Soul-Real" or self is in the presence of another real, it reacts to this presence, and the encounter results in a presentation or idea. The "Soul-Real" is isolated and alone, does not think, is not conscious. Consciousness is a result of the conflict of reals. Ideals are born in this conflict, and consciousness is an aggregate of ideas, of presentations.

Presentations have an existence and a life all their own. They facilitate or hinder one another, seek to maintain their integrity, and are disturbed when threatened. Like presentations attract their kind to form "apperceptive masses." These masses strive to occupy the focus of consciousness and to expel antagonistic presentations into the unconscious.

The mind, for Herbart, is neither a *tabula rasa* upon which the senses write, nor is it a number of faculties that are to be trained to the limit of their possibilities. There is no mind without presentations. The mind is a construction of presentations; it is one's presentations organized into apperceptive masses, each pulling, pushing, challenging and being challenged, rising from and being pushed back into the unconscious. The mind is merely an indifferent point where presentations are held together by their very nature.

Knowing, feeling, and willing result from the relations between presentations. We know only that which results from the conflict of reals. The ideas, mental content, that we have are born of conflict between the "Soul-Real" and other reals. Feeling is a result of the relationships between presentations. When one presentation furthers another, pleasantness results. When a presentation is challenged or arrested, the result is unpleasantness. The intensity of feeling depends upon the degree of furtherance or challenge. Feeling, then, is the consciousness of the rising or sinking, the furthering or hindering of presentations. As such, feeling is secondary and derived, not original and basic.

Primary ideas are sensations. As they come into conflict, they produce feeling. When an idea drops below the threshold of consciousness, it becomes an impulse. An apperceptive mass dominating the focus of consciousness becomes a volition—one acts in terms of the prevailing mass of like ideas. When conflicting apperceptive masses are struggling for the focus of consciousness, one is disturbed, he cannot "make up his mind," he is unable to act decisively. In this situation the individual deliberates, weighs possible choices, and may or may not be able to come to a conclusion.

Herbart's theory of mental life helped destroy faculty psychology. It became evident that the mind cannot be thought of as a number of faculties waiting to be trained. Herbart showed that the mind is a unity, an arena of competition in which the victor takes over and determines feeling, will, and volition.

Here was one of the first attempts to make psychology scientific. For Herbart, psychology is the "statics and mechanics" of ideas. It must be treated mathematically. As we learn the nature of presentations, we can predict one's actions, thoughts, and feelings. For Herbart, psychology rests upon the same empirical basis as the natural sciences. No longer could students of the field be concerned with the nature of "the soul." Theology had to give way to science. Scholars and experimenters turned to a study of the content of consciousness, to a study of physical elements and their relations. Psychology became an atomism, similar to all other sciences, and man was able to make substantial progress in understanding himself and his fellows.

His Educational Theory

Herbart's philosophy and psychology were the bases for his educational theory. Added to these was his careful study of young learners placed under his care. From all this he constructed a theory of instruction that was scientific and clear.

What, he reasoned, is the fundamental goal of education? What is the meaning of schooling? Taking his cue from Schiller, he concluded that the purpose of all education is the production of the cultured man, one of taste, who by his very nature strives to attain true morality. In his thinking, "esthetic taste" is opposed to the baser elements in human nature and, if properly developed, will give one control over himself in the struggle to attain the good. Herbart recognized that man may be good by blind habit or by accident. Neither of these seemed to him of real value. The truly good man, he reasoned, is one who freely and consciously chooses the good because it is his very nature to do so. Education must so construct character that one becomes an individual who can do nothing but the good.

The teacher does not know the future. He cannot predict in detail what choices the youth will be forced to make in later life. Therefore, while aiming to develop the "esthetic man" with a character turned toward morality, the teacher cannot produce a machine which will automatically act as he foresees. The pupil must become one who acts upon principle. He must, first, desire the good at all times, whatever its specific form at any given time. Second, he must be prepared to attain the good that he naturally desires. This necessitates the development of "many-sidedness of interest." Correct education consists in giving the youth a broad range of experiences that will eventuate in many interests, all leading to morality.

Stating the goal of education as the development of wide interests, Herbart turned to the method of creating these interests. This he found in his philosophy and psychology. Interest is a result of the relationships existing between ideas in the mind. As the individual interacts with his environment, ideas are produced. To state the process in Herbart's terms, when the "Soul-Real," or Ego, comes in contact with another real, an idea is born. These ideas are the furniture of the mind,

organizing themselves into apperceptive masses that strive to dominate consciousness. The strength of an apperceptive mass to maintain
itself and control consciousness determines the will. One is interested
in that which is sympathetic with this apperceptive mass.

Development of interests, and thus will, is a process of experiencing
reals that produce ideas. The more often an idea and its apperceptive
mass comes to consciousness, the greater its power over consciousness.
Here we see a law of association of like ideas and a law of frequency
of return to consciousness. These are, for Herbart, the basic laws of
instruction.

This methodology places the teacher in the position of builder of the
youth's mind. Instruction becomes construction. As the teacher controls the child's environment, he determines the experiences the child
will have, the "reals" his "Soul-Real" will contact. The teacher constructs the mind of the child and in so doing determines the child's
interests, his will, and his character.

This is a theory of "educative instruction." As the teacher instructs
in the classroom, he is actually determining the mind of his pupils. He
is producing "right" thinking, and right thinking produces right action, action in line with thinking. Instruction imparts knowledge. It
also develops discipline, interest, desire, will, and character. The child
will become what he learns, what he is taught.

This theory of education resulted naturally in a methodology that
Herbart developed and that his followers, the Herbartians, formalized
and made determinative of educational practice. To develop character,
or stability of will, the instructor must bring his pupil to complete
absorption in a single idea to the exclusion of all contradictory ideas.
As one focuses his attention upon a single object of thought, he is able
to associate the idea with other like ideas from past experiences and
build a strong apperceptive mass. To allow attention to sweep over
many experiences of conflicting nature confuses the learner, sets up
conflicts among reals, and an unsteady will results.

Herbart's followers built this concept into the theory of "concentration," demanding that all studies in the curriculum be grouped around
one common subject. The method by which this "concentration" is
attained is "correlation." One subject, theme, or principle becomes
central, determining. It is the focus from which all others have meaning. History may be such a "concentration" about which all other areas
of learning—English, mathematics, music, art, and other subjects—are
"correlated." By this method, the child is enabled to build apperceptive
masses of like ideas rather than filling his mind with a jumble of
confused and confusing ideas.

Out of Herbart's philosophy and psychology came a lesson plan consistent with his basic principles and designed to give the teacher a clear and simple procedure for teaching any lesson at any time. Herbart suggested four steps in the process, each consistent with his theory of education. The Herbartians went further and produced five steps, which they then formalized into "the five formal steps of the recitation." These steps were accepted by teachers in both Europe and America during the closing years of the nineteenth and the early years of the twentieth centuries, and became the rigid form into which was cast much of the teaching in the classrooms of the western world.

The teacher is planning to instruct a class regarding a specific bit of material. Following the principles of Herbart's theory, he must first recall to the focus of attention whatever ideas and apperceptive masses the pupil already has developed consistent with the new material to be taught. This the Herbartians called *preparation.* He is preparing the mind to receive the new material. In this procedure, interest in the new material is aroused, and the pupil is prepared to concentrate his attention upon it. This being done satisfactorily, the teacher then proceeds to the *presentation* of the new material to be taught. Here he must use concrete objects or other means of making learning vivid and clear. He must begin with the simplest matters, the most easily understood, and move on to the more complex or difficult.

Herbart thought of these two steps as a unit that he called *clearness,* the teaching of facts, knowledge, in a manner that would be most clear for the learner. To attain this clearness, he said, the teacher must bring to consciousness pre-learned materials, or ideas, and give to the pupil the new in as concrete a form as possible.

The third "formal" step in teaching was called *association.* The new is apperceived by the old, assimilated into the apperceptive mass already existent, tied up with what the pupil already knows. The teacher points to likenesses and differences between the new and what is already known and helps the child incorporate this new into his mental furniture.

This must be followed by *generalization,* a process by which the new sensory experiences are analyzed, abstract features made understandable, and general concepts formed from relationships seen between the old and the new. Until generalizations are made, Herbart believed, learning remains at the low level of the concrete and the perceptive. Generalization lifts learning to the conceptual level.

Finally, learning must eventuate in *application,* use in specific situations. By using the material learned, the pupil makes it his own, sees its accuracy, and is prepared to make it available for further learning.

Now the pupil is prepared to make this new knowledge a tool for assimilation of new material; he has learned it thoroughly.

These five steps of teaching became a rigid formula for all classroom activity, a fact which Herbart would never have approved. Student teachers were required to divide lesson plans into five sections, each of the same length. In a fifty-minute lesson, the teacher was expected to devote ten minutes, no more or no less, to each step. If he lingered too long over one step or cheated at another step, his supervisor would criticize him severely. Teaching, in the hands of the Herbartians, became a formal process lacking both vitality and warmth.

THE HERBARTIANS

In his *Science of Education* Herbart wrote:

> I have for twenty years employed metaphysics and mathematics, and side by side with them self-observation, experience, and experiments, merely to find the foundations of true psychological insight. And the motive for these not exactly toilless investigations has been and is, in the main, my conviction that a large part of the enormous gaps in our pedagogical knowledge results from lack of psychology.

Convinced that he had cleared away the mythology that had weighted down the psychology he inherited, he constructed a pedagogy that seemed to him scientific and clear. Most thinkers in the Germany of his day were engrossed in the work of Fichte and Hegel and had no time to listen to Herbart. This caused him to cry, "My poor pedagogy has not been able to lift up its voice."

Gradually, scholars began turning to Herbart for inspiration and guidance. In 1856, W. F. Volkman, an Austrian, published a textbook on Herbartianism that contained an extensive review of the history of Herbartian psychology and education and a critique of the literature on the subject. Two years later, Gustav Adolf Lindner wrote a textbook on *Empirical Psychology* along Herbartian lines. This became a standard textbook in the teacher-training institutions of Germany and, in 1889, was translated into English by Charles DeGarmo. Soon the universities at Jena and Leipzig became centers of Herbartian thought. At the latter, Moritz Drobisch worked on the mathematical aspects of Herbartian psychology, taught Herbartian philosophy to G. E. Muller, and was instrumental in bringing to the institution Wilhelm Wundt. Gustav Hartenstein, at Leipzig, edited Herbart's *Works* in ten volumes. By 1865, Herbartian thinking had permeated much of European psychology and education, and scholars everywhere were studying Herbart's writings and elaborating his ideas.

Next to Germany, Herbartianism was most universally accepted in America. In the late nineteenth century, several educators, disturbed by the ineffectiveness of much of the teaching in elementary and secondary schools, traveled to Germany to investigate the cause of the educational renaissance that was taking place there. Among these educators were the McMurrays, Charles and Frank, Charles DeGarmo, and C. C. Van Lieu. They returned to introduce American educators to Herbartianism and to spark an interest in his educational theories and methodology that resulted in a flood of books and monographs on the subject, the almost universal adoption of his methods in the classrooms, and the organization, in 1892, of the *National Herbartian Society.*

In 1892, Charles McMurray published his *General Method,* an introduction to Herbartianism, and five years later, with Frank, issued *The Method of the Recitation,* a clear analysis of the "five formal steps." Literature coming from American presses during the next ten years dealt with all aspects of the subject and gave Americans a thorough understanding of Herbartianism. Soon after the turn of the century a new point of view began to appear upon the American scene to eclipse Herbartian thinking. This new theory was contained in the writings of John Dewey, William T. Harris, and G. Stanley Hall. By 1902, Herbartianism was disappearing as a substantial force in American education. The *National Herbartian Society* changed its name to the *National Society for the Scientific Study of Education.* Soon thereafter, the vocabulary of Herbartianism was forgotten, scholars and teachers were beginning to show keen interest in the "new education," and the first glimmerings of the progressive movements in educational thought were appearing.

The basic principles of Herbart's thinking remained to strengthen teaching and give direction to further experimentation. Herbart had given the death blow to faculty psychology, had introduced the scientific and mathematical approach to psychology, had stimulated interest in the careful training of teachers, and had made educators aware that methodology must be founded on clear philosophical theory and psychological knowledge. Later scholars added to these basic concepts and gave the modern world its "frontier" education.

CHAPTER 16

In the United States – Nineteenth Century

INTRODUCTION

The nineteenth century represents the most significant age in the history of American education. It shaped the educational institution in its conservative direction. At the start of the century, education in the United States was still patterned, to a great extent, after the European models. Educational independence from Europe came about as Americans developed national concepts, such as a feeling for their American heritage, a pragmatic philosophical posture, democratic ideals of equal educational opportunity, the belief that education was essential to successful living, the development of the common school movement, which led to compulsory attendance legislation, an extension upward of the average level of education, the development of the educational ladder, and the belief that parents control the curriculum and school policies.

The United States of the nineteenth century was both an educational importer and a creator. In the early decades of the century she depended heavily upon Europe for much of her social and economic thinking, for her basic philosophical orientation, and for her educational structure and outlook. Goods and ideas marked "European" were held by many to be superior to anything "home-grown." Leaders in the intellectual and political arenas learned much from the experiences of European nations. The thinking of leading European educators attracted considerable attention in the United States, and several interested schoolmen visited Europe, studied with those in the forefront of educational thought, and brought back many of their ideas and practices, weaving them into the fabric of educational development. Still, there was much opposition in America to European education.

At the same time, the United States was growing up. When the century opened, she was a fledgling nation emerging from the effects of a revolutionary war and struggling to hold together thirteen highly divergent colonies in a tenuous union. During the century, she changed from an agricultural to an industrial nation and fought a civil war to determine whether "this nation, or any nation, so conceived and so dedicated can long endure." As the century came to a close, her leaders were asserting that she had become an adult prepared to play an adult's role in the family of nations.

This growing up was singularly creative. Internally, the United States was developing ideas and institutions suited to her peculiar needs and genius. Out of the struggles among the conflicting interests represented in the population came an original concept of democratic government, a new approach to individualism, and a clear national consciousness. These reached into all phases of living and shaped both the thinking and behavior of the people. National pride and loyalty were developed democratically as the electors chose and followed their leaders. Europeans of many cultural backgrounds immigrated to the United States during the century, to contribute their strengths and talents to her growth and development. At the same time, students and leaders came to study and learn about this unique experiment in group living and to carry back to their nationals its secrets and lessons.

During the nineteenth century, an educational ladder was constructed out of the varied schools the early settlers and the immigrants brought from their homelands. As each became part of this structure, it was changed to serve the needs of the people. Where no school existed, the people created one to complete the pattern. Among those so fashioned were the academy, the junior high school, the English high school, and the junior college. A total education was being developed in the United States to serve all the people. This task was by no means completed by the end of the century, but certainly the foundations were established, which are now so difficult to change in the 1970s. A commendable beginning laid down the guidelines for later growth.

A faltering union at the beginning of the nineteenth century, the United States was well on her way to world leadership when the century came to an end. She had met and solved many of her major problems as a nation. She had fashioned a culture, a government, and an educational system flexible enough to face up to new challenges with confidence and courage, and vital enough to grow and mature as a responsible member of the world in the twentieth century.

RISE OF THE COMMON SCHOOL

DEFINITION

The term common school meant to nineteenth century America a school supported and controlled by the community and open to all children living in the area. Restrictions governing citizenship, the "rate bill," and the educational implications of indenture and apprenticeship severely limited the application of this ideal in many sections of the United States. As the nation moved toward a clearer understanding of democracy, these restrictions were removed, and its schools became more truly "common."

IN NEW ENGLAND

As conditions in New England became more favorable to the expanded community, the centrally located town school proved inadequate, and the district system evolved. Each community was authorized by the colony to organize and support a school to teach children to read and write. Although at times this did result in small, wholly inadequate, poorly staffed schools, it aimed at providing a common school within reach of every child in the colony. The period from 1789 to 1827 was characterized by confusion and fumbling. First the colony and then the state attempted to discover a formula for providing public education for all. The law of 1789, passed by the Massachusetts General Assembly, handed over to local school committees the task of supervising schools. This was followed, in 1801, by a law giving each community control over taxation for schools. Since the attitudes of communities toward schools, and taxation for their support, differed widely within the state, this decentralization of control resulted in a serious decline in schools and educational interest. This trend was brought to a halt by the law of 1827, which made support of schools by taxation compulsory, abolished the "rate bill," and opened the schools of the state to all children.

IN NEW YORK

Three approaches to education can be seen in colonial New York. The Calvinist concern for instruction, especially at the elementary level, determined the attitudes of the Dutch settlers. As the English strengthened their influence in the area, a strong sentiment grew for leaving education in the hands of private and church interests. There was also much interest in the French idea of a centralized authority controlling all educational and cultural activities. Leaders holding these concepts battled for control of education in New York until a compromise was worked out in which a part of each point of view was evident.

Under the leadership of Governor George Clinton, the legislature set aside, in 1784, land in each township for the support of schools and established *The Board of Regents of the University of New York* as the state's chief educational agency. Six years later, this body was authorized to use money derived from the sale of certain state-owned lands to assist local school districts. By 1795, the legislature asserted its authority over education by passing a far-reaching school law providing money for common schools, specifically regulating its use, outlining the curriculum to be taught, and determining the administrative pattern in each district. Although this law resulted in the rapid growth of public schools in the state and a general diffusion of elementary education, it was bitterly opposed as too authoritarian and smacking of old country centralization of power. The law was allowed to lapse in 1800, and education was turned over to private interests.

In 1805, the legislature set up, with money received from sale of school lands, lotteries, income from bank stocks, federal funds the state had received, and other state monies, a "Common School Fund" for the encouragement of elementary education. This same year, DeWitt Clinton, then mayor of New York City, organized the *New York Free School Society* to provide instruction for poor children not cared for by other educational agencies in the city. As governor from 1817 to 1822 and again from 1824 to 1828, Clinton sponsored legislation and used his prestige to move the state in the direction of free schooling for all children.

The law of 1812, passed after a commission appointed by Governor Tompkins had drawn up a plan for public education in New York, divided the state into school districts under boards of three trustees, provided for state aid on the basis of population, and placed the whole system of state schools under the State Superintendent of Common Schools. Later, in 1821, the office of superintendent was abolished.

When, in 1832, New York City incorporated the schools of the Free School Society into its system of common schools, all schools in the city became free. This set the pattern for other cities and communities and moved the country closer to the ideal of the common school.

HORACE MANN (1796-1859)

Horace Mann resigned from the presidency of the Massachusetts Senate in 1837 to accept the post of secretary of the newly established State Board of Education. While in this office, Mann initiated a sequence of events which significantly influenced the entire course of public education in the United States.

Born in Franklin, Massachusetts, on May 4, 1796, of poor parents, Mann's early schooling was limited to not more than eight to ten weeks a year. He was fortunate in attracting the interest of an able village pastor who taught him privately and passed him on to a college preparatory teacher. After six months' study with the latter, he was able to enter Brown University, from which he was graduated in 1819 with highest honors. After a period of legal apprenticeship and two years tutoring Latin and Greek at Brown, he entered Judge Gould's law school at Litchfield, Connecticut, where his brilliant legal mind led many to predict a great future for him in the profession. Admitted to the bar in 1823, he set about to build his law practice, first in Dedham, and later in Boston. In 1827, he was elected to the Massachusetts House of Representatives, where he remained until 1833, when he moved up to the Senate. He served this body for four years, two of these as its president. Among his major accomplishments was an act, supported by many of his colleagues, creating a state board of education.

Massachusetts had, from its earliest beginnings, maintained a position of leadership in education. The decentralization of educational control and the declining interest in schools on the part of many of the people stimulated members of the state's legislature to pass the law of 1827. It soon became evident that legal enactments were not sufficient to guarantee public involvement in better education. A movement was begun, under the leadership of James G. Carter, Edmund Dwight, Josiah Quincy, Jr., and the Reverend Charles Brooks, to have the state create a central educational agency responsible for winning mass support for good schools. Responding to the demand created by this movement, Governor Edward Everett persuaded the legislature to establish a state board of education with a secretary. Opponents of the board were able to deny it any authority to found or administer schools, enforce legislation, or distribute state funds.

It was clearly evident to those who had championed the act that success or failure of the board depended upon its secretary. This was no position for a professional educator or a successful politician. Only a statesman who understood education, the state, and the democratic hope could make the undertaking succeed. With these facts in mind, Edmund Dwight asked Mann to accept the post of secretary, a position with no prestige or authority and in which he would be subject to violent criticism. At first Mann was astonished. He wrote later, "I never had a sleeping or waking dream that I should ever think of myself, or be thought of by any other, in relation to that station." Dwight persisted, and by the end of June, Mann had consented, against the advice of most of his friends who saw him throwing away a brilliant career in public service for an undertaking far too advanced for his day. In a letter to a friend, written on July 2, Mann said, "My lawbooks are for sale. My office is 'to let'! The bar is no longer my forum. My jurisdiction is changed. I have abandoned jurisprudence, and betaken myself to the larger sphere of mind and morals."

The appointment of Mann to the secretaryship of the Massachusetts Board of Education in 1837 was a stroke of genius. The law gave no authority to the board or to its secretary. Their function was to collect and diffuse information about schools and education, persuade leaders and the people to support better schools, and advise those in authority who would play major roles in building an educational structure suited to the needs of an expanding society. Mann thought of himself as moving from the law, with its clear avenues of enforcement, into "the larger sphere of mind and morals" where men must be reasoned with and persuaded. Law may punish immorality, but it will never produce morality. Only education can accomplish this end.

To discharge his duties as he interpreted them under the law, Mann traveled widely, delivering hundreds of addresses dealing with educational matters. He organized county teacher-training institutes wherever possible and invited leading educators of the nation to conduct courses to upgrade those already in service. He was able to persuade the state legislature to establish three "normal schools," the first at Lexington, to better prepare new teachers. He corresponded with educators, teachers, and public officials throughout the United States, offering both advice and encouragement. He established the *Common School Journal*—ten volumes appeared during his administration—which presented a wide range of materials of interest to teachers and leaders inside and outside the profession.

During Mann's career as secretary of the board of education, he published twelve reports that have become classics in education. Here we find him discussing the need for better school buildings; more intelligent local school boards; a deeper involvement of the public in universal education; more competent teachers; more effective teaching of reading, spelling, and composition in the schools; and free public libraries in all schools. Mann advocated, among other things, health and physical education, the primacy of moral over intellectual education, "the *absolute right* of every human being that comes into the world to an education," and strong religious training.

In May, 1843, Mann went to Europe, where he spent five months studying educational developments. The results of this study are contained in the famous *Seventh Annual Report* issued near the close of that year. This is a study in comparative education, containing data and interpretations dealing with schools in England, Ireland, Scotland, Germany, Holland, Belgium, and France. It contains a glowing commendation of the Pestalozzian teaching then dominating Prussian schools. It evoked sharp, and at times vicious, criticism of Mann and involved him in a running battle with an *ad hoc* association of Boston schoolmasters. These men saw in his commendation of oral instruction, the word method of teaching reading, and abolition of corporal punishment, an eventual undermining of the teacher's authority and a pertinent slap at "true and tried" methods of instruction.

Mann was convinced that a truly democratic common school had to be nonsectarian. His advocacy of this position infuriated most orthodox churchmen. They believed that one purpose of the school was to teach "true" religion. Mann's argument seemed to him clear and convincing. He held that just as the child in school is taught "the elements of a political education," not to make him vote with any particular political party but to "enable him to choose for himself, which party he will vote," so religious education in the common schools "is not imparted to him, for the purpose of making him join this or that denomination, when he arrives at years of discretion, but for the purpose of enabling him to judge for himself, according to the dictates of his own reason and conscience, what his religious obligations are and whither they lead."

Mann was convinced that there was a body of religious truths that could be taught all children without demeaning their special religious convictions. This included the Bible, Christian doctrine and morals, belief in God, and respect for ministers. He saw no conflict between this position and religious freedom in a democracy.

The orthodox attacked Mann bitterly, calling him an atheist, an infidel, an advocate of ungodly schools, and anti-Christian. He responded with a series of pamphlets and addresses that played a part in gradually eliminating sectarian religious teaching from public schools.

On February 21, 1848, John Quincy Adams fell unconscious on the floor of the House of Representatives' chamber, and died two days later. Mann was persuaded to resign his post with the board of education and accept Adams' seat in Congress. He was a Whig of moderate antislavery views, opposed to Webster's position. He ran in 1852 as the Free Soil candidate for governor of Massachusetts but was defeated. The next year he accepted the presidency of Antioch College, nonsectarian and coeducational, in Yellow Springs, Ohio. There, after years of difficulty because of his religious views and the lack of adequate financing, he died in 1859. Just a few weeks before his death, he delivered the baccalaureate address at the college that contains the famous admonition, "Be ashamed to die until you have won some victory for humanity."

In the light of modern understanding of education and its function in society, Mann won many victories for humanity. Due in part to his efforts, by 1848, twenty-four of the thirty states had established a state school office and adopted the principles of local taxes and state aid for the support of an adequate common school. In Massachusetts, teachers' salaries had been increased more than fifty per cent, the average school term lengthened, and millions of dollars were being spent to improve school buildings and erect new ones. The state "normal school" had been firmly established in Massachusetts, and New York, Connecticut, and Michigan had founded similar institutions. In 1852, largely through Mann's leadership, Massashusetts passed a law requiring children to attend school. Religious freedom had become a fundamental principle of common school education. As important as anything mentioned, the downward trend of interest in schools and the lack of support of public schools came to an end. Through Mann's efforts, the state had definitely assumed its full responsibility for providing every child a common school education.

HENRY BARNARD (1811-1900)

While Horace Mann was by far the most outstanding leader of the common school movement in the nineteenth century, he was by no means alone. Henry Barnard, often referred to as the scholar of this movement, did for Connecticut and Rhode Island what Mann did for Massachusetts.

Born in Hartford, Connecticut, Barnard graduated from Yale in 1830. After graduation, Barnard taught school for a year in a Pennsylvania academy. He was admitted to the bar in 1835, but went immediately to Europe, where he studied education in general and different schools in particular. He was at this time greatly influenced by the Pestalozzian educational philosophy. He returned to Connecticut, where he was elected to the legislature, and was the author and chief proponent of a bill, passed in 1838, establishing a board of commissioners of common schools.

To see that the intent of this bill would be carried out, Barnard left his legislative post to become secretary of the board, devoting his energies, as Mann was doing in Massachusetts, to the creation of an adequate free school system in his home state. A young man of twenty-seven, he traveled widely through the state, addressing any who would listen, organized groups interested in his ideas, wrote annual reports, and founded the *Connecticut Common School Journal,* through which he gave wide publicity to his plans. Public opposition to the idea of free common schools grew in intensity in spite of Barnard's efforts, and in 1842 the education law of 1838 was repealed. He was thus left without office.

The governor of Rhode Island invited Barnard to undertake a study of that state's educational structure and recommend improvements. Out of this came legislation similar to that which had been passed by Massachusetts in 1837 and by Connecticut in 1838. A Rhode Island law of 1845 established the office of state commissioner of education with considerably more power and prestige than enjoyed by secretaries of the boards in Massachusetts and Connecticut. Barnard was made the state's first commissioner and was able to get increased appropriations for schools, develop teacher-training facilities, organize model and demonstration schools, found libraries in almost every town in the state, and keep a flood of educational propaganda pouring over the people.

By 1851, Connecticut was convinced of its need for a common school structure able to provide its children with adequate instruction. It invited Barnard home to head a new normal school and resume his duties as secretary of the board of education. During the next four years, he was able to do for his own state what he had done for Rhode Island. In 1855, broken in health, he had to resign the office and retire to an easier and less demanding life, but not from education.

Freed from the exacting demands of the office of secretary of the Connecticut Board of Education, Barnard helped organize the *American Association for the Advancement of Education.* As its president, he began editing the *American School Journal.* This ran through more than thirty massive volumes, treating of all phases of education in the United States and throughout the western world. Wherever Barnard found an educational reform which seemed to him to have real promise, he gave it the support of the *Journal.* Here was created a rich storehouse of educational information, debate, and evaluation. Scholars find it by far the most complete and accurate source of information regarding educational developments in the nineteenth century in the United States.

Unable to divorce himself from the educational life of his day, Barnard was persuaded, in 1859, to accept the chancellorship of the University of Wisconsin and function as agent for the state's normal school fund. This was followed by several years of rest and study, broken finally by acceptance in 1866 of the presidency of Saint John's College at Annapolis, Maryland. His study of education led him to the realization that the nation had no central agency to which one could go for authentic information about American education. He urged Congress to establish an office of education as part of the federal government. When the office was finally created in 1867, he was designated its chief executive—the first United States Commissioner of Education. Resigning from this office in 1870, Barnard spent the last thirty years of his life editing the *Journal* and working, when his health would permit, for better common schools throughout the country. His dedication was such that he spent his entire fortune, which at one time was considerable, to further educational developments and, on July 5, 1900, died almost in poverty.

OTHER EDUCATIONAL LEADERS

While New England was building a common school system under the leadership of Horace Mann and Henry Barnard, other parts of the country were feeling the impact of capable and dedicated leaders. These were struggling with hesitant legislators and antagonistic pressure groups to strengthen state authority over schools; eliminate sectarian religious teaching; make common school education free to all and supported wholly by taxes; raise standards set for teachers; and discover better methods of teaching, better principles of textbook writing, and better school architecture.

Calvin Stowe in Ohio, Caleb Mills, who became known as the "Father of the Common Schools of Indiana," Ninian Edwards in Illinois, Isaac Crary in Michigan, Robert Breckenridge in Kentucky, and Calvin Wiley, who brought up the level of education in North Carolina to be on a par with northern areas, all drew inspiration from Mann and Barnard and worked much as they had for educational reform.

PROPAGANDA FOR COMMON SCHOOLS

The work of dynamic educational leaders stimulated a flood of propaganda for better schools through the nation. European developments were reported in great detail. John Griscom, in 1819, described European education in his *Year in Europe,* a volume which had considerable influence upon American educational reform. The famous *State of Public Education in Prussia,* prepared by Victor Cousin for the French government in 1831, was translated into English in 1834 and circulated widely. Reports and discussions dealing with developments in Europe were circulated by William C. Woodbridge and Calvin Stowe. A flood of educational journals appeared during the first half of the nineteenth century advocating reformation of the country's elementary schools. These included the *Academician, The American Journal of Education,* and the *American Annals of Education.*

To supplement these, friends of the common school organized associations, agencies, and institutes to finance publications on education, hold conventions and inform the people, and exert pressure upon legislators for better school laws. These organizations proved to be a means of shaping public opinion and organizing those concerned with good schooling into effective bodies. Two of these groups were the *Western Academic Institute* and the *Board of Education,* established in 1829 in Cincinnati. The next year the *American Institute of Instruction* was founded in Boston.

CONSERVATIVE TEXTBOOKS

By the mid-nineteenth century, American textbooks had taken on a point-of-view which has continued in part for over a hundred years. History textbooks became highly nationalistic, glorifying and approving America's past actions. "Manifest Destiny" became an overriding justification. Other materials taught acceptable and desirable moral and spiritual values. Concepts taught via the material studied were respect for authority, the virtues of hard work, respect for one's status in life, natural pride, Protestantism, and national unity. This development grew out of the private publishing industry and not as a result of government influence. The public believed in "My Country, right or wrong." It had determined concepts or ideals it wanted taught to its children. Publishers and authors wanted to sell books, and this was the kind of book the country wanted. This conservative tendency in textbook writing has continued to the present. If a controversial issue divides the public in a manner that textbooks with editorial points-of-view might offend a particular area of the country, the tendency is to avoid taking a stand. The most common of these issues currently relate to treatment of the Civil War, of the United Nations, and of the interpretation of history to meet the demands of minorities.

Many authors contributed to the textbook scene in the nineteenth century. Two in particular will be noted: Noah Webster and William Holmes McGuffey.

Noah Webster (1758-1843) has had more influence on American spelling and pronunciation than any other American. Earlier reference was made to some of his work. Born in Connecticut and working in Massachusetts, Webster is best known for his *American Dictionary of the English Language,* first published in 1828. He believed in an American type of education rather than a European one. Educationally, his influence has related to his "blue-back spellers," which were the prime textbooks used from the latter part of the eighteenth century to the mid-nineteenth century. A few paragraphs from the Blue-back speller will give a good indication of what American youth was taught:

> A good child will not lie, swear, nor steal.—He will be good at home, and ask to read his book; when he gets up he will wash his hands and

COLLEGE Required Curriculum for College Admission	LIFE WORK Elective Courses of English Curriculum
Ancient Hist., State Hist., Latin, Greek, U.S. Govt., Botany, Trigonometry, Declaration	English grammar, Law, intellectual, moral, and mental philosophy, Declaration, Minerology, Pol. Economy, Principles of Teaching
Adv. Algebra, Latin, Greek , Literature, Declaration, Grammar, Chemistry, Botany, Natural Philosophy	Mapping, Surveying, Bookkeeping, Topography, Navigation, Astronomy, English, Advanced French
Geometry, Latin, Greek, English Grammar, World Hist., Literature	Natural Hist., Rhetoric, French, Drawing, World Hist.

Algebra, Latin, English, Geography, General Hist., U.S. History

HIGH SCHOOL GRADUATION REQUIREMENTS

Arithmetic, English Literature, Reading

U.S. History, State History Government, Ancient History

Natural Philosophy, Botany, Chemistry

Latin, Advanced Algebra, Geometry, Bookkeeping, Surveying

Geography, U.S. History, General History

GRAMMAR SCHOOL	8	Advanced Arithmetic, Elementary Algebra	
	7	Advanced Reading, Spelling, Word Analysis, Penmanship, Grammar, Composition, Declaration	COMMON
INTER- MEDIATE SCHOOL	6	Geography	SCHOOL
	5	Arithmetic	
	4	Elementary Grammar, Reading, Spelling, Writing	
PRIMARY SCHOOL	3	Counting, Reckoning, Numbers, Arithmetic	
	2	Reading, Accentuation	
	1	Spelling, Syllabification, Writing	

FIGURE 2

The Academy Curriculum, Mid-Nineteenth Century, Adapted from Various Schools

423

face clean; he will comb his hair and make haste to school; he will not play by the way as bad boys do.

As for those boys and girls that mind not their books, and love not the church and school, but play with such as tell lies, curse, swear and steal, they will come to some bad end, and must be whipt till they mend their ways. . . .

Webster had many interesting features in his "Old Blue-back" spellers. For instance, note these excerpts from this assignment covering "Precepts concerning the Social Relations," wherein the young girl is to "Be cautious in listening to the addresses of men. Is thy suitor addicted to low vices? is he profane? is he a gambler? a tippler? a spendthrift? a haunter of taverns? and, above all, is he a scoffer at religion?—Banish such a man from thy presence, his heart is false, and his hand would lead thee to wretchedness and ruin."

He also had suggestions for the married folks:

Art thou a husband? Treat thy wife with tenderness, reprove her faults with gentleness.

Art thou a wife? Respect thy husband; oppose him not unreasonably, but yield thy will to his, and thou shall be blest with peace and concord; study to make him respectable; hide his faults.

Included in the "Old Blue-back" were a number of fables. One of the most famous was "Of *the* Boy *that stole* Apples," which went as follows:

An old Man found a rude Boy upon one of his trees stealing Apples, and desired him to come down; but the young Sauce-box told him plainly he would not. Won't you? said the old Man, then I will fetch you down; so he pulled up some tufts of Grass and threw at him; but this only made the Youngster laugh, to think the old Man should pretend to beat him down from the tree with grass only.

Well, well, said the old Man, if neither words nor grass will do, I must try what virtue there is in Stones: so the old Man pelted him heartily with stones, which soon made the young Chap hasten down from the tree and beg the old Man's pardon.

MORAL

If good words and gentle means will not reclaim the wicked, they must be dealt with in a more severe manner.

An example from another edition had many sentences similar to the few quoted here.

The man can put on his wig.
I love the young lady that shows me how to read.
Vipers are bad snakes, and they bite men.
I saw a rill run down the hill.
Visitors should not make their visits too long.
Style not in verse is called prose.
The birds fly from branch to branch on the trees and clinch their
    claws fast to the limbs.
Wolves howl in the woods, in the night.
Never pester the little boys.
The lark will soar up in the sky to look at the sun.
Forks have two or three tines.
Shut the gate, and keep the hogs out of the yard.
The dysentery is a painful disease.
Our blood is often chilled at the recital of acts of cruelty.
When large hailstones fall on the house they make a great
    racket. . . .
The chewing of tobacco is a useless custom.
Many kings have been thrown down from their thrones.
The rainbow is a token that the world will not be drowned again.
Christ is a mediator between an offended God and offending man. . . .
Friday is just as lucky a day as any other. . . .

William Holmes McGuffey (1800-1873) may have had even a greater
influence on American education than did Noah Webster. His readers
featured concepts of honesty, integrity, obedience, and patriotism. He
was an Ohio teacher who wrote his *Eclectic Readers* because of his
dissatisfaction with existing materials. According to the publishers, the
books were "moral and religious" in character, but, in the 1844 edition
of the *Fourth Reader,* the publishers explained that it contained no
sectarian material. Actually, the morality of the readers is Puritan in
concept, i.e., no matter how much pain or sorrow one has to endure, it
is all for the best. The material is deeply religious, yet materialistic and
worldly. The books emphasized a system of punishment and rewards.
Virtue does not win necessarily—at least not because of virtue. The
readers were mature, cosmopolitan, and their impact upon American
youth was terrific.

THE COMMON SCHOOL IDEA TAKES SHAPE

As dedicated leaders worked through conventions, associations, reports and other publications, wide correspondence, and persuasion of
legislators, state after state moved to establish free public schools for
all children. In 1827, Massachusetts abolished the "rate bill" and de-

clared all elementary schools free. Other states made this law a model for common school legislation: Pennsylvania (1834), Rhode Island (1848), Vermont (1864), Connecticut (1868), and New Jersey (1871). Prohibitions of the teaching of sectarian religion in public schools appeared either in newly enacted state laws or in the constitutions of states entering the union. By the time of the Civil War, the country had moved well toward adopting the policy of a tax-supported secular school system serving children of all citizens.

Ohio, the first state admitted to the union from the Northwest Territory, received from Congress one section of land in each township for the support of schools. The law of 1825 organized the state into school districts, required taxation for schools on a county basis, and placed the certification of teachers in the hands of county examiners. By 1853, all public schools in the state were made free. By 1852, Indiana had made its public schools free, as had Illinois by 1855. While North Carolina created a permanent school fund in 1825 and established a state system of elementary schools in 1839, most southern states, because of social and economic factors, did not accept the common school idea until well after the Civil War.

Before the nineteenth century, it was generally accepted that education should be made available for those individuals whose status in society demanded it. As it became generally recognized that all people needed some formal education, the number of schools was increased by churches, states, and individuals. The leaders of nineteenth century education in the United States were convinced that our democratic social structure, including the government, could not survive unless children of all citizens received a minimum of formal schooling. It was but a short step from this to the conviction that each child should be compelled to attend school. Providing the means of instruction was not enough. Ignorant, vicious, or uninterested parents could deny their children the right to education. Horace Mann found compulsory school attendance in Germany, appreciated its logic, and campaigned for its acceptance in Massachusetts. In 1852 the state decreed that all children must attend school. Other states followed this example. By the close of the century, thirty-four states had made school attendance compulsory. Slower to accept progressive educational ideas, the southern states waited until the early years of the twentieth century to join their sister states in this move. All states in the union had compulsory school attendance laws by 1918.

Due to the work of Mann, Barnard, and thousands of other perceptive leaders in nineteenth century America, the nation experienced an educational revolution at the elementary level. Turning away from their European traditions, the people of the United States created a common school system, in which centralization and decentralization were delicately balanced. They made the support of this system the duty of all citizens through taxation. All children were required to attend free schools, which were growing in quality to challenge the best that private education could offer. Many had come to believe that this system could teach morals and religion without being sectarian, and that a nation's crime and delinquency were inversely proportionate to the number and efficiency of its schools.

RISE OF THE AMERICAN HIGH SCHOOL

THE BOSTON HIGH SCHOOL

By the opening of the nineteenth century, it was evident that an ever-increasing number of boys were taking up "mercantile or mechanical pursuits" rather than looking toward a college education. These boys had to rely upon apprenticeship for their education and training. In 1820, a group of Boston businessmen proposed the establishment of an "English Classical School" that would accept boys with a knowledge of reading, writing, English grammar, and simple arithmetic, and prepare them for the jobs developing in the industrial and business life of the city. In May of 1821 such a school was opened. It set the minimum age for admission at twelve and offered a three-year curriculum, in which the boy studied composition, grammar, declamation, theoretical mathematics, navigation, surveying, geography, history, logic, and moral and political philosophy. No foreign language was included. English was the only language used, and the school was free to all boys wishing to attend, its support coming from the public treasury.

After three years, John Pierpont, secretary of the Boston School Committee, proposed that the school be renamed "The English High School." His idea was accepted and the school so named. After several years, "English" was dropped, and the school became known as the high school.

In 1826, encouraged by the popularity of the high school, a similar institution for girls was opened with the noted teacher Ebenezer Bailey in charge. John Quincy, then mayor of Boston and later president of Harvard, opposed the move bitterly. He was outvoted, and the school opened with wide public acclaim. Applications far exceeded the school's facilities. After two years of phenomenal success, the city fathers refused to vote funds for its maintenance, and its doors were closed. Quincy declared the whole project a failure, although many citizens did not share his opinion.

The success of the high school in Boston so convinced the people of the state of its value that, in 1827, the state legislature passed a law requiring a high school in every town of 500 householders and a Latin grammar school in towns of 4,000 inhabitants.

SPREAD OF THE HIGH SCHOOL IDEA

The need which created the Boston high school existed in many parts of the country, and communities were quick to follow Boston's example. Portland, Maine, established a high school in 1821, and three years later Worcester, Massachusetts, established its high school. Others followed in quick succession as the idea caught on and the popularity of the institution grew. The first high school outside of New England was organized in New York City in 1825.

While the high school idea had its beginning in the United States in Boston, and the enthusiasm which brought about its spread was based on the success of this first venture and on a growing consciousness of the need, other high schools were not carbon copies of their Boston ancestor. Experimentation was general. The age of admission ranged from nine through thirteen years, with the average at twelve. The curriculum varied as local needs dictated. Many academies, sensing public interest, were changed into high schools or offered high school subjects along with their original programs.

THE KALAMAZOO CASE

Problems of the high school were both educational and economic. After the Latin grammar school proved unsuited to American life, the academy grew in importance and came to dominate the secondary field. This was a private institution serving the public but representing an investment of large sums of money, from which it was in the American tradition to expect a reasonable profit. The free high school threatened this profit. Academies saw their clientele drifting away to the high schools and their investments threatened by public competition. It was natural for those interested in the academy to challenge the very existence of the high school.

Many taxpayers were disturbed by mounting taxation for education. They had become convinced that elementary education, to a certain level only, should be tax supported, but the addition of a high school to the tax burden was more than they wanted to accept.

When Kalamazoo, Michigan, voted public money for the support of a high school, a group of citizens brought suit to test the legality of this procedure. This was not the first suit concerning the use of tax money to finance high schools. The fame of this particular suit rested in the fact that Chief Justice Thomas M. Cooley of the Michigan Supreme Court, which received the case, approached the problem with the idea of a complete system of education, from elementary school through state university, free to all citizens of the state. Justice Cooley agreed with the Pennsylvania decision of 1851, and with similar decisions of the courts in other states, that public funds for education could not be restricted to certain grades or ages. In his decision, handed down in 1874, Cooley pointed out that legislation dealing with common or public schools set no limits as to the number of years that could be included, nor did it restrict the number of offices or officers that might be necessary to its proper functioning.

Since the Constitution of the United States, as interpreted by the courts, left education in the hands of the states, each state was free to decide this issue of tax-supported high schools as it saw fit. The unanimity of decisions handed down by state supreme courts, as they received similar cases, was clear testimony to the fact that free education for all was well on its way to becoming part of the nation's educational tradition.

CREATING THE EDUCATIONAL LADDER

BACKGROUND

One of the great educational achievements in the nineteenth century was a public educational system, beginning with the simplest instruction of the child in the ABC's, mounting grade by grade through the elementary school and the high school, and culminating in the state university. Each unit was correlated with the others and its subject material arranged in terms of the pupil's intellectual growth. This was the American educational ladder, which each child was free to climb as his capabilities and interests dictated.

Not one of the schools incorporated into the ladder was created as a segment of some educational whole. Each had taken form to meet a specific need and proposed to care for complete preparation of its pupils.

The home was the beginning school in America. It offered instruction at various levels and for many reasons. When the parents reached the limits of their ability as teachers, a tutor would be brought in to complete the educational development of the child. Soon many schools were functioning in the colonies to supplement the teaching of the home. The dame school, a combination nursery and primary school, taught children the alphabet, domestic skills, and some religion. Teachers able to instruct in reading, writing, and arithmetic appeared on the American scene very early, opened private schools, and set about to attract a clientele. The Latin grammar school, transplanted from Europe, prepared boys for college by grounding them in Latin and Greek. As this school proved unsuited to the American scene, the academy appeared to offer needed preparation in a variety of areas. To offer specialized training to youths who might become leaders in church and state, the settlers established colleges modeled after those they had known in England.

Originally, each of these was a discrete institution enrolling young boys and preparing them as promised. Although some "higher" schools required certain basic knowledge and skills for admission, they did not think of any other school as preparatory.

Usually these schools were taught by a single teacher who instructed each boy individually, beginning at his level of accomplishment upon entrance and continuing his education at a pace suited to him. The student might leave whenever he wished or remain until he had completed the generally accepted course of study for that kind of school. There were no grades, no classrooms, and no specialized teachers.

SEPARATE ATTEMPTS TO DEVELOP EDUCATION

During the first decades of the nineteenth century, there was no clear distinction between "private" and "public" schools. The private academies and the private colleges received state aid. The towns and cities often subsidized the "charity schools," which were apt to be private in nature. In giving financial assistance to private schools, the states adopted the position that education was a necessity, and thus financial assistance was in the public interest. The concept was not too different from the voucher system currently receiving support. This overlapping of public and private interests in schools was a demonstration of a similar situation found in the lack of sharp lines between sectarian and nonsectarian education. Many publicly supported schools taught the Puritan ethic, or at least a Protestant persuasion. Most sectarian schools admitted the children of the poor regardless of religious background.

A characterization of colonial American schools had been their religious, social, or vocational nature. In spite of the fine principles resulting from the Revolutionary zeal for democracy, conditions did not change much during the first few decades following independence. Philanthropists brought to America from England the idea of the secondary school for poor working children. Americans needed a rationale for any social innovation. So it was that the Sunday School movement started. As churchmen saw it, children who worked in the factories all week made deplorable use of the Sabbath. Hundreds of Sunday Schools developed whereby working children were given some education. These spread throughout the land. Even New England adopted them. It was the belief of New England educational leaders that the state could capture the schools, but it worked the other way. The Church captured the Sunday Schools to the point that they became religious in nature and no longer served the interest of public education.

Another import from England was Robert Owen's Infant School. This school served youngsters from ages three to ten. The program had a good start, but no "legs." In other words, the schools had little retaining power. The Infant School was concerned with the fundamentals of reading, writing, arithmetic, and state and national history. Recognizing that there had not been much history to learn as yet, this program at least put American history into the curriculum. The *Connecticut Courant,* in describing an open house demonstration of a Hartford Infant School, gave this report:

> ... the Centre Church ... was filled with one of the most respectable assemblies, both of our own citizens, and of strangers, that we have ever seen on any public occasion. The Governor, Lt. Governor, and most of the members of the two branches of the Legislature, were present ...
>
> We have not time to give a minute description of the various lessons which were recited. The scholars read and spelt, and showed that they understood the elementary principles of arithmetic, and of the most simple ones of geometry. They were examined with regard to their knowledge of religious truth, and of moral obligation, and manifested that this was not a mere repetition by rote ... They were questioned, also ... on the history of our own State, with which they showed an accuracy of knowledge with regard to facts, the names, and dates, that was truly surprising.

For a short period of time, there was a flurry of action in the eastern cities in the form of the monitorial schools. Many cities organized "free school societies" for the education of the children of the poor. Monitorial schools adopted the Joseph Lancaster program whereby masses of youngsters could be educated cheaply. The plan was somewhat in the order of present-day programmed instruction. If the room was big enough, there might be a thousand youngsters in a room. The students would be seated in rows of six to ten. The assignments would be developed and pre-taught to a group of monitors, who in turn would teach the students. There were monitors to take attendance, to teach various subjects, to take care of equipment, and even monitors to supervise monitors. The procedures were precise and exacting; the course of study emphasized only cognitive materials. Memorization was the teaching strategy. Discipline was severe and enforced by physical punishment.

Before the high school was developed, the private academy was the popular educational secondary institution. Prior to the Civil War, there were over 6,000 such academies in the nation, enrolling more than 265,000 students. While these academies were licensed or chartered by the state, they were run by private boards of trustees. Many of the private academies were publicly subsidized.

Nevertheless, schools were in poor shape everywhere. New England bragged of the idea that all New Englanders could read, but it was not even close to being true. The facilities were poor, there was little by way of texts and materials to work with, and the teachers were a sorry lot. James G. Carter of Massachusetts was a leader in the "revival" of education in that state. He wrote at some length about the decline of education and made suggestions for ways to rectify the shortcomings. In his essays entitled *Letters . . . On the Free Schools of New England,* published in 1824 and republished in 1969 by Arno Press, he wrote of incompetent teachers, poor books, and the lack of any understanding of the art of teaching. Concerning the New England school scene he stated:

> Two principal causes have operated from the first establishment of the free schools, to impair and pervert their influence. 1st, Incompetent instructers; 2d, Bad school books. It is not a little surprising, that a public so deeply impressed with the importance of the system of schools, and so resolved to carry it into full operation, by liberal appropriations, should stop short of their purpose, and stop precisely at that point, where the greatest attention and vigilance were essential, to give efficacy to the whole. . . .
>
> 1. The employment of incompetent and inexperienced instructers has probably arisen more from the peculiar situation of the country, than from any negligence or indifference on the subject. So many opportunities are open for industrious enterprise, that it has always been difficult to induce men to become *permanent* teachers. This evil, although a serious one, is one, which cannot at present be removed; but its bad effects may be more qualified, by raising the character and acquirements of instructers to a higher standard. The whole business of instruction, with very few exceptions, has hitherto been performed by those, who have felt little interest in the subject, beyond the immediate pecuniary compensation stipulated for their services. And even that has been too inconsiderable, to render a want of success in the employment, a subject of much regret. This remark applies to almost all instructers from the primary schools up to the higher schools; and it has no very remote bearing even upon some of the instructers in our colleges. Three classes of men have furnished the

whole body of instructers. 1st. Those have undertaken to teach, who had no better reason for it, than that the employment is easier, and perhaps a little more profitable, than labour. No doubt many excellent instructers belong to this class. A college education is by no means essential to a good teacher of a primary school. But it must be confessed, that many of this class have been most lamentably deficient in those literary qualifications, which *are essential* to any instructer; and perhaps, still more deficient in their notions of decency and propriety, which never approach to refinement in manners. . . .

2. A second class are those, who are acquiring, or have attained a publick education; and who assume the business of instruction as a temporary employment, either to afford a pecuniary emolument for the relief of immediate necessities, or to give themselves time to deliberate and choose some more agreeable and profitable profession. This is, probably, the most useful class of instructers; although their usefulness is much impaired by a want of experience and engagedness in the business. The thought that the employment is temporary, and that their ultimate success in life is not much affected by their success as teachers, cannot fail to weaken the motives to exertion, and discourage the sacrifices necessary to the successful teacher. . . .

3. The third class is composed of those, who from conscious weakness, despair of success in any other profession, or who have been more thoroughly convinced by unfortunate experiment, that they cannot attain distinction, perhaps even subsistence, by any other means. There may no doubt be found individuals among this class, who are respectable and useful instructers. But as a class, they are the most exceptional of the three. . . .

In another book, *Essay on Popular Education* (Boston, 1826), Carter wrote of teachers:

> The teachers of the primary summer schools have rarely had any education beyond what they have acquired in the very schools where they begin to teach. Their attainments, therefore, to say the least, are usually *very moderate.* But this is not the worst of it. They are often very young, they are constantly changing their employment, and consequently can have but little experience; and, what is worse than all, they never have had any direct preparation for their profession. . . .
>
> But I must return to the examination of the qualifications of the female teachers of the primary summer school. . . . They are a class of teachers unknown in our laws regulating the schools unless it be by some latitude of construction. No standard of attainments is fixed. . . . So that anyone *keeps school,* which is a very different thing from *teaching school* who wishes to do it, and can persuade, by herself, or her friends, a small district to employ her. And this is not a very difficult matter, especially when the remuneration for the em-

ployment is so very trifling. The farce of an examination and a certificate from the minister of the town, for it is a perfect farce, amounts to no efficient check upon the obtrusions of ignorance and inexperience. As no standard is fixed by law, each minister makes a standard for himself, and alters it as often as the peculiar circumstances of the case require. And there will always be enough of peculiar circumstances to render a refusal expedient. . . .

Many of the above remarks upon the character and qualifications of the teachers of the summer schools apply with equal force to the young men, who undertake the instruction of the primary winter schools, which now constitute the highest class of schools, to which the whole population of the state have free access. . . .

The young man, who lays down his axe and aspires to take up the "rod" and rule in a village school, has, usually, in common with other young men, a degree of dignity and self-complacency, which it is dangerous to the extent of his power to disturb. And when he comes to his minister, sustained by his own influence in the parish, and that of a respectable father and perhaps a large family of friends, and asks of him the legal approbation for a teacher, it is a pretty delicate matter to refuse it. . . . This is truly martyrdom. And martyrs in ordinary times are rare. . . .

It is the intention of the school-law to secure good, moral characters in the public instructors by requiring the approbation, as to this qualification, of the selectmen of the town, where the school is to be taught. . . . If a young man be moral enough to keep out of the State Prison, he will find no difficulty in getting approbation for a school-master. . . .

In another state we get a glimpse of the low esteem in which teachers were held. The Governor of this state declared that the willingness to teach was prima facie evidence of inability of the person to be able to do anything else. New England had the best prepared teachers but not by much. Pay might be only $2 or $3 per month, plus board and laundry.

Roots of the Graded School

Educational leaders in Europe had experimented with graded schools for centuries and found them wholly successful. Sturm's gymnasium founded at Strassburg in the sixteenth century, was organized in ten classes. Comenius, in the seventeenth century, organized schools with grades adjusted to the child's development and with a teacher for each class. Pestalozzi had insisted that grading be carefully determined by growth in ability and understanding. By the late eighteenth century, Germany had a graded school system that attracted interest everywhere.

Horace Mann, in his *Seventh Annual Report* of 1843, advocated the German system of graded schools. His enthusiasm was shared by Barnard, Stowe, and a number of others. By 1820, experiments were being undertaken to determine the advisability of grading American schools. As educators of the stature of Mann and Barnard came to champion the idea, more graded schools appeared. John Philbrick, a Boston schoolmaster, was so impressed by these early experiments that he organized the Quincy Grammar School to grade instruction and learning. Three years later, in 1850, when he became city superintendent of Boston, he introduced the graded pattern in all Boston's schools. This began a trend that soon resulted in the general acceptance of the graded school pattern.

CORRELATION OF DISCRETE SCHOOLS

Along with experiments in grading went an equally significant move to bring the discrete schools of American tradition into a correlated pattern of instruction that would eventually erase all marks of demarcation and create the American educational ladder. Boston is typical of this development.

While Latin grammar schools were, from very early times in New England, given some support by the towns, the teaching of the ABC's and reading and writing was left in private hands—either parents or teachers whose services could be obtained for a fee. In time, some communities subsidized teachers of these "baser" subjects or established schools to teach them. The Massachusetts law of 1647 was an attempt to make the teaching of reading and writing a recognized responsibility of the community. By the close of the eighteenth century these schools, under public auspices were to be found throughout the country.

In 1789, Boston established three reading schools and three writing schools for children between the ages of seven and fourteen. Usually a child would attend a reading school for half the day and then travel to a writing school for the remainder of the day. Realizing the inefficiency of this practice, the school committee in the early nineteenth century erected a two-story building capable of housing several hundred children. The writing teacher, with his assistants, taught on the ground floor, while the reading teacher and his assistants worked on the floor above. During the morning half the children were busy studying writing, while the other half were engaged in learning to read. At noon these groups would exchange places for the remainder of the day. It was not long before other communities adopted this plan, and the "elementary school" became a reality—a combination of the reading school and the writing school.

Although this school was primarily for boys, in some places girls were allowed to attend when the boys were working in the fields during the summer months. In other areas the boys were taught in the downstairs rooms and the girls confined to the upstairs.

This elementary school accepted pupils around seven years of age and expected them to be familiar with the rudiments of spelling and reading. This training was usually left to the parents or private teachers. Feeling that the latter were not preparing children adequately, the Boston School Committee, in 1818, appropriated $5,000 and appointed the Primary School Committee to establish schools for children between the ages of four and seven. The first of these primary schools was opened in 1819, separate from the elementary schools and under its own board. As the need increased, other schools of this type were established.

The final step in lacing all early education together into a system came in 1848, when the Quincy Grammar School was erected, a handsome two-story, twelve-room structure, designed to house a primary school, a reading school, and a writing school. John D. Philbrick was the principal. Four rooms housed the primary school, divided into four grades with a teacher for each. The other two areas, reading and writing, were graded in four rooms with a teacher for each grade. Here, at last, was an eight-grade school with the first four grades devoted to primary or basic subjects and skills and the second four years combining reading and writing. In 1855 this structure was adopted for all elementary schools. Pupils were promoted every half-year, as they progressed from the primary through the grammar school. That same year the special Primary Committee was disbanded and the whole system placed under the Boston School Committee.

Large cities and towns of the United States gradually adopted the Boston plan, and the eight-year elementary school became standard. In smaller communities and in the South, the practice of grading and the fusion of all schools concerned with early education had to be adjusted to conditions. Where there were few pupils or where teachers were difficult to obtain, the one-teacher school was continued. Where textbooks were scarce, it was impossible to grade subject matter. In the South, a seven-year school became normal, and classes were often combined when pupils were few.

The elementary school was not, in its original conception, thought of as preparatory to higher stages of learning. It aimed to give the child an elementary education sufficient for his needs, as a citizen in nineteenth century American society. It accepted him at five, six, or seven years of age, and usually "graduated" him at fourteen. This age, fourteen, was adopted from the German system and was the age at which the boy was confirmed by the church. During these years he received a common school education.

OTHER STEPS

By the middle of the nineteenth century, a graded elementary school organized as an educational ladder of seven or eight steps was fairly general throughout the United States. It was the opinion of most people that the completion of this work was all the education the masses of the population needed. Other schools, including the high school and college, were independent institutions serving only a small segment of the people. The high school accepted boys, or girls, at about twelve or thirteen years of age, prepared them for commercial pursuits, and graduated them into their chosen occupations three or four years later. While most high schools did require that the applicant for admission be able to read and write, have a knowledge of English grammar, and understand simple arithmetic, they designated no particular school as the accepted place for this preparation.

About the middle of the century, some high schools, especially in Massachusetts, established the practice of basing their entrance examinations on subjects taught in the elementary school. After the Civil War entrance examinations for high school admission were abandoned and children accepted upon the presentation of evidence that they had completed the elementary school work satisfactorily. These moves served to impose the high school directly upon the elementary school, no attempt being made to correlate the two institutions. In some instances elementary schools began looking at their curricula in the light of high school acceptance. The only immediate change resulting from this practice was to change the average age of high school entrance from twelve to fourteen or fifteen years, the age when most children completed the elementary school.

Another step toward realizing a complete educational ladder was taken when the high school began thinking of itself as a college preparatory institution. This was not the original intent of the high school. First the Latin grammar school and then the Academy served to fit boys for college. Since the high school curriculum did not include Latin or Greek, basic subjects for college admission, it could not hope to compete with either.

Very early, conditions arose that made it impossible for certain high schools to ignore the colleges. The prestige enjoyed by Latin grammar schools influenced some high schools to adopt part of the former's college preparatory curriculum in order to gain respectability. In communities which did not have a Latin grammar school, the high school came to serve the dual purpose of college preparation and training for mercantile pursuits. A move was made in 1826 to convert the Latin grammar school in Plymouth, Massachusetts, into a high school in which both classical languages and a practical English education would be available. In the 1830s, several communities, including Lowell, Massachusetts, and Portland, Maine, established high schools offering an English education and at the same time preparing boys for college. By 1850, the high school had become in fact a college preparatory institution, struggling desperately to maintain its status as a school for training boys in the practical activities of life. Gradually, two distinct courses appeared in the high school curriculum: the English course and the classical course.

Although high schools were offering courses needed for college entrance, it was some time before colleges gave attention to this fact. They continued to hold entrance examinations in Latin and Greek for all students applying. Many colleges had turned to written examinations by 1860, and were expanding these to include the subjects offered in the better high schools. Then, in 1870, the president of the University of Michigan proposed that graduates of approved high schools be exempt from entrance examinations. He suggested that a faculty committee be designated to inspect high schools and determine which should be so approved. His idea was accepted by many colleges throughout the country, and committees were busy inspecting and approving or rejecting high schools. The "approved list of high schools" soon became general, and institutions hastened to readjust their curricula in line with the demands of colleges. Here began a practice that was later challenged in many quarters—the domination of high schools by college interests rather than those of the student.

By 1900, the United States had built its educational ladder, an articulated pattern of instruction beginning with the ABC's and ending with a college education. This education was free to all who could meet the intellectual standards. While most colleges charged tuition, state institutions were appearing in ever-increasing numbers to offer tax-supported college and professional preparation to all who could qualify.

The completion of the educational ladder awaited the development of the kindergarten and its inclusion in the public school system. It is interesting to note that the first introduction of the kindergarten into the public school system took place during the 1870s. Now, just 100 years later, a movement is gaining ground to include preschool (early childhood education) into the public-supported educational program.

STRENGTHENING THE EDUCATIONAL LADDER

When Charles W. Eliot, president of Harvard University, addressed the department of superintendents of the National Education Association in Washington in 1888, he asked the question, "Can School Programmes be Shortened and Enriched?" This challenged educators at all levels to rethink the nation's educational structure and consider reforms that changing conditions demanded. Eliot was particularly concerned with the fact that young people were entering college at or near nineteen years of age and graduating around twenty-three. He contrasted this with the fact that the European systems graduated their young people three to five years earlier. At the annual meeting of the National Education Association in 1890, he returned to this issue in an address, "The Gap Between the Elementary Schools and the Colleges." He pointed to the inefficiencies rampant in both the elementary and the high school.

As a result of the questions raised in the minds of educators by Eliot's repeated attacks upon the educational ladder, the Association, in 1892, appointed a *Committee of Ten,* with Eliot as chairman, to study elementary and high schools and make recommendations for improvement. The committee chose nine subject-matter areas taught in the high school and organized subcommittees of ten experts each to study these areas and recommend necessary revisions in the method of teaching, the placement of the subject, and the length of time it should be given in the curriculum. All members of these committees were college professors, subject-matter specialists.

The Committee of Ten took all the recommendations of the subcommittees and correlated them into a report dealing with the American school system from the first grade through the high school. Their report to the Association, published in 1893, was based on the theory of mental discipline and concerned mainly with developing a uniform curriculum for admission to college. It was cautious and conservative.

Although many of the recommendations of this committee appear unjustified today, they did stimulate wide discussion, which resulted in many changes in the American school pattern. The committee held that some subjects should be taught earlier in the child's development. It felt that commercial and industrial subjects had no place in a college preparatory program. At the same time, it stressed the need for greater attention to English and history and recommended that all sciences include laboratory work.

To shorten the time spent in college preparation, the committee recommended that the four-year, lock-step curriculum of the high school be abandoned in favor of a credit system. In this way brighter pupils could accumulate the credits necessary for college entrance in a shorter time. It also recommended that summer schools be organized to allow these better pupils to move through the high school more rapidly.

This report triggered considerable controversy and many changes in the high school program. It also caused some to raise the question of the purpose of a high school education—was it to prepare young people for college or to meet their needs as citizens of the community? The report had clearly espoused college entrance.

In 1893, the National Education Association set up a *Committee of Fifteen* specifically charged with studying the elementary school in terms of organization, coordination of subjects, and teacher preparation. The report of this group stressed the need for allowing more flexibility for gifted children so that they might move ahead faster than the average.

To continue the study of the nation's educational structure, the Association organized the *Committee on College Entrance Requirements* to further standardize college entrance procedures. It recommended in 1899 that college preparation be confined to Latin, Greek, French, German, English, history, civics and economics, geography, mathematics, biology, and chemistry. Although the committee approved the elective system, since no student could be prepared in all the subjects recommended, it leaned heavily toward foreign languages. This is seen in its pattern of "constants": four years of foreign language, two years of mathematics, two years of English, one year of history, and one year of science.

The committee further recommended that all studies be equated. This was approval of the *Committee of Ten's* position that "all subjects are of equal educational value if taught equally well." In line with this position the committee suggested that if a student studied a subject four hours a week for one school year, he should be granted one unit of credit toward college admission. Ten of these units, it proposed, should be required as indicated above and the other six chosen from approved subjects.

PRIVATE COLLEGES AND THE STATES

INTRODUCTION

The first colleges in America were modeled after those of England, small institutions offering some literary training in the humanistic tradition, as well as morality and religious indoctrination. Only two colleges were established during the seventeenth century: Harvard and William and Mary. From the opening of the eighteenth century until the Revolutionary War, seven colleges were organized: Yale, Princeton, Pennsylvania, Columbia, Brown, Rutgers, and Dartmouth. All of these, save Pennsylvania, owed their allegiance to Protestant churches. Between 1780 and the close of the eighteenth century, eighteen new colleges were created. Of these, only eight were church motivated, while six were nonsectarian and four were state institutions.

These statistics indicate that new forces were becoming formative in the area of higher education. The religion-centered college was giving way to institutions with a more liberal attitude toward Christian doctrine. The newer colleges were religious, many training young men for missionary service, but their approach to religion was becoming less formal and restrictive. Creedal requirements for admission were being dropped, and complete religious liberty was becoming a practice on many campuses. States were entering the picture, providing higher education for their citizens at public expense. The nonsectarian and the state-supported colleges reflected a keen concern for the separation of church and state in the wake of increasing diversity in religious beliefs.

More than fifty new colleges and universities were established during the first quarter of the nineteenth century. Many of these were in the South and West, reflecting the fact that large numbers of graduates from eastern colleges were moving into these areas and carrying with them their concern for higher education. Some of these newer colleges were influenced by the agricultural theories of the French Physiocrats and Pestalozzi. Courses in agriculture were to be found in their curricula, some established farms in connection with their campuses, and many students were enabled to earn part of their expenses by working in the fields.

THE DARTMOUTH COLLEGE DECISION

After the Revolutionary War the newly formed states set about creating colleges, or universities, under their support and control, offering higher education more or less free to their citizens. North Carolina provided in its constitution of 1776 for "one or more universities." By 1789, it was able to open its own state university. Vermont, in 1777, made founding a state university part of its constitution. In 1801, Georgia opened its state university, and South Carolina followed in 1805. As states contemplated establishing publicly controlled institutions of higher education, it was logical that some would explore the possibilities of taking over successful private colleges. These private institutions were quasi-public agencies. Some were receiving subsidies from the state, and many had members of the state government sitting on their boards. It seemed logical to many that the state should step in and acquire one or more of these institutions for the educational welfare of all the people. Attempts were made to convert Yale, William and Mary, Pennsylvania, and Columbia into state institutions. Each college fought this move vigorously.

When the state of New Hampshire sought to take over Dartmouth College, a bitter struggle developed. This had significant political overtones. The Jeffersonians dominated the legislature and aimed to wrest control of the college from the Federalists. When the legislature changed the charter of the college to its liking and created the University of New Hampshire, the college administration refused to recognize the new institution. For a time, two colleges existed on the campus.

College authorities brought suit to retain the rights and privileges provided in the original charter granted by George III. The suit was eventually argued before the United States Supreme Court, Daniel Webster representing the college, his *alma mater.* In 1819 Justice John Marshall handed down the court's decision to the effect that a college charter was a contract, protected from invasion under the Constitution. This brought to an end attempts on the part of states to transform independent colleges into state institutions. It gave assurance to those donating funds that their wealth would remain in control of the institution designated. It also forced states to create their own colleges distinct from any pattern already part of the educational tradition. In 1868, New Hampshire established the University of New Hampshire, in no way connected with Dartmouth College.

THE UNIVERSITY MOVEMENT IN AMERICA

BACKGROUND

Until the nineteenth century, little was known in America of the university approach to higher education that Germany had been developing since late in the seventeenth century. A few settlers in German communities, especially in Pennsylvania, were products of German universities, but they had no voice in the development of higher education in this country. What they advocated was considered by most leaders in England and America as "the way to overthrow all colleges, cathedral churches, and places of learning."

The university, in German thinking, was characterized by freedom of investigation and teaching. German universities before the seventeenth century were medieval in outlook and scholastic in philosophy.

They were seats of sterile theological controversies, lacking in intellectual vigor, vitality, or progress. The Pietistic movement inspired Elector Frederick of Brandenburg to establish the University of Halle in 1694, "the first modern university." Here freedom of inquiry became a religion. Scholars drawn to the university turned from ancient authorities to investigate the universe as they found it. The teacher was a scholar adding to man's knowledge and leading his students to explore the unknown with him. Authoritative texts were abandoned for free discovery. University students were thought of as mature men free to do research, to think and challenge. Any limits that might be placed on these activities were believed to be destructive of the true purpose of a university.

As this approach to higher education grew in Germany, creative scholars became associated with the great universities that developed: Jena, Berlin, Heidelberg, Konigsberg, and others. In contrast, Roger Ascham's attempt to introduce research at Cambridge in England was bitterly opposed by the established church, forcing scholars such as Bacon, Locke, Darwin, Spencer, and Mill, to do their work outside the college community.

German universities looked to the gymnasium and other secondary schools to prepare young men for study and research at the college level. While England turned over the study of law and medicine to the apprenticeship system and offered in its colleges the A.B. degree in the liberal arts, German universities prepared students for the doctorate in medicine, law, philosophy, and theology. Here was graduate education as distinguished from undergraduate. These universities proposed to prepare investigators, scholars, thinkers, not mere technical experts or schoolmasters. Their faculties were staffed with specialists, not tutors, men elected not because of their ability to impart knowledge but because of their ability to push back the frontiers of knowledge. A student did not attend the university to "sit under" a teacher but to "work with" an innovator. He listened to lectures and read books, but his main purpose was to learn how to move freely and productively along the outer edges of knowledge.

DISCOVERING THE GERMAN UNIVERSITY

When Madame de Stael's *On Germany* came to the attention of George Ticknor in 1814, it fired him with a desire to visit Prussia and see for himself the universities she pictured. Finding no teacher of German in Boston, he had to dig out the language himself from a dictionary borrowed from a friend in New Hampshire. By 1835, when an English translation of Victor Cousin's *Rapport sur l'Etat de l'In-*

struction Publique en Prusse (Report on the State of Public Education in Prussia) appeared, many leading educators were ready to look to the German university for suggestions for bettering American higher education. This was followed by significant reports from American educators who visited Germany in an effort to understand what was happening there in the entire field of education: Horace Mann, Henry Barnard, Calvin Stowe, and others. During the nineteenth century an increasing number of American students enrolled in German universities—Gottingen, Berlin, Halle, Leipzig, Konigsberg—and returned home inspired with a desire to do research, think independently, and create in their homeland replicas of these centers of intellectual freedom. To hold a degree from one of these German universities gave one added respect in academic circles and assured him a choice professorship in colleges beginning to think in terms of freedom in study and teaching. Meanwhile, many German scholars were added to the faculties of American colleges; these were men able to represent the finest scholars from their native universities.

TAPPAN AT THE UNIVERSITY OF MICHIGAN

Among those who visited Germany during the nineteenth century, studied in German universities, and returned determined to reconstruct American higher education along lines pioneered in Germany were several who became presidents of American colleges. One was Henry P. Tappan, a graduate of Union College in New York State, who spent some time in Germany and recounted his experiences, along with his views on higher education, in *University Education,* published in 1851.

Tappan was convinced that the colleges in the American East were too wedded to the English tradition of general education to tolerate the German university idea. Consequently, he was eager to accept an invitation to become president of the University of Michigan in 1852. There the public school system had felt the impact of Victor Cousin's thinking, and founders of the university were convinced that their new institution "could be built only as an inseparable part, and a living member of a system of public instruction," "the culmination of a grand system of Education."

Tappan set about to create at Michigan "an association of scholars for scientific and educational purposes." By 1863, when he left the presidency of Michigan, this university had become the leading state university of the West, imitated by others that were taking shape.

THE CONTROVERSY

The work of Tappan at Michigan, and of others seeking to transform American higher education along German lines, stirred advocates of the English college idea to a vigorous defense of their position. This controversy reached a climax with the inauguration of Charles W. Eliot as president of Harvard in 1869. By this time the issues had become clear. Students were demanding that colleges offer preparation for secular vocations. Modern languages, applied sciences, and social studies were gaining in popularity, and pressures to give them a more prominent place in the college curriculum were increasing. Professional training could no longer be assigned to the apprentice system, and colleges were being urged to undertake this preparation. The German ideal of creative research was challenging traditional college orthodoxy. These developments brought into sharp relief the question as to which should dominate higher education in America—the traditional college or the university.

Impressed by the success of the university idea at Michigan and by the increasing numbers of students attending those institutions that had made provision for newer courses and practices, a number of college presidents advocated reforms. Among these were Andrew Dickson White at Cornell, Frederick A. P. Barnard at Columbia, Daniel Coit Gilman at Johns Hopkins, David Starr Jordan at Leland Stanford, and William Rainey Harper at Chicago. These men struggled to reshape their institutions to imitate more closely the Prussian example.

Their efforts were challenged vigorously by those who felt that they were destroying all that was good and wholesome in higher education. Chief among the champions of tradition was Noah Porter, soon to become president of Yale. In *The American College and the American People,* he attacked every proposal of the university group and pleaded for retention of that which had been proved good in the past. He espoused the fixed curriculum, the study of Latin, Greek, and mathematics, the lock-step four-year-class system, the textbook method of instruction, common dormitories, rigid supervision of student life, institutional religion, the college tutor, and strict segregation of boys and girls. He believed that should any of these practices be abandoned, the culture of the people would be so radically changed that "the existence of this country as a country" would be threatened.

Porter was answered by Andrew Ten Brooks, a member of the Michigan faculty, in *History of the American State University.* Brooks sought to show that the state university built along German lines was a natural capstone to a public school system and a necessary unit in the American educational ladder. He envisioned the child starting in a free public school that aimed to meet his needs as a citizen of a democracy, progressing by clearly marked steps through the elementary school, the grammar school, and into the high school and graduation. From there he saw the better minds moving into higher education and on to the frontiers of knowledge. He felt that the secondary schools of America should prepare young people for work in the university and that the university should prepare them for the professions and for self-motivated research.

THE NEW UNIVERSITY

Both sides in this controversy had merit. Gradually it became evident that neither the English college nor the Prussian university was suited to American culture. Each had a contribution to make, and each did contribute to the making of higher education in America.

The narrow, set curriculum of a few subjects was abandoned in favor of a pattern incorporating both elective and prescribed courses. Many newer subjects, including English, modern languages, the physical sciences, and the social studies, were introduced, along with more traditional subjects, as constituents of a liberal education. The small college was giving way to the large university with its laboratories, research centers, and professional schools. Secularism gradually forced the religious life of the campus into its "proper" position in a democratic society. Strict supervision of student life gave way to greater freedom as students became more mature and able to discipline themselves.

COEDUCATION

One of the more significant phases of the revolution that was taking place in higher education in America was concerned with the advanced education of women. The common school had made basic education available to girls as well as boys. High schools and colleges had no place for "females," and most people looked with horror at the possibility that they might demand more education.

As the nineteenth century opened, signs of a feminine revolution were beginning to appear. Sara Josepha Hale published the *Lady's Magazine* and eventually edited *Godey's Lady's Book.* Women were branching out from school-keeping to work in the mills, shops, and offices. In response to this change in "woman's function," Emma Hart Willard, a gifted woman, author of *Rocked in the Cradle of the Deep,* in 1807 opened a seminary for girls at Middlebury, Vermont. In 1821 she founded the Troy Female Academy. She held that while the majority of women would become housewives and mothers, they had a right to an education reaching beyond the niceties of the "finishing school." Catherine Beecher, sister of Henry Ward Beecher and Harriet Beecher Stowe, published in 1842 a *Treatise on Domestic Economy* designed to put the vocation of "housewifery" in teachable form. In 1828 she opened the Female Seminary in Hartford, Connecticut. Since her methods and goals were far ahead of the times, she was forced to close the institution and devote her energies to writing and lecturing in the interest of women's rights.

Mary Lyons, a child of poor parents who had been able to attend a female academy only by working for her keep and tuition, determined to develop a college for middle-class women equal to the best available to men. In 1837 she opened Mount Holyoke Female Seminary in Massachusetts. She stressed intellectual attainment, kept free from social "dalliance," and allowed the domestic subjects to serve poor girls who might use this knowledge to help pay their way in college. Here was a true college for women.

Slowly, since opposition to the education of women beyond the common school was severe, colleges for women were appearing, especially in the West and South. In 1836, the Georgia Female College was opened in Macon, Georgia. Others, often small and of little consequence, were founded and began conferring degrees on their graduates. In 1833, Oberlin College was opened in Oberlin, Ohio, with coeducation as its major innovation. When Horace Mann became president of Antioch College, he instituted coeducation at that institution. The West moved rapidly toward coeducation in both its private and state institutions for two reasons: it was socially sound as well as a source of increased revenue.

Eastern institutions resisted coeducation but eventually permitted establishment of colleges for women alongside or nearby colleges for men. Barnard College at Columbia, Radcliffe College at Harvard, and Sophie Newcomb College at Tulane were concessions to women on the part of institutions not ready to accept women on the same intellectual level as men.

THE GRADUATE SCHOOL

With the university came the idea of graduate study, a period of advanced work beyond the bachelor's degree. Feeble attempts to move along orthodox lines toward a higher degree were made early in the nineteenth century. As a result of a gift from the English philosopher George Berkeley, Yale, in 1814, boasted a small group of students who carried their education beyond the standard degree requirements, but the college did not confer its first doctorate until 1861. Stepping out rather ambitiously in its first moves to become a university in the German tradition, Michigan in the 1850s offered a "University Course" of some twenty subjects. This attracted a small number of students during the latter half of the century. Although Harvard made some exploratory attempts at graduate work in the early years of the century, it was not until Eliot became president that true graduate work was available there.

All these so-called "graduate schools" were in fact mere appendages of undergraduate colleges, subject to their tradition and imitative of their methods and ideals. The first true school for graduate study along German lines was Johns Hopkins University, opened in Baltimore, Maryland, in 1876 under the presidency of Daniel Coit Gilman. This was a new institution free from past tradition, unhampered by college thinking, and with adequate backing to insure research and creative scholarship. Gilman was a passionate apostle of the German university concept. There he was able to show the American educational community how a true university should and could function in the intellectual growth of the nation. Between 1882 and 1888, G. Stanley Hall, who had done graduate work at Bonn and Berlin, taught psychology and pedagogics at Johns Hopkins University. In 1888, he was chosen president of Clark University. Before assuming office he returned to Germany, and for nine months studied the advances made there in university education. Then, for thirty years, he was the center of a small but highly select group of inquiring minds who were possessed of the German university spirit. They concentrated many of their efforts in the fields of genetic psychology and education and contributed heavily to modern advances in these areas. Clark became known throughout the country as one of the freest centers for research scholars in America.

The University of Chicago, founded in 1892, launched into a program of graduate study that soon made it one of the nation's most noted centers of advanced instruction and research.

In Conclusion

The nineteenth century college was a replica of the English college, little better than a good secondary school. Stimulated by changing social and economic conditions and by the concept of the German university, the nation's educators battled to decide whether tradition or change would dominate higher education. From this came the American university. It developed into a great educational complex under one broad administration with each unit enjoying a high degree of independence.

The center of this pattern was the liberal arts college, humanistic in outlook and aiming to teach maturing youth the knowledge that had been handed down from the past. Above this was the graduate school, offering advanced work leading to the master's and doctor's degrees and demanding original research and free exploration. Around these were grouped a number of professional schools, aiming to prepare young men to serve these areas effectively. Each professional school set its own standards in terms of the demands of the area served. Students were admitted with a minimum of college training or with a full college background, this being governed by conditions within the profession. Degrees were developed in each professional school to designate the individual's status in terms of competency, and were only loosely related to degrees in other colleges or schools of the complex.

This pattern of university organization is a natural cause of academic antagonisms. Students of a graduate school, with its insistence upon research and exact scholarship, have difficulty in being civil to colleagues in professional schools who are concerned with employment, service, and effectiveness outside academic walls.

The American university is like nothing else in the world. It is a product of American life and need. It has taken from the colleges, universities, and secondary schools of Europe but has woven all into a truly American institution serving the divergent needs of a dynamic society.

FEDERAL CONCERN FOR EDUCATION

A Continuing Controversy

Although the general principle of state education was accepted throughout the country, repeated attempts were made during the nineteenth century to involve the federal government in schools at all levels. States were willing, and often anxious, to receive federal funds for strengthening their school structures, but feared federal control. At the same time, sentiment favoring more federal participation in education was reflected in bills introduced in Congress during the later years of the century. In 1870, Representative George F. Hoar of Massachusetts introduced a bill compelling the states to establish an efficient system of schools. Those failing to meet nationally determined standards were to be placed under the control of a federally-appointed superintendent of schools and his inspectors and taxed by the federal government for the support of their schools. This would have meant in effect a federal system of education and federal interference in any state failing to measure up to national criteria. The bill was opposed by powerful forces and did not come to a vote. In the same year, the Perce bill in the House and the Burnsides bill in the Senate provided for the use of income from the sale of public lands for education. Though both bills passed their respective houses, neither could be carried through both houses.

Senator Henry W. Blair of New Hampshire tried five times during the 1880s to persuade Congress to pass a bill granting states aid from federal funds for better schools, but failed on each occasion. His bills had the support of labor, some business groups, the Republican Party, many Protestant churches, and the National Education Association, but were opposed by private and parochial schools, especially those under Catholic administration, the Democrats, and several colleges.

THE GOVERNMENT AND SPECIAL EDUCATION

No one questioned the right of the federal government to support and control education for national defense. In 1802, a military academy was founded at West Point under the exclusive control of Congress. A similar institution for training naval officers was established at Annapolis in 1845. It was taken for granted that the federal government would educate its wards as part of its obligation to care for them. Thus there was little or no opposition to placing the education of the Indians under the Office of Indian Affairs in the Department of Interior. The work of the Freedmen's Bureau in educating former slaves was generally accepted as a function of the federal government.

Responding to advances in technology and the growing need for general dispersal of newer ideas and techniques in the area of agriculture, Senator Justin Morrill of Vermont sponsored a bill in 1859 proposing to award 20,000 acres of public land to each state for each of its congressmen to endow a college "to teach some branches of learning as are related to agriculture and the mechanic arts." President Buchanan vetoed the bill. In 1862, Morrill reintroduced the bill with significant changes. He raised the grant from 20,000 to 30,000 acres and included military science and tactics as required studies. President Lincoln saw in the bill a means of obtaining needed officer material for his war against the South, and signed it into law. This was the beginning of the "land grant colleges." Some states established new agricultural and mechanical colleges under the grant, while others used the income to strengthen their faltering state universities. Altogether more than eleven and a half million acres of land were distributed to forty-eight states, Alaska, Hawaii, and Puerto Rico.

FEDERAL DEPARTMENT OF EDUCATION

As the federal government became more involved in education, the need for some centralizing agency to administer phases of the program and serve as a clearing house for information became evident. In 1867, under the prodding of Henry Barnard and others, Congress created the Department of Education, and Barnard was chosen as its first commissioner. Fearing that this might prove to be the initial move toward federal control of education, many states objected vigorously and effected a compromise by which the office was reduced from a separate department of government to a branch of the Department of Interior. In 1870 it became the Bureau of Education. In 1930 its name was changed to the Office of Education. Nine years later it was incorporated into the Federal Security Agency. Eventually it was made a part of the Department of Health, Education, and Welfare. In spite of its many changes in name and affiliation, its function has remained fairly constant: to collect statistical data, conduct research, and disseminate information concerning the status and progress of American education.

EDUCATIONAL PHILOSOPHIES DURING THE NINETEENTH CENTURY

A CHANGING PICTURE

At the beginning of the nineteenth century, the United States looked to Europe for most of its philosophical orientation. As the century continued, European importations came under more careful scrutiny, while the nation began to assert its individuality and create new ideas and institutions that in time would influence Europe. During the first half of the century, French humanitarianism served to strengthen American democracy. English individualism and technological development were felt, especially by the middle classes. German idealism and transcendental philosophy were attractive to many.

After the Civil War, a spirit of nationalism began to be felt in many quarters, and the conviction grew that the nation had become mature enough to break with Europe intellectually and create its own patterns of thought. Since America was a melting pot of many European cultures, it was natural that it would incorporate much from each and that its distinctive culture would reflect this background.

REALISM AND MODERN SCIENCE

The idealism of the early nineteenth century came under heavy attack by those interested in advances in biological and physical sciences. Humanism, the classics, speculations so rewarding to the idealists, all seemed so much wasted effort to a people fascinated by material success in a society so recently characterized by the open frontier and now beginning to feel the certainty of modern industry. Realism was winning over idealism, and the security of science was more to be desired than arid speculation. A group of English scholars contributed to this development in America.

CHARLES ROBERT DARWIN (1809-1882)

Theories of the relationship of the parts to the whole are as old as man's thinking. The human mind is uncomfortable in a universe of discreteness and demands some pattern of oneness. The orthodox belief that God created all forms of life as unique individuals had been under attack for generations, and theories of evolution had received some attention. Hegel proposed a theory of cosmic evolution when he suggested that the universe is mind unfolding itself. Froebel's concept of "panentheism" was in this same idealistic tradition.

Although Hegelian creative evolution dominated much of philosophy during the nineteenth century and influenced the course of German nationalism, it was far too speculative for the scientific mind of the age. It lacked what the scientist treasured most, objective confirmation. Sir Charles Lyell's *Principles of Geology,* published between 1830 and 1833, suggested the theory that remains of life forms found in various strata of the earth's surface are evidence of an evolutionary process. The scientific mind could accept this as objective.

Then, in 1859, Darwin published his *On the Origin of Species by Means of Natural Selection, or the Preservation of Favored Races in the Struggle for Life.* This was the result of years of study and observation, including five years as a naturalist on the *Beagle.* In June of 1858 he had received from A. R. Wallace, then a Ternate in the Moluccas, a manuscript for his criticism. This proved to be "a complete abstract of his own theory of natural selection." After much consultation between Wallace, Darwin, Lyell and other scientists, it was decided that the *Origin of Species* be published as planned. Wallace had called the process "the struggle for existence," while Darwin called it "the survival of the fittest."

This work caused a revolution in human thinking. While it was condemned bitterly by the orthodox in both religion and science, it was evident that man had set out on a new avenue to the understanding of his universe. Almost every field of study was forced to revise its thinking. Since this theory provided man with a new approach to the nature of the child and his development, it reached deeply into education, challenging many of the earlier approaches to instruction.

Darwin published two other works, which have become scientific classics, developing more completely his original premises. These are *The Variation of Animals and Plants Under Domestication, 1868,* and *Descent of Man and Selection in Relation to Sex, 1871.*

The work of Darwin not only provided modern thought with a theory of evolution upon which it could build its house, but also it showed that the method of careful, unbiased observation could yield evidence that could not be challenged. It placed man squarely in the stream of material cause and effect and released his mind from the shackles of superstition and supernaturalism. With Darwin, science had won its battle against the past and was free now to attack the frontiers of knowledge confidently.

HERBERT SPENCER (1820-1903)

Spencer aimed to become the philosopher of the scientific movement in the nineteenth century. His friendship with many of the leading thinkers of the age gave him considerable insight into what was happening. Against this background he strove to express in a general formula the belief in progress that pervaded his age and to erect it into the supreme law of the universe.

His most notable contribution to education was contained in *Education, Intellectual, Moral, and Physical,* published in 1861. In this book he took the position that psychology is the only solid basis for a complete and exact pedagogy. "Education will not be definitely systematized," he wrote, "till the day when science shall be in possession of a rational psychology." The first chapter is entitled *What Knowledge Is of Most Worth?* In answering this question he asserted that the worth of any education must be determined by its function in preparation for complete living. In the modern world the knowledge of greatest value is that which one can verify for himself and use to solve his own problems. This is the knowledge given man through the sciences and the scientific method.

When Spencer attempted to apply this thesis to actual human experience, he was forced to analyze the activities in which man engages. These fell into five classes: (1) self-preservation, (2) securing the necessities of life, (3) rearing and disciplining of children, (4) maintaining proper social and political relations, and (5) leisure time occupations. To Spencer, this was also the order of their importance. An examination of these categories of activities convinced him that the traditional humanistic and classical education was useless and that only the sciences could prepare one to live effectively in all these areas.

The essay attained general popularity and was used in normal schools, teachers' institutes, and universities as a basic text in teacher training. In both the United States and England it enjoyed a status in educational circles accorded no other book of the generation. Its effect was to strengthen the instrumentalist or utilitarian philosophy of education. It placed the Darwinian faith in objective study and evaluation squarely in the field of education and helped lay the foundations for the philosophy of John Dewey.

THOMAS HENRY HUXLEY (1825-1875)

Born at Ealing, son of a schoolmaster, Huxley was self-taught. "I had," he tells us, "two years of a pandemonium of a school (between eight and ten) and after that neither help nor sympathy in any intellectual direction until I reached manhood." He was possessed of an insatiable curiosity and read widely. At seventeen, he began the study of medicine at Charing Cross Hospital graduating in 1854 at the age of twenty, and was admitted to the Royal College of Surgeons. As surgeon on *H.M.S. Rattlesnake* he made many biological observations and published papers in leading scientific journals. He was made a Fellow of the Royal Society in 1851.

He became convinced that the only sure method of discovery was inductive, and turned against deductive thinking. His studies led him to a belief in certain relationships between living things, but never to a clear theory of evolution. Herbert Spencer, with whom he became acquainted in 1852, was unable to convert him to evolution in its widest sense. In his first interview with Darwin, Huxley attempted to defend the belief that there is a sharp line of "demarcation between natural groups." Darwin is reported to have received his arguments "with a humorous smile."

Not only was Huxley a physician and a scientist, but he was also a devoted public servant, accepting civic responsibilities often to the detriment of his own research. Between 1862 and 1884 he served on ten Royal Commissions; from 1871 to 1880 he was secretary of the Royal Society and was its president from 1881 to 1885; and from 1870 to 1872 he was a member of the newly constituted London school board.

In this latter position he was able to make a contribution to elementary education by attacking scholastic methods and advocating an education that would prepare children "to take their place worthily in the community." This education, he argued, should include physical training, domestic "economy," drawing and singing to develop one's aesthetic sense, reading, writing, arithmetic, the physical sciences, and the Bible, which he called "the most democratic book in the world." He held that all sciences should be taught by the laboratory method.

Huxley could never be called a great scientist. His function was to popularize scientific knowledge. His posts of public service gave him ample opportunity to speak with authority in favor of the scientific approach. As a member of the London school board, he could champion a school structure "from the gutter to the university" and advocate the scientific approach at each level.

In *Science and Education,* he attempted to define clearly his conception of both science and education, pointing to the German university as much superior in research and academic freedom to anything in England. "As for works of profound research on any subject ... a third-rate, poverty-stricken German university turns out more produce of that kind in one year than our vast and wealthy foundations elaborate in ten," he charged. Referring to Grote, Mill, Faraday, Robert Brown, Lyle, and Darwin, Huxley concluded that "these men are what they are in virtue of their native intellectual force, and of a strength of character which will not recognize impediments. They are not trained in the courts of the Temple of Science."

In his defense of a scientific education he drew the thesis that "for the purpose of attaining real culture, an exclusively scientific education is at least as effectual as an exclusively literary education." Holding to this position, he believed that both scientific and literary studies were necessary for the truly educated man.

IMPACT ON AMERICA

Darwin, Spencer, and Huxley were Englishmen who developed within the English culture, though not necessarily in the English educational structure. They attacked the humanistic, classical education that had become solidly entrenched in their native land and that looked with disdain upon the claims of the sciences. They and their ideas about education were feared by most leaders of English thought.

In America these men found fertile soil for their point of view. Here was a democratic approach to schooling and a growing willingness to look at new ideas and incorporate them into the intellectual life of the nation. Traditional religion with its supernaturalism was being challenged successfully by Unitarianism, which had appeared very early in the century at Harvard. While William E. Channing was preaching that religion was not so much dogma and theology as ethical living, other Unitarians were urging their constituents to improve social conditions, champion social movements, and join in reform as a means of showing their Christianity.

When the theory of evolution appeared, it found many prepared to look at it scientifically and seek to adjust its implications to Christianity. Philip Schaff at Union Theological Seminary, Orello Cone at St. Lawrence University, and ministers of leading liberal churches— Henry Ward Beecher, Phillips Brooks, Washington Gladden, Lyman Abbott, and John Fish—actively supported the position that any religious belief that could not stand the searching study of a scientific mind was not suitable to the needs of man in this new age. Their position was attacked by the fundamentalists, and for more than a century the battle has raged from many American pulpits.

Meanwhile, there were appearing in America philosophers, psychologists, and scientists who challenged Hegelian idealism and developed the implications of evolution in the fields of ethics, political theory, history, economics, and social thinking. Out of this came a new philosophy, called pragmatism, for interpreting the world in terms of the new scientific outlook. Pragmatism looked at the universe as in the progress of evolving and at truth as dependent upon the consequences of men's actions. Education was interpreted as depending not on the authority of the past but rather on its ability to accomplish what is desired. John Dewey developed the implications of this pragmatic thesis in his philosophy of experimentalism or, as some would have it, instrumentalism.

It was in America rather than England that the work of Darwin, Spencer, and Huxley was understood and appreciated. With the rise of the graduate school and its allegiance to the German university concept, America was prepared to accept evolution with all its implications as a guide to thought and research. Darwin, Spencer, and Huxley were intellectually at home on American soil.

GRANVILLE STANLEY HALL (1846-1924)

Of the many scholars and educators in nineteenth century America to feel the effects of Darwin, Spencer, and Huxley and the German university ideal and to translate both into the American idiom, Hall was most debatable. Creative, adventurous, scholarly, and daring, he remains enigmatic. He wrote widely and significantly, gathered around him several who made telling contributions to man's understanding of himself, and traced in bold outline research that those who have followed him are yet working to complete. We are not prepared at this time to give a definitive answer to the question of his place in the history of American education.

HIS LIFE

Hall was born at Ashfield, Massachusetts, February 1, 1846, of Puritan parents who, though cultured and intellectually inclined, saw little need for a New England farm boy to waste his time at college. In spite of his parents' attitude, Hall was graduated from Williams College in 1867 and prepared for the ministry at Union Theological Seminary in New York City, from which he graduated in 1871. During his study at Union he was able to spend the greater part of two years studying philosophy and theology at Bonn and Berlin, where he came in contact with the finest of German universities. For the next four years he was a teacher of English literature and philosophy at Antioch College.

He became interested in psychology while at Antioch, and in 1876 resigned to study with William James at Harvard, where in 1878 he was granted the doctorate. From there he returned to Germany to study with Wilhelm Wundt, Hermann Helmholtz, and other noted scholars at Berlin, Bonn, Heidelberg, and Leipzig. These experiences made him familiar with the latest research in theology, philosophy, physiology, anthropology, biology, anatomy, psychology, and neurology, and able to cut across the lines of demarcation between these areas with skill and understanding.

He was professor of psychology at Johns Hopkins University from 1881 to 1888. There he established the first formal psychology laboratory in the United States. Several men destined to become frontiersmen in the fields of psychology and education were attracted to his classes and his laboratory. These included John Dewey, Joseph Jastrow, and J. McKeen Cattell. It was during this period that Hall made his now famous study of *The Contents of Children's Minds on Entering School.*

In 1888 he was elected president of newly formed Clark University. From 1889 to 1919, he engaged in educational and psychological research, teaching a small group of advanced scholars, and creating at Clark a true university in the German meaning of the term. There he developed his culture-epoch theory and wrote his famous study of *Adolescence* (1904). In 1887 he founded the *American Journal of Psychology,* which he edited until 1921, and through which he published many of his most significant papers. Although he resigned from Clark University in 1920, he continued to be active in research and publication until his death in 1924.

EVOLUTION OF THE MIND

Darwin had proved to Hall's satisfaction the evolution of the biological organism from its simplest forms to man. His *Origin of Species* made it necessary for scholars in all fields to rethink their data and place it clearly in the evolutionary process. Psychology, Hall felt, was faced with the problem of tracing the evolution of mental life. This he accepted as his mission, and to it he devoted the major portion of his adult life.

Hall concluded from his research that the development of physical life has been at all times accompanied by developing mind. In the untold millenia of the past when the first living cell took form, there was potentiality for mental behavior. Throughout the years from then until the present, psychic life has been taking shape. He held that hunger is the most primitive cause of activity, creating interest and curiosity. The hungry single cell reaches out for food, and this reaching marks the origin of mental life. So strongly did he believe this that he wrote, "The amoeba has a soul or else man has none."

As higher forms of life appeared, locomotion became more efficient. In time, the nervous system developed and mental life was lifted to a higher plane. This nervous system grew in complexity, cold-blooded reptiles gave way to warm-blooded mammals, and in due time man appeared. As the claw became a hand, the brain developed. The mind, he held, "is handmade." Through this entire process from primaeval ooze to man, mental life evolved along with the body. At various stages in this evolution appeared language, arts, the senses, the emotions, and eventually, in tribal society, the soul of man. This was Hall's theory of genetic psychology, a theory of the evolution of the psyche.

RECAPITULATION AND PSYCHIC EVOLUTION

Time and again, as scholars have studied the universe and man, there have been those who sensed a parallelism between the two. By the eighteenth century it was generally accepted that the human race, from its earliest forms to the present, had developed by stages that can be identified in the life pattern of any individual. Writers referred to the infancy of the race, to its childhood and youth, and finally to maturity passing into old age. The eighteenth century was, to many of these thinkers, the final stage in racial development.

Hall built on this tradition. The individual, he believed, will in his movement from birth to maturity repeat the evolution of the race. The embryo passes through stages of development characteristic of the earliest history of the race. The child, beginning at the moment of birth, repeats the periods of human development from primitive life to the present. Results of all these racial experiences are stored up in the individual and passed on through heredity. This explains man's instincts and impulses. At the earliest stages of growth these were needed to assure proper functioning and prepare for the next stage. Later they become vestigial, fossilized psychic habits, which may reappear in dreams or moments of fancy. Hall attempted to prove that just as the evolving organism retains vestigial organs, so the mind retains mental processes necessary in its past but no longer useful.

THE CHILD STUDY MOVEMENT

Hall's recapitulation theory was part of his more general thesis of child development, a thesis which he developed through the scientific observation and study of the growing individual. He held that to teach the child, one must know him thoroughly. A few studies of children had appeared in the late nineteenth century. Darwin had written his *A Biographical Sketch of an Infant* in 1877. Preyer's *The Mind of the Child* appeared in 1880. It remained for Hall to publish, the same year, the most definitive work on the subject to appear in the century, *Contents of the Child's Mind on Entering School.* Other studies by Hall and his students followed, creating a lively interest in child study, along with the realization that only as we know the child scientifically can we hope to develop curricula and methodology calculated to accomplish our goals.

Hall's major contribution to modern educational psychology was his two-volume work: *Adolescence; Its Psychology and Its Relations to Physiology, Anthropology, Sociology, Sex, Crime, Religion, and Education.* The title itself is evidence of the vastness of the author's ambition. Only a man with Hall's background and familiarity with all the sciences could have written the book. It proved to be epoch-making. The beginnings of the junior high school, changes in secondary school method and curricula, and more understanding attitudes toward adolescents on the part of parents, teachers, and social and religious workers all stem from this book and the studies that it stimulated.

TEACHING THE DEVELOPING CHILD

The child grows by distinct stages that represent eras of racial history. Education must be adapted to each stage to further its most complete unfolding, which is the best preparation for the next stage. *Infancy,* from birth to four, is the stage in which sense organs are most active, physical growth is rapid, and the child develops movements which are basic to self-preservation. *Childhood,* from four to eight, is the stage when imagination dominates. This must be stimulated by rich cultural experiences and freedom to work out the results of this imagination in play. Here the child is a savage living through the stages of myth-making, poetry and legend. *Youth,* from eight to twelve, is the stage in which intellectual powers develop while physical growth slows down. The child needs drill, repetition, ritual, and regimentation as means of stabilizing his character. At this stage he needs clearly defined authority to give him the security and certainty to carry him through the storm and stress of puberty. *Adolescence,* from puberty to full maturity, corresponds to the period of racial maturity. Here regimentation and authority give way to free play of interests. The young person's enthusiasms are to be fed and encouraged to develop to the fullest. Inspiration, appreciation, intuitive understanding, and enrichment are the methods and goals of learning. The individual must see the totality of things rather than concentrate on details. The emotional and intellectual phases of life "must be kept in close contact with each other."

Hall was in the great tradition that understood the educational significance of play. He held that play is in fact a repeating of the early activities of the race and serves to develop controls and skills. It is instinctive and has no conscious end. Early education must include much play, and throughout life the individual must engage in play to restore his energies.

Fancy, imagination, and make-believe are all "the play of the mind." Rather than introduce the very little child to scientific truth, Hall would have him enjoy the riches of fancy and imagination. As the mind plays, it reproduces experiences of the past and creates new experiences. Both serve to enrich the child's religion, morality, and art.

By using these natural factors, the teacher can instruct the child in the same manner as the race has learned. Employing play, imagination, myth, fancy, and sense experiences, he squares learning with racial development and effects the evolution of the mind in much the same way that the body evolves. Teaching the developing child then becomes truly scientific.

Toward a Scientific Philosophy of Education

Hall was a scientist in both method and attitude. He studied the child from every possible angle. He was convinced that all the sciences could help interpret child development and thereby throw light on a science of education. From his studies he drew inferences that served as the roots for a scientific philosophy of education.

All effective education, he believed, must have its foundation in the development of the child. Curriculum, methodology, discipline, environmental factors, goals, and texts must be determined by the capabilities, interests, and activities of the child at a specific stage in his growth. The end must be a well-balanced individual, all sides of whose nature have been given freedom to develop to their fullest.

Hall believed that he had laid the foundations for a truly scientific philosophy of education grounded on known facts about evolution. He made no claim to having completed the work. He saw clearly that his was the function of a pioneer, pushing into new territories, tracing out crude maps, exploring a few places, and directing those of the future to fill in the picture and complete the task he had begun. Many of his cherished ideas and theories have been attacked, and further study has proved some to be unfounded. This would not have disturbed Hall to any significant degree. What would have interested him more would have been the fact that his pioneering work has been carried on by others who have made creative breakthroughs toward an understanding of child development and the correct education to insure a fuller unfolding of the individual child's nature as a contributor to the future of the race.

ISSUES AND ANSWERS

A truly American system of education took shape during the nineteenth century. Discrete schools were built into an educational ladder. The states moved to create their own universities and professional schools as capstones of their free public school structures. The German-type university, concentrating on research and graduate study, appeared. Along with these came basic issues that had to be resolved if the system was to function as part of a democracy. Before the century came to a close the nation had wrestled with these issues and come up with some answers, which were in fact broad statements of policy determining the future of public education in America.

CENTRALIZATION AND LOCALISM IN CONTROL

Localism dominated colonial education. The school was a private or community institution. The law of 1647 sought to encourage local support of schools and brought the colony into the picture only when other agencies failed. As the value of public education became more evident, it was clear that local effort would have to be supplemented by centralized control and administration. As legislatures, responding to growing public pressure and the leadership of perceptive governors and members, began passing laws to effect greater centralization, they were opposed by those championing localism. Thus two approaches to the public school system vied for the voters' allegiance. During the nineteenth century these were incorporated into an administrative structure that took from both and effected a working balance between the two.

As states began to pass laws governing schools and to appropriate money or designate certain revenues for public education, it became necessary to administer these at the state level. In 1812, New York established the first state superintendency of public instruction and appointed Gideon Hawley to the post. Although Hawley worked diligently to bring some order out of the chaotic conditions which characterized education in the state, his office was abolished in 1821 and his duties placed in the office of the secretary of state. In 1854, the superintendency was reconstituted. Meanwhile, other states were organizing state departments of education, headed by superintendents, to enforce school laws, conduct research and make reports, supervise schools, disburse state funds, and establish minimum standards for buildings, curricula, qualifications of teachers, and support. It was generally accepted by the close of the century that state legislatures should pass laws governing the school system within each state and that a department of education administered by a state superintendent should supervise the system and advise the legislature on educational matters.

This did not mean that local control and support would be abolished. Each state granted considerable power to communities and considered state officials responsible for effective use of this power at the local level. Counties elected school boards and county superintendents to see that state provisions were carried out and that local initiative was encouraged. These officials gathered data for the state office, distributed state funds, and aided in determining and collecting school taxes.

As cities grew in size, the states turned over to them considerable authority to fashion and operate their schools. Buffalo, Louisville, Providence, St. Louis, and Springfield, Massachusetts, were among the first to elect school boards and establish the office of city superintendent of schools in the 1830s. Others followed, so that by the end of the century the country had accepted a pattern of school administration centralized in each state, but with considerable responsibility delegated to local boards chosen by the people and to local superintendents, usually designated by the boards. As some communities grew beyond the limits allowing for effective individual supervision, two new elements appeared. The superintendency became a large office staffed by assistant superintendents, experts in the different areas of education, and clerks, all responsible to the superintendent who in turn was responsible to the board. The board had a dual responsibility—to the people who had elected it and to the state under whose laws it functioned. The second new element was the school principal, who was given responsibility for a single building and was accountable to the superintendent.

At the opening of the twentieth century, the American school system had become an institution in which the issue of localism versus centralization had been resolved in a working pattern of divided responsibility. While the national government was barred from any direct interference in state educational matters, the states had assumed their responsibilities under the federal Constitution, as interpreted by the courts, and their own state constitutions. They had more or less strong state boards and skilled state superintendents. State legislatures had passed much intelligent legislation governing public schools. Local communities, including small districts, counties, and cities, had chosen their boards and superintendents under state laws and entrusted to them wide areas of responsibility. These boards had organized their local systems with teachers, administrators, experts, and clerks. This, with some polishing and reorientation due to changing conditions, was the administrative pattern of education carried into the twentieth century and down to the present.

RELIGIOUS SCHOOLS—PUBLIC FUNDS

The first amendment to the Constitution, as interpreted by the courts, established the principle of the separation of church and state. As the public school system developed during the nineteenth century and as increasing amounts of public money were made available for its support and expansion, those interested in religious schools felt that since these institutions were caring for the education of a sector of society's children, they should share in this bounty. Both England and Canada provided for public support of church schools, and it seemed logical to many that the United States should follow their example. Others came to believe that freedom of education would be guaranteed only if public funds were confined to public education, leaving each religious group free to educate its children as it saw fit and was able.

An early decision in this controversy came from New York State. The Free School Society, founded in 1805, and three religious and philanthropic societies, were receiving aid from the state legislature. As Catholics grew in numbers and began founding schools for the education of their children, their leaders turned to the state for assistance. In the early 1840s, Bishop John Hughes appealed to the state for tax funds. Failing to receive support, he proposed to take the matter to the people as an issue in state elections. In 1842, the legislature stated the concensus of the people when it ruled that "no school . . . in which any religious sectarian doctrine or tenet shall be taught . . . shall receive any portion of the school moneys to be distributed."

Massachusetts, in 1855, after a bitter struggle over the issue, ruled that

> all moneys raised by taxation . . . for the support of public schools, and all moneys which may be appropriated by the state for the support of common schools, shall be applied to . . . no other schools than those which are conducted according to law, under the order and superintendence of the authorities of the town or city in which the money is to be expanded. . . . Such money shall never be appropriated to any religious sect for the maintenance, exclusively, of its own schools.

The Illinois constitution of 1870 provided strict prohibitions against ever expending public money "in aid of any church or sectarian purpose." By the close of the century, the people of the United States had considered the issue of public financing of sectarian education carefully, debated it widely and often bitterly, listened to arguments developed and presented by the finest minds and tongues on all sides, and decided that the only way to guarantee a strong, free public educational system for all children, while protecting each religious group in its freedom to educate according to its conscience, was to devote public funds to public schools. The twentieth century was to see this position challenged effectively and the "wall of separation" pierced in many places.

COMPULSORY EDUCATION

The Massachusetts law of 1642 was a compulsory education law, requiring parents or guardians to see that each child received the minimum education. The law of 1647 was a compulsory school maintenance law, requiring that communities maintain schools to which children might go if their parents or guardians wished. Neither required children to attend school. The freedom of the individual to choose both the method of educating his charges and the amount of education beyond the minimum was protected even in colonial days.

Jefferson was convinced that the preservation of a free America rested upon a literate population. Martin Luther had argued that just as the state has the moral authority to draft citizens to defend it, so it must have equal authority to force children to receive an education. The western world came very early to accept Jefferson's thesis, but waited until well into the nineteenth century to implement Luther's position. As American culture demanded better education, and as thousands of immigrants came from all European nations, it became clear to many that some form of compulsory school attendance was necessary to prepare citizens to function effectively in the new society and to assimilate new citizens into the culture.

In 1852 Massachusetts, recognizing that voluntary measures were not adequate, passed the first compulsory school attendance law in the United States. This required that all children between the ages of eight and fourteen attend school twelve weeks out of each year, that six of these weeks be consecutive, and that parents failing to send their children to school be fined. Provision was made for exemption of the very poor, the mentally weak, those receiving adequate instruction elsewhere, and those already sufficiently educated. The law placed in the hands of the selectmen and a "truant officer" the responsibility for determining exemptions and forcing others to comply.

Other states followed the example set by Massachusetts. Those of the industrial East moved quickly to require school attendance. By 1875, Massachusetts had been joined by Connecticut, New York, the territory of Washington, Nevada, and California. The states of the South were the slowest to respond. Of the last twelve states to pass such laws, all were south of the Mason and Dixon line and all but two east of the Mississippi. Each state's law differed from the others, depending on the background of the state. The age for starting school, amount of education required, and methods of enforcement varied. These laws were gradually strengthened by lowering the age of entrance and raising the age of leaving, providing for stricter enforcement, and increasing the number of weeks or months of schooling required. By 1890, Massachusetts was requiring seven and one-half months a year between the ages of eight and fourteen. Ohio had the highest requirement, keeping children in school for twelve years—from six to eighteen.

These laws allowed reasonable exemptions for children who were ill, whose physical or mental condition made it impossible for them to profit from school work, who lived far from the nearest school, or who were receiving adequate instruction elsewhere. The latter exemption provided for attendance at private and parochial schools and for parents adequately prepared to teach their children at home. All laws limiting the right of parents to pick a school other than that under public control have been declared unconstitutional by the United States Supreme Court. The Oregon law, passed in 1922, requiring all children between the ages of eight and eighteen to attend a public school, a clear attempt to destroy parochial schools in that state, was struck down by the Court.

EDUCATION OF AMERICAN BLACKS

From time to time in this text, reference has been made to Negro education in the United States. Because, in general, educational opportunities for Blacks were so dismal prior to 1900, there is little positive that can be said. The history of education of Blacks in America has been of so low a level that it has raised questions of the quality and quantity of their cultural integration. As a result of centuries of slavery, followed by a hundred years of segregation and discrimination, Negro educational progress has been difficult. In many respects, the Negro has been in a cultural no-man's land. Cut off from his own religion, language, and other cultural backgrounds in Africa, he was not accepted on an equal basis in his new environment. He has not been in the mainstream of American life, whether economic, social, or intellectual. Lack of educational opportunity has been in large part responsible for his intolerable situation. There have been limited educational opportunities for the Black man, but these have been given to him as the result of outside forces and do not represent his own concept of an educational system that meets his needs.

NEW ENGLAND

Colonial America recognized that education was not compatible with the institution of slavery. Education of slaves could have resulted in the destruction of the slave system. Thus, any efforts toward educating the Negro were made mostly by individuals or by special philanthropic groups. In the last half of the eighteenth century, the Society for the Propagation of the Gospel in Foreign Parts began working with Southern Negroes. Missionaries sought to raise the level of living of the Blacks, to convert them to Christianity, and to teach them to read and write so that they could study the Bible. One of these humanitarian efforts was a school for Negroes established in Charleston, South Carolina. Missionaries organized the school, but the teachers were Black slaves owned by the Society.

New England did not have extensive contact with slavery. The Puritans favored introducing Negroes to Christianity. John Eliot was a Puritan who first worked with Indians, and then, around 1674, began instructing Negroes. A person as busy as Cotton Mather scheduled time for regular instruction of Negroes. In 1717, Mather started an evening school in Boston for Negroes and Indians. Another school for the instruction of Negroes in reading, catechizing, and writing was started in 1728 by Nathaniel Pigott. At about the same time, Paul Cuffee, a successful Negro businessman in Massachusetts, established a school for Blacks.

MIDDLE COLONIES

It was in Pennsylvania where the most conscientious effort was directed toward educating the colonial Negro. Not only were the Quakers interested in freeing the slaves, but they made strong efforts to teach them reading and writing. Leaders of the Quakers urged their followers to instruct the Negroes in religious matters. In the year 1700, acting under the leadership of William Penn, so-called monthly educational meetings were held in Philadelphia for Negroes. Many Quakers of this time were instructing their slaves in reading and writing.

John Woolman and Anthony Benezet were leading Quaker educators working with Negroes. In 1750, Benezet, a highly regarded intellectual, started an evening school in his home for Negroes, both free and slave. Since he was wealthy, he was able to keep this school going for over twenty years. His experience with Negro education led him to speak out against the concept of Negro inferiority:

> I can with truth and sincerity declare that I have found amongst the Negroes as great a variety of talents as amongst a like number of whites; and I am bold to assert, that the notion entertained by some, that the blacks are inferior in their capacities, is a vulgar prejudice, founded on the pride or ignorance of their lordly masters, who have kept their slaves at such a distance, as to be unable to form a right judgment of them.

The Quakers not only helped the Negro in fundamental education, they organized the Pennsylvania Abolition Society in 1776 with an aim toward ending slavery. Its members, including such men as Benjamin Franklin, Thomas Paine, and Noah Webster, later to become a leading educational writer, were active in Negro education.

New York also made minimum efforts to bring education to the Negroes. In 1704, a religious instruction school which included Negroes was started at Trinity Church. Elia Neau was its first instructor. In Maryland, the Reverend Thomas Bray was a leader in Negro education. At times, his schools included integrated teaching.

SPANISH AND FRENCH EFFORTS

In other parts of America, educational programs for Negroes developed with limited participation. The French and Spanish both took steps to teach reading and writing to the Negro. It was easier for the Spanish in the Southeastern part of present-day United States and for the French in New Orleans to attempt to educate Blacks because as Catholics they were most anxious to bring the Negroes and Indians into the Church. As an example, the Ursuline Nuns in New Orleans began educating Negroes and Indians as early as 1727, and established a school for them in 1734.

All of this colonial effort was meager, but it was somewhat better than nothing.

NEGRO EDUCATION IN THE NINETEENTH CENTURY

Strong resistance to Negro education was evident throughout the United States during the 1800s, both before and after the Civil War. Immediately following the American Revolution, there was initial support for improving the lot of the Negro. There were two major reasons for this attitude. The Negro had fought on the side of the Colonists, and had served in many other supporting capacities. He had remained with the Colonists in spite of the British promise of freedom. Further, the Declaration of Independence had been based on the concept of equality and the natural rights of man. These concepts led many Americans to favor abolition of slavery. Others favored giving the Negro a chance to upgrade himself. Benjamin Franklin, for instance, recommended that Negroes be offered a good education, including an academic education. On the other hand, Thomas Jefferson, while believing in education for Negroes, thought of this education as being industrial and agricultural. He did not believe Blacks were intellectually as capable as whites.

EDUCATION OF NEGROES FROM THE REVOLUTION TO THE CIVIL WAR

During the eighty-five years of slavery between the Revolution and the Civil War, education for the Negro was almost invisible. While numerous instances can be cited of self-educated Negroes or of the efforts of white individuals or groups to educate some Negroes, the Negro who received even a limited training in reading and writing was the exception. Much attention is often given to the talent of a few of the Blacks who received an education, but most were never given the opportunity to learn to read or write.

In the South, because of the fear of potential insurrection if the Blacks became educated, strong efforts were undertaken to prevent them from learning to read or write. Further, the belief was common, as expressed by John Calhoun, that the Negro was not capable of being educated. Still, some education for Negroes did exist in the South. John Hope Franklin, Negro historian, points out numerous instances wherein Southern slave owners educated their slaves. Contemporary Negro militants do not support this thesis. The film "Slavery and Slave Resistance" takes a different view. This film argues that the only education of Blacks in the South was self-taught. Nevertheless, Franklin's text cites numerous examples, the best known one being that of the former slave, Frederick Douglass, who was taught to read and write by his owner's family. One Mississippi slave holder claimed that all twenty of his slaves could read and write.

Most Southern states passed laws against educating the slave, although it appears Southerners did not take these laws seriously, since no records exist of any violators being brought to court. However, the danger of rebellion always hung heavy in the South. After the insurrections of 1800, this scare was translated into more rigorous enforcement of "no education" laws. From then to the Civil War, there was little prospect of the slave's being educated. Again, exceptions are to be noted. Several estimates exist concerning Negro education in the pre-Civil War South. One estimate for Georgia is that of the state's 400,000 slaves, about 5,000 were literate. Another estimate is that one out of every fifty slaves could read. John Hope Franklin concludes there is no way of knowing how many Blacks attended white schools.

In the years after the Revolution, Northern states began to establish educational systems. In the process of this development, the Negro made considerable progress along with the whites. Boston expended reasonable efforts in this process. Blacks were taught by whites in both private and public schools. In 1798, Primus Hall, a successful Negro businessman, established a school for Negroes in his own home. In 1800, a group of Negroes in Boston unsuccessfully petitioned the city for a separate Negro public school. Subsequently, the Negroes started a private school with two teachers from Harvard. The school was a successful example, with the result that, in 1820, Boston established a separate Negro public elementary school. The lead of Boston was quickly followed by other cities in Massachusetts so that separate schools for Blacks became a widespread development.

Black education made slow progress in Massachusetts. Several spectacular events occurred, but the overall picture was not good. In 1849, Charles Sumner, the northern abolitionist, argued before the Massachusetts Supreme Court, demanding the court set aside a local ordinance which required separate education for the races. In this case, *Roberts vs. The City of Boston,* Sumner's arguments failed, but six years later enough public support had been developed to force the passage through the Massachusetts legislature of a law prohibiting segregation in the public schools of the state.

Other New England states developed educational programs for Negroes. Connecticut and Rhode Island developed separate schools. By the time of the Civil War, both states were appropriating sizeable amounts of money for the support of these institutions. These segregated schools were not as effective as the Massachusetts schools, but neither was any kind of education.

Another landmark in Negro education was the establishment in 1787 in New York of the African Free School. The school began with an enrollment of forty children. Initially, there was much public opposition to the school; as a result, its student body increased slowly. By 1800, it had no more than sixty students. In that year, however, interest in the school picked up and enrollment increased rapidly. New impetus was given the school in 1810 when New York legislation required a master to teach slave children. By the end of the next decade, the school had grown to over 500 Black children. In 1824, the New York Common Council inaugurated financial support for African free schools. The city took over the free schools completely in 1834. Some communities continued to permit whites and Blacks to be educated in the same schools, but in 1841, the state legislature enacted a law making it permissible for any local school district to maintain separate educational facilities.

As might be expected, Quaker influences aided Negro education in New Jersey and Pennsylvania. Even before the American Revolution was over, New Jersey began educating Negro children. By the turn of the century, in addition to private education in Quaker homes, schools for Negroes had been established in numerous cities of the state.

Pennsylvania's contribution was more extensive. The education of Negroes by Quakers was widespread in Philadelphia. In 1774, a Negro school was started in that city. After the Revolution, Anthony Benezet provided money to build a school for Blacks. By 1790, Philadelphia had at least seven schools for Negro children. Most of the Pennsylvania schools were segregated, both public and private. As the population of Pennsylvania moved west, many Negro schools developed in the western parts of the state.

The frontiers kept moving westward, and with the new population came the Negro. The frontier was not always the most democratic place in America. Ohio at first excluded Negroes from public schools. This became law in 1829. By 1849, Ohio enacted legislation establishing separate schools for Blacks, but not enough money was ever appropriated to make this plan educationally effective. Indiana and Illinois were also indifferent to education in general and to Negro education in particular. The laws of Michigan and Missouri were more liberal toward Negro education, but financial support was little better. Nowhere in the West prior to the Civil War was there any real financial support for public education of the Negro.

NEGROES IN HIGHER EDUCATION PRIOR TO THE CIVIL WAR

Although the Negro was not involved in higher education to any great extent, considering the age and the obstacles, the ones who made it are worthy of note. Prior to the Civil War, Negroes could be found in numbers of one or two in most colleges. Typically, when a minority is no threat, it is easy to be tolerant. Bowdoin, Oberlin, Rutland, and Franklin Colleges have records of Negro graduates, as does the Howard Medical School. The American Missionary Association carried on a long experiment in coeducational integrated education at Berea College in Kentucky. Numerous Negroes held professorships at several white colleges. Perhaps Central College in McGrawville, New York, represents the best illustration. Here Blacks, notably Charles L. Reason, William G. Allen, and George B. Vashon, held the chair of Belles Lettres. It is stated that they wore the mantle of professor gracefully, "giving proof of good scholarship and manly character."

POST-CIVIL WAR

Freedom did not bring the Negro the expected educational opportunity. Opposition to the Negro continued in both the North and South. Southern leaders denounced the democratic tenet of equality explicit in public education. Opposition to Black education at times turned resentment into violence as Negro schools and churches were burned or destroyed. Students were often prevented from going to school and teachers were not permitted to teach. Nevertheless, it was during the post-Civil War years that an organized program of Negro education was developed. It was a serious problem in trying to bring education to four million free Blacks.

The various states in the South slowly produced educational programs that provided for Negro education. West Virginia, which had seceded from Virginia in 1863 during the war, established "equal though separate" education for the Blacks. In areas of the South where Union troops were stationed, efforts were made to establish educational programs for Negroes. This was true in parts of Florida, Louisiana, Tennessee, and Missouri. In most of these states, funds for this education came from funds supplied out of taxes paid by Negroes. The District of Columbia affords an example of this kind of support. In 1862, Congress passed legislation whereby ten per cent of all taxes collected from Negroes was to go toward public education of the Negro.

The Reconstruction period provided a battleground for Negro education. In the years following the war, attitudes of Southern whites toward Negro education can be classified into three groups: the image most often depicted is the traditional Southerner who refused to recognize the changed status of the former slave and hoped to return the Negro to his servile status. These whites opposed education of any type for the newly freed Blacks. The second group were whites who recognized that the institution of slavery was dead and that a new society was to come to the South. These liberals were in support of education for the Negro. In this group were many plantation owners and prospective industrialists who wanted peace and stability. They needed an effective labor supply. The third group, known in history as "scalawags," were the unpropertied whites, workers, and small farmers, who supported the North. These "renegades" supported Negro education, at the same time demanding it for their own children.

Black leader W. E. B. DuBois, in the *The Negro Common School,* credits the Reconstruction period with setting a precedent for the democratic right of all people to a publicly financed education. This principle was not totally accepted in the North even for white children, but it was rapidly developing as a universal concept. Equal opportunity for education seldom meant education in the same school. Some experiments in integrated education were attempted in the South, particularly in South Carolina and Louisiana, but the efforts were short-lived. White opposition and violence closed these schools. Further, Negroes did not indicate any particular opposition to segregated schools. The sophistication of racism was not an issue; decades of slave-master society had not prepared Blacks to challenge the practice of separation.

When the war came to an end and Lincoln was assassinated, Congress turned on the South and attempted to force Negro equality with the Civil Rights Act of 1866 and the Fourteenth Amendment to the Constitution two years later. Resistance to these measures in the South resulted in the Reconstruction Act of 1867. This required each state to reorganize its government, adopt a new constitution, purge itself of rebellion, and ratify the Fourteenth Amendment. All males of legal age, black and white, were allowed to vote. From the new legislatures came education laws that were unenforceable and that the weakened Southern economy could not implement. In Texas, a law was passed requiring that taxes "collected from Africans, or persons of African descent, shall be exclusively appropriated for the maintenance of a system of public schools for Africans and their children." Meanwhile, the South was being exploited by carpetbaggers from the North and by the anti-Southern whites, called scalawags.

While a vengeful Congress was devising ways to punish the South and force Northern culture upon the Southerner, and the unprincipled were milking what was left of the Southern economy in the guise of helping the Negro, groups of Northerners were organizing to help the

South and make available to Negroes training and education for their new status as citizens of a democracy. The Freedmen's Aid Society of New England, the Pennsylvania Relief Commission, and similar foundations were formed to supply Negroes with food, clothing, homes, and education. Many of these were eventually absorbed into the American Freedmen's Union Commission.

Postwar education for Negroes in the South received at least partial support when in 1865 Congress created the *Bureau of Refugees, Freedmen, and Abandoned Lands,* known popularly as the *Freedmen's Bureau,* under the War Department. Its function was to aid the Negro, protect his civil rights, and provide for his schooling. For five years the Bureau worked to educate and advance the Southern Negroes. During this time it spent approximately $6,000,000, organized and staffed 2,-500 schools, and educated some 150,000 Negroes, adults and children. The Bureau was not in tune with the South and failed to sense the grounds for the Southerner's attitudes. It urged coeducation of Negro and white, a proposal that frightened Southern whites and aroused misgivings even among the scalawags. Many Negroes were equally disturbed over this possibility. Teachers in Bureau schools were imported from the North and had no understanding of the South, even though their intentions were good. They hailed the Northern soldier as the Negro's liberator and the Southern white as his enemy. As a result, they were despised as troublemakers, and a few were stoned or whipped publicly, their belongings destroyed, and their schools burned.

One of the officers in the Bureau was John W. Alvord, Superintendent of Instruction, who became instrumental in the establishment of an educational system whereby the efforts of the states, and the financial support of individuals and groups, were funneled into an educational support system. The Bureau, several Freedmen's aid societies, and numerous philanthropists, combined to establish elementary and secondary schools. Religious groups also worked for Negro education. One outstanding organization was the American Missionary Association which set up schools in Washington, D. C., Newport News, Suffas, Portsmouth, and Yorktown in Virginia, as well as schools in Ohio. Important church groups supporting Negro education were the Quakers, Presbyterians, Methodists, Baptists, and Episcopalians. Their respective organizations went under these titles: The Friends Association for the Aid to Freedmen, The Board of Freedmen's Missions of the United Presbyterian Church, The Freedmen's Aid Society of the Methodist Episcopal Church, The Conferences of the African Methodist Episcopal Church, The American Baptist Home Mission Society, and The American Church Institute of the Episcopal Church.

In higher education, it was again the churches which led. They established Negro colleges in the South, although the level of work was at first little more than secondary education. This reputation for poor quality education in these colleges has remained to this day, even though there is little evidence to support this allegation. The American Missionary Association established a number of these colleges: Atlanta University (1865); Shaw University (1865) in Raleigh, North Carolina; Fisk University (1866) in Nashville, Tennessee; Talladega (1867) in Alabama; and Tougaloo University (1869) in Mississippi. The American Baptist Home Mission Society established and supported Virginia Union University (1865), Morehouse College (1867) in Atlanta, Georgia, and Benedict College (1870) in South Carolina. In Holly Springs, Mississippi, the Methodist Episcopal Church started Rust College. Barber Scotia College, first known as Scotia Seminary, and Biddle University, now known as Johnson C. Smith University, were established by the Presbyterians in North Carolina. The Centenary Biblical Institute, now known as Morgan State College, was started in 1866 in Baltimore by the Methodist Episcopal Church. Two other Negro institutions of higher education which are prominent today had their origin in the post-Civil War days; the Arkansas Agricultural, Mechanical, and Normal College at Pine Bluff, established in 1873, known originally as Branch Normal, and Howard College (1867) in Washington, D.C. Numerous financial leaders also contributed funds for education of Negroes. These funds, such as the Anna T. Jeanes Fund and the Daniel Hand Fund, earmarked exclusively for Negro education, were used for endowments, buildings, teacher education, scholarships, and industrial and agricultural education.

More effective help for the South came from other philanthropic interests. In 1867, George Peabody, a New England millionaire, established a fund of $2,000,000 "for the promotion and encouragement of intellectual, moral, and industrial education among the young of the more destitute portions of the southern and southwestern states of our Union." The money was channeled through the states and expended to aid struggling common schools, raise the standards of rural schools, provide normal schools to prepare better teachers, and raise the salaries of county superintendents. It also helped bring education to the Negroes, and, perhaps as important if not more so, enabled intelligent Negroes to receive training as teachers of their own people. In 1905, the trustees of the fund, feeling that its original purposes had been accomplished, used the $1,500,000 left in the fund to found the George Peabody College for Teachers at Nashville, Tennessee.

A similar project was initiated in 1882 by John F. Slater, another New England millionaire, with $1,000,000. While this fund was expended much as was the Peabody money, it laid greater stress on Negro industrial education. When the Peabody Fund was dissolved, the trustees gave $250,000 to the Slater Fund.

After the failure of the Freedmen's Bureau in 1870, attempts were made by Congress to provide federal funds to support education. The Hoar Bill in 1870, other bills in 1872 and 1879, and the Blair Bills, which came up repeatedly, were all defeated. Meanwhile, the question of co-racial education came to the front. Northerners advocated one public school system for all children. Although several Reconstruction governments in the South attempted to establish co-racial schools, by 1900 all southern states had declared, either in their constitutions or through legislation, in favor of two school systems.

The federal and state governments entered the higher education scene under authority of the Second Morrill Act of 1890 which approved land-grant colleges for Negroes. Under the provisions of this act, Negro land-grant colleges were started throughout the South. These institutions, supported by state and federal money, established further the practices of "separate but equal" education. This concept was further strengthened by the famous Supreme Court case of *Plessy vs. Ferguson* (1896). The *Plessy vs. Ferguson* decision recognized that racial segregation in education was practiced throughout the nation, not just in the South. With this decision, the "separate but equal" doctrine became the law of the land. It remained the official national position until *Brown vs. Board of Education of Topeka, Kansas* (1954) reversed *Plessy vs. Ferguson* by declaring that segregation of the races in public education in the United States was unconstitutional.

The great Negro educator of the nineteenth century was Booker T. Washington. Washington was an excellent product of post-Civil War social conditions. One of the most telling arguments against co-racial education was that the Negro did not need, and in fact could not succeed at, the kind of academic education offered white children. It was held that he needed training in areas fitting his intelligence and status in society. To provide this kind of education, General Samuel Chapman Armstrong, in 1868, founded Hampton Institute along lines suggested by Fellenberg's school at Hofwyl. Here he emphasized character building, farming, manual arts and crafts, and teacher training. Booker T. Washington was Armstrong's most famous pupil. He was the chief organizer of Tuskegee Institute, founded in 1881, where he served as president until his death in 1915.

Washington was convinced that the Negro could be best accepted if the type of education he received prepared him to provide services and produce for white society. In Tuskegee Institute, the curriculum emphasized agricultural, industrial, and vocational education, including domestic services. Some professional preparation was also introduced. In his speeches before white audiences, he insisted the Negro liked the whites, was not demanding social equality, but merely wanted to serve. These concepts pleased the whites, North and South. Booker T. Washington still represents the ideal as far as many whites are concerned: "Work your way up through the system."

While Armstrong and Washington, along with many others, were satisfied with a separate education for the Negro to prepare him for a life radically different from that of the Southern white, the younger Negro, aware of the industrial renaissance in the South and his own abilities, was not satisfied with this approach to education. As a strong white middle class grew, there was an increasing desire to forget the past and build a future in which the Southern Negro could live in dignity with whites. An expression of this attitude was the *Conference for Christian Education* in the South, founded in 1898 by the Reverend Edward Abbott. In 1901, the Conference created the Southern Educational Board to provide "free schools for all people." In 1903, the General Education Board was incorporated by an act of Congress to further education in all parts of the South.

Negroes generally have rejected the tenets of Washington's arguments. The leader in the opposition group has been W.E.B. DuBois, one of the founders of the National Association for the Advancement of Colored People. DuBois, after doing Bachelor's work at Fisk, received his Ph.D. from Harvard. He objected to Washington's educational program for Negroes because of its narrow vocational scope. It was a gospel of work and money. It ignored civil and human rights; it failed to provide the Negro a chance to reach out. Throughout his life, Washington was still the most influential Black educator, but today most Blacks look at Washington as an Uncle Tom, whereas DuBois represents an image they prefer.

RISE OF TEACHER EDUCATION

The first teachers in the colonies ranged all the way from scholars of the stature of Ezekiel Cheever to poor wives who taught a few children in their kitchens. Knowledge of subject matter and orthodoxy were prime requirements. By the early 1800s it was becoming evident that the pattern of schools developing in the United States demanded better-prepared teachers. To serve this end, normal schools under private auspices began to appear. Two of the most noted of these were Samuel R. Hall's school in Concord, Vermont, established in 1823, and James G. Carter's school at Lancaster, Massachusetts, founded in 1827.

These were called normal schools, from the French root of the word *normal,* meaning model or rule, indicating that teachers were given rules for teaching. The first state-supported normal school appeared in 1839 at Lexington, Massachusetts, a result of Horace Mann's efforts, and was presided over by Cyrus Peirce. By 1898, there were 167 public normal schools in the United States. Many of these schools were supported by counties and municipalities.

Most normal schools took their pupils directly from the elementary schools, and it was not until near 1900 that more than two years of high school training was required. The course of study ran for two years, and included the mastery of elementary school subjects along with some philosophy, history, and philosophy of education. In time, nearly all normal schools came to include observation and practice teaching either in "model" schools or in nearby public schools.

Foreign influences were evident in much of the normal school development. Victor Cousin's report on Prussian education, the reports of Mann, Barnard, Stowe, Brooks, Griscomb, and Woodbridge dealing with the advances in education in France and Germany, and the Oswego experiment of Edward Sheldon were among the events stimulating American concern for better teacher training. Sheldon had become a Pestalozzian enthusiast and introduced some Pestalozzian-trained teachers into the Oswego, New York, school system to help upgrade his teaching staff. In 1861, the city fathers of Oswego established a normal school to train teachers along the lines of Pestalozzi's thinking. Other normal schools were influenced by the work that went on there, and very soon Pestalozzian ideas about teacher preparation were spreading to similar schools throughout the country.

One of the functions of many academies was to prepare teachers for the several kinds of schools dotting America. Before the middle of the nineteenth century, some colleges began introducing "the art of teaching" into their curricula. Among these were New York University in 1832, Brown University in 1850, and Michigan in 1860. This was followed by professorships of pedagogy and departments of education in such leading institutions as Iowa, Michigan, Wisconsin, North Carolina, and Johns Hopkins. Graduate instruction in education was becoming popular by the end of the century in a number of institutions.

The New York College for the Training of Teachers was opened in 1888 with Nicholas Murray Butler as president. The same year, New York University offered graduate courses in teaching. Then, in 1892, the New York College changed its name to Teachers College and petitioned for affiliation with Columbia University. The University's council replied, "There is no such subject as education and, moreover, it would bring into the university women who are not wanted." By

1898, this attitude had changed considerably, and the college was accepted as part of the university under the leadership of Dean James E. Russell, who served the institution until 1927.

The work of normal schools, departments of education, and teachers' colleges was helped materially by teachers' institutes that came to be the fashion in almost every community or central town or city, the rise of numerous periodicals and journals dealing with different phases of education, and the many teachers' associations that were organized. Henry Barnard organized the first institute in 1839. Louis Agassiz, in 1837, initiated the practice at Harvard of holding summer institutes or "schools" for teachers. This was followed by extension courses to better prepare teachers already in service. Among the early educational journals keeping teachers informed of advances in the profession were the *Academician*, 1818, and Russell's *American Journal of Education*, 1855 to 1881. Added to these were the journals published and edited by Mann, Barnard, and other pioneers in American education. Organizations of teachers advocating better schooling and preparation were *The American Institute of Instruction*, 1830, and the *National Teachers Association*, 1857, which became the *National Education Association* in 1870.

Part Five

EDUCATION IN ONE WORLD

CHAPTER 17

In the Twentieth Century– Toward One World

INTRODUCTION

Life began in one world.

During millions of years this life spread over the face of the earth, took many forms, and developed diversified characteristics as it was determined by different environments. The evolutionary process eventually produced man, a creature who organized himself into groups, created cultures, and grew toward civilization. Where conditions were favorable, he was able to develop more or less closely-knit communities, attack and subjugate others, and employ his cleverness to protect himself and his values from "enemies." In time, he learned how to bring large areas under a single rule, create effective economic systems, develop patterns of commerce, and assemble codes of morality loosely related to a hierarchy of gods. Some of the more daring and perceptive dreamed of gathering all people under one government, one economy, and one god.

During the early centuries of history, great and powerful governments appeared, grew to fabulous proportions, were attacked by enemies from within and without, weakened, and disappeared. These were man's first attempts to create one world subject to the will of one sovereign and his gods.

As people in diverse parts of the world developed languages, economic systems, traditions, literatures, and religions suited to their local needs, smaller social groups took distinctive shapes. These were called nations. Gradually, each became a focus for loyalties and a base for fears and jealousies. This resulted in rivalries, offensive and defensive postures, and wars. Nations fought to control colonies and natural

481

resources, protect trade routes and markets, and gain advantages over others.

This divided world was tolerable when men traveled by horse and ship, plowed their fields with oxen, attacked with bows and arrows or cannons and guns, and could produce what was needed in their homes and in their own fields. As travel approached the speed of sound, as weapons deadly enough to depopulate the earth were developed, as industry grew into great factory complexes reaching throughout the world for raw materials and markets, and as populations grew beyond their ability to supply food locally, it became increasingly evident that an interdependence of mankind was developing that could not tolerate unbridled nationalism.

During the late nineteenth and early twentieth centuries, an increasing number of people were beginning to appreciate the fact that political, social, economic, scientific, religious, and ethnic developments had brought mankind to the point in history when a world unity had to be fashioned if human society was to continue on this planet. Events of the first half of the twentieth century drove this lesson home in no uncertain terms. While in the days of empires, unity could be maintained by force, it became evident that the one world that would save humanity from extinction could be created only through democratic consensus and guaranteed only by international good will and respect.

It was possible when studying past centuries to think of the historical and philosophical foundations of western education in terms of the western world, of the nations and people who shaped this segment of earth. Events leading to the twentieth century and happenings within the century have placed this western world squarely in the center of *one world* and brought to bear upon its education forces from the north, the east, and the south. Education in the western world of the twentieth century is determined, in part at least, by events that take place in Russia, China, Africa, and at the poles. When the assassination of an obscure Austrian archduke and his wife in Sarajevo could light the fires of a world war, when a *Sputnik* launched from Russia could cause the nations of the West to rethink their curricula, when a Communist take-over in China could deeply affect the other governments of the world, and when the two most powerful nations of the world could engage in a race to place men on the moon and explore the surface of the planet Venus, it became unrealistic to think of western education as something separate and distinct. It does have its uniqueness, as do all educational systems developed to serve people in different parts of the world. However, in the twentieth century all men must, despite their uniqueness and individuality, live as citizens of one world, and the education that serves them best will be characterized by one-worldness. To understand western education in the twentieth century, we must see it within the pattern of world events, not merely as a product of western culture.

THE WORLD OF THE TWENTIETH CENTURY

The First World War

From the union of Germany in 1870 until 1914, events in Europe and the East moved with the inevitability of a Greek tragedy. The plot became clear for all to see, but no one was able to stop the march of events to their logical conclusion. The rapid growth of industrial power, the ambition for national self-sufficiency, the need for colonies and markets, a sharpened sense of "national honor," and a creed of "peace through strength," all products of the nineteenth and early twentieth centuries, forced the nations of Europe and the East into powerful defensive alliances and placed upon them the staggering burden of an armaments race.

The long struggle between Austria and Serbia came to a head on June 28, 1914, when a member of a Serbian secret society called the Black Hand assassinated the Austrian Archduke Francis Ferdinand, heir to the throne, and his wife at Sarajevo in Bosnia. Austria declared war on Serbia over this incident and started a chain reaction that involved most of the nations of the world. Sides were chosen: the Central Powers, with Germany the leader, were arrayed against the Allies, grouped around Great Britain and France.

The war dragged on for two years, more a test of endurance than a measure of decisive strength. By 1916, a deadlock had developed. Both the Central Powers and the Allies were facing defections, weakening economies, and a terrible weariness. The United States remained neutral, profiting from trade with both sides. Eventually the game of playing both sides for economic gain became less profitable and too dangerous. Sentiment favoring the Allies was growing. When President Wilson's attempts at a negotiated peace failed, and when the German blockade of Great Britain and France threatened American trade routes, Congress, on April 7, 1917, declared war on Germany. By the spring of 1918, newly trained troops from the United States were fighting on the "western front."

The war had become truly worldwide. Although a few small nations, including Spain, Portugal, Holland, Switzerland, and the Scandinavian countries, were able to maintain neutrality, the war involved all of

Europe, reached the Far East to Japan, China, Australia, New Zealand, and India, and drew into its vortex Canada and many of the nations of Latin America. The future of each nation was to be determined not by what it planned and did alone but by what the world planned and did. Isolation was gone and one world was born.

Events moved rapidly after the United States' entry into the war. The Communists overthrew the Russian government in 1917 and made a separate peace with Germany. Wilson published his Fourteen Points to lure the nations of the Central Powers away from Germany and the German people from their leaders. The German offensive of 1918 failed, and nations of the Near East and the Balkans withdrew from the alliance. Then the German people rebelled, forced William II to abdicate, and on November 11, 1918, the new Socialist chancellor signed an armistice acknowledging the defeat of the Central Powers.

THE LEAGUE OF NATIONS

As early as 1907, nations attending the Second Hague Peace Conference came close to a general international organization. In 1914–1915, the League to Enforce Peace was organized under the leadership of former President William Howard Taft. In May, 1916, President Wilson espoused the cause of a league of nations, and by 1917 the idea was receiving support in other countries of the world. On March 20, 1918, a committee appointed by the British government under the chairmanship of Sir Walter G. F. Phillimore produced a draft of a world organization. This was sent to President Wilson, who turned it over to Colonel Edward House for study. House drew up a plan of his own. During the late summer of 1918, President Wilson, working with these various drafts, prepared a plan, which he took to the Paris conference, to write a peace settlement closing the First World War.

It soon became evident at Paris that, although the world was tired of war, it was not ready to build a peace "with justice for all." Greed, lust for vengeance, and fear characterized the conference. The victors were at war with each other over the spoils. President Wilson, working from his Fourteen Points, insisted that the first business of the conference should be the writing of a covenant to create an international body to promote international cooperation and maintain peace. He was supported by Great Britain, who had developed an official position on the subject from the Phillimore report. On January 25, 1919, the conference appointed a commission, with President Wilson and Colonel House representing the United States, to draft a covenant for a league of nations. A two-man subcommittee consisting of Cecil Hurst, legal expert of the British foreign office, and David Miller, legal expert of the

United States delegation, fused the British and the American drafts into a document that was adopted by a plenary session of the conference on April 28, 1919. On June 28 of that year it was signed by all delegates and became Part I of the Treaty of Versailles.

The entire treaty was rejected by the United States Congress. While this nation attended some sessions of the League of Nations as an observer and affiliated with some of the auxiliary bodies, it never sat as a full member or gave the weight of its prestige to any League decisions. As a result, the League's early period of growth from 1920 to 1929 was followed by six years of increasing difficulties, as member nations refused to cooperate in matters concerning them or held that their actions did not come under provisions of the covenant, then by a brief period of recovery from 1937 to 1939, and finally by eclipse and defeat from 1940 to 1946. When this world body proved impotent to deal with crises in Manchuria, Ethiopia, Spain, China, and central Europe, it became evident that this attempt at one-world cooperation had failed and that mankind must wait for a later day when a more earnest and honest world organization would try again.

THE RUSSIAN REVOLUTION AND AFTER

Although Russia was beginning industrialization by 1914, she was wholly unprepared to fight an industrialized and mechanized war of worldwide proportions. Her railroads were primitive. Her factories could not produce arms in the amounts needed. Turkey's entrance into World War I on the side of Germany isolated her from sources of supplies. An inefficient and corrupt government, headed by a ruler more interested in the health of his only son than in war and government, was unfit to hold its own in a world struggle.

By 1917, the people were disheartened, had lost faith in their government, and were smarting under the ruthlessness of Nicholas II in breaking the strike of factory workers in Petrograd and in dissolving the Duma, the national assembly elected by the people. An uprising on March 15, 1917, toppled Nicholas II from his throne and established the Provisional Government.

Meanwhile, another force was beginning to gain strength in Russia —the Soviet of Workers, Peasants, and Soldiers. This was a "council" composed of both moderate and radical socialists. The latter were Communists, called Bolsheviks. By 1917, the All-Russian Congress of Soviets had organized the Central Executive Committee, or parliament, to coordinate the work of the numerous local soviets. Soon the communists, although a minority, were in control.

As the war dragged on and conditions in Russia deteriorated, basic areas of disagreement developed between the Provisional Government, made up of conservatives and moderate liberals, and the Bolsheviks, representing the radicals. Nikolai Lenin, an intelligent and forceful man and a fanatically devoted Communist, was leader of the radicals. His slogan of "Land, Peace, and Bread" appealed directly to the masses. Under his leadership, the Provisional Government was overthrown on November 7, 1917, and the Communists took control. The new leaders made peace with Germany, Austria-Hungary, Bulgaria, and Turkey. They also embarked upon a propaganda move to rally all workers of the world to revolt, seize their governments, and take over the means of production. Against them were the White Russians and the Allies, who were angered over their separate peace treaties and advocacy of world revolution.

Lenin was a fanatical Communist; he was also a practical and perceptive man. This precipitated a struggle within himself between Communist theory and the hard facts of Russian life and economy. Theory lost, and in 1921 he announced the New Economic Policy, which incorporated many of the practices of capitalism. When he died on January 24, 1924, a vicious struggle for power emerged. In the confusion, Joseph Vissarionovich Stalin proved to be the outstanding leader of the Communist Party. By 1928 he was able to assume absolute power, junk the New Economic Policy, and return the Soviet Union to a planned society. His ideas were incorporated into the First Five-Year Plan, which outlined in detail the function of every phase of Russian life in producing an economically sufficient society. By way of introducing the plan, he wrote: "We are in a race. We are from fifty to one hundred years behind the advanced countries. We must run through the distance in ten years. Either we do this, or they will crush us." Stalin concentrated on the Soviet Union, leaving world revolution to a future date.

The menace of Adolph Hitler, who came to power in Germany in 1933, caused Stalin to scrap his Second Five-Year Plan and concentrate on producing guns, tanks, planes, and ammunition. His Third Five-Year Plan, begun in 1938, was almost entirely devoted to the military. Then, in the summer of 1941, the German armies poured into Russia. This was a master "double-cross," for in August, 1939, Hitler and Stalin had signed a nonaggression pact, which was in fact a plan to divide eastern Europe into spheres of influence. Hitler saw this as a way to keep Russia quiet while he conquered the West. Then he planned to turn on Russia and make it part of his world empire. Stalin saw the pact as a guarantee that there would be time to prepare to take over the West when the great powers were bled white fighting each other.

Hitler realized in 1941 that his plans for a short war had failed, and he turned on the Soviet Union before she could get ready for a major war.

Hitler's experience in Russia was disastrous. At Stalingrad, on February 3, 1943, the entire Russian wing of the German army was forced to surrender. From this moment the Soviet Union moved relentlessly against the German forces, driving them back into Poland. In 1944, the Soviets launched a gigantic attack along a 2,000-mile front and moved steadily west while other allied forces were moving east. As a result, the German armies collapsed, and on April 25, 1945, Russian and American armies met at Torgau, in Germany.

As the Soviets moved up through central Europe and Poland, they established Communist-controlled governments in Rumania, Bulgaria, Hungary, Albania, Yugoslavia, and Poland. By 1947, each of these had become a "People's Democratic Republic," which translated meant a Communist dictatorship. In the same year, the Communist international organization to foment world revolution, abolished in 1943, was reactivated as the Communist Information Bureau—Cominform. The Soviet Union had reentered the world with the avowed aim of destroying capitalism, elected governments, and religion, and establishing Communist regimes throughout.

Stalin died March 5, 1953, and Nikita S. Khrushchev became the first secretary of the Communist Party and, after some jockeying, dictator of all the Soviet Union. Between 1953 and 1957 he sought intermittently to frighten the world and to woo it with promises of "peaceful coexistence."

October 4, 1957, the Soviet government announced the successful launching of a *Sputnik,* or earth satellite, a ball twenty-two and a half inches in diameter weighing 184 pounds. At that moment, the world entered the space age and could under no conditions turn back. All areas of life were changed. Economics, politics, education, religion, philosophy, government could never be the same. Neutral nations were impressed by proved advances in Soviet science. The capitalistic powers suffered a rude awakening. Demands were heard for the immediate reform of education to prepare more scientists and engineers to rival Russia. The West hastened to review its defense spending and its protective complex. The entire world was shaken into a realization that, for the present at least, one world stood over against the universe.

In October of 1964, Khrushchev was toppled from power by the Presidium of the Central Committee of the Soviet Communist Party, and the government was placed in the hands of Leonid Brehznev as party chief and Aleksei Kosygin as premier. Leaders of the Soviet Union and the United States realize that the relationships worked out between these two great powers will determine the future of mankind on this earth and perhaps on other planets.

RISE OF FASCIST DICTATORSHIPS

Fascism is dictatorship by the right. It leaves the means of production in the hands of private individuals but under state management and regulation. It promises the industrialists prosperity, high profits, and freedom from labor troubles. It promises the workers uninterrupted employment, high wages, and a higher standard of living. It promises the nation a stable economy, a return to past glories, a reconquest of lost territories, and a place of honor.

Three nations turned to fascist dictatorships as a result of the First World War: Italy, Germany, and Spain. Thus was launched a strongly anti-Communist philosophy of government. The world had two extremes from which to choose: communism or fascism. Between these was democracy, a vague and adaptable philosophy that took many shapes and was revised from time to time as men with varied interpretations of world conditions rose to power in countries of the West and East.

Italy. Italy's problems after the First World War were tremendous. Her government, made up of many parties and forced to operate under tenuous coalitions, was helpless to solve these problems. The times were ripe for Benito Mussolini (1883-1945), son of a blacksmith, self-taught, and former member of the extreme left wing of the Socialist Party. When he returned from the war, he had shifted to the right and begun organizing his own party, the *Fascisti* or Fascist. He found much support from disillusioned veterans, discontented nationalists, businessmen, large manufacturers, and the lower middle class. He promised protection of private property and the middle class, anti-Communism and anti-socialism, full employment, public order, social security, and national glory. In 1922, the king was forced to make him prime minister. By the end of the following year the Fascists were in charge of the government, and their leader was dictator of all Italy. He assumed the title of *Il Duce,* The Leader.

Civil rights were abolished, a secret police organized, and the slogan "Believe! Obey! Work!" appeared everywhere. Conditions improved remarkably. A Charter of Labor was adopted, giving workers security and a high standard of living. Public order was restored, unemployment reduced, industry and agriculture prospered, and an ambitious program of public works, including draining the Pontine Marshes, undertaken. Education was greatly improved, with all children required to attend school until the age of fourteen. Literacy rose from sixty to seventy-five per cent.

In spite of these successes of the Fascist government, Italy was unable to maintain herself without outside help. Her wealth was unequal to the burdens of armaments and public works. There were too many people, too little food, and too few natural resources. Mussolini's solution was colonial expansion into North Africa and Ethiopia.

A border incident caused Mussolini to move into Ethiopia "to restore order." Emperor Haile Selassie appealed to the League of Nations to stop this aggression, but soon realized that he was talking to a body unwilling and unable to act. By the spring of 1936, Italian soldiers were in Addis Ababa, and Ethiopia was part of the Italian Empire with King Victor Emmanuel II its emperor. In the fall of 1936, Hitler's Germany recognized the Italian conquest and entered into an alliance with Mussolini, the Rome-Berlin Axis.

Germany. With the German defeat in 1918, the Weimar Republic was formed in an attempt to turn the nation into a "federal democratic republic." From its beginning, the new government was under attack by all those opposed to any form of republican government. By 1930, a total of twenty-seven parties vied for representation in the government. Unemployment, inflation, reparations, and depression dogged the nation and defied solution.

Adolf Hitler (1889–1945), an Austrian, the son of a minor customs official, and a frustrated artist, received the Iron Cross for bravery during the First World War and rose to the rank of corporal. When the war ended, he was bitter and disillusioned, smarting under the humiliating peace that the new government had signed. He joined General von Ludendorff's attempt in 1923 to overthrow the Weimar Republic, was captured, and spent almost a year in prison. While there he wrote *Mein Kampf* (My Battle), in which he outlined the methods necessary to restore Germany to her rightful place in the world.

On a June evening in 1919 he attended a meeting of the German Workers' Party and was persuaded to join as member number seven and become an active leader. His ability as a speaker and his violent denunciation of the Versailles Treaty, the Jews, and the Marxists drew great crowds, and in the acclaim of these multitudes "he found his soul." He changed the name of the party to the National Socialist German Workers' Party (called for short the *Nazi Party*) and proclaimed himself its *Fuehrer*. He promised repeal of the Versailles Treaty, restoration of Germany to equality in armaments, reconquest of lost territories and colonies, and creation of "Greater Germany" under control of a "master race," pure Aryan, destined eventually to rule the world.

The depression of 1929 increased the strength and prestige of the Nazi Party and *Der Fuehrer,* the man who promised prosperity, security, and national glory. In the elections of 1932 and 1933 the Nazis rolled up a large number of seats in the Reichstag, while both the Communists and the Socialists lost significantly. As a result, the German president, General Paul von Hindenburg, appointed Hitler chancellor and allowed him to form a cabinet. Once in command, Hitler seized power and became the dictator of Germany.

All opposition was ruthlessly silenced, the government centralized in the Nazi Party, the means of communication controlled, and the schools made propaganda agencies for the teachings of *Der Fuehrer* and his party. A program was begun to systematically destroy the Jews, whom Hitler had come to hate. Unemployment was reduced as a program of public works got under way, industry expanded, and Germany began armaments production under the slogan, "What Germany needs is not butter, but arms."

Hitler believed that Germany was ready, in 1936, to reclaim her lost glory. In the spring of that year he marched into the demilitarized Rhineland, while the nations of Europe stood by, unable and unwilling to check this illegal move. This was the first step. Its success drew Germany and eventually the entire world into the Second World War.

Spain. Spain was a poor country, its land largely barren, its wealth in the hands of the nobility and the Catholic Church, and its natural resources of no consequence. Its constitutional monarchy was harassed by strikes, political assassination, military plots, separatist movements in the provinces, and radicalism. Between 1923 and 1931, a military dictatorship, with the approval of the king, sought to stamp out all liberal and democratic movements. When it failed, Spain became a republic and undertook a program of social reforms, which were opposed by conservative elements as too radical and by liberal elements as too conservative. Land was taken from the Church and the nobles and given to the peasants, clergymen were denied tax support and ruled unacceptable as school teachers, and workers were given higher wages and the right to organize.

When the Loyalists, a coalition of liberals and radicals, won the election of 1936, the army revolted under General Francisco Franco Bahamonde (1892–   ) with the help of "volunteers" from Mussolini and Hitler. The Loyalists admitted Communists to the government and received aid from Stalin. The civil war that developed was a small world war, with Germany and Italy looking to Spain as a link in the chain around France, and Russia hoping to create in Spain another Communist state. Great Britain and France adopted a policy of "nonintervention," which proved to be a help to the rebels.

In March, 1939, Franco's forces were victorious. Spain had been bled white, her land devastated, and more than a million people killed. The

Spanish government established by General Franco was a dictatorship along Fascist lines. Franco became *El Caudillo,* the Chieftain, responsible "only to God and history." His party, the *Falange,* was the only political party permitted. The state was organized to resemble Fascist Italy, with the army in a privileged position, syndicates controlling all occupations and economic activities, and the lands and wealth of the country restored to the nobility and the Church.

When Italy entered the war, Franco decided upon "nonbelligerency," but after meeting Hitler on October 23, 1940, he sent "volunteers" to fight against Russia. When it became evident that the Allies would win the war, he proclaimed in October, 1943, "strict neutrality" and demanded a negotiated peace with Spain sitting at the conference table. This demand was ignored, and Franco turned to building his power as dictator of a Fascist state. In 1947 he persuaded the *Cortes,* the Spanish parliament, to pass the Succession Act, confirming him as head of the state for life and granting to him the right of naming his successor.

In Conclusion. This is the story of three European states between two world wars, how each tried democracy and failed, and how in desperation they turned to Fascist dictatorships. Problems left by the First World War proved too difficult for a free people to solve. When social, political, and economic chaos threatened, each turned to a dictator who promised security in exchange for freedom. Once in power, the dictator shaped the state to his philosophy, seized control of education, and set about to develop in each individual the Fascist mind. A new and frightening force was loosed upon the world to challenge liberal thinking and show that free men have neither the skill nor the will to rule themselves in times of crisis. Democracy, Fascist philosophy maintained, is a luxury that only the prosperous, the strong, and those under no threat from "foreign" enemies can afford.

JAPAN AND THE ONE WORLD DREAM

Marco Polo in the thirteenth century told the West what he had learned about Japan during his travels in the Far East. Much that he recorded was legend and folklore.

During the centuries that followed, traders and missionaries entered Japan from Portugal, Spain, Holland, and England. Christianity, represented by the Jesuits and Franciscans, moved in and made converts, challenging traditional Buddhism. Disagreements among members of these two great orders and, at times, their involvement in the political life of the country, caused the Japanese government in the seventeenth century to expel them. This was followed by a policy of exclusion that all but isolated Japan from the western world.

Industrial and economic changes in the western nations and Japan made isolation impossible. During the first half of the nineteenth century, attempts were made to make commercial contacts with Japan. American and British whaling and merchant ships, seeking shelter from storms or in need of supplies, stopped in her ports but were forced to move on after transacting their emergency business. The United States negotiated a limited trade treaty with Japan in 1853–1854. Great Britain, Russia, and other nations were able to get similar concessions, and Japan moved toward the West.

The people, under leadership of the younger and more progressive nobles, began to copy western methods in business, industry, and the armed forces. Foreign experts were invited to Japan, and groups of Japanese citizens, scholars, and students were sent abroad to study and bring back what lessons they could learn from the West. As a result, industrial development speeded up, trade expanded, and in less than half a century, Japan became a copy of the nations of the West. A new constitution was adopted in 1889, a strange mixture of democracy and dictatorship.

This new government, an absolute monarchy with a constitution, ruled Japan from 1889 to 1945. It had a parliament free to pass laws only on subjects submitted to it and powerless to legislate on matters of war, peace, and foreign policy. It was a dictatorship without a dictator, a government at the mercy of the military. As a result, Japan became industrialized, urban, and imperialistic. Her excessive population emigrated, experiencing legal discrimination while learning the ways of the West.

By 1914, Japan's record as a member of the family of nations was impressive. She was industrialized and westernized. She had avoided becoming another arena for colonial partitioning. She had defeated China and Russia and gained holdings in strategic areas of the East. She was ready to demand equality in the world struggle for power.

Honoring terms of the Anglo-Japanese treaty of 1902, she came into the First World War in 1914 on the side of the Allies. By this action she hoped to destroy the German Pacific fleet stationed at Kiaochow on the Shantung Peninsula. While this would aid the allies, it was actually a major move in Japan's ambitions to dominate the East. Her troops captured Kiaochow and occupied the entire Shantung Peninsula.

Japanese development since 1889 and her contributions to success of the Allies placed her among the five great powers who wrote the peace: Great Britain, France, Italy, the United States, and Japan. It also gave her a seat among the permanent members of the League of Nations.

On September 18, 1931, an explosion near Mukden, Manchuria, damaged the Japanese-controlled railroad. Japan immediately occupied Mukden on the pretext of "suppressing banditry." When China brought the matter to the League of Nations, the Japanese delegate claimed it was a mere "Chinese Incident," of no concern to other nations. When Japan occupied all of Manchuria, deposed its ruler, the Manchu emperor of China, and declared it an independent state under the name of Manchukuo, the League, acting under the guidance of a study made by Lord Lytton, voted to condemn this illegal action. Japan cast the only negative vote and withdrew from the League. This started a chain reaction that led to collapse of the peace the framers of the League had so fervently hoped to preserve.

The Japanese began an intensive program of naval shipbuilding and strengthened the army. A Monroe Doctrine of Asia was decreed, with Japan assuming exclusive responsibility for Eastern Asia. Although there was some indication that China might become a partner to this plan, when the Japanese announced their intention of moving into Inner Mongolia, Sinkiang, and the border provinces in which lay Peiping and Tientsin, opposing forces in China united in fear of a common enemy. This caused Japan to strike at China on July 7, 1937. By 1939, her troops had occupied one-fourth of China, including its seaports, the Yangtze Valley as far as Hankow, and many interior cities.

As tensions were building in the West, Japan was moving to grab additional territory. She captured Hainan Island, along with some islands along the coast of Indo-China, and began a determined march toward the Dutch East Indies. France and Britain were in no condition to interfere. The United States began a series of moves to protect her sources of raw materials in these areas, moves which eventually brought Japan and the United States to the brink of war. Then, on December 7, 1941, Japan made an all-out attack on the United States naval base at Pearl Harbor, Hawaii. The following day, the Congress of the United States declared war on Japan.

WESTERNIZATION OF CHINA

Kublai Khan organized the Mongols into a strong fighting force in the twelfth century and conquered China. It was the court of this warrior that Marco Polo visited. Time and again this vast land was invaded. For a period the invader ruled, but eventually his power weakened, and he was absorbed into the Chinese race and its culture.

Rich in natural resources, vast in extent, her people endowed with skill and understanding, China boasts a long and proud history. Records tell of an advanced civilization as early as 2,000 B.C. Her written language is one of the oldest. Her poetry and philosophy rank

among the world's greatest, her painting is exquisite, and her craftsmen in metal, stone, porcelain, clay, and silks show patience, skill, and
an unmatched sense of grace and beauty. Her scientists discovered the
art of making paper, invented block printing and produced gunpowder.
Her architects built with an eye toward both the practical and the
beautiful, while her scholars delved deep into mathematics and astronomy. She gave the world Lao-tze and Kung-fu-tze, whom westerners called Confucius, and made over Buddhism for the consolation of
the peasants.

In the mid-nineteenth century, China was isolated from the world
under the Manchu dynasty. Few foreign merchants visited her cities.
The outer world had only a vague knowledge of events within her
borders. Internally she was a vast land of small, isolated farming communities unacquainted with events in other sections of the country.
There was no industrial development, and western ideas and practices
were far removed from the thinking of the people. The Manchu dynasty
was feeble, its cycle about to run out. By the 1850s, Chinese progres-
sives were moving against the government—the Taiping Rebellion
took place in 1852, and the western powers, with Russia and Japan,
were making plans to split the country into spheres of influence. China's isolation came to an end with the Opium War, 1839–1842, when
she attempted to stop Great Britain from importing opium from India
and selling it in south China. The result was the first of a long list of
"unequal treaties" forcing China to open her ports to British ships,
grant extra-territorial privileges, and allow foreigners to be tried in
their own courts. France, the United States, Russia, and Japan, along
with other powers, began moving into China, taking possession of her
lands and gaining control of her natural resources. Defeated in the
Sino-Japanese War and forced to pay an unreasonable indemnity,
China had to borrow money from other countries, for which she gave
territory and privileges. The world was witnessing the humiliation and
destruction of a once proud and self-sufficient people by foreign materialistic greed dressed in garments of respectability. The Boxer Rebellion
was an outpouring of Chinese hatred for foreigners who were exploiting the nation. The defeat of the Chinese meant still heavier indemnity
and deeper humiliation.

Young Chinese leaders who had been educated in the West demanded changes that would be in effect a complete break with "old
China" and acceptance of the industrial revolution with all that it
meant. Their leader was Dr. Sun Yat-sen (1866–1925), who had lived
in the United States, attended school in Hawaii, and received a medical
degree from the newly formed medical school at Hong Kong. A Christian and a liberal, he believed that old China would have to go in order

that new China could face the world on equal terms. He founded the Chinese People's Party, the Kuomingtang. In February, 1912, the Manchus were forced to abdicate, and Dr. Sun proclaimed the Chinese Republic. In *The Three Principles of the People,* he stated his philosophy of government and his ambitions for his native land. These ambitions included political unification and the end of foreign influence, an eventual democratic government with full liberties and rights for all, and economic improvements, including land reforms and industrialization. He wanted to see China an equal among the nations of the world, giving and receiving, assuming her rightful and natural responsibilities in the one world he saw taking shape.

With the overthrow of the Manchus, Dr. Sun resigned the presidency in a move for unity, and Yuan Shih-k'ai, the new president, was empowered to organize the government. Although Yuan accomplished much, internal conditions plus foreign interference made success impossible. Civil war began, disagreements among the official family increased, and many people favorable to progressive ideas felt Yuan was moving too rapidly. When he died in 1916, the country appeared to unite behind Li Yuan-hung, who had been declared president by the Kuomintang at the urging of Dr. Sun.

With the outbreak of World War I, Japan moved to gain control of strategic areas in China on the pretext of eliminating Germany from the Far East. In January, 1915, she revealed her hand by presenting twenty-one demands to the Chinese government, ignoring China's neutrality and establishing herself firmly in control of much of China's economic life. With the West in no position to object, Japan humiliated China further and made a series of secret agreements with Great Britain, France, and Italy regarding disposal of German holdings in China after the war.

In February, 1917, the United States invited China to break diplomatic relations with Germany because of her submarine campaign. When, on March 14, the Chinese foreign office severed diplomatic intercourse with Germany, China was beset with civil strife over the question of her attitude toward the whole war. The result was that China was unable to play an active role in the war and confined her participation to sending 175,000 of her citizens as laborers to work behind the lines in France, Mesopotamia, and Africa.

After the war, Dr. Sun moved to develop Chinese nationalism along democratic lines. He had to face the fact that the Republic of China actually controlled only the regions around Canton. The rest of the country was in the hands of war lords, who ruled with little concern for the wishes of any centralized government. When Dr. Sun appealed to foreign interests for help in uniting all China under his democratic government, the United States, Great Britain, and most other powers of the world wanted no part of the struggle. Only Russia offered to send technical and political advisers. This strengthened the Communist Party in China, which was admitted to the Kuomintang, and won good will for Russia among progressive leaders of the new China. With this help, a strong nationalist army took shape under the skillful direction of a young general, Chiang Kai-shek. This force was able by 1926 to move against the war lords of the north and establish a center of democratic influence at Hankow. Meanwhile, the Communists were busy organizing workers in the factories of Canton and Shanghai and the peasants in the provinces to strengthen the revolution.

While Dr. Sun lived, it was possible to hold both conservative land-owners, merchants, bankers, and industrialists and left-wing Communists within one party, even though their philosophies and ambitions were poles apart. When he died in 1925, General Chiang made himself leader of the right wing of the party. In 1927, the Communists were driven from the party, Russian advisers were sent home, and two governments took shape in China, one at Nanking under Chiang and the other loosely put together in the provinces west of the great bend of the Yellow River under Communist control. This latter was little more than roving bands of Communists and left-wingers organizing the peasants and harassing the government at Nanking.

Chiang was dictator of China. He controlled the army, the Kuomintang, and policy-making agencies of the government. Beset by enemies and facing problems generations old, he was successful in keeping in balance the interests of the divergent groups in his party. He was able by 1937 to show considerable progress in westernizing China. Roads and railroads were improved significantly, the financial structure of the government was gaining strength, an educational system along western lines was taking shape, and industrialization was becoming evident everywhere. But the conservatives in the party and the weight of long tradition forced Chiang to move slowly in the areas of land reform and collection of taxes, two of China's most aggravating problems. Chiang realized meanwhile that he must make the nation strong and united before the inevitable day when Japan would strike. He diverted much of the revenue that might have been used for internal improvement to the military, feeling that if China were to survive, she had to be nationalistic, strong militarily, and have the undivided loyalty of all the people.

The long-expected invasion from Japan came in September, 1931, when she moved into Manchuria over the Mukden incident. Neither China, the League of Nations, nor the western powers could stop her aggression. China, though not united, with only an uneasy truce existing between nationalists and Communists, was able to hold out against the invaders until the involvement of Japan in the Second World War brought this struggle to a stalemate. When the United States, and later Russia, entered the war against Japan, the tide changed in favor of China. The United States furnished planes and supplies to fight the Japanese, while Russia made a pact with China guaranteeing restoration of Manchuria.

The Soviet Union invaded Manchuria and received the surrender of Japanese troops there at the end of the war. Since the Chinese Communists were nearer to Manchuria than were the nationalists, the Soviet Union turned over to them huge supplies of arms and ammunition taken from the Japanese. Soon the Communists, under the leadership of Mao Tse-tung, were in control of northern China. Their control spread gradually as their slogan, "Land for the Peasants," caught on. Numbers of nationalist troops came over to their side, while city after city fell to their armies. In spite of strong pressure from the United States, who furnished the nationalists more than $400,000,000 in aid, Chiang lost power steadily, while the peasants and some of his own personnel rallied around Mao and his Soviet advisers. By 1950, the nationalists had been driven off the mainland of China to Formosa and other coastal islands, and Mao and his followers had established the Central People's Government of the People's Republic of China. Mao was chosen president-dictator. Great Britain, India, the Soviet bloc of nations, and other world powers officially recognized the new Communist government as representative of the Chinese people. The United States was able to influence a significant number of western nations to remain loyal to the Formosa government.

THE NEW WORLD AND AFRICA

North Africa had for centuries been considered a part of Europe. There one of the oldest civilizations of the ancient world, Egypt, had developed and pushed inland along the valley of the Nile. In Roman days this area had been considered part of the empire. Many leaders of Roman life and of early Christianity had been born along these shores.

When the Portuguese began mapping a sea route to India around the southern tip of Africa, they explored the coastline and developed a thriving trade in Negro slaves, gold, and ivory, along with other tropical products fancied by the wealthy of Europe. This opened a period of imperialistic exploitation by the British, French, and Spanish in an effort to control their share of this trade.

Little was known of the interior of Africa until the nineteenth century. When explorers pushed into central Africa and brought back reports of great natural wealth, wide fertile fields, and climates friendly to the white man, western powers become increasingly interested in opening this new country to trade and colonization. Few whites actually settled in Africa. It was possible for a small contingent of Europeans, backed by supplies from their homelands and well-trained and equipped native armies, to maintain peace in large areas, control numbers of Black laborers at very low cost, and protect trade routes.

By 1914, the continent had been divided among the western powers —Great Britain, France, Germany, Belgium, the Netherlands, Italy, Spain, and Portugal. Three areas remained free from foreign domination, two of which were Black-controlled. Ethiopia had long been an independent state with a history that reached back into Greek and Hebrew folklore. Although it had welcomed missionaries and traders, engaged in several wars with foreign forces, and at times lost parts of its border territories, it remained a sovereign nation until Mussolini invaded it in 1934. The Republic of Liberia, established in 1847 by freed Negroes from the United States, was not subject to colonization. The Union of South Africa, settled first by the Dutch and later by the British, was a federated union of Cape Colony, Natal, Transvaal, and Orange Free State. It was white-dominated, but the whites felt themselves part of Africa, and accepted British protection unwillingly.

At the close of World War I, German holdings in Africa were divided among the victorious powers. This left Great Britain, France, Belgium, Italy, Portugal, and Spain in control of the continent. When Italy moved into Ethiopia in 1934, she was merely extending her imperial holdings into an area not claimed by any other western power. Since this independent area adjoined Somaliland, which Italy controlled, it seemed logical for Italian troops to assume authority in the vacuum.

Although some campaigns of World War II were fought in North Africa, the colonial pattern was not materially changed. The peace that followed created several knotty problems regarding areas of Africa. The Sudan, under British control, was allowed to become an independent republic. Libya was turned over to the United Nations, which granted it independence in 1952. While Great Britain moved against the Mau Mau in Kenya and held this colony under its authority, Northern and Southern Rhodesia and Nyasaland were organized into the Central African Federation and given almost complete self-government, and the Gold Coast and British Togoland were merged into the independent state of Ghana. In the Union of South Africa, the whites, fearing Negro domination, established the policy of *apartheid* (segregation). In 1956, both Morocco and Tunisia became independent of the French. Algeria, on July 3, 1962, became a republic and a member of the United Nations. Meanwhile Colonel Gamal Abdel Nasser, elected Egypt's first president in 1956, sought to put Egypt in the sphere of Arab influence by forming the United Arab Republic.

By 1964, there were forty-three African nations in the United Nations able to exert considerable pressure to gain for the Africans equality in the family of nations. While the forces of one world worked against colonialism in Africa, they produced in fact an increase of nationalism and a dangerous resurgence of regionalism. The problems spawned since the beginning of western imperialism and brought into focus by the upsurge of nationalism remain to challenge the skill and understanding of world and African leaders. Events in Africa will influence all phases of life in the modern world for some time to come. Neither the United Nations nor the Africans can be certain of the effects of these events upon the future of our one world.

THE SECOND WORLD WAR

The peace made at Versailles and subsequent "deals" with Austria, Hungary, Bulgaria, Turkey, and some of the minority groups of Europe solved some of the problems that led to World War I, failed to solve others, and created new problems which festered in the body politic of one world. The years that followed were marked by increased poverty, unemployment, revolution, unstable governments, and inflation. Beginning in 1929, a world-wide depression threatened to destroy the economies of western nations. Finding the League of Nations impotent to deal with these world problems, nations retreated to a narrow, super-patriotic nationalism. Each state sought to live within its own borders, build and support its own defenses, create its own government, shape its own foreign policy, and protect its economy by high tariffs.

Perceptive individuals in all nations understood what was happening and spoke out to warn the world, but again the world-encompassing Greek tragedy had to be played out. Although each character knew the plot and understood his role, none was able to stop the play or ring down the curtain. All attempts at peace and a fruitful organization of one world collapsed when Japan attacked Manchuria in 1931, Italy moved into Ethiopia in 1934, General Franco destroyed the Loyalists in Spain, and Hitler began his push through Europe. The world heard Emperor Haile Selassie I of Ethiopia from the rostrum of the League of Nations in 1934 warn of approaching danger, but no one was able to stop the march of events to their inevitable conclusion.

Neville Chamberlain, Great Britain's prime minister, tried appeasement, believing that he had assured "peace in our time," and failed miserably. When, on September 3, 1939, Great Britain and France found that they could no longer ignore Hitler's advances through

Europe, they declared war, and World War II was officially on. As nation after nation fell under the *blitzkrieg* tactics of Hitler, other countries joined the war. The United States was determined to remain neutral. The Neutrality Act, passed by Congress in 1939, stated that this country would trade with all belligerents on a "cash-and-carry" basis. Realizing that this was actually an unrealistic approach to world conditions, President Roosevelt moved steadily toward an alliance with Great Britain and internal preparations for war.

Then, on December 7, 1941, Japan attacked the United States naval base at Pearl Harbor, Hawaii, destroying most of the ships riding at anchor there and killing more than 2,000 American citizens. On December 8, Congress declared war on Japan. A series of quick declarations of war against enemies of the Allies followed, and the whole world was engaged in another one-world war far more costly and vicious than the first.

President Roosevelt died in 1945. One of the matters which President Harry S Truman found on his desk was the Manhattan Project, a secret from even the vice-president. In 1941, after almost twenty years of study and research, Albert Einstein had written President Roosevelt a letter outlining the results of his experimentation, describing the simple formula $E=mc^2$, and urging him to provide money for a crash program to produce an atomic weapon. Four years of secret work brought the world to August 6, 1945, and a new age, in which man was faced with the alternative of one world or self-destruction. On this day, an American bomber dropped an atomic bomb on Hiroshima, Japan, destroying 60 per cent of the town. Three days later, a second and more powerful atomic bomb was dropped on the city of Nagasaki.

On June 6, 1944, the Allies, under the command of General Dwight D. Eisenhower, landed in western Europe. At the same time, the Russians launched a gigantic attack against the Germans along the whole 2,000 miles of the eastern front. As these two prongs of a great pincers movement closed in on the Germans and their allies, country after country was "liberated." On May 8, 1945, the German high command surrendered unconditionally. On August 10, 1945, the Japanese sued for peace and on September 2, 1945, signed an unconditional surrender on board the American battleship *Missouri* in Tokyo Bay. Thus the most terrible war in all history came to an end.

THE UNITED NATIONS

Mankind was again in a position to try to build one world out of the chaos and misery of all-out war. During the summer of 1944, representatives of Great Britain, Russia, China, and the United States met at

Dumbarton Oaks in Washington, D.C., and prepared a provisional charter for a world organization to establish and maintain peace and security for the entire world through international cooperation. In February, 1945, at Yalta in southern Russia, President Roosevelt, Prime Minister Churchill, and Marshal Stalin discussed the charter and set April, 1945, for the first meeting of the General Assembly of the United Nations at San Francisco. There, representatives of fifty nations met in an atmosphere of idealism and hope and wrote a charter which, within four months, fifty-one nations ratified. On October 24, 1945, the charter became effective.

This was the concrete realization that the future of mankind could be secured only if all nations acted as members of one world. So compact had the world become, with high-speed transportation and communications, that happenings in a far distant part could shape the thinking and living of people everywhere. The atomic bomb had awakened the world to the realization that its science had given it a weapon deadly enough to destroy the planet. Thus, fifty-one nations were ready to pledge themselves to maintain peace and security, promote equal rights and self-determination for all people, develop international cooperation, respect each other's sovereign rights, settle disputes peacefully, abjure the use of force or threat of force for purposes contrary to the charter, and stand back of the United Nations in all its efforts to prevent aggression or threats to world peace.

In writing the charter of the United Nations, an earnest attempt was made to profit by experience with the old League of Nations. The new body was organized to provide workable facilities for preserving peace and international cooperation while allowing each member nation the greatest possible freedom as a sovereign power. All members sat as a General Assembly to debate issues freely and express world opinion. Its decisions were recommendations, not preludes to action. The Security Council determined action. It consisted of eleven members, five permanent and six elected for two-year terms. The former included the United States, Great Britain, the Soviet Union, France, and Nationalist China. Any decision of the Council required seven votes to become binding, and all five of the permanent members had to be included in the seven.

Much of the work of this body was done by the organizations and commissions constituting the Economic and Social Council. This body was charged with improving the economic and social conditions of all people. It had the power to make studies and offer recommendations, but no authority to enforce them.

One of the most significant bodies constituting the Economic and Social Council has been the United Nations Educational, Scientific, and

Cultural Organization, called UNESCO. The preamble to its charter begins, "Since wars begin in the minds of men, it is in the minds of men that the defenses of peace must be constructed." Here the framers of the United Nations stated their conviction that while political, economic, religious, and cultural factors divide men into nations with varying and often conflicting aims and purposes, the basic causes of wars and international conflicts lie in interpretations given to these in the thinking of people. To preserve peace and build one world, man's thinking must be properly oriented. The function of UNESCO is to develop the international intelligence basic to the realization of the one-world ideal.

The first years of UNESCO were lived in an atmosphere of idealism and hope. By 1948, the atmosphere had changed radically. Disillusionment and discouragement marked the years between 1945 and then. Old hatreds and jealousies returned to destroy post-war harmony. Gradually, the world was divided between East and West, democracy and communism, and the "iron curtain" separated the nations into two camps. Problems of starvation and devastation were more real to the masses of people than long-range plans for international goodwill. Russia and her satellites stood against the North Atlantic Treaty Organization (NATO), the European Defense Community (EDC), the Southeast Asia Treaty Organization (SEATO), and other groupings of nations for self-defense and regional cooperation.

At the biennial conference of UNESCO in 1948, it was made clear to all members that the success of the body lay in the slow process of hammering out a pattern for peace through persuasion, diplomacy, discussion, and education. Out of this meeting, new and more realistic plans were laid for the future. Many had come to think of UNESCO as an agency of the western powers to spread cultural imperialism and dominate the world. This had to be countered by building a truly international staff able to think and act freely while accepting the major proportion of its support from the West. The barriers of diverse languages and thought patterns had to be penetrated through face-to-face conferences and seminars in the major population centers of the world. UNESCO had to become truly international while adjusting its thinking and program to the realities of the post-war world.

To meet the needs of all the nations represented in the United Nations and the people under its trusteeships, UNESCO has, since 1948, developed a program that has resulted in considerable success. This has included (1) mass literacy training in countries where the majority of the people can neither read nor write, (2) a program of communication and cooperation within the natural sciences through aid to international scientific organizations, (3) a restoration of communication among scholars through libraries, museums, and societies of the arts and humanities, and (4) provision for technical assistance to member nations to plan and develop educational and scientific surveys.

One of the most successful and controversial programs of UNESCO is "Education for Living in a World Community." This has been an attempt to work directly for increased mutual understanding among people of the world. Seminars of teachers from different nations have met to consider how the teaching of history, geography, foreign languages, and other subjects might develop in students a "truer and more perfect knowledge of each other's lives." Textbooks of many nations were surveyed and criticized wherever narrow nationalism was discovered. To help shape the new Germany, UNESCO established institutes under this program in Hamburg, Munich, and Cologne.

School systems in western Europe, Latin America, India, Australia, and many other countries have reacted favorably to this program and encouraged teachers to make use of it as far as possible. In the United States, "Education for Living in a World Community" has had a mixed reception. The United States National Commission for UNESCO has given the program considerable publicity, and several schools have experimented with various phases of it. Others have opposed the program as "subversive," claiming that it seeks to destroy national loyalties and national religion in favor of a vague internationalism and atheism. Some communities have banned from their schools all materials dealing with the program. In 1954, President Eisenhower appointed Irving Salomom, an industrialist, to head a commission to study the issue. This group reported that UNESCO was not atheistic, antireligious, Communist-controlled, attempting to establish a world government in place of national governments, or undermining the loyalties of American children. A committee of the American Legion, chaired by National Commander Murphy, in 1955, reported findings similar to those of the President's commission. But the 1955 annual meeting of the Legion rejected the Murphy report and asked Congress to investigate UNESCO's activities in this country.

UNESCO represents an effort to create in the minds of all people international understanding, which will assure the desire to find ways of international cooperation to preserve peace and enhance the well-being of mankind. It has been forced to work in the real world of living people and to shape its program accordingly. Its future depends upon the ability of its leaders to meet the crises of modern living and win the minds of men. Only the history of tomorrow can tell us whether or not it will succeed.

PROBLEMS IN A POST-WAR WORLD—FRUSTRATION AND HOPE

Like the years after World War I, so the years following the unconditional surrender of the Axis powers and Japan were full of disappointment and frustration. Economic and political dislocations demanded
immediate and far-reaching decisions that the victorious powers were
not ready to make. Nationalism waxed, as each country turned to its
own internal problems and new nations took shape in Europe and
Africa. Germany was divided into spheres of influence resulting eventually in two nations, West Germany and East Germany, and two
Berlins, West Berlin and East Berlin. Symbols of the break of world
unity were the "iron curtain" and the Berlin wall.

Russia established Communist governments in the countries she had
"liberated" in her push west and began building a satellite empire.
Communism spread east to divide Korea and Indo-China between Communist and anti-Communist spheres of influence and control. Eventually the Communists gained control of the mainland of China, pushing
the Nationalists on to Formosa and other coastal islands. One world of
1945 had, by 1957, become two worlds, with a large bloc of neutral
nations caught between the jaws of the cold war.

To counter the aggressive moves of the Communist bloc, the West set
out to aid nations in danger of falling into Communist control through
the Truman Doctrine, a pledge of economic and technical aid to countries willing to help "contain" communism, and the Marshall Plan, to
furnish aid to save the economies of Europe from collapse. Steps were
taken to bring the West into closer economic and cultural unity and to
organize a strong defense complex against Communist aggression.

Events in defeated Japan were far more promising. Under the leadership of General Douglas MacArthur, this nation turned from military strength and imperialism to build a strong economy and take its
place in the struggle for peace and stability.

When the United States dropped the first atomic bomb on Hiroshima
on August 6, 1945, the world entered the Atomic Age. Scientists had
learned to release the energy of the atom. Slowly it dawned on men that
here was a power that could either destroy life on this planet or become
the instrument for creating a world guaranteeing mankind advantages
and opportunities beyond imagination. Then, on October 4, 1957,
Russia announced that she had put a man-made satellite, *Sputnik,* into
orbit around the earth. The world moved dramatically into the Space
Age. This resulted in crash programs in both the United States and
Russia to understand outer space, to explore some of the nearer planets, and to send instruments and men to collect data for further experimentation and the eventual use of space. The possibilities for space

travel and exploitation of the natural resources of space stimulate the imagination. At the same time, the realization that atomic bombs can be dropped from space vehicles on any part of the earth at a signal from a hidden control center is frightening.

Since World War II, the world has stood in fear of World War III. Realization that we now have a means of total destruction has stayed the conflict. There remains the haunting fear that either by accident or by design someone will push the button that will light the fires of the war to end all wars.

IN CONCLUSION

Education is created by the culture to serve its interests and must bear the marks of its creator. In the past, state and national cultures have produced educational systems to acculturate their young and preserve their integrity. While they have been influenced somewhat by events and conditions beyond their borders, their character has been determined largely by regional factors.

During the twentieth century, a new and determining factor has come into play—one world. We have traced in some detail the history of this new century to emphasize the fact that now world events have the greatest influence on education. No nation can live behind an iron curtain, a bamboo curtain, or any other instrument of isolation. Just as it is impossible for a country to stop "foreign" satellites from passing over its territory, so with even the best techniques of thought control, it is impossible to hide from the citizens of any nation events, ideas, and ways of life beyond its borders. Nationalistic educational systems can be strong instruments for warping the minds of the young into narrow, super-patriotic shapes, but as one-world pressures increase, knowledge and ideas will filter through to subvert and undermine intellectual and spiritual isolation.

As we turn to consider educational developments in the nations of the twentieth century, we must appreciate the fact that they are essentially products of one-world events and only secondarily the results of internal happenings. In this new century, the term "western education" designates the geographic locus of events being considered. A closer study of these events will reveal that they are the products of conditions and happenings throughout the world. This gives emphasis to the fact that if we are to understand the historical and philosophical foundations of western education in the twentieth century, we must add to the western tradition developments in Russia, China, Japan, India, Africa, and other areas of the world. As we move through this century and into the next, this fact will become clearer. We of the West have become part of one world, and there is no turning back.

CHAPTER 18

Twentieth Century Education: War Time and Peace Time

SCHOOLS OF THE EARLY TWENTIETH CENTURY

EDUCATION IN GREAT BRITAIN

Great Britain has known for generations a national unity rarely experienced elsewhere. Its history and ethos produced a oneness which reached into the farthest lands of the empire and caused the Englishman wherever he might be, to dress for dinner and remain devoted to English customs and traditions. Consequently, the British of the twentieth century did not feel it necessary to develop a nationalistic spirit through public schools, nor did they fear subversion as did less secure nations. They allowed a high degree of flexibility in their education, permitting private and religious agencies a fairly free hand. However, the British were not immune to the pressures of world events and one-world aspirations that marked this century.

Educationally, Great Britain throughout the first half of the new century continued to reflect her essential aristocratic social organization. Elementary education continued to serve the masses, while secondary education was designed to prepare upper class leaders for high places in church, state, and business.

The truth of these generalizations becomes clear when we look carefully at major educational developments in Great Britain during the first sixty years of the twentieth century. As the nineteenth century came to a close, the National Board of Education was formed to serve elementary, secondary, and technical education. It was authorized to make suggestions and offer assistance in matters of curriculum and method, set standards for teacher qualification, buildings, and equipment, and see that children attended school as prescribed by law.

The Balfour Act, passed in 1902, was a move to increase public control over schools. Local school boards were abolished, and supervision of schools placed in the hands of local governments empowered to collect taxes to support both elementary and secondary education. Under this act, two types of schools were legalized, those supported by public money and controlled by local councils, called *council schools,* and those supported and controlled by private or religious groups, called *voluntary schools.* These latter received some tax support along with other sources of financing. By 1905, the government was making public money available to these schools to buy meals for the poor, to provide free medical care and recreation, and provide for other needed facilities.

The First World War caused Parliament to pass the Fisher Act of 1918. By this act, governmental supervision, stimulation, and advice were restricted to allow for freedom and initiative at the local level. Attendance at school was made compulsory for all children to the age of fourteen, with part-time attendance until the age of sixteen. All existing fees imposed upon elementary pupils were dropped. To guarantee a complete and effective system of schools for the whole country at both the elementary and secondary levels, the National Board of Education was authorized to supplement funds raised by taxation in the local communities. Local authorities were empowered to establish nursery schools for children under five years of age, expand medical care, physical education, and recreation, and increase scholarship assistance to students in secondary schools.

Conservatives held that many of these moves were too socialistic and fought them vigorously. They were able to reduce appropriations designed to make the plan work and to place roadblocks in the way of further legislation to strengthen the Fisher Act. As a result, the provisions in this law to provide an education for every child to the limits of his abilities and needs remained largely inoperative.

As world conditions changed during the 1930s, pressures for educational reform grew. The Second World War changed much of the thinking about education in Great Britain. R.A. Butler, president of the National Board of Education, outlined in 1943 a broad program of educational reconstruction that he considered necessary to deal with the problems the nation could expect to face in the post-war years, and urged Parliament to take immediate action. This resulted in the Education Act of 1944, the most ambitious and extensive educational proposal ever accepted by Britain.

The act recognized that the Britain of the future would have to overcome political, economic, and social dislocations caused by the war, and that the only source of hope for success was education for all—to prepare each for his role in post-war reconstruction. The National Board of Education was abolished and a new Ministry of Education created with broad powers to concentrate the leadership, control, and direction of the nation's schools in this centralized authority. County councils and county-borough councils were ordered to submit to the ministry plans for developing their local school systems in the direction of an educational ladder.

Three levels characterized this ladder. At the base was a primary school serving children from two years of age through eleven. Day care and nursery schools were made responsible for children aged two through four. These were followed by separate schools for children from five through eleven. On top of this rested a secondary school enrolling children at twelve and offering them education through age eighteen. All were required to attend school through the age of fifteen. The third level was called "further education" and was designed to serve special situations. It included county colleges offering one full day or two half days per week of training to those who dropped out before finishing the ladder. It also provided adult education and special instruction in art, commercial subjects, and technical areas.

Control and support of these schools differed in terms of their origin, past history, and function. The council schools, now known as country schools, were the responsibility of local authorities. Some voluntary schools were left wholly in the hands of private groups, while others were supported in part by public funds. Those schools not under public control or support were subject to periodic inspection by the Ministry of Education.

Religious instruction was adjusted to the school and its needs. All schools were expected to offer some, but any child could be excused if his parents wished. While county schools were expected to provide nondenominational religious teaching, each school with a denominational background was free to teach the religion desired by the parents.

This reorganization of the educational system demanded a new look at the preparation of teachers. In the past, teachers in the elementary schools were graduates of these schools who had had either an apprenticeship of two to five years with an experienced teacher or special training in some school offering the needed preparation. Secondary school teachers were graduates of the secondary schools who had attended a university, where they studied academic subjects and some "education." While in the 1920s the government had maintained some control over the courses taken by prospective elementary school teachers, this was left to local initiative in the 1930s.

The Second World War depleted the ranks of the teaching profession alarmingly. To meet this teacher shortage, a national committee was appointed in 1944, under the chairmanship of Sir Arnold McNair, to draw up a long-range plan for teacher education. As a result of its study, emergency measures and more permanent plans were adopted by the Ministry of Education. To provide teachers immediately, a number of training schools offering a one-year intensive course were established. These, in a four-year period, prepared more than 18,000 young men and women to teach. In addition, Area Training Organizations were constituted to work with universities, teacher-training institutions, and school systems to provide curricula for prospective teachers and programs of in-service training for those already in the classrooms. To attract young people at all levels of instruction, a single salary scale was adopted for teachers at the elementary and secondary levels.

As a result of the Education Act of 1944, and additional laws and pronouncements by those in authority, the whole conception of elementary education changed. The class-centered elementary school was changed into a first step in the educational ladder for all children. The success of this revolution was different in the local communities of Great Britain. While some moved fairly easily into the newer program, others resisted the changes. Groups of mothers picketed in several communities protesting the breakdown of class segregation. Officially, there is a continuous educational structure in all British communities serving all the children. Actually, British individualism is strong, and class divisions are sacred to a great many.

At the secondary level, traditional "public schools" came under severe criticism after the Second World War. While they remained the primary source of leaders in government, business, and the church, their exclusiveness and classical curricula seemed unsuited to the more democratic trends of the age. Though the Education Act of 1944 set the pattern for a truly public secondary education, parents and leaders held to the notion that traditional secondary schools were superior and that graduation from one of them was a mark of distinction.

Following the Second World War, four new types of secondary schools were established, serving specific needs and interests. A few comprehensive schools appeared in some large cities in which students of varied interests could study the academic subjects they wished while mixing with those pursuing vocations. These schools usually offered academic subjects, vocational studies, and advanced technical training. A great number of grammar schools also appeared, resembling in curriculum at least the more traditional public schools. They offered a liberal arts education in preparation for college and the universities or professional schools. Here the emphasis was on foreign languages, English language and literature, mathematics, science, history, and geography. Although passing attention was given to the manual arts, domestic science, and physical training, the major emphasis was academic. To meet the vocational needs of young people and serve the occupational and social life of local communities, a large number of "modern schools" appeared. These grew out of the upper levels of the elementary school and, while stressing liberal arts in the lower grades, offered a practical training fitting the child to his station in life. Many of these schools provided work for students in businesses, shops, laboratories, or other places where they planned to seek employment after graduation. A fourth type of secondary school was the technical school. This provided specialized training in the sciences and technologies basic to the industries and businesses of the locality, preparing young people to move into key positions in the economic life of their area.

In higher education, Great Britain felt the pressures of the modern world and responded with a new type of institution little resembling the traditional Oxford and Cambridge patterns. While these two great universities neglected research and the newer approaches to the sciences in favor of those areas of instruction suited to the ruling classes of the country, a number of institutions appeared along the lines of the American state university. These included provincial universities in Birmingham, Manchester, Liverpool, Reading, Durham, Bristol, and Leeds. To these should be added the universities of Glasgow, Aberdeen, and Edinburgh in Scotland. In London, a huge, loosely coordinated complex took shape called the University of London. This included two undergraduate colleges, King's College and University College; schools dealing with special areas, such as the London School of Economics; the Imperial College of Science and Technology; the Institute of Education; and a number of research institutes, teacher-training schools, and graduate schools. In many ways the University of London resembled Columbia University in the United States.

Immediately following World War II, the student bodies of British universities more than doubled. As secondary schools became stronger and better able to prepare young people, higher education must expand to serve the needs of these young graduates. While the more traditional colleges hold to the classical curriculum and the education of the "English gentleman," the great body of higher education can be expected to move in the direction of world-wide needs and interests. The local community will be served, but only as this training is set in a one-world concept of education.

EDUCATION IN FRANCE

During the nineteenth and early twentieth centuries, France moved in the direction of nationalistic control of education in the interest of loyalty to the state. Napoleon knew that the educational system was an important agency of political control and set about to reinforce the national character of all schools. Throughout the nineteenth century, whether the government was monarchy, empire, or republic, its leaders hewed to the policy that a strongly centralized state school system is the best assurance of national unity.

The Third Republic, established in 1871, continued this policy until its overthrow by invading Germans in 1940. Although France remained a Catholic country, there has been a deep conviction that the Catholic Church is the chief deterrent to national unity. La Chalotais, in the eighteenth century, attacked Church education in his *Essay on National Education*. In 1871, Gambetta, a brilliant republican leader, had declared, "Clericalism, that is our enemy." In 1901, the prime minister, Waldeck-Rousseau, asserted that the Church was a rival power, hostile to the state. He secured passage of a law making religious orders illegal unless specifically authorized. This was followed in 1904 by a law excluding members of religious orders from teaching in public schools. The following year, separation of Church and state was made absolute, and both the French state and the French schools were completely secular. This did not eliminate religious education in France. Private schools, supported by the Church or other non-public sources, but subject to state minimum requirements, were permitted to flourish and attract children.

After the First World War, the traditional dualistic, class-conscious school structure came under attack. A strong case was made for a "ladder" system providing free education to all, better trade and technical schools, a substantial increase of continuation schools, and wider educational opportunities for girls. However, the strong conservatism which characterized French society was able to resist all pressures to destroy the two-track pattern.

On June 16, 1940, the Reynaud government resigned in the face of the German invasion, and Marshal Pétain became head of the government. The Germans, working through Pétain, used religious and class issues to divide France and weaken her ability to resist. The ban on religious teaching orders was lifted and state funds made available for private schools. By 1941, more than one and a quarter million children were enrolled in religious schools, while the nation was embroiled in a bitter controversy over the growing power of the Church in state and education. To further divide the nation, difficult examinations were given to children who wished to transfer from primary to secondary schools, and high tuition fees were charged for the secondary schools. This destroyed any possibility of bringing primary and secondary education into an educational ladder open to all children to the limit of their abilities.

The provisional government, established after the liberation in 1944, began to work for restoration of the pre-war secular school structure under centralized control. Its leaders recognized that reforms were necessary to deal with problems created by the war and economic and social conditions reshaping the world. In 1947, the government appointed a commission headed by Paul Langevin, a noted physicist, and Henri Wallon, an eminent psychologist, to make a comprehensive study of French education and the demands of the post-war world, with the intention of developing a program to move the nation into the modern world. The report of this commission recommended that the lines between classical education and technological studies be erased and all children move through three cycles: "basic"—from six to eleven years of age, "orientation"—from eleven to fifteen years of age, and "determination"—from fifteen to eighteen years of age. This last cycle was to be a period of specialization. It was proposed that children be required to remain in school until eighteen. Teachers in elementary schools, the committee recommended, should be required to have a diploma from a secondary school plus two years of pedagogical study, be able to use more progressive teaching methods, and have a broad academic background. The report proposed that adult education, at government expense, be extended to people living on farms and in villages.

This report was considered "too ambitious" even for the post-war period. It aroused the conservatives and many Catholics to vigorous opposition. As a result, it was rejected by the government. Official rejection did not mean that the suggestions contained in the report were without merit. Many of them had been made before, but never with the backing of so many distinguished leaders. Many of the advances made in French education after the war were sparked by this report.

The educational structure that emerged after World War II contained features of the pre-war system and some progressive ventures to meet new conditions. Primary, secondary, and university education were under the Ministry of National Education, while technical education, with sports, was administered by another governmental office. The country was divided into seventeen *circonscriptions académiques,* with a rector, appointed by the ministry and advised by a local council, in charge of each. A child began his education in a kindergarten, advanced to the elementary school, and finally into secondary education. At the third step there were three types of schools designed to meet the more specialized interests of young people: (1) the *lycées,* providing a classical and modern education, (2) the *collèges modernes,* where technical instruction was available along with some training in one or more trades, (3) technical institutions specializing in specific types of training.

In each *académie* was a state-administered university open only to the most brilliant, those who could meet strict qualifying tests. These were supplemented by other institutions for advanced study, teacher-training schools, and technical colleges specializing in agriculture, the sciences, engineering, and the like. The Catholics operated several institutions of higher education devoted principally to theology, law, and the humanities.

The state increasingly assumed financial support of all schools, leaving to the local communities the maintenance of buildings. Agitation for state subsidies to assist Catholic schools continued under the Fourth Republic but was bitterly opposed by the Radical Socialists, the Socialists, and the Communists.

The state also controlled the curricula through its examination system. French parents and employers emphasized the need for the youth's receiving the *brevet* or *certificat* at fourteen and the *baccalauréat* at seventeen. These were state diplomas. This strengthened the academic nature of French education as well as its inflexibility.

Although some advances were made in French education under the Fourth Republic, the instability of the government, severe economic problems, and constant harassment by the Catholic Church prevented the nation from moving forward as rapidly as might be expected. In spite of legal restrictions against them, Catholics schools increased rapidly with the tacit consent of the people. By 1951, the Church forced a compromise, by which the government provided scholarships to children in Catholic schools and gave direct aid to families of Catholic pupils. This resulted in a tremendous increase in Catholic education in France.

The Third Republic had drawn more distinctly than ever the class lines between teachers in elementary and secondary schools. The former were required to complete the elementary school, spend two years studying special preparatory courses, and finally devote three years to preparation in a primary normal school. The latter were graduates of a *collège* or *lycee* with two to three years of training in a school of education connected with a university, and had passed a series of difficult state examinations in their subject fields.

When the Fascists came to power, the conservatives moved to destroy all liberal and radical elements in teacher-training institutions and universities. In 1941, special primary normal schools were abolished as hotbeds of liberalism. The wave of anti-Semitism that engulfed the nation during the war made it almost impossible for Jews to enroll in normal schools or to teach.

During the later years of the Fourth Republic, some efforts were made to erase class lines between elementary and secondary teachers, but with only minor success. Those preparing to teach elementary pupils found their training placing great emphasis on methodology, while training for secondary school teachers stressed the humanities and sciences.

Pressures from within and without gradually began to destroy any stability that the French may have had in the past. Governments were created, only to fall before anything constructive could be accomplished. A major source of trouble was North Africa, where French nationalists and forces fighting for the liberation of Algeria were at each others' throats. Subversion, sabotage, violence, and open defiance of the French government reduced the people to desperation. The nation was threatened with open civil war when Charles De Gaulle formed a government pledged to solve the Algerian crisis and restore stability throughout the country. This was June 1, 1958. On December 21 of that year he was elected president of the Fifth Republic. France turned to an all-inclusive nationalism, and her institutions became instruments in De Gaulle's ambition to restore the nation to a position of world leadership.

During the De Gaulle years, education came under greater pressure to build nationalism in the minds of the young. This meant tighter regimentation of the schools with a greater concentration of control in the Ministry of Education. Loyalty to France and her ambitions and thorough mastery of subject matter were stressed in the lower schools. Textbooks were prescribed by the ministry, and its examinations determined the pupil's future. Attempts to liberalize elementary education and to incorporate more progressive methods were unsuccessful. Elementary schools were largely secular, and religious instruction was kept at a minimum.

During the early decades of the twentieth century, French secondary schools had moved slowly away from the predominantly classical curriculum to include modern languages and sciences, along with history, geography, and mathematics. This was fought by the conservatives, who felt that the best possible training for an upper-class boy was classical. Under the Vichy government, attempts were made to further modernize and "vulgarize" the secondary school curriculum.

Many progressive elements were introduced into French secondary education during the 1940s. Individual needs and the interests of the children became the determiners of learning, authoritarian methods and ideas were discouraged, and the curriculum was widened to include many of the "new" subjects. This move was resisted bitterly by the many who believed in more scholarly studies and strict discipline. Recognition of a need for technical training for both industrial and military security turned French thinking toward education for the modern world and lessened the emphasis upon humanistic and classical studies. De Gaulle moved the nation more in this direction. France was gradually joining the modern world educationally, but always on De Gaulle's terms.

France developed her own source of atomic power, her own industrial society, and her own secular philosophy. These required mastery of the sciences, penetrating understanding of the world that is, and a loyalty to ideals that could return her to the forefront of world leadership. She has lived for some time as a member of one world. After two world wars, during which she suffered much, her leaders became determined that she shall never again be unaware of the portent of what is happening.

EDUCATION IN GERMANY

During the nineteenth century, conservatism and extreme nationalism dominated German education. The liberalism sparked by Stein, Fichte, Humbolt, and Suvern faded soon after the Congress of Vienna when Frederick William III turned to religious and aristocratic control of education. He thought of the school as a means of developing loyalty to the king and peaceful contentment with one's station in society. Frederick William IV continued this policy, using the schools to counteract subversive religious or political ideas.

Under both William I and William II, from 1871 to 1918, education was an instrument for unifying the empire. Schools were conservative, nationalistic, and centralized under state administration. The two-track pattern was strengthened. As the twentieth century opened with William II firmly seated on the throne, German education was dedicated to combatting socialism and communism and shaping the nation into a nationalistic unity obedient to its ruler.

Three schools dominated German education at the close of the nineteenth century. The *Volksschule* was a free elementary school for children from six to fourteen years of age. Those who completed this level might, for a fee, enter the *Mittelschule,* an intermediate school providing six years of instruction in practical and commercial subjects and one modern language. Children of the lower classes received this training and moved into lesser positions in business and industry. The upper classes had several secondary schools preparing pupils for the *Abitur,* an examination taken at the age of eighteen or nineteen, which, if passed successfully, admitted the youth into a university or technical school. The oldest and most revered of these was the *Gymnasium,* offering a thorough grounding in Latin, Greek, and the humanities. The other schools at this level were the *Realgymnasium,* in which classical and modern subjects were available under one roof, and the *Realschule,* preparing youth in mathematics, science, and modern languages.

Within this pattern, the government sought to inculcate national loyalties, prepare each individual for his place in the state, and discover and train leaders. Children were forced to attend school from their sixth year through their fourteenth. Separate schools were maintained for boys and girls. Church influence was evident in all the schools in spite of the socialists and other liberal groups who opposed sectarian public schools.

This pattern was retained under the Weimar Republic with some slight reforms. Concerted effort of state authorities aimed at enforcing compulsory attendance at the *Grundschule.* Children who did not go on to higher levels of the system were required to attend part-time vocational continuation schools for two to three years. Some attempts were made to make free secondary education available to all children of ability, but the German was too well schooled in the belief that secondary education was the prerogative of the upper classes.

Denominational schools thrived throughout Germany, although many schools appeared in which only some religious instruction was offered, and there were a few that were entirely secular. Two new types of secondary schools were created under the Republic: the *Deutsche Oberschule,* stressing German tradition, and the *Aufbauschule,* suited to rural areas and offering a six-year elementary education for those who had to leave school after their twelfth year.

The Nazi period brought many reforms in the school structure, all aimed at concentrating control of education in the state and making the school an instrument of Nazi ideology. In 1934, the administration of schools was placed in the Reich and Prussian Ministry of Education. Denominational schools, though formally retained under the Concordat of 1933, were systematically undermined, so that by 1940 they faded from the picture. Hitler retained three of the secondary schools he found when he came to power. The *Deutsch Oberschule,* which emphasized German tradition, was strengthened as an instrument for inculcating pride in the nation and its history. The *Aufbauschule* was turned into a nationalistic agency serving the masses living on farms and in the country. The *Gymnasium* was, in Hitler's eyes, an institution of doubtful worth. It had certain values but might get out of hand if it emphasized too strongly the classic and humanistic traditions. Although it was retained, its function in secondary education was restricted severely.

In addition to reforming existing schools, the Hitler regime created a free four-year *Hauptschule* that offered technical training to selected pupils of superior physical ability and unquestioned racial purity. This was to take the place of the *Mittelschule. National Political Educational* institutions and the *Adolph Hitler* schools were established for training the party elite. The teaching in all these schools was consistent with Nazi doctrine, and the aim was always the production of a people with unquestioning loyalty to the regime. Jews and other suspect teachers were denied the right to teach.

German universities until 1810 were medieval and classical. The University of Berlin was established in an attempt to break this tradition and make the university a center of freedom to learn and to teach. Leaders of the Weimar Republic sought to open university education to students from all classes and sections of the country, but with only scattered success. German universities continued to attract upper class students and some from the prosperous middle classes. Freedom to teach degenerated into freedom to attack the democratic republic with nationalistic and antidemocratic propaganda. Numerous student organizations espousing Nazi-nationalistic causes appeared on the campuses as early as 1931.

Hitler appointed Bernard Rust minister of education responsible only to him. Rust, in turn, appointed university rectors, whose instructions were to purge their faculties of all Jews and any others suspected of opposing the theory that the main purpose of the university was to produce the new man, purely Germanic and Aryan. Curricula were revised to place major emphasis upon history and geopolitics and shape these subjects to the theory of German racial superiority.

At the close of World War II, the Allied leaders who met at Potsdam agreed that education in the occupied zones should aim at eliminating Nazi and militaristic doctrines and turn to democratic ideas and methods. It was discovered that a great number of Germans agreed with this approach and were willing to cooperate. Many schools had been destroyed during the war, textbooks along democratic lines were nonexistent, and only a small number of teachers could be found who were not loyal Nazis. Facing these problems, the occupying authorities began school reforms in each of their designated zones. The Control Council, in 1947, drew up a statement of general principles to guide the four powers concerned. These principles included equal opportunity for all, free tuition and school equipment, financial aid to non-public schools, compulsory attendance for children between the ages of six and fifteen and part-time attendance until eighteen for youths not attending an institution of higher education, an educational ladder, teacher education in universities or training schools of university status, and education for responsible citizenship in a democratic society for all Germans.

Serious attemps were made in the British and American zones to democratize the schools along the lines of the Council's suggestions. The British sought to build a school structure with a six-year *Grundschule* followed by a six-year secondary course. Allowance was made on the secondary level for adapting the work to student needs. The United States followed much the same pattern. Here free schooling became a reality.

The French returned the schools to the Weimar system with a four-year *Grundschule* and a nine-year secondary school. The Russians developed the most comprehensive school system of any zone, with education centralized at every stage. They instituted an eight-year elementary school, to be followed by a four-year period of instruction either in an *Oberschule* or a vocational school. Private schools were abolished, and no religious instruction was allowed. Schools in the Russian zone became agencies for Communist teaching.

German universities after World War II faced an almost impossible situation. Many of their buildings had been destroyed. The de-Nazification program undertaken in all zones removed from the faculties a large number of professors. Since this level of instruction had been neglected during the war, there was a flood of new students coming into university classrooms. To deal with these problems, a vast building program was inaugurated, rented quarters were used to deal with the immediate need, plans were laid to train as quickly as possible teachers with democratic leanings, and limits were placed on enrollments. By 1951, it was possible to remove these limits for all but medical education in certain universities.

Since the original University of Berlin was in the Russian sector of the city and was being transformed into a Communist propaganda center, a Free University of Berlin was founded in the western sector in 1948. Before the wall was built separating East Berlin from West Berlin, nearly forty per cent of the students attending the Free University came from the Russian sector, or Democratic Republic.

A mixed commission was constituted near the end of 1947 to study the university situation and recommend needed reforms. Its proposals included more independence from state administration, closer relationships between the universities and the communities involved, employment of professors skilled in teaching rather than research, and introduction of new materials into the curricula. Chairs of political and social science were founded in several universities, but little else was done to implement the commission's recommendations.

In East Germany, the Russians sought to make the university an institution reaching all classes of society. It was decreed in 1948 that sixty per cent of all students must come from the workers. When this number could not be attained, the percentage was lowered. Further, the university was construed as an instrument for Communist indoctrination, and professors were employed and advanced in terms of their political reliability. Since it was difficult to find enough adequately trained men and women who met this standard, the East German government was forced to wink at a degree of political apathy on the part of some members of the faculties.

Studies of universities in the Russian zone, called the Democratic Republic, have shown that higher education turned from the broad scholarship of earlier days to an excessive emphasis on Communist political theory and an overspecialization in technical subjects.

Because of Communist regimentation, excessive restrictions in the professions, and the avowed attempt of the Democratic Republic to use educational institutions as instruments for ideological indoctrination, a steady stream of teachers, scholars, doctors, and other professional and technical personnel flowed westward into the German Federal Republic, denuding the intellectual community of Communist Germany. Recognizing that it faced a crisis of major proportions, the government in East Germany decreed severe penalties for anyone leaving the country without permission. When this failed, the authorities, on August 13, 1961, began constructing a wall along the border between East and West Berlin and strengthened guard posts along the entire frontier separating East from West Germany. Restrictions were tightened to keep East Germans out of a three-mile strip along the border.

The loss of trained university teachers through defection to the West caused East Germany, in 1962, to abolish its "workers and peasant faculties" at all universities and technical colleges with the exception of two. To adjust to this dearth of instructors, the government required that all applicants for admission to these schools complete both their secondary education and their occupational training. This limited higher education and advanced technical training, restricting it to the intellectually superior. It was an abandonment of the earlier policy of bringing into all schools a larger number of students from the working and peasant classes.

As a result of World War II, Germany remains a divided country, not wholly trusted in either East or West and, in the light of her history during the twentieth century, feared as a potential enemy by many European and eastern nations. She is half free and half Communist. Two educational systems are to be found within her borders, one designed to serve free men in a democratic society, and the other striving to indoctrinate a whole people in Communist ideology. Though divided, the two Germanies have a common aim: to develop each its own kind of nationalism and loyalty to ideas. While conscious of the one world in which she must live, West Germany is nationalistic. Equally concerned with one world, the East German government is Communist, although the people are far more German than Communist.

EDUCATION IN THE SOVIET UNION

The Soviet Union comprises all those territories of the Eurasian continent within the Union of Soviet Socialist Republics. It is most important to bear this in mind when considering education in this vast area. Often, aims set in Moscow are incapable of realization in the far reaches of the Union. Whatever is written about Soviet education is not necessarily applicable in all of the republics constituting the Union.

Russia had nine universities in 1895, and a total enrollment of 13,976 students. Throughout all of the vast lands of the czar there were 29,241 primary schools with 1,937,076 pupils. It has been estimated that 75 per cent of the people could neither read nor write. Education was confined to a small elite group, while the government paid no attention to educating the peasants who formed the majority of the population.

Industrial expansion marked the last decade of the nineteenth century and the first of the twentieth. This stimulated the development of handicraft schools and communal schools able to train technicians to operate machinery. These, serving the needs of new industry in large population centers, did not alter in any significant way the educational poverty of the masses of Russians.

By 1964, the U.S.S.R. reported that approximately 2,000,000 teachers were instructing some 42,445,000 children in elementary schools. It further boasted that 1,390,000 students were enrolled in industrial institutes or were working as apprentices, while more than 2,668,000 were in the nation's secondary schools. The 738 institutions for higher education were serving 2,945,000, of which 1,658,000 were in attendance during the evenings or were learning through correspondence courses. It was claimed at that time that less than 10 per cent of the people in Russia could be termed illiterate, since most of the republics of the Soviet Union were making four years of elementary education available to their citizens.

This remarkable advance was due largely to a determination on the part of Communist leaders to use the schools as an instrument for ideological propaganda. They realized that a strong, modern, Communist nation could not exist where there was illiteracy and ignorance. On September 1, 1949, *Pravda* stated the Communist thinking clearly: "To bring up active fighters for the cause of Communism, all-round educated people, possessing thorough and firmly-based knowledge, such is the main task of our schools, such is the law of their life. All must be subordinated to this task: the process of education, extra-school occupations, propaganda among parents, the work of the Young Communist and Pioneer organizations in the schools." "All-round educated people," "thorough and firmly-based knowledge," and a Communist society are one in the thinking of Russian leaders. Thomas Jefferson wrote in 1816, "If a nation expects to be ignorant and free, in a state of civilization, it expects what never was and never will be." The Russians might well paraphrase this credo to read, "If a nation expects to be ignorant and communist, in a state of civilization, it expects what never was and never will be."

With the Revolution of 1917, an attempt was made to destroy all czarist institutions and systems. The Ministry of Education was replaced by two administrative bodies: the People's Commissariat for Education and the State Commission for Education. Anatoly V. Lunacharsky, head of the latter, published a statement of the basic aims of Communist education: (1) abolition of illiteracy and introduction of universal, free, and compulsory schooling, (2) immediate establishment of institutions for training the "people's teachers," and (3) abolition of all church schools in the interest of a "militant atheism."

In December of 1917, the state took over all church schools, seminaries, and academies. The next month it disestablished the church and ordered all schools to confine their teaching to secular matters. This was followed in May, 1918, by a decree making coeducation universal. In October of that year, another decree codified the many measures that had been introduced since the revolution. All schools under the People's Commissariat for Education were designated "united labor schools" and divided into two grades: Grade I—for children from eight to thirteen, and Grade II—for those thirteen to seventeen. Although the decree made the system free and compulsory, the shortage of teachers and lack of school buildings limited the numbers who might be enrolled. Old methods for discipline, homework, and examinations were abolished, and schools were run by soviets with pupils having considerable authority. Teachers were subject to control by these soviets.

On August 2, 1918, institutions of higher education were opened to all citizens over the age of sixteen. This was followed in September, 1919, by a decree directing all universities to provide special courses, called "worker's facilities," to prepare workers and peasants for higher education.

It had become evident by 1931 that new and more effective techniques of teaching and patterns of organization were needed. Several decrees followed, abolishing student control, localized freedom over the curriculum, and other measures that had seemed appropriate in 1917-1918. Russia turned to Europe for guidance and direction.

On May 16, 1934, the "united labor schools" were abolished and a new national system of "general educational schools" decreed. These were divided into three stages: (1) the elementary school with four grades, accepting children at seven years of age; (2) the secondary school with seven grades; and (3) the secondary school proper with ten grades. These schools were available to communities on the basis of facilities, teachers, population, and need. The most universal was the first stage, or four-year elementary school. In larger communities one might complete this elementary stage and move on into the "incomplete" secondary school. The third stage or "complete" secondary school, often called the ten-year school, was largely in the great cities. It accepted children at seven and graduated them at seventeen. This program was ideal on paper. Many schools were established, but the ten-year school was not common, even in towns of the most highly developed of the republics, and the seven-year school was almost unknown in less-developed areas.

The Soviet Union succeeded in developing the desire for general education far beyond its ability to provide teachers and school buildings and to the detriment of its agricultural and industrial development. Students were crowding the schools in vast numbers, neglecting farm and factory work and the military. To limit this, on October 2, 1940, a system of tuition fees was decreed for pupils in the senior year of secondary schools and in higher educational institutions. Subsequent decrees exempted students of outstanding ability, those in the military classes, in national theatrical and musical studios, in the national ballet schools in Moscow and Leningrad, children of noncommissioned members of the army and navy, and children of certain persons drawing invalid pensions. This restricted the number of students at these levels of instruction.

In 1943 an order came from the Council of People's Commissars to abolish coeducation and establish schools for the separation of the sexes as soon as possible.

Two patterns of advanced education were developed in the Soviet Union: specialized schools and universities. Pupils who completed the second stage, the seven-year "incomplete" secondary school, were eligible to advance to specialized schools, in which they could receive training as technicians, "middle grade" specialists, or elementary school teachers. They were granted free tuition, subsistence allowances, and a monthly income during training. Universities and certain institutes for the training of top-grade specialists were open only to those who had completed the third stage, the ten-year "complete" secondary school.

These were charged with the responsibility of training intellectuals, specialists in the management and direction of the state's industrial complex, and engineers.

An ordinance of July 17, 1928, faced squarely the country's need for skilled personnel and set the ambitious goal of producing twice as many engineers and specialists for heavy industry by 1932. After several years' experience, during which many experiments were tested, the Central Committee of the Communist Party and the Council of People's Commissars issued a decree on June 23, 1936, proposing a complete reorganization of higher education. Anyone admitted to an institution of higher education was now required to complete the full ten-year school and pass a state examination. Also, rigid requirements were laid down for members of the professional staffs and for receiving diplomas from these institutions.

For many years, people of "undesirable social origin" and children of parents with "limited social rights" had been banned from receiving higher education. In December, 1935, this ban was lifted as part of a move toward the abolition of proletarian class privileges, a move that culminated in the new Stalin constitution of 1936.

Stalin died in 1953. There followed a struggle during which Khrushchev rose to power and, in 1958, became Chairman of the Council of Ministers and Dictator of the Soviet Union. At the twentieth Congress of the Communist Party of the Soviet Union, held in Moscow in February, 1956, Khrushchev, as First Secretary of the party, delivered a bitter denunciation of Stalin and his "cult of the individual." This was the first serious attempt of the new Soviet leaders to divorce themselves from Stalin and his methods of rule. Since the schools were instruments of the state to inculcate the "party line," it was inevitable that education in the Soviet Union would be brought into line immediately. Textbooks had to be purged of all references to Stalin as the just and good father of the people, the leader who could do no wrong. Teachers had to be briefed, administrators had to be informed, pictures of Stalin in schools had to be removed, and the entire educational structure had to do an about-face. There was minor opposition because some felt the denunciation of their leader was unjustified, but the educational system of Russia changed rapidly. Textbooks, encyclopedias, journals, and reading materials were revised. Teachers and administrators, accustomed to sudden party shifts, fell in line.

The Central Committee of the Communist Party held several meetings during 1958. The November session tackled the question of educational reform in the light of the accumulated experiences of several years and the pressing problems of the moment. The Communist Youth League, meeting in April of that year, had previously pointed to defects in the school system detected by the young people. They were especially concerned with the lack of moral and social discipline and felt that weaknesses in the educational system were responsible. At that time Khrushchev told them reforms were under consideration. Then, in September, a plan for major changes in education was presented in the form of a memorandum signed by Khrushchev and approved by the Presidium of the Central Committee.

This plan was aimed at strengthening "the ties between school and life" and extending public education along several lines. It abandoned the earlier attempt to give every child a ten-year schooling and reverted to the practice of making a seven- or eight-year general education available to the majority. This was followed by various forms of advanced education aiming at raising the technical qualifications of youths for work in industry and agriculture. All children were required to participate in "socially useful work after finishing the seven- or eight-year school." Many had come to feel that the practice of admitting all graduates of secondary schools into higher education automatically tended to direct the attention of young people away from productive labor. Agricultural and industrial involvement on the part of youths, they held, would inculcate a sense of social responsibility and produce a moral commitment to the welfare of the nation.

In spite of considerable resentment on the part of parents, educators, and industrial managers, the program became general in large centers of population. It did not solve the basic problem that had stimulated its enactment. "Hooliganism" among Soviet youth in large cities continued to worry educators and leaders of the state. The Soviet press and writers in magazines and journals expressed the opinion that the entire Soviet educational system, including schools and all agencies of propaganda, was failing to inculcate Communist ideals in the young. They referred to ideological teaching as "colourless and unpersuasive." As such, it was failing miserably to combat "bourgeois nationalism," backward customs, parochialism, the influence of alien "ideology, cosmopolitanism, and political indifference," religion, lack of labor discipline and "contempt for labor," bureaucracy, bribery, speculation, and drunkenness. At a special meeting of the Central Committee in September, 1960, L. F. Ilyichev, propaganda chief, called for an intensive battle on the part of all Soviet educational agencies to combat "idlers and loafers, those who do not work but eat, private property and apolitical tendencies, revival of bourgeois nationalism, religious prejudices, and other manifestations of bourgeois ideology."

These developments indicated to many that the iron curtain failed to shut out the world, of which the Soviet Union must be a part, and that even the most carefully directed and prescribed education cannot deal with the problems of one world in transition.

With the increase of crime in the Soviet Union, the government decreed the death penalty for stated deviations from Communist ideology. Several were sentenced to death for currency speculation and embezzlement. By 1963, Soviet leaders were beginning to recognize that the "hooliganism" among youths was being matched by crime in places of high economic trust. In January, 1962, an Academy of the Social Sciences was established and immediately held a conference on social problems and their relation to education. At the same time, loud accusations were being heard against Russian literature, art, music, and other cultural areas. These arts were being charged with failing to teach Communist morals and ideals and thereby undermining the state. *Pravda,* in 1962, delivered a tirade against artists, writers, and composers who, it claimed, had come under western influence and were betraying socialist goals. Since many Jews were involved in these enterprises, a campaign was beginning to place much of the blame upon Jewish people living in the nation.

After the Revolution of 1917, Soviet Russia struggled to build an educational system that would serve communism and shape a vast nation according to Communist ideas and ideals. Many experiments were tried and abandoned. Schools were erected, teachers trained, and curricula developed with this goal in mind. Illiteracy was almost abolished. Basic education was made available to the entire population, with only a few minor exceptions. Scientists, industrialists, imaginative scholars, and leaders in every walk of life were developed, enabling the nation to take giant strides into the modern world. The West had to think and act in terms of what this people planned, accomplished, and hoped. One world became the arena for a cold war between East and West, and its atmosphere was permeated with a fear that man has never known before, a fear that someone might push a button that could destroy everything. The Soviet Union had become a major factor in western culture and western education.

EDUCATION IN CHINA

China has a population of 800,000,000. This is approximately one-fifth of all mankind. For centuries, most of the Chinese were peasants ruled by a small elite class that cared little for their welfare. They suffered starvation, diseases, exploitation, and ignorance. Today they are being re-educated and re-made under a totalitarian system. The major objective of their education under communism is the maximization of national power through industrialization. Within less than a half-century, China has marched into modernity and become a major force in the one world. Forces operating in present-day China are causing the West to change many aspects of its thinking and acting. The future of the West will inevitably be influenced to a large degree by developments in China, and education is basic to these developments.

Chinese education has been a function of the culture. Since the history of China is the history of three cultures, Chinese education must be studied as three types growing within these three cultures. These are traditional, western, and Communist.

In traditional China, education was considered the primary means for shaping the character of its people. One became worthy and good not by adherence to a religion but through proper education. Since China created no absolute god or blissful heaven to measure human character or determine the goals of life, the criteria of the good life were humanistic. One was judged by his relationships with others in this world. He learned the principles of right conduct and was motivated to follow them through his education in home, school, and environment.

The Great Learning, one of the Four Books of Confucian scripture, told the people that "what the Great Learning teaches is—to illustrate illustrious virtue, to renovate the people, and to rest in the highest excellence." One who studies, investigates things, will thereby extend his knowledge. In this way he becomes "sincere in [his] thoughts." Sincere thinking "rectifies the heart" and "cultivates" right character. One who has so cultivated his own person will be able to regulate his family, the state, and the kingdom. One is reminded here of Socrates' position that "knowledge is virtue," "to know the good is to do the good." Confucianism taught that knowledge is basic to right thinking and thus to right living.

The aim of all education, the Confucian believed, was the cultivation of *Jen,* the quality of humanness. Through education, or learning, the individual realizes his intrinsic value and dignity as a human being and strives to attain harmony between himself, others, and nature. When he has attained the state of *Jen,* he is a sage, a loyal subject of the ruler, a filial son, a faithful friend, and a just and righteous leader of men. At this point he becomes a *chun-tzu* or superior man.

China did not develop a hereditary aristocracy based on wealth, birth, or religion. The sole criterion for advancement to a position of power and leadership was, according to the Confucian teaching, proved ability through education. The scholar is the educated man, the good man. These terms are synonymous. The good man is the only one capable of ruling others. His moral life is an example for others to follow. A good society is one shaped by the moral superiority of its scholars, its "philosopher-kings." Since only a few can become superior men, the others are *hsiao-jen,* or mean men. They are to be ruled. The superior man rules only because of his moral superiority. Education brings responsibility, and the superior man must participate in government. The *Analects* hold that "when a superior man is well instructed, he is easily ruled." Education is for all, but some will through education become rulers, while others also through education will become the ruled.

Traditional China produced and selected its scholars through a system of schools and a pattern of examinations. Most Chinese received no formal education, learning what they needed to know by working and being instructed informally. Those who were able to obtain some formal education might attend one or more of the schools maintained by private groups or individuals. There were *family schools* found exclusively in the homes of the upper classes who were able to employ a tutor responsible for the instruction of their children. *Clan schools* were fairly widespread. These, operated and financed by clans, were open to children of clan members and were usually taught by some elderly member of the clan deemed qualified to give instruction. Often the leading families in a village would organize a *village school,* to which all children of the village might come upon payment of a fee determined by the financial status of the parents. In large cities or places of exceptional beauty were *private academies* where nationally famous scholars taught and students came on a voluntary basis.

In addition to these schools, there was a state school system consisting of a number of educational institutions located largely in county seats and prefectures. Scholars aspiring to higher degrees might attend these schools and listen to lectures by government educational officials. In the capital was the Imperial Academy, considered as the highest institution of learning but largely part of the imperial bureaucratic apparatus.

Although some of these schools have been thought of as comprising a state educational system, they were actually more or less discrete institutions in which one might prepare in part for the state controlled examinations. From the T'ang dynasty (618-906) until 1905, the imperial examination system was the principal means by which government offices were manned. One aspiring to government office might study where and as he wished or could afford. When he believed himself ready, he applied for admission to the examination held in the *hsien* or county. Success here meant that he could move on to the prefecture examination under the supervision of the provincial educational commissioner. If he passed this examination, he was granted the degree of *Sheng-yuan,* or licentiate. This was also called *Hsiu-ts'ai,* or budding talent. From here he might go on to the provincial examination held every three years in the provincial capital. The degree of provincial graduate was granted to all who passed this examination. They also were permitted to assume the title *Chu-jen* or elevated man.

Scholars earning the provincial degree might take the metropolitan examination held in the nation's capital triennially. The few who passed received the degree of metropolitan graduate and became *Chin-shih* or advanced scholar. There was then the palace examination, held in the presence of the emperor as a final phase of the metropolitan examination, which determined members of the *Han-lin Academy* who theoretically served as advisers to the emperor.

These examinations dealt wholly with classical learning and, in addition to supplying the state with administrators and leaders, served to preserve Confucian orthodoxy and the ancient traditions of the people. In so doing, they discouraged original thinking, critical analysis, and creative expression, while stressing imitation and memorization. The scholar was completely divorced from the practical. His love was "book-reading," which demanded all his time and talent. His long fingernails were proof that he had not stooped to engage in utilitarian pursuits.

Beginning in the 1840s, China yielded steadily in the face of advancing western power, until by the opening of the twentieth century she was reduced to the status of a semicolony. Chinese education was changed by this experience and reflected the nation's varied attempts to respond to the impact of the West. This second, or western, stage in Chinese educational history falls into three periods.

Beginning around 1860, China launched a program of school construction to prepare the nation to cope with western powers. The new schools existed along with traditional schools and the examination structure and were planned for specific needs. There were foreign language institutes to train diplomatic personnel, technical schools concerned with shipbuilding and navigation, and military academies to prepare officers and men for the army and navy. Although some significant developments took place during the years from 1860 to 1902, the national program of education was half-hearted, as though the leaders hoped the threats of the western powers might just go away.

The Sino-Japanese War of 1894-1895 was convincing evidence that China had to meet the outside world squarely and make whatever adjustments were demanded. The traditional examination system was abolished in 1905, and the government planned a new system of education that included modernized schools at all levels. Up to this time the Chinese had sought to preserve their traditional educational pattern while making minor adjustments to pressures from the West. Now they turned their backs on the past and determined to move wholeheartedly into the modern world. While it was impossible in the face of political, economic, and social conditions to make their plans a reality, the government of China had opened the floodgates of western influence. Chinese students were traveling west and returning with western knowledge and enthusiasm for change. Schools were springing up under the auspices of foreign missions, exposing larger and larger numbers of Chinese to western ideas and influences. The abolition of the examination system caused traditional schools to become obsolete and Confucian orthodoxy to fade. By 1920, the nation was ready to set about creating a western-type educational structure. By 1927, a national government had been established in Nanking, bringing to an end warlordism and disunity. Now was the time to begin to stabilize and rationalize the new education at which the nation had been stabbing since the 1860s. Professional guidance was sought in this endeavor, especially from the United States. American-trained educators helped form the National Association for the Advancement of Education to advance democratic concepts. Increased emphasis was put on science, technology, military training, vocational instruction, and teacher preparation.

Gradually, a new intelligentsia came of age and began influencing the nation and its schools. They were determined to create a scientific basis for education. John Dewey and Paul Monroe, symbols of western culture and education, were invited to lecture in China.

From 1860 to 1949, China moved from traditionalism to modernization. At first (1860-1900) she held tightly to her past, and made only those adjustments that could not be avoided. Language schools, technical schools, and military academies were poor seconds to the traditional schools and examinations which had been the backbone of Chinese education. Then (1900-1920) it became evident that the old had to go and the new put in its place. During these two decades, China was defeated by the Japanese, the Chinese Republic was formed, and the May Fourth Movement took place. Westernization was gradually becoming a reality, and leaders of new China were appearing, men and women trained in and inspired by the progressivism of western democracy.

During the third period (1920-1949), China accepted westernization as the only means of survival. Education was built around Dr. Sun's "Three People's Principles," with schools undertaking to give to as many people as possible civic training, instruction preparing them for citizenship and military service. As Japan began aggressive moves toward China after 1931, it became evident that even the western education sponsored by Dr. Sun and General Chiang was inadequate. The outbreak of hostilities in 1937 began a period of steady deterioration of social and economic conditions and was a prelude to the collapse of westernization that opened the way for the eventual Communist take-over.

The Communists moved in with a definite educational philosophy and clearly perceived plans for educating the masses to save themselves, develop a Chinese nationalism, and stride rapidly toward the modern world. Leaders in Communist thinking asserted that dialectical materialism was a world outlook founded on scientific truth and representing the forward-movement of history, while the idealistic philosophy of the West was reactionary, decadent, and opposed to human progress and scientific truth. They held that all knowledge begins with experience, moves into the theoretical, and returns to experience. First the individual acts. Through action he learns, reaches the theoretical plane. To be of value this knowledge must be "redirected to the practice of changing the world." This negated Chinese traditional education, which was wholly divorced from practice. Ideologically, China's new leaders broke with the metaphysical idealism of the West, an education that shunned practice, and all cultures developed out of imperialism or semifeudalism. These leaders would build on scientific truth, turn knowledge to the practical task of changing the world, and create a new culture out of the life and needs of the masses.

These ideological principles pointed, they believed, to an education that would be nationalistic, scientific, and of and for the masses. The Chinese people were to be taught to cherish their cultural tradition and avenge offenses against them by imperialists. All schools with foreign affiliations had to be destroyed, and the intellectuals had to profess faith in the new order. To develop modern science and technology, the Chinese Academy of Sciences was expanded, institutions of secondary and higher education were established to train engineers, technicians, doctors, and specialists in all fields, and schools for the "broad masses of the people" appeared everywhere, teaching reading and writing plus the rudiments of modern science and technology. These schools had but one purpose—to move China's 800,000,000 people into the modern world as rapidly as possible and to gain recognition as a distinct nation with its own history and tradition and national pride. The slogan "Intellectualize the proletariat; proletarianize the intellectuals!" governed this education.

By 1960, 90,000,000 pupils were in primary schools; 8,520,000 in secondary schools; 470,000 in technical schools; 810,000 in higher education; and 280,204 in teacher-training institutions. Children were placed in nurseries soon after birth and educated by the state. Youth were organized into Young Pioneers and a hundred other groups, and all means of mass communication taught rather than entertained. In addition to full-time schools, China created thousands of "spare-time" and "part-time" schools, in which the masses learned while continuing to labor at needed tasks. Education was being made available to the people in many ways, and each year more of the Chinese masses were reached by some form of instruction.

The Chinese Communists considered education primarily propaganda for teaching understanding of and loyalty to Communist principles. Schools and other agencies for teaching became concerned primarily with politics, the process of establishing the new national policy based on the leadership of the proletariat. Ideological indoctrination takes precedence over academic excellence. One must give evidence of political reliability if he is to progress through the schools.

Since China had been a backward nation, its leaders realized that production must be encouraged at all times in order to bring the nation abreast of the modern world. Therefore, all students are considered part of the work force of the nation. They are preparing to take their places in modern China, but they must devote holidays, evenings, and other released time to work that is clearly productive. Students labor in the fields, factories, and wherever production is progressing, to develop an understanding of work and remain free from any temptation to discredit those who work with their hands. The old Chinese education that immortalized the "book-reader" must never return.

This education is under strict party control. In all schools, the party secretary and party machinery are in absolute control. The party representatives determine curricula, student selection, teacher employment and pay, and examinations. The All-China Conference of Advanced Socialist Workers in Education, Culture, Health, Physical Education, and Press, meeting in Peking in 1960, affirmed that "the fundamental principle is that education and cultural work must serve proletarian politics and socialist economic construction. In order to accomplish this, education must be led by our Party."

In Communist China, all education has a purpose. There is no "education for education's sake." The philosophy of dialectical materialism is basic. Education must serve to bring China into the modern world as a People's Republic. The leaders of modern China have been phenomenally successful. There is a new and vital spirit among the people. They have surrendered their freedom and their children to the state, but they have received a meaning for life, a sense of accomplishment, and a security never before experienced. Members of the communes own nothing individually; but together they build homes, dams, and water systems; together they eat well and regularly, receive medical care, and protect their nation; and together they are developing a feeling of purpose that makes their living meaningful. Where a few years ago they were so many animals working on projects planned and built by foreign technicians, today they are planners and builders of their own nation.

China is on the way. Millions are as yet untouched by the new and modern. But the leaders have faith that time is on their side and that all China's 800,000,000 will be brought into the modern world eventually. In the past, those in charge did not hestitate to liquidate opposition, deviationists, or those who held on to the past. No longer do they cut off heads. Rather, they educate. One accused of deviationism is placed in a school where he is instructed, bombarded with slogans, and reasoned with until he comes to see the error of his ways.

In the old China, education produced the good man fit to rule lesser men. In Communist China, education is designed to produce a nation of people fit and able to rule themselves, not as free men, but as men bound to the group and finding the meaning of life in this group, this whole, this state. The West could not ignore this China even if it wished. Events here are changing the face of the one world of which the West is only a part.

THE UNITED STATES IN THE FIRST HALF OF THE TWENTIETH CENTURY

INTRODUCTION

By the close of the nineteenth century, it was becoming evident to many that the United States had reached adulthood and must take her place as a leader in the family of nations. In his inaugural address, Theodore Roosevelt said, "The problems are new, the tasks before us differ from the tasks set before our fathers who founded and preserved this republic." These new tasks included a growing responsibility for world leadership.

Since 1900, the United States has become involved in two world wars, for which she furnished armies, munitions, and money in fantastic amounts. She engaged in a costly "police action" in Korea, dispatched her battleships to numerous spots on the globe where danger threatened, developed a worldwide program of foreign aid to help nations bolster failing economies or fight threats of Communist domination, threw the weight of her prestige and power behind the creation of the United Nations, and in hundreds of other ways made herself a leader of one world.

This increasing involvement in one world has been a determining factor in the kind of nation the United States has become. It has shaped the lives of the population called upon to fight in the armed forces or man productive machinery on farms and in factories. It has determined how the nation shall spend its wealth. It has created issues upon which public officials have stood for election and has nurtured fears that spawned McCarthyism. It has reached into all phases of education, both public and private, from the nursery school through graduate work and research. We are what we are as individuals and as a nation because we have become totally and irrevocably involved in one world.

THE CULTURAL PATTERN

Two social outlooks marked the culture of twentieth century America and characterized the two major political parties in the United States. These were conservatism and liberalism. The first championed traditional capitalism and free enterprise with only minor changes to adjust to new conditions and new challenges. It held that government interference and planning should be kept at a minimum, leaving the individual and business free to compete in an open market. The second outlook was based on the conviction that conditions had changed so radically that capitalism needed major reforming to assure its functioning in the new industrial and urban society. It supported a planned economy—shaped by government, business, labor, and the consumer, and continually adjusted to changing circumstances—as the only means of guaranteeing to all economic and social security.

Other outlooks appeared during the century to challenge these, harass their advocates, and often to be absorbed in part into the structure of social thinking in the United States. Socialists, represented most clearly by Norman Thomas, proposed state ownership through democratic means of the instruments of production and distribution so that all might share in the nation's wealth and potential. Many of Thomas' ideas became planks in the platforms of either the conservatives or the liberals, and some of both. Communists, represented in the United States by the Communist Party, advocated revolutionary Marxism as the only road to true democracy. This thinking infiltrated both major trends, although it was more at home among liberals. Fascists branded liberalism and democracy as false ideals and taught that to assure the "great society," power must rest in the hands of an elite. It advocated violence, a hatred of minorities, authoritarianism, and world domination. Although fascist groups have attempted to align themselves with the more conservative forces in the nation, they have made some appeal to all groups that fear change.

Both communism and fascism were foreign imports and cannot be considered part of the American tradition. Their influence upon cul-

CHART 1
American Secondary Education

DATA TO BE EXAMINED	LATIN GRAMMAR SCHOOL	ACADEMY	TRADITIONAL HIGH SCHOOL
1. Years of Significant Influence	1635 until after the Revolutionary War	1751 until about 1875; still exists	1870 to 1940
2. Students in the School	Boys—select few of upper economic level and generally superior intellect	Both boys and girls; select few of upper economic level and generally superior intellect	Ever increasing percentage of boys and girls of America
3. The Curricular	Limited to college preparation	Started out broad but became narrow	Steadily broadening but dominated by college preparatory curriculum and in later years by vocational education
4. Articulation	School operated generally parallel to elementary school	School generally at level above elementary school	Next step in ladder above elementary school
5. Area of Location	Characteristically New England	Widespread throughout the entire country but located in the cities	At first in cities but later everywhere
6. Goals	College preparatory with emphasis on ministry	College preparatory with some preparation for life	College preparatory and incidental preparation for life
7. Source of Finance	Normally public	Normally endowed or private	Public, chiefly local at first, later state supported
8. Type of School	Normally public	Normally private	Public, local

CHART 1
American Secondary Education (*cont'd.*)

FUNCTIONAL AND LIFE ADJUSTMENT HIGH SCHOOL	COMPREHENSIVE HIGH SCHOOL	FULL EDUCATIONAL OPPORTUNITY SCHOOL
1940 to 1955	1955 to date	1970s
All American youth	All American youth	Disadvantaged youth
Quite broad education of all areas of living (citizenship, family life, vocational, etc.)	Curriculum in all areas with considerable ability grouping	Work-study program, vocational emphasis
Next step in ladder above the elementary school	Coordinated guidance under way; articulation at all levels (6th & 9th especially)	Continuous guidance program for all youths to 21: continuous progress
Existed everywhere, but more in urban than rural, more coast than other areas	Everywhere; large school the rule but experimental progress in large and small	Urban mostly
College preparation weak; primarily preparation for life	Every youngster in proper area; keep all ability levels going maximum	To bring better education to millions of disadvantaged youth; accountability
Public, local and state	Public, local and state but Federal entering picture	Federal government
Public, local (some state)	Public, mostly local (some state)	Local, under Federal restriction

ture in the United States has been seen in attempts by both conservatives and liberals to deal with them democratically while disavowing
allegiance to their beliefs. Fear that these undemocratic influences
might infect democratic culture caused federal and state governments
to pass laws and set up procedures to protect the people and especially
children in schools from "unAmerican ideas and ideals."
    These two major trends in American thinking are reflected in the
two major parties that have occupied the political arena. When the
Republicans have been in power in Washington, conservative factors
have been emphasized. When the Democrats have held the presidency,
the country has seen liberalism championed. In spite of the emphases
of the two parties, the United States has moved steadily toward a
stronger centralized government, social legislation, the regulation of
business in the interest of the masses, and a federal concern for the
needs of all the people.

JOHN DEWEY (1859-1952)

    American progressivism grew out of the desire to apply the Ameri-
can dream to the new urban and industrial society that began to take
shape after the Civil War. Progressive education was the educational
phase of this attempt, and sought to direct the schools toward improving the lives of individuals. This implied faith in the individual, a faith
that culture can be democratized without becoming vulgar, a faith that
instruction can be tailored to the needs of each individual without
destroying its essence or meaning, a faith in science as man's truest
guide to understanding the individual and his environment, and a faith
in the American future.
    John Dewey was the symbol of this faith, and his philosophy of
education was the clearest expression of this faith to be attempted
during the first half of the new century. He was born in Burlington,
Vermont, on October 20, 1859, and attended the local public school and
the University of Vermont, from which he was graduated in 1879.
After a less than successful experience as a teacher in a country school,
he returned to the university for a year's concentrated study of philosophy. From there he moved to Johns Hopkins University, where he
studied with G. Stanley Hall, Herbert B. Adams, a teacher of political
and institutional history, and the leading pragmatic philosopher of the
day, Charles S. Peirce.
    In 1884, with a Ph.D. degree, Dewey went to teach at the University
of Michigan, where he came in direct contact with progressivism and
where he began to integrate science into his ethical and philosophical
thinking. After a decade of teaching philosophy at the universities of

Michigan and Minnesota, he accepted the chairmanship of the department of philosophy at the University of Chicago.

After ten years at Chicago, Dewey moved to Columbia University, where he remained as America's leading philosopher and educational thinker until he died on June 1, 1952. During the years following his retirement from the Columbia faculty, which took place July 1, 1930, he was professor emeritus, maintained an office on the campus, and continued to work with graduate students and the faculties of both Columbia University and Teachers College.

Dewey's influence spread throughout the world. Not only did he attract thousands of students to Columbia to study with him, but he was in constant demand as visiting professor, lecturer, and adviser. In 1919, he lectured on philosophy and education at the Imperial University of Tokyo, Japan, and for two years he was visiting professor on the faculty of the University of Peking, China. He was invited to assist the governments of Turkey, Russia, Mexico, and other countries in reconstructing their educational systems.

Dewey has been called a pragmatist, an instrumentalist, a progressive, an experimentalist, and other names in an attempt to label his thinking. None of these is wholly accurate since each emphasizes only a phase of his philosophy. At Vermont he was influenced by Scottish realism, and at Johns Hopkins he was profoundly affected by Hegelian idealism. Around 1890 he read William James' *Principles of Psychology,* in which he discovered the evolutionary theory and the newer scientific outlook embodied in a truly American pragmatic philosophy. Always interested in education, he turned his major attention to educational experimentation, seeking to use the new knowledge, coming from developments in the field of psychology, about the individual, about man's evolution, and about the nature of society. In 1896, he established at the University of Chicago the University Elementary School to test his theories and ideas in an actual learning situation. In *School and Society,* a book in which he sought to explain the principles underlying his approach to education, the school is pictured as (1) bringing into closer relationships school, home, and community, (2) making subject matter of real significance to the child, (3) deriving learning of symbols from experiences of the learner, and (4) providing individual attention so that each child learns in terms of himself.

The philosophy basic to this approach to education is contained in many of Dewey's writings, chief among which is *Democracy and Education.* For Dewey, mind and knowledge were instruments for dealing with the situations of life. Just as man in his biological evolution has developed as a physical human being, so has he developed mind. An organism at any stage of evolution interacts with its environment and learns to control objects and situations.

Here is evidence that action, experience, and practice precede knowledge. The primitive action of the organism is a result of an inherited impulse or instinct. When this act takes place, experience results; the organism learns. Knowledge is the by-product of action and cannot be separated from the activity that produces it.

Since action results in experience, the organism comes to know what will happen if it acts in that way again. This knowledge directs future action. If the action does not result in the desired reaction on the part of the environment, the organism knows not to repeat that activity unless it desires an unfavorable reaction. If the action produces the desired reaction, it knows that when it desires this result, it must repeat the action. In this process of action and reaction the organism learns something about controlling its environment. From the lowest organism to the highest form of human life, knowledge modifies action either by inhibiting or redirecting it.

One acts only when he has a felt need. Therefore, knowledge results from felt needs. This is true of all knowledge, even that of the most primitive learner in primordial times. Human intelligence is a natural growth from these earlier times and has reached its present state through evolution.

Since the human individual lives among others and his environment is colored by others, knowledge is a social instrument, a tool by which he controls both his physical and social environments. One manipulates his environment in terms of himself and others. In his interaction with other human beings he learns how to manipulate his social environment; he sharpens this social instrument.

This is the instrumental theory of mind, the evidence cited to classify Dewey as an instrumentalist. It is carefully developed in one of his most provocative books, *How We Think.* There Dewey held that the individual thinks only when there is good and sufficient reason for thinking, when a change in his condition takes place, action no longer is satisfactory or is blocked, or one becomes uncertain as to the correct course to take. At that point he analyzes the situation to clarify the nature of the problem, calls to consciousness stored data or collects new data, makes hypotheses that he tests mentally until he finds one able to meet all his requirements, and acts as his hypothesis directs. If this activity is successful, he has learned how to deal with that situation. If the activity is not successful, he has learned that under this set of circumstances the hypothesis will not work. Then he must continue his search for one that will work. This is thinking, learning, building the instrumental mind. It has also been called experimentalism, since the individual is actually experimenting with ways of acting in an effort to find one that is successful.

Dewey's philosophy of education was the application of this instrumental philosophy of mind to education. He defined education in *Democracy and Education* as "that reconstruction or reorganization of experience which adds to the meaning of experience, and which increases ability to direct the course of subsequent experience." This concept of education differed significantly from those of the past. It did not divorce education from living, nor did it conceive of learning as the accumulation of knowledge for its own sake. Rather, it made education a process of experiencing. This is not confined to school years, but begins with birth, or perhaps before, and continues throughout life. Whenever one acts, he experiences, and this new experience reconstructs or reorganizes the experiences he already has, adds to their meaning, so that he is better able to direct the course of future experience. Education is living. The school is living in a specialized environment, but not one cut off from life. Education is not preparation for life. It is the most complete living at the moment.

It follows that the aims of education cannot be placed in some distant future but are within the process. The individual acts to solve an immediate problem, not one that may appear in adulthood. He learns by working with this problem, his problem, one that is significant to him now. The aim of education is the solution of the immediate problem. As one solves that problem, he learns and is better able to solve the next problem that arises. There can be no final goal of education, no time when one's education is complete.

Dewey affirmed in *Democracy and Education* that education "has all the time an immediate end, and so far as activity is educative, it reaches that end—the direct transformation of the quality of experience. . . . What is really *learned* at any and every stage of experience constitutes the value of that experience." This end for Dewey is growth. At every stage of life the individual is growing, and the end of growth is more growth. One grows today so that he may grow tomorrow. In the same way, education is growth, and one learns today so that he may learn better tomorrow. In the same volume Dewey wrote, "Since life means growth, a living creature lives as truly and positively at one stage as at another, with the same intrinsic fullness and the same absolute claims. Hence education means the enterprise of supplying the conditions which insure growth, or adequacy of life, irrespective of age. . . . Living has its own intrinsic quality and . . . the business of education is with that quality."

If we consider education in this light, we discover that two factors are involved, the individual or "psychological" and the other or "society." In the learning situation we have the child with his powers, capacities, impulses, and potentialities, and the social world with its customs, mores, institutions, activities, and attitudes. Education begins with "a psychological insight into the child's capacities, interests and habits." These must be interpreted, "translated into their social equivalents." We must be able to understand their roots in the past and project them into the future, to understand their meaning. One might be an organism, but he could not become human without society, "an organic union of individuals." As the child interacts with others, society reproduces itself in him; he comes to understand, appreciate, and appropriate as his own all the purposes, ideas, ideals, and attitudes of society. "Mind," says Dewey, "as a concrete thing is precisely the power to understand things in terms of the use made of them; a socialized mind is the power to understand them in terms of the use to which they are turned in joint or shared situations. *And mind in this sense is the method of social control.*"

The child is born into a society, the home. He learns within that environment since it furnishes him problem situations that he strives to solve at his level of maturity. This learning leads on to further learning as his environment widens from the home to the community. The school must continue this learning process by functioning as "that form of community life in which all those agencies are concentrated that will be most effective in bringing the child to share in the inherited resources of the race, and to use his own powers for social ends." When the individual leaves school, he continues this social process but is better able to deal with his environment because of the learning that has taken place at each previous stage of his life. The school is but one of the instruments furthering learning; it is not an end in itself or a part of life set off from living.

Since all learning is a by-product of action, method must be constructed out of action, experience, doing. All successful methods of instruction in the classroom "depend for their efficiency upon the fact that they go back to the type of the situation which causes reflection out of school in ordinary life. They give the pupil something to do, not something to learn; and the doing is of such a nature as to demand thinking, or the intentional noting of connections; learning naturally results." All method must be based on direct, concrete experience that is meaningful to the learner.

Dewey was a philosopher of one world. Ever-widening experience was the key to his philosophy and his philosophy of education. Although he symbolized the progressive trends in western, industrialized society, he was in no sense a nationalist or a regionalist. Learning, for him, could not be restricted to state or national boundaries. Growth and learning begin in the narrow confines of the home, move out into the community, and eventually encompass the entire world. Each individual in that world has the inalienable right to grow and learn to the fullness of his capacity. He is what he is because of the organic society of which he is a part. This society is at first the family, but it must become the world. That which is most human is most involved in all the world.

Not only did Dewey travel and teach throughout the world and draw to his classroom students from the entire world, but he also devoted his time and energies to the problems of this one world. When the Communists were accusing Trotsky and his followers, Dewey made it his business to travel to Mexico, interview many, and learn the truth. Throughout his life he was identified with local, national, and world organizations working for the freedom of the individual and a more complete sharing of experiences among all men. It was his firm conviction that anything that limited the sharing of experiences was evil and dangerous. He fought against all barriers that tended to separate men, lessen their ability to share with each other, and come to understand themselves and their fellows. Dewey was the embodiment of the one world concept in his thinking, teaching, and living.

EDUCATIONAL ISSUES (1900-1960)

The United States of the twentieth century raised many issues that involved the schools and the teaching profession. Two world wars, the Korean "police action," changes in social and political thinking, industrialization, urbanization, science and its plunge into atomic energy, flights into space, infiltrations by undemocratic theories, and other factors characteristic of this century posed problems that were either clearly educational or touched education at many places. Attempts to solve these problems divided the nation, threatened its educational structure, and called forth some of the best thinking that the nation had ever seen. Most of these issues remain unsolved, and some pose the question as to whether man, at his present level of intelligence, is ready even to face the problems honestly, much less settle them.

A major issue of this century was the *extension of educational opportunities* to more and more of the nation's population. To the extent that the schools of the United States were the responsibility of local communities, both the quality and extent of education were limited by the ability of those concerned to defray the necessary expenses. This resulted in a great diversity of educational opportunity. Poorer communities were able to offer less education to their citizens than the more wealthy.

This led to increases in state aid and the consolidation of school facilities. The principle that the wealth of the state should be used to support schooling for the entire population became general. Many formulae were experimented with in an effort to equalize educational opportunity throughout each state. Usually the formulae aimed at assuring a minimum quality and quantity of education for all while permitting wealthier communities to exceed this minimum. In several states smaller and less prosperous school districts consolidated into larger units able to offer better schooling to more people. Often children were transported long distances to these consolidated schools and, in some instances, kept at the school from Monday through Friday.

Although the federal government steadily increased its support of many schools, colleges, and specialized educational services, it was unable to provide funds for equalizing educational opportunities in the several states. Bills proposing direct federal aid to education were rejected for several reasons: (1) fear of federal control, (2) failure to provide money for private and parochial schools, and (3) allocation of funds only to those states that do not segregate Negroes and whites. As a result, the problem of equalizing educational opportunity between the states has not been solved. During 1963-1964, Alabama spent an average of $197 per public school pupil for education, Mississippi $217, and South Carolina $239. During the same period, New York was spending $791, Pennsylvania $564, and Illinois $545. The national average was $432. With the span of expenditures reaching from $197 to $791, it is obvious that in the Space Age, with its emphasis upon more and better education for all, many states were unable to offer their citizens the educational opportunities available to residents of sister states.

One of the most aggravating problems in the whole area of equality of educational opportunity has been that of racial segregation. As the nation moved into the twentieth century, the young Blacks of the South were on the march, helped by many understanding whites, toward equal opportunity in school and out. Events of the first half of this new century were but a fruition of forces created in the South during the last half of the nineteenth century. Even the term Negro changed to Black.

Black education has made great strides during the twentieth century. The Supreme Court decision in *Brown vs. Board of Education* (1954) is often taken as the starting point for the increased opportunity in education for Negro children. This is true as it pertains to the issue of integration and to educational participation, but not particularly so as to the quality of the results. The first half of the century saw startling qualitative gains. In the early decades of the century, vast amounts of private funds became available. The George Peabody Fund, the Anna T. Jeanes Fund, the Rockefeller Foundation, and the Julius Rosenwald Fund are examples.

A few facts may be cited to demonstrate the state of Black education in the early decades of the century. By 1900, approximately 1,500,000 Black children were in schools, being taught by nearly 30,000 Black teachers. Thirty-four Black institutions of higher education were servicing students, while Black students in increasing numbers were entering the colleges and universities of the North and West. Arkansas, Delaware, Virginia, and Georgia operated state colleges for Blacks. It was estimated that in 1900 the Black enrollment in college was about 700. Over 2,000 had graduated from colleges. In 1900, the average annual salary of white teachers was just under $200; the average annual salary for Black teachers was $100. By 1930 the average salary of white teachers was $900, while that of the Black teacher was $400. Something of holding power in the schools can be noted. In 1920, eighty-five per cent of all Black youth enrolled in Southern schools were in grade four or below. As late as 1916 there were only sixty-seven Black high schools, enrolling less than 20,000 students.

By the beginning of World War II, there were significant increases in the number of Black students, in the number of students enrolled, in teachers, and in improvement of the curriculum. These trends were in keeping with what was happening in all phases of education. The holding power of the schools was improved, which is demonstrated by large graduating classes from both high schools and colleges in the South as well as the North. Further, the quality of education also improved markedly as attested by a significant increase in accreditation of Negro schools.

The outstanding issue in Black education for the first half of the twentieth century continued to be the legal attacks on the segregated school. No real challenges to the "separate but equal" doctrine of the Plessy decision were made for nearly forty years. The first serious consideration arose in the case of Donald Murray, a Black student who applied for admission to the University of Maryland Law School. The Baltimore school refused Murray admission on the basis of Maryland's segregation legislation. Murray sued, on the complaint that Maryland had no law school for Blacks. The University had attempted to comply with the "separate but equal" doctrine by providing a limited number of scholarships for Blacks to attend law schools in other states. Murray argued that these scholarships did not provide adequate money to support oneself out-of-state. The Supreme Court upheld Murray's position on the basis that the Maryland system placed the Black student at an economic disadvantage.

In 1938, Lloyd Gaines sued for admission to the University of Missouri Law School. His suit was similar to Murray's, except he maintained that out-of-state scholarships did not meet the legal requirement of "separate but equal" doctrine. When the Supreme Court ruled in favor of Gaines, Southern states began developing graduate schools for Blacks, thereby hoping to maintain segregation. Southern states also began to upgrade Black elementary and high schools. State finance for Black education reached unprecedented levels. In 1950, the Sweatt case and the McLaurin case, forcing Texas and Oklahoma to provide higher education for Blacks, were still decided on the "separate but equal" principle. In 1954, it was estimated that more than 2,000 Negro students were enrolled in institutions of higher education in states where segregation was the law.

Improvement in financial support and curriculum did not impress the Negro. Comparisons in the quality of white and Black education continued. It was also realized that the test of the American dream of full educational opportunity for every boy and girl was about to be made. Segregation would be the basis of the attack. The first onslaughts had been in the field of graduate work, where separate was obviously not equal. New arguments began to appear. No segregated Black school was able to supply equal education. Blacks were equal in ability to whites. Segregation is harmful to the Black personality. Next the arguments developed that segregation in the elementary and secondary schools perpetuated the myth of inferiority of the Black. Segregation also included the other phases of life such as housing, justice, and employment. It was argued that segregation represented an outdated, undemocratic caste system. This attack on inequality was not on education alone, but it was an effective area, because a real lack of equal opportunity for Black children did exist.

Operating under the "separate but equal" provisions of *Plessy vs. Ferguson,* a number of states were placing Black children in substandard school buildings and providing poorly trained teachers and inadequate equipment for their instruction. Five cases challenging the "separate but equal" principle on constitutional grounds were received by the Supreme Court in December, 1952. Strong opposition to the idea of integration expressed by several Southern states caused the Court to delay its decision until May, 1954.

As discussed earlier, this landmark decision came out under the title of *Brown vs. the Board of Education, Topeka, Kansas.* In the Brown decision, school segregation was declared unconstitutional. With this decision, a new period of Black education developed. Certain arguments in the decision are worth noting:

In approaching this problem, we cannot turn the clock back to 1868 when the Amendment was adopted or even to 1896 when *Plessy vs. Ferguson* was written. We must consider public education in the light of its full development and its present place in American life throughout the Nation. Only in this way can it be determined that segregation in public schools deprives these plaintiffs of the equal protection of the laws.

. . . We come back to the question presented: Does segregation of children in public schools solely on the basis of race, even though the physical facilities and other "tangible" factors may be equal, deprive the children of the minority groups of equal educational opportunities? We believe that it does.

. . . Segregation of white and colored children in public schools has a detrimental effect upon the colored children. The impact is greater when it has the sanction of the law; for the policy of separating the races is usually interpreted as denoting the inferiority of the Negro group.

This decision set off a series of violent protests, resulting in use of federal troops to force integration. Some areas of the country abandoned their public schools, leaving education to private initiative. Others mounted campaigns of resistance that were more or less successful for a time. Gradually, token integration was permitted in areas of greatest protest, while other areas drew up plans for gradual integration. The *New York Times* of January 13, 1965, pointed out that, while the number of Blacks in desegregated schools in the eleven states of the "Old Confederacy" had increased from 34,000 in 1963 to 64,000 in 1964, Blacks attending desegregated classrooms represented only 2.14 per cent of the region's enrollment of almost 3,000,000 children. A survey quoted by the *Times* showed that of the 2,220 school districts having both white and Black children, only 604 had desegrated classrooms.

The issues of segregation, compulsory bussing, equal opportunity, and curriculum remain, and will be discussed separately.

Another growing problem in the area of equal educational opportunity was the substandard schooling available to large segments of the population in urban centers. During the first decade following the middle of the century, attention was increasingly focused on slum sections of cities, where school buildings were deteriorating, teachers refused to work because of poor conditions and danger to their persons, and juvenile crime was rampant. Demonstrations, boycotts, and other means of expressing discontent were used to call attention to the situation. While in the 1960s teacher education institutions began serious attempts to prepare teachers for these schools, various plans to reduce economic and racial segregation, called *de facto* segregation, were proposed in the face of determined opposition.

Equal opportunity was, in the middle 1960s, a goal expressed and aimed for but far from a reality. There was a growing realization that two important conditions had to be met before the goal could be attained: (1) basic changes in American culture that would free the Negro from the stigma of having been a slave without citizenship rights, and (2) sufficient money to attract and prepare the necessary personnel and provide equipment adequate to care for the growing population and those being channeled into schools because of their desire and need for more education.

A second major issue of the twentieth century was the extent of *federal participation* in education. The Constitution, as interpreted by the courts, placed education under the states and prohibited the federal government from interfering at any level. A fear of centralized control made the states jealous of this authority. Although land and cash grants for education and control and support of training for the military and other areas of federal employment were allowed, the direct expenditure of federal funds for public education was prohibited.

As the nation grew and expanded, problems arose which were not anticipated by writers of the Constitution. Resources within states were unequal, population grew at different rates in the several states, industry was concentrated in a few states, bringing taxable wealth not available in other states, and the more industrious and talented people tended to gravitate toward certain population centers, draining other areas of their potential economic leadership. By the 1930s, these facts were being driven into the nation's consciousness by the speed of social and economic change. Bills to provide federal aid to public schools were prepared by almost every Congress that followed but were either left in committee, passed by one house and not the other, or defeated. The issues upon which they were blocked continued to be religious and racial. While the old fear of federal control was evident, more specific and immediate deterrents were (1) insistence on the part of Catholic groups that any federal money voted for education be made available to parochial and private schools as well as to public schools, a position which most Protestant and Jewish groups opposed, (2) refusal on the part of some southern congressmen to accept a bill insisting on equal distribution of federal funds to white and Negro schools on the grounds that such would be illegal interference with states' rights, and (3) belief expressed by many that federal aid would weaken local and state initiative, which, if stimulated adequately, could support education at the level necessary.

Responding to emergency situations growing out of the two world wars and the depression of the 1930s, Congress provided money for an educational system that reached into every state and locality. This provision was contained in bills providing for the Civilian Conservation Corps, the National Youth Administration, the Servicemen's Readjustment Act, and other emergency measures. Fearing that these moves might be the beginning of a federal system of education that would eventually weaken state systems, the Educational Policies Commission of the National Education Association and the Problems and Policies Committee of the American Council on Education prepared jointly in 1945 a "white paper" warning of the dangers inherent in maintaining these federal agencies beyond the emergencies for which they were created and proposing a plan of federal aid without federal control. This plan called for the allocation of federal funds to each state on the basis of need, to be determined by the number of pupils enrolled and the wealth of the area. A simple audit and report of how the funds were spent was the limit proposed to federal control. The "paper" also demanded that federal control be limited to specific educational programs already in effect and that the function of the federal government be limited to leadership, research, compiling publications, and advising.

Various attempts to implement these proposals experienced varied success. Traditionally, the federal government had exerted leadership as suggested. The Office of Education, which in 1953 became a unit of the Department of Health, Education, and Welfare, had given leadership, published vast amounts of material dealing with education in the United States and throughout the world, conducted extensive research and campaigns for better education, and furnished expert help to states and local communities. The federal government had provided for the specialized training of officers in the branches of the military, the education of Indians and other wards of the government, and schools in many departments of the federal bureaucracy for the preparation of skilled personnel.

As specific needs arose, Congress moved in with a minimum of opposition. In 1914, the Smith-Lever Act was passed, making available federal funds to support a program of education in farming and home economics. Agricultural agents, through meetings, public lectures, classes in schools and out, publications, conferences, and demonstrations, worked to improve the productivity of the soil and insure better living on the farms and in rural areas of the country. The states accepting the program were required to match dollar for dollar the funds provided by the federal government.

Congress, through the Smith-Hughes Act in 1917, provided funds to finance vocational instruction in secondary schools. This included classes in agriculture, home economics, the trades, and industrial subjects. States were required to match federal appropriations, and the Federal Board of Vocational Education was organized to administer the funds and work closely with state organizations. In 1929, the George-Reed Act increased funds for these areas of instruction, while in 1936, the George-Deen Act extended the project to include distributive education in secondary schools.

The Vocational Rehabilitation Act of 1920 and the Social Security Act of 1935 aimed to provide opportunities for vocational rehabilitation of the handicapped.

As world conditions became more ominous in the 1930s, the federal government was forced to think in terms of education to provide defense against potential enemies. Vast funds were provided to train airplane pilots and defense workers. Courses in aviation mechanics, shipbuilding, welding, machine shop activities, radio, electricity, and other trades and skills necessary for the vast defense industry which was mushrooming throughout the country were set up in schools and colleges at federal expense. This program cost the government in the neighborhood of $500,000,000.

With the end of World War II, the nation faced the problem of helping the discharged soldier and sailor to readjust to civilian life and prepare himself for a productive future. The Servicemen's Readjustment Act of 1944, called the G. I. Bill of Rights, provided funds permitting more than 8,000,000 veterans to complete their education or train for specific trades or activities. In 1952, a similar act made provision for veterans of the Korean "police action."

Since World War II, the federal government has made more than half a billion dollars available to colleges and universities for the support of research in the sciences, agriculture, medicine, industry, and other areas bearing either on national defense or the inherent strength of the nation. The extent of this effort was such that many educators feared that grants of this nature would become in fact instruments determining the work of institutions of higher education. Some were convinced that college personnel were becoming so interested in the research that government funds made possible that they were neglecting classroom teaching. This problem became acute as an increasing number of institutions placed major emphasis on research and publication as a basis for faculty tenure and promotions.

In January, 1965, President Johnson sent to Congress a proposal for wide involvement of the federal government in matters affecting schools, colleges, and students. Among these were (1) one billion dollars in grants to states for the support of elementary and high schools, mostly in low-income districts, (2) 150 million to begin a program of preschool education for culturally deprived children from poor families, (3) one hundred million to help states purchase necessary library books and classroom texts, (4) a first-year appropriation of forty-five million to establish regional laboratories for educational research, teacher training, and experimentation with new techniques for teaching and learning, (5) one hundred million for supplementary centers for education in local communities, (6) 179 million to assist colleges in constructing classrooms, libraries, and laboratories, (7) twenty-five million for 4,500 graduate fellowships to train future college teachers, (8) the money necessary for 140,000 college scholarships for needy high school graduates, (9) 110 million for basic research, science fellowships, and science education at universities, (10) expansion of work-study programs to aid students from middle-income as well as poor families, and (11) money to pay part of the interest cost on government-guaranteed private loans to college students. The over-all program amounted to well over 4.1 billion dollars for the fiscal year beginning July 1, 1965, and aimed at a national goal of "full educational opportunity" for all children and young people in the nation. A feature of the proposal was that it made no distinction between public and parochial or private schools and colleges.

A third major issue of the first sixty years of twentieth century education in the United States centered around the *existence and support of a private school system* in the nation. Education in colonial America was predominantly private. As the public school structure took shape, private schools lost their clientele and many were closed, but there was no concerted effort to make them illegal. The public school grew alongside the private school, and the parent was free to choose either for the education of his children.

There was a growing conviction during the twentieth century that private and parochial schools posed a threat to the democracy of the public schools. James B. Conant, writing in *Education and Liberty,* took the position that the public schools "have served all creeds and economic groups within a given geographic area," bringing together children from divergent cultural backgrounds and shaping them into citizens of a democracy. With this in mind he wrote, "The greater the proportion of our youth who fail to attend our public schools and who receive their education elsewhere, the greater the threat to our democratic unity. To use taxpayers' money to assist private schools is to suggest that American society use its own hands to destroy itself."

This fear was basic to the Oregon law of 1922, requiring every child between the ages of eight and sixteen to attend a public school. This was a move to abolish private and parochial schools in the state. In 1925, the United States Supreme Court declared the law unconstitutional on two grounds: (1) the child is a creature of his parents, not the state, and they have the right to educate him in the school they think best, and (2) this law amounted to destruction of the value of the property of private schools without due process of law. The Court affirmed the right of the state to require children to attend school and to set minimum standards that all schools must meet, but it argued that parents should be free to choose among all the schools meeting these standards.

The Catholic Church during the twentieth century placed major emphasis upon parochial education. In 1929, Pope Pius XI issued his encyclical *On the Christian Education of Youth* in which he, repeating the instructions of Pius IX and Leo XIII, pointed out that attendance by Catholics at public schools is forbidden by canon law. "The school," he wrote, "if not a temple, is a den." This caused great numbers of Catholics to place their children in parochial schools.

As the public schools became more crowded, as a shortage of properly trained teachers developed, and as many of the schools in large cities became predominantly lower-class, with crime, narcotics, sex indulgence, and anti-social activities and attitudes on the increase, middle- and upper-class parents in increasing numbers and at great financial sacrifice placed their children in private schools. These schools increased in number, causing many to fear that the public schools might become lower-class institutions filled with "problem" children and failing to attract the better-prepared teachers.

Since many private schools found it difficult to finance a complete education for the children asking to be enrolled, plans were proposed during the 1960s to combine public and private education. It was suggested by some that the private schools confine their work to certain grades or certain subjects and send their students to public schools for the other grades and subjects.

As private schools multiplied in the United States, the question of support from tax revenue arose and resulted in considerable controversy. Many Catholics argued that their schools were supplying education for thousands of children who would otherwise be in public schools, necessitating greater expenditure of public money for their education. Since they were forced to pay for parochial education while being taxed for public schools which they did not use, they were in fact subject to "double taxation." Other Catholics and many Protestants and Jews argued that while the state was prohibited by the principle of the separation of church and state from giving direct aid to other than public schools, it was not denied the right to give indirect support for "auxiliary services." Among these "auxiliary services" were transportation to and from school, free textbooks, free lunches for the needy, free health and medical services within the school, and fire and police protection. Some suggested that public money could be given to the pupil to spend for his education in the school of his choice, public or private. Still others argued that either direct or indirect aid to private or parochial schools was clearly prohibited by law.

During the twentieth century, this issue became the center of extensive controversy, out of which came several serious cracks in what Jefferson believed was an impenetrable "wall of separation between Church and State" built by the First Amendment to the Constitution. In the case of *Everson v. Board of Education,* dealing with bus transportation at public expense to parochial schools in New Jersey, the United States Supreme Court in 1946 ruled in a five-to-four decision that such expenditure of public money did not violate the First Amendment. While in certain areas of instruction, Congress and most state legislatures provided public money for other than public education, the cracks in the "wall of separation" widened slowly. President Kennedy, though a Catholic, was convinced that the First Amendment prohibited the support of private or parochial education. President Johnson, a Protestant, began his administration with several programs of educational support that provided public money for all schools regardless of their affiliation.

Tied to this issue was the controversy over religious instruction in public schools. In 1947, the United States Supreme Court ruled, in the case of *McCollum v. Board of Education,* that it was illegal to conduct religious classes within the school buildings of Champaign, Illinois. This was an eight-to-one decision. In 1952, the Supreme Court ruled, five to three, in the case of *Zorach v. Clauson,* that providing "released time" from school activities for religious instruction was legal. Meanwhile, reading the Bible in public schools came under attack at the state level. Twelve states passed laws requiring Bible reading, while twenty-five permitted such reading under specified conditions. Since one version of the Bible was used, usually the King James version, Jews and Catholics argued that the practice violated the Constitution. Six state courts took the position that the Bible is and must inevitably be a sectarian document that cannot legally be read in public schools. When the issue was brought to the Supreme Court in 1952, the judges refused to make a ruling on a technicality. However, on June 17, 1963, the Court ruled in the case of *School District of Abington Township v. Schempp* that state laws requiring Bible reading in public schools violated the First Amendment. It also took the position that a prayer prepared by New York state education officials for reading in public schools violated the Constitution. The reaction to these decisions was immediate. States and church groups differed sharply as to their compliance with the ruling. The attorney general of Delaware defied the Court by ruling that so long as Bible reading and prayer sessions were not compulsory, they would be continued in the state. The Alabama state board of education passed a resolution making Bible reading compulsory in all schools of the state. The attorney general of New Jersey ruled that such exercises were unconstitutional.

As the United States moved through the 1960s, it became increasingly evident that the old issue of the proper relation between church and states in a democracy was becoming increasingly unsettled, as religious and other pressure groups intensified their demands for more governmental involvement in religious matters. In the words of Jeremiah S. Black, quoted by Justice Frankfurter in the case of *McCollum v. Board of Education,* "The manifest object of the men who framed the institutions of this country ... [was] to have a state *without religion* and a *Church without politics"* was being challenged, and the "wall of complete and perfect partition between the two" was being breached at many places.

A fourth major issue to embroil the public schools of the twentieth century in the United States centered around the question of *academic freedom.* It may be stated in this fashion: The public schools are instruments of the people for the acculturation of the young. They are supported by tax money and controlled by representatives of the people to accomplish certain specific ends. The public has not only the right but the obligation to determine who shall teach in its schools, what shall be taught, how it shall be taught, and what shall not be taught.

As the nation's thinking changed during the century, pressure groups were organized at local, state, and national levels to keep watch over the schools to see that they obeyed the "will of the people" as interpreted by each particular group. When patriotic fervor was high during wartimes, pacifist teachers or those suspected of alien ties or sympathies came under fire. When the nation was emphasizing peace and "normalcy," the militaristic-minded teacher was a target for criticism. When, during the 1920s, many sections of the country were centers of controversy between fundamentalists and those championing modern evolutionary science, it was possible to have laws passed making it illegal to teach the theory of evolution in public schools. The trial of John Scopes, a young teacher of high school biology in Rhea County, Tennessee, attracted international attention in the 1920s. It drew Clarence Darrow, one of the nation's most famous and colorful trial lawyers, to the defense, and William Jennings Bryan, former Secretary of State and three-time candidate for the presidency, to the prosecution.

The state law was clear—the legislature, acting within its legal right, had passed a law making it illegal for any teacher to teach atheism, agnosticism, Darwinism, or any theory that denied "the story of divine creation of man as taught in the *Bible.*" This law became effective in 1925. The judge hearing the case directed a verdict of guilty, since it was freely admitted that Scopes had taught the theory of evolution. The highest state court later affirmed the verdict, but the case died there, never reaching the United States Supreme Court.

As communism and the "red scare" became issues in the United States from the 1930s on, the nation began to shore up its defenses by demanding strict loyalty to American principles on the part of its public school teachers. By the early 1950s a total of thirty states had laws requiring teachers to take oaths of loyalty to state and federal governments. Professional bodies and others concerned with "academic freedom" opposed these laws on the grounds that (1) they were discriminatory against teachers, infringing upon their rights as citizens of a democracy, and (2) they were ineffective, since a subversive teacher would not hesitate to sign such an oath. In 1952, the United States Supreme Court, in the case of *Wieman v. Updegraff,* ruled the loyalty oath prescribed in Oklahoma unconstitutional, a violation of the First and Fourteenth Amendments to the Constitution.

In 1949, New York passed a law, called the Feinberg Law, to implement a provision of the Civil Service Law of the state, which provided that a member of any organization advocating the overthrow of the government by force, violence, or any unlawful means was ineligible for employment in any public school in the state. This law instructed the Board of Regents to prepare a list of organizations coming under provisions of the Civil Service Law. It also stated that membership in any of these listed organizations "shall constitute *prima facie* evidence for disqualification for appointment to or retention in any office or position in the school system." Before the state could disqualify any individual, it was required to give him a full and complete hearing under protection of all the laws of the state and nation. In 1952, by a six-to-three decision, the United States Supreme Court ruled the law constitutional. Justice Minton, writing the opinion of the Court, held:

A teacher works in a sensitive area in the schoolroom. There he shapes the attitude of young minds toward the society in which they live. In this, the state has a vital concern. It must preserve the integrity of the schools. That the school authorities have the right and the duty to screen the officials, teachers, and employees as to their fitness to maintain the integrity of the schools as part of ordered society, cannot be doubted. One's associates, past and present, as well as one's

conduct, may properly be considered in determining fitness and loyalty. ... we know of no rule, constitutional or otherwise, that pre-
vents the state, when determining the fitness or loyalty of such
persons, from considering the organizations and persons with whom
they associate.

A principle was stated in this case that came to dominate much of
the nation's thinking as regards the function of the teacher. Justice
Minton wrote: "It is clear that" persons employed or seeking employment in the public schools of the state of New York "have the right
under our law to assemble, speak, and think and believe as they will
... It is equally clear that they have no right to work for the State in
the school system on their own terms ... They may work for the school
system upon the reasonable terms laid down by the proper authorities
of New York. If they do not choose to work on such terms, they are at
liberty to retain their beliefs and associations and go elsewhere."

Various professional organizations have expressed opinions that
differ greatly. The National Education Association and the American
Federation of Teachers stated flatly that membership in the Communist Party should automatically disqualify one from teaching in the
public schools. At the other extreme were the American Association of
University Professors and the American Civil Liberties Union, who
took the position that the only criterion for the fitness of a teacher
should be competence in scholarship and teaching.

As a result of these attempts on the part of educational officials to
protect children from subversive doctrines and ideas, there developed
throughout the nation in the 1950s and 1960s, in the words of the *New
York Times,* "a subtle, creeping paralysis of freedom of thought." Cen-
sors were appearing in great numbers to pressure schools, the press,
radio, television, advertisers, and many others into conformity to their
standards and beliefs. Fear, suspicion, timidity, and anxiety were discovered among teachers at all levels. The National Education Association in 1953 expressed the opinion that there was a growing hesitancy
on the part of teachers everywhere to discuss controversial issues or to
raise questions that might be interpreted as expressions of disloyalty
or subversion.

At the same time, educators and leaders in political and social life
were working for an increase in freedom of teaching and learning as
the only defense against undemocratic ideologies. Speaking at the anniversary dinner honoring John Dewey on his ninetieth birthday,
Justice Felix Frankfurter said, "Without open minds there can be no
open society, and if there be no open society the spirit of man is muti-
lated and enslaved." One approach to this problem was expressed by

V. T. Thayer in 1960. Dr. Thayer, one of the leading progressive educators of the early twentieth century, pointed out that the schools and the public had to discover a policy that would "prevent public education from subversion within, at a time of national danger, without subverting the process of free education." At another point he said, "What is sought is a policy which distinguishes between an heretical ideology, on the one hand, and reprehensible conduct, on the other."

A glance back at the educational issues we have been discussing will reveal that while each is tied up with problems besetting the United States, it is at the same time in part a result of world conditions and thinking. Through the twentieth century the United States was forced by pressure of circumstances to see its problems in the perspective of one world. Isolation became impossible, and the nation was drawn into the world. As this happened, it was forced to look at its economy, its culture, its goals and aims, and its education differently. During the Kennedy administration world problems dominated the thinking of the White House and of the nation. The Peace Corps, created on March 1, 1961, was illustrative of the administration's interest in bettering the world and bringing the United States to an understanding of its true involvement in world problems. Although the Johnson administration began moving away from this involvement and concentrated its major activities on internal problems such as education, the elimination of poverty, adequate medical care, transportation, and the like, it was evident that even the planning along these lines was influenced deeply by world conditions.

JAMES BRYANT CONANT (1893-

A leading figure in public education in the United States during the middle decades of the twentieth century was Dr. James B. Conant, student of the nation's schools and counselor to school boards and college administrations. Born in Boston, Massachusetts, on March 26, 1893, and educated at Harvard University, he served for a time in the research division of the Chemical Warfare Service before becoming an instructor in chemistry at Harvard. In 1929 he became professor of organic chemistry and in 1931 was made chairman of the university's department of chemistry. On May 8, 1933, he was elected president of Harvard, succeeding A. Lawrence Lowell. As a chemist, he received some of the most honored awards for his work in this field: the Chandler Medal in 1932, and, later in that same year, the Nichols Medal of the American Chemical Society.

His administration at Harvard was distinguished for its forward-looking approach to higher education. Soon after he became president, he instituted a new degree, the Master of Arts in Teaching, offering to a liberal arts college graduate a legitimate short cut into public school teaching. Under his stimulus a committee was organized at Harvard to make an intensive study of American higher education. Its report, *General Education in a Free Society,* appeared in 1945. Its influence reached far beyond the Harvard campus to start programs of broad, generalized courses in the sciences, the humanities, the social sciences, and the arts in many universities and colleges of the country.

Retiring from the presidency of Harvard, he served as American High Commissioner in Berlin after the close of World War II. When, in 1956, the Russians launched their first man-made satellite, American secondary education came under severe attack for neglecting the sciences and failing to begin adequate preparation of young people to match the accomplishments of Russian scientists. At this time, Dr. Conant, with funds supplied by the Carnegie Corporation, began a study which resulted in *The American High School Today,* published in January, 1959.

In this volume he came out strongly for the comprehensive high school as the pillar of the American public school system. He also made twenty-one recommendations for improving secondary education. These included (1) standards for teaching English composition and foreign language, (2) ability groupings, (3) special programs for the academically talented, (4) standards for school counseling, and (5) special instruction for slow readers. He laid particular emphasis upon the need for identifying the most able students early and providing them with a challenging program of work at the level of their ability. This he believed should be done within the comprehensive high school, not in segregated special schools.

In 1960, Dr. Conant published an equally comprehensive and thought-provoking study of the junior high school, *Education in the Junior High School.* The junior high school, consisting of the seventh, eighth, and ninth grades, had been created to ease the transition from childhood to adolescence and to better articulate the child-centered elementary school and the subject-centered high school. During the years that followed its creation, the junior high school had come under severe attack by teachers and administrators. Conant's study was an attempt to appraise this institution and recommend moves to strengthen its offerings. Among his proposals were (1) more realistic preparation and selection of teachers, (2) a required core of English, social studies, mathematics, science, music, art, and physical education, (3) continuation of the basic skills when and where needed, (4) foreign languages and mathematics of high school quality for able students, (5) more attention to individual needs and abilities, (6) better guidance and testing, and (7) improvement of facilities for study, recreation, and experimentation.

The next year, 1961, he published *Slums and Suburbs,* a study of the contrasting educational problems faced by the schools in slum areas of large cities and those in fast-growing suburban areas. Here he stated, "I am convinced we are allowing social dynamite to accumulate in our large cities." This approach served to stimulate authorities and the general public to an awareness of some of the social and educational problems in disadvantaged sections of American cities and to inspire studies and programs aimed at achieving a better understanding of the situation and developing programs to deal with the needs of the children and young affected.

Then, in 1963, Dr. Conant published the results of his comprehensive study of teacher education, *The Education of American Teachers.* Advised by many of his friends to avoid this area as far too sensitive, he disregarded their suggestions, visited and studied several hundred institutions where teachers for the public schools were being prepared, and came up with recommendations that were received with mixed emotions by all who studied his book. He made a plea for greater freedom on the part of colleges and universities in designing and administering teacher-education programs. He would eliminate state certification requirements and leave this responsibility to the colleges and universities.

Other recommendations made by Conant were (1) preparation to consist of a bachelor's degree from a college or university plus evidence of successful teaching under the joint supervision of a good public school system and a clinical professor from the college or university, (2) certification based on an evaluation of the student by the whole college or university, not merely the education department, (3) five years of professional preparation for all teachers, (4) a four-year probationary period for beginning teachers during which they would work closely with experienced teachers, and (5) continuing in service training in academic rather than professional courses. Conant would place greater stress upon academic proficiency and less on "education courses."

All of Conant's writings proved controversial. Some of his recommendations were adopted and became general throughout the country. Others were bitterly opposed and failed to gain acceptance. Nevertheless, his general aim was, like many writers and educators of the twentieth century, to adjust the educational system of the United States to world demands so that it would better produce men and women able to work and live effectively in the one world of the age.

NATIONALISM AND INTERNATIONALISM

The twentieth century has been the century of internationalism, of one world. History reveals many attempts to organize a world society. The earliest empires, from the Babylonian and the Chinese through the Roman, brought people of diverse cultures and thinking under one rule, parts of a whole. This was accomplished by force of arms. Christianity and Mohammedanism are illustrations of internationalism through the force of religious faith. All these patterns took shape under strong and understanding leadership and weakened when such leadership was not available.

In the twentieth century, stimulated by the changes that characterized this age, two attempts were made to organize the world into one whole: the League of Nations and the United Nations. Both were products of experiences growing out of world wars. Leaders became convinced that the survival of mankind rested upon the ability of nations to live and work together in one world.

At the same time, the twentieth century was an age of nationalism. On January 1, 1964, there were 113 members of the United Nations. A large per cent of these were creations of the twentieth century. Many were former colonial possessions of Great Britain, others were the result of a surge of nationalism in Africa, while still others were former trusteeships of the League of Nations or the United Nations. To assure its integrity and continuity, each of these nations established some form of school structure and employed methods of general instruction to produce loyalties among their people. Often these loyalties came into conflict with the trend toward internationalism. Early in 1965, there were indications that nationalism was in the ascendency and internationalism threatened. President Sukarno of Indonesia had given notice of his withdrawal from the United Nations, the first such break in the ranks of that organization since its creation in 1945. Communist China was beginning a move to organize another international body in opposition to the United Nations, while Russia and several other countries were facing the loss of their votes because of nonpayment of assessments.

Coupled with these moves was a growing feeling on the part of many throughout the world that nationalism and internationalism were inherently incompatible. School authorities in many parts of the world came to fear that education in internationalism would undermine national loyalty and weaken the determination to defend national ideas and values. Since forty per cent of the world's population in 1965 was functionally illiterate, and almost half of the 500,000,000 children in the world lacked the opportunity for schooling, the more prosperous nations began plans to provide the education these people needed. In many cases this was interpreted as cultural imperialism and was resisted officially and by mobs excited by the authorities and allowed to destroy schools, information libraries, and consulates without interference from police or other constituted keepers of the peace.

These facts brought into bold relief one of the most serious issues of the mid-twentieth century. Robert J. Havighurst and Bernice L. Neugarten, writing in their *Society and Education,* held that international loyalties were the normal extension of national loyalties. Just as the little child learns first loyalty to his family and later loyalty to the wider community—neighborhood, city, state, and nation—without lessening his loyalty to the family, so with education people can be loyal to their nations while holding loyalties to one world. This education, Havighurst and Neugarten held, must aim at developing "open-ended loyalty" rather than "blind loyalty." They asserted that "A society that prepares its youth for loyalty in wider groups is one that gives children a satisfactory experience in the smaller, primary groups."

As the world moved through the first two decades after World War II, the most pressing educational problem was seen to be development of procedures and programs to employ the forces of nationalism in such a way as to strengthen internationalism. The conviction was strong that internationalism, the salvation of the future, must not destroy nationalism, the basis of one's security. This was a challenge to all education, western and eastern.

CHAPTER 19

Contemporary Education — Unifying Themes in Education Around the World

INTRODUCTION

The last decade has seen the expansion of educational opportunity in many parts of the world. Most countries have raised their compulsory attendance age. Early childhood education has been developing rapidly, while at the other end of the educational spectrum, higher education has become available to many more.

Most countries, particularly European, have attempted to democratize their school systems. This has been accomplished by opening new schools at the secondary level, eliminating barriers to admission, and making all schools free. The new common middle school has replaced many other forms. In most countries, comprehensive schools have been introduced and are making progress. What to do about curriculum changes is a polarized issue. Modernization has strong support, but so does retention of the traditional. While some peoples seem to favor the expansion of educational opportunity, there has been strong resistance to introduction of anything different from the academic.

Many factors contribute to these educational reform movements. The war completely disrupted a way of life. While it devastated much of Europe, peace gave a new level of aspirations to the people. The United Nations issued the Declaration of Human Rights. Many believe in the points of this document, including the right to an education.

Teachers and children of Europe have bounced back strongly in the years of peace since World War II. It was believed by large numbers that education could solve many of the political and social woes of the world. Confidence grew in education as an instrument for preservation of peace and the development of true democracy. This faith has been implemented widely. Social class origin for many is no longer a barrier to education at the secondary and higher levels. Curriculum and teaching methods have been updated, even if progress has not been rapid. By 1970, most countries have lost faith in the selection system at age eleven for secondary schools. Tests are less culture-oriented, but even so, evaluation remains. Defenders of the traditional still possess power, although their action is more rear-guard than holding back progress. It now appears that by the end of the 1970s, the comprehensive middle schools will be the prime educational institutions of most of the free world.

Until recently, European countries have shown little inclination toward curriculum reform. The traditional approach has been to permit teachers at all levels of education to make decisions. But new methods and new content are demanded for the 1970s. One of the problems is that, in general, contemporary educational theories require more expertise than the teachers are competent to give. However, much that was taught in the past two decades is still with us in the 1970s.

A big problem interfering with progress is the examination system. For example, in England the General Certificate of Education Ordinary Level became effective in 1951. This is a qualifying examination, developing information about a student's general education. It is administered after five years of secondary education, at the age of sixteen. An increasing number of students from all types of schools take this examination. The intent of the legislation was that the examinations would follow the curriculum, but like all tests, they direct it. Today, lay and professional opinion challenges the validity of tests, thus presenting prospects for revolution in testing philosophy. Most countries throughout the world are either eliminating testing altogether as a basis for advancement into higher education, or are combining these tests with the student's school record in order to make decisions as to the student's educational future. In addition, most countries provide alternative means for a student to enter the field of his choice.

Another characteristic that can be noted that tends to be common is the effort to make education relate more closely to real life. In the United States, the words "relevance" and "work experience" typify this movement. In European countries, it is an effort to develop a more functional general program. Educators in the Soviet Union, in the Balkans, and in Western Europe all express as a prime concern the need to relate education more directly to the kind of life the child will live. However, it should be noted that these words in the legislation appear better phrased than does the actual curriculum.

A general raising of the age of compulsory education is to be noted. While figures vary from country to country, and within each country, the general age of compulsory education is sixteen, and is going higher. In this regard, it should also be noted that the trend universally is for a large percentage of young people to continue education beyond the compulsory age. It should also be pointed out that the holding power of the schools is, in general, significantly greater than previously. For instance, in Communist countries, failure in school is almost nonexistent, and near 100 per cent holding power exists through the compulsory ages. There may be other reasons for this than simply a good educational program, but it is a fact. Interestingly, at the very time European schools are making such progress in getting the masses of students into higher education, the concept of a university education for such a higher percentage of students is being challenged in the United States. However, one big difference exists: European countries have far more technical and vocational institutes for higher education than does the United States. Thus, there exists this variation in the contemporary point of view.

The goals of education are quite similar throughout much of the world. The institutions are different; the procedure is not the same, but the aims and objectives are quite alike: equal opportunity for all, promotion of minority interests, and life-related education. Much emphasis is being placed upon cultural understandings of other countries, but all within the framework of nationalistic settings. The Communist countries are excellent examples of this. While talking and teaching internationalism, these countries work diligently at promoting the student's appreciation of his own historic past, emphasizing great respect for his heritage, and, in general, promoting nationalism. European countries push much harder at dignifying, even glorifying, the national history than does America.

While the evidence is not readily available, the trend is toward the child-centered classroom. Educators preach that the important element is the child, not the subject, not the teacher. Most countries emphasize that they are helping the youngster learn to inquire, to discover, to create, rather than work with textbooks and factual knowledge. Again, this is an educational theory in advance of practice in the classroom. Analysis of a limited number of classroom observations does not support this trend, though it appears to be an honest goal and will be fulfilled as rapidly as teachers and resources can be prepared.

Recognition exists that a new kind of education is essential for the technical world of today. New images are being developed for vocational and technical education. In some countries like France, England, and the United States, it is an uphill battle, because vocational education is so often equated with stupidity, failure, or lack of ambition. Other countries are having greater success in these areas, but by the end of the 1970s it is apparent that all countries will have made strides in this direction.

Closely allied with all of these trends in education rests the understanding that education is essential to modernity. America has long recognized the essentialness of education for all. Now the concept exists universally and much more money and manpower is being directed into the educational enterprise. China and the Soviet Union are prime examples. The pace is being accentuated in newly developed countries and the gap is being narrowed between education in advanced nations and in the so-called backward areas. Unfortunately, effort is not all there is to it; resources still favor the advanced countries.

GREAT BRITAIN

No country has been involved in a more exciting or innovative contemporary educational program than has England. The innovations extend from the British Infant School, through the free secondary school, to the Open University. If the casual observers of the English educational system are often confused, it is not surprising. So are the English. Reforms and rapid developments of the 1960s left the public bewildered. It must be recognized that the establishment of a paper plan to democratize educational opportunity did not make it effective. Side by side with the development of new institutions the old ones remain, and especially attitudes toward elitist education.

A characteristic of English education in the 1970s is that all British children can now have the opportunity of equal education regardless of social or financial constraints. The British no longer use the term elementary education because of its long association with a type of education which was deliberately inferior. British children today have access to free infant school education (ages five through seven); to free primary education (ages eight through eleven); to free secondary education (ages eleven through fifteen, or as old as eighteen if they desire to continue and have demonstrated their ability to do so); to free higher education in all technical and commercial schools; and to free admission to the University if they qualify and come from a family with less than average income. Extracurricular activities are encouraged in all levels but are particularly important in the secondary grammar schools. Physical education plays a strong role in the curriculum, as does the sports program.

All English children begin school shortly after reaching the age of five. There is no national curriculum at this level. Teachers and school administrators are relatively free to prescribe the method and content

Years in School					Years of age

Further and Higher Education

- 16 — 21
- 15 — 20
- 14 — 19

Universities (Higher Education)

Higher Technical Colleges

Further Education (Vocational, Adult)

- 13 — 18
- 12 — 17
- 11 — 16
- 10 — 15
- 9 — 14
- 8 — 13
- 7 — 12

The Secondary Stage

Secondary Grammar Schools

Secondary Technical Schools

Secondary Modern Schools

Comprehensive Secondary Schools or Bilateral Schools (increasing rapidly; now 25–30% of total and goes to age 18.)

(The secondary stage begins at age 12, leaving four years until the school-leaving age, but contains a program of two or three additional years for those who wish to continue.)

(over 3,000,000 pupils)

- 6 — 11
- 5 — 10
- 4 — 9
- 3 — 8
- 2 — 7
- 1 — 6
- — 5

The Primary Stage

Special Education (mental/physical disabilities)

Junior Schools (Middle Schools)

(Approximately 3,000,000 pupils)

Infant Schools

(Over 2,000,000 pupils; 3 years in length)

All-age-school (almost completely disappeared)

Nursery Schools (Ages 2–4)

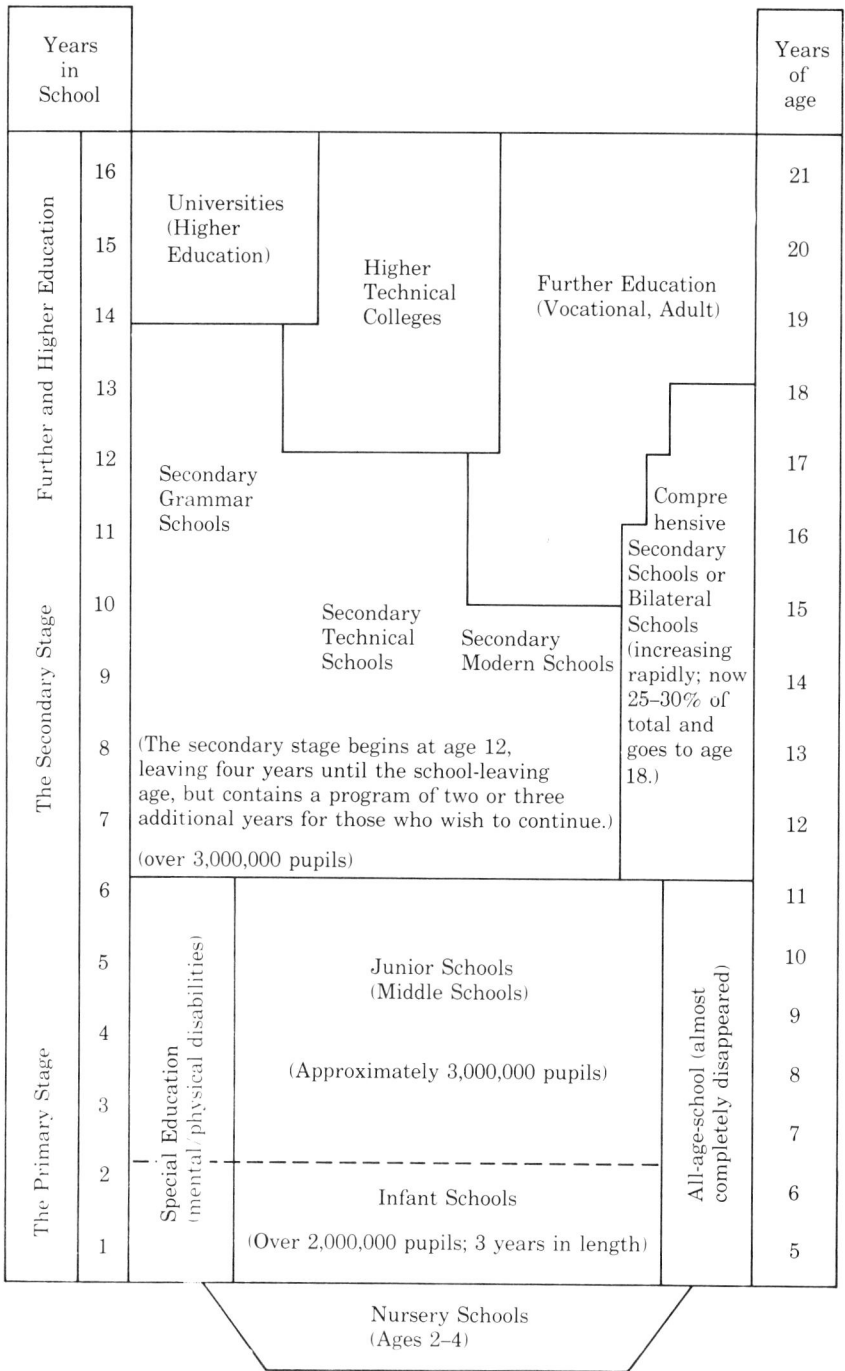

CHART 2   Organizational Chart of the Schools of England

of instruction best fitted for each child. Grouping is based upon reading ability. The normal rate of progress for the child by the age of six is to be able to read simple books and do simple arithmetic problems. By that age they can usually write. The most imitated British schools are infant schools (ages five through seven) and junior schools (ages eight through eleven). About the only thing in these schools American educators do not wish to imitate is the forty- to fifty-member classes. The work progresses steadily, and perhaps rapidly, until the youngster is eleven (grade six). Most authorities feel the work being done in a British junior school, grade six, is quite equal to the American grade seven. By grade six, the relationship between student and teacher has become quite formal, partly because the British think this is the way it works best and partly because this is the age of 11-plus examinations.

11-Plus Examinations

Historically, this examination has been the basis for advancement into the grammar school, the academic and prestigious form of secondary education. Admission has been a status symbol in England. The 11-plus examination covers formal English, mathematics, and standardized intelligence tests. No problem has had a sharper effect upon the curriculum of the junior schools than has the cramming sessions demanded by students and parents. Until recently, the British have had confidence in testing, but now there are those arguing that tests are class-biased, experience oriented, and narrow. In the early 1970s, some schools abandoned the 11-plus examination in favor of grades, records, and recommendations. Still, some form of evaluation is required in most instances, and, regardless of the method whereby it is done, all students are placed in a secondary school of some type, usually at age eleven, but it can be at age twelve or thirteen.

The basic school approach has been that the junior school tends to be child-centered and oriented toward an activity approach to learning. If the 11-plus examination had not interfered, the junior schools could be more innovative in the total curriculum.

While secondary education in England is not as spectacular as in the infant and junior schools, it does represent the most meaningful change in any form of British education. Prior to World War II, secondary education was primarily limited to the privileged few; since then, it has not only become open to all students, it has become compulsory.

In the last few years, many forms of secondary schools have developed. The most important ones are the grammar schools, the technical schools, the secondary modern schools, and the bilateral schools. The secondary grammar school is the status type. In the United States it would be the college prep program. The student attends for either six or seven years before he goes on to the university or to business. The curriculum is typically college prep. The secondary technical school also has a background, but it was not a first class institution until after the Butler Act of 1944, which accorded it the status of a fully accredited secondary school. In this school the students prepare for technological fields such as engineering, electronics, aeronautics, navigation, the trades, home economics, and many other areas. As in the United States, the vocational aspects of this school have not proved popular. The public still likes to approach education via the prestige-oriented grammar school.

The type of secondary institution carrying the heaviest enrollment is the secondary modern school. The students in these schools correspond to what might be called the "invisible students" if they were in the comprehensive high schools of the United States. They represent England's future work force. These schools are encouraged to avoid the testing programs which characterize the grammar school. The secondary modern schools are for "average" youngsters, but the British parents do not think of their youngsters as only average.

As of 1965, England had thirty-five universities; Scotland had six; Wales had six, and Northern Ireland had one. Not all of these were universities, since some were in reality only colleges. The universities tend to be small. The University of London is largest, with about 30,000 enrollment. Basically all of these universities are private, although supported by public money. Academic freedom is carefully protected.

THE OPEN UNIVERSITY IN GREAT BRITAIN

One of the newest experiments in higher education is the Open University. Educational leaders throughout the world are currently watching the British experiment with the Open University. Its origins are to be found in 1964 in the pre-election campaign of Harold Wilson, leader of the Labor Party. It was first called in the campaign literature the University of the Air. The name quickly disappeared because the connotation was that the method of instruction would be primarily television and radio broadcasting. This was an incorrect interpretation, although the method of instruction combines the use of many forms of electronic media, study centers, tutorials, summer sessions, night classes, residential weekends, and correspondence courses. From 1964 to 1969, plans were forged to make this plan a reality. It became a real university with its own research facilities and its own degrees. In 1969, The University was formally chartered, but it was not until 1971 that the Open University began its operation with its first program. It is

now an independent institution, closely allied with the British Broadcasting Corporation.

Often referred to as the University of the Second Chance, it utilized
an approach to higher education never before attempted on so wide a
basis. Enrollment is open to any person over the age of twenty-one
under certain restrictions. An evaluation is made of the capability of
the student to profit from higher education. Its students are persons
who have never had an opportunity to go to college or have not been
able to attend as much as they need or want to. Most are part-time
because they are employed in full-time work or homemaking. Specific
or formal education is not necessarily required for admission, merely
a judgment that the candidate can benefit from and succeed in the
courses needed for the degree. A second category of students are older
persons who have a desire or need for higher education. Thus the Open
University does not compete with existing universities for its students
because they are part-time and not necessarily adequately prepared for
the intensive work required in the British university system.

The University is "open" because of its enrollment practices, its
methods of instruction, and new ideas of curriculum. It does not feature
specialized work as does the university system. It tends to be concerned
with an explanation of basic concepts and principles. Much of the work
is interdisciplinary in nature. For example, a course may be concerned
with the interrelationships between science, technological developments, and the problems of society. The individualized mathematics
areas such as algebra, calculus, computation or statistics give way to
a general view of mathematics. Liberal arts classes are combined with
science. These are only examples of the many curriculum directions.

The Open University has as its prime responsibility the same major
functions expected of the traditional university system, although the
assignment of these responsibilities differ from the normal university
procedure. These functions are separated into individual assignments
to staff members. The function of the Open University falls into these
four categories: it provides information and knowledge; builds the criti
cal thinking powers; directs the process of learning; and orients the
enrollee to the culture of the university.

The five main branches of study are: arts, technology, mathematics,
science, and social science. In 1972, there were over 8,000 students in
each of the social science and arts foundations courses and some 7,000
in each of science and mathematics series.

The four foundation courses represent the first level of the academic
program and are thirty-six weeks in length. Advanced work is offered
only every other week and is valued at one-half credit. Completion of
a course gives one credit. Six credits are required for a bachelor of arts

degree. An honors degree is awarded for eight credits, providing two advanced courses are offered. Six years are normally required for the degree, although it could be longer or shorter, depending upon previous work. The cost of this university program is approximately one-third that of a traditional university. The university is about to become the world's first profit-making public university. By 1972, thousands of persons were in the program who did not plan for a degree but instead were there for updating information.

Certain characteristics of the Open University are being imitated throughout the world. In the United States, the State University of New York has created off-campus degree programs even more radical than the Open University. A student may enroll in courses at any of the seventy campuses of this university. Fees are low and students can work at home at their own pace via correspondence work, television programs, and cassette tape recorders. By 1972, several hundred students were already enrolled.

In California, the nineteen-campus State College System is progressing with similar plans for home self-study programs. In 1972, the University of California on certain of its campuses started part-time evening Master of Arts in Teaching programs for working students.

Another contemporary American experiment is the University Without Walls, a highly individualized and flexible alternative form of university education. Some twenty American universities have combined in an experiment to develop a new concept in higher education. While these universities are combined in a common goal, each campus determines its own admission policies and procedures. Most have employed an open-admission, self-selection policy. The ages of the students currently range from sixteen to seventy-one. The program for each student is tailor-made by the student and his advisor. Students use a variety of learning experiences to achieve their objectives: regular class work, independent study, projects, travel, programmed material, media, apprenticeships, and whatever. There is no prescribed curriculum or uniform time schedule for completing the degree. Graduation takes place when the student has achieved the learning objectives agreed upon with his advisor, whether it be one, five, or twenty years. In 1972, there were 3,000 students enrolled in the University Without Walls, including many Blacks, Puerto Ricans, Chicanos, and American Indians.

FRANCE

French education is administratively centralized in Paris, and as the French say, Paris is France. It operates under a number of general provisions. School attendance is required for all children between the ages of six and sixteen. Public education is free and is nondenominational. All diplomas and official titles are conferred by the state based on a public examination. Although the government guarantees free education to all children, private schools do exist. In these, students obtain their diplomas and similar certification from the state after public examination. While private schools can issue diplomas, they have no official value. There is a slight exception in that the diploma of a limited number of private technical schools are officially recognized by the state. Higher education degrees from some private universities have prestige today because of difficulties in the public universities. Private schools can receive state aid. Higher education is not free in France, but fees are low. In practice, over half of the students have their fees waived. More than 30 percent in secondary and higher education receive scholarships covering food, school supplies, and books.

The latest French reform in education was promulgated in 1959. Its goal has been to establish schools in which various types of education will fit the needs of children in terms of their individual aptitudes. France is trying to develop a system that suits the needs of children rather than catering to social criteria, traditions, status of family, and other factors long in existence in French schools.

The first schools are maternal or preschool. These are not compulsory. They cover the ages from two to six and their programs call for the common care necessary to develop the child physically, intellectually, and morally. The preschools include the Montessori and Decroly methods. While preschool is not compulsory, 92 percent of youngsters ages five to six are in preschool and 80 percent of the ages four to five are enrolled. The French have great confidence in and concern for this phase of early childhood education.

The next form of public schooling is primary education for children aged six to eleven years. Curricula and teaching methods are determined by regulations of the French Ministry of Education. The teaching is common to all children. The primary program is divided into three component parts. First is the preparatory course, covering ages six and seven. The second division is the elementary course, covering ages seven to nine years. The third is the middle course for children ages nine to eleven. The main theme of the elementary program is cultural. Formerly it was terminal, encyclopedic, and accumulative in nature, but now it prepares the student for the secondary schools. The curricula includes French, moral teaching (French patriotism, values and heritage), reading, natural science, physical education, and elements of drawing, singing, and manual work. There are special schools and classes for the various types of handicapped.

Secondary education has as its purpose provision of a general education which will develop the entry skills for higher education as well as for careers. During the four years from ages eleven to fifteen, students are in courses called "the first cycle" of lower secondary education. In the first cycle, the classes are numbered the opposite of American classes: the lowest class in this cycle is the sixth class and the highest class is the third class. Thus, when students from the primary school enter the first cycle, teaching begins with sixth level classes and goes through third level classes. During the four years of the first cycle, all students, without exception, enroll in one of the various sections of a particular class. Ability grouping is developed, with the sophistication level varying from one section to another. No vocational training is permitted. The several programs call for parallel courses and stay as close to each other as the ability of the students will permit. Transfer from one level to another is open but not advocated.

Since 1968, sixth level classes have divided into three different groupings. Sixth level classes I and II have a common curriculum, the distinction resting in the teaching method used. Sixth level class III is for other types of students with less ability.

Beginning with the fifth level class, there are four sections. The first section is a classical section featuring the study of Latin and Greek, although the latter is not started until the fourth class. The second section is what is called Modern I, and features a more thorough program in the study of French, along with two other living languages, usually English and German. The second foreign language does not start until the fourth class. The third section, called Modern 2, is characterized by the requirement of only one living language. The fourth section is known as the transition group, and is characterized by its flexibility to meet the needs of the students in the program. These classes were formerly known as "primary-schools leaving" classes. This program may well serve as an introduction to subsequent vocational training after the student reaches the age of fifteen years. However, the program in the "practical cycle" classes, or transition classes, is general-education oriented.

Another feature of lower secondary education is the development of a counseling system. Throughout the four years, from the sixth class to the third class, a guidance committee made up of inspectors, teachers, a representative of the parents, and possibly others, regularly review the records of a student and report their recommendations to the parents. These recommendations include a statement as to the type of school for which the student is best suited. This counseling includes the students in the "transition classes" and the "practical classes." At the end of the third level class, if the family supports the suggestions of the counseling report, the student is automatically free to enroll in the class that is recommended. If the family wishes the youngster to go to a different type of school not recommended in the report, the student is required to take an entrance examination.

Starting at the fourth or third class level, special classes, known as "reception" or "adaptation" classes, are organized which will admit students now ready for such schooling, but whose aptitude or school record had prevented entrance into the program at the sixth class level. These "bridge" classes permit easy transferring from one course to another and permit a recognition of the late-developing capacities of the child.

From the ages of fifteen to eighteen years, the student probably will be enrolled in upper secondary education. When the lower secondary course is ended, students are guided into either the "long" type school, lasting three years, or the "short" type, which does not last beyond two years. The decision as to which school to attend will be based upon a combination of school record and aptitude and achievement tests. The "long" courses give vocational training supported by general training.

The short upper secondary course provides vocational training of two years duration or one year of highly specialized training or work experience education wherein the student works part-time and goes to school part-time. This training can complete the student's compulsory education even though he may not have reached the age of sixteen.

GHOST OF THE BACCALAUREATE

The long upper secondary course has as its essential mission providing general culture and preparing for the baccalaureate, which has historically been the examination which determines the direction of the student's next educational move. The long courses have several sections offering students a variety of routes to follow which relate both to their individual aptitudes as well as to the principle forms of culture. These sections have been classified as follows:

Section A—literary studies;
Section B—economic and social studies;
Section C—mathematics and physical sciences;
Section D—sciences of nature; and
Section T—industrial sciences and techniques.

The plan has not worked well. Regardless of the ability level of the students, the big push has been for the students to get into the prestigious Section C. Much parent education needs to be done to popularize or make acceptable the other sections. The counseling structure that was started in lower secondary education is maintained throughout upper secondary education.

ABOVE THE AGE OF EIGHTEEN: HIGHER EDUCATION

Above the age of eighteen, the student may be in higher education. The French university does not attempt to develop applied or professional curricula such as law, medicine, engineering, or business. Characteristically, the curriculum is theory-oriented, with emphasis on the development of analytical ability. The mission of the university is to contribute to the progress of science, the training of research workers, the development of scientific, literary, and technological research, to dispense a high level of artistic and literary culture, and to prepare for professions requiring both broad culture and extensive knowledge. Particularly, it must develop graduate work at the highest level. One out of every ten students in the university is a foreigner; one out of every one hundred is American.

Admission to the university is based upon the secondary education baccalaureate. For persons twenty-one to twenty-five years, special admission examinations are offered. While the ghost of the baccalaureate remains, there is no real selection process for the French university. The French are opposed to any process of selection. Therefore, they developed what is known as the I.U.T., which corresponds somewhat to the American junior college, though the level of its program is probably more advanced. The I.U.T. was intended to solve the selection problem. It was believed students would select it as an alternative to the university since it was work-oriented. But French students and parents have not responded, and the I.U.T. has had a disappointing acceptance.

ISSUES IN FRENCH EDUCATION

With all this reform, French education is beset by huge problems. In France, as in numerous European countries, most citizens have only an elementary education. As late as 1962, relatively few had an education higher than elementary and most of those who possessed more had only "secondary" experience.

Since the compulsory attendance age has been raised to sixteen, many more have had some secondary education. Parents believe the school is to develop the intellect and they support the schools accordingly. The schools do not legally assign homework for children under eleven years of age. The "eleven-year-old" examinations have disappeared from France, except for marginal cases where parents will not accept the counseling decision.

Years of School						Years of Age
	Levels I and II 12% enrollment					
	Level III 8% enrollment			Traditional and Special Colleges		18 Years and Older
	Level IV 15% enrollment		I.O.T. (Junior College)			
12	Level V 40% enrollment			Second Cycle Secondary (Long)		17
11	Level VI 40% enrollment	Second Cycle Secondary (Short)				16
10						15
9						14
8		First Cycle — Secondary 100% enrollment				13
7	Handicapped Children					12
6						11
5		Elementary School 100% enrollment				10
4						9
3						8
2						7
1						6
						5
		Preschool (maternal) 73% eligible attend				4
						3
						2

CHART 3   Organizational Chart of the Schools of France

French education is highly examination-oriented. Numerous medical reports indicate the young French students suffer from overwork, but little is done about it. Centralized control of examinations continues, but today the grading of these examinations is more humanized; not softer, merely more flexible. The most abiding criticism represents the unequal preparation youngsters have who take these examinations. Equality of education does not exist when comparing backward provinces with metropolis schools, and of course, there are social disadvantages. Still, the system is a great improvement.

Curriculum has not changed much in France. Little has been added, even though organizationally the schools have changed considerably. There is educational conflict between the traditionalists, who favor a basic two-track system of academic and technical, and the newer reformers, who support a unitary system in organizational structure, in curriculum content, in modes of teaching, and *l'enseignement,* as the French call it. This element of the population opposes ability grouping.

In either approach, the French continue to place confidence in the intellectual function and to emphasize the importance of culture. However, they have much concern with what to learn. Since one cannot learn it all, the complexity and amount of knowledge available forces a choice. One curriculum advancement has been the development of the science of communication. A number of the traditional subjects, and some new courses, are indispensable "communicators" which have to be mastered before additional knowledge can be learned. These communicators are: ability to use effectively the mother tongue; mathematics, which is the symbolic language of science; technical drawing, which is the key to technology; and a mastery of one or more classical or modern languages, which add a further dimension to the ability to think. Probably the French concept of this foundation program is as defensible as any other basic curriculum, but such a cultural orientation is not adequate to meet the needs of the 1970s. Thus, the direction of the curriculum of the future is not clear.

Organization and operation of the *lycées* have begun to change from their long established regimentation and military-like discipline. Still, schools are intended as places for the development of intellectual ability. Since the student strike of 1968, students have had a part in determining school policy or government.

The French have innovated in numerous teaching procedures: smaller classes, directed work, individualized instruction, special work with underachievers and slow learners, pupil activity in the daily sessions in the basic subjects, language laboratories, and audio-visual methods of teaching language. Yet, the more it changes, the more it is the same thing. The author noted on a recent visit to French schools that the typical teaching methods are authoritarian, memory oriented, and teacher dominated, although a few schools were quite relaxed and flexible. There is student resistance and it is beginning, in some areas, to make the schools and teachers more sensitive to the needs and desires of youth. The French have provided money for research in the areas of teaching techniques and curriculum development, but this observer feels that the planners of the changes are far ahead of the teachers in their thinking.

In the *lycées,* the student is tested on each subject area once a term. The tests, called *compositions,* are an hour long and are given during class time. Students tend to resent these examinations, as do the teachers. The correctional work is extensive. At the conclusion of the academic secondary school experience, the student must take the baccalaureate (examination). The French are currently in harsh debate as to the function and type of the examination to be required. It is argued by one group that the examination should guarantee a minimum of general culture. Others maintain it should merely be considered the completion of secondary studies. A third group is concerned with what influence the test should have upon university admission. All tend to be concerned with the lack of jobs for college graduates, either now or in the foreseeable future.

WEST GERMANY

Germany has had significant influence upon American education. The educational ladder concept is one example. Yet, with all its historic contributions, German education can be characterized only in a general way. The description in the next few paragraphs relates to West Germany only. Control of West German education rests with the state governments. Although the laws differ from one state to another, there is enough uniformity to refer to it as a German educational system.

Education is complusory throughout West Germany from the ages of six through eighteen. The terminal age for full-time attendance varies from one state to another, but it is either fourteen or fifteen. Those who, for one reason or another, finish school before eighteen go to a continuation school one day a week.

Organizationally, West German schools divide into elementary, intermediate, and secondary. There are kindergartens, but these are not generally part of the regular school system. The elementary school is organized on an eight- or nine-grade basis. Usually the first four years are called the basic schools, although in the city states of West Berlin, Bremen, and Hamburg the basic schools cover the first six years. The next cycle above this basic school is the upper level school, varying from three to four years. Students must successfully finish the basic school for admission into intermediate or secondary schools. Approximately 80 percent of German children finish their education in the elementary school. However, this school-leaving route differs from the program of regular promotion and theoretically is equivalent to the first years in the West German intermediate or secondary schools.

Students go to school from 8:30 A.M. to 1:30 P.M., six days a week. The elementary schools are usually coeducational, while the secondary schools separate the sexes. Compulsory education is free to the students. Higher education is also free in some areas.

The intermediate schools in the West German system are difficult to classify. They represent an alternate form of education which does not lead directly to admission to institutions of higher education. It is secondary education that provides the regular route of admission. The grade span covered by intermediate schools begins at grade five or seven and continues through grade ten. The intermediate schools are of a terminal nature. They have a purpose of their own which does not include preparing for the upper secondary. It is quite different than the American junior high, which is an articulated part of the educational ladder. The terminal education aspects of the intermediate school include preparation for career opportunities at medium-level occupations such as government workers, technicians, or business. Some instances do exist wherein a student can transfer from the intermediate school to the secondary school, but not often.

One of the newer developments in West German schools is the unified school system, which is basically a six-year elementary school followed by differentiated upper level programs conducted in the same schools. These schools do not represent an actual change in subject matter, merely a basis of organization. The program has had so many difficulties it cannot be predicted as the pattern of the future.

The secondary school is the gymnasium. Over the years its curriculum has traditionally featured classical languages. If a change in curriculum is decided upon, a new school is established without changing the old. West Germany's program for the secondary education is relatively long, covering seven to nine years, with nine the more typical. West Germany has three kinds of secondary schools. The first and most prestigious is the classical school. It remains a rigorous system of academic work, with heavy stress on mental discipline and cognitive knowledge. The program of studies is based upon Greek and Latin, although at present it includes German, mathematics, history, a modern foreign language, science, and physical education. All of this study, which is continuous in each grade, culminates in a comprehensive examination to determine eligibility for the university.

The classical gymnasium is being replaced by other types of schools. Thus the second type of secondary school is the modern language school. It has now become West Germany's leading secondary school. This school has a curriculum emphasizing Latin studies and two foreign languages, along with science and mathematics.

The third type of secondary school is known as the mathematics-science school. As the name suggests, the emphasis is on mathematics and science, but it offers work in two foreign languages. There are numerous variations of these secondary schools which serve special purposes, such as the "build-up school" and girls' schools.

German universities (called *hochschulen*) are primarily supported by the public. The professors are civil servants. These universities resemble American graduate schools. Admission is based upon the certificate of maturity, granted after successful completion of the gymnasium comprehensive examinations or their equivalent. The only degree awarded by the university is the doctorate, based upon a dissertation.

SOVIET UNION

Soviet education needs to be examined carefully, since it influences such a large segment of the populations around the world. Differing from education in many countries, Soviet education is well-articulated. There is continuity from start to finish, and superior orientation to the various youth organizations which provide much of the extracurricular activities for children. Differing sharply with the American and British system of the extracurricular, the Soviet extracurricular is done outside of school by political youth groups. These youth organizations are: the Octobrists (grade one through three and one-half, ages seven through nine); the Pioneers (grades four through eight, ages ten through fifteen); and KOMSOMOL or Young Communist League (ages sixteen through twenty-eight). Many of the restored palaces have become resource centers for the youth clubs, providing opportunity for much creative work by brilliant students. The Soviet has no screening or ability grouping in the schools (beyond that of physically handicapped or mentally retarded), but it does provide just about the world's best opportunity for the gifted to create and become better-informed or more proficient than the slower children. The vast array of palaces provide fine settings for increased inter-scholastic and inter-collegiate events. Incidentally, sports programs do exist in Soviet schools, including volleyball, ice hockey, and soccer football. In addition, various secondary sports schools exist which specialize in various sports along with the regular education program.

There has been a steady movement in the Soviet Union toward universal general education for all children. In the 1920s, the general education level was four years; in the 1940s, seven years; in the 1960s, eight years; and its goal for the 1970s is a full secondary education for all children through ten grades. A new emphasis in curriculum is being placed on communication. It is interesting to note that the Soviet Union, like the United States, is introducing new methods of teaching —i.e., new grammar, new mathematics, etc. The Soviet Union has many youngsters being taken care of and tutored by retired grandparents (since both parents work). This "grandparent education" is being renovated because grandparents do not know the new way of doing things in the schools. They are not the help to the child they once were.

PRESCHOOL EDUCATION IN THE SOVIET UNION

A prime characteristic of Soviet education is that it is prescriptive. Further, the Soviets teach everything at as early an age as possible. Precocity not only is a value, it is inevitable for most. The basic rudiments of vocalization and discrimination of sounds is begun with the child of four months. Toilet training is started at eight months. By the end of the first year, formal education is underway. The core curriculum for these one-year-old infants consists of toilet training, neatness, obedience, self-reliance, self-control, speech development, music appreciation, games, dramatizations, and exercise. A nurse and an assistant are the teachers.

The daily schedule is firm for the one-year-old. The children learn to follow a definite pattern. The Soviets believe that whatever ought to be learned ought to be learned early. This is a similar issue in the United States, though why earlier is better is not necessarily clear.

At the end of the second year of life children are moved from the infant groups to the first preschool group. In the third year, the teacher's prime function is to build the child's health; much attention is given to physical development via physical training. The school aggressively works on the development of good speech patterns. Esthetics through music appreciation, art appreciation, and the beauties of nature are areas of emphasis at this age. Much time is devoted to play, utilizing educational toys. Art work, particularly drawing, is also important. Building materials are used widely.

The educational objectives for children from age three to seven progress systematically in sophistication as the youngsters learn what they are expected to learn. Because the program is influenced by intentional environmentalism, it relates to reality. The child learns about the work of the people on the collective farms and about jobs in the city. There is training in morality, speech development, appropriate work, health education, and the material objects of Soviet culture. At the same time, youngsters are deeply involved in value education: they begin study in their native language, develop a feeling of love for their country, and build up a favorable attitude towards hard work. Other curriculum areas include: arithmetic operations, art education (drawing, modeling, cutting and pasting); music (singing, dancing, and appreciation); and reading and writing. While reading and writing are in the kindergarten program, they are emphasized with the seven-year-old. However, Soviet authorities have recently informed the nation that 70 percent of the youngsters can read when they enter grade one, and most know considerable arithmetic at that time.

The Soviet Union has always used communal facilities for bringing up its children. A little over a decade ago, however, a new type of preschool program was instituted. It was the creche-kindergarten, developed for the purpose of rearing Soviet children from the time they are two months old until the age of seven. At this age they enter the regular school program. The kindergarten represents group upbringing. The kindergarten "teacher" follows faithfully in detail a prescribed program of daily procedure, including methods, curriculum, and activities. Believing that what the child will be is determined in the early years, the kindergarten is devoted to extensive character education, primarily Communist morality. This includes love of country, appreciation of things Russian, obedience, self-discipline, and manners, as well as firm preparation for formal school.

The majority of Soviet youngsters are in standardized educational programs from ages seven to fifteen. This includes primary education, grades one through four, and an "incomplete" secondary education, grades five through eight. Organizationally, the primary grades may be taught either in a four-year primary setting or in an eight-year school or in a ten-year school. The Soviet is experimenting with a one-through-three primary organization, and this is expected to be the plan for the future. Actually, experiments are being conducted wherein at six years, six months, the child will begin moving into first grade work. Differing from the American structure, the Soviets do not have separate middle, junior, or senior high schools. The plan for Soviet education is that by the latter part of the 1970s, compulsory education will include the ten-year secondary program and that this will be Soviet-wide.

The primary classrooms are self-contained, each with only one teacher through grade three. At grade four, subject matter specialists begin to take over. The curriculum of the primary grades includes heavy emphasis upon fundamentals—reading, writing, and arithmetic, but also includes art, music, natural science, physical education, and manual training. The primary schedule for the students is a four-hour day, six days a week. Since 1971, the Soviets have been experimenting with a three-year primary program, but it is not yet general and it does not change the total eight-year program.

The program in grades five through eight is normally a five-hour day for six days a week. An alternate provision exists in the fourteen non-great Russian Republics and in certain minority nationality regions in the SFSR, for lengthening this time two or three hours a week for instruction in local language, culture, history, and literature. Mathematics and language study represent the heaviest curriculum demands for these grades. Mathematics instruction includes algebra and geometry. Language studied is Russian, although some other native languages are permitted. Also included will be a foreign language begun at grade five. Other subjects studied include biology (from grade four on), geography (from grade four on), physics (from grade five on), history (from grade four on), drafting (from grade seven on), labor lessons (grades one through ten), and physical education. The early emphasis on music and art drops off after the sixth or seventh grades, giving way to chemistry at grade seven. The traditionally academic curriculum for the eight-year school is influenced by contemporary technological scientific society. Foreign language begins in grade two at the language schools (i.e., English school). These language schools are like all secondary schools except the emphasis is rearranged.

For the young Soviet students of fifteen who have completed the eight-year school, there are three routes open for additional education. If one desires to go on into higher education, the normal path would be to complete the ten-year secondary general education, which includes grades nine and ten. If he wishes to enter technical work, he may attend "technicums," or secondary technical schools. If he wishes to enter a trade or a factory, he can attend one of the various factory or trade schools.

Since in the Soviet there are no separate secondary schools, in some rural areas students have difficulties if they wish to continue in grades nine and ten. The separate four-year primary school exists in certain rural areas where there is no opportunity for the eight-year school. The one-through-eight schools exist in areas of concentration of population. The ten-year schools are generally even more restricted to urban areas. Thus, these schools become difficult for rural students to attend. To equalize opportunity for rural children, evening schools, called Schools for Rural Youth, are organized, using the buildings of the eight-year schools.

Many Soviets are working parents. The relatively short school day does not coincide with the working day. In the years after World War II, an effort was made to solve this problem by establishing boarding schools. This program proved too costly and has since disappeared, except for quite special needs. To meet the problem of the working parent, "extended day schools" have been set up which provide recreation and study opportunity.

The State controls most functions of the schools. The State prescribes textbooks, curriculum, teaching methods, and standard national achievement examinations. Classrooms tend to be boring, with often long, uninterrupted lectures, recitations that are rote and memorized, and traditional classroom arrangements such as rows of fixed bench desks. Most schools are poorly constructed, with poor ventilation, lighting, and heating.

Recent years have seen changes in upper secondary education. Most significant has been an increase in numbers and types of schools. During the five years prior to 1964, the secondary school was extended to grade eleven. The curriculum consisted of about two-thirds general education and one-third vocational training, along with experiences in industrial production. In 1964, the Soviet educational program was cut back. Much vocational training was eliminated and the eleventh year was dropped. Since 1971, industrial-production education has been almost entirely discontinued. Elective opportunities have become a part of the contemporary scene.

SOVIET HIGHER EDUCATION

Higher education has been primarily responsible for the emergence of the Soviet Union as a leading scientific, industrial, and military power. It has accounted for the Soviet status in atomic energy, military weaponry, space programs, computer technology, and radio electronics. It is of two general types—the university and specialized institutes. The Soviet Union currently has approximately eight hundred institutions of higher education, scattered throughout all areas of the country, although there is a heavy concentration in the Moscow-Leningrad areas. Some two million regular day students are enrolled in these schools, another two million are enrolled in correspondence-extension classes, and another million are in evening classes. The Soviet Union is second only to the United States in student enrollments.

Only fifty-two of the eight hundred institutions of higher learning are at university level. And they enroll less than 20 per cent of the students in higher education. Moscow State University is the largest, with an enrollment of approximately 30,000. Science facilities are first rate; humanities are second class. The basic curriculum is quite similar to that of a major university in the United States.

University students are part of the Soviet manpower system. The program is tuition-free, and about 80 per cent of the students receive monthly support from the government. In return for this free education, the student, upon completion of his training, works for the state for three years. The state may provide some choice of work assignment, but in any event, the three years are compulsory. Even the awarding of the degree is held up until one year of the work assignment is completed.

The Soviet Union is experimenting in many phases of education. One of the newest is that of university admission processes. The Soviets have not been satisfied that testing is the answer. Neither is the student's past academic record alone adequate. It is now recommended that both factors be considered on a 50-50 basis.

JAPAN

Japanese education took on a change toward the modern after World War II. During the latter part of the war, most secondary schools were closed because the young were at work in war industries or on farms. Thus, when the war ended, education was in serious shape. Few schools were open; at least one-fifth were damaged; many were heaps of rubble.

When American occupation began in 1945, it had as its task the elimination of excessive nationalism and militarism. Japan set about establishing a new educational system with new goals, but with ample American advice. Contrary to the historical background of Japanese education, the new system featured decentralized control. However, in spite of high intention, there has been a gradual return to centralized control. By the mid-1960s, financial control was centralized and even curriculum was taking on a national flavor. In 1947, a single-track 6-3-3-4 system was established, with the first nine years compulsory. The high schools might be either technical or general or both. Vocational education has developed rapidly, even for girls.

Another major issue has been training in the elementary schools in patriotism, or what the Japanese call moral education. It was eliminated at first, but, as centralization has returned, so has moral education. In 1958, the central government officially restored moral education, although the teacher's organization was in opposition. The result has been one of moderation. No effort has been made to resurrect the fanatical national policy of pre-war Japan.

American occupation ended when a peace treaty was signed in 1952. Many feared Japan would return to her old pre-war nationalism, but

Years in School			Years of Age

Universities

18 Years and Older

Higher Education

Technical Schools (5 years)

Junior Colleges

Vocational Schools

12			17
11	Upper Secondary Schools		16
10			15
9			14
8	Lower Secondary Schools		13
7			12
6			11
5			10
4			9
3	Elementary Schools		8
2			7
1			6

Kindergarten
3–5 years of age

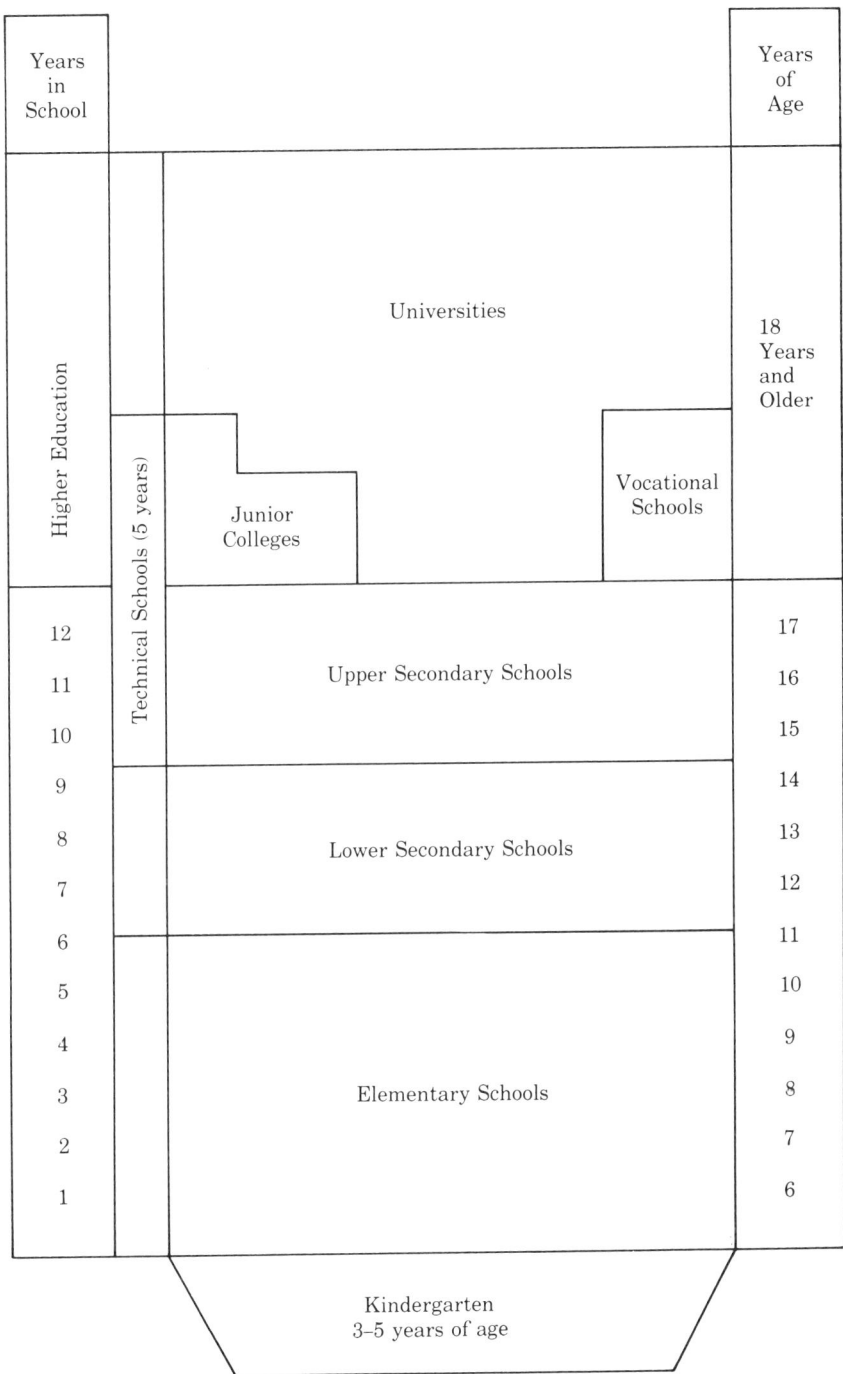

CHART 4   Organizational Chart of the Schools of Japan

to date it has not done so. The last Japanese report issued in the 1960s indicates the system has remained primarily democratic.

Japan faces numerous problems. Finance and improved school facilities are two. Language reform is another. The Japanese language has four systems of writing. Some reform has taken place, but the issue is still open. A bigger problem facing the schools, however, is psychological and quite subtle. If Japan is to continue to operate a democratic school program, the school must compete with the home. The home has the children far more hours per day than does the school. Old family habits do not change easily.

CHINA

The educational system in ancient China was directed toward educating civil servants. The curriculum emphasized the classics. The method was memorization, and questions for examinations were primarily objective in nature. This was the kind of educational heritage the Chinese Communist government has disavowed. With school traditions deeply embedded in school faculties and in communities, with a huge diversified land mass, with a tremendous population, with numerous spoken languages, with a difficult written language, and with a generally poor communication system, the Communist change-over has been difficult. The problems faced by Communist China are quite similar to those of the USSR.

But the Cultural Revolution has taken place. Mao Tse-tung has had much influence, but a great deal of work remains. In 1965, sixteen years after the Communist take-over, the Great Proletarian Cultural Revolution began. It grew during the next two years, as Mao and his followers eliminated those in the party "taking the capitalist road." Moral-political education became a central concern. The purpose of the Cultural Revolution was not only to demolish all the old ideology and culture, but also to create and cultivate among the masses entirely new proletarian customs, habits, ideology, and culture.

In an official document entitled *Decisions of the Central Committee of the Chinese Communist Party Concerning the Great Proletarian Cultural Revolution* (Peking: Foreign Languages Press, 1966), which set up guidelines for the Cultural Revolution, we read:

> In the great proletarian cultural revolution a most important task is to transform the old educational system and the old principles and methods of teaching.
> In this great cultural revolution, the phenomenon of our schools being dominated by bourgeois intellectuals must be completely changed.

In every kind of school we must apply thoroughly the policy advanced by Comrade Mao Ze-dong of education serving proletarian
politics and education being combined with productive labour, so as
to enable those receiving an education to develop morally, intellectually, and physically and to become workers with both socialist consciousness and culture.
     The period of schooling should be shortened. Courses should be
fewer and better. The teaching material should be thoroughly transformed, in some cases beginning with simplifying complicated material. While their main task is to study, students should also learn
other things. That is to say, in addition to their studies, they should
also learn industrial work, farming and military affairs, and take
part in the struggles of the cultural revolution to criticize the bour-
geoisie as these struggles occur.

Education in China is not compulsory at any level. However, there
are more students wanting to go to schools than there is space. This is
particularly true in the cities.
     The Chinese school system is made up primarily of the full-time first,
second, and third level schools. The first level schools are what may be
called the primary schools. These are divided between kindergartens,
which enroll students ages three through seven, and the junior schools,
which enroll students ages seven through thirteen.
     The kindergartens operate generally from eight to ten hours per day.
Like the Russian system, some of the schools are boarding schools. The
schools are poorly equipped. The curriculum includes language arts,
physical education, and general information. Reading is not normally
part of the kindergarten curriculum. The junior school might be government, private, or voluntary. The curriculum of these schools is
determined by the Ministry of Education, both as to content and to
time. The course work includes language, arithmetic, history, geography, natural science, agriculture, manual labor, physical education,
singing, and drawing.
     Second level schools are secondary. They are divided between junior
and senior high school, ages thirteen through sixteen, and seventeen
through nineteen respectively. The objective of the secondary school is
to provide an academic education. The curriculum in the junior high
schools is general to all, while the senior high schools are more specialized with either academic, teacher education, or vocational directions.
The curriculum differs little from what is found in other high schools
around the world, although communism intrudes at many places.
     Third level schools are institutions of higher education. Higher edu-
cation has the responsibility of training advanced technical personnel,
with principal emphasis upon defense and production. Throughout it
all, the student must have a thorough knowledge of Marxism-Leninism

and the philosophy of Mao Tse-tung. In 1965, there were 664 third-level institutions reported to be in operation.

The over-all intent of Chinese education is to develop the "new socialist man." This means new minds and new attitudes, a new way of life. The making of the "new socialist man" forces education to develop several characteristics: absolute selflessness, obedience to the Communist Party, class consciousness, versatility (a person serves in various capacities), love of labor, contribution to production, and above all, "Red expert" (the new socialist man is expected to be both Red and expert).

Under the Chinese Communist administration there has been a significant improvement in literacy. The best estimates today indicate that approximately 80 per cent of the Chinese population can read and write, whereas twenty-five years ago less than 20 per cent were literate.

CANADA

No single pattern of education in Canada can be developed, since each province has its own deviation. A typical organization is an articulated educational ladder giving a continuous program from grade one through the university. Throughout most of Canada, public education covers the years from kindergarten through grade twelve. Most Canadian students are in schools for eleven or more years. The compulsory education ages vary from fourteen to sixteen years of age, normally the latter. Consideration is being given in some areas (Ontario, for example) toward extending the compulsory age beyond sixteen.

Canadian public schools are what may be called traditional. This is true in organization as well as in curriculum. Most elementary schools consist of eight grades, even though only the first seven are considered elementary in some provinces. The elementary curriculum is oriented toward factual academic material, with memorization a prime method. The provincial subject-matter examinations cast a long shadow on the elementary curriculum. Canadian officials make much of their experimentation with "the newer concepts of education via the computer, the child centered school," "activity programs," and "enterprise education." These kinds of programs are aimed at "greening the curriculum," but they have not been powerful enough to offset the traditional concepts of subject-matter concentration, provincial examinations, and standards. Current efforts are also being made to relate more effectively with the community. The schools are providing more opportunity for athletic and social activities.

Another characteristic of contemporary Canadian elementary education is that of better attention to handicapped children. An interesting program of correspondence courses for all grade levels has developed. Quebec has several types of school organization worked out to meet the interests of a large French and Catholic population.

Secondary education in Canada has traditionally been separated according to academic, commercial, agricultural, home economics, or vocational abilities or interests. Recent years have seen a development similar to the American comprehensive high school. In Canada, this school organization is called the "composite high school." Academic schools are becoming less disciplined and academically oriented, whereas vocational schools are including more elective work. These directions have permitted the development of the composite school. The larger cities still favor the separate school, but in general the composite high school is the popular institution. Girls and boys are educated together, except in Quebec, where the Catholic influence brings about separate schools above grade seven.

Canada has approximately 5,600 secondary schools. The typical secondary organizational pattern is either grade eight through eleven, grade nine through twelve, or the five-year high school of grades nine through thirteen. Only a little over a quarter of the students finish grade twelve. A few provinces provide a thirteenth grade, which may be used as a freshman level course if a student goes on to a university. In spite of much interest in secondary education in Canada, and in spite of considerable broadening of the vocational school opportunity, there is a sharp drop in school attendance after grade seven.

UNITED STATES

Many severe issues continue to plague contemporary American education. The most difficult is the disenchanted youth that make up some of the student population. Included in this general category of issues are student power, student unrest, teacher militancy, polarized parent populations, drugs, sex, alternate education, and racism. A second series of problems is a combination of minority education, disadvantaged students, inner-city schools, and forced integration. A third grouping in the way of the great American democratic dream of equal educational opportunity relates to the curriculum, including relevancy, ability grouping, open classrooms, value education, and intelligence testing. Another source of controversy relates to behavioral objectives, accountability, and standardized tests. Big business, as represented in some instances by large textbook publishing houses, but more generally by electronic firms, has invaded and pressured in the field of computers, individualized and programmed instruction, instructional systems, educational machinery, media, and other technological tools. Foundations, the federal government, and other funding agencies have encouraged a system of grantmanship which, through the power of their money, have developed a new type of program and new private companies set up to capitalize on the availability of grant money, i.e., performance contracting. Other issues include innovations such as differentiated staffing, the child-centered classroom, computerized flexible scheduling, alternate schools within a given school, bilingual and bicultural education, and career development education.

Education in the United States is a major economic enterprise, second only to the military for money out-lay each year. The education industry in the United States employs more personnel, totals more investment, and serves more people than any other single business, yet it is perhaps the least modernized of any major industry. It remains a sprawling state-controlled business. Its bigness and its lack of central administration has led to much bureaucratic inertia. Public education is in deep trouble.

Contemporary American education is beset by gigantic problems. Perhaps the prime one is its brute size. Most institutions can survive weakness and mistakes when these errors can be absorbed in a growth program. This happened in education during the 1960s. Toward the beginning of the seventies, the growth pattern leveled off and currently is on the decline. Now the errors can no longer be hidden, absorbed, or justified.

Sources from the various states and from the U.S. Office of Education indicate interesting data as to the schools of the United States in 1969. Public and non-public day schools in operation totaled 113,659. Of these, 16.4 percent, totaling 18,600 schools, were non-public. There were 82,868 elementary schools and 29,228 secondary schools. The total school enrollment in 1969 showed an increase of approximately six million over seven years earlier, but over the same seven years the number of schools had dropped by nearly 14,000. Thus there has been a steady increase in the size of schools, primarily because of unification of school districts. During these seven years the decrease has been in public schools, since the number of private schools actually increased.

Statistics show the employment of teachers to be at an all-time high of nearly two million. The overall pupil-teacher ratio is on the decline, being twenty-three to one. Nearly 10 percent of public school children are in California, while New York is second with 8.5 percent of the total.

Today, major issues surround the question of what are the proper goals and directions for education, questions of emphasis that leave confusion in the determination of what the schools are supposed to be doing. On one extreme is the so-called liberalist, who believes that factual information is not important; content is not the main purpose of education. Facts change rapidly with new discoveries, so why learn them? Rather, learn how to solve problems and prepare students for change. This is the purpose of education.

On the other hand, there is a large conservative element of the population that believes the function of education is to maintain the values of the status quo, to recognize and learn the eternal values that have influenced the development of mankind. This education is obtained by storing up knowledge, and one of the best methods for doing this is memorization. Most educators fall between these two extremes, but there are significant divergent views on the goals of education.

There are numerous kinds of classifications of contemporary public educators. In general, these educational thinkers can be placed into five categories. The first group are those conservative thinkers who believe the function of education is to turn back to the timeless humanistic values of classical education. This group has been characterized by the words "retrenchment" or "traditionalism." These educators do not respond to the demand for relevancy or for education for change. They consider these problems as transitory and fleeting. Education should be concerned with the core of wisdom which has been recorded from the past. This curriculum is book-oriented. These educators can trace their ancestry back to the private academies and the old Latin Grammar School. Their sole concession to contemporary civilization is to recognize the need of science and mathematics education. Their prime target throughout the last forty years has been progressivists, but they have found plenty of others to fight as well.

At the other end of the spectrum are the advocates of free schools, alternate education, or imitators of A. S. Neill's Summerhill school. These experiments are deliberately non-structured, based upon a romanticist concept of individual freedom, self-motivation in education, doing what one wants to do when one wants to do it, and characterized by lack of rules and controls. This kind of educationalist claims these procedures promote creativity. This kind of educational orientation developed from the Summerhill ideas but now appears in many forms. The demands of students for a voice in their own curriculum and the belief that the justification of a curriculum is its obvious relevancy have found the Summerhill school an excellent example of how it should be. Numerous private schools have developed to cater to students who are not happy with the greater rigidity of the public schools. Another example is the free school movement, composed primarily of public-school dropouts who meet in vacant stores or what-not to do their "thing," which they call education. Harlem Tech, a private school for dropouts in New York, is an example. To numerous influential thinkers and writers, these schools are defended as responses to the inflexible, monolithic educational establishment. They have opposed the public school in many of its present forms because of rigidity in organization, obsolete teaching methods, non-relevant curriculum, and the role of the institution as it applies to the individual child.

Another contemporary group has been called educational engineers. These have such great faith in education that they believe its function is to solve the problems of mankind. They see the goals of education as the attacking of human ills and bringing about appropriate change. Education might be expected to change attitudes, values, or to bring about physical improvement. Examples of the social ills the engineers believe can be solved by education are racial intolerance, discrimination, unemployment, poverty, ghetto issues, and the environmental crisis.

The educational engineers tend to look at education as a system, as a mechanical manipulation. Rather than seeing education as a humanistic endeavor of a relationship between student and teacher dealing with abstraction, they turn to the use of statistical compilation, manipulation of numbers, graphical analysis, programmed instruction, teaching machines, and computers. Their evaluations rest upon quantity and efficiency rather than upon quality. In the earlier history of American education we have reported on the Lancaster "monitorial" schools. The engineers have much this same point of view. Lessons are programmed in some manner: texts, machines, or computers. Students can then be self-taught at their individual pace. Vast amounts of money have been invested in these ideas by the federal government and private foundations. While business and some educational leaders still pursue this concept, there has been in the early 1970s a teacher reaction against the mechanization of the teaching act. With a redirection of attention to the learner and his needs, humanistic teaching is again in demand. This is particularly true with programs that are honestly trying to do effective educational work with minority children.

The social engineers have developed a new breed of teachers. From the technical minds have come concepts of classrooms without teachers in the old sense of the words. The teacher becomes a manager, as students use electronic devices such as media and computers, employing a cafeteria of learning materials called software.

A fourth group, and by far the largest group operating within the establishment, are the innovationists. Most of the new ideas and approaches which have developed in school management, in teaching strategies, and in staff utilization are of this nature. These people do not wish to undo the educational system, merely kick it around until it works. The innovationist has confidence in the present system; it just needs reforms to make it work. Many gadget-type changes in school procedure have resulted. Most innovations disappear within three years (usually about the length of a grant). Some of the projects started by the innovationists that are still working are team teaching, large-small class organization, modular-flexible scheduling, teacher aides, the non-graded school, and such curriculum approaches as inquiry, new math, transformational grammar, new science curricula, and accountability.

A fifth group may well be called the child-centered group. These educationalists base their thinking on love for children. The basic concept is that the teacher is a facilitator of learning. The new role is not that of imparting knowledge in a changing society, but rather, helping students to learn how to learn. The humanistic teacher loves and knows her pupils. Personal meanings rather than facts become the objectives. The person in the process is primary. The most important aspect of learning lies not in the giving of information, but in discovering its meaning. Experiences in the affective domain are more significant than those in the cognitive domain. This kind of teacher has an answer to alternate schools, and that is the open school or open curriculum, sometimes referred to as schools without walls. The idea of this "openness" is that a child learns only when he is motivated and only about the things in which he has or develops an interest. There may be a planned structure for the curriculum, but in the classroom, the teacher responds on the spot to any interest which may develop. The time to develop a learning situation is to take advantage of any opportunities which may develop in the classroom.

The library, the field trip, and the community become a part of the extended classroom. Involved in this thinking is the idea that teachers should harness the unused teaching powers of students themselves through cross-age tutoring, which is the idea of "each one teach one." Students in a given class can be effective in working with other students in the class, and it is good for each type of student.

The most difficult contemporary issue which plagues American education is dealing with youth who refuse to accept any part of the present school program. This discontent generates from several sources. High school students, who are in large numbers dissatisfied with what they are expected to achieve or who have no real love for learning, have done little more than tolerate the twelve years of education. These students have completed their high school experience with considerable compartmentalized knowledge, but with a low level of communication skills and with little ability in the area of problem solving. Many have failed so completely to function effectively in the school system that they have finished their formal schooling battle scarred and disillusioned.

Student dislike of school has led to student unrest; so has racism as practiced by both the minority and the majority. Unrest has led to demands, to strikes, to violence. Students have demanded and are obtaining the right to the exercise of power over their own education. Student activism has resulted in militant teacher organizations.

Parents have also become antagonistic. Much of this parent reaction is beyond the sphere of influence of the school system. Examples can be cited in reaction to high taxes, polarized racial situations, forced integration, turned-off youngsters, and political extremists as far as curriculum content is concerned (sex education, inquiry methods in social sciences, phonics methods in the teaching of reading, content of textbooks, ad infinitum). In fact, the mid-seventies show no real agreement on what education should be about.

America's long struggle to make democracy's dream of equal educational opportunity for all has been nearly completed. While pockets of educational poverty exist, the most widely accepted figure for school enrollment is 95 percent of all school-age children. The present decade is shifting its emphasis from the quantitative aspects of education to concerns of equality. Hence educational accountability. Since the fadeout of the issue of boom enrollments, the products of schools are being looked at with a careful eye. Parent groups are demanding a say in what is happening to their children. Minority groups, students with divergent backgrounds, interests, and abilities, the disadvantaged, and the gifted are demanding individualizing of the programs.

In order to combat its many critics, public education through the 1960s and on into the 1970s has expended great efforts toward improving the quality and efficiency of its program. It has been highly innovational. To finance these innovations, money has been allocated by private foundations and by the federal government. These projects have included new managerial approaches, improving instruction, utilization of developing technology, differentiation of staffing patterns, assessment of student achievement via a national testing program, and eventually, accountability. Public education now views itself as a mirror and as an agent of change. Because change characterizes all of life —people, social institutions, political institutions, and the physical world—education must become involved with it. Whereas, in the earlier decades, education generally looked backward at the classical approaches, the traditional, the maintenance of the status quo, it is now the ally of change. This is the hallmark of the 1970s.

New managerial approaches have generally been directed toward breaking the rigidity of the school day and the Carnegie unit. The terms most used are modular-flexible scheduling, instruction in large groups/small groups, individual or independent study, and greater opportunity for laboratory experience.

The last few years of the 1960s saw great strides in innovation. Much of the innovation was piecemeal and in differing directions. Innovation corresponds to a sailboat trying to make progress through the bay. If there is no wind, nothing happens. But if there is any wind, no matter from what direction, progress is possible. This was the course of innovations in the sixties. The 1970s have seen the culmination of many of these innovations into workable, viable programs and models.

The concept involved is that students learn in various ways. Some things are better done in large groups. (Examples might be in a guest-lecture situation, a motion picture, or some other use of media.) Small-group instruction gives much greater opportunity for communication. Individual instruction permits diagnosis and correction. Flexible scheduling based on time modules breaks the lockstep of uniform time for each class, characteristic of the past, regardless of whether or not the time was needed, and equal credit, whether it be academic or otherwise. Flowing from modular scheduling have been new ideas on staff utilization. Once the class size and time allocations have been broken, there are numerous methods for developing instructional strategies. Newer approaches include interns, tutors, assistant teachers, and teacher aides. Mini courses have been used to develop more interest in the curriculum. Team teaching has become a prime innovational procedure, particularly in the elementary school, where the self-contained classroom and its all-purpose teacher is giving way to team operations which permit areas of specialization in the elementary teaching program. Elementary teacher education programs are now involving many students with academic degrees in mathematics, in foreign language, in dance, in music, and in art, who are entering the elementary field, hopefully to operate in a team situation.

Another development has been the non-graded school. The concept here, found in both the elementary and secondary school, is that the conventional grade-level designation does not permit the individual student to advance in accordance with his individual capabilities. The concept of the non-graded approach permits multi-age groupings with no reference to grade levels. This approach provides the opportunity for the student to make "continuous progress" at his own pace. It comes head-on with the traditional concept of classifying students by grade level and ability level grouping.

The 1960s and 1970s marked the widespread use of technology in the classroom. Planned objectives for instruction were carried out by the use of technology. Included in the technological devices were such familiar software items as tapes, records, slides, filmstrips, transparencies, motion pictures, programmed instruction, and textbooks, and such hardware items as language laboratories, television, teaching machines, and computers. Much more would have happened with computers had there been more money. Computers were expensive and school districts were broke. In spite of the financial pinch, the early 1970s saw the devices of technology used in a move toward educational automation. Much controversy developed over the machine teacher and the human learner. The resulting impact heralded a return to the humanistic teacher who loved young people.

INNOVATIONS IN ELECTRONIC METHODS

Television instruction to date has been only reasonably successful. This is particularly true of open-circuit television. Closed-circuit television has been more effective. Programmed learning continues to hold interest as a teaching strategy to meet individual differences and to allow students to progress at their own pace. Unfortunately, to date the programmed material is basically boring.

The computer remains a formidable ally of education for the seventies. The big problem of putting the computer to work in the public schools has been lack of trained teacher personnel and lack of money. Computerized education is still financially a long distance away.

INNOVATIONS IN CURRICULUM PLANNING

Courses are now different in the schools, particularly high schools. Survey courses are generally being replaced by mini-courses which are organized to run from two weeks to six weeks or perhaps even a semester in duration. An example can be in the teaching of United States history. Courses may run on a six-weeks basis on a particular topic and then change to another six-weeks course on a different topic; the students have considerable elective opportunity in these courses. English is doing the same thing, i.e. mini-courses in poetry, literary criticism, creative writing, short story, ad infinitum.

Some schools are experimenting in the elimination of course requirements as such. These courses are being replaced by establishing as a guide for graduation the information or skills that a student should have. Thus the student's graduation will not hinge upon the number of courses taken or which courses were taken, but rather upon the objectives concerning which the student should have knowledge. This program is known as performance-based curriculum.

Another attempt at solving the complexities of education has been a development called the open curriculum, or the open classroom. The essence of the open classroom is that curriculum originates in some happening—an idea or a human encounter. The teacher takes her cue from the encounter. From this background of teacher awareness, a different classroom curriculum can develop. This awareness can focus in such a way that it enlarges the classroom environment in which a child can respond.

The "Open-Space Plan" in public education represents a slightly different direction. Open-space might mean either an attitude or physical arrangements; in any event, it represents an approach to teaching rather than the buildings in which teaching takes place. It is a reconstruction of the curriculum and of the teacher-learner scene.

The "Open-Space Plan" has taken on many forms. Its origin generally traces to the British Infant School. In America, it is usually called the "open classroom" or the "open school." Basic to the open curriculum is the concept of individualization of instruction. It represents the antithesis of the formal classroom in which the teacher stands in front of the class, directing activities, dominating activity, and in a learning situation in which all of the thirty or so students are exposed to the same information at the same time.

Of the two words that make up the term "open-space," "open" is the more important concept. Several conditions need to exist to have meaningful openness: approachability, relaxed discipline, fluidity, flexibility, ease of communication, some kind of mobility, supportiveness of student by the teacher, vice versa, and a stimulating learning environment. The addition of space to the expression adds something only when it can be utilized to provide optimum educational advantage for each student.

A chief characteristic of the open-space classroom is that the emphasis is on the child's learning rather than on the teacher's teaching. Many open-space plans exist. One may be the learning center, wherein the students have easy access to appropriate materials, software (tapes, records, films, cassettes, slides), hardware (typewriters, tape recorders, record players, projectors), and perhaps computer terminals. Raw materials (such as sand, rocks), laboratory equipment, art materials, books and artifacts are but a few of the items which may be available.

Other open-space schools may have media laboratories wherein the students produce their own materials. These centers are sometimes called intensive learning centers. Math laboratories and reading skills centers are other methods of individualizing instruction.

FREE SCHOOL OR ALTERNATE SCHOOL

Another contemporary development is the free school. It is an alternate to public education, established within communities, usually with little or no tuition, and as a result of a perceived inequality or in-humanity. As those involved in the movement see it, the free school is an alternative to the monolith of the public schools. In the seventies, these new schools are springing up by the hundreds throughout the nation.

The first of the free schools were patterned mainly after the English Summerhill school, a private boarding school wherein the children have freedom, and do much as they please, except as controlled by their peers. Curriculum is "open." Numerous creative opportunities are offered, as is regular academic work. Students take classes when they are ready. Discipline is open. The American counterparts differ consid-erably. They are not boarding schools. The curriculum is seldom aca-demic. The schools are "free" in matters of curriculum and close to being free insofar as expenses are concerned.

Alternate education is unique in American educational history. The "free school," or street academy, is the outstanding example of alter-nate education. It is not simply another educational innovation such as progressive education, life-adjustment education, ability grouping, flexible scheduling, the voucher system, or differentiated staffing. Free schools are a solution to problems of education outside of the public school. They represent a rebellion against the regular curriculum, against the bigness of the establishment, against conformity. These free schools are small do-it-yourself schools; they are non-institutional. Free schools were brought into existence by parents and teachers, and at times by students themselves. These students hate the public schools, but they want to find for themselves a meaningful learning environment. Like the students who are dropouts from the public schools, so are most of the teachers. The teachers are ones who could not accept the "system," but are now working for "starvation wages." Perhaps the teachers are college students working on a volunteer basis. The "schools" are in deserted stores, in basements, in churches, in old buses, or in "underground" meeting places, "floating" around. At times the students build their own schools.

"Free schools" tend to have certain identifiable characteristics. They usually are non-authoritarian, even democratic. They are unstruc-tured in the sense of formal organization or having a body of knowledge for which the student will be responsible; and they have no minimum requirements. In most such schools, non-directive behavior becomes a value. They also value unity of life; sensory, ethical, aesthetic, and affective experiences are a large part of what learning is all about. Particularly, there is opposition to a formal curriculum such as science, mathematics, and foreign language. They are almost always politically radical in the context of leftist opposition to the dominant culture.

They are made up of youth who are rebelling against what regular education has to offer. The students claim to be attuned to people, to the earth, in the sense of peace, love, land, ecology, altruism, and to a concern for global matters.

Most "free" schools are private. The "free" schools choose to be independent. Since enrollments tend to be made up of dropouts and minorities, money remains a problem. The schools exercise no control over the students; lay people rather than professionals develop the curriculum and control the schools.

The curriculum is completely open. More often than otherwise it is in the affective area, since these students hold a disdain for cognitive concern. The curriculum varies from hobbies to social issues. It may be cybernetics, or it can be at the potter's wheel, or ethnic conscious-raising trips for Chicanos or Blacks, or just store-front drop-in centers.

Opportunities in higher education for minority students have been increasing steadily since 1965. Educational Opportunity Programs, developed to assess more accurately the academic potential of minority students, are to be found on nearly every college or university campus in the nation. The purpose of the Educational Opportunity Program is to enroll able people from minority and/or low-income backgrounds, finance their education when need exists, and make available academic support (in the form of tutoring and counseling) to help insure their success as university students. Students from minority and/or low-income backgrounds are encouraged to apply for admission to colleges and universities. Particularly sought out are those students who may not meet existing admission requirements, but who can offer evidence supporting their ability to achieve at the college or university level. The number of minority students wishing to make use of these opportunities far exceeds the capacity of these programs, and this discrepancy increases yearly.

The impact of the 1970s is a focus on "opening things up," on the greening of curriculum. The greening is in the form of a new consciousness sweeping the nation as a reaction to the machine-made environment. It is this consciousness that has encouraged alternate curriculum designs which are beginning to undermine the hard-rock, formal traditional curriculum of the public schools.

The American public school of the seventies is apt to range from the ultra-conservative to the alternate school on a regular campus. There are schools in several areas, for example, in California and Wisconsin, where the old moralistic McGuffey Readers are used in teaching reading. At the other extreme are the "free schools" of many cities. Between these two extremes are traditional schools, basically unchanged in the last forty years, as well as innovational schools which may be modular-scheduling schools, open-classroom schools, the all-year school, continuous-progress schools, individually prescribed instruction child-centered schools, differentiated-staffed schools, or "schools without failure." Instruction methods will vary from teacher centered, textbook oriented to utilization of individualized instruction, large group/small group instruction, team teaching, differentiated staffing, open curriculum, mini-made courses, cross-age tutoring, computerized instruction, programmed instruction, performance objectives, or performance contracting. Most innovations have tended to disappear in less than five years, but some of these seem to be more permanent.

Selected Bibliography

Ahlstrom, Winton M. and Robert J. Havighurst. *Four Hundred Losers: Delinquent Boys in High School.* San Francisco: Jossey-Bass, Inc., 1971.

Alexander, Thomas and Beryl Parker. *The New Education in the German Republic.* New York: The John Day Company, Inc., 1929.

Alston, Patrick L. *Education and the State in Tsarist Russia.* Stanford: Stanford University Press, 1969.

Altbach, Philip G., Robert S. Laufer, and Sheila McVey, eds. *Academic Supermarkets.* San Francisco: Jossey-Bass, Inc., 1971.

Anderson, Lewis F. *Pestalozzi.* New York: McGraw-Hill Book Company, 1931.

Aquinas, Thomas. *Basic Writings.* New York: Random House, 1905.

Archambault, Reginald Donat, ed. *Dewey on Education: Appraisals.* New York: Random House, 1966.

Archer, R. L. *Secondary Education in the 19th Century.* Cambridge: Cambridge University Press, 1921.

Aristotle. *Works of Aristotle.* Translated by St. George Stock. Oxford: The Clarendon Press, 1925.

Armytage, W. H. G. *The American Influence on English Education.* New York: Humanities Press, 1967.

————. *Four Hundred Years of English Education,* Rev. ed. Cambridge: Cambridge University Press, 1970.

Ascham, Roger. *The Schoolmaster.* Edited by D. C. Whimster. London: Methuen, 1934.

Bacon, Martha. *Puritan Promenade.* Boston: Houghton Mifflin Company, 1964.

Baird, Hugh, et al. *A Behavioral Approach to Teaching.* Dubuque, Iowa: Wm. C. Brown Company Publishers, 1972.

Barclay, William. *Educational Ideals in the Ancient World.* London: Collins, William, & Sons, 1959.

Barlow, Melvin L. *History of Industrial Education in the United States.* Peoria, Ill.: Charles A. Bennett, 1967.

Barnard, Henry. *German Teachers and Educators.* Hartford: Brown and Gross, 1878.

Barnard, Henry C. *The French Tradition in Education.* London: Cambridge University Press, 1922.

Beck, Frederick A. G. *Greek Education: 450-350 B.C.* New York: Barnes and Noble, 1964.

Becker, Carl. *The Heavenly City of the Eighteenth Century Philosophers.* New Haven: Yale University Press, 1932.

Bennett, Charles A. *A History of Manual and Industrial Education Up To 1870.* Peoria, Illinois: Manual Arts Press, 1926.

Berelson, B. *Graduate Education in the United States.* New York: McGraw-Hill, 1960.

Bernard, Harold W. *Psychology of Learning and Teaching.* New York: McGraw-Hill, 1972.

Bernbaum, Gerald. *Social Change and the Schools, 1918-1944.* New York: Humanities Press, 1967.

Best, John Harding, ed. *Benjamin Franklin on Education.* New York: Bureau of Publications, Teachers College, Columbia University Press, 1962.

Bibby, Cyril. *T. H. Huxley: Scientist, Humanist, and Educator.* London: Horizon Press, 1959.

Blewett, John, ed. *John Dewey: His Thought and Influence.* New York: Fordham University Press, 1960.

Bloom, Benjamin S., et al. *Handbook of Formative and Summative Evaluation of Instruction.* New York: McGraw-Hill, 1971.

————, ed. *Taxonomy of Educational Objectives. Handbook I: Cognitive Domain.* New York: David McKay Co., Inc., 1956.

Bolgar, R. R. *The Classical Heritage and Its Beneficiaries.* London: Cambridge University Press, 1954.

Bolton, F. E. *The Secondary School System of Germany.* New York: Appleton-Century, 1905.

Bond, Horace Mann. *The Education of the Negro in the American Social Order.* Englewood Cliffs, N.J.: Prentice-Hall, 1934.

Bonner, S. F. *Roman Declamation in the Late Republic and Early Empire.* Berkeley: University of California Press, 1950.

Bosanquet, Bernard. *The Education of the Young in the Republic of Plato.* Cambridge: Cambridge University Press, 1908.

Bowers, C. A. *The Progressive Educator and the Depression: The Radical Years.* New York: Random House, 1969.

Boyd, William, ed. and trans. *The Emile of Jean Jacques Rousseau, Selections.* New York: Bureau of Publications, Teachers College, Columbia University, 1962.

————, ed. and trans. *The Minor Educational Writings of Jean Jacques Rousseau.* New York: Bureau of Publications, Teachers College, Columbia University, 1962.

Brickman, William W., and Stanley Lehrer. *Education and the Many Faces of the Disadvantaged: Cultural and Historical Perspectives.* New York: John Wiley and Sons, 1972.

Brown, E. E. *The Making of Our Middle Schools; an account of the development of secondary education in the United States.* New York: Longmans, Green and Company, 1907.

Brubacher, John S. *The Courts and Higher Education.* San Francisco: Jossey-Bass, Inc., 1971.

————. *Henry Barnard on Education.* New York: McGraw-Hill Book Company, 1913.

Bruce, G. M. *Luther as an Educator.* Minneapolis: Augsburg Publishing House, 1928.

Bruner, Jerome S. *The Process of Education.* Cambridge, Mass.: Harvard University Press, 1960.

Bullock, Henry A. *A History of Negro Education in the South.* Cambridge, Mass.: Harvard University Press, 1967.

Burgess, Charles, and Merle L. Borrowman. *What Doctrines to Embrace: Studies in the History of American Education.* Glenview, Ill.: Scott, Foresman and Company, 1969.

Burnet, John. *Aristotle on Education.* Cambridge, Mass.: Harvard University Press, 1928.

Burston, W. H., ed. *James Mill on Education.* Cambridge: Cambridge University Press, 1969.

Butler, J. Donald. *Four Philosophies, and Their Practice in Education and Religion.* New York: Harper & Row, Publishers, 1957.

Cahn, Steven M. *The Philosophical Foundations of Education.* New York: Harper & Row, 1970.

Calhoun, Daniel H., ed. *The Educating of Americans: A Documentary History.* Boston: Houghton Mifflin Company, 1969.

Castiglione, Baldassare. *The Book of the Courtier.* Translated by L. E. Opdycke. New York: Liveright Publishing Company, 1929.

Chambliss, J. J., ed. *Nobility, Tragedy, and Naturalism: Education in Ancient Greece.* Minneapolis: Burgess, 1971.

Childs, John. *American Pragmatism and Education.* New York: Holt, Rinehart & Winston, Inc., 1956.

Cohen, S. Alan. *Teach Them All To Read: Theory, Methods, and Materials for Teaching the Disadvantaged.* New York: Random House, Inc., 1969.

Cohen, Arthur M. and Associates. *New Perspectives on the Community College.* San Francisco: Jossey-Bass, Inc., Publishers, 1971.

Cole, Percival R. *Herbart and Froebel, an Attempt at Synthesis.* New York: Bureau of Publications, Teachers College, Columbia University, 1907.

Compayre, Gabriel. *Herbart and Education by Instruction.* New York: Thomas Y. Crowell Company, 1907.

————. *Pestalozzi and Elementary Education.* Translated by R. P. Jago. New York: Thomas Y. Crowell Company, 1907.

Conant, James Bryant. *Education in a Divided World.* Cambridge, Mass.: Harvard University Press, 1948.

————. *The Education of American Teachers.* New York: McGraw-Hill Book Company, 1963.

Cooper, James M., ed. *Differentiated Staffing.* Philadelphia: W. B. Saunders Company, 1971.

Cornill, Carl H. "The Education of Children." In *The Culture of Ancient Israel.* Chicago: Open Court Publishing Company, 1914.

Counts, George S. *The Challenge of Soviet Education.* New York: McGraw-Hill Book Company, 1957.

――――. *Social Foundations of Education.* New York: Charles Scribner's Sons, 1938.

Cramer, J. F., and A. S. Brown. *Contemporary Education: A Comparative Study of National Systems.* New York: Harcourt, Brace & World, Inc., 1956.

Crane, Theodore Rawson, ed. *The Colleges and the Public, 1787-1862.* New York: Bureau of Publications, Teachers College, Columbia University, 1963.

Cremin, Lawrence A. *The American Common School.* New York: Bureau of Publications, Teachers College, Columbia University, 1951.

――――. *The Republic and the School, Horace Mann on the Education of Free Men.* New York: Teachers College, Columbia University, 1957.

――――. *The Transformation of the School, Progressivism in American Education, 1876-1957.* New York: Alfred A. Knopf, Inc., 1961.

Cruickshank, M. *Church and State in English Education: 1870 to the Present Day.* New York: St. Martin's Press, 1963.

Curti, Merle. *The Social Ideas of American Educators.* Rev. ed. Patterson, N.J.: Littlefield, Adams, 1965.

Curtis, S. J. *History of Education in Great Britain.* London: University Tutorial Press, 1950.

Curtius, E. R. *European Literature and the Latin Middle Ages.* New York: Harper & Row, 1963.

Dabney, Charles W. *Universal Education in the South.* Two vols. Chapel Hill: University of North Carolina Press, 1936.

Daly, L. J. *The Medieval University.* New York: Sheed & Ward, 1961.

Davidson, Thomas. *Aristotle and Ancient Educational Ideals.* New York: Franklin Burt, 1969.

――――. *Education of the Greek People.* New York: Appleton-Century Company, 1904.

Dearborn, Ned H. *The Oswego Movement in American Education.* New York: Bureau of Publications, Teachers College, Columbia University, 1925.

DeGarmo, Charles. *Herbart and the Herbartians.* New York: Charles Scribner's Sons, 1895.

De la Fontainerie, F. *The Conduct of the Schools of Jean Baptiste de la Salle.* New York: McGraw-Hill Book Company, 1935.

――――. *French Liberalism and Education in the Eighteenth Century.* New York: McGraw-Hill, 1932.

Dennison, G. *The Lives of Children: The Story of the First Street School.* New York: Random House, Inc., 1969.

Descartes, Rene. *Discourse on Method.* New York: P. F. Collier and Son, 1910.

Dewey, John. *Democracy and Education.* New York: The Macmillan Company, 1916.

——. *Experience and Education.* New York: The Macmillan Company, 1938.

——. *How We Think.* Boston: D. C. Heath & Company, 1933.

——. *Individualism Old and New.* New York: G. P. Putnam's Sons, 1930.

——. *Liberalism and Social Action.* New York: G. P. Putnam's Sons, 1935.

——. *Philosophy and Civilization.* New York: G. P. Putnam's Sons, 1931.

——. *Problems of Men.* New York: Philosophical Library, 1946.

DeYoung, Chris, and Richard Wynn. *American Education: Foundations in Education.* 7th ed. New York: McGraw-Hill Book Company, 1972.

Dickinson, G. Lowes. *The Greek View of Life.* New York: Doubleday & Company, Inc., 1927.

Dobson, J. F. *Ancient Education and Its Meaning to Us.* New York: Longmans, Green, 1932.

Donohue, John W. *St. Thomas Aquinas and Education.* New York: Random House, 1968.

Drever, J. *Greek Education: Its Practices and Principles.* London: Cambridge University Press, 1912.

Duckett, Eleanor S. *Alcuin, Friend of Charlemagne.* New York: Macmillan, 1951.

——. *Anglo-Saxon Saints and Scholars.* New York: Macmillan, 1948.

Dunkel, Harold B. *Herbart and Education.* New York: Random House, 1969.

——. *Herbart and Herbartianism.* Chicago: University of Chicago Press, 1970.

Dworkin, Martin S., ed. *Dewey on Education: Selections.* New York: Bureau of Publications, Teachers College, Columbia University, 1959.

Easton, Stewart C. *The Era of Charlemagne.* Princeton, N.J.: Van Nostrand, 1961.

Ebner, Eliezer. *Elementary Education in Ancient Israel.* New York: Bloch Publishing Company, 1956.

Eby, Frederick. *Early Protestant Educators.* New York: McGraw-Hill Book Company, 1931.

Emerson, Ralph W. *Essays—First and Second Series.* London: J.M. Dent and Co. 1906.

Fantini, Mario D., and Gerald Weinstein. *The Disadvantaged; Challenge to Education.* New York: Harper & Row, Publishers, 1968.

Farrington, F. E. *French Secondary Schools.* New York: Longmans, Green and Company, 1910.

——. *The Public Primary School System of France.* New York: Bureau of Publications, Teachers College, Columbia University, 1906.

Fellman, David, ed. *The Supreme Court and Education.* New York: Bureau of Publications, Teachers College, Columbia University, 1960.

Fenelon, F. de S. *On the Education of Girls.* Translated by Kate Lupton. Boston: Ginn and Company, 1891.

Fitzpatrick, E. A. *La Salle, Patron of All Teachers.* Milwaukee: The Bruce Publishing Company, 1951.

———. *St. Ignatius and the Ratio Studiorum.* New York: McGraw-Hill Book Company, 1933.

Fleming, W. G. *Ontario's Educative Society: A Comprehensive Study of Ontario's Educational System.* 7 volumes. Toronto, Canada: University of Toronto Press, 1971-1972.

Flournoy, Don M., and Associates. *The New Teachers.* San Francisco: Jossey-Bass, Inc., 1972.

Ford, Paul L. Introduction to *The New-England Primer.* New York: Bureau of Publications, Teachers College, Columbia University, 1962.

Frankena, William K. *Three Historical Philosophies of Education: Aristotle, Kant, and Dewey.* Chicago: Scott Foresman, 1965.

Freeman, K. L. *Schools of Hellas from 600 to 300 B.C.* London: Macmillan and Company, 1912.

Full, Harold. *Controversy in American Education: An Anthology of Crucial Issues.* New York: Macmillan Company, 1972.

Furth, Hans G. *Piaget for Teachers.* Englewood Cliffs, N.J.: Prentice-Hall, Inc., 1970.

Gay, Peter, ed. *John Locke on Education.* New York: Bureau of Publications, Teachers College, Columbia University, 1964.

Georgeoff, Peter John. *The Social Education of Bulgarian Youth.* Minneapolis: University of Minnesota Press, 1968.

Gifford, Walter J. *Historical Development of the New York High School System.* Albany, N.Y.: J.B. Lyons Company, 1922.

Ginzberg, Louis. *Students, Scholars, and Saints.* Philadelphia: Jewish Publication Society, 1928.

Grant, Michael, ed. *The Birth of Western Civilization, Greece, and Rome.* New York: McGraw-Hill Book Company, 1964.

Grant, Nigel. *Soviet Education.* Baltimore: Penguin, 1964.

Grattan, C. Hartley, ed. *American Ideas About Adult Education, 1710-1915.* New York: Bureau of Publications, Teachers College, Columbia University, 1959.

Green, F. C., *Jean-Jacques Rousseau: A Critical Study of His Life and Writings.* New York: University of Cambridge Press, 1955.

Green, J. A. *Pestalozzi's Educational Writings.* London: Edward Arnold, 1916.

Grizzel, E. D. *Origin and Development of the High School in New England Before 1865.* New York: Macmillan, 1923.

Guilford, J. P. *Intelligence, Creativity, and Their Educational Implications.* San Diego, California: Robert R. Knapp, 1968.

Gutek, Gerald L. *The Educational Theory of George S. Counts.* Columbus, Ohio: The Ohio State University Press, 1970.

———. *Pestalozzi and Education.* New York: Random House, 1968.

Gwynn, Aubrey Osborn. *Roman Education From Cicero to Quintilian.* Oxford: Oxford University Press, 1926.

Hadas, Moses. *Humanism: The Greek Ideal and Its Survival.* New York: Harper & Row, 1960.

Halls, W. D. *Society, Schools and Progress in France.* New York: Pergamon Press, 1965.

Hambly, W. D. *Origins of Education Among Primitive Peoples; a Comparative Study in Racial Development.* London: Macmillan, 1926.

Handlin, Oscar. *John Dewey's Challenge to Education.* New York: Harper & Row, 1959.

Hans, Nicholas A. *History of Russian Educational Policy (1701-1917).* New York: Russell and Russell, 1964.

Hansen, A. O. *Liberalism and American Education in the Eighteenth Century.* New York: Macmillan, 1926.

Harcleroad, Fred F., ed. *Issues of the Seventies.* San Francisco: Jossey-Bass, Inc., 1970.

Haring, Norris G., and E. Lakin Phillips. *Analysis and Modification of the Classroom Behavior.* Englewood Cliffs, N.J.: Prentice-Hall, Inc., 1972.

Harris, J. Henry. *Robert Raikes: The Man and His Work.* New York: E. P. Dutton and Company, 1899.

Harrison, John F. *Quest for the New Moral World: Robert Owen and the Owenites in Britain and America.* New York: Scribner, 1969.

Heafford, M. R. *Pestalozzi: His Thought and its Relevance Today.* London: Barnes & Noble, 1967.

Herbart, J. F. *Outlines of Educational Doctrine.* New York: The Macmillan Company, 1901.

———. *The Science of Education.* Boston: D. C. Heath & Company, 1908.

Heslep, Robert D. *Thomas Jefferson and Education.* New York: Random House, 1969.

Hinsdale, B. A. *Horace Mann and the Common School Revival.* New York: Charles Scribner's Sons, 1898.

Hoffding, Harald. *Jean Jacques Rousseau and His Philosophy.* Translated by William Richards and Leo E. Saidlar. New Haven: Yale University Press, 1930.

Hofstadter, Richard, and Walter P. Metzger. *The Development of Academic Freedom in the United States.* New York: Columbia University Press, 1955.

Hollis, Andrew P. *The Contribution of the Oswego Normal School.* Boston: D. C. Heath & Company, 1898.

Holman, H. *Pestalozzi: An Account of His Life and Work.* London: Longmans, Green and Company, 1908.

Holmes, D. O. W. *The Evolution of the Negro College.* New York: Bureau of Publications, Teachers College, Columbia University, 1934.

Holmes, P. A. *Tercentenary History of the Boston Public Latin School 1635-1935.* Cambridge, Mass.: Harvard University Press, 1935.

Honeywell, R. J. *The Educational Work of Thomas Jefferson.* Cambridge, Mass.: Harvard University Press, 1931.

Houle, Cyril O. *The Design of Education.* San Francisco: Jossey-Bass, Inc., 1972.

Howell, W. S., ed. *The Rhetoric of Alcuin and Charlemagne.* Princeton, N.J.: Princeton University Press, 1941.

Hu, Chang-tu, ed. *Chinese Education Under Communism.* New York: Bureau of Publications, Teachers College, Columbia University, 1962.

Huebener, Theodore. *The Schools of West Germany; A Study of German Elementary and Sunday Schools*. New York: New York University Press, 1962.

Hughes, J. L. *Froebel's Educational Laws For All Teachers*. New York: Appleton-Century, 1898.

Hughes, Thomas A. *Loyola*. New York: Charles Scribner's Sons, 1904.

Hurlock, Elizabeth. *Child Development*. 5th edition. New York: McGraw-Hill, 1972.

Hutchins, Robert M. *The Higher Learning in America*. New Haven: Yale University Press, 1936.

Hurwitz, Emanuel, Jr., and Charles A. Tesconi, Jr., eds. *Challenges to Education: Readings for Analysis of Major Issues*. New York: Dodd, Mead, & Company, Inc., 1972.

Hyma, Albert. *Erasmus and the Humanists*. New York: Croft Educational Services, 1930.

Illich, Ivan. *DeSchooling Society*. New York: Harper & Row, 1972.

Inglis, A. J. *The Rise of the High School in Massachusetts*. New York: Bureau of Publications, Teachers College, Columbia University, 1911.

Jackson, George L. *The Development of School Support in Colonial Massachusetts*. New York: Bureau of Publications, Teachers College, Columbia University, 1909.

Jacobsen, J. V. *Educational Foundations of the Jesuits in Sixteenth Century New Spain*. Berkeley: University of California Press, 1938.

James, William. *Pragmatism*. New York: Longmans, Green and Company, 1907.

Jelinex, Vladimir, trans. and ed., *The Analytical Didactic of Comenius*. Chicago: University of Chicago Press, 1953.

Jenkins, Ralph C., and Gertrude C. Warner. *Henry Barnard, An Introduction*. Hartford: The Connecticut State Teachers Association, 1937.

Jerome, Saint. *Letters*. Cambridge, Mass.: Harvard University Press, 1933.

———. "On Female Education," *American Journal of Education,* V, 593-598.

Johnson, Clifton. *Old Time Schools and School Books*. New York: Macmillan & Co., 1904.

Johnson, George M. *Education Law*. East Lansing: Michigan State University Press, 1969.

Johnson, James A., Harold W. Collins, John H. Johansen, and Victor L. Dupuis. *Foundations of American Education: Readings*. Second Edition. Boston, Mass.: Allyn and Bacon, Inc., 1972.

Johnson, William H. E. *Russia's Educational Heritage*. New York: Octagon Books, 1969.

Joncich, Geraldine M., ed. *Psychology and the Science of Education: Selected Writings of Edward L. Thorndike*. New York: Bureau of Publications, Teachers College, Columbia University, 1962.

Jones, Lloyd. *The Life, Times, and Labours of Robert Owen*. London: Swan Sonnenschein and Company, 1905.

Keatings, M. W. *Comenius*. New York: McGraw-Hill Book Company, 1931.

Kelly, Thomas. *George Birkbeck, Pioneer of Adult Education.* Liverpool: University of Liverpool Press, 1957.

Kibre, P. *Scholarly Privileges in the Middle Ages; the Rights, Privileges, and Immunities of Scholars and Universities at Bologna, Padua, Paris, and Oxford.* Cambridge, Mass.: Medieval Academy of America, 1962.

———. *The Nations in the Medieval Universities.* Cambridge, Mass.: Medieval Academy of America, 1948.

Kilpatrick, W. H. *The Dutch Schools of New Netherland and Colonial New York.* Washington, D.C.: Government Printing Office, 1912.

———. *Froebel's Kindergarten Principles Critically Examined.* New York: The Macmillan Company, 1916.

———. *Heinrich Pestalozzi: The Education of Man: Aphorisms.* New York: Philosophical Library, 1951.

Klain, Zora. *Educational Activities of New England Quakers: A Source Book.* New Brunswick, N.J.: New Jersey College for Women, 1928.

Kline, George L., ed. *Soviet Education.* London: Routledge & Kegan Paul, 1957.

Kneller, George R. *The Educational Philosophy of National Socialism.* New Haven: Yale University Press, 1941.

Kogan, Maurice. *The Government of Education: Informal Schools in Britain Today.* New York: Citation Press, 1971.

Kohl, H. *Thirty-Six Children.* New York: New American Library, 1968.

Korol, Alexander. *Soviet Education for Science and Technology.* Cambridge, Mass.: Technology Press of M.I.T., 1957.

Krathwohl, David R., Benjamin S. Bloom, and Bertram B. Masia. *Taxonomy of Educational Objectives. Handbook II: Affective Domain.* New York: David McKay Co., Inc., 1964.

Krug, Edward A., ed. *Charles W. Eliot and Popular Education.* New York: Bureau of Publications, Teachers College, Columbia University, 1961.

Laurie, S. S. *Studies in the History of Educational Opinion from the Renaissance.* New York: Humanities Press, 1968.

Lawrence, Evelyn, ed. *Friedrich Froebel and English Education,* by P. Woodham-Smith, et al. New York: Philosophical Library, 1953.

Lawson, John. *Medieval Education.* London: Routledge and Kegan Paul, 1968.

———. *Medieval Education and the Reformation.* New York: Humanities Press, 1967.

Lee, Gordon C., ed. *Crusade Against Ignorance: Thomas Jefferson on Education.* New York: Teachers College, Columbia University, 1962.

Leff, Gordon. *Paris and Oxford Universities in the Thirteenth and Fourteenth Centuries: An Institutional and Intellectual History.* New York: Wiley, 1968.

Lee, J. Murray. *Elementary Education: Today and Tomorrow.* 2nd edition. Boston: Allyn and Bacon, Inc., 1972.

Lightfoot, Alfred. *Inquiries Into the Social Foundations of Education: Schools In Their Urban Setting.* Chicago: Rand, McNally & Company, 1972.

Lindsay, T. M. *Luther and the German Reformation.* New York: Charles Scribner's Sons, 1900.

Listokin, David L. *Funding Education: Problems, Patterns, Solutions.* New Brunswick, N.J.: World Distribution by Transaction Inc., Rutgers University, 1972.

Locke, John. *An Essay Concerning Human Understanding.* Abridged and edited by A. S. Pringle-Pattison. Oxford: The Clarendon Press, 1928.

Lockwood, George B. *The New Harmony Movement.* New York: Augustus M. Kelley, 1969.

Lodge, R. C. *Plato's Theory of Education.* New York: Harcourt, Brace & World, Inc., 1947.

MacIver, Robert M. *Academic Freedom in Our Times.* New York: Columbia University Press, 1955.

Mangum, V. L. *The American Normal School: Its Rise and Development in Massachusetts.* Baltimore: Warwick and York, 1928.

Marique, Pierre J. *History of Christian Education.* New York: Fordham University Press, 1924.

Marrou, H. I. *A History of Education in Antiquity.* New York: Sheed & Ward, 1956.

Marsh, Leonard. *Alongside the Child: Experiences in the English Primary School.* N.Y.: Harper & Row, 1972.

Martin, G. H. *Evolution of the Massachusetts Public School System.* New York: Appleton-Century, 1894.

Mayer, Frederick. *A History of Educational Thought.* 3rd edition. Columbus: Charles E. Merrill, 1973.

Mayer, M. H. *The Philosophy of Teaching of St. Thomas Aquinas.* Milwaukee: Bruce Publishing Company, 1929.

McCabe, Joseph A. *A Candid History of the Jesuits.* London: E. Nash, 1913.

McClure, M. T. *Bacon Selections.* New York: Charles Scribner's Sons, 1928.

McClusky, Niel G. S. J., ed. *Catholic Education in America: A Documentary History.* New York: Bureau of Publications, Teachers College, Columbia University, 1964.

McMurrin, Sterling M., ed. *The Conditions for Educational Equality.* New York: Committee for Economic Development, 1971.

―――, ed. *Resources for Urban Schools: Better Use and Balance.* New York: Committee for Economic Development, 1971.

Medsker, Leland L. *The Junior College: Progress and Prospect.* New York: McGraw-Hill, 1960.

Meriwether, Colyer. *Our Colonial Curriculum 1607-1776.* Washington, D.C.: Capitol Publishing Co., 1907.

Meyer, Adolph E. *An Educational History of the Western World.* 2nd edition. New York: McGraw-Hill, 1972.

Miller, Richard I. *Evaluating Faculty Performance.* San Francisco: Jossey-Bass, Inc., 1972.

Minnich, H. C. *William Holmes McGuffey.* New York: The Macmillan Company, 1936.

Monroe, Paul. *Founding of the American School System.* New York: The Macmillan Company, 1940.

Monroe, Will S. *Comenius and the Beginnings of Educational Reform.* New York: Charles Scribner's Sons, 1900.

———. *Comenius' School of Infancy.* Boston: D. C. Heath & Company, 1896.

———. *History of the Pestalozzian Movement in the United States.* Syracuse, New York: C. W. Bardeen, 1907.

Moore, Ernest C. *The Story of Instruction: The Church, the Renaissance, and the Reformation.* New York: The Macmillan Company, 1938.

Mullinger, J. Bass. *The Schools of Charles the Great and the Restoration of Education in the Ninth Century.* New York: Stechart, 1911.

Nash, Paul, ed. *History and Education.* New York: Random House, 1970.

———. *Models of Man: Explorations in the Western Educational Tradition.* New York: John Wiley & Sons, 1968.

Nettleship, R. L. *The Theory of Education in Plato's Republic.* London: Oxford University Press, 1935.

Nietz, J. A. *Old Textbooks: Spelling, Grammar, Reading, Arithmetic, Geography, American History, Civil Government, Penmanship, Art, Music as Taught in the Common Schools from Colonial Days to 1900.* Pittsburgh: University of Pittsburgh Press, 1961.

Norlin, George. *Isocrates.* Cambridge, Mass.: Harvard University Press, 1966.

Norton, A. O. *Readings in the History of Education: Medieval Universities.* Cambridge, Mass.: Harvard University Press, 1909.

O'Neil, J. M. *Religion and Education Under the Constitution.* New York: Harper & Row, Publishers, 1949.

Painter, F. V. N. *Luther on Education.* St. Louis, Missouri: Concordia Publishing House, 1928.

Parker, Ronald K. *The Pre-School in Action: Exploring Early Childhood Programs.* Boston: Allyn and Bacon, Inc., 1972.

Parks, E. P. *The Roman Rhetorical Schools as a Preparation for the Courts Under the Early Empire.* Baltimore: The Johns Hopkins Press, 1945.

Parry, A. W. *Education in England in the Middle Ages.* London: W.B. Clive, 1920.

Paulsen, F. *The German Universities and University Study.* Translated by Frank Thilly and William W. Elwang. New York: Charles Scribner's Sons, 1906.

Perry, Leslie R., ed. *Bertrand Russell, A. S. Neill, Homer Lane, W. H. Kilpatrick: Four Progressive Educators.* New York: Macmillan, 1967.

Piaget, Jean. *The Moral Judgment of the Child.* New York: The Free Press, 1965.

Pidgeon, Douglas A. *Evaluation of Achievement.* New York: Citation Press, 1972.

Plato, *Works of Plato.* Translated by several scholars in the Loeb Classical Library. London: William Heinemann, several dates.

Potter, Alonzo, and George B. Emerson. *The School and the Schoolmaster.* Boston: W.B. Fowle and N. Capen, 1843.

Price, R. F. *Education in Communist China.* New York: Praeger, Publishers, Inc., 1970.

Quick, R. H. *Educational Reformers.* New York: Appleton-Century, 1960.

Randall, John Herman, Jr. *The Career of Philosophy: From the Middle Ages to the Enlightenment*. New York: Columbia University Press, 1962.

Rashdall, H. *Universities of Europe in the Middle Ages*. Three vols. New York: Oxford University Press, 1936.

Reisner, E. H. *The Evolution of the Common School*. New York: The Macmillan Company, 1930.

Rice, E. W. *The Sunday School Movement, 1780-1917, and the Sunday School Union 1817-1917*. Philadelphia: American Sunday School Union, 1917.

Rippa, S. Alexander, ed. *Educational Ideas in America: A Documentary History*. New York: David McKay Co., 1969.

Rist, Ray C., ed. *Restructuring American Education: Innovations and Alternatives*. New York: E. P. Dutton & Co., Distributors, 1972.

Roberts, A., and James Donaldson. *The Ante-Nicene Fathers*. Especially Vol. II, the writings of Clement of Alexandria, and Vols. III and IV, the writings of Tertullian. New York: Charles Scribner's Sons, 1917-1925.

Robinson, J. H., and H. W. Rolfe. *Petrarch: The First Modern Scholar and Man of Letters*. New York: G. P. Putnam's Sons, 1909.

Ross, Dorothy. *G. Stanley Hall: The Psychologist as Prophet*. Chicago: University of Chicago Press, 1972.

Sadler, John E. *J. A. Comenius and the Concept of Universal Education*. New York: Barnes and Noble, 1966.

Salmon, D. *Joseph Lancaster*. London: Longmans, Green and Company, 1904.

———. *The Practical Parts of Lancaster's Improvements and Bell's Experiments*. Cambridge: Cambridge University Press, 1932.

——— and W. Hindshaw. *Infant Schools, Their History and Theory*. London: Longmans, Green and Company, 1904.

Sampson, George. *English for the English: A Chapter on National Education*. Cambridge: Cambridge University Press, 1970.

Samuel, R. H., and R. Hinton Thomas. *Education and Society in Modern Germany*. London: Routledge & Kegan Paul, 1949.

Scanlon, David G., ed. *International Education: A Documentary History*. New York: Bureau of Publications, Teachers College, Columbia University, 1960.

———. *Traditions of African Education*. New York: Bureau of Publications, Teachers College, Columbia University, 1964.

Schevill, Ferdinand. *The First Century of Italian Humanism*. New York: Russell and Russell, 1967.

Schwickerath, Robert. *Jesuit Education: Its History and Principles*. St. Louis, Missouri: B. Herder, 1903.

Scott, Emmett J., and Lyman B. Stowe. *Booker T. Washington, Builder of a Civilization*. Garden City, N.Y.: Doubleday, 1916.

Seagoe, May V. *The Learning Process and School Practice*. Rev. ed. San Francisco: Chandler Publishing Company, 1970.

Sexton, Patricia Cayo. *School Policy and Issues in a Changing Society*. Boston: Allyn and Bacon, Inc., 1971.

Shoemaker, Ervin C. *Noah Webster: Pioneer of Learning*. New York: Columbia University Press, 1936.

Sikes, J. G. *Peter Abelard.* Cambridge, England: The University Press, 1932.
Silber, K. *Pestalozzi: The Man and His Work.* 2nd ed. New York: Humanities Press, 1965.
Silberman, Charles E. *Crisis in the Classroom: The Remaking of American Education.* New York: Random House, Inc., 1970.
Silver, Harold. *Robert Owen on Education.* Cambridge, England: Cambridge University Press, 1969.
Simmons, George C., ed. *Education and Western Civilization: Greece, Rome and the Middle Ages.* Arlington, Va.: College Readings Inc., 1972.
Sizer, Theodore R., ed. *The Age of the Academies.* New York: Bureau of Publications, Teachers College, Columbia University, 1964.
Smail, W. M. *Quintilian on Education.* New York: Oxford University Press, 1938.
Small, W. H. *Early New England Schools.* Boston: Ginn and Company, 1914.
Smith, Frank. *History of English Elementary Education Since 1760.* London: University of London Press, 1931.
Smith, L. Glenn, and Charles R. Kniker. *Myth and Reality in School and Society: A Reader in Educational Foundations.* Boston: Allyn and Bacon, Inc., 1972.
Smith, Preserved. *Erasmus.* New York: Harper & Row, Publishers, 1923.
Smith, W. A. *Ancient Education.* New York: Philosophical Library, 1955.
Spencer, Herbert. *Education.* New York: Appleton-Century, 1860.
Stettbacher, Hans, ed. *Pestalozzi, a Pictorial Record for the Centenary of His Death.* Zurich: Zentralbibliothek, 1928.
Stone, James C., and Donald P. De Nevi. *Teaching Multicultural Populations.* New York: Van Nostrand Reinhold Co., 1971.
────── and Frederick Schneider. *Teacher in the Inner City.* New York: Thomas Y. Crowell Co., 1970.
Swift, Fletcher J. *Education in Ancient Israel.* Chicago: Open Court Publishing Company, 1919.
Talbott, John E. *The Politics of Educational Reform in France, 1918–1940.* Princeton: Princeton University Press, 1969.
Tewksbury, D. G. *The Founding of American Colleges and Universities Before the Civil War.* New York: Bureau of Publications, Teachers College, Columbia University, 1932.
Tharp, Louise Hall. *Until Victory: Horace Mann and Mary Peabody.* Boston: Little, Brown, 1953.
Thompson, Alexander H. *Bede: His Life, Times and Writings.* Oxford: Clarendon Press, 1935.
Thorndike, L. *University Records and Life in the Middle Ages.* New York: Columbia University Press, 1944.
Thursfield, Richard. *Henry Barnard's Journal of Education.* Baltimore: The Johns Hopkins Press, 1946.
Totah, K. A. *Contribution of the Arabs to Education.* New York: Teachers College, Columbia University, 1926.
Toynbee, Arnold. *A Study of History.* New York: Oxford University Press, 1939.

Tsanoff, Radoslav. *The Great Philosophers.* New York: Harper & Row, Publishers, 1953.

Tuer, Andrew. *History of the Horn-book.* New York: Charles Scribner's Sons, 1897.

Ulich, Robert. *The Education of Nations: A Comparison in Historical Perspective.* Cambridge, Mass.: Harvard University Press, 1967.

————. *Sequence of Educational Influences Traced Through Unpublished Writings of Pestalozzi, Froebel, Diesterweg, Horace Mann, and Henry Barnard.* Cambridge, Mass.: Harvard University Press, 1935.

Walch, M. R. *Pestalozzi and the Pestalozzian Theory of Education.* Washington, D.C.: Catholic University of American Press, 1952.

Waller, George M. *Puritanism in Early America.* Boston: D. C. Heath & Company, 1950.

Warfel, Harry Redcay. *Noah Webster, Schoolmaster to America.* New York: Macmillan, 1936.

Washington, Booker T. *Tuskegee and Its People.* New York: Appleton & Co., 1908.

Watson, Foster. *English Grammar Schools to 1660.* London: Cambridge University Press, 1908.

Weber, Evelyn. *The Kindergarten: Its Encounter with Educational Thought in America.* New York: Teachers College Press, 1969.

Wells, Guy F. *Parish Education in Colonial Virginia.* New York: Teachers College, Columbia University, 1923.

West, A. F. *Alcuin and the Rise of Christian Schools.* New York: Charles Scribner's Sons, 1892.

Westaway, K. M. *The Educational Theory of Plutarch.* London: University of London Press, Ltd., 1922.

Wieruszowski, Helene. *The Medieval University.* Princeton, N.J.: Van Nostrand, 1966.

Wilderspin, Samuel. *Infant Education; or Practical Remarks on the Importance of Educating the Infant Poor.* London: Simpkin and Marshall, 1929.

Wilmot-Buxton, E. M. *Alcuin.* New York: P. J. Kennedy & Sons, 1922.

Williams, E. I. F. *Horace Mann, Educational Statesman.* New York: Macmillan, 1937.

Wilson, J. Dover, ed. *The Schools of England; A Study in Renaissance.* Chapel Hill: University of North Carolina Press, 1929.

Wilson, John A. *Signs and Wonders Upon Pharaoh. A History of American Egyptology.* Chicago: Chicago University Press, 1964.

Wilson, Louis N. *Granville Stanley Hall.* New York: G. E. Stechert & Co., 1914.

Wilson, William E. *The Angel and the Serpent. The Story of New Harmony.* Bloomington: Indiana University Press, 1964.

Wirth, Arthur G. *John Dewey as Educator: His Design for Work in Education.* New York: John Wiley & Sons, 1966.

Woock, R. P., ed. *Education and the Urban Crisis.* Scranton, Pa.: International Textbook Company, 1970.

Woodward, William H. *Desiderius Erasmus, Concerning the Aim and Method of Education.* A reprint from a 1904 edition. Foreword by Craig R. Thompson. New York: Bureau of Publications, Teachers College, Columbia University, 1964.

———. *Studies in Education During the Age of the Renaissance.* Cambridge: Cambridge University Press, 1906.

Woody, Thomas. *The Educational Views of Benjamin Franklin.* New York: McGraw-Hill Book Company, 1931.

———. *History of the Education of Women in the United States.* Lancaster, Penn.: Science Press, 1929.

———. *Life and Education in Early Societies.* New York: The Macmillan Company, 1949.

Zahorik, John A. *Toward More Humanistic Instruction.* Dubuque, Iowa: Wm. S. Brown Company, Publishers, 1972.

Ziemer, Gregor A. *Education for Death; The Making of the Nazi.* New York: Oxford University Press, 1941.

Zweig, Stefan. *Erasmus of Rotterdam.* New York: The Viking Press, Inc., 1934.

Zyskind, Harold, and Robert Sternfeld. *The Voiceless University.* San Francisco: Jossey-Bass, Inc., 1971.

INDEX